WRITING ACROSS
THE CURRICULUM

The Bedford/St. Martin's Series in Rhetoric and Composition

Assessing Writing: A Critical Sourcebook, edited by Brian Huot and Peggy O'Neill

Computers in the Composition Classroom: A Critical Sourcebook, edited by Michelle Sidler, Richard Morris, and Elizabeth Overman Smith

Disability and the Teaching of Writing: A Critical Sourcebook, edited by Cynthia Lewiecki-Wilson and Brenda Jo Brueggmann

Feminism and Composition: A Critical Sourcebook, edited by Gesa E. Kirsch, Faye Spencer Maor, Lance Massey, Lee Nickoson-Massey, and Mary P. Sheridan-Rabideau

Literacy: A Critical Sourcebook, edited by Ellen Cushman, Eugene R. Kintgen, Barry M. Kroll, and Mike Rose

An Open Language: Selected Writing in Literacy, Learning, and Opportunity, edited by Mike Rose

Second-Language Writing in the Composition Classroom: A Critical Sourcebook, edited by Paul Kei Matsuda, Michelle Cox, Jay Jordan, and Christina Ortmeier-Hooper

Selected Essays of Robert J. Connors, edited by Lisa Ede and Andrea A. Lunsford

Style in Composition and Rhetoric: A Critical Sourcebook, edited by Paul Butler

Views from the Center: The CCCC Chairs' Addresses 1977–2005, edited by Duane Roen

Visual Rhetoric in a Digital World: A Critical Sourcebook, edited by Carolyn Handa

Writing and Community Engagement: A Critical Sourcebook, edited by Thomas Deans, Barbara Roswell, and Adrian J. Wurr

Writing on the Margins: Essays on Composition and Teaching, edited by David Bartholomae

On Writing Research: The Braddock Essays 1975–1998, edited by Lisa Ede

WRITING ACROSS THE CURRICULUM

A Critical Sourcebook

EDITED BY

Terry Myers Zawacki
George Mason University

Paul M. Rogers
George Mason University

BEDFORD / ST. MARTIN'S   Boston • New York

For Bedford / St. Martin's

Executive Editor: Leasa Burton
Developmental Editor: Allie Goldstein
Production Associate: Ashley Chalmers
Marketing Manager: Marjorie Adler
Project Management: DeMasi Design and Publishing Services
Text Design: Anna Palchik
Cover Design: Donna L. Dennison
Composition: Jeff Miller Book Design
Printing and Binding: Haddon Craftsmen, Inc., an RR Donnelley & Sons Company

President: Joan E. Feinberg
Editorial Director: Denise B. Wydra
Editor in Chief: Karen S. Henry
Director of Marketing: Karen R. Soeltz
Director of Production: Susan W. Brown
Associate Director, Editorial Production: Elise S. Kaiser
Manager, Publishing Services: Andrea Cava

Library of Congress Control Number: 2010940842

Manufactured in the United States of America.

6 5 4
f e d

For information, write: Bedford / St. Martin's, 75 Arlington Street, Boston, MA 02116 (617-399-4000)

ISBN: 978-0-312-65258-6

To my many generous colleagues and friends in the WAC field and to my husband, Bob.

—Terry Myers Zawacki

To Charles Bazerman and Susan McLeod for their expert guidance and unwavering support.

To Brandice and Estella, the lights of my life.

—Paul M. Rogers

CONTENTS

A History of Inquiry: The Resilience of Writing Across the Curriculum

For nearly forty years, faculty associated with writing across the curriculum (WAC) have purposefully investigated the multifaceted roles writing and language play in higher education. This sustained inquiry into writing as a tool of teaching, learning, and communication has produced a distinctive student-centered pedagogy, an influential reform movement in modern higher education, and a field of scholarship covering a wide range of developmental, pedagogical, and administrative issues. In the articles collected in this sourcebook and here, in our introduction, we lay out the central areas of inquiry and activity that have contributed to WAC's impact, highlighting how, through the engagement of WAC leaders and scholars, this educational reform movement has thrived across a wide array of college and university contexts. In choosing and organizing the readings, our goal has been to provide a resource that captures the breadth and depth of scholarship in the field of WAC for students, as well as for faculty and administrators currently engaged in developing and leading WAC programs. Taken together, the contents show how and why WAC has been successful in improving teaching and learning in the challenging environment of higher education.

Almost from the outset, WAC program leaders and researchers have been interested in charting the progress of the movement to discover the ways in which programs are structured and administered and what factors might account for their growth or demise. As early as 1985, C. W. Griffin published the results of his first survey of WAC programs, which was followed four years later by Susan McLeod's "Second Stage" article reporting WAC programs at 427 of the institutions that responded to her survey. She and Eric Miraglia extended this survey in 1995 to ask why some programs had "staying power" and others did not. Those with staying power, they found, had more curricular elements, engaged in more assessment, and enjoyed faculty support and strong, consistent leadership. There has also been some effort to map WAC at community colleges, starting with Barbara Stout and Joyce Magnotto's 1987 survey, which described WAC programs at 121 community colleges and, over twenty years later, Leslie Roberts's 2008 survey of WAC and writing centers at two-year colleges (see p. 351 in this volume). The most recent effort to map

1

WAC programs across institutional levels was begun in 2007 by Chris Thaiss and Tara Porter, who circulated a web-based survey to update McLeod's data and gather information on WAC-like programs in institutions internationally. Of the nearly 1,400 institutions that responded to their survey, 625 have WAC programs and 152 have plans to start a program. Thaiss and Porter conclude that WAC is "alive and well," measured not only by the greater number of programs and institutions planning programs but also by the growth and diversity of WAC scholarship (527–28).

Viewed over time, these surveys demonstrate an enduring interest in WAC among higher education administrators, faculty across disciplines, and WAC professionals. At the hundreds of institutions that have programs, whatever their shape, the impulses for educational reform and the need to engage in this work remain as strong as ever, and the major themes of WAC continue to resonate with faculty interested in improving their teaching and student learning. Notwithstanding WAC's record of achievements, however, implementing, maintaining, expanding, and passing on strong WAC programs to the next generation of leaders continues to be difficult work, even for the most accomplished scholars and practitioners in the field. In the area of faculty development, for example, a considerable gap exists between faculty writing practices and the way they teach writing to students in the major (Thaiss and Zawacki). Amid economic, time, and resource pressures such as increased class sizes and teaching loads, many faculty feel hard-pressed to attend workshops on best practices for teaching with writing, no matter how dedicated they may be as teachers. Even in the best of times, faculty often express concern about the additional workload that comes with assigning and grading writing, especially when there may be little professional incentive to do so. Clearly, much work remains to be done in addressing these concerns, particularly now with the rapidly growing numbers of multilingual writers in our institutions and the increasingly important role writing plays in a global economy.

In 1996, Barbara Walvoord cautioned program leaders that WAC must "dive in or die," a directive that is as relevant today as it was then. To us, this means that first of all WAC leaders must continue the vigorous inquiry into language, learning, writing, and teaching that lies at the heart of the WAC movement. Further, program leaders must continue to work with faculty from across the disciplines and develop close relationships with writing centers, centers for teaching excellence, composition programs, and assessment offices to support faculty in meeting new demands and to prepare diverse student writers for the equally diverse workplaces and graduate degree programs they will enter. Finally, perhaps now more than ever, new and experienced WAC leaders alike must be willing to act in entrepreneurial ways, move beyond their comfort zones, and engage with sometimes unlikely partners and projects, such as quality enhancement plans (QEPs), mandated writing assessments, and institutional strategic plans, which, increasingly, envision a globalized future. For, as the articles in this sourcebook show, it is through wide-ranging, persistent, and disciplined engagement that WAC practitioners find ways to lead and participate in cross-curricular initiatives and reforms.

As a contemporary educational movement, WAC's roots can be traced to the holistic approaches to language and learning that emerged in England at the London Institute of Education in the early 1970s, where James Britton, Nancy Martin, and their colleagues conducted intensive cross-sectional research on writing in secondary schools. This groundbreaking research clearly showed the extent to which writing was narrowly used in schools, for few purposes and limited audiences. Britton and his colleagues argued convincingly that students should use writing for much more than regurgitating knowledge to teachers as examiners; they should instead employ writing extensively across content areas as a tool of exploration and discovery, a practice Britton called "the expressive function of language." This insight into writing as a tool of learning stands today as the most widely known and enduring contribution of the early work by Britton and his colleagues to WAC. Yet their work also contained many other seeds that would come to fruition in the WAC movement over time.

In addition to writing-to-learn pedagogy, the British researchers also advocated for educational policies that fostered the integration of language across content areas, decentering writing from its home in studies of literature and situating each curricular subject as "a distinctive mode of analysis" (see Bullock, p. 47). Moreover, Britton's rich theoretical work situated the development of writing abilities within a wider educational context, thereby enriching mandated teaching and assessment practices. Thus, we find in the very foundations of WAC a deeply nuanced view of language and language development, pedagogical practice, and a respect for disciplinary distinctions, epistemologies, and practices within and across the disciplines. We also find a strong interest in general education and its relationship to disciplinary specialization.

Unlike the original work in the UK, the WAC movement in the United States has, with notable exceptions, found its primary home in institutions of higher education, perhaps due to the ubiquity of the first-year composition (FYC) course in American colleges and universities. WAC histories date the beginning of the movement to the informal cross-disciplinary workshops conducted at Carleton College in the early 1970s, which inspired Elaine Maimon to apply for a National Endowment for the Humanities grant to institute a series of faculty development workshops and seminars, and to Michigan Tech, where Toby Fulwiler and Art Young used a grant from General Motors to support faculty retreats, a program they discussed in the influential *Language Connections: Writing and Reading Across the Curriculum*. Meanwhile, Barbara Walvoord had organized the Baltimore Area Consortium for Writing Across the Curriculum that brought together faculty from thirteen colleges and community colleges for retreats and WAC planning sessions. Participants in these various workshops also included college teachers of writing well versed in writing-process pedagogies; as Maimon explains, many of these composition teachers began to question whether it "made sense to work in isolation from their colleagues in other disciplines" or to ask students "to write outside of the context of the rest of their academic lives" (70).

Cross-disciplinary exchanges focused on writing, as exemplified by these early workshop approaches, remain a hallmark of WAC practice. The workshop approach, with its teacher-centered view of professional development, grew alongside another inquiry-based educational reform movement, the National Writing Project (NWP). Like WAC, the NWP was rooted in broad and somewhat minimalist theoretical underpinnings. Rather than subscribing to restrictive pedagogical prescriptions, faculty involved in WAC and the NWP shared values and reflective approaches that lent themselves well to local adaptation: in particular, the belief in writing as a powerful tool of learning, communication, and contribution for both students and teachers. WAC scholarship provided rich input for the NWP, while the NWP provided an avenue for the spread of WAC ideas through its growing network of sites across the country. Always located on university campuses but including teachers at all grade levels, the NWP, like WAC, centered around an interactive workshop approach in which teachers shared pedagogical practices through presentations of actual classroom activities and student work. Many early WAC leaders, such as Fulwiler, Young, Thaiss, Walvoord, and Mary K. Healy, either directed or helped direct Writing Project sites. Word of this work was spread early on in Fulwiler's *The Journal Book*, Thaiss's *Writing to Learn: Essays and Reflections on Writing Across the Curriculum*, and Fulwiler and Young's *Language Connections*.

In his 1982 introduction to *Teaching Writing in All Disciplines*, the earliest collection of WAC articles to be published, C. W. Griffin called WAC, which had become synonymous with writing-to-learn (WTL) pedagogy, a "quiet revolution" — one that was proving persuasive to educators across the curriculum and across institutions. The revolution was not without its critics, however. John Ackerman, for example, argued that WAC scholars had to move beyond reflective inquiry into WTL practices to provide empirical evidence for the enthusiastic claims being made for this pedagogical approach. Meanwhile, other scholars, most notably Charles Bazerman, had begun to take a rhetorical approach that focused on writing in the disciplines (WID), leading Sue McLeod and others (Jones and Comprone; Walvoord; Bazerman) to argue for a "second stage" reformulation of WAC that would include both WTL and WID, which by then had come to be seen as different entities, partly as a result of Maimon's and Bazerman's textbooks, *Writing in the Arts and Sciences* and *The Informed Writer*. At the same time that WAC leaders were trying to repair the purported WTL-WID split in the still nascent movement, others, like Anne Herrington, were showing how both approaches are integral and necessary to effective WAC practice. Despite these second-stage reformulations, some WAC critics continued to focus on the perceived shift to WID. Drawing on critical and cultural studies pedagogies, they argued that WAC had not lived up to its promise of reform (Mahala), that it simply instantiated already dominant and exclusionary disciplinary discourses (Malinowitz; Villanueva), that it had turned its back on student discourses and discursive practices, and that a "third stage" was needed to recover its lost emphasis (see LeCourt, p. 69). Still later, genre and activity theorists and researchers (Miller;

Russell and Yanez; Bazerman; Thaiss and Zawacki; and others) rejected fixed, stable definitions of WID and argued instead that disciplines, genres, teaching practices, and expectations for student writers all work within dynamic and fluid "activity systems" that will differ from institution to institution, teacher to teacher, and course to course.

Qualitative research investigations associated directly with the WAC movement began to occur in the early 1980s, notably with Herrington's and McCarthy's studies of student writers in disciplinary contexts and the case studies presented by Young and Fulwiler in *Writing Across the Disciplines: Research into Practice*. David Jolliffe's 1988 edited collection *Writing in Academic Disciplines* presented empirical studies that attempted to account for the "myriad of contextual variables" around writing in disciplines. As a framework for these studies, Chris Anson's "Toward a Multidimensional Model of Writing in the Academic Disciplines" organized WAC research into three domains: WID, writing as a mode of learning, and students' acquisition of disciplinary writing practices. Anson's framework still pertains today, encompassing, since the 1980s, qualitative and longitudinal studies of student development (e.g., Walvoord and McCarthy; Jolliffe and Brier; Herrington; Herrington and Curtis; Carroll; Sommers; Sommers and Saltz; Beaufort), investigations into the efficacy of writing as a tool of learning (e.g., Sternglass; Marsella, Hilgers, and McLaren; Hilgers, Hussey, and Stitt-Bergh, p. 261), and the nature of disciplinary discourses (e.g., Bazerman; Geisler). Thus the focus of WAC inquiry now includes all subject matter areas, the work of genres as social action, disciplines as complex activity systems (e.g., Bazerman; Russell's "Activity Theory" and "Rethinking Genre"; Russell and Yanez), and the relationship of language and academic enculturation across disciplines (e.g., Fishman and McCarthy; Leki; Casanave). Moreover, from the outset, WAC anthologies have included chapters from faculty across disciplines (e.g., Fulwiler and Young's *Language Connections*, Thaiss's *Writing*, and Herrington and Moran's *Writing, Teaching, and Learning*), embodying the cross-disciplinary principles and practices that have guided the movement from the outset. That these principles are still firmly in place can easily be seen by scanning the tables of contents in issues of *Language and Learning Across the Disciplines*, *academic.writing*, the *WAC Journal*, and *Across the Disciplines*.

This dynamic investigation into language, writing, and learning across all of these established areas of inquiry has contributed tremendously to WAC's staying power. Today, WAC scholarship includes strong contributions in the areas of institutional and classroom assessments; the teaching and learning of English as a second language; the role of WAC in university writing and learning centers, and community colleges; and WAC's place in higher education programs like service learning, learning communities, and writing fellows programs. Perhaps one of the most visible and constantly changing areas of WAC inquiry is "WAC wired," to echo the title of Donna Reiss and Art Young's chapter in *WAC for the New Millennium*. In 1998, Reiss, Dickie Selfe, and Young coined the acronym ECAC — electronic communication across the curriculum — to recognize the new modes of writing and teaching with writing that were emerging from new technologies such as e-mail, synchronous/asynchronous conferencing, multimedia, and the Web. Now, in a moment when the very definitions of writing are changing as disciplines expand and transform in response to Web 2.0 and new writing technologies, we need to know so much more about writing in digital environments, including, for example, the role of mobile devices and cloud-based computing. Evidence is emerging that many students in this new media landscape are doing a great deal of writing beyond the curriculum. We have much to learn about how, when, and why they are writing, and how literate activity in the twenty-first century is changing the writing that both teachers and students do in the curriculum.

WAC has grown enormously as a field over the past forty plus years, thanks to the strong foundation laid by its pioneers and the valuable guidance they've given in such publications as McLeod and Margot Soven's *Writing Across the Curriculum: A Guide to Developing Programs* and McLeod's follow-up collection *Strengthening Programs for Writing Across the Curriculum*. In addition, the National Network of WAC Consultants was formed in 1981, with Chris Thaiss as coordinator. The role of the network was not to make policy statements or to define "WAC," but rather to help those interested in starting programs on their campuses — programs that would mirror local institutional cultures and exigencies rather than conform to larger national trends or the structures of the most prominent programs. In 1993, the first WAC conference was convened at the College of Charleston; the conference proved to be so popular that it is now a biennial event, often drawing more than a thousand participants from the United States and other countries. To signal its inclusiveness of WAC efforts outside of the United States, in 2008 the organization became the International Network of Writing Across the Curriculum Programs (INWAC).

WAC's reach has extended to international audiences in part because of the robust growth of the WAC Clearinghouse website, which was created in 1998 by Mike Palmquist and a project team to provide open access to scholarly WAC work. In 2000, when it became clear that the original vision for the site was not feasible because scholars were typically not rewarded for website publication, the Clearinghouse was converted into the journal *academic .writing*. In 2002, however, the Clearinghouse was relaunched as the go-to WAC resource when back issues of *Language and Learning Across the Disciplines* (*LLAD*) were added to the site, along with other online journals and journal archives, including the *WAC Journal*, *RhetNet*, and *Across the Disciplines*, which joined *academic.writing* and *LLAD* into one publication. More recently, it also became home to INWAC and a digital book series featuring both landmark and new publications. For anyone interested in WAC, the Clearinghouse is an invaluable resource, as it was for us as we compiled this sourcebook.

In addition to the resources available on the Clearinghouse, an abundance of WAC-focused articles have been published in major journals such as *College English*, *College Composition and Communication* (*CCC*), *Written Communication*, and *Research in the Teaching of English*. Articles on the WAC movement, WTL pedagogies, and research on teaching, learning, and WID have also been well represented in field-specific journals, WAC anthologies, and research monographs. These include Herrington and Moran's *Writing, Teaching, and Learning in the Disciplines*, Bazerman and Russell's *Landmark Essays on Writing Across the Curriculum*, McLeod et al.'s *WAC for the New Millennium*, and the many open-access resources of the WAC Clearinghouse, among these the digital book series and, notably, Bazerman et al.'s Web-based *Reference Guide to Writing Across the Curriculum*. Certainly, anyone interested in expanding their understanding of WAC will want to familiarize themselves with these resources, many which are listed in our extended bibliography.

To narrow WAC's rich and advancing scholarship to only thirty-one key readings that represent the entire field to new WAC scholars, program leaders, administrators, and college teachers has proven to be a daunting task. Nevertheless, given the current higher education environment and the lessons learned from the trenches of forty years of activity, a WAC resource that charts our history, theory, research, and future directions is long overdue. In making our final selections, we aimed to provide as comprehensive an introduction to the field as possible within the page limits allowed. Being comprehensive, however, meant that we had to leave out many of the voices and perspectives that have enriched WAC studies and added depth and complexity to the array of issues and concerns represented here. Even as we wrote this introduction, we were still weighing the merits of including one article over another, one issue over another, one prominent program voice over another. We also came to the difficult realization that we could not even begin to represent the body of scholarship on WID, which, as we suggested to the Bedford/St. Martin's editors, would fill a sourcebook of its own. In our introductions to each of the parts, we explain in more detail our rationale for the articles we've included.

The sourcebook is divided into five sections, the first of which includes foundational texts that chart the history and stages of the WAC movement and point to future directions. In a second section, we feature representative "how-to" articles — pieces that offer concrete strategies for using writing to learn and facilitating cross-disciplinary dialogue in faculty seminars and that describe ways writing is being assigned across the curriculum. In the third section, we include a small sample of research studies and theoretical pieces that have influenced the development and direction of WAC work. In section four we include articles that show some of the ways WAC has expanded its reach over the years. The articles illustrate how WAC is "involved with or already has adapted to and informed recent initiatives in higher education," as McLeod notes (4, 2001), and how, increasingly, WAC-like initiatives are being developed in other countries, such as the UK. Finally, in section five we treat the topic of WAC and assessment. At the end of the book we provide an extended bibliography covering all of these areas, as well as a section entitled "How to Do WAC," which includes a list of essential readings for starting and sustaining WAC programs and resources for teaching writing across the disciplines. We trust readers will see the threads of inquiry that cut across all of these areas, and that these articles will assist current and future WAC leaders in finding ways to engage effectively in this inquiry at their own institutional settings.

As we wrote in our proposal for this collection, there has been a demonstrated and enduring interest in writing across the curriculum as a vehicle for pedagogical reform. Higher education administrators and faculty across disciplines continue to focus on WAC as a way to achieve literacy goals for all students in the increasingly diverse and globalized world of higher education — even as these goals are subject to intense debate and scrutiny. "Change is a journey, not a blueprint," McLeod and Miraglia observe in their introduction to *WAC for the New Millennium* (20), and this sourcebook is intended to help map that journey. This collection builds on the other compilations of WAC material and the rich resources of the WAC Clearinghouse by bringing together a new set of touchstone pieces, written by many of the leading voices in WAC, and providing the next generation of leaders with the broadest possible vision of WAC theory, practice, and research. We hope this sourcebook will be of interest to constituencies in all of these areas, but especially to the future leaders of WAC, including graduate students, teachers across disciplines, and faculty and administrators charged with building and/or resuscitating a WAC program.

We are grateful to Bedford/St. Martin's for producing this volume and to our editors Leasa Burton and Sarah Guariglia Macomber and their editorial assistant Allie Goldstein for their support and patience throughout the process. We were guided in that process by our reviewers — Susan McLeod, Mike Palmquist, Joan Mullin, Jeff Galin, and Jason Tougaw — who affirmed our selections and suggested several additions. Each provided advice and insights that led to the final shape of the sourcebook.

WORKS CITED

Ackerman, John. "The Promise of Writing to Learn." *Written Communication* 10.3 (1993): 334–70. Print.

Anson, Chris. "Toward a Multidimensional Model of Writing in the Academic Disciplines." *Writing in Academic Disciplines*. Ed. David Jolliffe. Norwood: Ablex, 1988. 35–88. Print.

Bazerman, Charles. "What Written Knowledge Does: Three Examples of Academic Discourse." *Philosophy of the Social Sciences* 2 (1981): 361–87. Print.

Bazerman, Charles, and David Russell, eds. *Landmark Essays on Writing Across the Curriculum*. Davis: Hermagoras, 1994. Print.

Bazerman, Charles, Joseph Little, Lisa Bethel, Teri Chavkin, Danielle Fouquette, and Janet Garufis. "Chapter Nine: New Programmatic Directions." *Reference Guide to Writing Across the Curriculum*. West Lafayette: Parlor; and WAC Clearinghouse, 2005. Print, eBook.

Beaufort, Anne. *College Writing and Beyond: A New Framework for University Writing Instruction*. Logan: Utah UP, 2007. Print.

Britton, James, Tony Burgess, Nancy Martin, Alex McLeod, and Harold Rosen. *The Development of Writing Abilities (11–18)*. London: Macmillan, 1975. Print.

Carroll, Lee Ann. *Rehearsing New Roles: How College Students Develop as Writers*. Carbondale: Southern Illinois UP, 2002. Print.

Casanave, Christine Pearson. *Writing Games: Multicultural Case Studies of Academic Literacy Practices in Higher Education*. Mahwah: Erlbaum, 2002. Print.

Fishman, Stephen, and Lucille McCarthy. "When Writing-to-Learn Is Not Enough." *Crossing the Curriculum: Multilingual Learners in College Classrooms*. Ed. Vivian Zamel and Ruth Spack. Mahwah: Erlbaum, 2004. 145–62. Print.

Fulwiler, Toby. *The Journal Book*. Portsmouth: Boynton, 1987. Print.

Fulwiler, Toby, and Art Young, eds. *Language Connections: Writing and Reading Across the Curriculum.* Urbana: NCTW, 1982. *The WAC Clearinghouse.* Web. 22 Apr. 2010.

Geisler, Cheryl. *Academic Literacy and the Nature of Expertise.* Hillsdale: Erlbaum, 1994. Print.

Griffin, C. Williams, ed. *Teaching Writing in All Disciplines.* San Francisco: Jossey-Bass, 1982. Print.

Herrington, Anne J. "Classrooms as Forums for Reasoning and Writing." *College Composition and Communication* 36.4 (1985): 404–18. Print.

Herrington, Anne, and Charles Moran, eds. *Writing, Teaching, and Learning in the Disciplines.* New York: MLA, 1992. Print.

Herrington, Anne J., and Marcia Curtis. *Persons in Process: Four Stories of Writing and Personal Development in College.* Urbana: NCTE, 2000. Print.

Hilgers, Thomas, Ann Shea Bayer, Monica Stitt-Bergh, and Megumi Taniguchi. "Doing More Than 'Thinning Out the Herd': How Eighty-Two College Seniors Perceived Writing-Intensive Classes." *Research in the Teaching of English,* 29.1 (1995): 59–87.

Jolliffe, David, ed. *Writing in Academic Disciplines.* Norwood: Ablex, 1988. Print.

Jolliffe, David, and Ellen M. Brier. "Studying Writers' Knowledge in Academic Disciplines." *Writing in Academic Disciplines.* Ed. David Jolliffe. Norwood: Ablex, 1988. 35–88. Print.

Jones, Robert and Joseph Comprone. "Where Do We Go Next in Writing Across the Curriculum?" *College Composition and Communication* 44.1 (1993): 59–68. Print.

Leki, Ilona. "Meaning and Development of Academic Literacy in a Second Language." *Multiple Literacies for the 21st Century.* Eds. Brian Huot, Beth Stroble, and Charles Bazerman. Cresskill: Hampton, 2004. 115–28. Print.

Mahala, Daniel. "Writing Utopias: Writing across the Curriculum and the Promise of Reform." *College English* 53 (1991): 773–89. Print.

Maimon, Elaine. "WAC: Past, Present and Future." *Teaching Writing in All Disciplines.* Ed. C. W. Griffin. San Francisco: Jossey-Bass, 1982. 67–82. Print.

Malinowitz, Harriet. "A Feminist Critique of Writing in the Disciplines." *Feminism and Composition Studies: In Other Words.* Eds. Susan Jarratt and Lynn Worsham. New York: MLA, 1998. 291–312. Print.

Marsella, Joy, Thomas Hilgers, and Clemence McLaren. "How Students Handle Writing Assignments: A Study of Eighteen Responses in Six Disciplines." *Writing, Teaching and Learning in the Disciplines.* Eds. Anne Herrington and Charles Moran. New York: MLA, 1992. 174–88. Print.

McCarthy, L. "A Stranger in Strange Lands: A College Student Writing Across the Curriculum." *Research in the Teaching of English* 21 (1987): 233–65. Print.

McCarthy, Lucille, and Stephen Fishman. "An ESL Writer and Her Discipline-Based Professor: Making Progress Even When Goals Don't Match." *Written Communication* 18.2 (2001): 180–228. Print.

McLeod, Susan H., ed. *Strengthening Programs for Writing Across the Curriculum.* San Francisco: Jossey-Bass, 1988. *The WAC Clearinghouse.* Web. 22 Apr. 2010.

McLeod, Susan. "Writing Across the Curriculum: The Second Stage, and Beyond." *College Composition and Communication* 40.3 (1989): 337–43. Print.

McLeod, Susan, Eric Miraglia, Margot Soven, and Chris Thaiss. *WAC for the New Millennium: Strategies for Continuing Writing-Across-the-Curriculum Programs.* Urbana: NCTE, 2001. Print.

McLeod, Susan. "The Pedagogy of Writing Across the Curriculum." *A Guide to Composition Pedagogies.* Eds. Gary Tate, Amy Rupiper, and Kurt Schick. New York: Oxford UP, 2001. 149–64. Print.

McLeod, Susan H., and Margot Soven, eds. *Writing Across the Curriculum: A Guide to Developing Programs.* Newbury Park: Sage, 1992. *The WAC Clearinghouse.* Web. 22 Apr. 2010.

McLeod, Susan, and Eric Miraglia. "Writing Across the Curriculum in a Time of Change." *WAC for the New Millennium: Strategies for Continuing Writing-Across-the-Curriculum.* Eds. Susan H. McLeod, Eric Miraglia, Margot Soven, and Christopher Thaiss. Urbana: NCTE, 2001. 1–27. Print.

Miller, Carolyn R. "Genre as Social Action." *Quarterly Journal of Speech* 70 (1984): 151–67. Print.

Miraglia, Eric, and Susan McLeod. "Whither WAC? Interpreting the Stories/Histories of Enduring WAC Programs." *Writing Program Administration* 20.3 (Spring 1997): 46–65. Print.

Reiss, Donna, and Art Young. "WAC Wired: Electronic Communication Across the Curriculum." *WAC for the New Millennium: Strategies for Continuing Writing-Across-the-Curriculum.* Eds. Susan H. McLeod, Eric Miraglia, Margot Soven, and Christopher Thaiss. Urbana: NCTE, 2001. 52–85. Print.

Reiss, Donna, Dickie Selfe, and Art Young, eds. *Electronic Communication Across the Curriculum.* Urbana: NCTE, 1998. Print.

Russell, David R. "Activity Theory and Its Implications for Writing Instruction." *Reconceiving Writing, Rethinking Writing Instruction.* Ed. Joseph Petraglia. Hillsdale: Erlbaum, 1995. 51–78. Print.

Russell, David R. "Rethinking Genre in School and Society: An Activity Theory Analysis." *Written Communication* 14 (1997): 504–54. Print.

Russell, David, and Arturo Yanez. " 'Big Picture People Rarely Become Historians': Genre Systems and the Contradictions of General Education." *Writing Selves/Writing Societies.* Eds. Charles Bazerman and David R. Russell. Fort Collins: WAC Clearinghouse and Mind, Culture, and Activity, 2003. 331–62. *The WAC Clearinghouse.* Web. 22 Apr. 2010.

Sommers, Nancy. "The Origins of *Shaped by Writing* and *Across the Drafts.*" *The Harvard Study of Undergraduate Writing.* Harvard College, n.d. Web. 25 Aug. 2006.

Sommers, Nancy, and Laura Saltz. "Across the Drafts." *College Composition and Communication.* 58:2 (2006): 248–57. Print.

Sternglass, Marilyn S. *Time to Know Them: A Longitudinal Study of Writing and Learning at the College Level.* Mahwah: Erlbaum, 1997. Print.

Stout, Barbara R., and Joyce N. Magnotto. "Writing across the Curriculum at Community Colleges." *New Directions for Teaching and Learning* 36 (1988): 21–30. Print.

Thaiss, Christopher, ed. *Writing to Learn: Essays and Reflections on Writing Across the Curriculum.* Dubuque: Kendall, 1983. Print.

Thaiss, Chris, and Tara Porter. "The State of WAC/WID in 2010: Methods and Results of the U.S. Survey of the International WAC/WID Mapping Project." *College Composition and Communication* 61:3 (February 2010): 535–70. Print.

Thaiss, Chris, and Terry Myers Zawacki. *Engaged Writers and Dynamic Disciplines: Research on the Academic Writing Life.* Portsmouth, NH: Boynton/Cook-Heinemann, 2006. Print.

Villanueva, Victor. "The Politics of Literacy Across the Curriculum." *WAC for the New Millennium: Strategies for Continuing Writing-Across-the-Curriculum.* Eds. Susan H. McLeod, Eric Miraglia, Margot Soven, and Christopher Thaiss. Urbana: NCTE, 2001. 165–78. Print.

Walvoord, Barbara, and Lucille McCarthy. *Thinking and Writing in College: A Naturalistic Study of Students in Four Disciplines.* Urbana: NCTE, 1990. Print.

Walvoord, Barbara Fassler. "The Future of WAC." *College English* 58 (1996): 58–91. Print.

Young, Art, and Toby Fulwiler, eds. *Writing Across the Disciplines: Research into Practice.* Upper Montclair: Boynton, 1986. Print.

PART ONE

Charting the WAC Movement

Introduction to Part One

As we have argued in our introduction, the history of WAC is one of inquiry into language and learning — a history deeply situated in the institutional structures and dynamics of higher education. As the readings in this section show, the WAC movement has always responded to and moved in line with changing exigencies for institutional reform, as well as advances in theory and research in education, linguistics, psychology, and composition. The ongoing efforts to chart the progress of the WAC movement speak to this dynamism and also to a certain self-consciousness among program leaders about the role of WAC in the context of other higher education reforms.

We begin Part One with David Russell's "The Writing-Across-the-Curriculum Movement: 1970–1990," which describes the birth of WAC in the early 70s. Russell shows how the growth of the WAC movement corresponded with a need to rethink language instruction in the midst of other cultural, political, social, and educational "upheavals," among which were pressures for greater access to higher education for those who had previously been excluded. As he explains, these "waves [of reform] met in a dramatic burst of interest in writing instruction and produced what is certainly the most widespread and sustained reform movement in cross-curricular writing instruction."

Following Russell, we turn to Alan Bullock's "Language Across the Curriculum." James Britton served as a lead member on the Committee of Enquiry responsible for the report, which presents a compelling case for the complex interrelationship of learning and language across grade levels and disciplines. While focused on K–12 classrooms in the UK, the chapter is prescient in laying out many of the vital areas of inquiry WAC practitioners in the United States have addressed over the years. Bullock clearly anticipates what Russell refers to as WAC's two central, pedagogically focused questions: how will students use writing, and how can we equip them to enter different discourse communities?

In "The Pedagogy of Writing Across the Curriculum," Susan McLeod describes the centrality of pedagogy to answering these questions. Invoking the rich history of WAC practice, she describes the field's fundamental concern for student and faculty learning processes, the former as writers and the latter as teachers of writing in the disciplines. She also addresses the relationship of WAC pedagogy to first-year composition courses, general education, and collaborative learning. McLeod explains how genre and activity theory are informing WAC approaches to teaching and learning. Additionally, she sharply refutes those who have sought to portray writing to learn and learning to write in the disciplines as contradictory approaches, arguing that the two are "complementary and even synergistic." (In this collection, we too have sought to avoid such false dichotomies by framing WAC as an inquiry-based approach to language and learning that supports both of these central positions and the other streams of activity that have emerged from the movement.)

Donna LeCourt's "WAC as Critical Pedagogy: The Third Stage?" takes us in another direction, that of critiques of WAC, which have tended to occur in response to different theoretical moments in composition studies. LeCourt's article is but one example of many calls for WAC to embrace a more critical pedagogy. Her critique and others have served over the years to sharpen and refine WAC, as they are taken up and responded to by scholars in the field. Most valuable in LeCourt's argument, from our point of view, is the notion that student writing should be valued as a genre of its own alongside established knowledge within the disciplines, which, as Charles Bazerman and others have argued, are not monolithic "communities," but rather contested spaces constructed by individuals with rhetorical motives.

We conclude Part One with Chris Thaiss's "Theory in WAC: Where Have We Been, Where Are We Going?" which presents an overview of WAC theory, highlighting the complexity of its most basic terms: *writing*, *across*, and *curriculum*. This selection, taken from McLeod et al.'s collection *WAC for the New Millennium*, affirms the roots of WAC theory, examines its shortcomings, and challenges practitioners to consider the complex ways technology and the fluid nature of disciplines are shaping WAC's future.

1

The Writing-Across-the-Curriculum Movement: 1970–1990

DAVID R. RUSSELL

C̲ross-curricular writing programs were almost always a response to a perceived need for greater access, greater equity. They set out to assimilate, integrate, or (in the current phrasing) initiate previously excluded students by means of language instruction. So, it is not surprising that the greatest efforts came as the pressure for access increased. The cooperation movement and the first general-education initiatives began just after the turn of the century, when middle-class, rural, and immigrant students were clambering for admission; the core-curriculum experiments at Chicago and elsewhere, as well as the correlated curriculum movement, flourished in the 1930s when economic pressures forced students out of the job market and back into school — and when social agitation for egalitarian reforms was at its height in modern America; the communications movement and the postwar reforms in general education were explicit responses to the massive influx of GI's into higher education; and the current WAC movement was born in the early 1970s, when open admissions in universities and racial integration in secondary schools forced educators to rethink language instruction.

When pressures for greater access abated in the late 1950s and early 1960s, writing in the disciplines received little attention within English, as pressures for disciplinary excellence increased. At the secondary level, English, like the sciences, was immediately influenced by Jerome S. Bruner's emphasis on the structure of the disciplines. In the early 1960s, federally funded Project English centers pursued a disciplinary model, strongly influenced by the new-critical approach to literature, and had distant relations with other disciplines.[1] However, the emphasis on disciplinary rigor, higher standards, and education of the "gifted" students ignored Bruner's deeper theorizing on the process (rather than on the product) of education and on the role of language in all learning.[2] Once again, writing remained largely transparent. Only later, in the 1970s, would composition teachers begin to explore his work on the unique role that writing plays in learning.[3] And only in the 1980s did writing

From *Writing in the Academic Disciplines: A Curricular History*, 2nd ed. Carbondale: Southern Illinois UP, 2002. 271–307.

teachers and researchers begin to investigate the ways in which students can gradually and systematically acquire "the underlying principles that give structure to a subject" through writing in the disciplines.[4]

Higher education also had more pressing matters to attend to than writing instruction. It accomplished a vast building program while bearing much of the brunt of America's social and political upheaval. The "baby boomers" entering college allowed old institutions to keep both enrollment and admission standards high. And the system built a host of new institutions or expanded old ones into "regional universities" to meet the demands for higher education of excluded students. Indeed, the 1960s saw massive cutbacks in general-composition courses; and despite a few isolated experiments, writing instruction stayed in its usual places. Almost one-third of all four-year colleges and universities dropped or reduced their composition requirements, with many of them abolishing freshman composition altogether.[5]

Yet the 1960s set into motion the forces that produced the current writing-across-the-curriculum (WAC) movement, or rather amplified those waves of reform that, moving in several different directions, had successively rocked American language instruction for a century. In the 1970s those waves met in a dramatic burst of interest in writing instruction and produced what is certainly the most widespread and sustained reform movement in cross-curricular writing instruction.

One legacy of the 1960s for writing instruction was ideological. The political and cultural upheaval of the decade revived the communitarian vision in American social and educational thought that had spurred previous generations of curricular reformers, but it had its own antiauthoritarian, utopian, and romantic cast. Such theorists as Peter Elbow, Ken Macrorie, Donald Graves, and James Moffett profoundly influenced the generation of teachers and curricular reformers who were nurtured in the 1960s and gave to the WAC movement its focus on the classroom as community; its student-centered pedagogy, often with a subversive tinge; and its neoromantic, expressivist assumptions, reprising themes familiar among child-centered progressives of the 1930s.[6]

There were also crucial foreign influences. At the 1966 Dartmouth Seminar, a meeting of NCTE leaders with their counterparts in Britain's National Association of Teachers of English (NATE), Americans pursuing rigid disciplinary or industrial models were fundamentally challenged by the British emphasis on the linguistic, social, and personal development of the student, "a personal growth model, based on principles of language in operation and creative expression."[7] Loosely structured classroom "talk," dramatic improvisation, and personal response to literature took precedence over disciplinary knowledge embodied in literary classics and rhetorical or grammatical principles. Students' own creations were valued as literature and treated as texts worthy of serious analysis. The British were also reprising themes from the American progressive tradition — Dewey, in a broad way, but mainly expressivists in the "sentimental" progressive tradition, such as Hughes Mearns and Harold Rugg. However, the British, like Bruner, also had Continental influences, notably Jean Piaget and Lev Vygotsky, who had studied the relationship between language and cognitive development in children. One British educator at the Dartmouth Seminar, James Britton, would shortly provide an influential theoretical framework to link the development of writing in the disciplines with personal writing, a connection the American progressives had not yet systematically explored.

But the communitarian and expressivist vision, though broadly influential, could only have shaped WAC through another legacy of the 1960s: the newly professionalized writing instructor. During the 1960s, the interest in writing instruction that had been evident in the communications movement coalesced into a "revival of rhetoric," which not only gave composition teachers a professional identity apart from literature (the MLA had shown diminishing interest in composition teaching since disbanding its pedagogical section in 1903) but also provided institutions with recognized experts who could design and implement curricular reforms in writing instruction.[8] The CCCC outgrew the communications movement to become a large professional organization for writing teachers, with its own traditions of research that increasingly went beyond freshman-composition courses to investigate wider issues of writing and learning.

The decade of the 1960s left its greatest legacy, however, in less obvious, though far more important changes in the structure and social role of mass education. The first was racial integration. As America's secondary schools and colleges haltingly moved during the 1960s to implement *Brown v. Board of Education of Topeka, Kansas,* the social differentiation of schooling became glaringly apparent, especially so in language policy. In the wake of the civil rights movement and the race riots of the late 1960s, as the nation began to take affirmative action to rectify educational inequality, schools and colleges faced — many for the first time — the task of teaching the dominant language to excluded populations.

The second was the massive boom in higher education, which created far more — and more differentiated — institutions of higher learning, preparing students from increasingly diverse backgrounds (primarily first-generation college students) for increasingly diverse roles. By 1980 there were 3,125 institutions, up from 2,006 in 1960. Significantly, many were open admission. Like integration, the rapid growth in numbers forced colleges to face the task of initiating students whose language background was radically different. For example, one of those new institutions, City University of New York (CUNY), began project SEEK in 1965 to prepare students whose grades excluded them from admission. Social and political upheavals in the late 1960s forced CUNY to begin open admissions in 1970, five years earlier than planned. Out of that experience, Mina Shaughnessy, a former copy editor and part-time writing instructor at CUNY, founded the study of *basic writing,* a new, more politically and pedagogically sensitive approach to "remedial" writing instruction, which would become important in the growth of the WAC movement.[9]

Moreover, the new institutions, and increasingly the old ones as well, came to be managed by a new class of academic executive. These managers —

like their secondary-school counterparts half a century earlier — adopted the techniques and attitudes of industrial management in an attempt to make the institutions more effective in instruction and more accountable to the society that supported them and employed their "products." In the late 1970s the new academic executive would discover in WAC a tool for curricular reform and faculty development.[10]

Finally, in the wake of the social upheaval of the 1960s — much of it focused in schools (through integration) and colleges (through student political movements) — government and industry became directly involved in those social aspects of education that bore on language and culture. Though the post-Sputnik National Defense Education Act had been belatedly extended to the humanities and social sciences in the early 1960s, federal and private granting agencies had paid little attention to writing instruction until the educational crises of the late 1960s and 1970s. But as pressures for widening access increased, new public and private funds fueled the WAC reform efforts of the coming decades and encouraged their spread.[11]

In the early 1970s, these social and institutional factors produced the widest social and institutional demand for writing instruction since the mass-education system had founded composition a century earlier to solve the problem of integrating new students into academia. An outcry against "illiteracy" in the 1970s, like those of the 1870s, 1910s, and 1950s, coincided with the attempt to broaden access to schools and colleges for students who had formerly been excluded from them; though the 1970s crisis, like its predecessors, almost ignored the complex political issue of rising social expectations and focused instead on the popular issue of declining standards. Like the earlier literacy campaigns, the new one became a cause célèbre of the reformist press. The national press greeted with shock and indignation the release of the 1974 National Assessment of Education Progress (NAEP) results on writing ability, a study of actual student writing (not another multiple-choice test) conducted every five years by the Education Commission of the States. The 1974 NAEP showed an apparent decline in some areas of secondary students' performance since the test was first administered in 1969. *Newsweek*'s 9 December 1975 cover story, "Why Johnny Can't Write," brought to a head the national discussion — some said crisis — over literacy, particularly writing instruction, with its inflammatory conclusion: "Willy-nilly, the U.S. educational system is spawning a generation of semi-literates." Even NEH Chairman Ronald Berman fanned the flames with his warning that the results presaged "a massive regression toward the intellectually invertebrate." The next NAEP administration (1979) revealed an all-time high in many of the very areas that had shown the greatest decline five years earlier, leading the Education Commission to conclude that "changes in overall writing quality are basically undramatic for any particular age group" and to recommend "caution in making global statements about writing."[12] But the nation was already aroused, and the educational establishment had already mobilized to meet the crisis. As in previous decades, with the coming of heretofore excluded groups to academia, there were also fresh attempts to broaden responsibility for language instruction. This time, though, the resources were greater, the organization more flexible, and the theoretical basis firmer.

THEORETICAL BASES: JAMES BRITTON AND THE BRITISH

In 1975, as the newest American literacy crisis reached a fever pitch, two new British books were published that gave researchers and reformers in composition a name and a theory to catalyze disparate experiments into a full-fledged educational movement. *A Language for Life* (the Bullock Report) and James Britton's *Development of Writing Abilities (11–18)* both came out of the British tradition of educational reform, which had its first impact on America at the 1966 Dartmouth Seminar.[13]

In 1972 Margaret Thatcher, who was then secretary of state for education and science, asked Sir Alan Bullock, vice-chancellor of Oxford, to head yet another of the blue-ribbon educational commissions that Britain periodically forms to look into some current crisis in education. Britain had weathered its own literacy crisis only a few years before America's — also precipitated by pressure for widening access to comprehensive secondary schools and new universities. The commission was thus charged with reporting on "all aspects of teaching the use of English" in British education. In 1975 its six-hundred-page report reached a more informed conclusion than had most American educators about the extent and cause of the "crisis." While it is "extremely difficult to say whether standards of written and spoken English have fallen," the report said, changing patterns of employment and higher education are today "making more widespread demands on reading and writing skill and therefore exposing deficiencies that have escaped attention in the past."[14]

Its recommendations generally followed progressive lines instead of remedial lines, emphasizing informal classroom talk, especially in small groups; expressive writing; and teacher-student collaboration. The commission particularly listened to a theory of natural language acquisition and development propounded by James Britton, one of its members, whose 1970 book *Language and Learning* had argued that language is central to learning because through language we "organize our representation of the world."[15] Britton's study of children's language acquisition convinced him that, for students to learn language effectively, the classroom, like the home, must have a climate of trust and shared contexts for purposeful communication. Britton was a chief contributor to the Bullock Report's chapter entitled "Language Across the Curriculum," which emphasized the roles played by language in discipline-specific learning. "While many teachers recognize that their aim is to initiate students into a mode of analysis," the report concluded, "they rarely recognize the linguistic implications of doing so. They do not recognize, in short, that the mental processes they seek to foster are outcomes of a development that originates in speech."[16]

Britton also led the British writing-across-the-curriculum research project, which produced the other influential 1975 book, *The Development of Writing Abilities (11–18)*. Britton and his colleagues conducted a survey of student writing for the Schools Council, a prestigious advisory group composed of leaders from business, government, and education. That survey was based on Britton's theory that children develop writing ability by moving from personal forms of writing (what he calls *expressive* and *poetic*) to more public, workaday forms, which communicate information (what he calls *transactional*). Britton and his associates found that the overwhelming majority of writing in British schools was transactional, that students were given very few opportunities to do expressive or poetic writing, and thus, he argued, they had little chance of developing in a natural way their writing abilities. The Schools Council's writing-across-the-curriculum project recommended a thorough revamping of pedagogy to rectify the imbalance.[17]

On reaching America, Britton's theory and the British pedagogical reforms found a warm reception among reformers in composition who were doing research along similar lines. The British reformers gave the Americans a new theory, a new set of tactics, political and pedagogical, and, most important, a new title for their response to the most recent literacy crisis: writing across the curriculum. In the spring of 1977, America's leading researcher in writing development, Janet Emig, published a seminal essay, "Writing as a Mode of Learning," which wove together the British research, the Continental theories of Vygotsky and Piaget, and American theorists' ideas, from Dewey, Bruner, and George Kelly, to support the central contention of the nascent WAC movement: that writing has "unique value for learning."[18] Robert P. Parker and others organized an NEH seminar for college teachers at Rutgers in the summer of 1977 to introduce the new theories and pedagogical techniques to fifty American composition teachers in higher education. Future leaders of the WAC movement, such as Toby Fulwiler, were exposed to the works of Britton, Moffett, and others in a writing-rich workshop environment of the kind that would become the hallmark of the WAC movement. In the next few years, the CCCC and NCTE held convention sessions on WAC, and the journals in composition and English education published many articles on writing and language development, writing and learning. The movement had found its intellectual moorings.

The choice of Britton and the British is surprising in some respects. The British educational system, unlike America's, is based on external written examinations — essays that are graded outside the classroom, the school, even the country. Teachers across the curriculum must and do teach students to write for those exams, and they have a long tradition of doing so. British reform, then, did not aim to introduce or extend writing across the curriculum, as in America, only to modify the kinds of writing and its pedagogical uses.[19] America's rapid adoption of Britton's theory is surprising as well. The idea that language is central to learning forms a recurring theme in Deweyan progressives' thought, beginning with Dewey himself. And Britton was profoundly influenced by his American contemporary Bruner. Britton's discourse classification system is in many ways similar to the theories of Americans James Moffett and James L. Kinneavy. But Britton entered the American scene at a climactic moment. His student-centered pedagogy struck a deep chord within American reformers fresh from the 1960s' climate of experiment with radically student-centered education; but despite its domestic roots, Britton's work carried few of the "educationist" overtones of the discredited American progressive tradition. His theory was simple in its outlines and readily adapted to a student-centered pedagogy, without the complexities of rhetorical or communications theories, which had been the staple of the rhetoric revival in the 1950s and 1960s.

Perhaps most importantly, Britton and the British popularized a methodology that fit well with student-centered pedagogy: an adaptation of anthropological descriptive inquiry variously called *classroom ethnography, naturalistic inquiry,* or *qualitative research.* He and his associates entered classrooms to listen and observe, to learn from teachers and students, not to prescribe "teacherproof" methods and test them in controlled statistical trials. Broadly empirical, yet humanistic, these methods seemed to bridge the gulf in American academia between social science and the humanities, a gulf that English departments were encountering as composition research, with its social science (education department) model, encountered the departments' liberal culture.

WAC in Secondary Schools

In the 1970s, the ferment in public schools brought about by racial integration gave new life to the old industrial model, now transformed by a "systems approach" into the back-to-the-basics movement. Conceived as a corrective to the laissez-faire educational approaches of the late 1960s, the back-to-the-basics movement introduced competency-based education in the three R's — little more than the familiar remedial labs and workbooks, though supported now by computers and federal monies.[20] Administrators spoke of "accountability" and "behavioral objectives," and textbooks stressed mechanical drill and practice, reinforcing the remedial, atomistic "skills" conception of writing — as well as the myth of transience. The few writing-across-the-curriculum programs that this movement produced were, like their forebears in the 1910s, little more than "grammar and spelling across the curriculum."

But one program sympathetic to Britton's approach achieved national prominence and influenced cross-curricular writing instruction in secondary and higher education: the Bay Area Writing Project (BAWP). In 1971, administrators at the University of California at Berkeley, recalling the demise of the Prose Improvement Committee almost a decade earlier, began a program to improve the writing of college freshmen by improving their secondary-school writing instruction. In 1974, BAWP held its first summer institutes for area high-school teachers — primarily composition teachers, though disciplines from history to home economics were represented. The idea was not to supply them with "teacher-proof" materials or prescribe expert-developed methods but to provide a forum for successful teachers to share their insights and methods for using writing in the classroom. Participants presented their own methods, shared experiences, and, most importantly, wrote a great deal themselves. In this collegial environment, the BAWP staff, while disclaiming any single theory or methodology, could disseminate the results of composition theory and research that they considered most important: the work of Britton, Francis Christiansen, Moffett, Macrorie, and others.

Two years later, in 1976, the California Department of Education adopted BAWP as a model for staff development statewide and, as with some later WAC programs, funded it with federal monies (earmarked for compensatory education under Title IV C of the National Defense Education Act). In 1977 the NEH provided money for a National Writing Project (NWP) at sites in several states. By 1979 there were sixteen California sites and sixty-eight others nationwide, each offering summer institutes, a newsletter, and in-service follow-up visits in the schools by NWP staff members.[21]

In 1979, Arthur N. Applebee conducted a national survey of writing in the schools. He and his collaborators found that there was little extended writing, though a great deal of copying, filling in of blanks, and other "writing without composing," as he called it. Such extended writing as there was fit the pattern the British had found: transactional writing for an audience of the teacher in the role of examiner.[22] Further studies have confirmed these findings and sought to understand the resistance to secondary-school pedagogical reform in the structure of mass education. The American secondary-school system faces unique difficulties in implementing WAC programs. The system is organized on an industrial model, which uses writing primarily to assess students' performance, not to improve it. Teachers operating within this system lack the time and training necessary to integrate meaningfully process-oriented writing into their instruction. Even education departments have sometimes attempted to "reign in" such efforts as BAWP, for it challenges their research paradigm and their professional turf.[23] Furthermore, research into writing and learning in the disciplines has not yet formulated an analysis of the ways in which writing can be meaningfully integrated into discipline-specific learning activities to produce increasingly more sophisticated levels of understanding and writing performance — the kinds of pedagogical "scaffolding" that Bruner suggested in the 1960s.[24]

However, in the 1980s, with the spread of Britton's theories and the WAC movement in higher education, many secondary schools and school districts began successful WAC programs despite the obstacles. With support from administrators, curriculum coordinators in some districts began in-service training programs for teachers in the disciplines, produced extensive materials to aid teachers in their efforts to incorporate meaningful writing activities into their content teaching, and provided ongoing support for these activities. In several states, school districts began cooperative programs with universities to reform writing instruction.[25] And some states passed regulations to encourage or even mandate writing instruction, though these efforts have been more prevalent in elementary schools and secondary-school English courses than in the disciplines. Several of the content areas (particularly social studies) have also begun to investigate uses of writing in secondary-school teaching, and a small but growing literature on secondary-school writing in the disciplines now exists.[26] These efforts suggest that, during its first decade in the secondary schools, WAC has had an increasing influence and in some districts has become part of the institutional structure. Although secondary education resists deep pedagogical and curricular change, WAC programs have survived and grown, building on BAWP's collegial approach to reform.

THE BIRTH OF WAC IN HIGHER EDUCATION

Though WAC projects in the United Kingdom were almost exclusively concerned with elementary and secondary education and James Britton's first American followers were secondary-school reformers, his most visible influence was on higher education. The first WAC programs in higher education appeared in small, private liberal arts colleges with selective admissions, where general education and other interdisciplinary programs had always found a more congenial atmosphere. In the 1970s, enrollment and affirmative action pressures sparked a renewed interest in literacy issues and produced experiments in cross-curricular writing instruction. Carleton College in Northfield, Minnesota, faced problems of rising enrollment (a near doubling in five years) and "the diversity in ability that accompanies the increase in numbers of students," as one faculty member tactfully put it.[27] The college first responded by reducing the composition requirement and exempting more students, as other "abolitionist" colleges had done in the 1960s, and like many colleges in the early 1970s, it established special sections to allow for that "diversity in ability." But the college also instituted what it called "the college writing proficiency requirement" to give "formal recognition of the fact that teachers in departments other than English may assume the responsibility of judging a student's ability to read and write well" (Larsen 8). Volunteering faculty attended a two-week conference on improving and evaluating student writing in all courses, beginning in the summer of 1974. The faculty then developed criteria that allowed students to satisfy the proficiency requirement through writing in courses from several departments. Moreover, a Carleton administrator, Harriet W. Sheridan, set up a program of "writing fellows" to tutor fellow undergraduates on writing assignments for their courses in the disciplines, an idea that would be developed elsewhere in the coming decade.

Further south, Central College, a liberal arts institution of twelve hundred students in Pella, Iowa, began a similar program, which embodied most of the central features of what came to be called the writing-across-the-curriculum movement: faculty development workshops, a faculty-wide supervisory committee, a writing lab with a writing specialist as coordinator, student tutors, departmental responsibility for students' writing proficiency, a system of student writing portfolios, and external funding (federal and corporate) to defray start-up costs.

Faced with rising numbers of students whose reading and writing skills the faculty considered inadequate, a group of Central College faculty, led by Barbara Fassler, began in 1971 a weeklong seminar, held once each semester, to discuss student writing. In 1975, as part of curriculum restructuring, the college opened a writing lab and trained upper-division students to tutor writing. With a grant from HEW for "Special Services for Economically Disadvantaged Students," the college hired a full-time "skills coordinator" to supervise the program, recruited a "skills council" from the faculty to oversee the program, and in 1976 voted to give each department responsibility for teaching and certifying the reading, writing, and oral communications skills of its students. Central College then obtained further funding from the Exxon Corporation to expand its peer-tutoring program.[28] The skills coordinator organized workshops to train faculty from other disciplines to foster (and evaluate) student writing in their classes.

The most influential of the early private, liberal arts college WAC programs — inspired in large part by the Carleton College experiment — was at Beaver College in Glenside, Pennsylvania (with some eight hundred students). In December 1975, the *Newsweek* exposé led the dean to call in the new composition director, Elaine P. Maimon, and charge her with the task of improving student writing in conjunction with the Educational Policy Committee (EPC). Rather than adopting a remedial approach, as some advocated, she and several colleagues from psychology, anthropology, and biology interested in student writing began sharing ideas and collaborating on research and pedagogy to "galvanize scholarly and research interests" in composition.[29] By 1976, the ground of argument had moved away from remediation, and the EPC endorsed wider-scale faculty involvement in writing instruction. Maimon obtained outside funding to organize workshops for faculty, beginning in 1977, which treated writing as a serious intellectual and scholarly activity (Harriet W. Sheridan from Carleton led the first one, using as the first text Aristotle's *Rhetoric*). A $207,000 NEH grant in 1977 funded a program to create "a liberal arts college committed to teaching writing in all parts of the curriculum." The earlier informal collaboration among colleagues led to a college-wide "course cluster" experiment. In each cluster, three instructors (one from the English department) met to plan ways to make writing, in Maimon's words, "a natural part of each class meeting." In these clusters, loosely organized around a few themes or a text — such as Charles Darwin's *On the Origin of Species* for a history-biology–British literature cluster — students wrote projects acceptable in two courses.[30]

The Beaver College program emphasized the connections between writing instruction and faculty research. Writing and its teaching were treated as serious intellectual activities intimately related to disciplinary inquiry, activities that go beyond mere skill building or correction of surface features. As Maimon put it, "The teaching of writing is scholarly not scullery."[31] At one level, of course, the emphasis on research and scholarship simply reflected the growing seriousness of the new writing professionals who came out of the revival of rhetoric in the 1960s. Maimon was deeply influenced by Shaughnessy, Britton, Emig, and others, who valorized composition as a field of study. But there were also political advantages. The attempt to recreate the role of writing instruction in higher education by giving it the mantle of academic respectability (research) was an essential element of WAC's success in institutional settings where research was valued over teaching.

At the deepest level, reconceiving writing as a serious intellectual activity, worthy of study and consideration by academia, was a means of breaking down the century-old academic notion of writing as an elementary mechanical skill or a romantic inspiration and replacing it with transactional theories and student-centered pedagogies in the Deweyan progressive tradition. (Maimon called Dewey the "presiding ghost" in her early efforts.) The workshops gave many faculty their first opportunity to discuss writing and teaching in an environment of communal scholarship, without the "educationist" stigma or the belletristic assumptions of the English department determining the ground. In a collegial, interdisciplinary atmosphere, a faculty member could explore the relationships between the structure of the discipline, as revealed in its discourse, and the ways in which students learned that structure and discourse.

Such dialogue was not without its conflicts, of course. There were interdisciplinary battles over the nature of "jargon" and of "proper" academic writing. The ambiguous role of the English department, where many faculty had taught writing but few had studied or taught it in contexts outside their own field, produced other jurisdictional battles — an experience repeated often elsewhere.[32] But in this new forum, writing could not remain transparent. And the specialization of academic discourse, the dependence of writing on discipline-specific contexts and genres, could no longer hide behind unexamined notions of a universal "plain English" or a "general reader." Discussions of the various contexts of academic writing and the genres that those contexts produced was deeply stimulating, by all accounts. Out of the collaboration of Maimon and her colleagues grew an influential composition textbook, *Writing in the Arts and Sciences*, one of the first texts to portray students wrestling with the intellectual complexities of assignments from many disciplines, and federally funded seminars at Beaver drew faculty from across the country who founded WAC programs at many kinds of institutions.

WAC at Public Colleges and Universities

The mid 1970s' literacy crisis also prompted several public colleges and universities to institute programs that spread the WAC movement to this, the largest segment of American higher education — and the segment most affected by pressure for widening access. Some programs grew out of the abolition of freshman composition. For example, at Eastern Oregon State College, a four-year college of seventeen hundred students, the faculty reduced the composition requirement in 1965. In 1975, during the national debate over students' writing proficiency, the faculty abolished the course requirement in favor of a proficiency exam. Although most students continued to take optional composition courses to prepare for the exam, some faculty in other disciplines added or increased writing assignments and instruction in their courses. Three years later the college began a voluntary summer training workshop for faculty, though it was discontinued in 1983 as the program struggled to maintain the commitment of faculty.[33]

The most famous of the WAC programs at public institutions is at Michigan Technological University (with some six thousand students). The program began after the usual complaints from faculty about student writing, complaints bolstered by the *Newsweek* article and other national publicity. There were demands for higher standards, specifically a junior-level objective examination over grammar and mechanics, with English department remediation for those who failed. Instead of adopting the usual belletristic and remedial approaches, the head of the humanities department, Art Young, and the new composition director, Toby Fulwiler, set about designing a program more appropriate to a technical university, one that would involve many faculty in improving student writing. At the 1977 CCCC convention, the two learned of programs at Central College, Oregon State, and elsewhere; and at the Rutgers NEH summer seminar, Fulwiler was exposed to the new British and American composition research and, more importantly, to the writing-rich workshop environment of the NWP used by such seminar leaders as Lee Odell (a NWP meeting was also going on in a nearby room). There Fulwiler conceived two central elements of the Michigan Tech approach: writing workshops to change faculty attitudes toward the role of language in the classroom and journal writing across the curriculum. Young and Fulwiler then convinced the Michigan Tech faculty to provide opportunities for student writing, supported by a writing lab in the humanities division. In October 1977 Fulwiler and Young led the first of their influential faculty writing retreats (at a mountain lodge in northern Michigan). They borrowed Britton's fundamental notions of the importance of language — particularly expressive language — for active, student-centered learning and his focus on teachers as the agents of curricular change. They borrowed their methods primarily from the expressivist pedagogical tradition of the 1960s: free writing, personal journal writing, and dialogue, from Peter Elbow (*Writing Without Teachers*), Donald Murray, James Moffett, and others. But they also stressed what had come to be known as "the writing process": an emphasis on heuristic invention or "prewriting" and conceptual revision rather than mere proofreading for mechanical correctness.[34]

Art Young described the response of the fifteen volunteer faculty as "heart warming if not epidemical."[35] The most enthusiastic faculty described it in terms of a conversion experience: it restored a sense of their mission as teachers and their identity as part of a collegial academic environment. During the following year, the retreatants revised their courses to incorporate more writing, with the help of several two-hour follow-up sessions and a WAC newsletter. More faculty retreats, this time funded by the General Motors Corporation, spread the word across campus, and the English department's commitment to hiring writing specialists and their ongoing research and evaluation of WAC further drove the program.

Elsewhere, large research universities were forced to approach WAC with more complex organization and less dependence on the faculty consciousness-raising model, as Richard Lanham has described Michigan Tech's approach.[36] The most common model at large research universities was and is a campus-wide writing requirement administered by a committee of faculty from several disciplines, which students satisfy by taking a certain number of "writing intensive" (WI) courses offered in several — sometimes all — departments. Faculty in each discipline agree to assign a specified amount of writing, sometimes with a revision requirement, and to guide the students in writing the assignments. These WI courses usually have fewer students than typical sections so that faculty will have time to grade assignments. Often the university also requires one or more general-composition courses of most freshmen and makes a writing lab available to students in the WI courses. For example, at the University of Michigan at Ann Arbor, the first large research university to adopt the model, the interdisciplinary English Composition Board oversees a large number of WI courses, approving syllabi, providing training for faculty and teaching assistants, and administering a writing lab, which supports the WI's.[37]

Realizing that faculty in large research universities often give undergraduate teaching lower priority, other institutions have revived (without realizing it) the plan of the 1950s Prose Improvement Committee and focused their efforts on training graduate assistants or adjunct faculty to teach writing in support of regular courses — often large-enrollment lecture classes. In 1975 the University of Washington began a program of linking writing courses to large lecture classes — usually lower-division general-education or honors classes. It was expanded in 1978 with a Fund for the Improvement of Post-secondary Education (FIPSE) grant and grew to its present level of twelve Writing Link sections, as they are called. Students enrolled in specified lecture courses have the option of also taking its Writing Link course: prepared, taught, and graded separately by a TA or an adjunct instructor who attends the lecture course and structures the Writing Link assignments around the lecture course's material and schedule. About 10 percent to 15 percent of the students in the participating lecture courses also enroll in the Writing Link. Contact between the two instructors may be minimal or extensive, depending on their relationship. But any such contact between writing instructors and other faculty promotes discussion of writing and learning issues, which would likely not exist otherwise. Similar programs at UC San Diego, UCLA, and elsewhere use the linked-course concept in upper-division classes, often with support from a peer-tutoring program, a writing lab, or some combination of other models.[38]

A less common model for WAC in some public midsize and large institutions is peer tutoring, another means of getting around the problem of recruiting faculty whose time and interests may not allow them to restructure their courses to include more writing. In 1972 programs began at Brooklyn College and at California State College, Dominguez Hills.[39] Peer tutors were recruited from undergraduates through a competitive program, trained in writing instruction, then assigned to a particular course (as at Cal State) or to a writing lab (as at Brooklyn College). Based on research in group process conducted in the 1960s, the peer-tutoring model addresses what Burton Clark and Martin Trow concluded in 1966 was a central problem of mass higher education: to overcome students' "indifference to ideas, and the irrelevance of their education to their associations and relationships with other students." The research of Kenneth A. Bruffee of Brooklyn College on group process in writing and learning was particularly influential in the development of this aspect of WAC.[40] Paired courses and peer tutoring are what Tori Haring-Smith calls "bottom-up" approaches, attempts to influence faculty to use and value writing in their teaching by creating an atmosphere among the students where writing is used, valued, and expected.[41]

EVOLVING MODELS

In the 1980s, the movement spread to many more institutions. Theories, methods, and organizational models of the pioneering programs gained currency among administrators and faculty in a multitude of ways: through sessions devoted to WAC at professional conferences such as NCTE and CCCC; through summer workshops at Beaver College, the University of Chicago, and elsewhere; through hundreds of retreats and workshops nationwide, led by Fulwiler, Young, Maimon, Fassler, and others; and through articles in the pedagogical journals of several disciplines. In time, some administrators, as well as composition specialists, came to see these programs not only as ways of improving student writing but also as faculty development efforts, a means of initiating discussions of pedagogy among faculty and increasing contact between faculty and students.

Just as WAC gained momentum, however, the political climate of educational reform changed profoundly. Enrollment at traditional four-year colleges and universities decreased as the baby boom generation left college, though enrollment increased in community colleges (as did WAC programs).[42] Pressure for affirmative action and integration subsided; minority enrollment began to decline in higher education. The literacy crisis of the 1970s, with its impetus for school writing reforms, became in the 1980s a return to general-education core courses. In a spate of highly publicized reports on secondary and higher education, several national commissions recommended a return to "common learnings" or "core curricula," and while each of the commissions recommended strengthening programs to improve students' writing skills (and in some cases specifically praised WAC efforts), they had little to say about discipline-specific writing instruction and, indeed, criticized the increasing specialization of education. In the absence of social pressures for widening access, the focus of language policy shifted to the agenda of liberal culture, now under the rubric of *cultural literacy*. In the curricular ferment that accompanied the publication of the reports, WAC became only one of many reform movements, though it served as a model for several: speech communications, critical thinking, ethics, computer literacy — all "across the curriculum." WAC also became part of a general rethinking of pedagogy and assessment, as institutions sought to increase student "involvement in learning," as one of the reports put it, through faculty-student mentoring programs, offices of faculty development and teaching, "freshman experience" programs to retain students in an era of dwindling enrollment, and a host of other programs.[43]

The change in climate had an immediate effect on the fledgling WAC movement: federal and corporate funding became more scarce, forcing programs to find ways to move beyond the initial enthusiasm of retreats or workshops or pilot programs that had begun with outside funding to permanent curricular structures in the institutions. WAC programs entered their "second stage," adapting (and sometimes succumbing) to the increasing pressures.[44] Some institutions took over full funding of WAC or found permanent endowments when outside funding ended. Other institutions reduced their programs, attaching them to a writing center or to English department writing courses. Still others merged WAC efforts with one or more of the other curricular reforms of the 1980s. Capitalizing on the renewed popularity of general-education core programs, some WAC programs focused their efforts on writing in core courses. George Mason's Plan for Alternative General Education (PAGE) program, for example, grew out of a WAC program. Other WAC programs became "critical thinking" programs or evolved into consulting services under the auspices of faculty development offices.

Despite these changes, the WAC movement far surpasses any previous movement to improve writing across the curriculum, both in the number of programs and in the breadth of their influence. Susan H. McLeod's 1987 survey of 2,735 institutions of higher education found that, of the 1,113 that replied, 427 (38 percent) had some WAC program, and 235 of these had had a program in existence for three years or more. The persistence of so many programs and their ability to secure ongoing internal funding (rather than external grant funding) suggests that WAC programs have found a secure place in many institutions.

The range of activities that WAC programs embrace suggests that WAC is having a diverse impact on higher education. McLeod's respondents reported efforts to encourage individual departments to make writing a part of their teaching, through departmental faculty workshops and through the recruiting and training of faculty writing consultants within individual departments. Some institutions have begun interdisciplinary discussions of rhetoric, through workshops on discipline-specific uses of language and through cooperative research projects to describe and classify discipline-specific conventions of written discourse. Other institutions have organized workshops or made consultants available to help faculty with their own writing. Still others have sponsored faculty debates on writing issues, organized national teleconferences on WAC, and published faculty handbooks, videos, newsletters, anthologies of student writing in the disciplines, and many other materials. Some WAC programs have even reached beyond faculty involvement to sponsor writing-to-learn workshops for administrators.[45]

REFORM AND RESISTANCE

The WAC movement has clearly had a broad and growing influence on American higher education over the last fifteen years. By conservative estimate, tens of thousands of faculty, students, and administrators at hundreds of institutions have been exposed to the movement, and many have made it an important part of their work. Yet the same attitudes and organizational structures that ended or marginalized earlier reforms continue to place large, often insurmountable obstacles in the way of current efforts to make writing a central part of American education. And without minimizing the unprecedented success of the WAC movement in the 1980s, it is important to understand the historical roots of the resistance that the movement faces as it enters the 1990s.

WAC challenges deeply held institutional attitudes toward writing, learning, and teaching: attitudes that are reinforced by the differentiated structure of knowledge and education. Faculty who grew up with the century-old notion that writing is a generalizable mechanical skill, learned once and for all at an early age, have difficulty experimenting with alternatives, even when teaching loads might permit time to be spent on their students' writing. Ideas of "correctness" inherited from the nineteenth century make some instructors reluctant to accept writing (even in drafts, notebooks, or journals) that is not edited by the teacher. The instructor's role as examiner is difficult to step out of because it is assigned to faculty by the institutional hierarchy. Assumptions about the nature of writing in their disciplines may also make faculty reluctant to assign personal or expressive writing (again, even in drafts, notebooks, or journals). Faculty who are accustomed to complete autonomy and authority in the classroom often feel threatened by reforms in pedagogy that necessitate personal and intellectual involvements with students and colleagues.

WAC is therefore sometimes perceived as an attempt to take time away from content and thus lower standards. Specialized instruction is, by its very nature, elitist, in that it is carried on by specialized communities with certain powers, sanctioned by the wider society, to regulate areas of public knowledge and life. When WAC programs threaten those elites — by asking them to change the pedagogical practices that form new members, or by altering the examination processes by which those entering a discipline or profession are selected and credentialed — then resistance comes. An instructor (or discipline or institution) may consider it a violation of her professional role to cover less material in a course to make room for more writing (particularly since the almost-ubiquitous standardized tests primarily measure such coverage).[46] Fulwiler and Young note that high-school administrators have even reprimanded teachers "for asking students to write before they completed workbook exercises — the required preparation for an upcoming [objective] test" (292).

Moreover, the instructor's role has been traditionally (and logically) defined in terms of "discipline": showing students the "right" way within the constraints of that discipline. Thus, he may find his identity as a teacher of a discipline challenged by student responses that propose answers or use evidence or methods of inquiry not accepted by the discipline. Even simply allowing students to revise drafts is sometimes seen as lowering standards. Faculty are naturally hesitant to risk a reexamination of their roles as teachers and as representatives of a discipline. Thus, relatively few faculty commit themselves to WAC.

Not surprisingly, some of the most entrenched opposition to WAC has come from English departments, who see programs challenging liberal culture's view of writing as an unteachable gift or infringing on the department's century-old institutional prerogatives. Most WAC programs began with (and are still led by) composition teachers in English who reach out to like-minded colleagues in other disciplines, and many English departments actively support WAC programs. But the claims of discipline are as strong in English as they are in any other department, and if writing is perceived as a threat to the department's literary mission, then it can be marginalized or ended. Fulwiler and Young again report that a number of programs have been "dismantled by a change in departmental administration or by the curricular or personnel decisions of unsympathetic English faculty" (289).

Perhaps more surprising is the controversy among composition specialists over whether students should be taught the conventions of specific disciplines, though this controversy is understandable given the historical divisions within the progressive tradition of writing instruction. An expressivist element in composition studies today, like its forebears in the "sentimental" progressive tradition of the 1920s, sees the teaching of disciplinary conventions as a denial of students' "authentic voice" and a rejection of the possibility of true academic community in a reformed institution, where knowledge and discourse will not be controlled by disciplinary elites. Expressivists, such as Kurt Spellmeyer, argue that students should be encouraged to do personal writing (the personal essay of the belletristic tradition, mainly) *instead of* learning to write in the public genres of the disciplines, a practice that in his view "encourages both conformity and submission" through a naive and formulaic "cookie cutter" approach to composition.[47] Proponents of writing in the disciplines argue that, as did Dewey, this line of reasoning rests on "a badly formulated opposition — a wrongly forced choice," in Joan Graham's words.[48] They insist that the student's experience, individual and personal, must interact in complex ways with disciplinary discourse, communal and public, in order for meaningful learning — and writing — to take place in academia. Britton, Maimon, Fulwiler, and Charles Bazerman, as well as other WAC proponents espouse varying theories and pedagogical approaches, but all favor students doing both personal and public writing at various stages of their writing and learning. They agree that learning to write is part of a dialectic between self and society, which can transform both, but only if students learn how disciplines are constituted through their discourse.[49]

Thus, given these reductive notions of writing among academics in all quarters, a central theme of many versions of WAC today is the transformation of faculty attitudes toward writing and an emphasis on the intrinsic motivation of more successful, satisfying teaching. The WAC movement, unlike most of its predecessors, attempts to reform pedagogy more than curriculum. In most of its theory and much of its practice, writing to learn overshadows learning to write. This is one reason WAC has eclipsed all of its predecessors. It asks for a fundamental commitment to a radically different way of teaching, a way that requires personal sacrifices, given the structure of American education, and offers personal rather than institutional rewards (perhaps this explains the religious metaphors common in the movement).[50] A group of faculty who are personally committed to WAC can ride out any administrative changes (and perhaps increase their number), for the reforms are personal not institutional, and their success depends on conversion not curriculum. But on an *institutional* basis, WAC exists in a structure that fundamentally resists it.

Faculty tend to retain narrow attitudes toward the role of writing in pedagogy not only because of disciplinary constraints but because those attitudes reflect the priorities of academia and are reinforced by its structure of rewards.[51] Even faculty who recognize the importance of writing for improving learning may not have the time to restructure their courses and pedagogies to incorporate writing more effectively, for faculty must work within institutional and disciplinary contexts that embody competing values. The century-old complaint of faculty that they do not have time to assign and respond to student writing is frequently a just one, but it begs deeper questions of institutional values. At research institutions, for example, undergraduate instruction typically holds a lower priority than graduate teaching or research. And responses to WAC reflect those priorities, despite jeremiads on the crisis in undergraduate education. Faculty at such institutions have little extrinsic motivation for introducing or continuing to incorporate writing in a course if it takes time away from research or graduate teaching; and there are many extrinsic motivations for dropping it. To initiate WAC programs, institutions have therefore had to offer release time, smaller classes, or other forms of compensation as carrots, but these are, of course, very expensive and easily cut when priorities or personnel change. What is less common is a deeper change in the way teaching is assessed and rewarded in the institution. If WAC is to become more than a marginal activity, criteria for promotion, tenure, or merit pay must measure and value the kinds of teaching and learning that WAC promotes, though this, like measuring and valuing writing itself, is far more difficult than looking only at more easily quantifiable "outcomes."

Without a strong base of support from faculty who see writing and learning in less reductive terms — and are committed to using writing in their teaching — WAC efforts easily fall victim to the institutional inertia of academia's differentiated, hierarchical structure. The myth of transience reasserts itself, and WAC programs, like composition courses, tend to become marginalized. This reassertion of the status quo takes many forms.

Some WAC programs never progress beyond (or may revert to) remedial labs, outside the curricular structure. Today many universities carry on the tradition of writing police and remedial labs; faculty prescribe treatment (often using computers), administered by a staff member or tutor — but rarely by a tenure-line faculty member. Responsibility remains outside the disciplinary communities, dropout rates are high, and the status quo is preserved. Many labs are attempting to shake the remedial image (and some are succeeding) by encouraging students of all backgrounds in all courses to use their services. Writing tutors have become "writing fellows"; labs have become "centers"; and at some institutions faculty members are encouraged to consult the center for help with their own writing. Yet the exclusionary attitudes remain. Some campuses have even attempted to overcome the stigma by separating a writing center from a remedial lab — further marginalizing the students who most need intellectual contact with students and faculty who use language in the approved ways.

WAC programs are also marginalized when writing "in the disciplines" is confined to general-composition courses. One of the most common models of WAC amounts to a revised general-composition course, usually taught by English department graduate students or by junior faculty trained in literary analysis. This model simply shifts the emphasis of composition courses toward reading (and writing about) nontechnical, often belletristic essays collected in "WAC readers," on topics from the sciences and social sciences, as well as from the humanities: Stephen Jay Gould, Loren Eiseley, and so on.[52] Such a program need not require (or even ask for) the active involvement of faculty from across the curriculum or even those in the English department outside the composition staff.

Writing intensive courses, sometimes supported by a lab, are another common curricular model for WAC, but these WI's may also tend to marginalize writing in the disciplines.[53] WI courses again concentrate in a few professors or TA's the responsibility for initiating students into the discourse community, while freeing most faculty resources for other activities which the community views as more important. As Tori Haring-Smith points out, when a few courses are labeled *writing intensive*, students sometimes object when other courses require writing. Writing is viewed as an adjunct to a course, even a punishment, not as an accomplishment valued by the community. And WI's do not necessarily provide students with more writing (as a recent survey of such courses at Cornell indicated) because faculty are not always held accountable for writing instruction in these courses.[54] Moreover, WI courses often substitute for one or more semesters of composition, further decreasing the little formal writing instruction that students typically receive.

Even when WAC programs attempt to make writing part of every class, every discipline, the writing can be marginalized if it is perceived as an additional burden rather than as an intrinsic part of learning. At some institutions, administrators have attempted to impose WAC by fiat, sometimes without providing training and support for faculty or securing their consent. Naturally, faculty resent and resist the imposition, considering it "doing the English teacher's job" or "adding writing" of the traditional evaluative kind, often a research paper divorced from the "real" content and activity of the course.[55] For the new generation of upwardly mobile career administrators, advancement often depends on their ability to initiate and support visible, innovative programs. WAC easily becomes part of administrators' curricular and pedagogical reform initiatives. As one administrator recently remarked to me, "WAC is the cheapest faculty development program you can buy." But the danger is that these "top-down" programs may simply reinforce the myth of transience. As Fulwiler points out, "Many administrators believe or want to believe that writing across the curriculum is a quick fix. They seek the immediate gratification of a visibly successful program, one that quiets legislators and enhances administrative careers."[56] Christopher Thaiss, coordinator of the National Network of WAC Programs, sees these administratively mandated programs as one of the most troubling trends in WAC in the 1980s, for it destroys the grass-roots efforts of faculty and breeds resentment.[57]

Without deep changes in the ways that disciplines and institutions approach writing, the WAC movement will, in all likelihood, remain on the margins of the curriculum at many, perhaps most, institutions. What Rudolph said of interdisciplinary programs in the past is no less true of WAC today: "Unless handsomely funded and courageously defended, efforts to launch courses and programs outside the departmental structure [have] generally failed."[58] There is no specific constituency for interdepartmental programs within the structure of the American university, much less for interdepartmental programs that incorporate writing, because the academic community is fragmented, and there is thus no permanent defense against the slow erosion of programs under the pressure of well-defined departmental interests. Until individual disciplines accept the responsibility of studying and teaching the writing of their community to students, WAC programs will continue to be marginalized, subject to the vagaries of existence in an institutional no-man's-land. Writing will continue to be transparent and the myth of transience powerful among those who do not understand or acknowledge the relationship between writing and the creation and acquisition of knowledge.

RHETORIC, RESEARCH, AND REFORM

Like its many predecessors, the current WAC movement encountered an institution whose very structure eroded meaningful reforms. But unlike its predecessors, the current WAC movement has elements within it that do not ignore or attempt to supplant institutional divisions; rather they work through the disciplines to transform not only student writing but also the ways the disciplines conceive of writing and its teaching. The WAC movement (and, with it, elements within the academic disciplines themselves) are attempting to develop new traditions of inquiry into writing and its pedagogy that examine the structure of academia's divisions and the ways that students and faculty may learn to travel among them, not transcend them.

In the late 1970s and 1980s, research into rhetoric and writing has taken a new direction. Instead of examining writing as a single set of generalizable skills and its teaching a set of generalizable principles and techniques, new lines of investigation have examined writing as a constituent of communities, differentiated by the structure of knowledge and the activities of each community. Drawing upon such diverse fields as the history of science, anthropology, sociology, and social psychology, these investigations attempt, as Steven Weiland recently put it, to "assemble the rudiments of rhetorical interpretation and instruction in composition on a field-by-field basis."[59] After a century of working under reductive nineteenth-century assumptions, this research may at last give academia an intellectual foundation on which to construct pedagogies, one that acknowledges the differentiation of written knowledge in modern academia and, indeed, the modern world.

Appropriately, this new direction in rhetorical research began within composition studies as an attempt to resuscitate the research paper, the oldest tradition of extended student writing in the modern university. In the mid-1970s, CUNY professor Charles Bazerman revised his freshman course to strengthen its research-paper component and found that there was almost no research on the rhetorical conventions of various disciplines or on the relationship between college-level reading and writing. His 1979 article on the "conversation model" of academic discourse and his 1981 textbook, *The Informed Writer*, approached writing as a means of drawing students into "wider public, professional, and academic communities." He and others began research into disciplinary rhetorics, the differing ways communities use written discourse in their activities.[60] He found that other disciplines, such as the sociology of science, were also investigating the social and rhetorical dimensions of knowledge. By the mid-1980s, research in disciplinary rhetorics was going on in many fields, both among composition scholars and among scholars in philosophy, anthropology, literary theory, economics, biology, business, history, law, and other fields. Even physics, that most theoretical of the modern disciplines, is engaged in a lively debate over whether it should change the conventions of its written discourse to acknowledge the social dimensions of research.[61] It is by no means clear if those who view knowledge in social and rhetorical terms will prevail in their disciplines, but at least the role that writing plays in shaping knowledge is now an issue. Writing cannot so easily remain transparent.

This is a crucial step. For unless disciplines first understand the rhetorical nature of their own work and make conscious and visible what was transparent, the teaching of writing in the disciplines will continue to reinforce the myth of transience and the current WAC movement may share the fate of its predecessors. Writing in content courses will be seen merely as a further opportunity for evaluation or remediation, a means of introducing pedagogical variety, or as a favor to the English department and not as a central part of disciplinary research or teaching.

What is most promising about this line of investigation for those interested in improving student writing and learning is that faculty now have an intellectually respectable avenue for investigating and discussing writing, an avenue that acknowledges the institution's curricular and structural differentiation, instead of lamenting academia's fall from the homogeneous community of the nineteenth-century college and longing for some linguistic homecoming. However, understanding the rhetorical nature of a discipline is no guarantee that the discipline will find and embrace pedagogies for teaching its rhetoric more effectively (or to more students). We must not only understand how a discipline constitutes its discourse but also understand how students learn the discourse of a discipline, how writing plays a role at various stages in their initiation into that community.

A second line of research has begun to investigate these pedagogical implications of disciplinary rhetorics. Faculty from English departments and their colleagues across the curriculum have in the last decade begun to study in specific, concrete ways how students learn the discourse of various disciplines. This research has grown directly out of the WAC programs as participating faculty from many departments have become interested in tracing the development of writing ability in its relation to learning in specific disciplinary and classroom contexts. Such research uses qualitative *and* quantitative methods; it traces the relationships between a discipline's texts, its pedagogy, and its students' texts; it reassesses the old notions of writing as a generalizable skill; it even addresses those central issues of evaluation that have been neglected under the reign of machine-scored tests. For example, some departments and institutions are experimenting with portfolios of student writing, gathered over several months, even years, to measure and promote students' intellectual and communicative development through time.[62]

Through this research, disciplines may eventually be able to design the pedagogical "scaffoldings" that Bruner theorized, curricular structures built of meaningful experiences with language, which will lead students toward progressively more sophisticated engagement with the activities of each discipline through its discourse. And the dream of Dewey — a curricular balance between the interests of the learner and the demands of the disciplines — may be realized as disciplines at last come to grips with the concrete ties between language and the process of learning. After more than a century of complaints and recriminations, the mass-education system may bridge the old rift that has divided student-centered from discipline-centered education and marginalized writing in both.

But discipline-specific rhetorical and pedagogical research is still in its infancy, and it faces major obstacles in translating its results into pedagogical reform. To influence scholarly activity and pedagogy deeply, such research must be valued and supported by the disciplines themselves — not merely by individual scholars inspired by a WAC program, as has largely been the case thus far. By its very nature, WAC research challenges the convenient notion that disciplines are static repositories of knowledge and replaces it with a model of disciplines as communities that are continually being reformed through their discursive practices, including those of students. It opens for criticism the structures of disciplinary formation and initiation, and those critiques can threaten the central assumptions that the members of a discipline have come to take for granted (as faculty participants in WAC research have discovered).

Yet these are the very obstacles WAC must overcome if it is to achieve its ultimate goal: reforming American pedagogy. Reform efforts will continue to depend largely on the goodwill of individual faculty and administrators until disciplines assume responsibility for making writing a central part of their pedagogy. As the fundamental unit of academic organization, disciplines have many means for assuming this responsibility: through their professional associations, their training of graduate students, their accreditation procedures, their support of pedagogical research, their relations with secondary teachers. Some few disciplines have taken small but important steps in this direction. The accrediting body for engineering schools, for example, has made comprehensive writing instruction one of its criteria.

Ultimately, these efforts in the disciplines will themselves depend on broader changes in the structure of secondary and higher education to overcome institutional inertia, which has eroded previous reforms. If writing is to become a central focus of pedagogy, then it must be structurally linked to the values, goals, and activities of disciplines; faculty must see a connection between encouraging better writing among their students and advancing the value and status of their disciplines — and of their own individual careers. Disciplines must find or create places where student writing matters to the disciplinary community. The oral communal performance of the old college is of course unworkable and irrelevant in a writing-based academic culture, but written forums for opening student discourse and its teaching to the communal discussion and criticism of disciplines are possible. For example, if student writing is critiqued by a faculty member's disciplinary peers outside the individual classroom, outside the institution even, then standards for student writing and its teaching will inevitably develop, as will pedagogical traditions for preparing students to meet those standards. European systems provide models of external evaluation of student writing by faculty in a discipline, though the traditional autonomy of American academics in the classroom and the diversity and independence of American institutions in setting curriculum will make such peer review difficult. "Lifting the veils that normally shroud the teaching behavior of individual professors and departments," says Clark, is "perhaps the best way to improve teaching competence in large systems," but it is immensely threatening.[63] Even so, a few institutions have begun programs in which faculty in a WAC program or a discipline review student portfolios. One institution, Swarthmore College, has even begun external reviews of senior honors theses.[64] Such attempts, along with the renewed efforts to improve the evaluation of writing, may again allow written performance to become a viable complement (or in some contexts, even an alternative) to machine-scored tests.

Administrative structures can play an important role in encouraging disciplines to value writing — not by mandating writing or its teaching but by setting up structurally integrated forums that open writing to discussion and critique within and across disciplines. Faculty workshops, WAC committees, writing centers, and consultants provide forums, of course; but these are structurally independent of the fundamental disciplinary organization of institutions and therefore easily dispensed with. If writing is to become a valued part of teaching and learning, then the evaluation of student writing and its role in curricula must become integrated into the disciplinary structure of the academic system: through departmental reviews, teaching evaluations conducted by peers, promotion and tenure procedures, and so on. Peer review of faculty-written texts forms the very basis of disciplinary structure, organizing each disciplinary community's energies toward greater efforts and higher standards. Applying some analogous process to student-written texts may allow the American system to evaluate (and thus value) students' writing performances across a discipline or even across institutions.

Finding ways to harness the efforts of the disciplines — where the faculty's primary loyalty and interest lie — will perhaps achieve more in the long run than structurally separate programs, no matter how well intentioned and well financed. Here again there are political costs and trade-offs. The energies that departments and disciplines expend on student writing might be spent elsewhere, and the critique of learning and teaching that writing opens will challenge both students and faculty. WAC will become part of the ongoing negotiation among the many interests that comprise the system (as Robert Morris College recently discovered when WAC became an issue in contract talks with the faculty union). But without structural changes to integrate writing into the disciplinary fiber of institutions, without a commitment to permanent change in the way academia values writing in pedagogy, WAC programs will always work against the grain.

Despite these formidable obstacles, there are reasons to believe that academia will support research and reform in writing — perhaps even evolve traditions of writing instruction in the disciplines that are fully integrated into the structure of academic work. Industrial society, which gave birth to composition courses a century ago — with its compartmentalization of roles and knowledge, its alienating bureaucratic management, its separation of mental and manual labor — is evolving, some say, into postindustrial society, where new knowledge is created through disciplinary and interdisciplinary collaboration, where competitive advantages are derived from more effective communication (often written) among workers at all levels, and where new management structures replace the rigid hierarchies of the past. Writing instruction may be part of this shift, as it was part of the shift in the American economy a century ago. For example, the recent interest in collaborative-writing and student-writing groups within academia may reflect and support, more or less consciously, collaborative management and worker productivity circles within the business community. WAC may also reflect and support a postindustrial economy in subtle, but crucial ways. Writing instruction is potentially a way of making connections between individual scholars and disciplines, either directly, through the contact many WAC programs encourage among faculty, or indirectly, through research into the discourse of various disciplines, which opens their central assumptions, methodologies, and rhetoric to examination and invites useful comparisons and interactions with others. Unlike many previous cross-curricular writing programs, most versions of WAC today do not posit a unified structure of knowledge, a "theology of education," as did Hutchins' neo-Thomism. But WAC may nevertheless forge links between scholars and disciplines, without attempting to create and impose a single overarching discourse community on academia.[65]

WAC also may have profound implications for preparing students to enter a postindustrial economy (as granting agencies acknowledge, more or less explicitly, through their funding of it). Those who study employment trends generally agree that in fifteen years most jobs will involve information processing, in one form or another, almost always with computers. But in the electronic office of the information age, "computer literacy" may mean much more than mechanical or clerical skill. The productive capacity of America — and perhaps its social cohesion as well — may increasingly depend on rhetorical skill, the ability of an ever-growing portion of the work force to communicate in writing, both in and out of an organizational unit, not only from one person to another but also from one community to another.[66] The rising demand for writing skill, which the Bullock Report noted fifteen years ago, will not likely be reversed, and the growth of information technology may continue to increase it. WAC is one way to prepare students for the complex new roles many of them will play in professional communities. Ideally, cross-curricular writing instruction would initiate students into the discourse of one professional community and give them extensive experience in negotiating the discourse of several other communities, other disciplines. While students cannot be fully initiated into the discourse of all the communities to which they are exposed in their schooling, making writing central to the whole curriculum may give students, in Maimon's phrase, "a sense of intellectual tact," a kind of liberal education that would encourage students to take an intellectual interest in several communities and to respect the logic and diversity of written conventions they find there.[67]

There is indeed much that is new and promising in the current WAC movement, but it would only be reinforcing the myth of transience to assume that these differences, as important as they are, will guarantee WAC's survival. When cross-curricular programs seek to modify the attitudes and compartmental structure of academia, when programs seek to broaden access to professional discourse communities, they become forms of resistance, threats to the institution (or to the century-old conceptions of it). Thus, as with all movements to extend literacy, WAC has political, economic, and social consequences. The empowerment that literacy affords demands power sharing. In composition studies, the identity of the field — perhaps its existence as a discrete discipline — is negotiated in WAC. Will writing specialists be tenure-track faculty, members of a department, or will they primarily be administrative staff consultants, temporary instructors, support personnel? In the postmodern education system, how will various kinds of knowledge and instruction be organized and funded? It is worth contemplating the fate of Great Britain's "new universities," which were founded in the 1960s as innovative centers of interdisciplinary teaching and research but are now suffering from a bureaucratic malaise caused in large part by budgetary and administrative strictures of the present government, a government that discourages the intellectual risk taking that interdisciplinary innovation requires.[68] And finally, WAC has implications for the wider society. If the educational system teaches greater numbers of students to enter academic discourse communities and, through them, coveted professional roles, there may be increased competition, economic dislocation, and political conflict. If, however, the system frankly acknowledges that it is excluding students from professional communities on the basis of their language rather than committing its resources to teaching the linguistic forms of those communities to those students, the results might also be painful. The recent rioting in France over access to higher education (determined there primarily by written examinations) should give one pause. In any case, there are powerful reasons for preserving the myth of transience and equally powerful reasons for reformers to construct alternatives, consciously, deliberately, with some attention to their historical precedents, and great regard for their long-term consequences.

For in historical perspective, WAC is not a single trend or movement; it is, like its predecessors, a collection of often-conflicting approaches to the problem of linguistic differentiation in the modern world. It offers no panacea, but it need not support the myth of transience either. Seen in its full dimensions, WAC can become a convenient tool for focusing our attention in a very practical way on the contradictions of American secondary and higher education, a means of examining rather than skirting the deepest problems. With WAC, the old battles between access and exclusion, excellence and equity, scientific and humanist worldviews, liberal and professional education, all come down to very specific questions of responsibility for curriculum and teaching. WAC ultimately asks: in what ways will graduates of our institutions use language, and how shall we teach them to use it in those ways? And behind this two-part question lies a deeper one: what discourse communities — and ultimately, what social class — will students be equipped to enter? That is an extremely complex question in our heterogeneous society. It is a question that Americans have consistently begged because it forces us to face painful issues of opportunity, of equality, of democracy in education. But underneath the buzzwords and the bustle of programs, it is the question we will inevitably answer by pursuing WAC.

NOTES

1. Two notable exceptions were a pioneering curriculum for the "disadvantaged," Gateway English, at Hunter College, and the Northwestern University curriculum materials, which focused on the process of writing. See Kenneth J. Kantor, "The English Curriculum and the Structure of the Disciplines," *Theory into Practice* 22 (1984): 175.

2. Berlin, *Rhetoric* 122–23.

3. See Myrna J. Smith, "Bruner on Writing," *College Composition and Communication* 28 (1977): 129–33.

4. Bruner, *Process* 31. For Bruner's influence in WAC research in the 1980s, see, for example, Arthur N. Applebee, *Contexts for Learning to Write: Studies of Secondary School Instruction* (Norwood, NJ: Ablex, 1984) esp. 177–78; and Bazerman, *Shaping* 306.

5. Ron Smith, "Composition Requirements: A Report on a Nationwide Survey of Four-Year Colleges and Universities," *College Composition and Communication* 25 (1974): 139.

6. On expressivist writing instruction in composition during the 1960s, see Berlin, *Rhetoric* 145–55.

7. John Dixon, *Growth Through English: A Report Based on the Dartmouth Seminar, 1966* (Reading, UK: National Association for the Teaching of English, 1967), qtd. in Kantor, "English" 176.

8. On the "revival of rhetoric," see Berlin, *Rhetoric* chap. 6; on the MLA, see Donald Stewart, "Status of Composition."

9. On the CUNY experience, see Blanche Skurnick, "Basic Writing at the City University of New York," in *Options for the Teaching of English: Freshman Composition*, ed. Jasper P. Neel (New York: MLA, 1978) 10–15. On Mina Shaughnessy, see Robert Lyons, "Mina Shaughnessy," in *Traditions of Inquiry*, ed. John Brereton (New York: Oxford UP, 1985) 171–89.

10. On the rationalization of university administration, see Clark, *Academic Life* chap. 6; and Clark, *Higher Education System* chap. 4.

11. The National Defense Education Act was belatedly extended to English in 1964 (see Applebee, *Tradition* 198–204).

12. Quotations are from Daniels 138.

13. *Language for Life* (The Bullock Report) (London: HMSO, 1975); James Britton, Tony Burgess, Nancy Martin, Alex McLeod, and Harold Rosen, *The Development of Writing Abilities (11–18)* (London: Macmillan, 1975).

14. *Language for Life* 6.

15. James Britton, *Language and Learning* (London: Penguin, 1970) 214.

16. *Language for Life* 395–96. For Britton's assessment of The Bullock Report, see his essay, "Reflections on the Writing of The Bullock Report," in *Prospect and Retrospect: Selected Essays of James Britton*, ed. Gordon M. Pradl (Montclair, NJ: Boynton, 1982): 185–90.

17. On the Schools Council Project, see Michael Marland, *Language Across the Curriculum: The Implementation of The Bullock Report in the Secondary School* (London: Heinemann, 1977).

18. Janet Emig, "Writing as a Mode of Learning," *College Composition and Communication* 28 (1977): 127.

19. See Roy, 1–18.

20. See Applebee, *Tradition* 232–36.

21. For an account of the early years of BAWP, see "Bay Area Writing Project/California Writing Project/National Writing Project: An Overview," University of California at Berkeley, School of Education. Urbana: ERIC, 1978 (ED 184123).

22. See Applebee, *Writing*.

23. See Clifford and Guthrie 317–18.

24. See Applebee, *Contexts* 187–88; Judith A. Langer and Arthur N. Applebee, *How Writing Shapes Thinking: A Study of Teaching and Writing*, NCTE Research Report no. 22 (Urbana: NCTE, 1987) 138–39; and Deborah Swanson-Owens, "Identifying Natural Sources of Resistance: A Case Study of Implementing Writing Across the Curriculum," *Research in the Teaching of English* 20 (1986): 69–97.

25. Among the university and secondary-school cooperative programs (often associated with the NWP) are those at Beaver College, University of Michigan, University of Washington, Rutgers, Indiana University, George Mason University, and the original at UC Berkeley. See Mary A. Barr and Mary K. Healy, "School and University Articulation: Different Contexts for Writing Across the Curriculum," in McLeod. *Speaking and Writing, K–12: Classroom Strategies and the New Research*, ed. Christopher Thaiss and C. Suhor (Urbana: NCTE, 1984). Christopher Thaiss, *Language Across the Curriculum in the Elementary Grades* (Urbana: NCTE, 1986).

26. In the social studies, see especially Barry Beyer and Anita Brostoff, eds., "Managing/Evaluating Writing and Social Studies," *Social Education* 43 (1979): 194–97.

27. Recounted in Erling Larsen, "Carleton College," in *Options for the Teaching of English: The Undergraduate Curriculum*, ed. Elizabeth Wooton Cowan (New York: MLA, 1975) 8.

28. See "The Development of the Communication Skills Program at Central College, Pella, Iowa," 1985 (CCA); and Barbara Fassler, "The Interdepartmental Composition Program at Central College," in Neel, *Options* 84–89.

29. Elaine P. Maimon, personal interview, 23 Apr. 1990.

30. Elaine P. Maimon, "Writing, Learning, and Thinking at Beaver College," College English Association Annual Meeting, Savannah, Mar. 1979 (ED 175054).

31. Maimon, "Writing, Learning, and Thinking" 4.

32. On Maimon's experience, see "Writing, Learning and Thinking"; Maimon, "Beaver College," in Fulwiler and Young 142–43; Maimon, "Cinderella to Hercules: Demythologizing Writing Across the Curriculum," *Journal of Basic Writing* 2 (1980): 3–11. On conflicts elsewhere, see Toby Fulwiler, "How Well Does Writing Across the Curriculum Work?" *College English* 46 (1984): 113–25.

33. See Lois Barry, "Eastern Oregon State College," in *New Methods in College Writing Programs: Theories in Practice*, ed. Paul Connolly and Teresa Vilardi (New York: MLA, 1986) 33–39.

34. This account is drawn primarily from Toby Fulwiler, "Writing Across the Curriculum at Michigan Tech," *Journal of the Council of Writing Program Administrators* 4 (1981): 15–20; *Writing Across the Disciplines: Research into Practice*, Art Young and Toby Fulwiler, eds. (Portsmouth, NH: Boynton, 1986); and Toby Fulwiler, personal interview, 24 Mar. 1990.

35. Art Young, "Teaching Writing Across the University: The Michigan Tech Experience," College English Association Convention, Savannah, Mar. 1979 (ED 176 928).

36. Richard Lanham, "Urgency and Opportunity: Implementing Writing Across the Curriculum," address, University of Georgia faculty, Athens, 25 Apr. 1985; reported in *Writing Across the Curriculum* 3 (1985): 5–6.

37. See, for example, Patricia Stock, "University of Michigan, Ann Arbor," in Connolly and Vilardi 117–21; and Milton D. Glick, "Writing Across the Curriculum: A Dean's Perspective," *WPA: Writing Program Administration* 11 (1988): 53–58.

38. On Washington's program, see Joan Graham, "University of Washington," in Connolly and Vilardi 143–48; and Joan Graham, "What Works: The Problems and Rewards of Cross-Curricular Writing Programs," *Current Issues in Higher Education* 3 (1983–84): 16–26.

39. Kenneth A. Bruffee, "The Brooklyn Plan: Attaining Intellectual Growth through Peer-Group Tutoring," *Liberal Education* 64 (1978): 447–68. On California State's program, see Marilyn Sutton, "The Writing Adjunct Program at the Small College of California State College, Dominguez Hills," in Neel, *Options* 104–9.

40. Burton Clark and Martin Trow in *College Peer Groups*, ed. Theodore M. Newcomb and Everett K. Wilson (Chicago: Aldine, 1966) 67, qtd. in Bruffee, "Brooklyn Plan" 449.

41. *A Guide to Writing Programs: Writing Centers, Peer Tutoring Programs, and Writing Across the Curriculum*, ed. Tori Haring-Smith, Nathaniel Hawkins, Elizabeth Morrison, Lise Stern, and Robin Tatu (Glenview, IL: Scott Foresman, 1987) 7–27.

42. For community college perspectives on WAC, see Barbara R. Stout and Joyce N. Magnotto, "Writing Across the Curriculum at Community Colleges," in McLeod 21–30; and "Prince George's Community College," in Fulwiler and Young 65–81.

43. National Institute of Education, *Involvement in Learning: Realizing the Potential of American Higher Education* (Washington, DC: NIE, 1984). See also William J. Bennett, *To Reclaim a Legacy: A Report on the Humanities in Higher Education* (Washington, DC: NEH, 1984). For the student-personnel perspective, see, for example *The Freshman Year Experience: Helping Students Survive and Succeed in College*, ed. John M. Lee Upcraft (San Francisco: Jossey, 1989).

44. The term *second stage* was coined by Susan McLeod, "Translating Enthusiasm into Curricular Change," in McLeod. For a range of models and perspectives, see the other essays in McLeod.

45. Susan H. McLeod, "Writing Across the Curriculum: The Second Stage and Beyond," *College Composition and Communication* 40 (1989): 339–41.

46. See Langer and Applebee 146.

47. Kurt Spellmeyer, "A Common Ground: The Essay in the Academy," *College English* 3 (1989): 266.

48. Joan Graham, "Writing Conferences in Disciplinary Contexts: Students Working Out What They Think," CCCC Convention, Chicago, Mar. 1990.

49. See the responses to Spellmeyer's essay by Bazerman and Susan Miller in "Two Comments on 'A Common Ground: The Essay in Academe,'" *College English* 52 (1990): 329–38; and Elaine P. Maimon, "Reexamining False Dichotomies," CCCC Convention, Chicago, Mar. 1990, esp. 6–7.

50. Thaiss, in McLeod (91), notes the prevalence of religious metaphors in discussions of WAC.

51. See Fulwiler, "How Well" 120.

52. For a critique of this approach, see Thaiss in McLeod 91–102.

53. For the 1987 survey, see Susan H. McLeod and Susan Shirley, "National Survey of Writing Across the Curriculum Programs," in McLeod 103–30.

54. See Haring-Smith, "What's Wrong"; and Thaiss in McLeod 94–95. Kitzhaber (*Themes* 102, 153n) noted similar attitudes in 1963.

55. See Thaiss in McLeod 94.

56. Art Young and Toby Fulwiler, "The Enemies of Writing Across the Curriculum," in Fulwiler and Young 293.

57. Thaiss (in McLeod 94–96) lists administrative mandate as one of the three major difficulties that WAC programs must overcome.

58. Rudolph, *Curriculum* 251; see also Bell 25.
59. Steven Weiland, "History Toward Rhetoric," *College English* 49 (1987): 816.
60. Charles Bazerman, "A Relationship between Reading and Writing," *College English* 41 (1980): 656–61; and Charles Bazerman, *The Informed Writer* (Boston: Houghton, 1981).
61. See "Letters," *Physics Today* (May 1989): 9–11; and (Feb. 1990): 11–15, 156.
62. For a useful overview and theoretical discussion of this research, see *Writing in Academic Disciplines*, ed. David A. Jolliffe (Norwood, NJ: Ablex, 1988); and Lucille Parkinson McCarthy and Barbara F. Walvoord, "Models for Collaborative Research in Writing Across the Curriculum," in McLeod 77–90. See also Graham, "Writing Conferences"; Catherine Beyer, "Making Knowledge in Political Economics," CCCC Convention, Chicago, Mar. 1990; David S. Kaufer and Cheryl Geisler, "Novelty in Academic Writing," *Written Communication* 6 (1989): 286–311; Barbara F. Walvoord, ed., *Thinking and Writing in College: A Naturalistic Study of Students Writing in Four Disciplines* (Urbana: NCTE, 1991); Anne Herrington, "Writing in Academic Settings: A Study of the Contexts for Writing in Two College Chemical Engineering Courses," *Research in the Teaching of English* 19 (1985): 331–61; Anderson, et al.; Berkenkotter, et al.
63. Clark, *Higher Education System* 246.
64. See Patrick J. Hill, "Communities of Learners: Curriculum as the Infrastructure of Academic Communities," in Hall and Kevles; and "Swarthmore College," *Liberal Education* 73 (May/June 1987): 32–33.
65. For theoretical perspectives on interdisciplinary study, see Raymond Williams, *Writing in Society* (London: Verso, 1984): 213–26; Sherif and Sherif; and Fish.
66. See Chris M. Anson, "The Classroom and the 'Real World' as Contexts: Re-examining the Goals of Writing Instruction," *MMLA* 20 (1987): 6–9.
67. Elaine P. Maimon, personal interview, 23 Apr. 1990.
68. For critical views of British education in the 1970s and 1980s, see David Bouchier, "Universities and the Government: A Lesson from Britain," *Chronicle of Higher Education* 14 Jan. 1987: 120; and John Carswell, *Government and the Universities in Britain* (Cambridge: Cambridge UP, 1985).

WORKS CITED

Anderson, Worth, Cynthia Best, Alycia Black, John Hurst, Brandt Miller, and Susan Miller. "Cross-Curricular Underlife: A Collaborative Report on Ways with Academic Words." *College Composition and Communication* 41 (1990): 11–36.
Anson, Chris M. "The Classroom and the 'Real World' as Contexts: Re-examining the Goals of Writing Instruction." *MMLA* 20 (1987): 1–16.
Applebee, Arthur N. *Contexts for Learning to Write: Studies of Secondary School Instruction.* Norwood, NJ: Ablex, 1984.
———. *Tradition and Reform in the Teaching of English: A History.* Urbana, IL: NCTE, 1974.
———. *Writing in the Secondary School: English and the Content Areas.* NCTE Research Report No. 21. Urbana, IL: NCTE, 1981.
"Bay Area Writing Project/California Writing Project/National Writing Project: An Overview." University of California at Berkeley, School of Education. Urbana, IL: ERIC, 1978. ERIC, ED 184123.
Bazerman, Charles. *The Informed Writer.* Boston: Houghton, 1981.
———. "A Relationship Between Reading and Writing." *College English* 41 (1980): 656–69.
———. *Shaping Written Knowledge: The Genre and Activity of the Experimental Article in Science.* Madison: U of Wisconsin P, 1988.
Bell, Daniel. *The Reforming of General Education: The Columbia Experience in Its National Setting.* New York: Columbia UP, 1966.
Bennett, William J. *To Reclaim a Legacy: A Report on the Humanities in Higher Education.* Washington, CD: NEH, 1984.
Berkenkotter, Carol, Thomas N. Huckin, and John Ackerman. "Conventions, Conversations, and the Writer: Case Study of a Student in a Rhetoric Ph.D. Program." *Research in the Teaching of English* 22 (1988): 9–43.
Berlin, James A. *Rhetoric and Reality: Writing Instruction in American Colleges 1900–1985.* Carbondale: Southern Illinois UP, 1987.
Beyer, Barry, and Anita Brostoff. "Managing/Evaluating Writing and Social Studies." *Social Education* 43 (1979): 194–97.
Beyer, Catherine. "Making Knowledge in Political Economics." CCCC Convention. Chicago, Mar. 1990.

Bouchier, David. "Universities and the Government: A Lesson from Britain." *Chronicle of Higher Education* 14 Jan. 1987: 120.

Brereton, John, ed. *Traditions of Inquiry.* New York: Oxford UP, 1985.

Britton, James. *Language and Learning.* London: Penguin 1970.

———. *Prospect and Retrospect: Selected Essays of James Britton.* Ed. Gordon M. Pradl. Montclair, NJ: Boynton, 1982.

Britton, James, Tony Burgess, Nancy Martin, Alex McLeod, and Harold Rosen. *The Development of Writing Abilities (11–18).* London: Macmillan, 1975.

Bruffee, Kenneth A. "The Brooklyn Plan: Attaining Intellectual Growth Through Peer-Group Tutoring." *Liberal Education* 64 (1978): 447–68.

Bruner, Jerome S. *The Process of Education.* Westminster, MD: Random, 1963.

Carswell, John. *Government and the Universities in Britain.* Cambridge: Cambridge UP, 1985.

Clark, Burton R. *The Academic Life: Small Worlds, Different Worlds.* Princeton: Carnegie Foundation for the Advancement of Teaching, 1987.

———. *The Higher Education System: Academic Organization in Cross-National Perspective.* Berkeley: U of California P, 1983.

Clifford, Geraldine Joncich, and James W. Guthrie. *Ed School: A Brief for Professional Education.* Chicago: U of Chicago P, 1988.

Connolly, Paul, and Teresa Vilardi. *New Methods in College Writing Programs: Theories in Practice.* New York: MLA, 1986.

Cowan, Elizabeth Wooton, ed. *Options for the Teaching of English: The Undergraduate Curriculum.* New York: MLA, 1975.

Daniels, Harvey. *Famous Last Words: The American Language Crisis Reconsidered.* Carbondale: Southern Illinois UP, 1983.

Dixon, John. *Growth Through English: A Report Based on the Dartmouth Seminar, 1966.* Reading, UK: National Association for the Teaching of English, 1967.

Elbow, Peter. *Writing Without Teachers.* New York: Oxford UP, 1973.

Emig, Janet. "Writing as a Mode of Learning." *College Composition and Communication* 28 (1977): 122–28.

Fish, Stanley, "Being Interdisciplinary Is So Very Hard to Do." *Profession* 1989: 15–22.

Fulwiler, Toby. "How Well Does Writing Across the Curriculum Work?" *College English* 46 (1984): 113–25.

———. "Writing Across the Curriculum at Michigan Tech." *Journal of the Council of Writing Program Administrators* 4 (1981): 15–20.

Fulwiler, Toby, and Art Young, eds. *Programs That Work: Models and Methods for Writing Across the Curriculum.* Portsmouth, NH: Boynton, 1990.

Glick, Milton D. "Writing Across the Curriculum: A Dean's Perspective." *WPA: Writing Program Administration* 11 (1988): 53–58.

Graham, Joan. "What Works: The Problems and Rewards of Cross-Curricular Writing Programs." *Current Issues in Higher Education* 3 (1983–84): 16–26.

———. "Writing Conferences in Disciplinary Contexts: Students Working Out What They Think." CCCC Convention. Chicago, Mar. 1990.

Hall, James W., and Barbara L. Kevles, eds. *In Opposition to Core Curriculum: Alternative Models for Undergraduate Education.* Westport, CT: Greenwood, 1982.

Haring-Smith, Tori, ed. *A Guide to Writing Programs: Writing Centers, Peer Tutoring Programs, and Writing Across the Curriculum.* Glenview, IL: Scott Foresman, 1987.

———. "What's Wrong with Writing Across the Curriculum?" CCCC Convention. Atlanta, Mar. 1987.

Herrington, Anne. "Writing in Academic Settings: A Study of the Contexts for Writing in Two College Chemical Engineering Courses." *Research in the Teaching of English* 19 (1985): 331–61.

Jolliffe, David A., ed. *Writing in Academic Disciplines.* Norwood, NJ: Ablex, 1988.

Kantor, Kenneth J. "The English Curriculum and the Structure of the Disciplines." *Theory into Practice* 22 (1984): 174–81.

Kaufer, David S., and Cheryl Geisler. "Novelty in Academic Writing." *Written Communication* 6 (1989): 286–311.

Kitzhaber, Albert R. *Themes, Theories, and Therapy.* New York: McGraw, 1963.

Langer, Judith A., and Arthur N. Applebee. *How Writing Shapes Thinking: A Study of Teaching and Writing.* NCTE Research Report No. 22. Urbana, IL: NCTE, 1987.

Language for Life. (The Bullock Report). London: HMSO, 1977.

Lanham, Richard. "Urgency and Opportunity: Implementing Writing Across the Curriculum." Address. University of Georgia faculty. Athens, 25 Apr. 1985. Reported in *Writing Across the Curriculum* 3 (1985): 5–6.

"Letters." *Physics Today* Feb. 1990: 11+.

"Letters." *Physics Today* May 1989: 9–11.

Maimon, Elaine P. "Cinderella to Hercules: Demythologizing Writing Across the Curriculum." *Journal of Basic Writing* 2 (1980): 3–11.

———. "Reexamining False Dichotomies." CCCC Convention. Chicago, Mar. 1990.

———. *Writing in the Arts and Sciences*. Boston: Little, 1981.

———. "Writing, Learning, and Thinking at Beaver College." College English Association Annual Meeting. Savannah, Mar. 1979. ERIC, ED 175054.

Marland, Michael. *Language Across the Curriculum: The Implementation of the Bullock Report in the Secondary School*. London: Heinemann, 1977.

McLeod, Susan H., ed. *Strengthening Programs for Writing Across the Curriculum*. San Francisco: Jossey, 1988.

———. "Writing Across the Curriculum: The Second Stage and Beyond." *College Composition and Communication* 40 (1989): 337–43.

Neel, Jasper P., ed. *Options for the Teaching of English: Freshman Composition*. New York: MLA, 1978.

Newcomb, Theodore M., and Everett K. Wilson, eds. *College Peer Groups*. Chicago: Aldine, 1966.

Roy, Walter. *The New Examination System*. London: Croom, 1986.

Rudolph, Fredrick. *Curriculum: A History of the American Undergraduate Course of Study Since 1636*. San Francisco: Jossey, 1978.

Sherif, Muzafer, and Carolyn W. Sherif, eds. *Interdisciplinary Relationships in the Social Sciences*. Chicago: Aldine, 1969.

Smith, Myrna J. "Bruner on Writing." *College Composition and Communication* 28 (1977): 129–33.

Smith, Ron. "Composition Requirements: A Report on a Nationwide Survey of Four-Year Colleges and Universities." *College Composition and Communication* 25 (1974): 138–48.

Spellmeyer, Kurt. "A Common Ground: The Essay in the Academy." *College English* 3 (1989): 262–76.

Stewart, Donald C. "The Status of Composition and Rhetoric in American Colleges, 1880–1902: An MLA Perspective." *College English* 47 (1975): 734–46.

Swanson-Owens, Deborah. "Identifying Natural Sources of Resistance: A Case Study of Implementing Writing Across the Curriculum." *Research in the Teaching of English* 20 (1986): 69–97.

"Swarthmore College." *Liberal Education* May/June 1987: 32–33.

Thaiss, Christopher. *Language Across the Curriculum in the Elementary Grades*. Urbana, IL: NCTE, 1986.

Thaiss, Christopher, and C. Suhor, eds. *Speaking and Writing, K–12: Classroom Strategies and the New Research*. Urbana, IL: NCTE, 1984.

"Two Comments on 'A Common Ground: The Essay in Academe.'" *College English* 52 (1990): 329–38.

Upcraft, M. Lee, ed. *The Freshman Year Experience: Helping Students Survive and Succeed in College*. San Francisco: Jossey, 1989.

Walvoord, Barbara E., et al. *Thinking and Writing in College: A Naturalistic Study of Students Writing in Four Disciplines*. Urbana, IL: NCTE, 1991.

Weiland, Steven. "History Toward Rhetoric." *College English* 49 (1987): 816–26.

Williams, Raymond. *Writing in Society*. London: Verso, 1984.

Young, Art. "Teaching Writing Across the University: The Michigan Tech Experience." College English Association Convention. Savannah, Mar. 1979. ERIC, ED 176928.

Young, Art, and Toby Fulwiler, eds. *Writing Across the Disciplines: Research into Practice*. Portsmouth, NH: Boynton, 1986.

2   *Language Across the Curriculum*

ALAN BULLOCK AND THE
COMMITTEE OF ENQUIRY

I t has been claimed that at no time in the life of an average person does he successfully achieve a more complex learning task than when he learns to speak, a task which is substantially completed before he is five years old. It has also been suggested that during the period from early infancy to five years old a child makes more rapid progress in learning about his environment than in any subsequent five-year span. The two processes cannot be independent. The effort a child needs to apply in learning language must derive from the satisfaction of evolving from helplessness to self-possession. Conversely, that very evolution must owe a great deal to the developing power of language as its instrument. What we advocate here is no more than that this interlocking of the means and the end should be maintained, if possible, throughout the years of schooling. To achieve this we must convince the teacher of history or of science, for example, that he has to understand the process by which his pupils take possession of the historical or scientific information that is offered them; and that such an understanding involves his paying particular attention to the part language plays in learning. The pupils' engagement with the subject may rely upon a linguistic process that his teaching procedures actually discourage.

The primary school teacher responsible for the whole or most of the schoolwork of his class already has it in his power to establish a language policy across the curriculum. Whether or not he is taking that opportunity will depend upon the extent to which the various uses of language permeate all the other learning activities, or to which, on the other hand, language learning is regarded as a separate activity. The distinction is a crucial one, and a great deal follows from it. For language to play its full role as a means of learning, the teacher must create in the classroom an environment which encourages a wide range of language uses. The effectiveness of this context for the purpose can be judged by the answers to a number of questions. For example, how often does a child share his personal interests and learning discoveries with others in the class? How far is the teacher able to enter such

From *Language for Life* (The Bullock Report). London: HMSO, 1975. 188–93.

conversations without robbing the children of verbal initiative? Are the children accustomed to read to one another what they have written, and just as readily listen? Are they accustomed to solving co-operatively in talk the practical problems that arise when they work together? How much opportunity is there for the kind of talk by which children make sense in their own terms of the information offered by teacher or by book? What varieties of writing — story, personal record, comment, report, speculation, etc. — are produced in the course of a day? Over a longer span, what varieties occur in the output of a single child? These are straws in the wind. What they indicate is the degree to which learning and the acquisition of language are interlocked. We have argued elsewhere, and particularly in connection with reading, the need for a consensus among the staff of a primary school on matters of language learning. The individual teacher is in a position to devise a language policy across the various aspects of the curriculum, but there remains the need for a general policy to give expression to the aim and ensure consistency throughout the years of primary schooling.

By his training and experience, the primary school teacher is likely to conceive of his task in terms of integrated rather than subject-oriented work. In the secondary school, however, it is traditional practice to move more or less directly into a programme of specialist teaching and a subject timetable. Clearly it is here that the proposals to be made in this chapter principally apply. A primary school teacher may happen to be unaware of new conceptions of the role of language, but he would not generally regard them as matters outside his concern. However, they are certainly regarded in this way by secondary school teachers of most subjects. The move from an integrated to a specialist curriculum constitutes in itself a considerably increased demand upon the linguistic powers of the pupil, but the most obvious demand, that for a wider and more specialised vocabulary, is not the principal difficulty. In general, a curriculum subject, philosophically speaking, is a distinctive mode of analysis. While many teachers recognise that their aim is to initiate a student in a particular mode of analysis, they rarely recognise the linguistic implications of doing so. They do not recognise, in short, that the mental processes they seek to foster are the outcome of a development that originates in speech. A person's impulse to talk over a problem that his thinking has failed to solve is a natural one; what he is doing is to regress to an earlier, simpler form of problem-solving situation. Every teacher has known occasions when a child has solved his difficulties in the act of explaining what they are. Face-to-face speech is a very direct embodiment of the relationship between the speakers. If the relationship is one that gives the speaker confidence he will be understood, it acts as a powerful incentive to him to complete the train of thought he has begun. It has even been claimed that goodwill is enough in a listener, without understanding.

When we consider the working day in a secondary school the neglect of pupil talk as a valuable means of learning stands out sharply. To bring about a change will take time and persistence. Where pupil talk has been accorded little status in teaching methods, it is not surprising that when the opportunity does occur it tends to be filled by pointless chatter. But the cycle can be broken, as experience has amply shown. There is no need to repeat here the points we have made earlier about the role of exploratory talk in the classroom. For such talk to nourish, the context must be as informal and re- laxed as possible, and this is most likely to occur in small groups and in a well-organised and controlled classroom. Once the practice has been estab- lished in such groups there is no reason why the exploratory talk should not succeed in due course with the whole class and the teacher together. The prin- ciple to be recognised, however, is that good "class discussion" cannot be had simply on demand; it must be built up on work in small groups, and continue to be supported by it.

If the value of expressive talk is commonly overlooked in many subject areas, expressive writing often finds no place at all. In a recent research study[1] it was found that the teachers of a number of subjects did not encourage such writing, and this can be taken to mean that the children were often being asked to run before they could walk. They were being required to report con- clusions in writing, their own or other people's, but not to produce the kind of writing that most effectively helps them to arrive at conclusions. The follow- ing passage[2] will illustrate the point. Asked to give an account of how to set up a wormery, a thirteen-year-old wrote:

> I fetched a bucket of soil and a cup. A jar of sand and some chalk. I fetched a wormery glass which you can see through. I made layers of soil then sand and then powdered chalk. I continued like that. Then I put some water in it. I have marked with biro where the water ran. Then I placed four worms in the wormery. They did not stir when they were on top of the soil but later they will. I put the wormery into a dark cupboard which is closed.

At thirteen a writer might have been expected to produce a simple and practi- cal statement in the style of a manual of instructions. In this light the comment made by his teacher, "Not very good," can be said to have been merited. What the pupil wrote, however, was an expressive statement reflecting his personal involvement. It is from such writing that the transactional must grow, and what the pupil wrote may have been appropriate to him at that particular stage.

We believe that expressive writing shares some of the virtues of expres- sive talk in helping a pupil to find his way into a subject. Moreover, it is an important stage on the way to a range of differentiated kinds of writing. To quote from the language policy document prepared by a secondary school we visited:

> As well as providing opportunities for purposeful oral work within a given context, other subject areas might consider how they can enlist the personal involvement and interest of children in any writing required of them.

Or as Rosen[3] has put it: "The demand for transactional writing in school is ceaseless, but expressive language with all its vitality and richness is the only possible soil from which it can grow."

There is a sequence of ways, fairly obvious in themselves, in which children gather information. They can be listed in ascending order of difficulty as follows:

finding out from observation and firsthand experience;

finding out from someone who will explain and discuss;

finding out by listening to a spoken monologue, for example a radio talk;

finding out by reading.

These are not, of course, four independent processes; on the contrary, they must be seen as variants of a single activity, likely to be used in close conjunction. Moreover, it must be recognised that the child's speaking and writing are essential means by which he appropriates and uses the information he has gathered. This places reading firmly in a context of the use of language. "Finding out by reading" puts the emphasis where we feel it belongs; the child reads because there is something he wants to find out, and this can be made to apply in any or every lesson on the timetable. This quest for information will call upon and promote [a] wide range of reading skills, but the child must be given the right kind of help. Subject teachers need to be aware of the processes involved, able to provide the variety of reading material that is appropriate, and willing to see it as their responsibility to help their pupils meet the reading demands of their subject. The variety of written forms a child encounters in reading will be an influence upon the development of his writing abilities. To restrict the first can result in limiting the second.

Furthermore, just as different tasks call upon different reading skills so also they demand a variety of modes of recording. Note making and other forms of record keeping associated with a pupil's reading can be valuable ways not simply of learning, but of "learning to learn." In the past attempts at teaching the art of learning have too often consisted in a few stereotyped methods of study, so generalised as to be of little value when applied in a real context. Subject teachers who know both the particular demands of their subjects and the individual needs of their pupils have an important contribution to make in this area.

This brief survey of language across the curriculum would not be complete if we failed to take account of the teacher's own language. There is no doubt that a well-prepared, extensive presentation by the teacher is sometimes the best way of handling a topic, particularly in the introductory stages of a course of study. It is likely to begin with the circulation of some material in the form of evidence, or data upon which conclusions can be based. The teacher marks out an area of concern and allows for a variety of approaches to it, and he does this through open-ended questions which elicit from his pupils the ideas and experiences upon which to work. The presentation is thus newly developed on each successive occasion. What the teacher is shaping by his probing is something to which both he and his pupils contribute. It may at the conclusion be an incomplete and modified version of what he intended, but it will be a truer representation of the understanding the group has reached than could have been derived from any direct exposition. In the course of working upon new concepts the teacher is bound to introduce new terms, but he can make good use of the pupils' own views and experiences to help them assimilate these. It is what the pupils do in following up the presentation that realises its value, and this is best achieved by the teacher's interaction with individuals and small groups. Getting children to talk to them is an art that most teachers acquire without giving the matter any thought. When it becomes evident to a teacher that his professional teaching relationship requires mutuality rather than distance, he is likely to find little difficulty in making the adjustment. The problem is that of reconciling this relationship with his role as a keeper of the peace, for he cannot avoid his responsibility for maintaining in the group an atmosphere in which learning may go on. There exist the two distinct roles of teaching and control, and the constant aim should be to develop the first to a point where it encompasses the second.

The notions we have been discussing here are gradually gaining currency, and we are encouraged by what has been achieved in the comparatively short time since their inception. The documentation has grown considerably in the last six years and now covers principles and practice, teaching and organisation. One of the earliest initiatives came from the London Association for the Teaching of English, which organised a series of conferences leading to the publication in 1969 of a discussion document,[4] "A language policy across the curriculum." A number of schools responded to the suggestions this contained, and there followed valuable contacts with other subject associations, notably the Association of Teachers of Mathematics. The topic was taken up by the National Association for the Teaching of English, which invited teachers of all subjects to its 1971 annual conference[5] and devoted the programme to a series of working groups on various aspects of language across the curriculum.

A teacher of mathematics afterwards reported:

> as children talk or write . . . in a mathematics lesson, or in the playground when they are sorting out the rules of a game of marbles, they are "doing mathematics." It is not just that language is used in mathematics: rather, it is that the language that is used is the mathematics. It was perhaps on this account that I did not feel myself too much of an eavesdropper when I went to Reading for the NATE conference: the discussions were directly relevant to my own concerns.

And a teacher of biology:

> How might further developments take place? There was a strong feeling that local follow-up was essential, perhaps in Teachers' Centres. Objectives should be much more restricted, for example "Reading" or "Projects" or "Discussion," and it will be necessary to consider the practical problems of small group work in the classroom. We all felt that other subject associations should become involved.

The next major development was a series of Department of Education and Science short courses, beginning in 1972, which brought together on successive occasions heads of schools, advisers, heads of subject departments, and representatives of subject associations. The courses were planned as working parties, and a number of stimulating papers were produced on language across the curriculum. Another focal point for teacher activity has been the Writing Across the Curriculum project,[6] at present being conducted for the Schools Council at the University of London Institute of Education. Several local authorities are now co-operating with the project team, and a large number of teachers are making a valuable contribution.

We have chosen these developments to illustrate the growth of interest in the notion of language across the curriculum, but it cannot be inferred from this that it has taken root in large numbers of schools. Despite such initiatives, and similar ones at [the] local level, there are still comparatively few schools which have introduced it as a policy. This is understandable, for it cannot be pretended that a policy of this kind is easy to establish. The need is not obvious to every teacher, and the head of the school can best influence others if he is himself informed and convinced. This, however, is only the beginning, and the head cannot achieve alone the introduction and maintenance of the policy. We have considered various ways in which it might take effect, but to endorse any one would be to produce a prescription that would not suit the circumstances of every school. One possibility is for the responsibility to lie with a senior member of staff, experienced and appropriately qualified, whose status is at least equal to that of the heads of department with whom he will be working so closely. The advantage of such an appointment is that the teacher concerned would be able to concentrate his efforts upon the policy and carry the weight to enable him to persuade and exercise influence. The difficulty might be that it would not be easy to argue for another post to be added to the senior level of the school management structure. In some schools it would be possible for the function to be taken on by a member of the staff already occupying a senior post, for example, a director of studies or curriculum coordinator where he was qualified for the role.

Whatever form it took it would be important to establish a proper working relationship with the head of [the] English department, whose own contribution to the policy must clearly be a considerable one. It could, of course, be argued that the head of [the] department and his English specialist colleagues are in an ideal position to take on the responsibility themselves, and this is another possibility to be considered. The virtues are obvious, but we have argued elsewhere that English departments — and particularly the teachers in charge of them — are hard-pressed. To expect them to add this important task to their existing commitments would be asking a great deal. Moreover, it is conceivable that in some schools such an arrangement might make it harder for the concept to win acceptance among the staff. One approach might be to place the responsibility with a committee composed of heads of department, with the head teacher and the head of English giving a strong lead. This has the advantage of continuous consultation and collective responsibility, but it could be countered that it takes an individual hand to give real leadership. Clearly a great deal depends upon the circumstances of each school, not least its size and its present administrative structure. We strongly recommend that whatever the means chosen to implement it a policy for language across the curriculum should be adopted by every secondary school. We are convinced that the benefits would be out of all proportion to the effort it would demand, considerable though this would undoubtedly be.

REFERENCES

1. *The Development of Writing Abilities (11–18)*, Writing Research Unit. Schools Council: 1974.
2. Reproduced in "Language Across the Curriculum" *English in Education*, Vol. 5, No. 2: 1971.
3. D. Barnes et al. *Language, the Learner, and the School*, revised edition. Penguin Education: 1971.
4. Reproduced in D. Barnes et al.: op. cit.
5. Reported in *Language Across the Curriculum*: op. cit.
6. See *From Information to Understanding*, University of London Institute of Education: 1973.

3

The Pedagogy of Writing Across the Curriculum

SUSAN McLEOD

Origins of WAC

Chances are good that if you are in the field of rhetoric and composition, you have heard of writing across the curriculum. As an educational reform movement, it has been around more than twenty-five years — about as long as the National Writing Project,[1] its counterpart in elementary and secondary schools. It was born in the 1970s during a time of curricular and demographic change in higher education, when college teachers found themselves with students who struggled with college writing tasks. The widespread use of the "objective" multiple-choice/true-false test in public education meant that many students had little practice with extended writing tasks by the time they got to college; at the same time, the rapid growth of higher education coupled with open admissions at some institutions brought a new population of first-generation college students to the institution. Faced with what looked like declining skills, faculty felt the need to do something, anything, about the state of student writing. The first WAC faculty seminar came about in 1969–70 at Central College in Pella, Iowa (Russell, *Writing* 283), when Barbara Walvoord's Chaucer seminar didn't make; to fill the void she organized a regular meeting of faculty to discuss issues of student writing. She went on to write the first book on teaching writing that was aimed at faculty in the disciplines, *Helping Students Write Well: A Guide for Teachers in All Disciplines*, first published in 1982. This book, now in its second edition, is still the standard reference for teachers in fields outside of English who need a guidebook to help them understand how to assign and respond to student writing. True to its title, the book is for those who want to help students learn to write well, as most faculty do.

All of us who have been involved in WAC since its beginnings have a story to tell about how we got started facilitating faculty seminars. The story usually involves faculty colleagues like Barbara's who were at their collective

From *A Guide to Composition Pedagogies*. Eds. Gary Tate, Amy Rupiper, and Kurt Schick. New York: Oxford UP, 2001. 149–64.

wits' end trying to deal with the student writing problems they were encountering. Here's mine. One day I was cornered just outside my office by a friend who taught history, who was furious with me and with (it appeared) not only the English Department but the entire discipline of English. "Why can't you people teach these students how to write?" he thundered. I was defensive — of course I was teaching them how to write. I had stacks of papers waiting to be graded to prove it. After we had both finished harumphing and started to listen to each other, I asked to see the papers he was so distressed about. Among them was a paper from a former student of mine, one who had done reasonably well in my freshman comp class the previous semester. He was right; it was abysmal. He had asked for analysis and discussion of historical data, and she had responded with vague generalities and personal opinion. Like all progressive writing teachers at that time, I was trying to help my students find their authentic voices. But my history colleague was not interested in this student's authentic voice; he wanted her to try to think and write like a historian. My class, based as it was on literary notions of what good writing was, had not helped her figure out how to do that. Out of cross-disciplinary faculty conversations like this one, out of seminars like the one Walvoord started, the WAC movement was born.

WHAT IS WAC?

Like the term *general education, writing across the curriculum* has come to have an aura that is vaguely positive, something that is good for students. Like general education programs, WAC programs are defined in part by their intended outcomes — helping students to become critical thinkers and problem-solvers as well as developing their communications skills. But unlike general education, WAC is uniquely defined by its pedagogy. Indeed, one might say that WAC has been, more than any other recent educational reform movement, one aimed at transforming pedagogy at the college level, at moving away from the lecture mode of teaching (the "delivery of information" model) to a model of active student engagement with the material and with the genres of the discipline through writing, not just in English classes but in all classes across the university. WAC draws on many pedagogical techniques used in general composition classes, but unlike those classes (for example, freshman composition) it focuses around a particular body of information. Where freshman composition might focus on teaching the general features of what we term "academic discourse," WAC focuses not on writing skills per se, but on teaching both the content of the discipline and the particular discourse features used in writing about that content.

When we speak of WAC pedagogy, we are talking about two somewhat different approaches: we may think of these under the headings of "writing to learn" and "writing to communicate."[2] The former is the pedagogy most identified with WAC programs, one that caught on quickly in the form of one of its most popular assignments, the journal. Based on the theories of language and learning articulated by James Britton and by Janet Emig in her article "Writing as a Mode of Learning," this pedagogy encourages teachers to use ungraded writing (writing to the self as audience) in order to have students think on paper, to objectify their knowledge and therefore to help them discover both what they know and what they need to learn. The latter approach, writing to communicate, is pedagogically more complex. It is based on theories of the social construction of knowledge, best summarized in Kenneth Bruffee's article "Collaborative Learning and the 'Conversation of Mankind.'" The most obvious pedagogical manifestation of this approach is the use of peer groups in the classroom and approaches to teaching that take into account analysis of the discourse of the disciplines and genre theory. The rest of this essay will be devoted to these two pedagogical approaches for classrooms — writing to learn and writing to communicate — and will in addition consider the appropriate pedagogy for one of the most important elements of a WAC program, the faculty workshop.

Before reviewing these approaches, however, I feel it necessary to warn readers away from a view of writing to learn and writing to communicate somehow in conflict with each other. There are two articles in the WAC literature that present such a view: C. A. Knoblauch and Lil Brannon's "Writing as Learning Through the Curriculum," and more recently, Daniel Mahala's "Writing Utopias: Writing Across the Curriculum and the Promise of Reform." The former article appeared in *College English* before it became a refereed journal; it presents a vision of then-existing WAC programs as being largely "grammar across the curriculum," a claim that is not backed by any proof and certainly not borne out by the results of national WAC surveys that I have now twice conducted (McLeod; Miraglia and McLeod). The authors' discussion of the textbook *Writing in the Arts and Sciences* by Elaine Maimon and her colleagues (mentioned below) is a good example of what I see as a false dichotomy, characterizing that text as an introduction to mere forms and formats and opposing it to "writing to learn." The same approach is taken by Mahala, who sets up a dichotomy between "American formalism" and "British expressivism," again misrepresenting the approach of Maimon and colleagues by quoting out of context from their work in order to argue his case. Neither of these articles is taken seriously by the WAC discourse community at large. On the contrary, most of us who have been involved in WAC programs from the beginning see "writing to learn" and "writing to communicate" as two complementary, even synergistic, approaches to writing across the curriculum.

WRITING TO LEARN

Writing to learn pedagogy encourages teachers to use writing as a tool for learning as well as a test for learning, or as James Moffett would say at workshops, "writing to *know* as well as to *show*." This branch of WAC has its roots in the language across the curriculum movement in British secondary schools, sparked by James Britton and his colleagues and associated in the United States with Toby Fulwiler and his colleagues at Michigan Technological University.

In *Language and Learning*, Britton argued that language is central to learning because it is through language that we organize our representations of the world (214). His research called for the use of more "expressive" writing in the curriculum — writing that will help students explore and assimilate new ideas, create links between the unfamiliar and the familiar, mull over possibilities, explain things to the self before explaining them to others. The analog for this kind of student writing is the expert's notebook — the scientist's lab book, the engineer's notebook, the artist's and architect's sketchbook (the journals of Thomas Edison and of Leonardo da Vinci are prototypical examples). It is not polished work intended for an outside audience; sometimes it is comprehensible only to the writer.

For such writing to be useful in the classroom as a tool for learning, it must be ungraded. The teacher does respond, but as a facilitator and coach rather than as a judge. As I mentioned earlier, the most popular writing to learn assignment, one that caught on very quickly across the curriculum, is the journal. In *The Journal Book*, Toby Fulwiler has gathered together more than forty accounts from teachers across the disciplines who use journals in their classrooms. The actual assignments vary. Ann Berthoff describes the dialectical notebook — a double-entry notebook, with summaries of readings or passages copied out on one side and the student's responses (or metacomments) on the facing page (11–18). Jana Staton discusses the dialogue journal, in which elementary school students comment and the teacher responds, creating a private conversation between teacher and student about course content (47–63). French teacher Karen Wiley Sandler describes the use of the journal in the foreign language class as a place to experiment and make mistakes (as we all do when learning a language) without fear of penalty; the journal becomes a place to approximate, to play with the new language (312–20). Catherine Larson and Margaret Merrion describe the music journal, used to help students understand and describe the aesthetic experience of listening to music (254–60). Stephen BeMiller describes the mathematics notebook, in which students do their practice work — explorations of possible solutions to problems, discussions of the course challenges, questions, outlines of concepts, and self-tests of comprehension (359–66). All the descriptions have one thing in common: student use of informal, speculative, personal writing to make sense of the course material with the teacher acting as prompter and guide.

Of course, the journal is not the only assignment teachers have integrated into their pedagogical repertoire. Another way to facilitate writing as a mode of learning is the "quick write" or "focused freewrite" that has become popularized by Thomas Angelo and K. Patricia Cross in *Classroom Assessment Techniques*[3] as the "minute paper" (148–58). Where the journal is more suitable for smaller classes in which the teacher can collect and respond to student writing periodically, the minute paper has been used successfully in classes of all sizes, including large lecture classes. The technique is simple: at some point in the class, the students write for one minute answering a question that asks them to evaluate their learning in some way. For example, at the end of a lecture, students might be asked to jot down the two or three most important points of the lecture, and also what puzzled them about the material. These jottings, usually no more than half a page, give the teacher instant feedback as to the success of the lecture and show her what issues may need clarification. Angelo and Cross give this example: a history teacher might ask students two questions: "What is the single most significant reason that Italy became a center of the Renaissance?" and "What one question puzzles you about Italy's role in the Renaissance?" Because they are writing anonymously, students are free to express their genuine puzzlement, and the teacher can see immediately how to address their confusion about cause and effect in the next lecture. The minute paper is not only a mode of learning for the students, it is also for the teacher a window into their learning, a method of establishing communication between teacher and student in large classes.

There are many other ways to use writing to learn assignments. John Bean, in *Engaging Ideas: The Professor's Guide to Integrating Writing, Critical Thinking, and Active Learning in the Classroom*, devotes chapter 6 to twenty-five varieties of what he calls "exploratory writing." These include versions of the journal and the minute paper as well as creative approaches (having students write an imaginary dialogue between historical figures) and practice pieces for what will eventually be graded writing (for example, dry run essay exams). Bean also answers the common objections teachers have to using this kind of writing (it will take too much time; students will regard it as busy work; if it's not corrected it will promote bad writing habits), and provides useful suggestions for responding to the assignments and managing the paper load.

Two major characteristics of WAC write-to-learn pedagogy should be clear by now. First, such pedagogy is student centered. College faculty who focus on and are concerned about their students' learning are those who pick up WAC techniques and use them successfully; they are quick to see the value of assignments like those described above that promote active learning and critical thinking. Second, it is reflective. These exploratory writing assignments are all ones that provide a feedback loop to the teacher as to the progress of student learning, allowing her or him to adjust the teaching accordingly. It also takes the teacher out of the role of judge for awhile, allowing her to play the role of coach. As the now-famous active learning mantra goes, the teacher moves from being the sage on the stage to the guide on the side.

Writing to Communicate

Writing to communicate is the other branch of WAC. It is closely related and interconnected with writing to learn, but has these important differences: it focuses on writing to an audience outside the self in order to inform that audience, and the writing therefore is revised, crafted, and polished. Writing to communicate is reader based rather than writer based, and uses the formal language of a particular discourse community to communicate information. This branch of WAC is sometimes called WID, writing in the disciplines. It is most closely identified with Elaine Maimon's WAC program at Beaver

College, which started about the same time as Toby Fulwiler's program at Michigan Tech. Maimon's program, like Walvoord's and Fulwiler's, also grew out of a close collaboration of faculty colleagues, faculty talking to each other in a series of workshops about how to help students with their writing. Out of that program grew a textbook, *Writing in the Arts and Sciences*, now out of print.[4] In that text, Maimon (who invited Kenneth Bruffee, among others, to help lead the faculty workshops at her institution) articulates not only writing-to-learn principles, but also what has become known as the "social turn" in teaching writing: "Writing in every discipline is a form of social behavior in that discipline" (xii).

The notion of discourse communities is a commonplace now in the field of rhetoric and composition, but was not so obvious to composition teachers in the 1980s. In my own experience, at least, conversations with faculty in other disciplines helped me understand the nature of the differences in disciplinary discourses. Permit me another story. I was working with a group of graduate students in our American Studies program at my institution, students who shuttled back and forth between seminars in English and in history. Some of them were having mysterious difficulties with their papers for those classes; both history and English professors were circling their verbs and writing "tense" in the margins. The students were stumped. They had never had such problems as undergraduate history or English majors. I sat down with a history colleague, and together we discovered what should have been obvious. In English, we use the present tense to quote the words of authors long dead: "As Shakespeare says . . ." For us, these authors live on in their texts; they are not of an age but for all time. But in history dates are very important, and one must mark the tense accordingly to indicate which authors are current and which are historical (e.g., dead). A historian would never write, "Gibbon says." The question was not just one of verb tense, but of epistemology.

WAC as writing to communicate, as differentiated from writing to learn, puts the teacher in a somewhat different but related pedagogical situation. The teacher is still a guide, but is focusing now on helping students learn the discourse of the discipline; the relationship is that of seasoned professional to apprentice, or in anthropological terms, of tribal elder to initiate. The person who knows best how to initiate the newcomer is not the composition teacher, but the teacher who is already grounded in the content of the field and who is fluent in the disciplinary discourse — the history teacher, the biology teacher, the math teacher.

This is not to say that we as writing teachers can't make students aware that there are different discourse communities and teach them some strategies for asking the right questions about discourse expectations in their other classes. Patricia Linton and her associates, in an excellent (and too little known) article on the role of the general composition course in WAC, describe how such a class might be set up: teaching students to observe disciplinary patterns in the way discourse is structured, helping them understand the various rhetorical moves that are accepted within particular discourse communities, explaining conventions of reference and of language. Composition teachers, the authors argue, are no strangers to teaching discourse analysis; we just need to enlarge our notions of what discourse we should be helping students analyze. Linton and her associates, this time with Madigan as the lead author,[5] demonstrate in another article how one might go about analyzing the language of psychology; in this article they suggest something far more complex than teaching students how to cite sources in APA as well as MLA style in first-year composition. Instead, they demonstrate convincingly that APA style is the embodiment of social science epistemology; the style reflects the values of the discipline. I think of a student I had recently, a theater major named Ginger, who was given to large dramatic gestures in class and double exclamation points in her prose. One day she brought in a draft of a paper she was writing in her introductory psychology class. She was researching child abuse in the United States, and had written "the statistics are horrifying." The teacher had circled the last word and written in the margin "diction." In a conference with the teacher Ginger had been told she couldn't use such a word in APA style. She came to me to vent: Why couldn't she???? What was wrong with saying that, since it was true???? After she had calmed down somewhat, we discussed some of the values of psychology, in particular the detached, objective tone. Although she wasn't happy about it, Ginger saw the point and changed "horrifying" to "cause for concern."

Having said that composition teachers can make students aware of disciplinary differences, of the fact that "good writing" (in academe as elsewhere) is a relative term, I must go on to state that such a course is only a first step toward helping students write to communicate in their own disciplines. The person who has the disciplinary knowledge base and writes the discourse as a mother tongue is the person who can best serve as mentor in this professional-apprentice relationship.[6]

The fact that academics are so grounded in their own disciplinary discourse conventions presents an immediate challenge, however, precisely because the conventions seem so natural to those fluent in them that it is difficult for them to see why students struggle as they learn them, or why writing in other disciplines has different but equally valid conventions. The psychology teacher is so used to the passive voice as a signal of objectivity in social science writing that she thinks of it as the norm, and of writing in the humanities as "flowery." I will say something in the final section about how WAC directors might approach this issue of disciplinary ethnocentrism in a WAC workshop; for now let us assume that faculty in the disciplines are aware of these differences and wish to demystify their own disciplinary discourse for students, helping them learn appropriate ways to write to those in their field as well as to audiences outside their field. How might they go about it?

There are various resources for teachers in the disciplines, many of them written by colleagues in those disciplines. I will mention just a few here. *Mathematical Writing*, edited by Donald Knuth and his associates and published by the Mathematical Association of America, is a book by and for mathematicians. It consists of lecture transcripts and handouts from a course of the same name offered at Stanford University in 1987. The course involved various star guest lecturers, and it focused on writing in computer science as well as in mathematics.[7] Robert Day's *How to Write and Publish a Scientific Paper* is a readable and lively book which at first glance seems to deal only with forms and formats, but in fact deals with the way knowledge is created in scientific fields; the chapter entitled "How to List the Authors," for example, deals with the thorny issue of who is really an "author" when a team of scientists has contributed to the findings. Perhaps the ultimate disciplinary discourse may be found in the foreign language curriculum, where the discourse to be learned is indeed an entirely different language. Claire Gaudiani's *Teaching Composition in the Foreign Language Curriculum* focuses on the issue of developing fluency in prose written in the target language, focusing on how learning to write in a foreign language differs considerably from learning to write in one's native language. Finally, there are a number of sites rapidly developing on the Web for teachers in the disciplines to consult. The most useful of these from my point of view is the WAC Clearinghouse at http://wac.colostate.edu. The site has answers to questions frequently asked about WAC and provides links to other WAC sites on the Web.

These and other resources like them for faculty in the disciplines may be thought of in light of genre theory. As Carol Berkenkotter and Thomas Huckin say in their book *Genre Knowledge in Disciplinary Communication*, "[g]enres are the media through which scholars and scientists communicate with their peers. Genres are intimately linked to a discipline's methodology, and they package information in ways that conform to a discipline's norms, values, and ideology" (1). Teaching the genres of the discourse community is therefore inseparable from teaching the disciplinary knowledge of the discipline. The pedagogy connected with such teaching is not one of forms and formats; it involves setting up various practice sessions for students to model the writing behaviors and practices they will need as members of particular discourse communities. This means doing away with the usual kinds of school assignments, writing only for the teacher as examiner, and having students try out as much as possible writing to real audiences for real professional purposes.

Teachers have known for some time that there is something wrong with the "school" writing assignment; in 1965, W. Earl Britton had this to say:

> I believe that in all too many instances, at least in college, the student writes the wrong thing, for the wrong reason, to the wrong person, who evaluates it on the wrong basis. That is, he writes about a subject he is not thoroughly informed upon, in order to exhibit his knowledge rather than explain something the reader does not understand, and he writes to a professor who already knows more than he does about the matter and who evaluates the paper, not in terms of what he has derived, but in terms of what he thinks the writer knows. In every respect, this is the converse of what happens in professional life, where the writer is the 'hority; he writes to transmit new or unfamiliar knowledge to some-who does not know but needs to, and who evaluates the paper in of what he derives and understands. (116)

The pedagogy of WAC as writing to communicate invites teachers to think about how they might place students in rhetorical situations that approximate those they will encounter as professionals in their fields and learn to use the appropriate genres and discourse conventions. For example, the College of Engineering at my institution has a capstone course in which students form teams that become consulting firms; they must go out into the community, find a client, and work up a project for that client, who then has a say in their final grade for the class. Business schools pioneered the use of the case method for situated learning, giving students a narrative describing a realistic scenario in which they might find themselves in their work and asking them to provide possible solutions to the problem described; this method has been used successfully by teachers in other disciplines to create writing assignments like the ones students will encounter in their professions.[8] Teachers in fields that are not charged with preparing students for such specific professions (for example, the liberal arts) are nevertheless able to create writing assignments that have audiences other than the teacher as examiner and have some purpose other than testing student knowledge and comprehension.

Genre theory also brings with it the promise of a pedagogical approach aimed at helping linguistically marginalized groups in academe — those whose home language is not standard English. Using a functional linguistics approach developed by M. A. K. Halliday at the University of Sydney (and promulgated by Gunther Kress in the United Kingdom), researchers in Australia have developed an "explicit pedagogy for inclusion and access" (Cope and Kalantzis 63), one that focuses explicitly on the teaching of genre as a way of teaching academic literacy. According to Bill Cope and Mary Kalantzis, this approach has been very successful with aboriginal children in Australia. Such a pedagogy is not without its critics, however; Berkenkotter and Huckin provide a useful examination of the issues in chapter 8 of *Genre Knowledge in Disciplinary Communication* (a chapter they title "Suffer the Little Children"). Their most telling critique is this: "It may be that a genre approach to the teaching of writing does not fit many language arts and composition teachers' conception of their role, given their training, ideological loyalties, and professional allegiances. If this is the case, rethinking the training of language arts and composition teachers as well as the current curricula in language arts and university writing courses may be what is called for" (163). Russell's article "Rethinking Genre in School and Society: An Activity Theory Analysis" also provides a useful overview of the issues involved in explicit teaching of genres.

Writing in the disciplines involves more than just learning genres and discourse conventions, however. It also involves learning the processes by which experts in the field develop and disseminate knowledge. Russell, in a 1993 article, argues the matter thus: "[Since writing is] a matter of learning to participate in some historically situated human activity that requires some kind(s) of writing, it cannot be learned apart from the problems, the habits, the activities — the subject matter — of some group that found the need to write in that way to solve a problem or carry on its activities" ("Vygotsky" 194).

What are some of the "habits and activities" Russell refers to that might be translated into pedagogical practice? One obvious answer is collaborative learning techniques, which are based on assumptions about the social nature of learning as well as of the collaborative construction of disciplinary knowledge. Donald Finkel and G. Stephen Monk's "Teachers and Learning Groups: Dissolution of the Atlas Complex" was an early resource for teachers in the disciplines. This piece encourages teachers to view their classrooms as social systems, and offers suggestions about how to get out of the two-person model of interaction (teacher-student) and encourage interaction among students that models the mode of debate and intellectual exchange among colleagues in the discipline. Finkel and Monk do not advocate exclusive use of group work, but differentiate among teaching functions (lecture, Socratic questioning, guided group work) and encourage teachers to think about which particular function suits each part of the course. Once teachers in the disciplines begin to see the teacher/student relationship as one of professional/apprentice, and once they also begin to view their classrooms as social systems that model the methods and the discourse of their particular discipline, it is not a large step for them to see that it makes sense for apprentices to follow the same process that the experts do when writing papers. If the experts draft papers and revise according to readers' and editors' comments, students should become familiar with this process. One of the most interesting quiet revolutions that has taken place on college campuses as a result of successful WAC programs is the use by many teachers in the disciplines of what we have come to think of as the "process approach" in teaching writing — not only allowing revision of student work, but requiring it, often using peer groups in the classroom to respond to drafts.

The increased use of peers for responding to student writing is most obvious in that now-familiar unit on campus, the writing center. It is not coincidental that WAC and writing centers have grown up together during the past twenty-five years, since they are natural partners and in many institutions mutually dependent on one another. One early (1984) article by Bruffee, "Peer Tutoring and the 'Conversation of Mankind,'" ties the theory of peer tutoring to the notion of the disciplinary conversation, showing how tutoring from a knowledgeable peer can help model the "habits and activities" (to use Russell's term again) of the knowledge-constructing processes in the disciplines. Ray Wallace's "The Writing Center's Role in the Writing Across the Curriculum Program: Theory and Practice" discusses not only theory but also gives some practical guidelines for tying the writing center firmly to a WAC program — including a helpful outline of a WAC tutor-training course.

SHOWING, NOT TELLING, AT A WRITING WORKSHOP

I have borrowed the heading for the final section of this essay from Toby Fulwiler's early article on how a WAC faculty workshop should be run because it summarizes the main point to be made about all such workshops: they must model the pedagogy they are promulgating. Faculty don't like being told what to do in their own classrooms, and rightly so — not every technique is workable in every class. Faculty need to try out various techniques and decide for themselves how to adapt them to their own teaching and achieve their own pedagogical ends. Would-be facilitators of WAC faculty workshops should think carefully about how to use the pedagogical techniques they are suggesting in order to demonstrate their power. There are two rules of thumb: faculty should themselves write, and faculty should have opportunities to talk to each other about writing. Both writing-to-learn and writing-to-communicate pedagogies should be integral parts of every WAC faculty workshop. I said at the beginning that WAC programs grew out of cross-disciplinary faculty conversations, and that faculty workshops are at the heart of any WAC program. The reason for this is rather simple: faculty tend to teach as they were taught. The lecture mode is still one of the most common modes of instruction at research institutions, where faculty get their degrees. The faculty workshop is a place for faculty to learn other modes of instruction by experiencing these modes themselves and understanding from the inside out, as it were, how something other than a lecture-quiz approach to learning might work.

If you wish to set up and facilitate a faculty workshop, there are two sorts of resources available to you: those of the "how to" variety, which are of most use to the workshop facilitator, and those that can be used in the workshop as texts or resources for the workshop faculty. Fulwiler's article, mentioned earlier, is of the first sort, explaining how various types of workshops may be set up and managed. Anne Herrington's "Writing to Learn: Writing Across the Disciplines" also lays out some of the issues one needs to think about in planning a faculty workshop. For example, workshops often ask faculty to write out their course objectives and expected learning outcomes for one of their classes to bring to the workshop, so that they can design writing assignments connected to those course objectives. Often college faculty, most of whom have had no formal pedagogical training, find this small exercise one of the most useful parts of the workshop, since they have thought about course objectives and expected outcomes only tacitly. Joyce Magnotto and Barbara Stout have written the most direct and comprehensive piece on how to run a faculty workshop; it is full of advice on all aspects of such an event, and includes a sample syllabus. Some books that can be very helpful to the would-be WAC workshop leader are now available from commercial presses. The most useful of these is *The Harcourt Brace Guide to Writing Across the Curriculum* by Christopher Thaiss. Thaiss deals not only with conducting a workshop but also with how to launch a WAC program, WAC options for the curriculum, assessment, and research. It is the most compact, comprehensive book on WAC to date; this is not surprising, given the fact that Thaiss is the head of the Board of Consultants of the National Network of Writing Across the Curriculum Programs.* The Board meets once a year as a Special Interest Group at the Conference on College Composition and Communication and consists of

*Now the International Network of Writing Across the Curriculum. — Eds.

seasoned WAC directors who can be brought to campus as consultants. If you are asked to start a WAC program on your campus, the outside consultant is a time-honored way of getting faculty involved. I should also mention here the book that I co-edited with Margot Soven, *Writing Across the Curriculum: A Guide to Developing Programs*; this book, with chapters from some of the members of the Board of Consultants of the National Network of WAC programs, gives advice on starting and sustaining WAC programs and is intended for administrators as well as faculty.

There are several books that may be used as texts for a workshop and resources for teachers in the disciplines, books that have been written by experienced workshop facilitators and based in large part on their own versions of the WAC workshop. The earliest of these, *Improving Student Writing: A Guidebook for Faculty in All Disciplines* by Andrew Moss and Carol Holder, is short, affordable, and full of practical tips for teachers; its virtue is that parts of it (for example, the chapter on designing writing assignments) may be used as a basis for a segment of a seminar, but it is also a useful reference book for teachers after the seminar. True to its title, it really is a guidebook. More recently, Margot Soven has published a similar short guide, *Write to Learn: A Guide to Writing Across the Curriculum*. Soven's book provides instructions and models for academic assignments that are sequenced from journal writing to more formal academic assignments. (Bean's useful book, mentioned earlier, is a good resource for a faculty seminar, but probably too expensive to order copies for all participants.) Fulwiler's *Teaching with Writing* grew out of the many workshops Fulwiler has facilitated and may be used either as a text for a workshop or as a sort of workbook to be used by an individual teacher interested in learning more about using writing as a pedagogical tool.

As I said above, WAC workshop pedagogy should model both write-to-learn and write-to-communicate pedagogies. Let me give just two examples. I always begin a WAC faculty workshop with an exercise I saw modeled long ago at a WAC conference. First, I ask participants to write for a few minutes about the student writing problems they encounter; there is no lack of interest in this topic, and participants write busily. We then discuss what they have written and try to come to a consensus about the most important writing problems (the discussion invariably focuses on conceptual problems as being more important than the grammatical issues). I then give them a truly dreadful student paper and ask them to mark it as if it were a paper for one of their classes; then I ask them to tally up the sorts of marks they have made. Even though we have just discussed the fact that conceptual issues are more important than grammatical ones, they find that most of their marks are for spelling and punctuation errors. I then ask them to write for a few moments about how they might establish a hierarchy of problems to respond to in student writing, and we discuss possible grading rubrics. Finally, I ask them to step back and think about the way we used writing in this particular segment of the workshop — to begin the discussion, to think through the issue of responding to student papers, and we talk about possible applications to their own classes. We discuss writing to learn only after they have used it as a technique for their own thinking and learning.

To get at the issue of disciplinary discourse and get participants out of their disciplinary ethnocentrism a bit, I hand out a one-page student paper and ask faculty to grade it, using whatever criteria they wish — but they have to articulate their criteria for the rest of us. Invariably, teachers from the humanities grade it low, saying "lack of development" is the problem. Teachers from the sciences and from business grade it high, saying it is "concise." This always leads into a lively discussion of discourse values and of articulating those values for students. One of the more interesting discussions I have heard among faculty on this issue had to do with the use of headings: the engineering faculty member said he graded a paper down if it didn't have headings, since these were important signposts for the reader of technical material. Technical reports are not read front to back, but readers skip around to find the most important and relevant information. The history teacher said he graded papers down if they *did* have headings; history involves writing a careful, analytical narrative. Clearly, a student who relied on headings for this narrative hadn't yet learned how to use transitions gracefully. Hearing discussions like these helps teachers understand why students can be confused about disciplinary discourse conventions.

FINAL THOUGHTS: THE FUTURE OF WAC

A recent thread on the Writing Program Administration listserv was titled "Is WAC dead?" A lively discussion ensued in cyberspace, with those of us who have been involved in WAC most of our professional lives saying "Of course not!" and pointing to the record attendance at the last (1997) national WAC conference. But on reflection, I can see why the question was asked. In the early days of WAC, funding was readily available for programs; outside funding for WAC programs is now rare. Book publishers are no longer slapping a WAC subtitle on their more popular composition textbooks, hoping to push their sales higher. WAC is no longer the new initiative that deans want to claim on their CVs as they climb up the administrative ladder toward a position as provost.

But the interesting thing about the WAC reform movement is that over the decades it has been able to tie into and become part of whatever new initiative was thrust upon higher education. For example, the 1980s may be thought of as the decade of assessment and accountability in higher education. Institutions of higher learning were being pressured by legislators and by the taxpaying public to show that they were really doing what they claimed to do. Many of us involved in WAC programs had already developed extensive assessment tools to examine student writing; WAC and the assessment movement became allies in many universities. At my own institution, for example, we were called upon to present baseline data for freshmen writing skills, mid-point data, and end-of-program assessment data. Because our WAC program already involved a placement test for freshmen and a rising junior writing portfolio, we were able not only to provide the data but to track students longitudinally and show improvement in their writing between entry and mid-point assessment. I mentioned the book by Angelo and Cross earlier; that book is a good example of WAC techniques that are cast as assessment techniques — not necessarily in the sense of testing student knowledge but of assessing where students are, how well the instruction as well as the learning is progressing.

If the decade of the 1980s was one of assessment, that of the 1990s has been the decade of technology. Legislators and administrators alike are backing technology initiatives not only in the classroom but beyond; many institutions (my own included) are investing heavily in distance learning technologies, creating virtual classrooms and interacting with students on-line as well as (or often instead of) in person. WAC is part of this movement, although that fact may not be apparent. The most interesting recent WAC book doesn't even have the word "writing" in the title: it is called *Electronic Communication Across the Curriculum* (Reiss, Selfe, and Young). WAC has become ECAC.

What is the future of WAC? I am confident that it will continue as it has for the last twenty-five years, as an educational movement aimed at transforming college pedagogy and encouraging active learning as students understand and become part of the construction of knowledge in the disciplines. In the next twenty-five years, the term *writing across the curriculum* itself may disappear. Who cares? As long as there are teachers focusing on writing to learn and writing to communicate in the disciplines, WAC will continue to be part of the landscape of higher education.

NOTES

1. The educational reform movement now known as the National Writing Project began in 1974 as the Bay Area Writing Project; by 1976 it was a model for statewide staff development, and by 1979 it had become the National Writing Project. See Russell, *Writing* 280–82.

2. James Britton and his associates called these "expressive" and "transactional" in his influential book *The Development of Writing Abilities* (11–18).

3. Although their book does not have WAC in its title, Angelo and Cross describe many pedagogical techniques and assignments that are drawn from WAC pedagogy.

4. The book is available in some university libraries. Maimon coauthored a new text (with Janice Peritz), *A Writer's Resource: A Handbook for Writing and Research*, that she says is a second-generation *Writing in the Arts and Sciences*.

5. Madigan is the psychologist of this interdisciplinary team; putting his name first is an example of the very style the authors are discussing, in which the lead author is put first to ensure that he or she will get the citation.

6. Here I would be remiss if I did not mention my own mentors as I attempted to enter the discourse community of writing across the curriculum. When I set up my first WAC workshop, Carol Holder of California Polytechnic University, Pomona, was extremely generous with her time and materials, even coming down to run one session for me. Later, an administrator sent me to one of the meetings on WAC held at the University of Chicago to meet Elaine Maimon, who was a speaker at the meeting. In spite of her busy schedule, she met with me and gave me invaluable advice. Both Carol and Elaine urged me to call Toby Fulwiler, who likewise helped generously, coming out to my present institution when I started a WAC program here. I continue to be grateful to these three early leaders in WAC for their help and encouragement as I was learning my way in the field.

7. Videotapes of the class sessions are in the Mathematical and Computer Sciences Library at Stanford.

8. For further information about the case method, see Hutchings, *Using Cases to Improve College Teaching*.

BIBLIOGRAPHY

Angelo, Thomas A., and K. Patricia Cross. *Classroom Assessment Techniques: A Handbook for College Teachers.* 2nd ed. San Francisco: Jossey-Bass, 1993.

Bean, John. *Engaging Ideas: The Professor's Guide to Integrating Writing, Critical Thinking, and Active Learning in the Classroom.* San Francisco: Jossey-Bass, 1996.

Berkenkotter, Carol, and Thomas N. Huckin. *Genre Knowledge in Disciplinary Communication: Cognition/Culture/Power.* Hillsdale, NJ: Erlbaum, 1995.

Britton, James. *Language and Learning.* London: Penguin, 1970.

Britton, James, et al. *The Development of Writing Abilities (11–18).* London: Macmillan, 1975.

Britton, W. Earl. "What Is Technical Writing?" *College Composition and Communication* 16 (1965): 113–16.

Bruffee, Kenneth A. "Collaborative Learning and the 'Conversation of Mankind.'" *College English* 46 (1984): 635–52.

———. "Peer Tutoring and the 'Conversation of Mankind.'" *Writing Centers: Theory and Administration.* Ed. Gary Olson. Urbana, IL: NCTE, 1984. 3–15.

Cope, Bill, and Mary Kalantzis. "The Power of Literacy and the Literacy of Power." *The Powers of Literacy: A Genre Approach to Teaching Writing.* Ed. Bill Cope and Mary Kalantzis. Pittsburgh: U of Pittsburgh P, 1993. 63–89.

Day, Robert. *How to Write and Publish a Scientific Paper.* Phoenix: Oryx, 1994.

Emig, Janet. "Writing as a Mode of Learning." *College Composition and Communication* 28 (1977): 122–28.

Finkel, Donald L., and G. Stephen Monk. "Teachers and Learning Groups: Dissolution of the Atlas Complex." *Learning in Groups.* Ed. Clark Bouton and Russell Y. Garth. New Directions for Teaching and Learning 14. San Francisco: Jossey-Bass, 1983. 83–97.

Fulwiler, Toby. *The Journal Book.* Portsmouth, NH: Boynton/Cook-Heinemann, 1987.

———. "Showing, Not Telling, at a Writing Workshop." *College English* 43 (1981): 55–63.

———. *Teaching with Writing.* Upper Montclair, NJ: Boynton/Cook, 1987.

Gaudiani, Claire. *Teaching Composition in the Foreign Language Curriculum.* Washington, DC: Center for Applied Linguistics, 1981.

Herrington, Anne J. "Writing to Learn: Writing Across the Disciplines." *College English* 43 (1984): 379–87.

Hutchings, Pat. *Using Cases to Improve College Teaching: A Guide to More Reflective Practice.* Washington, DC: American Association of Higher Education, 1993.

Knoblauch, C. A., and Lil Brannon. "Writing as Learning Through the Curriculum." *College English* 45 (1983): 465–74.

Knuth, Donald E., Tracy Larrabee, and Paul M. Roberts. *Mathematical Writing.* MAA Notes 14. Mathematical Association of America, 1989.

Linton, Patricia, Robert Madigan, and Susan Johnson. "Introducing Students to Disciplinary Genres: The Role of the General Composition Course." *Language and Learning Across the Disciplines* 1 (1994): 63–78.

Madigan, Robert, Susan Johnson, and Patricia Linton. "The Language of Psychology: APA Style as Epistemology." *American Psychologist* 50 (1995): 428–36.

Magnotto, Joyce Neff, and Barbara R. Stout. "Faculty Workshops." *Writing Across the Curriculum: A Guide to Developing Programs.* Ed. Susan H. McLeod and Margot Soven. Newbury Park, CA: Sage, 1992.

Mahala, Daniel. "Writing Utopias: Writing Across the Curriculum and the Promise of Reform." *College English* 53 (1991): 773–89.

Maimon, Elaine, et al. *Writing in the Arts and Sciences.* Cambridge, MA: Winthrop, 1981.

Maimon, Elaine, and Janice Peritz. *A Writer's Resource: A Handbook for Writing and Research.* Boston: McGraw-Hill, 2003.

McLeod, Susan H. "Writing Across the Curriculum: The Second Stage, and Beyond." *College Composition and Communication* 40 (1989): 337–43. Rpt. in *Landmarks in Writing Across the Curriculum.* Ed. David R. Russell and Charles Bazerman. Davis, CA: Hermagoras, 1994. 79–86.

McLeod, Susan H., and Margot Soven, eds. *Writing Across the Curriculum: A Guide to Developing Programs.* Newbury Park, CA: Sage, 1992.

Miraglia, Eric, and Susan H. McLeod. "Whither WAC?: Interpreting the Stories/Histories of Mature WAC Programs." *WPA: Writing Program Administration* (1997): 46–65.

Moss, Andrew, and Carol Holder. *Improving Student Writing: A Guidebook for Faculty in All Disciplines.* Dubuque, IA: Kendall Hunt, 1988.

Reiss, Donna, Dickie Selfe, and Art Young, eds. *Electronic Communication Across the Curriculum.* Urbana, IL: NCTE, 1998.

Russell, David R. "Rethinking Genre in School and Society: An Activity Theory Analysis." *Written Communication* 14 (1997): 504–54.

———. "Vygotsky, Dewey, and Externalism: Beyond the Student/Discipline Dichotomy." *Journal of Advanced Composition* 13 (1993): 173–97.

———. *Writing in the Academic Disciplines, 1870–1990.* Carbondale: Southern Illinois UP, 1991.

Soven, Margot K. *Write to Learn: A Guide to Writing Across the Curriculum.* Cincinnati: South-Western, 1996.

Thaiss, Christopher. *The Harcourt Brace Guide to Writing Across the Curriculum.* Fort Worth: Harcourt, 1998.

Wallace, Ray. "The Writing Center's Role in the Writing Across the Curriculum Program: Theory and Practice." *The Writing Center Journal* 8.2 (1988): 43–48. Rpt. in *Landmark Essays on Writing Centers.* Ed. Christina Murphy and Joe Law. Davis, CA: Hermagoras, 1995. 191–95.

Walvoord, Barbara Fassler. *Helping Students Write Well: A Guide for Teachers in All Disciplines.* New York: MLA, 1982. 2nd ed. 1986.

4

WAC as Critical Pedagogy: The Third Stage?

DONNA LeCOURT

A Personal/Professional Dilemma

Whenever I am approached by a faculty member, department chair, or college dean about the way they could improve writing instruction in their classes, I inevitably walk them through two related options that should be addressed: how writing can help students learn course content and how writing prepares their students to become better professionals in their fields. The two, of course, are always related in my discussion. I emphasize how learning to write according to the disciplinary norms of a certain profession is inextricably linked to encouraging the type of thinking valued within that discipline. Writing-to-learn activities, I explain, have the ability to not only make disciplinary concepts more familiar to students but also to serve as preparation for more transactional writing about these concepts. This approach has served me well as one of the primary WAC people on two different campuses . . . until recently.

I'm almost embarrassed to admit, however, how recently my perspective changed. During my involvement with WAC — almost eight years now — I had moved from a rather expressive pedagogical practice to one more informed by critical pedagogy, cultural studies, and poststructuralist theory. While my teaching in both first-year and advanced writing classes has represented the more critical approach to discourse encouraged by these theories, my WAC practice did not change at all. Somehow I blithely assumed that WAC was and had to be different than teaching writing within my home department. Herein lies the irony. I had revised my pedagogical practice wholesale over the past six years to focus on cultural studies because I firmly believed that discourse has the power to inscribe individuals such that it marginalized and silenced voices which threatened its monopoly on ways of thinking and modes of expression. Because much of my research and past teaching experience focused on multicultural education, a concern for student difference, particularly cultural difference and alternative literacies, has

From *Journal of Advanced Composition* 16.3 (1996): 389–405.

pervaded all my professional work, except, it seems, for WAC. I never once turned this ideological lens toward my WAC work with faculty.

Given the re-examination of approaches to writing across the curriculum currently taking place within composition (e.g., Herrington and Moran; McLeod 1989), now seems an ideal moment to examine not only what should take place in writing across the curriculum but also how the goals of such efforts respond to the field's concerns about writing instruction in other contexts, particularly first-year and advanced writing instruction. While I realize the field has by no means come to a consensus on how first-year writing should be taught, my hope is that examining WAC through the lens of the post-structural and cultural theories currently gaining a voice in these conversations will allow us to view WAC critically, thus opening up new possibilities.

From this perspective, it seems that the field's approaches to WAC are subject to the same description and critique of how academic discourse seeks to inscribe students as subjects that has been forged against composition instruction in English departments (e.g., Clifford; Faigley). Ironically, through WAC, we have presumed a clear mission for writing instruction in our effort to accommodate other disciplines that is not nearly so evident in our own approach to advanced literacy. While much of the work in first-year writing presumes that writing instruction should study how cultural discourses position those who seek to be a part of them and offer strategies of resistance to such discursive positions, WAC focuses upon accommodating students to that discourse. In particular, we seem to have forgotten the concern for alternative literacies and voices Other to the academy that permeates much of our discussion of writing courses in an English department. Yet, writing instruction in the disciplines is perhaps even more dangerous to representations of difference or challenges to the dominant than even first-year programs because their localized, specific articulations of a more generalized academic discourse have the potential to be even more restrictive and totalizing, particularly when a student sees the immediate effects rejecting these norms could have on their future livelihood. In sum, a close examination of how WAC has been theorized points to some disturbing possibilities which include (1) the acculturation of students into already normalized discourses, (2) the reproduction of dominant ideologies that these discourses support, and (3) the silencing of difference, particularly cultural, socio-economic, and gender differences as well as alternative literacies and other ways of knowing. While this reading of WAC may seem harsh, there are many reasons for the disparities which seem to emerge between approaches to WAC and first-year writing. The most obvious of these is the different position we hold within the institution as WAC consultants. In our role as consultants, rather than faculty with control over our pedagogies, we cannot simply foist our ideology of writing instruction onto other disciplines — the "missionary" approach. This institutional position must, indeed, affect our approach to other disciplines, but it need not, I argue here, result in an accommodation to that discipline.

In this essay, then, I propose first to examine representative samples of WAC theory and pedagogy through the lens of first-year writing. Rather than engage only in critique, however, the essay concludes by offering yet another alternative WAC model, which I call the critical model, that addresses not only the concerns about an accommodationist model but also the institutional position we are forced into when we work with other departments. In other words, I hope to offer a model which mediates between the binary of "missionary" and "accommodationist" while still retaining some of the critical sense about discourse and ideology which pervades our approaches to writing instruction in our home departments. As Susan McLeod notes in a 1989 Staffroom Interchange, the challenge of WAC programs in the "second stage" is no longer simply to "convince" but to "provide for veterans" and resist the idea that institutionalization indicates success (Second Stage 339). Instead, McLeod argues, we need to stay open to experimentation, lest we lose the vitality and opportunities for changing institutional structures opened up by the unique interdisciplinarity of WAC programs (Second Stage 342). It is in this vein of resisting the rigidity and homogenization of administrative structures that I offer up a possibility for WAC in its "third stage."

A CRITICAL READING OF THE "SECOND STAGE"

As a result of the re-examination of how WAC programs have situated themselves within composition theory, an intriguing disparity has presented itself between writing to learn and writing in the disciplines. These two threads of WAC theory and practice provide a useful rubric for my purposes here. As McLeod points out, these two approaches, which she designates the "cognitive" and the "rhetorical," respectively, exist in most programs simultaneously despite their radically different epistemological assumptions. What I suggest in this essay, however, is that despite the two approaches' seeming epistemological differences, they work toward a similar goal: the accommodation or inscription of (student) subjects into the various disciplinary strands of academic discourse. If we examine both these models from the more critical perspective that pervades many of our discussions of first-year writing, we see that the goals of both these models function as a coherent technology of subject production. Writing-to-learn exercises provide a discursive space in which students learn to write themselves as subjects of the discourse, using the writing space to "practice" an integration of self with a disciplinary subjectivity. The rhetorical model reinforces such an integration even more strongly, providing explicit instruction in how the discursive subject must write herself in order to produce "effective" prose which mirrors the texts of other "speaking" subjects of the discourse.

   Although there is an expressivist side to writing to learn (and I will return to this articulation later in the essay), this approach has more often drawn upon the way writing-to-learn activities focus on learning itself. James Britton describes this function in terms of a "predisciplinary theory" which is disinterested in the subject being taught and more interested in how "a teacher comes to an understanding of what will result in an understanding on someone else's part" (60). Yet such an argument about predisciplinarity becomes suspect when we consider that writing-to-learn activities are always used in the service of particular curricular goals by particular teachers in particular contexts. As John Ackerman has recently argued, writing-to-learn activities can never be only about learning. "Each program or classroom instance," he writes, "in some way, reproduces or challenges ecologies of academic and professional discourses as well as cultural values and routines" (351).

The way in which a writing-to-learn focus can become particularized into a disciplinary ideology has become more overt in recent years as arguments about its viability come in the form of connecting it to a writing-in-the-disciplines approach. In this reinterpretation, writing-to-learn activities provide an effective way to learn content in the disciplines. This emphasis on learning content knowledge is perhaps most clear in McLeod's designation of this approach as "cognitive" because of its emphasis on individual knowledge construction. As she explains, "writing to learn demonstrates that knowledge is not passively received, the theory goes, but is actively constructed by each individual learner; these constructions change as our knowledge changes and grows. . . . We might think of writing to learn as a 'knowledge-transforming' rather than 'knowledge-telling' task" ("Introduction" 4). Other applications of writing-to-learn activities characterize them as preparation for more transactional writing. In fact, the emphasis of most of the recent work on WAC is on how writing-to-learn activities can serve the goals of more disciplinary-centered WAC instruction. For example Robert Jones and Joseph Comprone see writing to learn as developing "conventional knowledge" of a discipline, while writing in the disciplines joins that knowledge with "rhetorical acumen" (61). Another characterization focuses less on content knowledge and more on the process of making knowledge. Judy Kirscht, Rhonda Levine, and John Reiff present writing-to-learn activities as "a way not only to interact with declarative knowledge, but also to develop procedural knowledge concerning the field — to learn *how* knowledge has been constructed as well as *what* that knowledge is" (374).

Given the way that writing-to-learn activities are increasingly seen as either a way to learn content, preparation for more disciplinary writing, or both, these cognitive or process-based activities serve to reinforce the ways of thinking and status of particular knowledge emphasized in the writing-in-the-disciplines approach. As such, an analysis of writing in the disciplines might be said to include these more content-based approaches to writing to learn since the latter work to further the goals of such programs.

The "writing in the disciplines" approach brings the work on discourse communities and social construction to a conception of WAC. As Charles Bazerman explains, "critical commonplace now has it that disciplines are socially and rhetorically constructed and that academic knowledge is the product of sociolinguistic activities advancing individual and group interests" (61). In short, the "writing in the disciplines" approach recognizes that forms of writing do not become conventional innocently; instead, they serve as reflections and are constitutive of the ways of knowing and the modes of inquiry valued within certain disciplines. This approach recognizes a dialectical relationship between texts and disciplinary epistemologies: that knowledge and discursive practices are inseparable. Adherence to certain discursive practices ensures that the knowledge generated within a text will be reflective of disciplinary epistemologies, thus writing practice serves to perpetuate epistemological assumptions. Similarly, it is these epistemological assumptions that generated the forms of discourse most appropriate for their expression. As epistemology changes so does writing practice, yet it is through writing and other linguistic practice that epistemologies can change.

The emphasis on "writing in the disciplines" has led to calls for more research into disciplinary writing by both English-trained and content-area instructors (e.g., Bazerman; Jones and Comprone; Farris and Smith), an emphasis on rhetorical analysis as a way of making conventions explicit (e.g., Peterson), and the need, as Judith Langer puts it, to "look beyond generic terminology about thinking and reasoning in discipline-based writing . . . to finding more specific vocabulary to use in discussion with students . . . that can be used to talk about the shapes of knowledge within a discipline" (85). As the Langer quote illustrates, a "writing in the disciplines" approach does not mean teaching blind subservience to disciplinary conventions; instead, in most articulations of this approach the emphasis is on creating rhetorical situations in assignments that encourage disciplinary ways of thinking, and/or connecting, as Kirscht, Levine, and Reiff argue, "discussions of methodology to concrete inquiries in various contexts, and especially to the languages of their conduct" (Nelson et al., qtd. in Kirscht, Levine, and Reiff 370).

Although the writing-in-the-disciplines approach does not immediately seem an accommodationist enterprise, its possibilities for accommodating students to a normalized discourse become clearer when we examine the goals of the approach more closely. While making the process by which knowledge is made more explicit has critical potential, the goal of such an approach is almost always put in terms of teaching or initiating the student into a certain way of thinking valued by the discipline. In sum, to "train" students to think and write within a certain discourse community. Consider the variety of ways such goals have been articulated within work in WAC below (all emphases are mine).

> The rationale for adopting this model (a rhetorical analysis approach in first-year comp.) might be articulated as follows: Professionals within a discipline share a knowledge of the conventions of written discourse used by that discipline. Such knowledge needs to be shared with students, too. English faculty can, with the help of others, encourage this sharing by introducing students to the written work of professionals in various disciplines, by showing them how to read that work for conventions as well as content, and then *by asking students to try their hands at apprentice versions of such writing.* (Peterson 61)

> This dialogue [between faculty in the humanities and other disciplines] must work toward balancing humanistic methods of encouraging more active and collaborative learning [writing-to-learn activities] in WAC courses with *reinforcing the ways of knowing and the writing conventions of different discourse communities.* (Jones and Comprone 61)

> In writing-intensive courses focused on disciplinary writing, students achieve an understanding of "the relationship between writing (the writing in the assigned texts and the writing prepared by students) and what

it means to become *members of that discipline's intellectual community."* (Slevin 13)

Although this approach [the rhetorical of "writing in the disciplines"] does not exclude writing-to-learn assignments, it emphasizes more formal assignments, teaching *writing as a form of social behavior in the academic community.* (McLeod, "Introduction" 5)

[From studies of writing-intensive classes] We are able to say that the thinking students are able to engage in their writing for WI [writing-intensive] courses is contextually determined and includes assumptions of the discipline, belief systems of the instructors, and the extent to which those instructors have reflected these in constructing class assignments and activities. We have a much better understanding of how WI instructors' classrooms really function as "interpretative communities." . . . More important, perhaps, we have a much fuller sense of what [course] goals mean to the *members of that classroom's and that discipline's "culture."* (Farris and Smith 83–84)

If we put these various statements about the goals of writing in the disciplines together, we are presented with several metaphors and concepts which intersect directly with our discussions of first-year writing: (1) the metaphor of apprentice/expert; (2) the concept of reinforcing and supporting dominant epistemologies, and thus, the ideologies which support them; (3) a concept of community which is constituted as separate from others, with clearly marked boundaries and characteristics which delineate terms of "membership"; and, (4) a concept of such communities as "containing" not only epistemological assumptions but also cultural and social norms of behavior and values.

While the references to "culture" and "social behavior" most explicitly invoke the reacculturation aspect of initiation into discourse communities that has been so vehemently criticized in our own field, the focus of such a critique centers on the way in which communities are described as demarcating clear boundaries between one community and the next, boundaries constituted through the differing consensus reached by different communities. Such a consensually based and rather codified notion of community can be seen operating clearly not only in these quotes but also in the way I have summarized the "writing in the disciplines" work thus far. Disciplinary communities exist as entities to be studied in and of themselves because of the uniqueness of their epistemological and discursive practice. Thus, the many calls to investigate disciplinary discourses without the presumption that language functions the same way in any discipline. Students learn how the conventions and discursive practices of a discipline relate to the consensus reached about modes of inquiry, what counts as knowledge, and the best way to express the two.

It is precisely this consensual characterization of community and discourse that has been so vehemently criticized within the conversation about first-year writing. Such critiques demonstrate clearly how this reified concept of community merely serves to reproduce dominant ideology and to accommodate students in the ways I have been arguing. Greg Myers, for example, points out that focusing only on the consensual workings of a discourse community ignores the wider social discourses that influence that consensus as well as the differences a consensual discourse is designed to silence, prohibit, and marginalize.[1] In short, focusing on consensual practice enables the discourse to operate as a Foucauldian technology of power, privileging and excluding certain types of knowledge, perspectives, ways of thinking, values, and voices. Lester Faigley echoes this point in *Fragments of Rationality*: "A holistic and closed notion of community encourages a simplified view of a discursive field, where the influences of contradictory and multiple discourses that one encounters in daily life are minimal" (226).

John Trimbur, however, is perhaps the most clear about the way acceding to an already constituted consensus allows the discourse to appear natural and pragmatic, and thus ideologically free. In his critical reading of Kenneth Bruffee's alignment of collaborative learning with teaching the normal discourse of the academy, Trimbur points out how referring to the " 'real world' authority of such consensual practices neutralizes the critical and transformative project of collaborative learning, de-politicizes it, and reduces it to an acculturative technique" (612). Although the writing-in-the-disciplines approach focuses only on epistemology in its references to ways of thinking, epistemological concerns cannot be separated from ideological ones. An uncritical approach to disciplinary communities — the assumedly reified authority of already constituted practices — only serves to perpetuate and instantiate the worldview and ways of knowing already valued within the dominant professional ideology. In sum, teaching conventions as reflective and constitutive of epistemology still acculturates students into certain ways of thinking, providing a specific venue for ideology to replicate itself. If we define ideology as giving people "the structures through which they make sense of their world," teaching "ways of knowing and writing conventions" perforce suggests adopting the ideological position inherent in those ways of knowing (Myers 156; see also Williams and Freire).

Admittedly, replication of ideology or initiation into appropriate ways of thinking may not seem an entirely accurate way of characterizing the goal of writing in the disciplines since most of these approaches emphasize the active and social nature of such disciplinary communities. As Jones and Comprone put it, research into disciplinary conventions "does not mean that those conventions need to be slavishly imitated. Rather, it means that students should learn these conventions in ways that encourage them to fit their own intentions and the varying demands of rhetorical situations together in their writing" (65). For others, making the relationship between epistemology and writing allows the "field" of discursive practice to become more opaque, providing students with the ability to more easily explore new ideas of their own. Kirscht, Levine, and Reiff put it this way: "The forms and conventions of the disciplines become, in turn, tools used consciously to aid students in moving beyond the boundaries of previous belief systems and in exploring new perceptions" (374). The ability to create an intention or perception that is more personally located seems to provide the opportunity for students to bring alternative literacies and ways of knowing into the discursive realm of a particular discourse.

If we take the Marxist critique of community and consensus seriously, however, such new perspectives and/or personal intentions will be constructed in accommodation with the discipline's ideology rather than providing a space for students to "name" the discipline or construct knowledge in terms other than those already laid out. The seeming range of discursive intentions students can construct matter little because their seeming choices are, themselves, ideologically constituted through the disciplinary discourse. As John Clifford has argued via Althusser, "the myriad ways in which writing subjects can make the world intelligible have already been carefully proscribed so that the dutiful subject, true to ideals already internalized, believes it is possible to inscribe his own ideas as a free subject in the action of his material practice" (43). Put simply, writers perceive their discursive options as being naturally those created by the discursive context. In many ways, we give ourselves over to the discourse by presuming, as we've been taught, that to do so will help us realize our intentions. Once the student accepts the role she is to play within the disciplinary discourse, her own "free" actions will themselves be determined by the options she perceives as viable.

Yet we need not turn only to Marxism for this critique. Even in the initial explanation of a rhetorical situation, Lloyd Bitzer contends that intention is constituted through the exigence brought about by the rhetorical situation. In other words, the rhetorical context itself — lodged firmly within the disciplinary discourse — creates intention, or at least, limits the ways in which the writer can conceive of his intention. Further, the insider/outsider or apprentice/expert language of many of the goals of writing in the disciplines sets up the discursive options for the student as seemingly only "accept or reject." As Min-zhan Lu has illustrated in her critique of basic writing, setting up such rigid boundaries of seemingly unitary paradigms "might also lead students to focus their energy on accommodating their thoughts and actions to rigid boundaries rather than on actively engaging themselves in what to [Gloria] Anzaldúa is the resource of life in the borderlands: a continual creative motion which breaks entrenched habits and patterns of behavior" (899).

Lu's use of Anzaldúa here is telling in that it points us toward the direction needed in order to make disciplinary writing less of an accommodation to dominant ideologies and ways of thinking. What we need is a way to present and discuss such discourses that allows both the discourse and the student to be envisioned as sites of conflict wherein competing discourses interact, allowing the student writer the possibility of resisting and/or changing the constitution of the discourse through her subject positions in other discourses. As Joseph Harris and Lu have shown, our students are always located at points of conflict among discourses whether writing in WAC courses or those in our own department. In fact, as Jim Henry demonstrates in his narratological analysis of student writers in a Landscape Architecture course, these are the positions in which our students frequently find themselves in WAC courses. Henry's research highlights the student writer as an "intratextual self," pointing to the numerous discursive identities the student brings with her from cultural, personal, and other disciplinary discourses that compete for authority within a particular disciplinary, rhetorical situation.

Despite the reality that Harris, Lu, and Henry assert of the writer as always already a site of conflict and multivocality, the critiques cited here also point to how this conflict can be sublimated in favor of ways of thinking and writing already constituted by disciplinary communities unless we become more explicit about how discourse not only constitutes epistemology but also the ideological positions that come with that epistemology. Henry's narratological analysis points to just this possibility. The assignment he focuses upon to illustrate how student writers write from an intratextual self is one that all the writers have difficulty with because it explicitly asks for the personal within the disciplinary realm. The students, he points out, "had difficulty meeting the [discursive] scene's mandate to embrace the personal as both theoretically valid and discursively viable" (817). In other rhetorical contexts, students have less difficulty because of the more unified disciplinary self called for in the writing. Examples like Henry's point to the very real possibility that students, eager for acceptance and validation in their chosen fields, will allow the disciplinary discourses to name their reality for them by internalizing its ways of thinking, accepting them as more authoritative and viable than alternatives they may already possess.

MOVING TOWARD A CRITICAL WAC MODEL

Altering such an accommodation to disciplinary ideology necessitates, I believe, two changes in our current conceptions of WAC theory and practice. The first must alter the ways in which we conceive of disciplinary communities. The second must position the student as an active partner in a dialectic with such communities, making space for the personal — for difference — within the disciplinary.

Reconstituting Community

The critiques forged by Myers, Trimbur, Faigley and others point not only to the problematic of a reified concept of community but also to how community can be reconceptualized to be less hegemonic. Their work suggests that a more open and critical approach to disciplinary discourses would (1) recognize the continual conflicts currently being played out within the discourse, (2) examine the influence of wider social discourses on their construction, and (3) interrogate how a discourse's constitution is both productive and silencing.

Some moves are already being made in these directions, although they are few. Bazerman arguably provides the most comprehensive argument for how disciplinary writing can be reimagined in the ways I outline above. In "From Cultural Criticism to Disciplinary Participation" (see p. 239 in this volume), Bazerman argues for rhetorical study of the disciplines with attention to the "locales of heteroglossic contention that they are" (p. 240). Such analyses would look closely at the historical constitution of a current consensus not to justify it but to "open up exclusions and enclosures of discourse to see how and why they are deployed and to question their necessity in any particular case" (p. 241). Pedagogically, Bazerman suggests that instructors teach a disciplinary discourse in these very terms, holding what is taught "up for inspection" (p. 242), providing students with a critical initiation into the discourse which opens up avenues for "active, reactive, and proactive" participation (p. 244). "With a sense of individual power," he explains, students "can constantly press at the bit of the disciplinary practices they are trained into or run up against" (p. 244).

While I find Bazerman's suggestions extremely persuasive because of his emphasis on opening up discourses so that students are provided with ways to resist as well as accommodate disciplinary epistemologies and ideologies, there are also some problems that need to be addressed in his suggestions. First, his pedagogical suggestions may be difficult to institute because they require, as he admits, significant research commitments from both disciplinary and language professionals (p. 244). Second, and more importantly, he locates the possibility for student resistance in the ability of the instructor to present the discourse itself as a site of contention and possibility. While such a presentation is preferable to a reified concept of community, it still subjects the student to a professional reading of such debates, perhaps limiting the critiques her own multiple positions in culture might be able to offer to the discourse. Further, locating the starting point for resistance and action in the discourse itself rather than in the student's multiplicity still subjects the student to the effects of power exacerbated by the discipline's cultural status.

These problems, however, are manageable. The challenge is to attend to student difference without falling back on a banking concept of education and without necessarily putting us in the unenviable position of the one who analyzes another community's discourse or convinces our colleagues to engage in such rhetorical criticism. Instead, what seems both pragmatic and a viable way to facilitate students' critical consciousness about disciplinary discourses would be to have students conduct such investigations themselves. At my own institution, I have been making moves in this direction in more subtle ways than those that Bazerman proposes. The first has been to start students off in such investigations in first-year writing courses, the only writing instruction over which I can exercise more overt control. Thanks to the hard work of our composition staff, particularly Laura Thomas, Jon Leydens, and Steve Reid, our first-year writing course now focuses upon cultural criticism and includes a critical component of disciplinary discourses. The final "unit" in this course asks students to investigate and perform a rhetorical analysis of the discourses of their chosen majors in collaborative groups using the techniques of cultural criticism they learned earlier in the course. While such investigations are similar to those proposed by others seeking to connect first-year writing more closely with WAC efforts, the assignment goes one step further than preparing "students to attend to the writing demands of new situations and thus speed[ing] their enculturation into new communities"

(Linton, Madigan, and Johnson 65). In our course, students are also asked to investigate disciplinary discourses critically, with an eye toward what the discipline's rhetorical practices include and exclude in terms of knowledge. In my role as WAC consultant and facilitator of faculty workshops, I propose and model similar rhetorical investigations as possibilities for assignments in my colleagues' courses. I meet little resistance to this idea since we already use rhetorical criticism in these workshops to help faculty gain metaknowledge about discursive norms.

I want to emphasize here that I do not turn to student analyses only as a way to mediate institutional realities. Instead, by making students the rhetorical critics, we ensure that students are attending to such criticism themselves rather than only receiving another's knowledge. As Bazerman himself argues, "it is not the serious attention to disciplinary discourse that restricts our intellectual options but the refusal to attend that fosters the hegemony of narrow discourses" (pp. 209–10). Such practices as those I recommend here rely on the presumption that in attending to how discursive norms both include and exclude certain types of knowledge and perspectives, students can learn how to perform their own critical reflections on discourse, an ability that they will hopefully carry with them beyond the institution into their chosen professions. Such a critical consciousness will not, however, take place if students must rely on discourse or disciplinary experts to perform such critiques for them.

Student Difference within Disciplinary Discourses

While "opening up" discourse communities to critical examination is a necessary first step to a more critical model of WAC, it remains too focused on the internal workings of the community itself. Given our institutional constraints, this might be the best we can do, but I am not as confident as Bazerman that allowing for critical reflection on disciplinary discourses will necessarily in and of itself open up routes for action, for change and resistance in student writing. I fear such attempts will fail unless there is a concomitant focus on the writer's multiple discursive positions as a way of allowing for student difference and alternative literacies to find a space within disciplinary discourses. Further, allowing for student difference might open up the even more critical version of discourse communities that Trimbur points to, one whose goal is "not simply to demystify the authority of knowledge by revealing its social character but to transform the productive apparatus, to change the social character of production" (612). In short, in order to avoid the power of disciplinary discourses to prescribe discursive positions that only reinforce its ideology, we also need to provide ways to let students negotiate these positions via authority gained in discourses not necessarily constituted in relationship to the discipline. For example, a Native American student majoring in history should be able to resist the discursive convention of past tense, which implies a certain epistemological and ideological version of time that he may not be willing to accept, and construct an authority based in a different cultural conception of time and history. In so doing, his forms of resistance need not rely on the dissensus within the discursive community itself; instead, his writing can create such a dissensus. As such, student difference provides a viable way to help us situate disciplinary communities within the larger social discourses that also influence their construction, using students to bring critiques to disciplinary discourses that might elude experts without the cultural experiences our increasingly diverse classrooms offer.

Ironically enough for someone who has been taking a Marxist perspective throughout this essay, I find the most viable opportunities for this component of a critical WAC model in a return to an expressivist concept of writing to learn. By expressivist, I refer to the ways writing to learn was once characterized as a way of helping students develop a meta-awareness of how disciplinary knowledge impacts them personally. As Toby Fulwiler explained it over 10 years ago, writing-to-learn strategies encourage "writers to become conscious, through language, of what is happening to them, both personally and academically" (17). Admittedly, invoking Fulwiler here also brings with it romantic conceptions of the autonomous individual who controls language and speaks with a "natural" voice that are antithetical to the WAC model I propose. As Janice Peritz has shown in her historical analysis of writing to learn, such expressivist practices are equally open to the ideological critique I forge against cognitive writing-to-learn strategies above. What I want to retain from expressive concepts of writing to learn, however, is not this focus on autonomy but the ways in which such practices suggest an orientation that, as C. H. Knoblauch and Lil Brannon have recently argued, is amenable to a more critical version of literacy instruction. Specifically, the ways in which expressivist concepts of writing to learn "honor the linguistic resources" students already possess and value what "learners already know" are particularly useful in a critical WAC model (Knoblauch and Brannon 128). It is this sense of the personal as valuable to writing that has been occluded by reinterpretations of writing to learn to fit disciplinary models.

It is also this sense of the personal which may provide a means for students to interact proactively with disciplinary discourses. Of course, how we define "personal" would necessarily have to be reconstituted for such a concept to work in a critical WAC model. The personal in this context more accurately refers to the multiplicity of voices and discursive positions constructed in contexts other than school. What a focus on the personal defined in this way gives us is a way to imagine a space within disciplinary discourse for alternative literacies to interact with the discourse: a way for the personal and disciplinary to *interact* in a dialectical fashion rather than one in which one voice must be silenced for the other to speak. Such a dialectic not only provides the student with a means to speak an alternative literacy or worldview but also a way to speak it without sacrificing his investment in a disciplinary discourse necessary to his professional reality. In sum, it becomes critical literacy in the truest sense of the term: the ability to recognize ideological structures within language while still interacting with them to produce texts that express difference in terms the discourse must take seriously.

Henry's study of a Landscape Architecture course points to just how "productive" such a space might be. In addition to suggesting how easily the multiplicity of a student's subject positions and voices can be silenced by disciplinary writing, Henry points out how this multiplicity emerges as both natural and viable within the disciplinary discourse in an assignment which merges the personal and the theoretical. In fact, Henry attributes the ability to construct an "intratextual self" to the nature of the assignment: "By locating the expressive instances of writing among the forms of transactions, we allow students to perceive the many discursive contingencies with which they are always already contending when writing" (822). While Henry makes no explicit connection between an intratextual self and critical literacy, such an intratextual self is precisely one which engages the multiplicity of a student's discursive positions with the disciplinary discourse in the ways I have been arguing for here. Henry's analysis points to how a return to the personal within the disciplinary might be just the way to allow students to write from a multiplicity of positions rather than only the unified voice constructed in the disciplinary discourse.

Similarly, Bonnie Spanier points to the value allowing the personal in the disciplinary has for achieving a critical perspective on disciplinary knowledge. In "Encountering the Biological Sciences: Ideology, Language, and Learning," she discusses the difficulties "students trained in the sciences" have in overcoming "a *passive, nonexpert* stance and plac[ing] their views into assignments about science in social context" (204, my emphasis) when responding to her assignments which explicitly ask for the students to personally situate their knowledge. On the other hand, her feminist students, "educated to take themselves seriously" and to place their knowledge and values at the center of their education achieve a "balanced intersubjectivity" in these assignments (204). Significantly, Spanier points out how such an intersubjectivity allows students to more clearly perceive the ideology in the discourse and practice of science. This critical sense, however, does not come with feminism alone; instead, Spanier links it with the writing assignments themselves in her indication that students trained in a passive stance also perform well on such assignments with encouragement. Making a space for the personal, in other words, counteracts the students' perceptions that their alternative voices must be silenced within a disciplinary discourse.

Admittedly, asking our colleagues in WAC workshops to enact an explicit ideological analysis in the way Spanier does of her work in the biological sciences is not a viable option. Such a suggestion would definitely position us as ideological missionaries attempting to convert the masses. On the other hand, presenting the option for the personal within the disciplinary does not seem so radical a move. While I call such writing resistance, it is also an ideological production in itself, a conscious reflection on the ways in which ideology constitutes our world and an action upon it. It is, in this sense, enacting knowledge by reconstituting it through the multiplicity of a discursively situated self. Such a textual production would produce "new" knowledge in the best sense: new for the student in her creation of disciplinary subject positions which can productively interact with others, and new for the discipline in the challenges it poses to see our knowledge, and thus our discursive practice, in different ways. Such writing, if we attend to it closely, might also help us meet one of the primary challenges Herrington and Moran locate within writing in the disciplines: the challenge "to reflect critically on our teaching and our disciplinary values" and "to understand discourse practices and values that may be different from our own" (238, 239). Using student writing as a form of challenge to disciplinary norms also presents a more effective way of opening up a space for student difference than asking teachers to reflect on the effects of disciplinary norms through their writing assignments in a workshop (see Peritz).

Despite the potential combining the expressive and transactional has for changing the discipline from within, in the end, the writing produced is also simply good writing emerging out of learning through writing. It seems to me that this move is what WAC has always been about — the mutual concern for student learning and thinking through writing that brings all of us, no matter the discipline, to the workshop. A critical model of WAC simply redefines thinking and learning through writing in terms that recognize the viability of the students' discourses as much as disciplinary ones.

CONCLUSION

When I first discussed my ideas for this essay (originally a CCCC presentation) with colleagues from my own and other institutions, I was met with much resistance. Surprisingly, the resistance didn't come from my insistence that many writing-in-the-disciplines approaches to WAC were too accommodationist. Instead, everyone I spoke to, all WAC practitioners themselves, found it impossible to believe that faculty in other disciplines would be amenable in any way to a critical WAC model. Others were disturbed by what they saw as a return to the "missionary model" of early WAC programs, suggesting that it was not my role to foist my ideology onto my colleagues in other disciplines. Although my rather glib reply at the time was "we do that anyway, no matter how we run a WAC workshop or consultation," I'd like to suggest more seriously in this conclusion that these reactions are based in metaphors about our role as WAC consultants and impressions of our colleagues that need to be re-examined.

While I believe the reactions to the model I propose here are appropriately cautionary, I also think they do a disservice to faculty in other disciplines. As McLeod has argued in a recent essay, there are multiple ways to imagine our role as WAC consultants, ranging from "conquerors" who force institutional change via curricular mandates to "missionaries" who presume they must bring their superior knowledge to the "unenlightened" ("Foreigner" 109, 111). Presuming that colleagues in other disciplines would automatically reject a critical WAC model in effect positions them as the "unenlightened" and the WAC consultant as missionary. Not only are there examples out there of faculty in other disciplines engaging in such work already — Louise Dunlap's course in urban planning is an excellent example —

but such reactions also ignore the pervasive influence postmodern theories are having in disciplines other than our own. I've encountered many faculty members engaged in ideological critique and/or political questioning of epistemological practices for whom my suggestions are only "new" in their application to discursive practice rather than content. Most persuasive for me, however, is the attitude toward student learning of the faculty members who attend WAC workshops. Most of the faculty members I've worked with are willing to put time and energy into writing across the curriculum because they honestly care about helping their students learn better and providing egalitarian access to their disciplines, particularly for those who have been traditionally excluded from them. Suggesting that discursive practices can serve to include some students and exclude others finds fertile ground in such educators.

While the use of the metaphor missionary not only prescribes an inaccurate picture of our colleagues, presuming that we should resist *any* attempt at change in our colleagues' ideological investments similarly masks the investments we already make in WAC work and leads to an inaccurate picture of our position. What I think we fail to realize when we express concern about foisting our agenda on our colleagues is that any WAC work involves initiating both pedagogical and theoretical change. If change is not included as part of WAC work, we effectively silence ourselves as much as the missionary model silences our colleagues. As McLeod argues, the ostensible aim of WAC workshops is to improve student writing, yet such a goal always includes suggesting changes in classroom practice, which, in the end, means changing "theories about teaching and writing" ("Foreigner" 113). When we set out to convince colleagues from more foundational disciplines that knowledge and language may not be neutral or objective (i.e., the writing-in-the-disciplines approach), we are already setting out to change theory; when we suggest peer workshops we not only suggest a change in practice but also theories of how knowledge is made and/or learning happens. Given that, in McLeod's terms, it is virtually impossible not to act as a "change agent" when doing WAC work, we might be better served by considering what the consequences of the changes we advocate will be rather than denying our role in such changes. Seen in this light, a critical WAC model is a much smaller step than those we've already taken, but, I'd argue, a very large step in terms of the consequences it might have for our students.

NOTES

1. Please note that I am deliberately invoking work, such as Myers and Trimbur, with which many may already be familiar to highlight the disparity between discussions of composition applied to our own teaching versus writing across the curriculum.

WORKS CITED

Ackerman, John. "The Promise of Writing to Learn." *Written Communication* 3 (1993): 334–69.
Bazerman, Charles. "From Cultural Criticism to Disciplinary Participation: Living with Powerful Words." Herrington and Moran. 61–68.
Bitzer, Lloyd. "Rhetorical Situation." *Philosophy and Rhetoric* 1 (1968): 1–14.

Britton, James. "Theories of the Disciplines and a Learning Theory." Herrington and Moran. 47–60.

Clifford, John. "The Subject in Discourse." *Contending with Words: Composition and Rhetoric in a Postmodern Age.* Eds. Patricia Harkin and John Schilb. New York: MLA, 1991. 38–51.

Dunlap, Louise. "Advocacy and Neutrality: A Contradiction in the Discourse of Urban Planners." Herrington and Moran. 213–30.

Faigley, Lester. *Fragments of Rationality: Postmodernity and the Subject of Composition.* Pittsburgh: U of Pittsburgh P, 1992.

Farris, Christine, and Raymond Smith. "Writing-Intensive Courses: Tools for Curricular Change." McLeod and Soven. 71–86.

Freire, Paulo. *Pedagogy of the Oppressed.* New York: Continuum, 1993.

Fulwiler, Toby. "The Personal Connection: Journal Writing Across the Curriculum." *Language Connections: Writing and Reading Across the Curriculum.* Eds. Toby Fulwiler and Art Young. Urbana: NCTE, 1982. 15–32.

Harris, Joseph. "The Idea of Community in the Study of Writing." *College Composition and Communication* 40 (1989): 11–22.

Henry, Jim. "A Narratological Analysis of WAC Authorship." *College English* 56 (1994): 810–24.

Herrington, Anne, and Charles Moran, eds. *Writing, Teaching, and Learning in the Disciplines.* New York: MLA, 1992.

———. "Writing in the Disciplines: A Prospect." Herrington and Moran. 231–44.

Jones, Robert, and Joseph J. Comprone. "Where Do We Go Next in Writing across the Curriculum?" *College Composition and Communication* 44 (1993): 59–68.

Kirscht, Judy, Rhonda Levine, and John Reiff. "Evolving Paradigms: WAC and the Rhetoric of Inquiry." *College Composition and Communication* 45 (1994): 369–80.

Knoblauch, C. H., and Lil Brannon. *Critical Teaching and the Idea of Literacy.* Portsmouth, NH: Boynton/Cook, 1993.

Langer, Judith A. "Speaking and Knowing: Conceptions of Understanding in Academic Disciplines." Herrington and Moran. 69–86.

Linton, Patricia, Robert Madigan, and Susan Johnson. "Introducing Students to Disciplinary Genres: The Role of the General Composition Course." *Language and Learning Across the Disciplines* 1 (1994): 63–68.

Lu, Min-Zhan. "Conflict and Struggle: The Enemies or Preconditions of Basic Writing?" *College English* 54 (1988): 887–913.

McLeod, Susan. "The Foreigner: WAC Directors as Agents of Change." *Resituating Writing.* Eds. Joseph Janangelo and Kristine Hansen. Portsmouth, NH: Boynton, 1995: 108–16.

———. "Writing Across the Curriculum: An Introduction." McLeod and Soven. 1–11.

———. "Writing Across the Curriculum: The Second Stage, and Beyond." *College Composition and Communication* 40 (1989): 337–43.

McLeod, Susan, and Margot Soven, eds. *Writing Across the Curriculum: A Guide to Developing Programs.* Newbury Park: Sage, 1992.

Myers, Greg. "Reality, Consensus, and Reform in the Rhetoric of Composition Teaching." *College English* 48 (1986): 154–74.

Peritz, Janice H. "When Learning Is Not Enough: Writing Across the Curriculum and the (Re)turn to Rhetoric." *Journal of Advanced Composition* 14 (1994): 431–54.

Peterson, Linda H. "Writing Across the Curriculum and/in the Freshman English Program." McLeod and Soven. 58–70.

Slevin, James, et al. "Georgetown University." *Programs That Work: Methods for Writing Across the Curriculum.* Eds. Toby Fulwiler and Art Young. Portsmouth, NH: Boynton, 1990. 9–28.

Spanier, Bonnie B. "Encountering the Biological Sciences: Ideology, Language, and Learning." Herrington and Moran. 193–212.

Trimbur, John. "Consensus and Difference in Collaborative Learning." *College English* 51 (1989): 602–16.

Williams, Raymond. *Marxism and Literature.* New York: Oxford UP, 1977.

5   *Theory in WAC: Where Have We Been, Where Are We Going?*

CHRISTOPHER THAISS

F irst, a rationale for this chapter: Why talk about "WAC theory"? After all, every chapter in this book deals with "theory" in some fashion since theory provides reasons, based in scholarship and teaching practice, for the methods it describes. The focus of this chapter, however, will be on first principles: the assumptions behind the reasons — the theories beneath the theories, if you will. Moreover, in the almost three decades since explicit workshops on writing across the curriculum began, the shape of WAC has undergone significant change. It is therefore reasonable to attempt to define both (1) a core of consistent WAC principles over that span, and (2) the theoretical influences that have worked changes on the concept.

I proceed as follows: in keeping with the notion of first principles, I work toward extensive definitions of the three terms — "writing," "across," and "the curriculum," — that make up the operant phrase. Each term is defined historically within the context of WAC programmatic and teaching practice; changes are explored and trends emerge. Where appropriate, I cite other essays . . . that further illuminate my observations. I close by speculating, in the spirit of this millennial volume, about a few further developments in WAC theory.

And so . . .

"WRITING"

The public, including many academics, talks about writing as if it were a simple concept and as if everyone meant the same thing by it. Sweeping pronouncements, usually negative, are made: "Students can't write," "The writing is poor," and so forth, and generalizers rarely specify, nor are asked to specify, exactly what the trouble is. Nevertheless, anyone who studies writing is familiar with the surprise of reading allegedly "poor" and "good" samples and wondering on what bases the evaluator reached the judgment. When I

From *WAC for the New Millennium: Strategies for Continuing Writing-Across-the-Curriculum Programs*, Eds. Susan McLeod, Eric Miraglia, Margot Soven, and Chris Thaiss. Urbana: NCTE, 2001. 200–326.

conduct discussions of standards with my colleagues, we routinely fill the chalkboard with criteria for successful writing of experienced-based essays; we disagree about priorities, even though we are discussing, mind you, only a single — though varied and complex — genre.

Writing does appear simple to define: the use of graphic characters, "letters," to render language. This illusion of simplicity and consensus may explain the consternation of the faculty at Harvard who after 1870 felt it necessary to make composition a required, remedial course in its own right (Berlin, *Writing*; Halloran) and thus set in motion the U.S. composition industry. The illusion is also responsible for the easy acceptance of "good writing," an equally elusive term, as a virtue and as a goal of education. Most pertinent to this chapter, this illusion helps to explain why writing across the curriculum has gained such widespread acceptance — at least in concept — in colleges and schools. Faculty and administrators readily pay lip service to the "need" for students to "write well," and they tend readily to pass motions and even earmark funding for various forms of faculty inservice training and curricular mandating. Yet, as always, the devil is in the details, and programs bog down when the significant differences in real definitions become apparent. (I would speculate that schools that have faced the most difficulty in even starting WAC programs have been those that have addressed the definitional question at the outset, and the resulting conflict of definitions has stalled any initiative.)

What most safely can be said is that "writing" in writing-across-the-curriculum programs has been many things, not all of them compatible, exemplifying Naisbitt's theory of the "trends and countertrends" that he saw as characteristic of the movement of ideas in a society (Naisbitt and Aburdene). Even within one institution — even, I would argue, in the deliberations of a single teacher — we can almost perceive definitions and goals of writing moving in opposite directions.

Conformity versus Originality

I will label these opposite directions the "drive to conformity" and the "drive to originality." These are certainly nothing new — the basic yin/yang, tree/serpent of the cultural anthropologists — but how they are played out in the teaching of writing, and especially in WAC programs, helps us understand the variety of meanings given to such spin-offs of "writing" as "good writing," "learning to write," and "writing to learn."

First, the drive to conformity. Some faculty and governing boards are attracted to WAC because it promises greater conformity: to these advocates, "learning to write" means learning correct usage of Standard English, the learning of modes and formats characteristic of a discipline, consistency of documentation, and consistency of application of disciplinary research methodology.

Conversely, others see in WAC the potential for the student's growth as thinker and stylist; this direction is toward the more individual, less easily defined or prescribed, more evanescent development of style and confidence characteristic of insiders in a discourse. David Bartholomae's notion of "inventing the university" involves this more profound theory of "learning to write" ("Inventing"), similar to Kenneth Bruffee's adaptation of the age-old notion of university education as allowing one to "join the ongoing conversation" of ideas. Several common aspects of "good writing" exemplify this trend: among them, (1) the ability to integrate the writings of others into one's own vision, (2) the ability to envision how one might adapt one's writing to the needs of diverse readers, (3) the ability to take a writing project through an unpredictable "process" that encourages revisioning and reshaping, and (4) the ability to cross conventions — reinvent them, as it were — in order to make connections with styles and genres of other fields. Genre theorists (e.g., Bishop and Ostrom) explore this process, and this growing research field clearly will have more and more impact on WAC development in coming years.

It is in this less-conformist sense of "learning to write" that the definition of "writing" includes that other epigrammatic notion popular in WAC: "writing to learn." Although "writing to learn" has been frequently isolated from "learning to write" in workshops, often by means of a split between so-called "formal" ("learning to write") and "informal" ("writing to learn") assignments, conscientious workshop leaders try to keep the connections before the minds of participants. Certainly the work of the theorists who were most influential in the rise of WAC integrated these ideas. For example, Mina Shaughnessy's (1977) developmental progression from "fluency" to "correctness" saw the conformist goal of "learning to write" as dependent on the use of writing as a tool of thought, as did James Britton's earlier formulation (1975) of the "expressive" mode of writing (for the self, as an exploratory tool) as the "matrix" out of which grew the ability to write "transactionally" to others (Britton et al.). I count it one of the failings of theory in recent years that our sense of the connectedness of "writing to learn"/"the expressive"/"the informal" and of "learning to write"/"the transactional"/"the formal" has been lost to some extent in the drive of some scholars to stress the distinctions between theories more than their connections. This loss may have been best illustrated by the 1995 "debate" between Peter Elbow and David Bartholomae in the pages of *College Composition and Communication*, but this focus on the disconnect, rather than on the profound links, between concepts is played out continuously in uninformed, off-the-cuff critiques of the expressive as "soft," "touchy-feely," and "self-indulgent" and of the transactional/formal as "rigid," "formulaic," and "superficial." While it has been useful analytically for composition theorists to specify differences between, as Patricia Bizzell described them, so-called "inner"- and "outer"-directed theories, the loss of a unified theory has not been helpful to teachers trying to plan a coherent course.

While I have characterized "writing to learn" as related to the growth of the student as thinker and stylist, I should also point out opposing trends in this aspect of WAC. On the one hand, "writing to learn" includes the conforming goals of recall and memorization, manifest in note-taking and journaling exercises directed to better performance on standardized tests. This "lower-order" thinking (Perry) contrasts with, and to some extent runs counter to, "higher-order" uses of writing, also often pursued in some form of regular writing such as a journal, including doing synthetic or divergent writing, thought experiments, metaphorizing and other creative invention, and what cultural studies theorists (see Berlin and Vivion, for example) call "critical work" — examining and questioning ("deconstructing," if you will) those very terms and concepts that one strives so conscientiously to memorize and assimilate. The annual symposia on "Writing and Higher Order Thinking" at the University of Chicago in the 1980s have been thus far the most explicit attempt to relate WAC theory and practice to these theories of psychological development, but they are played out tacitly in the variety of assignments arrayed under the "writing to learn" umbrella.

Overall, what we mean by "writing" and by "learning to write" and "writing to learn" varies from school to school, teacher to teacher, class to class, assignment to assignment, even from thought to thought within a teacher's response to a group of papers or to a single paper.

Dominance of the Transactional

Nevertheless, the concept can be narrowed to some degree. The "writing" that is most often meant in the phrase "good writing" can be safely, if nebulously, defined as what James Britton and his colleagues called "transactional" writing, or what Janet Emig in 1971 termed "extensive" writing: "the mode that focuses upon the writer's conveying a message or a communication to another; the domain explored is usually the cognitive; the style is assured, impersonal, and often reportorial" (*Composing* 4). Further refining the term to the school context, we can accept Bartholomae's definition of successful academic writing in "Inventing the University":

> What our beginning students need to learn is to extend themselves, by successive approximations, into the commonplaces, set phrases, rituals and gestures, *habits of mind*, tricks of persuasion, obligatory conclusions and necessary connections that determine the "what might be said" and constitute knowledge within the various branches of our academic community. (145; emphasis added)

The conformist vision clearly dominates in this definition; however, in the phrase "habits of mind," which I have italicized, lurks the drive toward originality. Bartholomae later in the essay explains one of the key "habits" of the successful academic writer: "The key distinguishing gesture . . . is the way the writer works against a conventional point of view, one that is represented within the essay by conventional phrases that the writer must then work against" (152). Nevertheless, since this type of originality marks the successful academic, it too is an expected part of the transaction.

This greater emphasis on the transactional has been consistent in WAC. Even though the informal and the expressive have received considerable attention in WAC programs, as best illustrated by Toby Fulwiler's early work on journals (e.g., in *The Journal Book*), the earliest impetus to WAC was signaled by the 1970s furor created by concern about correctness. The 1975 *Newsweek* cover story, "Why Johnny Can't Write," is typically cited as epitomizing the mood at that time; "Johnny's" explicit shortcomings were in syntax, spelling, vocabulary, and organization. Moreover, the assessment/accountability fashion of the 1990s, part of the many-faceted reaction to the free-spending 1980s, has made "transaction" far more emphatic in WAC programs than "expression." Certainly, the increase in the number of writing intensive requirements illustrates this trend. Where "writing to learn" exists as a key element of the definition of "writing" in WAC, more and more it exists as a stage of student progress toward that transactional "good writing," rather than as an end in itself.

Technology: Changing All the Rules

But if traditional concerns have kept the definitions of "writing" and "good writing" somewhat narrow, the force of technological advancement is expanding those definitions and will no doubt continue to do so. When Janet Emig wrote "Writing as a Mode of Learning" (1977), which helped conceptualize "writing to learn" as theory, she carefully distinguished between writing and three other language modes — speech, reading, and listening — in order to support the "uniqueness" of writing. But the "writing" she assumed was of words as conventionally defined; to wit:

> Making such a case for the uniqueness of writing should logically and theoretically involve establishing many contrasts, distinctions between (1) writing and all other verbal languaging processes — listening, reading, and especially talking; (2) writing and all other forms of composing, such as composing a painting, a symphony, a dance, a film, a building. (7)

Emig's formulation antedates the emergence of other tools, such as the computer monitor, invisible storage on disks, and the mouse, that have changed in still undetermined ways the relationship between writer and text. (One question, for example: does the operation of the hand on the mouse, as one imports text from one source into another or moves text around in a document, still reinforce learning to the extent claimed by Emig for the physical act of writing using old tools?) Even more profoundly, Emig's definition antedates the virtual fusion — at least hybridization — of talk and writing by means of e-mail (Spooner and Yancey). Anyone attempting to define first principles of WAC must confront the e-mail explosion. Some practical questions, for example: In determining the prevalence of WAC at a school, does one "count" the e-mail exchanges between student and professor regarding answers to test questions or ideas for a presentation? Does one count — and how might one count, even if one wished to — e-mail exchanges between students preparing for that same test or presentation?

When WAC was new in the 1970s, surely no one foresaw the difficulty of distinguishing writing from other modes of communication that exist today. Talk was talk and writing was writing — indeed, it can be argued that the concept of writing across the curriculum grew up in this country precisely because writing seemed so clearly different from talk. Interestingly, the British, our predecessors in identifying both writing and talk as subjects for study across the curriculum (Martin et al.; Martin), persistently linked the two in the term "language across the curriculum." In the United States, however, where the preeminence of multiple-choice and short-answer testing had devalued both writing and speaking in curricula (Russell), most teachers had little practical experience of the mutually reinforcing effects of the two, and so their differences were much more obvious than their connections. In the late 1970s, a few U.S. writers (e.g., Goodkin and Parker) argued for synthesis, but "language across the curriculum" or "communication across the curriculum" — the sense of a reforged link between speech and written composition — has yet to take hold in institutions, except in rare instances (Thaiss and Suhor; Sipple and Carson), whereas WAC has flourished. Hence, e-mail poses a conceptual difficulty for WAC planners, a difficulty that will disappear in an integrated language-across-the-curriculum (LAC) environment, one which, I predict, technology is forcing us to conceptualize and eventually accept.

The Multimedia Swamp

If e-mail muddies the definition of writing, consider the swamp created by multimedia composing. When I try out different colors for the background of a Web page and ask one of my sons, a visual artist, to design a logo, am I "writing"? If another son, in tenth grade and a guitarist, attaches an alternative rock music file to an e-mail message to a friend in order to illustrate a point about that rock group, where does the "writing" end and something else take over? If the final product in an electrical engineering course that meets a school's writing intensive requirement (see Townsend, ["Writing Intensive Courses and WAC"] for definitions of "writing intensive") is a multimedia (video, sound, words) Web page designed by a six-person team of students from three universities, how and how much does that work count, how does the teacher evaluate it, and is it "writing"? Should the university WAC committee question its validity and demand something different, or does the entity demand new theory? (See ["WAC Wired: Electronic Communication Across the Curriculum"] by Reiss and Young and the volume by Reiss, Selfe, and Young for more on this issue.)

If we define "writing" conventionally as words, sentences, paragraphs, pages, and so forth, then multimedia composing creates problems for the teacher/evaluator and the administrator. If program guidelines say, for example, that for a course to be writing intensive every student must write four thousand graded words, then the teacher and the committee must do some clever rationalizing to justify the product. But if the definition of writing is broadened to, let's say, "creative use, for communicative purposes, of the various tools available to the electronic composer," then the challenges change.

The teacher of a dramatic literature course must, for example, weigh the comparative communicative power within a critical essay of a video clip from a production of *Hamlet* versus a written description of the same excerpt. Using the clip may make the essay a clearer, more emphatic piece of "writing"; but if we define writing in this more inclusive, technologically current way, then we are setting up new standards for "good writing" that have many consequences. Among these, "teaching writing" will now include teaching a broad range of computer skills — an issue even now facing all administrators of writing programs; hence, teaching these skills means that all students must have access to sophisticated hardware and software, and teachers must be well-"versed" (to use an old-tech metaphor) in them. The broader definition will now mean that the act of writing means choosing among a huge array of images and forms, only some of which are "words." Ideas such as "syntax," "organization," "accuracy," "clarity," "style" — the list includes all the conventional criteria and more — will all come to be defined in multimedia terms. "Style," for example, would come to mean the distinctive way a writer designs and organizes sound, video, static visuals, spoken words, and so forth. How quickly are we approaching the day when the class of "good writers" will not include anyone who composes only with words, even if that person is a virtuoso on the instruments of "mere" literacy?

A More and More Inclusive Definition

Of course, the broader definition of "writing" may make the notion of "good writing" much broader. Rather than simply raising the bar, so that only those with the most eclectic, omni-media skills are rewarded, technological choice might allow a much greater variety of "written products" to succeed in the context of the academy. This multiplicity of media already flourishes outside the academy and there is no reason to believe that schools won't adapt, though they will never catch up to the commercial marketplace in technical or conceptual innovation — unless universities, through corporate funding, become (or become once again) the research arms of industry (e.g., Bleich). Just as printed books, visuals-and-text magazines, radio, television, CDs, live theater, Web sites, MOOs, and so on coexist today as venues for "writing" in the marketplace, so school parameters of "good writing" should broaden as these varied technologies continue to become cheaper and easier to use.

This technological broadening of the definition of writing is helped along, I would argue (as I have elsewhere [Thaiss, "WAC Theory"]), by the hesitancy (or neglect, possibly benign) of program directors and committees to impose detailed definitions of writing on WAC, or to enunciate detailed, narrowing criteria. As I stated at the beginning of this chapter, this lack of close definition is largely responsible for the growth of WAC programs. Allowing, even encouraging, different parts of a faculty to maintain divergent, often conflicting, goals for writing does serve the growth of the program, and it also serves the tendency of a concept to grow and change with technology. An intriguing paradox in the history of WAC has been that most programs have been funded because of deep and wide concern about the quality of student writing; nevertheless, few programs have systematically studied just what is wrong and what is good with that writing, nor prescribed in detail what is needed (as Condon, ["Accommodating Complexity"] shows). Consciously or not, WAC theorists and program leaders have encouraged almost unlimited variety in terms of what counts as writing and how it is evaluated, and therefore have kept the door open for a vigorous, intimate relationship between technological advance and writing. Walvoord et al. argue that assessment of WAC programs should honor this diversity of teachers' definitions of "what works for them"; they criticize a potential tendency of program leaders and their supervisors to assess programs in terms of a narrow range of criteria. I would argue that the relative lack of rigorous assessment of WAC programs (again, see [Condon]) demonstrates that the vast majority of WAC programs already honor this laissez-faire principle, at least tacitly. Almost everyone agrees that "good writing" is hard to find among students, but most program participants also agree that definitions of good writing are best left to them, to individual teachers and members of professional groups trying to achieve meaningful, workable standards within shared contexts.

The Assessment Caveat

Hence, while some powers-that-be (presidents, boards of regents, state legislatures) may be calling for more rigorous assessment, we need to keep in mind that such accountability always carries with it the risk of making programs and instruction obsolete by making them inflexible. As Sosnoski argues in a recent volume about grading writing, the electronic writing environment calls into question all conventional assumptions about academic assessment:

> Yet as hazardous as grading in print environments is to the psyche of teachers, how much more perplexing it becomes in electronic environments where teacher/student roles characteristically shift. In computer-oriented classrooms, students often teach their teachers. When boundaries of authority blur, grading can become an arbitrary use of power. (157)

I used the term "laissez-faire" deliberately in the previous paragraph because critics of WAC's indeterminacy have focused on the relationship between writing and economics. Regardless of one's views of and desires for that relationship, it is hard to ignore the usefulness of what has been variously called the "social-epistemic" (Berlin, "Rhetoric"), "cultural studies" (e.g., Berlin and Vivion), or "new historicist" approach to defining "writing," "good writing," "teaching writing," and so forth. As explained in Russell's essay, ["Where Do the Naturalistic Studies of WAC/WID Point? A Research Review,"] an ongoing element of some WAC research (e.g., by Bazerman; Myers) has been to highlight the ways by which "learning to write" in a discipline means reproducing the existing hierarchies of power. As Mahala contended, the willingness of WAC directors to allow departments and faculty to define standards of good writing in their own areas actually determined that the status quo would be maintained. To Mahala, the status quo meant that "instead of addressing the most contentious issues, WAC programs have often maintained a political invisibility, tailoring theory to institutional divisions . . . rather than really interrogating prevailing attitudes about knowledge, language, and learning" (773). In a rebuttal, Patricia Dunn argued that, given the diversity of disciplines and teachers, it was inaccurate and reductive to characterize faculty monolithically and as committed to the status quo: "they would not be involved in WAC if they believed they had nothing to learn" (732; see also the rebuttal of Mahala's arguments by McLeod and Maimon). I would argue that regardless of one's view of the motives of faculty, and regardless of one's view of how economic power is held and distributed, "writing" in WAC always is defined in terms of the relationship between what happens in academia and what happens in the "economy" of which it is a part and into which colleges graduate students. Moreover, WAC is a powerful concept precisely because it addresses that relationship.

The Marketplace as Driving Force

To show how WAC-defined "writing" directly addresses the question of economy, we might contrast it to writing as defined in the first-year (FY) composition class. When we seek to define writing in WAC, we should keep in mind that as a political movement, writing across the curriculum in the United States has meant "writing not only in required English composition courses." Implicitly manifesting awareness of the social construction of knowledge, WAC researchers and planners saw the teaching of writing in the typical FY comp class as disconnected from (1) the disciplines in which students would be writing later on (if not at the same time as they were taking the comp class), and (2) the careers for which, one presumed, the disciplines were preparing them (see, for example, Maimon; Thaiss, "WAC and General Education"). The basic rationale for WAC has always been that writing cannot be the same in an FY comp class as it is in a course in the major because all the key environmental factors differ:

- Ways of knowing (hence logic, evidence, organization) differ among disciplines — indeed, we define disciplines by these differences. (I use the term "disciplines" for convenience here; later I take up the difficulties with this term.)

- Terms are specialized, and even the connotations of familiar words change from discipline to discipline.

- The purposes of writing are different because of when the student takes the course and who teaches it. Basically, the FY comp class is part of the student's acclimation to the discourse of the academy only in its most general features; the writing is an end in itself, the teacher usually a specialist in language or literature. Conversely, writing in a course in the major is usually a means to the end of developing and demonstrating knowledge of methods and materials in the discipline; it is not an end in itself. The teacher is a specialist in those materials and methods.

- Further, even if the course in the major is also part of the student's acclimation to the academy, it primarily prepares the student for life after school, presumably within the marketplace, in a way that the FY comp course cannot approach.

In summary, then, writing within WAC can be defined historically in contrast to the British language across the curriculum. It can also be defined dynamically and unpredictably in terms of advances in technology, as well as somewhat more narrowly in terms of its distinction from writing in FY comp class. But even this "narrower" definition ineluctably admits of great variety since it is founded on the (antifoundational!) assumption that "writing" and its ethical corollary "good writing" differ from discipline to discipline, context to context.

"Across"

I don't want to make too much of this little word, but focusing on it briefly can help to clarify some points and make others helpfully cloudier. After all, "across" is not the same as "in" or "throughout" (not to mention "against," "over," "behind," or other delicious prepositions that conjure up intriguing ironies). The term "writing across the curriculum" has had remarkable staying power,[1] for which I think there are good reasons. "Across" connotes movement from place to place, time to time. It implies coverage, but not necessarily depth. "They moved across the country" means something very different from "They moved through the country." "Across" need not be profound; it can imply visited but did not stay.

Of course, its connotation depends on subjects and verbs. "The plague spread across Europe" feels very different from "The train sped across Europe." But even if it's a deadly disease that is "crossing," "across" feels less permanent and thorough than "The plague spread throughout Europe."

Why then does "writing across the curriculum" have staying power even though "across" is not a "stay-put" kind of word? I think it's because it sounds nonthreatening. Unlike "writing throughout the curriculum," which implies 100 percent compliance, "writing across the curriculum" implies an even presence, but not control. Variants such as "writing across the disciplines" and "writing across the university" have a similar feel. Note that when governing bodies want to get tough about the idea, the language becomes more aggressive: "writing intensive requirement" is the best example. "Writing across the curriculum" says to faculty, "See how this works in your own teaching and how it might work; no pressure."

A second connotation of "across" is best illustrated by contrast with "in," specifically in the phrase "writing in the disciplines." "Across" suggests a link — "hands across the sea," "telephone lines across the continent" — whereas "in" suggests presence but not connection, certainly not movement. Writers over the years have commented on the messianic, or at least peripatetic, nature of WAC (see Walvoord), and "across" expresses this dynamic character well. That the signal event of WAC programs has been the multi- or cross-disciplinary workshop, marked by discussions and exchanges of information, also fits with "across." ("Sharing," a 1960s word, was the vogue term for this mode until the 1980s backlash. We now "interact," but we don't "share.")

"In," as in the phrase "writing in the disciplines," suits well that aspect of WAC which is more concerned with the specific, differentiating features of disciplinary discourse than in their intersections or in the effort to establish a community of interest among faculty. As I explored in my attempt to define "writing," the notion that each discipline has its own distinctive epistemology and discourse has been a central argument in support of a cross-curricular writing movement. Without the "in" there is little argument for the "across." Or, to give a different answer to the old question, "Why did the chicken cross the road?" — because there really was another side.

"THE CURRICULUM"

"The curriculum" is not the same as "curriculum"; in fact, these two might be more different than "the curriculum" and "the disciplines," at least as WAC has evolved in practice. In my first draft of this chapter, I planned to define "curriculum" as the third term of the phrase, but having discovered the resonance of "across," I became fascinated by the even smaller word "the." So please bear with me.

I have never heard the phrase "writing across curriculum"; what might it mean? I have heard National Writing Project colleagues who teach K–12 say, "I'm writing curriculum," as in "I'm writing a plan of study or designing a sequence of courses." But "curriculum" without the definite article implies tentativeness, a draft perhaps of what might, if all the officials sign off on it, become "the curriculum," at least until the next batch of standardized test scores comes in. "The curriculum," particularly in the context of colleges and universities, evokes hallowed halls, festoons of ivy, Greek lettering, and all the other trappings of surety, permanence, even immortality. "Writing across the curriculum," especially when paired with "writing in the disciplines," reinforces this emotion. ("Writing across the disciplines" is a nice conflation that captures this feeling and some of the flavor of both "in" and "across.")

Actually, "the curriculum," like an unambiguous "writing," is an illusion, an idyll of some rapidly receding golden age. I'm not sure for whom we continue to peddle phrases such as "the curriculum" or "the disciplines," since higher education, like every other aspect of culture, is in flux, and has been as far back as we can study it (Halloran; Ohmann). Even if the definite articles sustain some selling power with parents — usually concerned that the college experience provide at least some stability — and with some prospective students, I assume that faculty, at least those who have been around a while, automatically see through "the curriculum" and "the disciplines" to such fluctuating administrative expediencies as "the departments" or "the majors."

"The curriculum" is subject to the same destabilizing forces that make the definition of "writing" so volatile. Indeed, if we see "the curriculum" as embodied in its documents and its processes of communication (the postmodern versus Platonic perspective as [Victor] Villanueva points out in ["The Politics of Literacy Across the Curriculum"]), then changes in "writing" and "curriculum" must go together. Speaking practically, a theory of mutual change in "writing" and "the curriculum" implies, for example, that we should not look for fixity in a roster of courses labeled "writing intensive," just as we should not try to define our criteria for "writing intensity" too specifically. The theory also implies that changes in curriculum should signal to writing researchers and administrators changes in the writing environment and in forms of writing. Even the smallest change, say approval of a new course, may represent a deep change in faculty feeling about the discipline, about students, about technology, and about the outside community that can affect every facet of "writing" for those faculty, from purpose, to format, to potential audience, and so forth.

The Elusive WID

If "the curriculum" is a misleading term, "the disciplines" is no less so. Although our sense of the social construction of "writing" has advanced from our reliance on the one-size-fits-all composition course to the recognition of basic differences across disciplines, our sense of categorical differences does not yet extend within the so-called disciplines themselves. In the relatively short history of writing-in-the-disciplines (WID) research (Bazerman; Myers; Herrington; Henry; McCarthy), areas of study tend to be given traditional disciplinary names: chemistry, philosophy, biology, engineering, architecture, and so forth, and researchers continue to seek generalizable characteristics within those broad categories. Certainly WID textbook publishers have reinforced this level of generality (e.g., the several textbooks on "writing in psychology" or "writing in political science"), when they aren't dealing at an even more abstract level: e.g., "writing in the sciences." Although researchers have conscientiously explored the great differences from context to context within alleged disciplines, overall theory has basically ignored both (1) the proliferation of subspecialties within so-called disciplines (e.g., composition within English)[2] that render communication among "colleagues" almost nil, and (2) the rise of so-called interdisciplinary specialties that correspond to emergent professional descriptions in the workplace: e.g., law enforcement, recreation and leisure studies, career counseling. The usual notion of WID, when applied to program design and assessment, fails to question the level of generality that is either possible or meaningful. To cite an absurdly obvious example, if I record that the Department of Modern and Classical Languages has designated ten courses as "writing intensive," participation by those faculty looks different than if I record that for each of the ten languages taught in that department there is one WI course, different still if the ten break down into five in the Spanish literature of South America, none in the rest of Spanish, and five scattered among the nine other languages. Categorizing the distribution of writing in other disciplines, such as computer science, might not be so easy, and the difficulty points up the shortcomings of our current theory of WID, as well as WAC.

Helpful to our understanding of "the disciplines" would be the comparatively sophisticated theory of research in workplace writing (see Alred). This research has moved beyond such general categories as professions (e.g., writing by lawyers or engineers) and industries (e.g., textiles, aerospace) toward the definition of context based on multiple factors, such as "Electronic Mail in Two Corporate Workplaces" (the title of an essay by Brenda Sims, in Sullivan and Dauterman), in which technology ("electronic"), genre ("mail"), and setting ("two corporate workplaces") confine the study and its pretensions. The definition of writing assumes ethnographic limitations: the research does not presume to generalize about whole genres, technologies, or fields (in this case telecommunications and computers) based on the findings, but merely to compare features of the technology and the genre in two specific locales. If readers wish to extrapolate analogies to other contexts, such as to the entirety of "the computer industry," they may, but it is not the intent of the essay to do so.

FROM WID TO WIC

This is not to say that many WID-type studies have not already adhered to this ethnographic lack of pretension; nevertheless, the fact that the WID category still exists shows that we have not yet moved beyond the so-called discipline as a meaningful marker of difference. More useful in looking at writing cultures in academia might be the notion of "WIC" — or "writing in the course" (analogous to "writing in the workplace"). This concept would allow researchers to observe the richness of each course context without having to fit that context within the arbitrary category of a so-called discipline. Certainly part of the research data might be the teacher's and the students' senses of how the course fits within their concepts of the field — which one would expect to differ from one another — but the theory would never assume that the course in any way represents a consensus definition of "the discipline." By removing the assumption of disciplinary "fit," the theory also allows other influences to be observed. If, for example, we look at a course called History 130 — The New South and do not assume that the prefix "History" is essentially meaningful, then we can more openly question the origins, purposes, and methods of the course. We may find that the teacher draws theory from texts usually categorized according to other nebulous disciplines — public policy, economics, literature, sociology, not to mention popular media — and uses methods drawn from participants and guest lecturers at cross-university workshops. We would definitely not assume that, whatever we find, History 130 represents in any way the methods, purposes, and materials of any other course also prefixed "History." We might discover, with further research, that such a link does exist within the particular institution, but we would not be able to generalize about "the discipline" — nor, I should add, about the characteristic behaviors or attitudes of any disciplinary group of faculty toward writing. I have often heard WAC program leaders say things like "English faculty are hard [or easy] to work with," as if it were possible to make such "disciplinary" generalizations, and I invariably find these generalizations contradicted by the next conversation.

As theory, "writing in the course" operates on an ethnographic basis close to that of another subfield of composition studies, "teacher research" (see, e.g., Goswami and Stillman; Mohr and McLean). Teacher research also sees the relationship between the individual teacher and a group of students as the most meaningful locus of study about writing in the academic context. Teacher research goes further, of course, to see the teacher as the key researcher in the context, because the primary goal of the research is the teacher's knowledge, with the long-range objective being improved teaching and learning. While I believe that WAC research has benefited — and will benefit further — from applications of teacher research principles (e.g., the studies of Fishman ["Writing to Learn," "Writing and Philosophy"]), the most useful principle is the primacy of the individual course as the focus of the study of writing in an academic setting, regardless of the researcher.

Although I suggest here that the notion of "writing in the disciplines" has diverted attention from the most meaningful context of "writing across the curriculum," I would stress that most WAC programs, in their most common activities, support the theory of "writing in the course." The most common event of the WAC program has been some form of faculty development workshop, usually open to teachers from many departmental units. Even when workshops are conducted within single departments or among smaller units, the preponderance of workshop materials and topics has centered on the individual course, irrespective of discipline. Such common teacher concerns as workload, student motivation, productive feedback to students, and grading dominate both workshop discussion and the most popular workshop materials. Moreover, the typical "genre" of the inhouse WAC newsletter (Thaiss, "Newsletters"), the "teacher practice" essay (although most of these hardly qualify as conscientious ethnography), is based on the theory of the individual course as a more meaningful locale of study about the role of writing in academia. Though writers of such essays routinely invoke their concept of "the discipline" as part of the rationale for their methods, the burden of such essays is usually to explain methods in relation to the teacher's goals. The audience for these essays is usually faculty across the institution, and the essays are published in order to inform and encourage this heterogeneous group to make individual adaptations, much as the workshop does.

CONCLUSION: THEORY FOR A NEW MILLENNIUM

In defining "writing," I made some predictions about the future of WAC theory, primarily in response to advances in technology. By changing every facet of what we currently mean by "writing," technology will ineluctably change every aspect of "the curriculum" and what we mean by the dynamic term "across." In addition, I don't see any reason why the trend in higher education to adapt to the career interests of prospective students should be interrupted. As pointed out earlier, new degree programs correspond to emerging careers; why should this trend change? Further, just as electronic technology is bridging the physical separation of "the university" and "the community," so technology will facilitate further interplay between "student," "professor," "worker," and "manager," with blurring and perhaps eventual merger of aspects of these roles. For example, it is easy to see service learning, as explored by David Jolliffe in ["Writing Across the Curriculum and Service Learning: Kairos, Genre, and Collaboration"], evolving from a college outreach program to an intrinsic part of education. There is no reason for this not to be so: technology facilitates communication by students working at an off-campus site with other students, the professor, and onsite supervisors. Inevitably, roles and lines of authority will blur and in some cases vanish, just as the concept of "distance education" is drastically changing the notions of "campus" and "classroom."

Theory will both respond to these changes and help to encourage them. I predict that the ethnographic similarity between "writing in the course" and "writing in the workplace" will enable further blurring of the differences between school and community. As the concept of "writing in the disciplines" gives way to theory that encourages a more open exploration of the influences on what and how we teach, curriculum will be freer to grow symbiotically with changes in work.

NOTES

1. In the preface to Martin et al. (1976), the term is dated to as early as 1971.

2. Composition studies, of course, has developed its own rich literature on methods and style in the field itself — Asher and Lauer; Kirsch and Sullivan; Kirklighter, Vincent, and Moxley; etc. I use comp within English as an example, familiar to many readers of this essay, of "disciplinary" subdivisions that appear in all so-called disciplines and that likewise have developed their own literatures of method.

WORKS CITED

Alred, Gerald. *The St. Martin's Bibliography of Business and Technical Communication.* New York: St. Martin's, 1997.

Asher, William, and Janice Lauer. *Composition Research: Empirical Designs.* New York: Oxford UP, 1988.

Bartholomae, David. "Inventing the University." *When a Writer Can't Write: Studies in Writer's Block and Other Composing-Process Problems.* Ed. Mike Rose. New York: Guilford, 1985. 135–65.

———. "Writing with Teachers: A Conversation with Peter Elbow." *College Composition and Communication* 46 (1995): 62–71.

Bazerman, Charles. *Shaping Written Knowledge: The Genre and Activity of the Experimental Article in Science.* Madison: U of Wisconsin P, 1988.

Berlin, James. "Rhetoric and Ideology in the Writing Class." *College English* 50 (1988): 477–94.

———. *Writing Instruction in Nineteenth-Century American Colleges.* Carbondale: Southern Illinois UP, 1984.

Berlin, James, and Michael Vivion, eds. *Cultural Studies in the English Classroom.* Portsmouth, NH: Boynton/Cook, 1992.

Bishop, Wendy, and Hans Ostrom, eds. *Genre and Writing: Issues, Arguments, Alternatives.* Portsmouth, NH: Heinemann, 1997.

Bizzell, Patricia. "Cognition, Convention, and Certainty: What We Need to Know about Writing." *PRE/TEXT* 3.3 (1982): 213–43.

Bleich, David. "What Can Be Done about Grading?" *Grading in the Post-Process Classroom: From Theory to Practice.* Ed. Libby Allison, Lizbeth Bryant, and Maureen Hourigan. Portsmouth, NH: Boynton/Cook, 1997. 15–35.

Britton, James N., et al. *The Development of Writing Abilities, 11–18.* London: Macmillan, 1975.

Bruffee, Kenneth. "Collaborative Learning and the 'Conversation of Mankind.'" *College English* 46 (1984): 635–52.

Condon, William. "Accommodating Complexity: WAC Program Evaluation in the Age of Account-ability." *WAC for the New Millennium: Strategies for Continuing Writing-Across-the-Curriculum Programs*. Eds. Susan McLeod, Eric Miraglia, Margot Soven, and Chris Thaiss. Urbana: NCTE, 2001. 28–51. Print.

Dunn, Patricia. "Response to 'Writing Utopias.'" *College English* 54 (1992): 731–33.

Elbow, Peter. "Being a Writer vs. Being an Academic." *College Composition and Communication* 46 (1995): 72–83.

Emig, Janet. "Writing as a Mode of Learning." *College Composition and Communication* 28 (1977): 122–28. Rpt. in *Cross-Talk in Comp Theory: A Reader*. Ed. Victor Villanueva, Jr. Urbana, IL: NCTE, 1997. 7–15.

———. *The Composing Processes of Twelfth Graders*. Research Report No. 13. Urbana, IL: NCTE, 1971.

Fishman, Stephen. "Writing to Learn in Philosophy." *Teaching Philosophy* 8 (1985): 331–34.

———. "Writing and Philosophy." *Teaching Philosophy* 12 (1989): 361–74.

Fulwiler, Toby, ed. *The Journal Book*. Portsmouth, NH: Heinemann, 1987.

Goodkin, Vera, and Robert Parker. *The Consequences of Writing: Enhancing Learning in the Disciplines*. Upper Montclair, NJ: Boynton/Cook, 1987.

Goswami, Dixie, and Peter Stillman, eds. *Reclaiming the Classroom: Teacher Research as an Agency for Change*. Portsmouth, NH: Heinemann, 1987.

Halloran, S. Michael. "From Rhetoric to Composition: The Teaching of Writing in America to 1900." *A Short History of Writing Instruction*. Ed. James J. Murphy. Davis, CA: Hermagoras, 1990. 151–82.

Henry, Jim. "A Narratological Analysis of WAC Authorship." *College English* 56 (1994): 810–24.

Herrington, Anne. "Writing in Academic Settings: A Study of the Contexts for Writing in Two College Chemical Engineering Courses." *Research in the Teaching of English* 19 (1985): 331–61.

Jolliffe, David A. "Writing Across the Curriculum and Service Learning: Kairos, Genre, and Collaboration." *WAC for the New Millennium: Strategies for Continuing Writing-Across-the-Curriculum Programs*. Eds. Susan McLeod, Eric Miraglia, Margot Soven, and Chris Thaiss. Urbana: NCTE, 2001. 86–108. Print.

Kirklighter, Christina, Cloe Vincent, and Joseph Moxley, eds. *Voices and Visions: Refiguring Ethnography in Composition*. Portsmouth, NH: Boynton/Cook, 1997.

Kirsch, Gesa, and Patricia Sullivan, eds. *Methods and Methodology in Composition Research*. Carbondale: Southern Illinois UP, 1992.

Mahala, Daniel. "Writing Utopias: Writing Across the Curriculum and the Promise of Reform." *College English* 53 (1991): 773–89.

Maimon, Elaine. "Writing Across the Curriculum: Past, Present, and Future." *Teaching Writing in All Disciplines*. Ed. C. W. Griffin. San Francisco: Jossey-Bass, 1982. 67–74.

Martin, Nancy. "Language Across the Curriculum: Where It Began and What It Promises." *Writing, Teaching, and Learning in the Disciplines*. Ed. Anne Herrington and Charles Moran. New York: MLA, 1992. 6–21.

Martin, Nancy, et al. *Writing and Learning Across the Curriculum, 11–16*. London: Ward Lock, 1976.

McCarthy, Lucille. "A Stranger in Strange Lands: A College Student Writing Across the Curriculum." *Research in the Teaching of English* 21 (1987): 233–65.

McLeod, Susan, and Elaine Maimon. "Clearing the Air: WAC Myths and Realities." *College English* 62 (2000): 573–83.

Mohr, Marian, and Marion McLean. *Working Together: A Guide for Teacher-Researchers*. Urbana, IL: NCTE, 1987.

Myers, Greg. *Writing Biology: Texts in the Social Construction of Scientific Knowledge*. Madison: U of Wisconsin P, 1990.

Naisbitt, John, and Patricia Aburdene. *Megatrends 2000: Ten New Directions for the 1990's*. New York: Morrow, 1990.

Ohmann, Richard. *English in America: A Radical View of the Profession*. New York: Oxford, 1976.

Perry, William G. *Forms of Intellectual and Ethical Development in the College Years: A Scheme*. New York: Holt, 1970.

Reiss, Donna, Dickie Selfe, and Art Young, eds. *Electronic Communication Across the Curriculum*. Urbana, IL: NCTE, 1998.

Russell, David. "American Origins of the Writing-Across-the-Curriculum Movement." *Writing, Teaching, and Learning in the Disciplines*. Ed. Anne Herrington and Charles Moran. New York: MLA, 1992. 22–42.

———. "Where Do the Naturalistic Studies of WAC/WID Point? A Research Review." *WAC for the New Millennium: Strategies for Continuing Writing-Across-the-Curriculum Programs*. Eds. Susan McLeod, Eric Miraglia, Margot Soven, and Chris Thaiss. Urbana: NCTE, 2001. 259–98. Print.

Shaughnessy, Mina. *Errors and Expectations.* New York: Oxford, 1977.

Sipple, Jo-Ann, and Jay Carson. "Reaching Out to the Business and Professional Community." *Composition Chronicle* 10A (1997): 9–10.

Sosnoski, James. "Grades for Work: Giving Value for Value." *Grading in the Post-Process Classroom: From Theory to Practice.* Ed. Libby Allison, Lizbeth Bryant, and Maureen Hourigan. Portsmouth, NH: Heinemann, 1997. 157–76.

Spooner, Michael, and Kathleen Yancey. "Postings on a Genre of Email." *Genre and Writing: Issues, Arguments, Alternatives.* Ed. Wendy Bishop and Hans Ostrom. Portsmouth, NH: Boynton/Cook, 1997.

Sullivan, Patricia, and Jennie Dauterman, eds. *Electronic Literacies in the Workplace: Technologies of Writing.* Urbana, IL: NCTE, 1996.

Thaiss, Christopher. "Newsletters." *The Harcourt Brace Guide to Writing Across the Curriculum.* Fort Worth: Harcourt Brace, 1998. Chap. 4.

———. "WAC and General Education Courses." *Writing Across the Curriculum: A Guide to Developing Programs.* Ed. Susan McLeod and Margot Soven. Academic.Writing Landmark Publications in Writing Studies: http://aw.colostate.edu/books/mcleod_soven/2000. Originally published in print by Sage (Newbury Park, CA), 1992. 87–109.

———. "Writing-Across-the-Curriculum Theory." *Theorizing Composition: A Critical Sourcebook of Theory and Scholarship.* Ed. Mary Lynch Kennedy. Westport, CT: Greenwood, 1998. 356–64.

Thaiss, Christopher, and Charles Suhor, eds. *Speaking and Writing, K–12: Classroom Strategies and the New Research.* Urbana, IL: NCTE, 1984.

Townsend, Martha A. "Writing Intensive Courses and WAC." *WAC for the New Millennium: Strategies for Continuing Writing-Across-the-Curriculum Programs.* Eds. Susan McLeod, Eric Miraglia, Margot Soven, and Chris Thaiss. Urbana: NCTE, 2001. 233–58. Print.

Villanueva, Victor. "The Politics of Literacy Across the Curriculum." *WAC for the New Millennium: Strategies for Continuing Writing-Across-the-Curriculum Programs.* Eds. Susan McLeod, Eric Miraglia, Margot Soven, and Chris Thaiss. Urbana: NCTE, 2001. 165–78. Print.

Walvoord, Barbara. "The Future of WAC." *College English* 58 (1996): 58–79.

Walvoord, Barbara, et al. *In the Long Run: A Study of Faculty in Three Writing-Across-the-Curriculum Programs.* Urbana, IL: NCTE, 1997.

"Why Johnny Can't Write." *Newsweek* 8 Dec. 1975: cover and 58ff.

PART TWO

Practicing WAC

Introduction to Part Two

Leaders in the WAC field are "agents of change," as Susan McLeod argues in her 1988 collection on designing WAC programs, and, as such, these leaders must practice WAC from the ground up by sharing knowledge and experience, learning from colleagues in the disciplines, collaborating on cross-disciplinary ventures, and enlisting the cooperation of faculty and administrators. This focus on improving teaching and student learning at the programmatic level, and therefore in practice, in many ways has guided WAC theory, development, and research. In this section, we provide key articles that describe in detail practical ways to engage in faculty development, enhance classroom teaching practices, and impact the culture of learning at the institutional level. (The "How to Do WAC" section of our extended bibliography includes special subsections devoted to starting and sustaining a WAC program, and resources for teaching with writing across the disciplines.)

From the outset of the movement, WAC practice focused on the faculty development seminar as the central activity for engaging educators from across disciplines in efforts to improve teaching and learning in higher education. We begin, then, with Toby Fulwiler's classic "Showing, Not Telling, at a Writing Workshop," which provides five detailed descriptions of model WAC workshops and encourages seminar facilitators to tap into the "wealth of knowledge about writing" that faculty across the disciplines already possess. The experiential approach he advocates has become a WAC commonplace, both for interdisciplinary faculty interactions and classroom pedagogy. In Anne Herrington's "Writing to Learn: Writing Across the Disciplines," we see the results of Fulwiler's approach as she describes the outcomes of actual WAC workshops in which model courses, assignment sequences, and assessment tools were developed and later implemented. Incorporating student feedback and some empirical investigation of texts, Herrington provides a powerful example of how WAC workshops illuminate for faculty a number of critical pedagogical issues: assignment sequencing, the linking of assignments to course objectives, and the need for "clear and relevant assessment criteria." Her admonition that "the time given to working out the purpose of an assignment and preparing students for it is much more important than the time given to evaluating the finished product" suggests the importance of faculty colleagues reflecting deeply on course objectives and activities.

Dan Melzer's "Writing Assignments Across the Curriculum: A National Study of College Writing," which presents the results of his study of more than 2,000 writing assignments from college courses across disciplines, provides ample data for such reflection. Writing assignments, Melzer argues, are "revealing classroom artifacts," a rich source of information about teachers' disciplinary, course, and classroom goals and values. His quantitative and qualitative analysis of the rhetorical features and contexts for writing assignments is modeled on the studies of secondary school essays carried out by James Britton and his colleagues in 1975 and by Judith Langer and Arthur Applebee in 1987; however, Melzer expands on Britton's multidimensional rhetorical taxonomy to include an analysis of assignments from a genre-as-social-action perspective. As Melzer finds, students in WAC courses are more likely to be asked to "use writing to explore" — and more likely to write, period — than their counterparts in regular courses.

Several articles in this section outline exciting ways in which practitioners have used WAC pedagogy effectively in their classrooms. John Bean, Dean Drenk, and F. D. Lee's article, "Microtheme Strategies for Developing Cognitive Skills," offers an early preview of Bean's best-selling *Engaging Ideas: The Professor's Guide to Integrating Writing, Critical Thinking, and Active Learning in the Classroom*. The article provides practical suggestions for faculty across disciplines who are interested in transforming their pedagogy by incorporating low-stakes writing-to-learn exercises. We include an example of innovative WAC pedagogy as Art Young, also drawing on Britton's work, describes ways he and his colleagues at Clemson employed poetry writing in non-composition classes. In "Writing Across and Against the Curriculum," Young argues that informal and ungraded writing provides students from across the disciplines with opportunities to use written language to engage with all kinds of course content in personally meaningful ways.

Valuable writing-in-the-disciplines instruction can also occur in an introductory composition course, as Patricia Linton, Robert Madigan, and Susan Johnson explain in "Introducing Students to Disciplinary Genres: The Role of the General Composition Course." While English faculty are not typically experts in the genres and methodologies of various disciplines, they can help students understand how and why discourse conventions differ from discipline to discipline. The authors suggest that there are three categories of conventions that occur in all academic genres — conventions of structure, reference, and language — and that these reflect the differing epistemological values of the humanities and the social and natural sciences.

In "One Size Does Not Fit All: Plagiarism Across the Curriculum," Sandra Jamieson also calls for an emphasis on teaching the "whys" of disciplinary conventions, in this case, conventions of reference, if our goal is to invite students into the discourse communities of their majors rather than to discipline them for their failure to understand source use as a reflection of that community's epistemological values. Jamieson describes the confusion that arises over conventions of reference — on the part of both faculty and students — when correct source use is assumed to be a simple matter of rote learning of the rules rather than a context-specific discursive practice. How might we reread student plagiarism, Jamieson asks, if we reject the idea that "one size fits all" and focus instead on developing WAC policies and pedagogies that attend to the underlying "intentions" of source use in the "real work of disciplines." Jamieson concludes her article with a reflexive rereading of her own use of sources, demonstrating an approach we might use with students to help them see the seemingly transparent textual differences that mark novices and disciplinary insiders.

Moving from classroom practice to the practice of WAC institution-wide, Joan Mullin offers a way forward for WAC leaders who inevitably confront difficult obstacles when working to transform the culture of teaching at their institutions. In "Interdisciplinary Work as Professional Development: Changing the Culture of Teaching," she stresses the importance of active listening and suggests that WAC faculty development activities should foster a shared inquiry into the systems of literate activity through which students and teachers move rather than cheerlead or evangelize for WAC. Mullin describes how active listening can draw out subtle differences in the ways faculty understand writing and how illuminating these differences can positively impact students and teaching (see also Zawacki and Genteman in Part Five of this volume). Rather than providing templates or new teaching strategies for using writing to foster learning in the disciplines, she argues that WAC leaders too must examine their definitions and assumptions, work to decenter their understandings from their home disciplines, and attend carefully to the way writing is dynamically situated in the departments and programs at particular institutions.

WORKS CITED

Britton, James, Tony Burgess, Nancy Martin, Alex McLeod, and Harold Rosen. *The Development of Writing Abilities (11–18)*. London: Macmillan Education, 1975. Print.

Langer, Judith, and Arthur Applebee. *How Writing Shapes Thinking: Studies of Teaching and Learning*. Urbana: NCTE, 1987. *The WAC Clearinghouse*. Web. 10 June 2010.

McLeod, Susan H. "Translating Enthusiasm into Curricular Change." *Strengthening Programs for Writing across the Curriculum*. Ed. McLeod. San Francisco: Jossey-Bass, 1988. 5–12. *The WAC Clearinghouse*. Web. 10 June 2010.

6 Showing, Not Telling, at a Writing Workshop

TOBY FULWILER

How does a teacher of writing encourage colleagues in other disciplines to pay more attention to student writing? And, once encouraged, what specifically can teachers of history, biology, or business do in their classrooms to foster student writing? One approach, of course, is to tell them what they ought to be doing: "Look! You should require those history students to keep journals." You can mail out broadsides, write editorials, and deliver seminars on the virtues of "writing across the curriculum." If your colleagues have strong self-concepts and are not scared off by your enthusiasm, some will actually try what you suggest. But *telling* teachers how to use writing in their classes is very close to telling them that you know a better way to teach their subjects. Very touchy business.

A more politic way, it seems to me, is to *show* other teachers some writing techniques and exercises that work but allow them to pick and choose among them, making up their own minds about what is useful and what not. Showing, not telling, is a principle often taught in freshman English classes; readers can make up their own minds about the narrative's importance. So too is this idea effective at writing across the curriculum workshops. Most teachers in disciplines other than English understand well that writing, like reading and mathematics, cannot be the sole province of teachers in any one discipline. As Dan Fader and James Britton have argued before me, writing is an interdisciplinary learning activity with a place in every classroom. But not all teachers know how to integrate writing instruction easily into their pedagogy, nor are they comfortable "teaching" it outright. Each teacher is already a professional, practicing writer in his or her own field, yet few have ever been trained to teach writing to others.

There is a wealth of knowledge about writing in the pool of teachers who do not teach writing or who think they do not know how to teach writing. Who knows better than the geographer whether or not first person narration is acceptable in professional geography publications? Who knows better than the physics teacher whether or not to use passive construction in laboratory

From *College English* 43.1 (1981): 55–63.

reports? Furthermore, most teachers have a fairly solid grasp, themselves, of the "elements of style" according to Strunk and White or Turabian; it matters little that they cannot label a particular modifier as "free" or "dangling"; it does matter that they can identify writing appropriate to good work in their field.

If you want to encourage all teachers to teach more writing in their classes, then start with the knowledge of writing which they already possess and build from there. The best way that I have found to do this is through an off-campus, overnight, retreat-like writing workshop. A place where teachers are on neutral ground, removed from mailboxes, telephones, students, classes, secretaries, and families. In this setting writing can be explored slowly, thoroughly, and experientially among colleagues who are interested because they are mutually concerned with the quality of student writing.

During the last several years I have helped plan, set up, and staff half a dozen writing workshops for teachers at Michigan Tech, where I teach writing; I have also worked with high school and college instructors from schools other than my own. The principles of good writing workshops are remarkably consistent whether the participants are high school English teachers or university engineering professors. Showing works better than telling; induction better than deduction. By introducing workshop participants to the complex nature of "the composing process," experientially rather than through lecture, I have been able to draw consistently on knowledge and ideas already present among the participants. I avoid, wherever possible, appearing to be the resident expert among a crew of novices, for these teachers are, in fact, my peers in every important sense. The writing workshops work because all lessons are learned through personal experience or an appeal to common sense.

In the rest of this article I will describe five workshops designed to introduce content-area teachers to the theory and practice of writing across the curriculum. These workshops, with minor variations, have worked with teachers from almost every grade level and academic discipline.

WORKSHOP I, EXPLORING

Many teachers who attend writing workshops believe, initially at least, that they will learn how to banish forever bad spelling and comma splices from student papers. These teachers are usually disappointed because I teach them no such tricks. Instead, during the first five minutes, I ask people to write about the student writing problems they perceive as most common, serious, or troublesome. According to the teachers, who take turns reading their entries, students have these problems:

1. outlining and organizing
2. spelling correctly
3. being interested in a topic
4. finding information about a topic

5. specifying rather than generalizing
6. writing good sentences
7. practicing good study habits
8. thinking maturely
9. punctuating correctly
10. reading critically
11. using a library
12. developing a college-level vocabulary
13. understanding the writing assignment
14. supporting an argument
15. writing a thesis statement

The list may go on even longer, sometimes extending to twenty-five or thirty items. I ask people to take a few more minutes and see if they can simplify and condense the list into fewer, more general categories. The next list of writing problem categories looks something like this:

1. motivation
2. mechanics
3. style
4. reading
5. critical thinking
6. cognitive maturity
7. assignments

Teachers suggest, in turn, strategies they have found successful in dealing with these problems. One teacher defers grading until a lab report is properly complete, a second teaches outlining, while a third hands out written copies of all assignments to eliminate confusion. A genuine dialogue now begins, with participants addressing writing problems with concrete, practical suggestions — the result of years of classroom experience. The teachers are sharing ideas, contributing to the general pool of knowledge, and talking to each other about an issue of mutual concern.

This first session is "exploratory"; during this first hour of an extended workshop it is not too important what particular solutions are offered. Some suggestions might be less useful than others — such as giving automatic "Fs" to papers with five mechanical errors. The primary purpose of this workshop is to get the participants talking to each other, sharing ideas, and recognizing that writing is a rather complicated activity. No participant who helped shape the preceding list can comfortably hold on to the notion that "spelling or grammar drills" will cure all or most writing problems. The "solution" to a "motivation" problem is far different from (though perhaps related to) an "editing skills" problem. Student "skill" problems (outlining, punctuation) require of the teacher a response different from student "developmental" problems (cognitive maturity, reading background); teacher-centered problems (poor assignments, vague feedback) differ from institutional problems (credit hours, course loads, grades). The whole concept of "writing problems" opens up and teachers begin to understand both the complexity and diversity of the composing process. At the conclusion of this sixty-minute session, the teachers write a short summary of the ideas which have emerged during this workshop, ideas which, in most cases, are broader and more complex than they were an hour earlier.

Workshop II, Journal Writing

Participants at writing workshops keep journals for the duration of the workshop. At the very first session participants are asked to write out their reasons for attending the workshop; later on they are given a variety of writing assignments, such as the listing and summary activities described in Workshop I. The journal is the place for participants to record their thoughts, feelings, impressions, insights, and ideas as they travel through the workshop. By the end of the first day, everyone has written eight or nine assigned journal entries.

Journals prove to be active catalysts for stimulating both personal insights and small-group discussions at a writing workshop just as they are in individual classrooms. In addition to the initial journal writing I ask the teachers to do the following tasks:

1. Summarize a particular session by writing about it, to give verbal shape to the session as well as provide a written record for later perusal.

2. Interrupt a discussion with a five-minute journal write to refocus your thoughts and gain perspective about the topic.

3. Clarify difficult concepts in your own words; for example, "What, exactly, does James Britton mean by the term *expressive writing*?"

4. "Free write" about a topic in order to use this entry, later, as the basis for a short paper.

5. Brainstorm for ten minutes to see how many assignments you can think of for using "peer critics" or "journals" in your classrooms.

6. Reflect personally and privately on the course of the workshop and record your thoughts about being here.

At some point, usually at the end of the first day, we talk about the importance of this personal writing in a formal academic environment. Participants usually are quick to point out a number of possible uses for the journal, especially to reinforce the learning of subject matter and to aid small-group discussions. In particular, however, the teachers want to know: (1) how to give directions for using journals, (2) how often and when to read the journals, and (3) how to evaluate and "count" them as part of the course requirements. Once the discussion reaches this point, the workshop has already turned a corner; the workshop leader can then provide a handout on journal use, discuss his or her personal means of handling the journal in class, or generate guidelines on the spot by drawing on the participants' own experience with journals that day.

The journal-writing activity at the workshop really serves more than one purpose. The journal is a concrete, practical writing assignment for teachers to take back to their history or biology classes. It is a means of introducing the workshop participants to the importance of writing to oneself in order to invent, clarify, interpret, or reflect. Journal writing usually helps relax group members by giving them time, periodically, to get their bearings and examine their thoughts as they participate in workshop exercises. Finally, journal-writing time is an invaluable aid to the workshop leader to help monitor the course of the workshop — by using those five-minute writing "time-outs" the leader is able to continually and quietly evaluate the mood, progress, and problems of the group and make cuts, additions, and revisions where necessary. The journal, then, is the workhorse writing assignment throughout the whole workshop experience; after the workshop is over, each participant's journal provides a lasting written record of insights and ideas gained during the experience.

WORKSHOP III, THEORY

In *The Development of Writing Abilities, 11–18* (London: The Schools Council, 1975), James Britton develops the idea that "expressive writing" is the matrix from which other writing modes evolve. Expressive writing is close to speech or thought; it is informal, personal, speculative, discovery writing which one does for oneself, to try out new ideas and see what's on one's mind. First drafts, diaries, and journals are places where such writing can be found. Britton's other two function categories of writing are already familiar to academic audiences: "transactional" writing (communicating messages to audiences) and "poetic" writing (creative writing, language as an art). Prior to this workshop, most participants will not have considered expressive writing important.

Britton argues, as the workshop leader can explain in a brief lecture, that expressive writing is very close to the thinking process itself — thinking on paper. Students who learn to use it gain a powerful, dependable "learning tool" with which to speculate, discover, argue, brainstorm, and invent — by themselves, independent of teachers or classmates. Expressive writing is also one of the easiest, quickest means of overcoming writer's block and "the terror of the blank page." Once teachers are aware of its potential, they can use expressive writing as a means to stimulate student thought and reduce student anxiety at the same time.

Understanding expressive writing is important for the success of the writing-across-the-curriculum program as Britton conceives it. This writer-based prose, as Linda Flower calls it, can be used in any discipline where thinking is important — whether or not the teacher makes other, more formal writing assignments. Expressive writing should not be critically judged by the teacher nor graded in any traditional sense, a feature attractive to teachers in any discipline where large classes are common or where paper work is excessive.

This theoretical discussion about the value of expressive writing works well at the end of a day in which teachers have been actively writing in their journals. In other words, the participants have been practicing expressive writing all day — and most recognize that they have used it often in the past when rough-writing professional articles or grant proposals at home. Examined by the light of personal experience, this mode of writing — at once familiar and foreign — sells itself.

Once sold, the nature of the rest of the workshop changes dramatically. The question ceases to be, "So what can you tell us that we do not already know?" and becomes, "What are some concrete ways that I can incorporate expressive writing as a learning activity in my classroom?" The workshop activities which follow this theoretical session all build on Britton's notion of expressive writing and its root relationship to more transactional modes.

WORKSHOP IV, "RESPONDING TO WRITING"

In this workshop participants are asked to read and respond to a piece of student writing. First (ten minutes), teachers evaluate the writing on their own and jot down initial observations about the paper: (1) where it is strong, (2) where weak, and (3) what specific suggestions might help the student writer to improve the paper. Second (twenty minutes), teachers are asked to form groups of three, share their personal commentaries, and agree on a consensus response which would help the student most in rewriting. Third (thirty minutes), teachers come together as a whole group and share, once again, the consensus responses to those papers. During this third activity the director can stand at the chalkboard and outline briefly each group's response, which might include suggestions about thesis statements, outlines, mechanical errors, grades, oral versus written responses, praise versus criticism, and various suggestions for revision.

Finally (fifteen minutes), teachers compare, visually, the responses of the various groups and note similarities and differences. It is important, at this point, for the workshop director to be as non-directive as possible; there really isn't a "right" answer, after all, but rather more and less helpful suggestions. In my experience, any time a group of these teachers talk about a piece of writing, with the purpose of helping a student do better next time, their eventual response is reasonable and helpful. Most teachers understand well the value of such basic helping strategies as positive reinforcement, rewriting, and individual conferencing, even though many of us do not always take the time to practice what we understand. The final consensus list often looks something like this one, which comes from a workshop for biology teachers:

1. Point out strengths, as well as weaknesses, in each paper handed back.

2. Focus on one or two problems at a time rather than insisting that students learn and correct everything in one draft.

3. Be specific when commenting about what is wrong on a paper; what, exactly, can a student do to make it better?

4. Ask for revision prior to grading if you want the student to keep on learning.

5. Be aware when you make a writing assignment whether you want to (a) find out what the student already knows or (b) enhance his or her learning experience.

6. Hold conferences with students who have the most difficulty writing your assignments.

The value of this particular workshop, however, goes beyond generating a list of helpful hints for responding to student writing; equally important is the self-confidence teachers gain from sharing perceptions and opinions among colleagues. Teachers in content-areas often feel insecure about responding to and evaluating writing; many remember being penalized by error-conscious English teachers and some retain the view that writing, along with responding to writing, is an arcane craft, the precise practice of which belongs exclusively to teachers of English. This exercise puts that notion nicely to rest. Teachers see common-sense practices used by colleagues and approved by writing teachers and so are more likely to trust their own judgments next time.

A variation of this workshop, used later in a several-day workshop, asks participants to respond from "peer critique sheets," which are simply written-out guidelines for students to critique from. Sometimes these critique sheets are used in stages. Critique I asks questions such as: (1) What is the thesis of the paper? (2) Who is the audience for the paper? (3) Where is the strongest writing? (4) Where is the weakest writing? Critique II, used a draft later, asks more particular questions: (1) Is each point well supported by evidence, fact, or example? (2) Does the paper avoid clichés, generalizations, and stereotypes? (3) Are any phrases awkward, vague, or unclear? (4) Are any words repetitious or unnecessary? (5) Can you find errors in spelling, punctuation, or grammar? Colleagues from scientific and technical fields have modified these sheets to reflect their particular needs, adding, for example, questions about mathematical computation or diagram accuracy. Guidelines such as these can help both teacher and novice writer focus more pointedly on different stages in the writing process.

One final note. I think it is important to solicit and use for workshop exercises papers written in subjects other than English. This can be done easily by asking participants, when they sign up to attend the workshop, to send samples of what they consider to be "good" and "bad" writing. The workshop leader can then choose some representative short writings from science and social science areas with which most of the faculty audience can identify; I usually include two different papers and allow groups to choose either one.

An obvious extension of this workshop, when time permits, is to do a similar exercise with discipline-specific materials, where social science teachers form one cluster, science teachers another, humanities teachers a third and, perhaps, engineers a fourth. In this way specific types of writing, such as "lab reports" or "term papers," especially appropriate to each area can be studied in detail.

WORKSHOP V, COMPOSING

Perhaps the most important sessions at a faculty workshop require the teachers themselves to write something. Whether the workshop is one day or five weeks, teachers must generate a piece of writing based on personal experience and share that writing with other participants. They must also listen to critical commentary about their efforts.

An easy way to start participants writing is to follow Peter Elbow's suggestion in *Writing Without Teachers* (New York: Oxford University Press, 1973) and ask everybody to do a ten-minute "freewrite." I ask people to "focus" the freewrite and concentrate on "one experience you had with writing — either good or bad," or "a learning experience you remember well." Faculty members find these topics easy to write about, coming as they all do from school environments; the assignment results in fast, furious narrative writing by all, including me. (For the sake of credibility, workshop directors must do all the assignments along with participants.)

Next, participants spend twenty minutes reshaping and revising this piece of personal writing to make it suitable to share with an audience. I tell them to cut out the fat and dead ends, to amplify, explain, and add detail, to edit the parts which might embarrass. Writers then form response groups of three and share in turn their writing according to these guidelines:[1]

A. First Reader: Read your paper out loud twice to the two persons in your group.

B. Audience: Listen to the reader carefully. After the second reading, respond orally only in these two ways:

1. What struck you as interesting?

2. Where did you want more information?

Immediately this exercise creates a hive of activity in the room. Anxiety levels among participants first soar, then drop, as people become more comfortable with their response group. More than any other workshop exercise, this one places the participant back in the role of the student who is asked to write on demand and then submit that writing for some form of evaluation. In this case, however, the responses are deliberately uncritical; the listener practices giving help without saying what was "good" and "bad," what he or she liked or didn't like. The point, of course, is to set up the anxiety-producing situation (reading your writing out loud) and then defuse it by creating a non-threatening environment (small, non-judgmental response groups).

Participants regroup and do a short journal write about what they felt at various stages of the exercise. Finally, people share their observations and talk about the possible "lessons" for teachers who make writing assignments to students: (1) the value of writing for idea generation (freewriting); (2) the importance of shaping toward an audience (revision of freewrite); (3) the benefits of the non-judgmental peer response; (4) the difficulty (and excitement) of creating under pressure; and also (5) the stimulation which results from having one's writing well-received.

In workshops of more than a day's duration participants revise their writing overnight, in the privacy of their quarters, and write it on ditto masters for duplication the following day. It is then possible to form larger writing groups, five or six each, and read and respond to a visible piece of writing, which creates a different kind of anxiety, but more precise suggestions for revision. I encourage these groups to meet for about two hours and to set up their own response guidelines. For a four- or five-day workshop this same group can meet several times and discuss the progressive revisions of each paper; for longer workshops, such as the five-week Bay Area Writing Projects, these groups can meet regularly each week and talk about several pieces of writing. When the group mix is good, the sharing of writing becomes an important ritual.

In any case, this personal writing activity is often cited by participants as the most memorable workshop experience. One engineering teacher told me that he hadn't "done any personal writing since 1951" — and now he was determined to try more. After sweating through this condensed composing process most teachers admit to having more empathy for student writers. After this exercise few teachers who begin the workshop with hard-line responses still retain that attitude. The process of writing, reading, and responding seems to humanize us all.

At the conclusion of the workshop it is important for participants to return briefly to that list of "writing problems" with which the workshop began. I often ask how many of these have we now addressed through the course of the various workshops — and participants are often surprised to find out that we have, in fact, generated numerous suggestions to handle motivation, organization, stylistic and mechanical problems, and so on. In reviewing their journals, which I ask them to do at the end of the workshop, teachers discover personal insights on how journals, multiple drafts, or peer-editing would work in their particular classes. Some insights are "planted": "Write one way you could use journals in your classroom." Other insights depend strictly on the mind of the writer: "Summarize what you learned in the afternoon sessions." Each teacher takes from the workshop what is useful; for a history teacher it may be "book-review journals"; for a biologist it might be "peer-response groups." One accounting teacher did not think he could use any particular activity in his classes, but said he had learned important things about his own writing process.

How do you influence your colleagues to pay more attention to student writing? Ask them to write, to examine what they do when they write, and to share their insights with each other. After all, that's really what a writing workshop is — a time and a place for sharing among teachers who care.

NOTES

1. I learned this exercise from Lee Odell of the State University of New York at Albany.

7   *Writing to Learn: Writing Across the Disciplines*

ANNE J. HERRINGTON

In "Writing as a Mode of Learning," Janet Emig develops the single most powerful rationale for using writing in all courses, no matter what the discipline. She asserts that "writing represents a unique mode of learning — not merely valuable, not merely special, but unique." By identifying the correspondences between the act of learning and the act of writing, she develops a persuasive theoretical argument for writing as a "central academic process."[1] While Emig's argument provides an important foundation for the use of writing across the curriculum, it does not address the related problem of teaching students who are not yet prepared for the intellectual demands of the courses they enter. In this context, Lee Odell asks that teachers from all disciplines use writing to help "students gain some control of the process of discovery in writing" and, even more important, to relate "the process of writing to the process of learning a given subject matter."[2] He goes on to suggest some specific ways teachers can use writing to teach students strategies for thinking.

Taken together, the arguments developed by Emig and Odell offer a far more positive reason for using writing in all disciplines than the negative rationale of mounting a school-wide campaign to eradicate the problems of poor writers. This latter rationale, which is all too pervasive, implies that English teachers are only asking their colleagues to assume a burden which rightfully belongs with the English faculty: improving the surface features of the written product. Don Graves decries this same faulty emphasis when he notes that for too many people, "the eradication of error is clearly more important than the encouragement of expression. Clearly underlying this attitude toward the teaching of writing is the belief that most people, and particularly students, have nothing of their own to say."[3] In contrast, the "writing as learning" approach implies that students do have something to say and that the process of writing provides at once the way for them to discover and communicate it.

This approach underscores a responsibility that all teachers rightfully share: creating situations that stimulate student learning. Consequently, we

From *College English* 43.4 (1981): 379–87.

English teachers can approach our colleagues more positively. We can encourage them to use writing more often in their courses to serve their own pedagogical ends, not their preconceived notions of writing teachers' ends. We can also go beyond mere exhortations and suggest some specific ways to use writing to meet these ends: by designing assignments linked to course objectives and by responding to student writing in ways that stress its value as a process of discovery. My purpose in this article is to explain some of the specific strategies which my colleagues from other disciplines have found effective. To provide a context, I will first describe briefly the interdisciplinary project from which these strategies evolved.

For the past two years, I have directed a project supported by a grant from the Fund for the Improvement of Post-Secondary Education to train faculty from a variety of disciplines (e.g., art, economics, chemistry, history, and sociology) to use writing as an integral component of their courses. Each year a group of twelve faculty participants received release time from one course to participate in a one-week summer seminar and monthly meetings each semester and to redesign one course each semester experimenting with the ways writing could be used in that course. The intent was not to develop writing courses in these disciplines, but to experiment with ways writing can be incorporated into courses to help students meet course objectives.

The goal of the summer workshop was for each faculty member to determine the sequence of writing assignments to use in his or her model course and the strategies to be used in responding to student writing. To reach this goal, the faculty worked from their statements of course objectives to define writing assignments which would help students reach these objectives. The workshop leaders introduced the participants to different types of assignments, ways to define an assignment in a full rhetorical context (topic, purpose, and audience), and techniques for responding to student writing. A considerable amount of time was spent actually drafting and critiquing assignments and critiquing student papers.

The regular semester meetings were essential to reinforce the faculty's efforts and to share different assignments and evaluation techniques. For some sessions, each participant would bring a draft of a future assignment (specifying topic, purpose, audience, intellectual demands, evaluation criteria) which would then be critiqued by the group. For other sessions, we would focus on one specific assignment and three or four student responses to this assignment. For these sessions the purpose would be to try to apply the specified evaluation criteria and to discuss how successful the assignment was and how each response should be evaluated. In sum: the two purposes of all of the sessions were to encourage the participants to be more analytic about their assignments and to provide them with specific strategies for evaluating writing.

The model courses were designated by the participants from their regular teaching load. They included such courses as "Introduction to Economics," a laboratory in physics, a literature survey, "Literature for Youth," "Theories of Society," "How to Survey," a course in United States history, "Introduction to

Psychology," and a course in state and local government. For each course, the instructor designed not only the course objectives but also the sequence of writing assignments in advance.

The student evaluations of these courses indicate that the writing was a powerful way of learning for them. In fact, ninety percent of the students reported that the writing added at least in some degree to their understanding of course material. The faculty participants agreed that the writing definitely enhanced their courses. As one noted, the students "had to learn more about what they were doing before they could write." In the remainder of this article, I will report on the strategies used in some of the most successful of the courses, that is, ones in which both students and faculty felt the writing added much more to the students' understanding of the course material. All of these strategies underscore the emphasis which the faculty placed on writing as a way of learning and communicating what had been learned.

When the purpose of using writing is to help students learn, it is only logical that assignments be linked to course objectives, preferably ones that emphasize more than just recall of facts. The writing assignments should be used as opportunities to learn to use the particular patterns of inquiry of a discipline, whether they be processes of observation and generalization or a problem-solving process of applying a general principle to specific situations. For example, if one objective of "Introduction to United States History" is "to see connections and contrasts between events," then a useful assignment might be to compare and contrast the goals and achievements of the Plymouth and Jamestown colonies so that the reader of a college-level text would know which was more successful in reaching its goals. An assignment which asked the writer only to summarize the goals and achievements of each colony would not be as useful because it would not ask the writer to discern significant relationships between the events.

One of the model courses offers a more comprehensive example. The primary course objectives of "Theories of Society" were "(1) to familiarize [the students] with some of the most important contributors to sociological thought, and (2) to develop what C. Wright Mills called the 'sociological imagination' which 'enables us to grasp history and biography and the relations between the two within society.'"

In preparation for the discussion of each theorist, the students were to write a 200–300 word paper summarizing the theorist's important biographical background, significant socio-cultural influences, and major theoretical contributions. The summaries were to be written for an informed but curious audience. This assignment went beyond mere recall since it required selecting from a mass of information the significant factors that influenced the theorist, making inferences about the relationships among the factors, and distilling the information into a limited number of words. Throughout, it emphasized making informed judgments about the relationships among the biographical data, the socio-cultural setting, and the theory. This same assignment was used for the entire semester. The students responded to it very positively because the assignment helped them understand the new material continually introduced into the course and because the process of writing the paper enabled them to participate more actively and knowledgeably in class discussions.

The course evaluations of "Theories of Society" provide instances of two of the correspondences Emig notes between learning strategies and writing (p. 128). One correspondence is that writing, like learning, "provides connections." The student comments clearly state the value of having to synthesize the material and work out relationships: "It encouraged me to think, to relate the material, and not merely memorize it." "Examining the biography, sociocultural background, and the work of each theorist made me understand how each factor influenced the other."

A second correspondence which Emig notes is that writing "is active, engaged, personal — notably self-rhythmed." In all of the student comments there was a sense of "I" actively doing something — something difficult which they might not otherwise have done, but something rewarding: "I was forced to think about the material thoroughly in order to write a comprehensive paper. By doing this, I obtained a much greater understanding of the material." "It forced me to really understand the specific theorist before I could write about him." These comments underscore the powerful role the writing played in learning for these students and by implication suggest what they would have missed without it. The act of writing led beyond mere memorization to understanding — selecting and reconnecting material, digesting it, and translating it into one's own meaning and words.

If a course uses a variety of assignments instead of just one kind, the assignments should be so sequenced that each one prepares students for the next; that is, they should move from less to more complex conceptual tasks. This point is especially crucial in an introductory course where a student is being exposed to the particular methodologies and jargon of a discipline for the first time. To illustrate these observations in more detail, I will describe the writing assignments used in another of the interdisciplinary project courses, "Introduction to Economics," taught by Don Tobey.[4]

The specified goals of "Introduction to Economics" were: (1) to acquaint the student with the fundamentals of economic theory and the terminology; (2) to develop in the student the ability to analyze and to apply basic theory to solving economic problems; and (3) to provide the student with the background for evaluating rudimentary recommendations in the field of governmental economic policy. As one can see, each of these objectives is more complex and assumes mastery of the previous one: the first only requires knowledge of terms and basic principles, while the second requires application of this knowledge to new situations, and the third requires both selection and application of appropriate measures to solve broad economic problems.

The writing assignments paralleled this sequence. The first ones asked primarily for a restatement of terms explained in the text and lectures. For example:

> What is meant by the assumption of "rationality" in economics? Do you feel that the consumer's behavior is rational? Why or why not?

The assignments given midway through the semester assumed an understanding of basic principles and asked the students to apply a given principle to a specified situation. For example:

> You are talking with your parents, who wish to know what you're learning at college. Explain the term "leakage" as it relates to the circular flow concept. Then describe a type of leakage taking place in your own (or your parents') household. Be specific and explain how that example of leakage effects Aggregate Demand.

The final two assignments were much more demanding in that they presented a more complex problem and did not specify the economic measure to be applied. Thus, the students were expected to decide on the appropriate economic measures and develop a convincing rationale for their choice. For example:

> You have been hired as an economic speech-writer for President Carter. His political advisers (and image makers) have concluded that preventing recession — and its related unemployment of eight percent or more — is the top priority and the key to getting Carter re-elected in 1980. Thus, the majority of voters will tolerate inflation of nine or ten percent if they have jobs.
>
> Identify which measures fall under which category, recommend two measures of monetary policy (other than discount rate) and two measures of fiscal policy to be used in combination to prevent recession and to help re-elect Carter. Include a description of how each measure would function, which would be the fastest and slowest to take effect (and why), and whether your policy mix would yield a budgetary balance, deficit, or surplus. Why?
>
> Your answer will be evaluated by these criteria:
>
> - Effective application of concepts.
> - A clear, integrated (not piecemeal) answer encompassing all components of the question.
> - Development of an organized and persuasive case.

The instructor prepared students for these assignments in a number of ways. First, class readings and lectures were planned for each assignment. The readings were used primarily to introduce terminology and concepts. During lectures, by using frequent references to current events, the instructor illustrated the meaning of important terms and concepts and showed how they apply to specific contemporary problems. The students were then asked in the assignments to apply these same terms to different situations. Second, each assignment itself prepared students for its successors since they proceeded from simpler, more defined, recall-oriented tasks to more complex, less defined, analytic tasks. In-class discussion of each assignment on the day it was due and written responses from the teacher gave the students frequent evaluation of how well they had understood and applied the material. During the discussions the instructor tried to elicit a number of possible responses and lead the class to critique them and decide on the most accurate or convincing ones.

Regardless of whether one, three, or twelve different assignments are used in a course, each assignment should be carefully planned in advance. The actual designing of the assignment should be viewed as a two-part task to include, as Odell advocates in the essay I have previously cited, defining the assignment in a full rhetorical context and identifying its intellectual demands. First, the assignment should be constructed to specify not only the topic, but also the purpose and audience. This specificity will help the writers understand what is required of them and usually will challenge them to something more than restating information for no purpose.

For example, the following assignment was designed by R. Gordon MacGregor as the first in his "Introduction to Psychology" course:

> Short Paper 1: The Biological, Intra-Psychic, and Social/Behavioral Viewpoints.
>
> *Question:* Choose one aspect of your behavior or an aspect of general human behavior which lends itself to being explained from each viewpoint which McConnell [the text] elucidates in Chapter 1. Write a short paper in which you explain the *causes* of each behavior from the perspective of each viewpoint. In your concluding paragraph, state which viewpoint offers the most plausible explanation of the behavior and why you believe that explanation is best. If you select one viewpoint as best, you must discredit the other two viewpoints. If you decide that an eclectic viewpoint is best, you must incorporate two or three viewpoints into a plausible, coherent, single explanation of the behavior.
>
> *Audience and Purpose:* Write this paper for a friend to help him/her acquire understanding of your or others' behavior, trying to convince him/her that one explanation is superior.
>
> *Evaluative Criteria:* Your instructor will evaluate your paper with these criteria in mind:
>
> 1) Did you clearly understand each viewpoint?
>
> 2) Did you present a plausible explanation of the behavior from each viewpoint?
>
> 3) Did you thoroughly explain the cause of the behavior from each viewpoint?
>
> 4) Did you support your conclusion with convincing evidence? That is, did you satisfactorily discredit the other two viewpoints or did you present a plausible, coherent, eclectic viewpoint?

It is clear that the task is to do more than restate lecture material. It requires the students to use this material to gain an insight into various explanations of behavior. By specifying the audience and purpose, the assignment also defines the writer's role: that of a friend providing a convincing explanation in nontechnical terms.

Second, the teacher should identify the intellectual demands of the assignment and develop ways to teach students to meet these demands. Clarifying these demands in advance will help the teacher decide if the assignment relates to the course objectives and, if it does, what instruction students will need in order to meet these demands.

For example, the above psychology assignment requires the writers to: (1) understand the central trait of each viewpoint and how it differs from the other two viewpoints; (2) apply theoretical knowledge to a specific behavior; (3) shift perspectives; and (4) make a comparative judgment. Since this assignment was given early in the semester, the instructor was most concerned that the students master the first three of these demands. Thus, most of the preparatory work focused on them. MacGregor spent a good deal of class time clarifying the meaning of each viewpoint (biological, intra-psychic, social/behavioral) and showing how it could be applied to specific behaviors. He provided a series of examples in the following sequence: first, he explained the cause of a behavior from the perspective of each viewpoint, explicitly naming the viewpoint as he proceeded. Then he explained the cause of a behavior from one viewpoint and asked the class to identify which behavior it was. After working through a number of these examples, he divided the class into small groups to work through a similar process. First, each group was to reach agreement on the appropriate explanations of the cause of a behavior from the three viewpoints. Once they reached agreement, they presented their explanations to the rest of the class for critique or for them to identify the viewpoints. These rehearsals were successful in preparing students because they consistently focused on the demands of the assignment (know the term, apply it, shift perspectives) and because they actively involved the class in explaining their judgments to their peers.

In an interview James Britton commented that "The way the teacher receives what the child writes is highly influential in the attitude the child has in the next piece of writing."[5] The Johnson State College interdisciplinary project certainly validates this observation in reference to college students as well. No matter how creative the assignments, if the teacher treats the resulting writings as unimportant, or merely samples of writing, then the students begin to resent having to write. In one of our project courses, the teacher had well-conceived assignments, but his manner of responding to the writings suggested he saw them only as burdens. Once the writings were collected, he would keep them for awhile unread, then go through them hastily making limited comments, and return them with no further discussion. As a result, the students commented in the course evaluations that the writings were of little value and they resented having to do them. In contrast, if the teacher treats the student writings as important to the course and as worthy of substantive response, then the students can be expected to feel more positively about future assignments and to invest more in them.

The specific ways teachers respond to writing also affect the degree to which students perceive writing as a means of learning. The Johnson State College interdisciplinary group found three response strategies to be particularly effective. All are common to most writing classes.

First, a teacher should evaluate a writing in terms of a limited number of criteria which evolve from the task, purpose, and audience of the assignment. These criteria should be established when the assignment is designed and given to the students as part of the assignment. This will help students and the teacher focus on the specific conceptual demands of the assignment. To illustrate, here are an assignment and the evaluation criteria used in the "Introduction to Economics" class:

> As a candidate for the U.S. Congress, you are speaking to a local Rotary Club, most of whose members have a practical, working knowledge of economics. You are attempting to persuade the members that you know economic principles and have practical ideas for the application of those principles. Describe the two measures of fiscal policy that you recommend in combination to reduce the rate of U.S. inflation to 4% per year. Explain how each measure will function in reducing inflation. Also explain any risks (economic, not political) or drawbacks which potentially accompany either of your recommended measures.
>
> Your response will be evaluated by these criteria:
>
> - accurate use of economic terminology;
> - effective application of economic principles to the inflation problem;
> - consideration of both gains and risks from your two policy recommendations;
> - development of a persuasive case for your two recommendations as practical solutions to the problem, notwithstanding the risks.

In this assignment, the four criteria clearly define for the students the demands of the task. Paralleling the increased level of difficulty of the assignment over the previous ones, the criteria show that the assignment goes beyond explanation and application of a principle to much more complex intellectual tasks: making a judgment as to the best among many options, weighing gains against risks, and persuading others to one's viewpoint.

The third short paper assigned for "Introduction to Psychology" provides another example:

> Short Paper 3: Erik Erikson's Theory of Psychosocial Development.
>
> The Senses of Trust, Mistrust; Autonomy, Shame/Doubt; Initiative, Guilt; Industry, Inferiority; Identity, and Role Confusion.
>
> *Question:* Using the definitions and the causes of each "sense" for the first five stages of psychosocial development, indicate which "sense," e.g., trust or mistrust, is more characteristic of you and why you believe that sense is more characteristic of you than its opposite. Write your essay as if you were writing an Eriksonian autobiography to facilitate someone's understanding of your psychosocial development.
>
> *Requirements:* In order to write this assignment, you must:
>
> 1) know Erikson's definition of each sense;
> 2) know the cause of each sense as seen by Erikson;
> 3) be able to recognize each sense in yourself; and
> 4) be able to provide concrete examples of each sense in yourself.

Evaluative Criteria: Your instructor will evaluate your essay with these criteria in mind:

1) Did you clearly understand Erikson's conceptualization of each sense, i.e., Erikson's definition of the sense and his assertions about its cause?

2) Did you provide lucid examples of how each sense is evident in your psychosocial development?

Note: Your instructor will evaluate each short paper for content only. You will be allowed to write one revision of the content of your paper in order to try to earn a higher grade. Your instructor will note your grammatical, spelling, and typographical errors which you must correct in pencil on your paper. Correcting your errors is mandatory. However, correcting your errors will not raise your grade. If you fail to correct your errors, a grade of F will be assigned to your short paper.

In this example, the statement of requirements very clearly outlines, step by step, what the students will have to do to prepare the paper. The evaluation criteria underscore that the success of the paper will be determined by the degree to which these "content" requirements are met. The note, which actually appeared on the course syllabus, makes it very clear that while the writing must be grammatically correct and free of editing errors, these features will not be the basis for evaluation.

Such criteria underscore the primary purpose of any writing assignment, which is to learn, because they clearly state that success will be measured by how well the writers apply what they are learning, not by how well they spell or punctuate. They also lead the teacher to clarify in advance what he or she expects for acceptable responses and thus provide a standard for consistent evaluation of all papers. More specifically, they focus the teacher's attention quite sharply not just on a general sense of accuracy and thoroughness, but on application of knowledge to a specific task and purpose. Thus, when the teacher evaluates a paper, it should be primarily on these criteria and secondarily on such superficial factors as grammar and spelling.

In addition to establishing clear and relevant criteria for assignments, a teacher should stress that writing is, above all, a process of discovery. As a means of communication, it is more than a one-step act of writing a finished copy; and as an intellectual process, it is more than merely putting down on paper what is already known. The process begins by defining what the task requires, moves through formulating one's ideas and shaping these ideas by writing successive drafts, and ends with stating them coherently in the final written product. The teacher can help the student writer learn to use this process by structuring opportunities to intervene in the process before the written product, or even a final draft, is received.

For example, for major projects, a number of the project faculty find it particularly helpful to talk with students at the initial point of deciding on the scope of the task (issues to be addressed, type of information needed). It is also useful to discuss the project when the students are ready to analyze and synthesize information they are using. At this point the teacher can suggest critical questions to guide their inquiry and to assess their work to date. While it is useful to review a draft of the final product for form and coherence, at that point most of the process of inquiry and analysis has passed and there is little time left for further research or formulation of central ideas.

And lastly, a teacher should create opportunities to share writings in class. A number of the project faculty would occasionally duplicate student writings which were particularly insightful or controversial and use them for class discussions or supplemental reading. To stress the process of writing, one psychology teacher held in-class small group critiques of the rough drafts of writings. Such in-class publication not only gives public recognition to the writers, but also stimulates the interchange of ideas among the class. It stresses in the most graphic way that writing is a way of learning for the individual writer and for the readers.

In this article I have given most attention to the design and presentation of writing assignments since the time given to working out the purpose of an assignment and preparing students for it is much more important than the time given to evaluating the finished product. No matter what our discipline, we should be using writing in our courses, as one student commented, "not for writing improvement, but for focus on course material." Writing has an integral role to play in any course as a medium for learning and for teaching how to learn. For these goals to be realized, we as teachers must first believe in the value of writing as a discovery process and be willing to commit our efforts to teach this process to our students.

NOTES

1. *College Composition and Communication*, 28 (1977), 122, 127.
2. "Teaching Writing by Teaching the Process of Discovery: An Interdisciplinary Enterprise," in *Cognitive Processes in Writing: An Interdisciplinary Approach*, ed. Lee Gregg and Erwin Steinberg (Hillsdale, N.J.: Lawrence Erlbaum, 1980).
3. *Balance the Basics; Let Them Write* (New York: Ford Foundation, 1978), p. 18.
4. For further explanation see Professor Tobey's "Writing Instruction in Economics Courses: Experimentation Across Disciplines," forthcoming in *Journal of the Northeastern Agricultural Council*.
5. Lois Rosen, "An Interview with James Britton, Tony Burgess, and Harold Rosen," *English Journal*, 67 (November 1970), 55.

8 Writing Assignments Across the Curriculum: A National Study of College Writing

DAN MELZER

Writing assignments are revealing classroom artifacts. Instructors' writing assignments say a great deal about their goals and values, as well as the goals and values of their discipline. Writing assignments are a rich source of information about the rhetorical contexts of writing across the curriculum: a resource that composition researchers have yet to make the focus of a significant study. Consider, for example, the following assignment from a European history course at Cornell University:

Essay 2: Documentary Analysis
This assignment requires you to play the detective, combining textual sources for clues and evidence to form a reconstruction of past events. If you took A.P. history courses in high school, you may recall doing similar document-based questions.

In a tight, well-argued essay of two to four pages, identify and assess the historical significance of the documents in one of the four sets I have given you.

You bring to this assignment a limited body of outside knowledge gained from our readings, class discussions, and videos. Make the most of this contextual knowledge when interpreting your sources.

Questions to consider when planning your essay:

- What do the documents reveal about the author and his audience?
- Why were they written?
- Can you discern the author's motivation and tone?
- Does the genre make a difference in your interpretation?
- How do the documents fit in both their immediate and greater historical contexts?
- Do your documents support or contradict what other sources have told you?
- Is there a contrast between documents within your set?
- What is not said, but implied?

From *College Composition and Communication* 61.2 (2009): W240–61.

- What is left out? (As a historian, you should always look for what is not said, and ask yourself what the omission signifies.)

Because of the nature of the assignment, you will probably not have an overarching thesis, as you would in most papers. Instead, your essay will consist of two parts: the IDENTIFICATION and INTERPRETATION sections.

Even though this assignment is brief, it reveals a great deal about rhetorical contexts for writing such as purpose, audience, and genre. The assignment requires "analysis" and "interpretation," and both of these thinking strategies are defined in ways that are specific to the discipline of history. Although the primary audience for the assignment is the teacher, the implied audience can be seen as fellow historians, since students are asked to play the role of disciplinary insiders ("As a historian, you should always look for what is not said, and ask yourself what the omission signifies"). The genre of the assignment is also associated with the work of historians, and throughout the description of the assignment the instructor reminds students that a documentary analysis is more than just a template: it's a fundamental part of the work of historians. What is valued in this genre, and in this instructor's notion of the work of historians, is clear from the questions students should consider when planning their essays: quality of analysis, integration of contextual knowledge, and close and careful interpretation.

An assignment such as this documentary analysis provides a snapshot of writing in the disciplines, but only a snapshot. The purpose of this study is to provide not just a snapshot but a panorama: an overview of college writing through a large-scale survey of writing assignments across disciplines. From 2002 to 2006, I visited the websites of 100 postsecondary institutions in four categories based on the Carnegie Classification of Institutions of Higher Education: Doctoral/Research Universities, Master's Comprehensive Colleges, Baccalaureate Colleges, and A.A. Colleges. I collected 2,100 writing assignments from 400 undergraduate courses across disciplines (100 courses in the natural and applied sciences, 100 courses in the social sciences, 100 courses in business, and 100 courses in the arts and humanities).[1] A number of these courses were connected in some way to a Writing Across the Curriculum program or initiative (a writing-intensive designation, a writing fellows program, a writing link, etc.), allowing me to make comparisons between courses explicitly linked to a WAC program or initiative and those that are not. In order to aim for an arbitrary and geographically disperse sample, I visited institutional websites through an index of the home pages of all accredited colleges in the United States, which is found at www.utexas.edu/world/univ/.[2]

In both a quantitative and qualitative discourse analysis of the rhetorical features and contexts of the assignments, I explore the following research questions in this essay:

- What purposes are students asked to write for in different disciplines?
- What audiences are students asked to address? What role are they asked to play as writers? What role do instructors play as audience?

- What kinds of genres are students asked to write in? How do these genres vary from discipline to discipline and instructor to instructor? What is the rhetorical context for these genres?

- How do assignments vary across types of institutions, between upper- and lower-division courses, and between courses associated with a WAC program or initiative and those courses not connected to WAC?

In subject and scope, my research emulates James Britton and his research team's study of 2,122 essays from British secondary schools reported in *The Development of Writing Abilities (11–18)* and Arthur Applebee's study of 603 essays from 200 American high schools. I use Britton's multidimensional taxonomy of function and audience to analyze and discuss the rhetorical situations of the assignments in my study, but I also include in my taxonomy the assignments that are common responses to recurring rhetorical situations — genres. Aviva Freedman and Peter Medway argue that Britton's taxonomy is limited because it fails to consider the complexities of genre (12). I draw on recent work in genre studies in order to analyze not just the rhetorical situation of individual assignments but also assignment genres: groups of assignments that respond to similar, recurring rhetorical situations.

Britton's taxonomy, which will be familiar to most readers of this journal, divides writing into three functions, which roughly correspond to different points on the rhetorical triangle of writer (the expressive function), text (the poetic function), and audience (the transactional function). Expressive writing is informal and exploratory, with the self as audience. Poetic writing is imaginative, with a focus on the text as art form. The primary purpose of transactional writing is to inform or persuade an audience. Based on Timothy Crusius's critique of Britton's categories, which Crusius feels lack a place for informal writing for an audience beyond the self, I added a fourth function to Britton's taxonomy: "exploratory." Like expressive assignments, exploratory assignments are informal and focus on exploring ideas, but the audience is public. Common examples in my study of writing with an exploratory function are reading responses posted on an electronic bulletin board that are read and often responded to by peers and the instructor. Borrowing from Britton, I divide the audience categories into the self, the teacher, peers, and wider audiences. The "teacher" audience category is further subdivided into "Student to Examiner," in which the student provides the "correct" information to the teacher, and "Student to Instructor [General]," in which the student is not required to merely regurgitate information. Like Britton, I coded for the dominant function or audience when more than one was evident. As I discuss in detail later in this essay, rather than classify genres by formal features, as former surveys of college writing have done (Bridgeman and Carlson; Eblen; Harris and Hult; Sherwood), I follow the lead of recent work in genre studies (Bazerman and Paradis; Miller; Swales) and define genres as responses to recurring rhetorical situations rather than merely templates of form and format.

My taxonomy of the rhetorical situation (Britton's function and audience model) and responses to recurring rhetorical situations (genres) provides a more authentic and extensive method of analyzing writing assignments than taxonomies from the surveys of college writing cited previously. In addition to providing a more complex taxonomy, I present a more complex analysis than prior surveys of college writing by looking at the assignments through the multiple lenses of the two primary approaches to WAC: "writing to learn" and "writing in the disciplines." Most readers of this journal are familiar with the contrast between the "writing-to-learn" approach to WAC, with its focus on bringing expressivist pedagogies to instructors across disciplines, and the "writing-in-the-disciplines" or "learning-to-write" approach and its emphasis on investigating writing in different academic discourse communities. A number of prominent WAC theorists have argued that this writing-to-learn/ writing-in-the-disciplines split in WAC research and practice is artificial, and they argue for a dialogue between the two approaches (McLeod and Maimon; McLeod and Miraglia). Rather than viewing my results though a single "terministic screen," to use Kenneth Burke's phrase, I take a multiple-lens approach and consider the assignments in my study from both writing-to-learn and writing-in-the-disciplines perspectives. This multiple-lens approach is especially valuable in my research because my findings suggest the influence and value of both approaches, as well as points of connection between the two approaches. For example, my research reveals a dominance of short-answer exam writing that writing-to-learn and writing-in-the-disciplines approaches can address in unison, and my research indicates that both the writing-to-learn and writing-in-the-disciplines approaches have had a powerful and positive influence on instructors who are teaching in courses explicitly linked with a WAC program or initiative. In the following study, then, I provide a model for analyzing writing assignments as well as a way to interpret that analysis that takes into account multiple approaches to understanding and evaluating writing across disciplines. I also provide evidence for the influence of WAC and for the effectiveness of WAC initiatives such as writing-intensive courses and writing fellows programs.

THE FUNCTIONS OF COLLEGE WRITING

Both Britton and Applebee found that transactional writing, and especially writing to inform, dominated in the assignments they collected. Eighty-four percent of Britton's samples were transactional, with the informative function accounting for 62 percent of transactional writing. Seventeen percent of assignments were poetic, and only 5 percent were expressive. Transactional writing was even more predominant in Applebee's research. Surveys of college courses by Bridgeman and Carlson and by Eblen reveal similar results: writing to transact, and in particular, writing to inform, was the dominant function.

My research shows results similar to prior studies, as Table 8-1 outlines. Of the 2,100 assignments I collected, transactional writing makes up 83 percent, and most transactional assignments (66 percent) are informative rather than persuasive. Although a significant amount of the writing is exploratory

TABLE 8-1   Distribution of the Functions of Writing

Function	Number of Assignments	Percentage of Total
Transactional (total)	1,751	83
Informative	1,399	66
Persuasive	352	17
Expressive	62	3
Exploratory	279	13
Poetic	9	.4

(13 percent), poetic writing and expressive writing are almost non-existent. These distributions are similar across types of institutions and at both the lower and upper divisions. Sixty-four percent of upper-division writing was informative, with only 3 percent of writing expressive and 0.4 percent poetic. At the "elite" colleges in my study (institutions such as University of California at Berkeley, Duke, and Cornell), 69 percent of writing was to inform, and only 1 percent of writing had expressive or poetic functions. At every type of institution and at each level — from community colleges to "elite" institutions, and from introductory courses to senior seminars — writing to inform is the dominant function.

It's important to emphasize that much of the informative assignments in my study present students with an extremely limited view of academic discourse, asking them simply to display the "right" answer or the "correct" definition to the instructor through a recall of facts — what Applebee calls "writing without composing" (18). Typically the required information comes from lecture material or the textbook, as these exam questions illustrate:

> In your textbook, Steven Smith describes three different roles legislators might play in representing their constituents. List and describe each of these three.

> Describe the major factors causing changes in food consumption (see Chpts. 1–4) and describe the marketing channel for a chosen commodity (see Chpt. 12).

> From my outline on earthquakes, explain the "effects" of earthquakes.

Short-answer and essay exams make up 21 percent of the assignments, and the majority of informative writing is for an audience of "teacher-as-examiner." Only 17 percent of transactional writing in my study asks students to write for persuasive purposes for an audience other than the teacher-as-examiner.

Expressive and poetic writing were even rarer than persuasive writing. Just 62 of the assignments in my research call on students to produce expressive writing. These assignments are "freewrites" written to an audience of the self, with the goal of invention. Toby Fulwiler and Art Young argue that "expressive writing is the primary means we have of personalizing knowledge"

(4), a sentiment shared by other writing-to-learn theorists such as Britton and Applebee. Writing-to-learn theorists also see creative writing — the poetic function — as a valuable way for students to make personal connections with disciplinary content and "broaden their repertoire of language tools for thinking and communicating" (Young par. 5). Britton found that 17 percent of British secondary school writing was poetic, but my sample contains only nine assignments whose dominant function is poetic. Beginning with Janet Emig's *The Composing Processes of Twelfth Graders*, researchers who have investigated student writing habits in school and out of school have found that in their self-sponsored writing, students are more likely to write for expressive and poetic functions. Writing-to-learn theorists would view the dominance of informative writing and the lack of expressive and poetic writing in my sample as evidence of the limited uses teachers across disciplines make of writing, and of the continued need for WAC practitioners to bring writing-to-learn approaches to the disciplines.

The dominance of informative writing and absence of expressive and poetic writing in my research is similar to the results of previous studies. Where my findings differ from prior research is the number of journaling assignments, which typically asked students to explore ideas for an audience beyond the self. Most previous researchers found that the genre of the exploratory journal was rare. In my research, however, exploratory journals and their computer-age equivalent, the electronic discussion board, are a common phenomenon. Although, in general, assignments that called on students to use technology like blogs, hypertext, wikis, etc., were rare in my research, the use of electronic discussion boards for exploratory writing was frequent. The instructors in my research see exploratory writing as a way to encourage students to invent arguments, make connections, reflect on personal experience, and take risks. The following passages from journaling assignments illustrate this use of exploratory writing:

> The journal is a space for you to investigate your own thoughts, reactions, and feelings on particular art ideas and art works. I'm asking you to make connections between what you are learning and what you have already experienced.

> Logs are designed to keep you up to date with the readings, to stimulate class discussion, and to encourage you to think about the class materials as both psychological scholarship and as personally relevant.

> Treat the e-mail messages as an opportunity to express freely your own thoughts, opinions, observations, and questions. You may also use them to float preliminary ideas for your essays. Because they are informal you needn't be overly concerned with structure, organization, and rhetorical polish.

I found that exploratory writing is being assigned across disciplines. The previous passages are from journaling assignments in courses in art history, psychology, and environmental studies, respectively. Although there were no personal diary journals in my study, journals are more or less the only genre in my research that allows students to test ideas and take risks, to use personal experience, and to respond to peers. As the passages above reveal, instructors were using journals for both writing-to-learn and writing-in-the-disciplines purposes.

THE AUDIENCES FOR COLLEGE WRITING

Both Britton and Applebee found that most of the assignments they collected were written for the teacher, and most commonly the teacher-as-examiner. Eighty-six percent of Britton's samples were written for the teacher, and in 48 percent of those the teacher played the role of examiner. In Applebee's study, 55 percent of school writing was directed to the teacher-as-examiner. As Table 8-2 indicates, the audience distributions in my study are similar to Britton's and Applebee's. In 64 percent of the assignments, the teacher-as-examiner is the audience for student writing. Just as informative writing dominates at all levels of instruction in my study, the dominant audience for the assignments at all levels of instruction is "Student to Examiner." In upper-division courses, 61 percent of writing has the audience of teacher-as-examiner. The prevalence of the examiner audience held across types of institutions as well. The instructor played the examiner role in 64 percent of the writing in the "elite" colleges in my survey.

TABLE 8-2   Distribution of the Audiences for Writing

Audience	Number of Assignments	Percentage of Total
Student to Examiner	1,343	64
Student to Instructor [General]	388	18
Peers	117	6
Self	111	5
Wider Audience (total)	142	7
Informed	89	4
Novice	29	2
Generalized Reader	24	1

Coding assignments "Student to Examiner" wasn't difficult: nearly two out of every three assignments is directed to the audience of the teacher-as-examiner, and nearly one out of every four assignments is a short-answer exam. This kind of emphasis on providing the correct answer to the teacher-as-examiner isn't limited to short-answer exams, however. The "informal" response journals in a British literature course represent a vivid case of writing to inform as writing to provide a correct answer. In the assignment description for a journal asking students to interpret an ode from Wordsworth, the instructor writes:

> I see only one way to interpret these stanzas. You may interpret some of the details in a slightly different way, but there is a well-established way to interpret the stanzas that makes perfect sense, that explains <u>all</u> of the details of the lines, and that is consistent with the ideas explained in the introduction to the poem and conveyed elsewhere in the poem. Yes, I'm looking for a specific and correct answer here!

This teacher-as-examiner approach is seen again in the grading rubric of a sociology instructor. The instructor includes in his rubric an explanation of essay response marks, including the symbol "?" for "Do you really think so? I doubt it"; "??" for "Are you serious?"; "x" for "This is not correct"; and "No" for "You have badly misinterpreted the reading. I'm unhappy." Britton and Applebee, along with other writing-to-learn theorists, argue that this kind of emphasis on the instructor as examiner has a negative effect on student engagement, a sentiment shared by an agricultural economics instructor in my study who asks students, "Are you a learner or a sponge? Classes are a lot more interesting and productive for learners than for sponges."

In most of the assignments I placed in the "Student to Instructor [General]" category, there's evidence of a dialogue between instructor and student. Assignments that I placed in this category are often done in stages, with the instructor collecting and commenting on a draft of the essay. The instructors who comment on drafts appear to be trying to establish a dialogue with students that place them in a "coaching" rather than an "examining" role. This passage from a political science assignment is representative:

> For the term paper listed in your syllabus, you will first submit a draft to me. I will review your essay and suggest ways to improve the argument and style. These comments will raise questions, suggest changes, and provide you with a valuable resource for revising your material for the final draft.

Robert Jones and Joseph Comprone argue, "Teaching process in a single class — freshman comp — cannot ultimately be successful unless the writing in that course is reinforced by the same kind of approach to learning in other courses" (59). Anecdotal evidence from WAC workshop leaders suggests that prior to exposure to WAC pedagogy, few teachers in disciplines outside of English engage students in a writing process. In my research, 50 of 400 instructors collected at least one rough draft from students. In their assignment descriptions, these instructors usually give students the kind of encouraging message about process that a political science instructor gives in a political philosophy essay assignment:

> You will turn in a first version of the essay. This initial essay will be read and critiqued but will be ungraded. I would be more than happy to read a draft of your essay at any time prior to the class period it is due and give you feedback.

These instructors respond to drafts and hold one-on-one conferences and peer response workshops because they feel, to quote two business course syllabi, that "writing involves frequent drafting and revising" and "no one writes the final version of anything on the first draft."

In both Britton's and Applebee's research, writing to peers was negligible. Considering the results of previous studies, the fact that 6 percent of the assignments I collected have the stated or implied audience of peers is significant. It's not surprising that courses that use what Paulo Freire disparagingly refers to as the "banking method," where instructors "deposit" information to students through lectures and then test them for the information on exams, rarely require writing to peer audiences. It seems that instructors who require writing to a peer audience do so in order to take the emphasis off of the teacher-as-examiner. In an American history course, for example, students write a series of research essays that have to be "credible to both peers and instructors." The culmination of the essays is an in-class presentation where students explain the results of their research to peers. A number of instructors use electronic bulletin board journals as a space for writing to peers, and this emphasis on writing to peers is reinforced by assignments that described these journals, as one British literature instructor says, as "a conversation in writing."

In my study, there are three general types of assignments written for the audience of the "self": freewrites, a self-assessment written at the beginning or end of the course, or an assignment that requires students to relate the content of the course to their own lives. A self-evaluation assignment from an environmental studies course is an example of an assignment from the second category. The instructor writes in his description of the assignment: "This is your education, you must be an active participant in it, and it is only you who can determine its value to you, through self-evaluation and reflection." An example of the third type of writing for the self comes from an anthropology course. Students compare their diet to that of a caveman, partly to "analyze the nutritional quality of the diet of a hunter gatherer" and partly to "analyze the nutritional quality of your own diet" and "give you a broader perspective on the relative quality of your own diet." These are the kind of assignments that writing-to-learn scholars such as Fulwiler and Young feel can "personalize knowledge" (4) and "represent our experience to our own understanding" (x). In their meta-analysis of writing-to-learn studies, Robert Bangert-Drowns, Marlene Hurley, and Barbara Wilkinson found that these kinds of metacognitive prompts in which students could "reflect on their current knowledge, confusions, and learning processes proved particularly effective" (50). Unfortunately, in the courses I surveyed students were not often called upon to relate course content to personal experiences and interests or to use personal experiences to develop and support their arguments.

In sharp contrast to assignments written to the teacher-as-examiner, assignments written to a wider audience almost always provide students with a rhetorical situation and a genre with a social context beyond the student writing to the teacher-as-examiner. This is especially true of assignments in the "Wider Audience: Informed" category. Some of the audiences students write for in this category are company CEOs, Democratic Party organizers, and readers of the *New England Journal of Medicine*. Usually these rhetorical situations mirror the kind of writing students will encounter in the workplace. For example, the management course assignment that asks students to "provide group recommendations as if you were a consulting team offering suggestions on how to improve management practices" and the finance course assignment that instructs students to "assume that you are just hired as a CFO for a major corporation. The CEO would like you to review some of the major financial decisions for the company." Instructors who assign only writing to the teacher — and especially writing to inform the teacher-as-examiner — neglect to provide students with the kind of meaningful rhetorical purposes and social contexts found in assignments aimed at wider audiences.

THE GENRES OF COLLEGE WRITING

Previous surveys of the genres assigned in courses across the curriculum (Bridgeman and Carlson; Eblen; Harris and Hult) have shown that instructors claim to assign a variety of genres, both academic and professional. Despite this variety, however, these surveys also reveal a dominance of two genres: the term paper and the short-answer exam. My results are similar to previous studies in that a variety of genres are assigned. Lab reports, executive summaries, book reviews, ethnographies, feasibility reports, essay exams, abstracts, annotated bibliographies — the list is truly extensive. There was, in fact, such a variety of genres, and such a difference in the way these genres were defined in their various disciplinary contexts, that I resist the urge to classify, to merely categorize genres by their formal features and their distribution. As genre studies theorists argue, genres are impossible to deduce from just the structure of the discourse act itself (Bazerman and Paradis; Miller; Prior; Swales). Rather than imposing static categories on dynamic uses of language by classifying genres by formal features, as previous surveys of college writing have done, my aim is to get a sense of the rhetorical context of the genres in my study: the functions and audiences for genres, their social exigencies, and how they vary from discipline to discipline and instructor to instructor. In order to do this, I focus on the two genres found to be most common in previous surveys of college writing: the research paper and the short answer exam.

I focus on the research paper because as a genre it is representative of almost all of the genres I found in my research: it is too various to classify by formal features, and too discipline-specific and even classroom-specific to be considered as a type of writing without also analyzing its social context. Based on the research paper assignments in my study, I agree with Richard Larson's (1982) argument that the "research paper" cannot be classified as a genre, since research writing varies to such a degree from discipline to discipline and even from instructor to instructor. Prior surveys that have used the label "research paper" or "term paper" use it artificially, as a too-convenient way to classify a broad range of research writing.

Despite the variety of "research papers" in my study, I did find a pattern in my analysis of research writing that leads me to make at least one broad distinction that I think is valuable. Robert Davis and Mark Shadle divide research papers into two broad categories: "modernist" and "alternative." The modernist research paper is the "traditional" research paper. It's informative in function, logical, thesis-driven, and objective. Modernist research papers value "detachment, expertise, and certainty" (417). The purpose of a modernist research paper is "not making knowledge so much as reporting the known" (423). A research paper assignment from a psychology course contains many of the features Davis and Shadle would call "modernist":

Research Paper Guidelines

Purpose: The purpose of this project is for the student to (1) become familiar with a particular area of research activity in the field of human development, (2) by learning referencing techniques for this discipline, (3) gleaning information from the primary psychological literature, (4) summarizing this information clearly in a written report, and (5) practicing the format of scientific writing in this discipline.

Format: The format of the paper is a term paper about research, not an original research report. Each paper presents a summary of a single article.

Evaluation: The grade is based on content and form, including: Organization of the paper as a whole and of each section, adequacy of the summaries and interpretations of literature, the explication of controversial issues when appropriate, your conclusions and defense of your conclusions, grammar, punctuation, neatness, listing and citing of bibliographic references.

The grade will be lowered ten points for each of the following:

    errors in citation format

    errors in reference format

    failure to use APA format

    excessive spelling, grammatical or punctuation errors

    inaccurate information

This is a "term paper," not an "original research report." Students merely "glean" and "summarize" information. The evaluation criteria are focused mostly on the correctness of information, citations, and grammar.

Perhaps a religious studies instructor from my research provides the best description of the way alternative research writing differs from the modernist research paper. In a handout on writing essays, this instructor writes:

Remember when you were in grade six and your teacher told you to write a report on such and such or so and so, and you went to the library, opened up the encyclopedia, and tried to put the information into your own words? You should be past that now. A university essay is not a standard report that uses a few more books!

Alternative research writing values the creation of new knowledge, and not just "amassing of brute facts," in Robert Connors's words (321).

Compositionists from Larson to Davis and Shadle have bemoaned the staying power of the traditional research paper, so I fully expected that the majority of the research writing in my survey would fit Davis and Shadle's modernist category. I was surprised to find that the religious studies instructor is right, as far as the research writing in my study: the majority of college "research papers" are closer in spirit to alternative than modernist research writing. Take, for example, this research project from a psychology course:

> **Integration Project:** As an integration course, cross-cultural psychology seeks to involve students in exploring the interrelationships between two or more disciplines. The purpose of the project is to help you do just that. The format of the project is open to your creative ideas as long as the project looks at culture from two or more disciplinary perspectives. Some options might be:
>
> - A cross-cultural comparison on some topic of interest in psychology as well as another discipline (e.g., family structure, ceremonies and/or rituals, child-rearing practices, delinquency, artistic expression, mental health, religiosity, therapy). Discuss how cross-cultural differences and similarities would be viewed and handled from the perspectives of a psychologist and a professional from the other field.
>
> - A report of the cross-cultural psychological observations you made in a place where you had exposure to another culture (e.g., a church, a theatre, a refugee center, an office) while being involved in an activity/job related to other disciplines (e.g., religion, art, social work, business administration).
>
> - A critique of your own major or minor field of study (if you are not a psychology major or minor) from the point of view of cross-cultural psychology. You might discuss how inclusive and culturally sensitive the field of study is, citing specific research and theoretical examples.
>
> - An analysis of a movie, a piece of music, or some literature from another culture. Using our textbook information, explain how the concepts in the text are depicted in the piece you are analyzing and/or how the piece can be explained by some of the concepts in the text.

The goal of this research project is not to report the known, but to encourage exploration, synthesis, and creativity. Students choose from a variety of genres, all of which require analysis, argument, or evaluation. The instructions for most of the research paper assignments in my study echo this psychology assignment's insistence on exploration and argument, as these passages from research paper assignments illustrate:

> The goal of the project is to provide you with an opportunity to integrate, synthesize, and apply the material we are studying in class in a real-world context, gain experience with group decision making, research a topic in greater depth, and connect with a larger community.

> The purpose of this paper is to stimulate your thinking about "social or distributive justice." You are to develop your own position on this topic. Specifically, what principles should guide government in determining what to guarantee its citizens.

> You'll begin to create your corporate portfolio by writing a corporate mission statement and corporate profile or image brochure, and you'll also begin to research the cross-cultural communication differences you uncover in your case. Next, you'll collaborate to write a consulting report. The report must identify the international, cross-cultural communication problems in the case (supporting your conclusions with research), identify possible solutions to the primary problems (after comparing and contrasting the possibilities), and propose a solution to the appropriate audience (i.e., offer recommendations, and offer an implementation plan, and reasons).

Although I'm using Davis and Shadle's category of "alternative research writing" as a way to make distinctions between two broad types of research writing, a closer look at the research papers in my study reveals a deeper truth about the genres in my study. The differences among disciplines — and even among instructors within the same discipline and subdiscipline — in terms of the purposes and audiences for research writing, research methods, what counts as evidence, how research papers are structured, and the persona the writer is asked to take on make it difficult to generalize about the research paper as a genre, just as it would be difficult to generalize about the "lab report" or the "journal" without considering both disciplinary and classroom contexts.

Consider, for example, what it means to conduct research and what counts as evidence in the research papers in my study. A political science research project asks students to "research every aspect of the political background of the incumbent" for a presentation before the local Democratic Party organization. This will require primarily textual research, and the instructor recommends that students do a thorough search of sources such as *Congressional Quarterly* and *The Almanac of American Politics*. The research has a public audience and must be persuasive to Democratic Party insiders, who will have certain expectations for any research of this kind (for example, the use of data from polls). In another course from the social sciences, a political psychology course, the method of investigation for the research paper includes "administering a questionnaire," "participant observation," and "database analysis," all of which require a different set of research skills and have different research expectations than the presentation to the local Democratic Party.

In an American history course, students are asked to approach research and evidence in a way that is different in kind from these two social sciences courses. Student must "empathize with the person, place, or event you are writing about. The goal here is to use your understanding of the primary and secondary sources you have read to 'become' that person." This approach aligns with the instructor's notion that history is socially constructed: that "historians come to a socially negotiated understanding of historical figures and events" (a view of the way knowledge in history is created that is not always in accord with the views of other history instructors in my research, especially those who assign only short-answer exams). What counts as evidence in this history course is far more broadly defined than in the political science courses: "old family photos, a grandparent's memories, even family reunions allow people to understand their lives through an appreciation of the past." Evidence is explicitly connected to the discipline of history: "These events and artifacts remind us that history is a dynamic and interpretive field of study that requires far more than rote memorization."

Research papers in the business courses in my study value research and evidence that is, as one business instructor puts it, "quantitative and concise." Research and evidence in a marketing course mean "a table with a frequency distribution with counts and percentages" as well as "at least three pages of chi-square analyses" and "one page of a correlation/regression analysis." Another business instructor advises students to "make your descriptions and analyses precise and factual. Specific data about costs, market shares, time to market, and so on will enrich your work. In other words, what do the numbers tell us?" Just as historical figures and artifacts told the story for the American history course, here numbers tell a story. Despite the ubiquity of this emphasis on using quantitative data to tell the story in business courses, the form in which this research story is told differs dramatically from business course to business course. Business research genres in my study include executive summaries, proposals, business plans, case studies, progress reports, company profiles, marketing campaigns — all of which used quantitative data in different contexts, for different purposes, and for different audiences. Christopher Thaiss's argument that WAC research should focus as much on "writing-in-the-course" as "writing-in-the-discipline" is born out in my analysis of the research paper as a genre (324).

Despite the apparent variety of genres in my study, and despite the variety of social contexts for writing from discipline to discipline and instructor to instructor, it's important to note that nearly a quarter of the assignments in my research were of the genre most lacking in rhetorical and social context: the short-answer exam. Although my urge is to avoid classifying genres by their formal features, perhaps short-answer exams are the one school genre that resists the application of current genre theory. As I collected and analyzed the assignments, the sheer force of exam writing became the most noticeable pattern in my research. The midterm and final exams are the only writing in one out of every four courses, and as genres these exams show little variation across disciplines. They almost always consist of questions that require rote memorization and recall of facts, and the instructor almost always plays the role of teacher-as-examiner, looking for "correct" answers. The short-answer exam is the genre with the least "social action," to use Carolyn Miller's term. Writing-in-the-disciplines theorists are right to insist on looking at genres in their social context, but in my research, it is unfortunately the genre with the least social context that predominates.

WRITING TO LEARN, WRITING IN THE DISCIPLINES, AND THE INFLUENCE OF WAC

Writing-to-learn theorists would find it disheartening that the functions and audiences for writing in my college-level study conducted in the year 2006 are as limited as those in Britton's and in Applebee's studies of secondary schools conducted over thirty years ago. The majority (66 percent) of the assignments are writing to inform the teacher-as-examiner, as opposed to writing to learn, and one out of four assignments is a short-answer exam. Writing-in-the-disciplines theorists would also find this emphasis on exam writing disheartening, considering that these short-answer exams rarely call on students to practice disciplinary ways of making meaning.

This is not to assert that the whole of academic discourse, as revealed in the assignments in my collection, is reduced to exam taking and "correct" answers. Writing-in-the-disciplines theorists would be interested in the predominance of alternative research writing in my study, and the ways research writing genres — and all genres beyond the short-answer exam — are tied so closely to discipline-specific ways of making meaning, even as they vary significantly from instructor to instructor within the same discipline. Another piece of hopeful news is that exploratory writing makes up a far larger percentage of the assignments in my study than it had in previous studies, due in large part to the popularity of journals, which are used by instructors for both writing-to-learn purposes and to introduce students to disciplinary ways of thinking. Another positive finding from my study is the fact that 50 out of 400 instructors respond to drafts. These positive revelations — the increase in exploratory writing, the absence of traditional research papers, the significant number of instructors intervening during the writing process — point to the most encouraging pattern in my study, and it is of interest to both writing-to-learn and writing-in-the-disciplines theorists — and to anyone interested in supporting writing in the undergraduate years.

The instructors in my research who assign the widest variety of purposes, audiences, and genres, who provide students with interesting and complex rhetorical situations rather than just the traditional lecture/exam format, and who teach writing as a process through peer response or responding to rough drafts are most often teaching in a course connected in some way to a Writing Across the Curriculum program. This may mean a writing-intensive course, a team-taught course with an English department faculty member, a learning community, or a course connected to a writing fellows program. Instructors from writing-intensive courses connected to established WAC programs at institutions such as the University of Missouri, University of Pittsburgh, Cornell, University of Hawaii, Duke, University of Massachusetts, and Stanford assigned the most writing, asked students to write for the greatest variety of audiences in the greatest variety of genres, and adopted common WAC pedagogical tools such as journaling, freewriting, grading rubrics, and peer response. Tables 8-3 and 8-4 reveal the significant difference between the distribution of functions and audiences for these WAC courses versus the courses as a whole.

TABLE 8-3   Distribution of the Functions of Writing for WAC Courses

Function	Number of Assignments	Percentage of Total
Transactional (total)	60	70
Informative	43	49
Persuasive	17	21
Expressive	5	6
Exploratory	20	23
Poetic	2	.2

TABLE 8-4   Distribution of the Audiences of Writing for WAC Courses

Audience	Number of Assignments	Percentage of Total
Student to Examiner	35	40
Student to Instructor [General]	13	15
Peers	5	6
Self	18	21
Wider Audience	16	18

Although my research leads me to conclude that college students write for limited purposes and audiences, even as they progress through their majors, WAC has certainly had a positive influence on many of the instructors in my study. As the tables below make clear, students in these WAC courses are far less likely to encounter only short-answer exams, and far more likely to use writing to explore. They are also more likely to write for wider audiences as well as to use writing to reflect. Students also encounter more writing assignments in these WAC courses. The average number of assignments per course in the study is 5.25, but the average number of assignments per WAC course is 8.7.

There is no doubt, then, that WAC has had a positive influence on the instructors in my study who have come into contact with it, whether that influence has resulted in writing-to-learn pedagogy, moving away from the lecture/exam format, or seeing the importance of immersing students in discipline-specific ways of making meaning through writing. The results of my research are both an argument for the need to continue to work to transform the writing done outside of composition courses — to bring writing-to-learn pedagogies to instructors across disciplines — as well as an argument for continuing to investigate writing in the disciplines and consider how what we learn from this investigation might transform our own composition courses: for example, by moving away from traditional, thesis-driven research papers and by teaching students to analyze and respond to multiple genres.

Most importantly, though, the results of my research are an argument for the importance and influence of the WAC movement and the need to continue to support WAC efforts as the most powerful antidote to the limited uses of writing I found in so many of the courses in my study.

Acknowledgments: I would like to give thanks to Richard Straub and Wendy Bishop, teachers who helped shape this study and who also helped shape me as a researcher and a teacher of writing. This essay is dedicated to their memory.

NOTES

1. The results of a pilot study of 770 writing assignments at forty-eight institutions was reported in Melzer (86–110).

2. Because I collected the assignments from the Internet, my research has one important advantage over previous surveys of writing across disciplines. Chris Anson says of these WAC surveys, "Because most surveys are responded to by choice, even a relatively good return may still represent a skewed sample" (12). As Anson points out, instructors filling out these surveys may exaggerate the importance of writing or the amount of writing in their classes, either to put themselves in a positive light or to attempt to give the researchers what the instructor thinks they want. Despite the advantage of the ability to collect a large amount of writing assignments without having to ask for samples from instructors, conducting research via the Internet brings with it its own set of problems. Although the assignments I collected were not given voluntarily, the fact that instructors published their assignments on the Internet means that they are aware of at least the possibility of a more public audience. Instructors who use class websites could be considered "early adopters" of technology, and it's possible that their assignments might be fuller or more explicitly laid out than the assignments of instructors who are not using websites. Despite these problems inherent in my study, I feel that the advantages of studying a large sample of assignments that is not given voluntarily outweigh the disadvantages of collecting data from the Internet. It's important to note that although I collected the assignments from course websites, none of the courses were delivered entirely online.

WORKS CITED

Anson, Chris. "Toward a Multidimensional Model of Writing in the Academic Disciplines." *Advances in Writing Research*. Vol. 2: *Writing in Academic Disciplines*. Ed. David Joliffe. Norwood, NJ: Ablex, 1998. 1–33.

Applebee, Arthur N. *Contexts for Learning to Write*. Norwood, NJ: Ablex, 1984.

Bangert-Drowns, Robert, Marlene Hurley, and Barbara Wilkinson. "The Effects of School-Based Writing-to-Learn Interventions on Academic Achievement: A Meta-analysis." *Review of Educational Research* 74.1 (2004): 29–58.

Bazerman, Charles, and James Paradis. *Textual Dynamics of the Professions*. Madison: U of Wisconsin P, 1991.

Bridgeman, Brent, and Sybil Carlson. "Survey of Academic Writing Tasks." *Written Communication* 1.2 (1984): 247–80.

Britton, James, et al. *The Development of Writing Abilities (11–18)*. London: Macmillan Education, 1975.

Connors, Robert. *Composition-Rhetoric: Backgrounds, Theory, and Pedagogy*. Pittsburgh: U of Pittsburgh P, 1997.

Crusius, Timothy. *Discourse: A Critique and Synthesis of the Major Theories*. New York: Modern Language Association, 1989.

Davis, Robert, and Mark Shadle. "Building a Mystery: Alternative Research Writing and the Academic Act of Seeking." *College Composition and Communication* 51.3 (2000): 417–46.

Eblen, Charlene. (1983). "Writing Across the Curriculum: A Survey of University Faculty's Views and Classroom Practices." *Research in the Teaching of English* 17.4 (1983): 343–48.

Emig, Janet. *The Composing Processes of Twelfth Graders*. Urbana, IL: National Council of Teachers of English, 1971.

Freedman, Aviva, and Peter Medway. "Introduction: New Views of Genres and Their Implications for Education." *Learning and Teaching Genre*. Ed. Aviva Freedman and Peter Medway. Portsmouth, NH: Boynton/Cook, 1994.

Freire, Paulo. *Pedagogy of the Oppressed*. New York: Herder and Herder, 1970.

Fulwiler, Toby, and Art Young, eds. *Language Connections: Writing and Reading Across the Curriculum*. Urbana, IL: National Council of Teachers of English, 1982.

Harris, Jeanette, and Christine Hult. "Using a Survey of Writing Assignments to Make Informed Curricular Decisions." *Writing Program Administration* 8.3 (1985): 7–14.

Jones, Robert, and Joseph Comprone. "Where Do We Go Next in Writing Across the Curriculum?" *College Composition and Communication* 44.1 (1993): 59–68.

Larson, Richard. "The 'Research Paper' in the Writing Course: A Non-form of Writing." *College English* 44.8 (1982): 811–16.

McLeod, Susan, and Elaine Maimon. "Clearing the Air: WAC Myths and Realities." *College English* 62.5 (2000): 573–83.

McLeod, Susan H., and Eric Miraglia. "Writing Across the Curriculum in a Time of Change." McLeod, Miraglia, Soven, and Thaiss. 1–27.

McLeod, Susan H., Eric Miraglia, Margot Soven, and Christopher Thaiss, eds. *WAC for the New Millennium: Strategies for Continuing Writing-Across-the-Curriculum Programs*. Urbana, IL: National Council of Teachers of English, 2001.

Melzer, Daniel. "Assignments Across the Curriculum: A Survey of College Writing." *Language and Learning Across the Disciplines* 6.1 (Jan. 2003): 86–110.

Miller, Carolyn. "Genre as Social Action." *Genre and the New Rhetoric*. Ed. Aviva Freedman and Peter Medway. London: Taylor and Francis, 1994. 23–42.

Prior, Paul. *Writing/Disciplinarity: A Sociohistoric Account of Literate Activity in the Academy*. Mahwah, NJ: Lawrence Erlbaum, 1998.

Sherwood, Rhoda. "A Survey of Undergraduate Reading and Writing Needs." *College Composition and Communication* 28.2 (1977): 145–49.

Swales, John. *Genre Analysis: English in Academic and Research Settings*. Cambridge: Cambridge UP, 1990.

Thaiss, Christopher. "Theory in WAC: Where Have We Been, Where Are We Going?" McLeod, Miraglia, Soven, and Thaiss. 299–325.

Young, Art. "Guest Editor's Introduction: A Venture into the Counter-Intuitive." *Language and Learning Across the Disciplines* 6.2 (June 2003). 1 April 2008 <http://wac.colostate.edu/llad/v6n2/guest.pdf>.

9

Microtheme Strategies for Developing Cognitive Skills

JOHN C. BEAN, DEAN DRENK,
AND F. D. LEE

G enerating faculty enthusiasm for a writing-across-the-curriculum effort is not an easy task. As long as content area instructors think of writing instruction as doctoring up the grammar of term papers, there can be little hope of progress. A successful writing-across-the-curriculum program therefore demands some conceptual blockbusting.

One of the best blockbusters we have discovered is the microtheme — an essay so short that it can be typed on a single five-by-eight-inch note card (Work, 1979). Capable of being graded rapidly and thus adaptable to large classes, microthemes can be designed to promote growth in specified thinking skills. Once content area instructors discover that a new kind of writing assignment can help their students become better learners and thinkers without adding a heavy paper-grading burden to their own work load, they become enthusiastic about writing-across-the-curriculum programs.

The microtheme method can be employed successfully in both large and small classes. Instructors who use the method generally give all students the same assignment, along with a description of the criteria by which the theme will be evaluated. Since writing is seen as a mode of learning, students are urged to work together outside of class as a way of expanding their active thinking time. The assignments are designed according to a principle that we call *leverage* in which a small amount of writing is preceded by a great deal of thinking. Not all microthemes need to be graded; some instructors, considering them practice for later graded exercises, simply record that they have been completed. When microthemes are graded, they can be scored rapidly according to a variety of strategies. Using simple rating scales (several examples are displayed later in this chapter) instructors report that they can grade between thirty and fifty microthemes per hour. In large lecture classes, graduate assistants or even top undergraduates can be trained to grade microthemes. Rather than writing comments on individual microthemes, the instructor can provide feedback to students by duplicating and distributing several of the best

From *New Directions for Teaching and Learning: Teaching Writing in All Disciplines*. Ed. C. W. Griffin. San Francisco: Jossey-Bass, 1982. 27–38.

microthemes, as well as a few of the less successful ones that exhibit representative writing or thinking problems. Class discussion of these microthemes provides adequate feedback; indeed, some students report that it provides better feedback than traditional comments on papers.

We have had success with four kinds of microtheme assignments. Each is designed to focus on a different cognitive problem.

THE SUMMARY-WRITING MICROTHEME:
THE PROBLEM OF COGNITIVE EGOCENTRISM

As anyone who has tried it knows, writing a good one or two hundred-word summary of an article is a cognitively difficult task. The writer must first determine the structure of the original article by locating the transitions and other cues that signal hierarchical relationships among specific details and various levels of abstraction. Then, the writer must condense the whole, retaining main and subordinate ideas while eliminating supporting details. Such a task builds students' reading comprehension skills and also gives students practice in writing concise, flexible prose. (Figure 9-1 shows a sample rating scale for summaries.)

The summary-writing microtheme can have another benefit for students — as a way of helping them combat what cognitive psychologists call *egocentrism*. According to Piaget, an egocentric thinker "sees the world from a single point of view only — his own — but without knowledge of the existence of [other] viewpoints or perspectives and . . . without awareness that he is the prisoner of his own" (Flavell, 1963, p. 60). As maturing thinkers develop toward formal operations — that is, toward the ability to think in abstractions by attending to the form of logical argument without dependence upon concrete or specific example — they gradually acquire the ability to imagine the points of view of other thinkers and thus to initiate the kind of dialectic interplay between opposing views that leads to intellectual growth.

Lunsford (1979) has used Piaget's concept of egocentrism to explain why basic writers, when asked to compose paragraphs analyzing objective data, frequently write instead about personal opinions provided by the data, apparently unaware that they have veered from the assigned topic. We have noted the same kind of egocentrism in students' first attempts at summary writing. For example, students frequently distort the ideas of authors whose views are unfamiliar or distasteful. These students either introduce their own opinions and observations into the summaries, or they turn disturbing ideas into comfortable ones. With repeated practice, however, students can learn to "listen" to the authors whom they are summarizing and consciously guard against the tendency to block out dissonant points of view.

The summary-writing microtheme, therefore, is particularly beneficial in courses where conflicting world views clash — sociology, ethics, political science, and so forth. Having students summarize articles that express opposing points of view urges them away from superficial one-right-answer thinking. One especially valuable procedure in such classes is to have students

FIGURE 9-1   Evaluation Criteria for Summaries

A summary should be directed toward imagined readers who have not read the article being summarized. The purpose of the summary is to give these persons a clear overview of the article's main points. The criteria for a summary are (1) accuracy of content, (2) comprehensiveness and balance, and (3) clear sentence structure with good transitions.

6   A "six" summary meets all the criteria for accuracy, comprehensiveness and balance, and clear sentence structure. The writer should understand the article thoroughly. The main points in the article should appear correctly in the summary with all main points proportionately developed (that is, the writer should not spend excessive time on one main point while neglecting other main points). The summary should be as comprehensive as possible and should read smoothly from beginning to end with appropriate transitions between ideas. The sentence structure should be clear and varied, without vagueness or ambiguity and without grammatical errors.

5   A "five" summary should still be excellent, but it can be weaker than a "six" summary in one area. It may have excellent accuracy, comprehensiveness, and balance but show occasional problems in sentence structure. Or it may be clearly written but somewhat unbalanced or less comprehensive than a "six" summary or it may show a minor misunderstanding of the article.

4   A "four" summary is one that is good but not excellent. It will reveal a generally accurate reading of the article with a clear sense of the main points, but it will be noticeably weaker than a "six" summary in one of the areas of criteria or somewhat weaker in two areas.

3   A "three" summary must have strength in at least one area of competence, and it should still be good enough to give a reader a fairly clear and accurate overview of the article being summarized. A "three" summary is generally either seriously unbalanced or fuzzily written and lacks the clarity and precision of a top-rated summary. The sentence structure of a "three" summary frequently prevents inclusion of enough ideas for good comprehensiveness.

2   A "two" summary is weak in all areas of competence, either because it is so poorly written that the reader cannot understand the content or because the content is inaccurate or seriously disorganized.

1   A "one" summary fails to meet any of the areas of competence.

summarize opposing articles while keeping a journal that allows them to explore their own subjective reactions to the material. In fact, it is only a short step from summarizing articles with varying viewpoints to accomplishing the kind of synthesis required for library research papers. A recent anthology on writing across the curriculum takes just this approach (Behrens and Rosen, 1982).

THE THESIS-SUPPORT MICROTHEME:
THE PROBLEM OF FOCUSED ARGUMENTATION

An essential concept for writers is the thesis statement, that is, the basic proposition or controlling idea of a piece of writing. Whereas a topic is a noun phrase by itself (for example, "the student revolutionary movement in the late sixties"), a thesis statement has a predicate that makes an assertion about some issue within the topic ("The student revolutionary movement in the late sixties resulted from the childhood permissiveness popularized by Benjamin Spock"). Because thesis statements generally take a stand on an issue, mature writers learn to imagine a doubting audience that needs to be argued out of a countering position ("The student revolutionary movement in the late sixties was not causally related to the permissiveness of Benjamin Spock"). Many student writers, however, have difficulty discovering issues within a topic or formulating thesis statements that take focused positions on issues. Either they write a diffuse thesis statement ("The student revolutionary movement in the late sixties had good points and bad points"), or they write a paper that has no thesis statement at all (for example, a research paper on the student revolutionary movement replete with historical facts but devoid of clear purpose or point — what one of our colleagues calls *data dumping*). Illogical or poorly focused papers, therefore, frequently stem from inadequate thesis statements, which stem in turn from an inadequate sense of the issue at hand.

Thesis-support microthemes are designed specifically to enable students to discover issues and create propositions within a content discipline. An assignment sequence designed by Dean Drenk for an upper division finance course in investments illustrates this strategy. Drenk assigns students ten issues from a list of more than sixty. Each issue is stated in terms of contradictory propositions or theses. Students must choose one of the alternative propositions for each issue and write a microtheme that defends the position. (Drenk allows students to write as many as two typed pages — slightly more than the other microthemes described in this chapter.) These propositions differ from most essay examination questions in that they take positions that are controversial and unproven in the field. Here are five representative issues:

1. The price-earnings ratio of a stock (does/does not) reflect the rate or return that an investor in that stock will achieve.

2. Professional management (is/is not) an effective means of achieving higher than average stock returns.

3. Random diversification (is/is not) more reliable than selective diversification.

4. The geometric mean of a return distribution (is/is not) an indicator of the risk of that investment.

5. Mutual fund performance (is/is not) superior to the average investor's performance.

In writing this kind of microtheme, students must stop being passive memorizers and become active thinkers. They must support their assigned propositions concisely, using empirical evidence, syllogistic reasoning, appeal to appropriate authority, and so forth — all the tools of argumentation used by professionals in the field. (Criteria for grading such microthemes are shown in Figure 9-2.) Because many of these propositions can be best supported through library research, students learn to seek out information for themselves, information that they must weigh, synthesize, and reshape in order to build a logical, cohesive argument. Moreover, the proposition not chosen — the alternative counter-proposition — continually reminds students that their task is not simply to utter facts but to defend a position. Finally, because the

FIGURE 9-2   Grading Criteria for Thesis-Support Microthemes

There are various types of support of theses, including the following: empirical evidence, theoretical argument, authority, and intuition. These types of support are listed in order of their strength. That is, empirical evidence outweighs theoretical argument, which outweighs authority, and so on. When using different types of support, students should take into account such factors as:

For empirical evidence:
- The past versus the future
- Precise pertinence of the data to the thesis
- The unbiased or biased nature of the data

For authority:
- The past record of the authority
- Qualifications of the authority
- The extent of concurrence with other authorities

Thesis-support microthemes should be written so that they are clear to those who are not members of the class or even in the same disciplines. They should not be written so that they can be understood only if the reader already knows the thesis and its support.

Grading Criteria

Support of Theses		*Other Feedback*
A. Clarity of support	_____	Grammatical errors are numerous enough to interfere with understanding your response. ( )
B. Logic (Relationship of support to thesis)	_____	The organization of your response is not clear. ( )
C. Sources of Support		The logic of your support is confusing or does not make sense. ( )
1. Quantity	_____	Your conclusions are not warranted by your support. ( )
2. Quality	_____	
Total Microtheme Grade	_____	Your support is too imprecise or too general to convince. ( )

thesis-support microtheme demands mastery of the principles covered in courses that rely on the textbook and lecture, students are actively learning central course material as they prepare their microthemes.

Drenk posits two immediate advantages to thesis-support assignments: Students become noticeably more skilled at focused argumentation as the course progresses, and students learn to see their discipline as a field of controversies, not as a body of facts to be memorized. Thus, students learn to understand the complexity of what is known and what is not known within their disciplines.

THE DATA-PROVIDED MICROTHEME: THE PROBLEM OF INDUCTIVE REASONING

The task of the data-provided microtheme is the obverse of the task of the thesis-support microtheme. Here, students are provided with data and asked to discover a thesis or general statement that gives meaning to the data. The data can be provided as a list of sentences (Figure 9-3) or as a graph or statistical table (Figure 9-4). Students must arrange the data in a logical order (in more complex assignments, students must select only the significant data and omit irrelevant data), connect the parts with appropriate transitions, and write

FIGURE 9-3   Example of Data-Provided Assignment (Sentence Method)

Using all of the data supplied below, write a brief essay on the topic "Is the Energy Crisis Real?"

1. 90 percent of the world's oil (2,100 billion barrels) is still in the ground.
2. The proportion of oil left in the U.S. is much less than 90 percent.
3. Experts estimate that the U.S. will ultimately produce a total of 204 billion barrels of oil.
4. The U.S. has produced and burned 110 billion barrels of oil so far.
5. 75 percent of America's potentially available oil has already been discovered.
6. Half of all the oil produced in the past 110 years was pumped and burned in the last ten years.
7. The Alaskan oil discovery added 35 billion barrels of oil to America's proven reserves.
8. The U.S. presently uses 30 billion barrels of oil per decade.
9. We have used 1.7 percent of the world's coal supply.
10. Coal contains a lot of sulfur, which vaporizes when burned and gives off noxious gas.
11. Coal burning leaves much ash, which poses a significant disposal problem.
12. Coal smoke is a serious air pollutant.
13. Coal mining can damage the countryside.
14. Miners are killed in mine accidents every year.
15. Many coal miners suffer from black lung.

FIGURE 9-4   Data-Supplied Microtheme Assignment (Table Method)

Your assignment is to write a paragraph using specific detail data from the table provided. You will notice that the death rates for some diseases have declined sharply from 1910 to 1966, while the death rates from other diseases have increased. To make your microtheme interesting, you might speculate as to why these changes have occurred. Your priority, however, is to explain clearly that the changes happened and highlight what you feel to be significant about the data.

You are to imagine a general audience who has never seen this table, and your task is to create an interesting and informative paragraph. This assignment will test your skill in creating a hierarchical structure that alternates between general statements and specific details in a clear, logical order.

The following is a chart depicting the death rates (per 100,000 population) and the causes of death from 1910 to 1966 in the United States. Fetal deaths are not included.

Death rates per 100,000 population

Year	All causes	Cardio-vascular diseases	Malignant neoplasms	Certain diseases of early infancy	Influenza and pneumonia	Diabetes	Bronchitis and emphysema	Accidents	All other
1910....	1,468	287	76.2	73.0	155.9	15.3	-	84.2	776
1920....	1,299	283	83.4	69.2	207.3	16.1	-	70.0	570
1930....	1,132	328	97.4	49.6	102.5	19.1	-	79.8	456
1935....	1,095	353	108.2	40.2	104.2	22.3	-	77.8	388
1940....	1,076	407	120.3	39.2	70.3	26.6	-	73.2	340
1942....	1,032	409	122.0	41.4	55.7	25.4	-	71.3	309
1943....	1,087	439	124.3	41.3	67.1	27.1	-	73.4	315
1945....	1,058	444	134.0	38.3	51.6	26.5	-	72.1	292
1948....	989	437	134.9	42.1	38.7	26.4	-	66.9	243
1949....	971	485	138.8	43.2	30.0	16.9	2.8	60.6	194
1950....	964	494	139.8	40.5	31.3	16.2	2.8	60.6	178
1951....	967	499	140.6	41.2	31.4	16.3	3.0	62.5	173
1952....	961	499	143.4	40.9	29.7	16.4	3.1	61.8	168
1953....	959	503	144.8	40.1	33.0	16.3	3.6	60.1	158
1954....	919	485	145.6	39.4	25.4	15.6	3.6	55.9	149
1955....	930	496	146.5	39.0	27.1	15.5	4.1	56.9	145
1956....	935	501	147.8	38.6	28.2	15.7	4.6	56.7	142
1957....	959	515	148.6	39.1	35.8	16.0	5.5	55.9	143
1958....	951	516	146.8	39.8	33.1	15.9	6.2	52.3	141
1959....	939	509	147.3	38.5	31.2	15.9	6.6	52.2	138
1960....	955	515	149.2	37.4	37.3	16.7	7.6	52.3	139
1961....	930	505	149.4	35.9	30.1	16.4	7.8	50.4	134
1962....	945	515	149.9	34.5	32.3	16.8	9.2	52.3	135
1963....	961	521	151.3	33.2	37.5	17.2	10.9	53.4	137
1964....	940	509	151.3	31.5	31.1	16.9	11.2	54.3	135
1965....	943	511	153.5	28.6	31.9	17.1	12.6	55.7	133
1966....	954	520	154.8	26.1	32.8	18.1	-	57.3	146

general statements showing the meaning that they have induced. In a sense, data-provided microthemes are to writing as scales are to piano playing or school figures to ice-skating. They de-emphasize individuality and creativity, forcing students to concentrate on technique — in this case, on the development of inductive reasoning powers and on the shaping of meaningful paragraphs by means of the transitions and generalizations that students must provide. Ideally, this kind of exercise helps students to learn the difference between a mere list of facts (the data as they are provided) and an assertion of meaning (the data reshaped into a logical microtheme).

Data-provided microthemes can serve a variety of purposes. At the most basic level, they can teach students to arrange paragraphs hierarchically and to signal the relationships with transitions. In these cases, the instructor can provide a tree diagram for the intended paragraph (see the "diet" assignment in Maimon and others, 1981, pp. 50–51). Lunsford (1979) uses data-provided assignments to help students to improve their skills in inductive reasoning. (For commentary on Lunsford's methods, see Bean, 1981–1982). At a more advanced level, instructors can use data-provided assignments to teach students how to write the discussion section of a scientific paper. The instructor can duplicate a chart or table from the findings section of a sample paper and ask students to write an appropriate discussion paragraph that analyzes the meaning residing within the raw data. Exercises of this nature can sometimes have a dramatic effect on students' understanding of how meaning is conveyed in written discourse.

THE QUANDARY-POSING MICROTHEME: THE PROBLEM OF COGNITIVE PUZZLES

Evidence is accumulating in scientific journals that nearly two-thirds of today's college students are not fully capable of abstract reasoning (Arons and Karplus, 1976). Among physics students, this problem frequently manifests itself as an inability to understand the differences between such concepts as weight and mass, or velocity and acceleration (although students can, of course, recall textbook explanations and perform formula computations). It is students' confusion about such concepts, in fact, that has led to the interest in Piaget among science educators and to the multiplication of Piaget-based science curricula throughout the country.

Recently, Arons (1981) reported that students can be guided toward mastery of a concept if a Socratic dialogue technique is used to urge them to articulate the concept in their own words. Apparently, the process of thinking out loud, of working to transform vaguely formed private thoughts into public words, enhances comprehension. Arons's report seems to bear out the professorial folk wisdom that one does not really understand a concept until one can articulate it clearly to someone else. In an effort to duplicate in a 400-student lecture course some of the benefits reported by Arons from face-to-face conferences with students, F. D. Lee designed a sequence of quandary-posing microthemes. These microtheme assignments asked students to solve puzzles involving velocity, acceleration, and other physics concepts and to teach their solutions in writing to an imagined learner, often in humorous case situations (Figures 9-5 and 9-6). The microthemes received a top grade only if, in the grader's opinion, they had explained the physics concepts clearly to the specified audience. Such microthemes can be sequenced if the difficulty of the cognitive puzzle presented is increased gradually, moving, for example, from simple mass and weight puzzles to complex puzzles — such as "Alaska, Land of the Midnight Sun," designed by Drumheller and others (1978) — that require students to think from multiple perspectives and to make transferences from analogous experiences.

Although we have not yet completed an empirical study of the effect of microtheme writing on students' comprehension of physics concepts, we

FIGURE 9-5   Quandary-Posing Microtheme for Introductory Physics

Suppose that you are Dr. Science, the question-and-answer person for a popular magazine called *Practical Science*. Readers of your magazine are invited to submit letters to Dr. Science, who answers them in "Dear Abby" style in a special section of the magazine. One day you receive the following letter:

Dear Dr. Science:

You've got to help me settle this argument I am having with my girlfriend. We were watching a baseball game several weeks ago when this guy hit a high pop-up straight over the catcher's head. When it finally came down, the catcher caught it standing on home plate. Well, my girlfriend told me that when the ball stopped in midair just before it started back down, its velocity was zero, but acceleration was not zero. I said she was stupid. If something isn't moving at all, how could it have any acceleration? Ever since then she has been making a big deal out of this and won't let me kiss her. I love her, but I don't think we can get back together until we settle this argument. We checked some physics books, but they weren't very clear. We agreed that I would write to you and let you settle the argument. But, Dr. Science, don't just tell us the answer. You've got to explain it so we both understand, because my girlfriend is really dogmatic. She said she wouldn't even trust Einstein unless he could explain himself clearly.

Sincerely,
Baseball Blues

Can This Relationship Be Saved? Your task is to write an answer to Baseball Blues. Because space in your magazine is limited, restrict your answer to what can be put on a single 5 × 8 card. Don't confuse Baseball and his girlfriend by using any special physics terms unless you explain clearly what they mean. If you think some diagrams would help, include them on a separate sheet.

know that the quandary-posing microthemes have generated vigorous discussions among students. At the very least, they have altered students' study habits and helped them to view writing as a learning tool. From the instructor's point of view, the microthemes have also laid bare problems in students' thinking patterns, revealing that what appears to be a writing problem in an unsuccessful microtheme is actually a problem in reasoning and understanding. Because many students have been unable to solve the puzzles presented (their microthemes revealed a baffling train of misconceptions and illogic), microthemes by themselves cannot ensure comprehension. Nevertheless, students do shift their emphasis from rote learning to an active struggle with concepts; moreover, many students report that the need to teach their ideas has helped them to understand the physics principles involved. We intend in

FIGURE 9-6   Quandary-Posing Microtheme for Introductory Physics

Suppose you put a big block of ice in a bucket and then fill the bucket with water until the water level is exactly even with the edge of the bucket. (The ice, of course, is now floating in the water.)

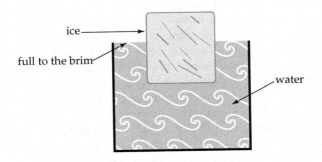

ice

full to the brim

water

Now we will wait for several hours for the ice to melt. Which of the following will happen? (Neglect evaporation.)

1. The water level in the bucket will remain exactly the same.
2. The water level in the bucket will drop.
3. Some water will overflow the sides of the bucket.

Your Task: After deciding upon your answer, explain it in writing. Imagine that you are writing to a classmate who doesn't yet understand flotation and who is arguing for what you consider the wrong answer. Your task is to explain your reasoning so clearly that your microtheme serves as a little textbook, *teaching* your classmate the physics principles involved. Thus, your microtheme will be judged *not simply* on whether or not you figure out the correct answer, but also on whether or not you can write clearly enough to *teach* a fellow classmate.

the future to assign students to collaborative learning teams, whose members will write a microtheme together as a group project. In this way, students can perhaps teach each other, which better approximates the Socratic technique; teams may also help to temper the isolation that students sometimes feel in large lecture courses.

CONCLUSION AND SUMMARY

We would like to conclude by making some brief connections between microtheme assignments and the general problem of designing a curriculum that better enhances cognitive development. Lochhead (1978) has identified a number of obstacles that hinder the development of such a curriculum, the foremost being general resistance to change among academics. In this regard, microthemes are particularly useful, because they are politically innocuous. They can be added to any instructor's syllabus without necessitating major changes in teaching style or course design. If teachers who currently require no writing simply add two or three microthemes to their course assignments — representing, we guess, a tolerable increase in an instructor's work load — students' writing output during a four-year college career will increase enormously.

Microthemes are also pedagogically appropriate. That is, they meet all the requirements for curricular reform cited by Lochhead: They are designed to develop students' intellectual maturity; they reward qualitative, not factual, knowledge; and they make students active learners. Moreover, since the level of difficulty of microthemes can be controlled, it is theoretically possible for a department to design a coherent sequence of assignments for a four-year curriculum. For example, instructors can design simple microtheme assignments for the freshman level, more complex assignments for the sophomore level, and longer analytical or research papers for students at the upper division level. Such a sequence could be designed to promote growth along Perry's (1970) intellectual maturity scale, which places students at points ranging from immature cognitive dualism (all questions have right or wrong answers), to relativism (all opinions are equally valid), to mature commitment within relativism (there may be no right answers, but a thinker must take a reasoned stand). Summary-writing and thesis-support microthemes do much to promote such growth, because they encourage openness to alternative points of view and foster the ability to see the world in terms of complex issues, not of right and wrong answers.

But, these are theoretical concerns that await further research and further experimentation in curriculum design. At this point, it is enough to say that across-the-curriculum microthemes are an attractive alternative to term papers and a decided improvement over no writing assignments at all.

REFERENCES

Arons, A. B. "Thinking, Reasoning, and Understanding in Introductory Physics Courses." *Physics Teacher*, 1981, *19*, 166–172.
Arons, A. B., and Karplus, R. "Implications of Accumulating Data on Levels of Intellectual Development." *American Journal of Physics*, 1976, *44*, 396.

Bean, J. C. "Involving Non-English Faculty in the Teaching of Writing and Thinking Skills." *International Journal of Instructional Media*, 1981–1982, *9*, (1), 51–69.

Behrens, L., and Rosen, L. J. *Writing and Reading Across the Curriculum*. Boston: Little, Brown, 1982.

Drumheller, J. E. and others. "Alaska, Land of the Midnight Sun." *Physics Teacher*, 1978, *16*, 380.

Flavell, J. H. *The Developmental Psychology of Jean Piaget*. Princeton, N.J.: D. Van Nostrand, 1963.

Lochhead, J. *Final Report: A Cognitive Development Project*. Amherst: Department of Physics and Astronomy, University of Massachusetts, 1978. (FIPSE Grant Number G007603206)

Lunsford A. A. "Cognitive Development and the Basic Writer." *College English*, 1979, *41*, 38–46.

Maimon, E. P., and others. *Writing in the Arts and Sciences*. Cambridge: Mass.: Winthrop, 1981.

Perry, W. *Forms of Intellectual and Ethical Development in the College Years: A Scheme*. New York: Holt, Rinehart and Winston, 1970.

Work, J. C. "Reducing Three Papers to Ten: A Method for Literature Courses." In G. Stanford (Ed.), *How to Handle the Paper Load: Classroom Practices in Teaching English*. Urbana, Ill.: National Council of Teachers of English, 1979.

10 Writing Across and Against the Curriculum

ART YOUNG

This year (2002) marks the thirtieth anniversary of attending my first Conference on College Composition and Communication (CCCC) convention. At the beginning of my career as a composition teacher, scholar, and program administrator, I joined CCCC, and its members have nurtured me and have been my primary collegial and intellectual community ever since. In 1972 I attended my first CCCC convention in Boston and chaired a session titled Innovations in Technical Writing. The next year, in New Orleans, I read my first conference paper, "Writing for Engineering and Technology," and I met a colleague, Don Cunningham, who asked me to revise the paper for a new journal he was editing for the recently formed group, the Association of Teachers of Writing (annual dues $3.00, including three issues of the journal). As a result, my first professional publication came out later that year in the inaugural issue of *Technical Writing Teacher* ("Technical Communications and Freshman Composition"). It didn't even matter to me (or apparently anyone else) that four pages of my manuscript were inadvertently omitted.

I was drawn to composition and to CCCC out of political activism for social justice in the 1960s. My dissertation was on British Romantic poetry and nonviolence (*Shelley and Nonviolence*), using the twentieth-century lens of nonviolence created by Mohandas K. Gandhi, Martin Luther King, Jr., and Cesar Chavez to reexamine the poetry of Percy Bysshe Shelley. I envisioned myself as a change agent working within the system to make a difference in "education as usual." In the 1970s and early 1980s, my colleagues at Michigan Technological University (MTU) and I became involved in new or rapidly growing movements in program and pedagogy: writing centers, writing program administration, technical and professional communication, computers and composition, and, most significantly for me, writing across the curriculum, all under the receptive and responsive umbrella of CCCC. Each successive CCCC meeting produced the excitement of working with colleagues from across the nation and renewed my commitment to return to my own campus and make a difference. For me, each of these movements in composition

From *College Composition and Communication* 54.3 (2003): 472–85.

theory and practice was nurtured at CCCC, which continues to be the one site that integrates my own continuing interest in these related areas.

In the 1970s, writing across the curriculum (WAC) with its faculty workshops and the resulting changes in teaching practices felt absolutely subversive to "education as usual." Promoting active learning strategies for students and interactive pedagogy for teachers while introducing what writing teachers knew to the rest of the campus certainly felt anti-establishment. This feeling was confirmed when the Faculty Senate at MTU, led by its officers who had never attended one of our writing workshops on the pedagogical uses of informal and formal writing, conducted a study of our WAC program and then debated a resolution demanding we stop suggesting to students and teachers that there are purposes for writing in which correct spelling, punctuation, and grammar are not essential ("the touchy-feely curriculum," remarked one senator). The resolution was narrowly defeated.

At roughly the same time, WAC, writing to learn, and interdisciplinary connections were flourishing nationally. Toby Fulwiler, Elaine Maimon, and Linda Peterson, among others, conspired at the 1978 CCCC convention in Denver to lobby Frank D'Angelo, the program chair for 1979 in Minneapolis, to make writing across the curriculum that convention's theme — and so it was. Later, D'Angelo recalled that every time he got on or off an elevator in Denver, someone would suggest to him that WAC be next year's theme. Since Minneapolis is "just" a seven-hour drive from MTU in Houghton, twenty-five of my colleagues and I were able to participate in that CCCC convention — yet another way that CCCC's inclusiveness supported the work we were doing on our own campus. Further direct support came in 1982 when NCTE published our book *Language Connections: Writing and Reading Across the Curriculum*, a collection by fourteen MTU faculty (Fulwiler and Young). We recognized the necessity for collegial collaboration centered on the teaching of writing that we had encountered at CCCC and attempted to replicate on our own campus.

However, no matter how much of an insider I was becoming in the field of composition, the "literature establishment" reminded me that I was an outsider in English departments when I suggested substantive change and reallocation of budgets or positions in support of writing programs — thus providing continual reassurance that I was, indeed, a provocateur. Like many of you, I enjoy teaching literature as well as composition, and WAC enables me to combine these two interests by focusing on writing across the literature curriculum. When I attempt to fully integrate writing in a literature course, such as the British Romantics or Victorians, I face the same issues that professors in chemistry or engineering face: how to cover the content — especially when the content of literature courses includes a canon that is continually expanding to include women's voices, ethnic voices, cultural studies, and newly recognized genres — and, at the same time, to regularly use writing to learn strategies, group exercises, electronic forums, and formal critical writing based on research, drafting, feedback, and revising. Currently, teaching literature enables me to better contribute to WAC by collaborating with colleagues on a new poetry-across-the-curriculum (PAC) project at Clemson University in which students develop their language abilities and learn course content by using all three of James Britton's functions for written language: expressive, transactional, and poetic (see *Language and Learning*). When students write poetry in an accounting, biology, engineering, literature, or psychology course, they are not writing *across* the curriculum nor writing *in* the discipline but writing *against* the curriculum. Downright subversive of "education as usual."

POETRY ACROSS THE CURRICULUM

The purpose of poetry across the curriculum, as we conceive it, is not to teach students to be better poets but to provide opportunities for them to use written language to engage course content in meaningful ways. For many students, creating a poem provides a way into disciplinary discussions in which the writers' own poetic language engages, recasts, and critiques disciplinary knowledge without having to conform to the conventions of what to them is often an alien discourse. For other students, who know the "formula" when they are required to write a lab report or book review, composing a poem occasions disequilibrium because they have learned to mimic the prose of familiar "school" discourse, and now to write poetry they must rethink form and content. As one colleague said recently in describing the academic writing of such students, "they just go on automatic pilot." Yet many of these students, both the novices and the automatic pilots, respond enthusiastically to writing a poem on an academic topic. As teachers, we seek to provide these inexperienced poets with writing tasks that are unpredictable — tasks that keep writers off balance, that shut off the automatic pilot.

For example, when people write poetically and express their ideas and values about science in nonscientific language, freedom from scientific discourse creates opportunities to make personal connections to what they are writing about. Writers are free to invent their own poetic language in order to find fresh insights into their learning as well as imaginative and innovative ways to communicate with others. Writers take the unfamiliar knowledge they are learning in the class and attempt to integrate it into the familiar — to integrate the new knowledge into what they already know — and thereby assimilate the new, or enrich it, or critique it. My colleagues and I consider the composing of poetry in the disciplines to be creative writing as a mode of learning — low stake but somehow risky, personal but somehow social, alien but somehow accessible. Brief poems, in particular, can easily be read aloud to classmates and used to enhance perspectives and collaborative participation on the content being studied.

Our primary theoretical framework draws on our understanding of the poetic function of language as developed in the work of Britton and his colleagues at the Schools Council Project in England, *The Development of Language Abilities (11–18)*. Britton asserts that poetic writing involves a kind of learning different from the learning in transactional or functional writing. In many instances, creative writing is connected to creative thinking and problem solving, to alternative and innovative ways of seeing and doing.

Britton speculates that both the freedom and the discipline of the artist's perspective enable us to express our values. For example, when we assume the artist's role in writing, we write in what Britton calls the "spectator" role. Writing in the spectator role frees the imagination to reflect on experience and to engage language in such a way that meaning is shaped and reshaped by an active but disinterested mind (not *as* interested in pleasing the teacher, getting an "A," or other "business" concerns). In *Language and Learning*, Britton writes: "As spectators, we use language to contemplate what has happened to us or to other people, or what might conceivably happen; in other words, we improvise upon our world representation — and we may do so either to enrich it, to embroider it, to fill its gaps and extend its frontiers, or to iron out its inconsistencies" (6). This activity is fundamentally different from composing transactional writing, the purposeful writing we do to transact the world's business in the vested "participant" role, that role in which we are actively or tacitly involved primarily in persuasion (selling a product, changing a mind, influencing a decision, or participating in the making of knowledge in a particular discipline — such as a scientific research report or journal article). This is not to deny rhetorical purposes for poetry but, rather, to recognize that poetic to transactional writing exists along a continuum where the writer's stance toward language and audience changes the more one writes in either the spectator or the participant role. Students often attest to the "freedom" of writing poetically once they develop trust that the teacher is encouraging creativity and risk taking rather than judging their artistic ability. "I never thought about science that way before," students say, or "I was able to say what I really thought," or "there is no one right way to write a poem."

WRITING ACROSS THE LITERATURE CURRICULUM

When I teach a literature class, in addition to critical essays, freewrites, and online discussion boards, students are required to write poetry in response to the literature they are reading. In asking them to do so, I have eight goals for students: (1) to experience literature as producers as well as consumers; (2) to read poetry carefully and imaginatively; (3) to gain new understandings and perspectives about how poetry works; (4) to develop a personal connection (feelings and values) to the literature they are reading; (5) to pay close attention to the possibilities of language; (6) to express voice and to make discoveries about their own voices; (7) to behave as writers serious about the writing they do; and (8) to surprise themselves, each other, and me.

In spring 2002, I taught The Romantic Period, a course devoted to British writers at the end of the eighteenth century and the first half of the nineteenth. After we read selections about slavery and the slave trade, including narratives by former slaves Olaudah Equiano and Mary Prince, students wrote a poem in response. A particularly effective and engaging example is this poem by Tara M. Hanshaw.

interracial

strong sable hands,
luminous white smile like
in my third grade textbook
(black face-rags-crosshatched back)
the green eyes he borrowed
from that white man with the whip
lifetimes ago,
the man that (beat) (raped) owned
the ghosts that still dwell in those
eyes-
so forgiving of my flesh (so pale)
and of my father's forbidding nudge
and silence,
the hard stares of strangers
(colors don't mix)
pointing fingers, good 'ole boys snicker,
flags flutter in the southern winds-
but the warm hugs from his mama
who lets me call her such,
the acceptance of his family,
the dinners to which i am invited
and the ones (at my parents') where he is not-
　　　　　　　who is savage?
Times have changed
　　　　　　　(we are free!)
　　　　　　　　　　but we are still slaves to
　　　　　　　　　　the oppression of ignorance,
　　　　　　　　　　the bigotry that claims
　　　　　　　　　　his filthy darkness taints my
　　　　　　　　　　innocent clean whiteness
　　　　　　　　　　where he clasps my hand
　　　　　　　　　　protectively,
　　　　　　　　　　with love.
(to be silent is to endorse it)

Tara's poem and those of many of her classmates moved me. Let me see if I can explain why, knowing as I do that a prose analysis does not fully capture a poem's essence. And let me do so in a way that does not critique the poem as a creative writing teacher or literary critic might because, like my colleagues in biology and psychology, my purpose for this assignment was to give Tara a writing-to-learn opportunity about the disciplinary content we were study-ing, not to provide her with direct instruction and feedback on how to write better poetry. Tara uses sophisticated poetic strategies not necessarily avail-able to all of her classmates, for example, a monologue with an internal dialog in parenthesis. In doing so, she displays imagination, personal engagement, and the close attention to language that I want to help develop in all of my students as readers and writers.

Tara's poem describes a contemporary interracial love relationship to which a white woman's parents are opposed, even hostile, while the black man's family is accepting and hospitable. The tale unfolds through the speaker's reflections, memories, feelings, and thoughts about race and interracial relationships. There is a historical emphasis with "Times have changed" — the black man is descended from slaves and apparently conceived in interracial violence "whip," "(beat) (raped)" — the white master raping the black man's ancestor. This historical reference connects the present reality directly to the slave narratives we have been reading. One subtle irony of the poem with its complex thoughts and feelings is that the black man whose ancestor was conceived in hatred and violence represents love.

I like the visual portrayal on the page — the way lines are arranged and the movement back in forth in time and then a movement to the future — where we, ironically, are still slaves ("not free at all") to that bigotry "that claims his filthy darkness" — a reference to her father's voice or that of the dominant white southern society. The last line "(to be silent is to endorse it)" is richer in ambiguity because of the textual representation. The speaker of the poem, in one sense, is speaking out against racism. Yet, why the parenthesis that implies this sentiment is an aside or a kind of silent dialog?

The poem draws me further into interracial experience through color imagery (black, white, green, pale) and "hand" imagery. Strangers stare and "good ole' boys snicker" because "(colors don't mix)," and that's what her parents apparently say with their "silence." But the truth is that colors do mix — his sable hands and white smile and their hands together "with love" at the end demonstrate that. His clasping of her hand "protectively" is ironic and profound within the context of this poem, for elsewhere the hand imagery is associated with white bigotry and violence, the hand that smacks the whip during slavery and the "pointing fingers" on the hands of contemporary racists. He protects her with love, but there is no escaping the "ghosts that still dwell" in those green eyes and the racial hatred and history that infuses and complicates their lives. Thus the poem begins with black/white imagery and ends with the irony of her "innocent clean whiteness" and "his filthy darkness," ironic because at times the white in this poem symbolizes hate, violence, and separation, and the black (he and his mama) enact community, love, and unity.

The overall impact of Tara's poem on me is compassion for the interracial couple living in a racist society. I have been invited into a world not my own as created by this poet, and I have been asked to consider the legacy of slavery on contemporary race relations from a new, immediate, and intense perspective. My understanding and my empathy are renewed and enlarged by this student's insight. Within the context of this course on British Romantic writers, the poet William Blake in "The Little Black Boy" provides readers with a similar experience, creating a dramatic situation in which to explore and express the often invisible toll racism takes on human aspirations. Such writing is the work of poets, whether the famous William Blake or the Clemson student, Tara Hanshaw, and this is a key point I want my students to learn and to experience through their own writing and our collective reading.

Some students in this course responded to the readings by creating poetic monologues set dramatically and historically in the time of slavery. In "Woman of the House," Kimaris Toogood writes from the point of view of a plantation wife whose husband brings a slave "domestic" into the home to do housework but then favors her and fathers children by her, as the plantation wife deteriorates into hatred, jealousy, and drunkenness. The poem ends "I have not given my husband an heir, his name will not live on./But his blood will." Chris Epting writes in "The Song of the Waves" from the perspective of a slave entrapped on a ship during the Middle Passage — dreaming of his wife left behind in Africa: "And when the salt water mingles with the air,/I shall breathe deep of you and hope that somewhere you are breathing me in also." Janice Holmes in "Tea at Bellamy's" writes from the point of view of a slave domestic expressing her anger at slave owners who believe they are doing God's work by bringing Christianity and Western values to their slaves. This poem ends, "They say the sun never sets on the British Empire,/I hope that the sun sets it on fire."

This ensemble of student voices resonates against one another and against the Romantic Period literature we are reading, thus creating for many students a richer personal connection and communal experience with literature, both canonical literature and the insightful, moving literature the students themselves are composing. Tara reinforces this connection when she writes in a reflective essay: "I have truly enjoyed the experience of expressing myself through poetry and in reading the poems of classmates. It gives each of us a voice and a chance to write of our own experiences, opinions, and emotions instead of simply reading and memorizing parts of others' writing." On the first day of class, Tara had responded to a prompt asking what contributions she planned to make to the class. She wrote: "I am pretty shy. Even if I don't speak much, please know that I am paying attention." And she was true to her prediction, not participating in class discussions but obviously paying attention and eventually contributing to our collaborative learning through the poetry she wrote. Her poetic voice is strong and confident, and it surprised me and others accustomed to her silence. Kimaris also surprised herself as well. On the first day of class, she had written: "I am not a huge fan of poetry: writing or reading." Two months later, in a reflective essay about her poem "Woman of the House" she wrote: "I had originally had several drafts of this one poem because I was writing it with divided opinions about the tone of the poem. But once I opened up to the idea that I was to put more of me, unedited, into the poem, it flowed like a river. The result was a piece that I truly admired, even stuck it on the Fridge!" As I reread the poems and the reflective essays my students wrote that semester and as I glance back at my eight goals for the poetry assignment, I am persuaded that these goals were fulfilled by the poems Tara, Kimaris, Chris, Janice, and their classmates wrote.

WRITING ACROSS THE PSYCHOLOGY CURRICULUM

Currently, thirty faculty are participating in Clemson's PAC project. They represent all five colleges and numerous academic departments, and they require students to write poetry in response to course readings and other content-related prompts. This ongoing project (2000–2003), a part of Clemson's broader Communication-Across-the-Curriculum program, involves faculty workshops and informal luncheons; an anthology of selected student poems gathered from each participating class; print editions of whole sets of poems from particular classes (among them biology, horticulture, music, and psychology); judging sessions by interdisciplinary groups of faculty; certificates of achievement and bookstore gift certificates awarded to selected authors; Web publication of selected poems <http://people.clemson.edu/~apyoung/>; and ongoing formative assessment.

One PAC teacher, Professor of Psychology Jan Murdoch, assigns students to write poems in the Clinical Practicum course. She writes: "For many students, this course is their first hands-on experience with individuals having diagnosed mental disorders. Writing poems, either from their own perspective or their clients' perspectives, provided students an opportunity to express their reactions to the unique client-therapist interaction." One of the poems Murdoch received was "I watch those hands . . ." by Amanda Oberdorff, a poem that moved her, Amanda's classmates, me, and an interdisciplinary faculty committee.

> I watch those hands that are still too small
> To grasp what I carry with ease.
> But while my own hands resign themselves
> To the tasks that comprise adulthood
> His move with frantic fascination
> To interpret the details of life.
> With black ink and pencil lead
> I record the Crayola spectrum of his day.
> And while he touches the worms and critters
> Whose sensation I've long since abandoned
> I look at my own hands and wonder
> Do my fingers point direction for him
> Or is his easy grip pulling me
> To the memories and excitement that age forgets?

Amanda's language beckons me into yet another world not of my own making, one in which her experience as a therapist colors my imaginings of growing older, childhood play, sense of loss, mental disorders, this clinician speaker as a reflective and responsible human being, this poet as a spectator on her own experience. I'm in awe that Amanda found the language to describe a part of her experience with this young child, to connect it imaginatively and quizzically to her course work in psychology, to portray the internal tension between clinical observer and compassionate human being, and to connect it to my world and the worlds of other readers — all this, and more, in fewer than one hundred words.

The poem describes the experience of an adult, perhaps a student clinician or a licensed therapist, recording clinical observations of a child at play. The poem sets up immediately a contrast between the adult and the child with the image of the little hands of the child and the larger hands of the adult. The speaker's hands are "resigned" while the child's move "with frantic fascination to interpret the details of life," a task we generally associate with an adult, perhaps a psychologist. While the child *interprets* the details of life, the adult *records* the details of this clinical session. The emotional and psychological distance between the child and the adult is further emphasized by the connotations of "black ink and pencil lead" contrasted with "Crayola spectrum." The child curiously touches "worms and critters," causing the speaker's hands to merge image and question: just who is pointing direction for whom?

This poem effectively illustrates "writing against the curriculum" in portraying the speaker's functional writing — the recording of the details necessary for a clinical evaluation, the rote writing as if on an automatic pilot while the mind wanders — and contrasting this professional writing with Amanda's own poetic writing. The functional writing is necessary for training clinicians; the poetic writing enables Amanda to reflect on her experience and learn from it. And in writing poetically, Amanda expresses through her speaker's voice some doubts about disciplinary knowledge and practice — a recognition that the professional life of a therapist is often perplexing and emotionally challenging, a life confronting situations in which there are no easy textbook answers. In the drama described in the poem, the speaker questions the adult's abandonment of youthful sensations and questions the clinician's authority to confidently point direction. Amanda can imagine what it would be like one day to be a therapist, but she doesn't have to imagine one day being a poet. She is a poet.

WHY POETRY?

My colleagues and I found that when students write poetry in response to a specific assignment carefully constructed to fulfill a course goal, under the tutelage of an encouraging teacher who makes students feel "safe" as they compose and share, most authors do express fresh perspectives on disciplinary knowledge and develop better understanding of multiple purposes, connections, and contexts for that knowledge.

But why poetry? I think that other forms of creative writing composed in the spectator role, such as short stories and plays, would provide students with similar opportunities for learning and expression. However, poetry's intensity of language and succinctness allow for pedagogical use in the disciplines in ways that longer and more time-consuming writing tasks do not. When poems are assigned as brief, informal, writing-to-learn activities, students are free to spend as much time writing them as they wish — and undoubtedly some writers spend less than ten minutes and others spend an hour or more — but the choice is theirs. Because the quality of a poem is not commented on critically or graded, teachers can set parameters on their own reading time as well. And short poems, like the two I've presented, can easily be read aloud to the class to enhance perspectives and collaborative participation on the content being studied.

In writing poetry students write outside the discourse of the discipline; at the same time, they often make connections to the discipline not typically available when they attempt to follow the discipline's rhetorical conventions. Usually they are being graded on how well they follow those conventions and how quickly they learn the discourse of an insider. Writing poems across the curriculum interrupts their expectations for disciplinary writing and thinking; for many poets it loosens the requirement to think inside the curriculum. Using the writing of poetry as a tool for learning should not be an esoteric activity but, rather, an important strategy for enhancing student learning and influencing campus culture.

Acknowledgments: I thank Tara Hanshaw and Amanda Oberdorff for permission to publish their poems; my colleagues at Clemson in the PAC project, particularly Patricia Connor-Greene, Jan Murdoch, Catherine Paul, and Jerry Waldvogel; Jonathan Monroe at Cornell for the concept of writing *against* the curriculum and our subsequent discussions; and Donna Reiss for her thoughtful responses to both this article and the 2002 CCCC Exemplar talk on which it is based.

WORKS CITED

Britton, James. *Language and Learning*, 2nd ed. Portsmouth, NH: Boynton/Cook, 1993.
Britton, James, Tony Burgess, Nancy Martin, Alex McLeod, and Harold Rosen. *The Development of Writing Abilities (11–18)*. London: Macmillan Education, 1975.
Fulwiler, Toby, and Art Young. *Language Connections: Writing and Reading Across the Curriculum*. Urbana, IL: NCTE, 1982.
Young, Art. *Shelley and Nonviolence*. The Hague: Mouton, 1975.
———. "Technical Communications and Freshman Composition." *The Technical Writing Teacher* 1.1 (1973): 10–14.

11   Introducing Students to Disciplinary Genres: The Role of the General Composition Course

PATRICIA LINTON, ROBERT MADIGAN,
AND SUSAN JOHNSON

Recent discussions of disciplinary writing have addressed the possibility that disciplinary genres cannot be taught. In particular, they have considered the proposition that if we understand disciplinary writing as a product of situated cognition, then it cannot be taught effectively by English faculty as part of a composition curriculum. David Russell, drawing on Vygotsky and Dewey, has argued this point forcefully:

> [Because writing is] a matter of learning to participate in some historically situated human activity that requires some kind(s) of writing, it cannot be learned apart from the problems, the habits, the activities — the subject matter — of some group that found the need to write in that way to solve a problem or carry on its activities. (194)

Russell recognizes that one logical consequence of this way of understanding writing might be "to drop the abstraction (and perhaps the institution) of general composition courses in higher education" (195).

Furthermore, it may be the case that even within the disciplines, skill in writing can be learned (as one component of apprenticeship) but not taught. Carol Berkenkotter and Thomas N. Huckin have observed that "generally the enculturation into the practices of disciplinary communities is 'picked up' in the local milieu of the culture rather than being explicitly taught" (485). They focus attention on the question of when this initiation into disciplinary practices actually occurs, suggesting that what undergraduate students acquire are pedagogical genres rather than disciplinary discourse models. In other words, most undergraduate students acquire transitional genres which share some of the features of disciplinary writing but are situated in classroom contexts. For this reason, Berkenkotter and Huckin argue that it may not be reasonable to expect undergraduates to acquire true disciplinary style and that modified teaching objectives may be more valid at the baccalaureate level. In support of this view, they suggest that writing-across-the-curriculum activi-

From *Across the Disciplines* 1.2 (October 1994): 63–78.

ties might reinforce the idea that classroom genres should not be assessed according to the standards for disciplinary genres (488).

Aviva Freedman raises the possibility that explicit teaching of disciplinary genres may be not only ineffective but even harmful. She argues that at best it may have little effect on students' development of the tacit knowledge needed to practice disciplinary writing. On the other hand, explicit teaching may lead students to overgeneralize rules which only partially encode the rhetorical practices of a discipline, and particularly when presented by writing specialists rather than faculty in the disciplines, may cause students to attend to the wrong things and thereby actually impede the process of enculturation (234).

We believe, with Joseph Williams and Gregory Colomb, that explicit teaching is beneficial, and we argue that it is particularly so for undergraduates, who are just at the thresholds of their disciplines. Most undergraduate writers lack contextualized knowledge of the disciplines to which they are being introduced. For them, the generative potential of disciplinary forms is especially important: When students try to practice the linguistic features of disciplinary genres, they must seek at the same time the kinds of substantive information those genres convey. As Williams and Colomb propose, even students who are not fully socialized are "compelled to focus on, perhaps even to generate, the knowledge for those generic moves" (262).

We suggest that in the process of introducing students to disciplinary genres, the roles of faculty in composition and faculty in the disciplines are distinct but complementary. English faculty can prepare the ground for acquisition of disciplinary style — which typically takes place gradually throughout the period of undergraduate and graduate study. Explicit teaching of writing by faculty within the disciplines can further ease the task undergraduates face as they move toward mastery. Our position rests on two fundamental propositions. First, even if "all" that general composition courses can accomplish is to introduce students to formal differences in the writing characteristic of different disciplines, that introduction is acquisition of disciplinary style nevertheless. Noticing the crucial surface stage in features of a disciplinary genre is not a trivial matter, but a subtle and extremely important one. Second, a focus on the acquisition of disciplinary style is desirable at the undergraduate level because of its pedagogical role in fostering students' enculturation into their chosen fields. Truly mastering a disciplinary style means mastering the reasoning, the conventions, and the epistemological assumptions of the relevant discourse community; because completion of the undergraduate major is typically the first stage in mastery of the discipline, it makes sense to incorporate explicit attention to writing at that level.

THE ROLE OF ENGLISH FACULTY

English faculty are in the best position to introduce students to the concepts of discourse communities and disciplinary style. Samples of writing across different disciplines can be used to illustrate to beginning college students how writing varies with the setting. This fact is an important discovery for students and becomes itself a conceptual tool to assist them in dealing with the varied writing assignments encountered during their lives. Unless they become academics, students are unlikely to practice in their careers the kind of writing they produce in college courses. But they will have to adapt to patterns in the form and style of writing in their professional settings. Job promotions, career changes, and avocational pursuits can all move individuals into new discourse communities and present them with writing challenges that cannot be anticipated by formal instruction. A successful introduction to disciplinary styles prepares students to attend to the writing demands of new situations and thus speeds their enculturation into new communities.

The undergraduate curriculum itself presents many writing challenges. Variations in academic writing are more numerous and more fundamental than we once perceived. Charles Bazerman has shown that what counts as knowledge differs across disciplines and that disciplinary writing styles have grown out of varying conceptions of what and how we know. Susan Peck MacDonald's work has extended that insight; she has identified systematic differences at the sentence level, demonstrating not only that disciplines privilege different kinds of information but also that those interests are reflected and reinforced in the syntax of the sentence. Disciplinary styles are not just frames or shells into which content can be cast, but habits of thought and communication grounded in the objectives, values, and "world view" of each discipline. To ignore these realities in a general composition course seems irresponsible. A decade ago, Elaine Maimon proposed that with help from faculty in the disciplines English faculty could "make explicit the tacit conventions of a variety of genres" (113). Similarly Leslie E. Moore and Linda H. Peterson have suggested, "[I]f English faculty cannot bring a knowledge of the content and methodologies of various disciplines to the composition classroom, they can bring something else that is essential: an understanding of how conventions operate in a piece of written discourse" (466–67).

THE GENERAL COMPOSITION COURSE

Composition courses can introduce students to ways in which writing produced in different disciplines can be expected to vary. Like most introductory courses, general composition courses should aim to survey material which will be developed more fully as students progress. One of the goals of Writing Across the Curriculum has been to counter the notion, in the minds of students and faculty alike, that a single composition course — or, more likely, a sequence of required courses — completes a program of instruction, that it prepares students to "go forth and write" without further formal instruction. The general composition sequence should inform students about the task that lies before them and prepare them to assimilate new genres (ideally with the help of explicit instruction from faculty in the disciplines).

Although academic writing is not monolithic, there are at least three categories of conventions which occur in all academic genres. Conventions of structure control the flow of the argument and, more importantly, determine the kinds of cues available to readers. Conventions of reference establish standard ways of addressing the work of other scholars; they encode the formal or public relationships among members of the discourse community. Finally, conventions of language guide phrasing at the sentence level: they reflect characteristic choices of syntax and diction. Undergraduates in the early stages of their academic careers — toward the end of their first semester and particularly during the second semester of a two-semester sequence — can understand the ways in which writing conventions reflect the values and serve the needs of specialized communities of writers, and they can begin to recognize patterns and variations in selected samples of academic texts.

Conventions of Structure

Students can learn to observe disciplinary patterns in the ways academic writing is structured. Although there is, as Freedman notes, danger in overgeneralization, it is valuable for students to know that there are certain rhetorical moves which are familiar and accepted within particular discourse communities. In empirical reports, it is conventional for detailed presentation of data to precede discussion of the conclusion to be drawn from them. In a literary essay, on the other hand, presentation of the author's central insight (the conclusion or endpoint of reasoning) typically comes much earlier and is followed by detailed discussion of supporting data. Handbooks for freshman composition courses generally offer students a menu of devices for the opening sentence or opening paragraph of an essay. It is important for students to know that particular options are more appropriate to one discipline than another. For example, opening a literary essay with an anecdote or a play on words or a quotation may be a sign of sophistication, but opening an empirical report in the same way would be extremely unconventional and would mark the writer as an outsider.

All academic writing exhibits patterns that Peter Elbow has called "conventions of explicitness" — that is, every mode of academic writing has ways of announcing its own structure and directing attention to its main points. "Even though there is a wide range of custom as to the degree of signposting in different academic discourses, signposting is probably the most general or common textual convention of academic discourse" (Elbow 144). For example, academic writing typically provides some sort of preview of its own objectives at or near the beginning of an article. In the humanities, as Elbow points out, it is particularly conventional to articulate the thesis near the start of an essay; the stress in many composition texts on announcing the thesis explicitly and early reflects the practice of their authors. The statement of thesis may be accompanied by even more detailed previewing: a listing of the principal stages in the development of the argument. In addition, academic writing in the humanities tends to be particularly attentive to signposting in the form of explicit sentence-level transitions, as well as mini-introductions and conclusions as the argument proceeds: here's where we've been and here's where we're going; thus . . . next. The use of headings and subheadings to announce subsections of the essay is optional but less common, certainly not required by convention.

The early introduction of an explicit thesis is by far the most common way of announcing in advance the point an essay will make. But in the humanities, another familiar strategy to cue readers to the writer's interests and strategies is the use of an epigraph. From the perspective of enculturated readers, epigraphs offer an especially elegant way of previewing because they accomplish more than one task: a well-chosen quotation both reveals and conceals, guides readers and challenges them; at the same time it often serves to establish the writer's scholarly credentials.

Writing in the natural and social sciences offers a preview of significant content, but not always by means of an explicit thesis statement early in the article. By convention, scholarly articles in these disciplines are preceded by an abstract or initial summary; before they begin the text of an article, readers have considerable insight concerning where it is going and how it expects to get there. Sometimes there is a true thesis statement near the end of the introduction, but more often what is stated in the introduction is a hypothesis, which focuses the issue yet preserves the possibility that the outcome may be unexpected.

Another convention of explicitness in the natural and social sciences is the nearly universal use of headings and subheadings to divide the text and announce its content. In empirical reports, the labeling and sequence of the major subsections are prescribed: introduction, methods, results, discussion. The specificity and universality of the convention are not trivial matters. These headings, in the order specified, signal not only the content or objective of each section, but the writer's commitment to one of the fundamental values underlying the empirical disciplines: the importance of shared, replicated methodology. Practitioners have long recognized that the genre of the empirical report is not so much a record of the actual process of thinking and doing as it is a rhetorical strategy for imposing a particular kind of order on experience (Gross, "Does" 437–39). By presenting their work in the conventional structure, with the customary signposting, researchers make the messiness of ordinary experience — which is more recursive, less linear, less neat than the model — conform to the ideal of the empirical method. Noticing and imitating this kind of rhetorical restructuring contributes to students' development of the values of the discipline.

Conventions of Reference

All academic discourse requires attention to the work of other scholars; the way references to other writers and texts are managed is governed by disciplinary conventions. These patterns encode differences in the ways disciplines conceive the nature and purpose of intertextual dialogue.

Strategic Use of Citations.   The incorporation of citations in a scholarly text accomplishes a variety of different purposes, as John M. Swales has observed

(6–7). First, writers need to establish their credentials as masters of the literature in the field. Second, they display strategic judgment in their choices from among a range of possible citations. It may be prudent or even necessary for publication to establish professional alignments by including certain citations. For academic writers, the choice of citations becomes a subtle argument for the centrality or prominence of particular sources; texts and writers that are cited frequently acquire status, while citation of new or less familiar work can bring it wider notice. Finally, writers use citation and discussion of particular sources as a means to establish the focus and stance of the present text. The relative importance of these rhetorical objectives varies by discipline.

In empirical reports, for example, selecting references effectively and incorporating them in the right places is more important than discussing them. Listing citations without detailed discussion of the work referenced is accepted practice. Merely naming the source serves as a subtle and highly condensed form of communication with other members of the discourse community. Indeed, it may be difficult for an uninitiated reader to tell from the context exactly what the publication cited is about or how it relates to the work under discussion. The function of the reference is not to say anything substantive about the work cited, but to encode other kinds of communication between writer and readers. At first, it may seem to students that being allowed to drop names is easier than extended discussion; they do not appreciate the importance of citing the right sources. It is true that English faculty won't know the relevant sources for other disciplines, but they can alert students to some possible missteps — for example, the risks in citing a source outside the particular target discourse community.

In other disciplines (for example, philosophy or literary criticism) a long string of unexamined citations is less common and likely to seem superficial, the strategy of a novice rather than an initiate. In the humanities, analysis (rather than identification) of previous work is often used strategically to anchor a discussion. One of the most common ways for writers to put an issue on the table is to select a particular precursor for extended discussion, focusing on points of convergence as well as points where the present text will diverge. While it is still true that the subtleties of the argument are inaccessible to an outsider or a neophyte, the conventional treatment of sources is obviously less telegraphic and more discursive.

Quotation.   In many freshman composition courses, considerable attention is paid to the mechanics of incorporating references to source material within a new text. Typically, students are expected to learn the phrasing and punctuation of direct and indirect quotation, the uses of block quotations as well as shorter quotations incorporated within paragraphs or sentences. In addition, students are taught to avoid dropping quotations or citations of sources into the text without analysis or discussion.

In fact, however, the use of frequent or extended quotation is a discipline-specific feature, more characteristic of the humanities than the sciences. A glance at the pages of a journal publishing literary criticism is likely to reveal quotations on every page; in journals publishing articles on cognitive psychology or archeology, quotations are quite rare. In such disciplines, students are expected to do extensive research and to master literature relevant to the problem they are addressing, but they are likely to lose points if they include the exact language of the original. Even a crucial insight, distinctively phrased, is more often paraphrased than quoted; block quotations are almost unknown.

A reliance on direct quotation is natural and essential in a discipline like literary criticism where the objects of study are texts. However, the habit of direct quotation is so common in the humanities and so uncommon in the empirical sciences that it seems to coincide, in practice if not in origin, with other differences in the relationships among members of a discourse community and the uses writers make of each other's work. In the humanities, the writer often defines a position by distinguishing it from that of others. New learning is as likely to result from revisiting old territory as from actually breaking "new" ground. Advances in understanding an issue or a text can be conceived as "thickening," elaborating, making more complex. Although literary scholars would be likely to agree that the "truth" toward which the discipline proceeds is multi-layered and encompasses a variety of different, often conflicting, contributions, the way an individual scholar presents a contribution is often by disputing or displacing work that has gone before. There is nothing particularly disturbing about standing apart or presenting work that represents a radical departure from the prevailing norms — perhaps a startlingly new reading of a literary text. Enterprises like literary criticism, philosophy, and history need revisionist thinking. The enabling fiction which justifies new contributions may be that previous work has been "wrong," "blind," or inadequate in a significant way.

Progress in the empirical disciplines, on the other hand, depends upon the cumulative, collaborative nature of the scientific enterprise. As Kuhn implies, the most common and perhaps overall the most satisfying kind of contribution is to add a brick to the wall without displacing parts of the wall that are already in place. Obviously, identification of a fundamental flaw or instability requires radical rebuilding, but tearing down the wall and starting over sets everybody back. Researchers who produce completely anomalous findings are likely, initially at least, to be distressed and to be concerned about the validity of their own work. While relationships among members of scientific communities are no less hierarchical and no less competitive than those of other intellectual communities, the governing myth is one of disinterested cooperation.

The habit of avoiding direct quotation is useful to this community in two ways. First, the practice of rephrasing minimizes explicit attention to the language in which ideas are expressed and contributes to what George Dillon has called "the rhetoric of objectivity." In theory, it is the core of the insight or observation which is available for restatement. Second, the convention of condensing and paraphrasing rather than quoting directly diminishes the need for public dispute or for the kind of clarification that sometimes seems quibbling. The narrow but inevitable distance between a statement and its paraphrase creates a useful space for redirecting language in ways that support new work. Although writers are expected to guard against actual distortion of another's point, a certain amount of accommodation is the norm.

Thus a relatively superficial difference in the texts produced in different disciplines, observable on the page, pointed out to students and imitated by them, suggests a crucial distinction in the assumptions of different disciplines about knowledge and knowledge-making. Dispensing with direct quotation assumes that ideas are separable from the language in which they are expressed. Conversely, heavy emphasis on direct quotation, particularly when quotation is accompanied by extensive explication, assumes that language and meaning are inextricable.

Conventions of Language

Preparing students to assimilate the conventions of language they will encounter in their disciplines is the most demanding and dangerous portion of a general composition course which addresses disciplinary genres. Useful information associated with conventions of structure and reference can be communicated to students as concrete examples and suggestions for practice. Students at an introductory level can examine texts to determine whether a discourse community typically uses — or doesn't use — quotations. They can be guided in observing the different functions references perform in disciplinary texts. They can compose texts which imitate the way typical written works in the discipline are organized. But with respect to the nuances of language, this approach is more difficult — for several fundamental reasons, not the least of which may be the inability of the typical English instructor to recognize and articulate such features.

Although analysis of disciplinary genres has been conducted largely by specialists in composition (for the most part faculty in English departments), the insight it has produced forces us to question whether English faculty are qualified to teach the language of academic writing in other disciplines. Composition instructors typically have little or no experience writing outside their own fields. In many colleges and universities, composition is taught by people steeped in the traditional English curriculum who have a sketchy understanding of and no admiration for the writing produced in other fields. Lester Faigley and Kristine Hansen observe that "the conventional four-part organization of a psychology report specified in the APA Style Sheet embodies a world view about how knowledge can be verified, a world view that few English teachers share or are willing to assimilate" (148). Many English faculty give students and colleagues the impression that they regard writing in other disciplines as pedestrian at best, because features they associate with fine writing (vivid metaphors, perhaps, or active verbs) are missing. On the other hand unfamiliar rhetorical moves may not be valued or even recognized. People who have never written lab reports or case studies cannot appreciate the way fully enculturated writers communicate with one another — the way they use and "manipulate" conventions, the way a particular choice of language may encode a subtext evident to readers in the discourse community — let alone coach students to attempt such writing.

Further, an English teacher venturing into these waters risks offending colleagues in the disciplines whose writing styles are addressed. Even scholars specializing in composition or rhetoric often fail to perceive how often their characterizations of intentions and practices in other fields strike a false note. It is hard for English faculty to appreciate how annoying it may be for writers in empirical disciplines to be told that they "manipulate conventions" when "manipulation" suggests not an appropriate and admirable mastery of the form but deviousness, deceit, or a lapse in the forthrightness valued in the discipline.

To be successful in preparing students to assimilate conventions of language, an English instructor must develop sensitivity to these issues and adopt conservative instructional objectives that can be reasonably achieved. He or she should not be placed in the role of "expert" in the nuances of language in other disciplines but rather should use appropriate examples to instill in students the basic principle that conventions of language differ among academic writing genres. We nominate three topics for use in making that point.

Language as a Medium or a Product.   In some disciplines such as literary criticism, texts not only communicate, they are unabashed celebrations of language. Vivid metaphors, dramatic sentences, and self-conscious phrasing distinguish these works from writing in other disciplines where words are chosen to make language appear to be a transparent medium for expressing ideas. Writing in the natural and social sciences is an example of the latter, where diction and syntax work together to keep the reader's attention on the phenomenon under study, not the language used to describe it. Metaphors are not at all uncommon in empirical reports (where, for instance, measurements may be discussed in terms of "floor" or "ceiling" values), but they are likely to be conventional metaphors so familiar to enculturated readers that they do not call attention to themselves. Undergraduate students can learn to appreciate fundamental assumptions about language which underlie differences in disciplinary styles. A collection of carefully selected samples can prepare students to attend to the ways language is used in their disciplines and thus aid them in assimilating the style of their chosen fields.

Expressing Disagreement.   Writers must sometimes disagree with others in their fields, and the ways in which disagreement is expressed differ dramatically among disciplines. This is another area where distinctive language patterns can be identified that are interesting to students and also serve to reinforce the idea that there are differences in language conventions among disciplines. In some fields such as literary criticism, disagreement may be sharply expressed. Another view may be described as "willful revisionism" (Bethea 232), or a colleague may be said to be "truculently persist[ing] in crediting the discredited" (Battersby 51). In the discipline of history, such assertive rhetoric is rare; disagreement is gently handled or ignored. An alternative position is described as "too simple" (White 874). A historian with a different interpretation may be said to "take a sunnier view of the material" (Rogin 1076). In empirical disciplines such as psychology, disagreement is focused on the details of the empirical process and away from other writers as individuals. The generality of another's proposal may be challenged as Tenpenny and Shoben do in asserting that ". . . this [theoretical distinction] is not able to deal with an increasing number of results . . ." (25), or methodology may be questioned as illustrated by Hirshman and Durante: "The primary criticism is that the threshold-setting procedures used in previous experiments are not adequate to ensure that . . ." (255).

These examples show different conceptions of etiquette in disagreeing with colleagues. Although the subtler nuances of such language conventions are beyond the scope of a general composition course, their basic forms and the issues they index can be presented by English faculty in a way that prepares undergraduates to be more thoughtful readers and writers in their disciplines.

The Language of Conviction.   Handbooks used in composition courses often give students blanket advice to be direct and to avoid redundancy or "clutter" by eliminating qualifiers ("probably," "maybe," "I think," "In my judgment") and making assertions forthrightly. In particular, students are advised not to allow the use of such qualifiers to become a mannerism. In literary criticism, for example, it is understood that the writer is presenting his or her reading of the work and it is usually unnecessary to repeatedly emphasize the tentativeness of the enterprise. Within this disciplinary context, an appropriate degree of assertiveness conveys conviction.

In the conclusions of empirical reports, however, "hedged" wording — for example "tend," "suggest," "may," "it is probable that," "it is reasonable to conclude that" — serves an important function. Because empirical reports typically relate the data of the study to the discipline's current understanding of a recognized problem, the author is faced with a rhetorical task that requires a delicate balance. On the one hand the author must convince peers that the results have substantive implications, but on the other, the conclusions must not appear to extend beyond the data. One indication of this rhetorical tightrope is the frequency with which hedged wording is used to discuss the conclusions of empirical studies. Hedged wording implicitly recognizes the uncertain flow of the ongoing stream of empirical studies investigating complex phenomena. New findings can and do cause old conclusions to be abandoned. As Alan Gross has observed, the language is designed to convey the impression that theories are more tenuous and less permanent than the data that generate them, an idea that has characterized empirical disciplines since the time of Bacon (*Rhetoric* 69–74). By communicating proper respect for the empirical process, such wording has the rhetorical effect of making a hedged conclusion more convincing than a stronger claim.

THE ROLE OF FACULTY IN THE DISCIPLINES

We should begin by saying that the role of other faculty in improving the writing skills of their students is, and will remain, outside of the purview of the English department. We expect that these faculty will continue to employ a wide variety of strategies designed to improve the writing of their students. Nonetheless, the approach to discipline-specific writing proposed here would change the model of writing instruction current on most university campuses. Presently, most faculty view writing instruction as the responsibility and the expertise of faculty in the English department (even writing across the curriculum programs often involve "outreach" by members of the English department who participate directly in the instruction and assessment of writing in disciplines other than English). Many faculty would be surprised at the disciplinary differences identified by studies in composition; they share with some English faculty the assumption that good writing is readily identifiable and that good writing in one setting is good writing in another. As English courses move to explicitly prepare students to acquire disciplinary style, the operative model of writing in an academic setting is likely to evolve as well to one where faculty in the other disciplines feel responsibility to help their students master the relevant disciplinary style. We believe this will be the case, if for no other reason, because students primed in the ways we suggest here will be asking more focused questions that faculty in the disciplines will find interesting to address. Many of these faculty may come to accept the proposition that mastery of a discipline's writing style helps students acquire the discipline's style of thinking and problem solving. It is likely that disciplinary writing could become a more important pedagogical objective for these faculty than it is at present. We believe that such changes could revolutionize not only the composition course but also the general role of writing in college instruction. The effect may be an increase in experimentation with pedagogical approaches to disciplinary writing, carried out by individual faculty members in many disciplines. These innovations are likely to involve explicit teaching strategies in many varied forms. They will no doubt draw on existing guidebooks (such as Gelfand and Walker's *Mastering APA Style*) and also develop new directions. English faculty cannot expect to direct such efforts. But they can expect that studies in composition and rhetoric will be enriched by mutual exchanges with colleagues in the disciplines.

CONCLUDING COMMENTS

Presently, students in composition classes are offered more models of writing in the humanities and more practice in producing that kind of writing than any other. The result is that much of what they learn in composition is not transferable to writing in their other classes, let alone to writing in their professions. We believe that this need not be the case. Students can learn the kinds of conventions that can be expected to change across discourse communities. They can practice the surface features of generic form — and can profit particularly from comparative exercises. For example, working from a set of readings, students can compose introductions for two different disciplinary genres, an assignment that requires them to attempt different rhetorical moves in their opening sentences, in references to source material, and in the establishment of focus. They can practice modifying an argument by using the language of conviction appropriate to different disciplinary genres. By careful selection of material and staging of assignments, the general composition course (particularly the second course in a two-course sequence) can prepare students to adapt to the discourse communities they will encounter later. In examining the crucial issue of whether writing skills acquired in one context can be applied successfully in other situations, Michael Carter draws upon a fundamental distinction between general and local knowledge: general or abstract knowledge of writing should be applicable across different contexts, while local knowledge is context specific; he argues for the importance of both general and local knowledge in writing, with general knowledge particularly critical when writers approach unfamiliar writing tasks (269–71). Heretofore, composition specialists have typically assumed that examination of disciplinary writing relies upon local knowledge and therefore is beyond the scope of the introductory composition course. The problem is that many of us have been offering local knowledge (the patterns of structure, reference, and language characteristic of writing in the humanities) as general knowledge. In fact, however, the required composition course presents a unique opportunity to equip students with heuristically useful general knowledge about writing conventions in the disciplines.

WORKS CITED

Battersby, James L. "Professionalism, Relativism, and Rationality." *PMLA* 107 (1992): 51–64.
Bazerman, Charles. *Shaping Written Knowledge: The Genre and Activity of the Experimental Article in Science.* Madison: U of Wisconsin P, 1988.
Berkenkotter, Carol, and Thomas N. Huckin. "Rethinking Genre from a Sociocognitive Perspective." *Written Communication* 10 (1993): 475–509.
Bethea, David M. "Exile, Elegy, and Auden in Brodsky's Verses on the Death of T. S. Eliot." *PMLA* 107 (1992): 232–45.
Carter, Michael. "The Idea of Expertise: An Exploration of Cognitive and Social Dimensions of Writing." *College Composition and Communication* 41 (1990): 265–86.
Dillon, George L. *Contending Rhetorics: Writing in Academic Disciplines.* Bloomington: Indiana UP, 1991.
Elbow, Peter. "Reflections on Academic Discourse: How It Relates to Freshmen and Colleagues." *College English* 53 (1991): 135–55.
Faigley, Lester, and Kristine Hansen. "Learning to Write in the Social Sciences." *College Composition and Communication* 36 (1985): 140–49.
Freedman, Aviva. "Show and Tell? The Role of Explicit Teaching in the Learning of New Genres." *Research in the Teaching of English* 27 (1993): 222–51.
Gelfand, Harold, and Charles J. Walker. *Mastering APA Style: Student's Workbook and Training Guide.* Washington, DC: American Psychological Association, 1990.
Gross, Alan G. "Does Rhetoric of Science Matter? The Case of the Floppy-Eared Rabbits." *College English* 53 (1991): 933-43.
———. *The Rhetoric of Science.* Cambridge, MA: Harvard UP, 1990.
Hirshman, Elliot, and Richard Durante. "Prime Identification and Semantic Pruning." *Journal of Experimental Psychology: Learning, Memory, and Cognition* 18 (1992): 255–65.
Kuhn, Thomas S. *The Structure of Scientific Revolutions.* 2nd ed. Chicago: U of Chicago P, 1970.

MacDonald, Susan Peck. "A Method for Analyzing Sentence-Level Differences in Disciplinary Knowledge Making." *Written Communication* 9 (1992): 533–69.

Maimon, Elaine P. "Maps and Genres: Exploring Connections in the Arts and Sciences." *Composition and Literature: Bridging the Gap*. Ed. Winifred Bryan Homer. Chicago: U of Chicago P, 1983. 110–25.

Moore, Leslie E., and Linda H. Peterson. "Convention as Connection: Linking the Composition Course to the English and College Curriculum." *College Composition and Communication* 37 (1986): 466–77.

Rogin, Michael. "Making America Home: Racial Masquerade and Ethnic Association in the Transition to Talking Pictures." *Journal of American History* 79 (1992): 1050–77.

Russell, David R. "Vygotsky, Dewey, and Externalism: Beyond the Student/Discipline Dichotomy." *Journal of Advanced Composition* 13 (1993): 173–94.

Swales, John M. *Genre Analysis: English in Academic and Research Settings*. New York: Cambridge UP, 1990.

Tenpenny, Patricia L., and Edward J. Shoben. "Component Processes and the Utility of the Conceptually-Driven/Data-Driven Distinction." *Journal of Experimental Psychology: Learning, Memory and Cognition* 18 (1992): 25–42.

White, Richard. "Discovering Nature in North America." *Journal of American History* 79 (1992): 874–91.

Williams, Joseph M., and Gregory G. Colomb. "The Case for Explicit Teaching: Why What You Don't Know Won't Help You." *Research in the Teaching of English* 27 (1993): 252–64.

12 One Size Does Not Fit All: Plagiarism Across the Curriculum

SANDRA JAMIESON

I first heard it when we revised our academic integrity policy a few years after I started teaching at my small liberal arts college, but I didn't comprehend its significance. I heard it again later in response to various cases brought to the Academic Integrity Committee by colleagues across the disciplines. What is interesting to me is that none of my colleagues said it directly until I sat down to talk one-on-one with them. When I did that, this is what they said: *Most of these rules about how to use and cite sources don't actually apply in my discipline.* My colleagues had worked with me through long faculty meetings in which we discussed and group-edited the new academic integrity policy, and they had brought cases of plagiarism and misuse of sources to the committee for hearing and sanction; but they did not follow those guidelines themselves, did not have any personal sense of ownership of them beyond general education, and could not afford to teach them to students who wanted to pursue graduate studies in their field. They could teach the principle that significant sources must be acknowledged, but they could not require that students in their disciplines remain within the rules of our policy in upper-level discipline-specific courses. We all agreed about paper mills and cheat sites, of course; about the paper, report, computer code, or work of art not authored by the student who submits it for a grade; and about cheating on tests. But it was impossible to generalize or universalize pretty much anything else — from what to cite to how one should indicate the work of others or even why one cites at all.

Interestingly, when I expressed my concern and desire to develop a new policy incorporating discipline-specific guidelines and conventions, to a person they defended the existing policy, arguing that in a liberal arts college we should have some universal standards and that it made sense for the English department to set them. They added that the rules were fine for first-year seminars and introductory and general education courses and that the existence of common rules taught in first-year composition meant that they did

From *Pluralizing Plagiarism: Identities, Contexts, Pedagogies.* Eds. Rebecca Moore Howard and Amy Robillard. Portsmouth: Heinemann, 2008. 77–91.

not have to try to teach the rules in introductory classes and that nonmajors did not have to learn the rules of each discipline as they fulfilled general education breadth requirements.

I remained mystified about this response until the publication of Chris Thaiss and Terry Myers Zawacki's fascinating study in *Engaged Writers and Dynamic Disciplines* (2006). Thaiss and Zawacki interviewed faculty and students about the kinds of writing assigned and its adherence to convention. In contrast to faculty in other studies (most notably Walvoord and McCarthy 1990), the faculty they interviewed did not believe the purpose of undergraduate education is to "train little psychologists, mathematicians, [or] biologists" (117) and argued instead that "good writing is good writing and hence good thinking, no matter what the discipline" (58). Yet Thaiss and Zawacki report that their responses to questions and their description of practice revealed significant differences in the way "common" terms they named as being at the heart of "good writing" (such as evidence, purpose, style, audience, and organization) are articulated in each discipline and explained to students. Even as the faculty claimed they were simply teaching "good writing" (89), all were found to assign and expect writing that matched the way they write (88), without noting the disciplinary embeddedness of their own writing. This matches what Lee Ann Carroll learned from the students in her study — namely what she calls the "gap between faculty fantasies about writing" and the struggles of their students (8). It also matches her major finding that faculty are not likely to understand the extent to which writing differs from discipline to discipline and, at times, class to class and professor to professor. Walvoord and McCarthy (1990) also discuss a mismatch between student and teacher expectations.

David Russell (1997) explains this gap or mismatch as the inevitable result of disciplinary apprenticeship through which fledgling members of a discipline "very gradually learn its written conventions as an active and integral part of their socialization in a community" (16), which makes learning to write in that discipline seem a "transparent" process. Hare and Fitzsimmons (1991) also observe that "literacy norms within most fields . . . remain . . . invisible" (144). According to Russell, this is because "the community's genres and conventions appear to be unproblematic renderings of the fruits of research" (17) rather than determining that research or interpellating its members into discipline-specific ideologies.

Aside from the intellectual implications of this lack of self-reflexivity, such as simplistic calls to break down the walls between disciplines, Russell's analysis has some serious pedagogical repercussions. If, as Thaiss and Zawacki (2006) put it, the faculty they interviewed "see academic writing as generic rather than discipline-specific" (123), they will pass that belief to students who then assume that what they learn in one class — including source-use rules — applies to all classes. This also will lead students to perceive variation from that assumed norm as "differences in teachers' personalities rather than . . . nuanced articulations of the discipline" (132). Such a mystification of the fundamental differences between academic discourse communities can only lead to problems for students who try to write for us.

Thaiss and Zawacki's (2006) findings and Russell's (1997) analysis all seem to explain exactly what I saw on my campus and perhaps also the "cluelessness" that Gerald Graff (2003) describes. If faculty are not intending to invite undergraduates into disciplinary discourse, but undergraduates are being interpellated by the values of that discourse and feeling the need to speak its language anyway, there is clearly "cluelessness" on both sides. As faculty, we think we are teaching general skills — hence our enthusiasm for one-size-fits-all policies and plagiarism checking programs. Yet students do feel the need, and desire, to "speak our language," understanding better than us that our passion for what we do and the answers our disciplines seek to uncover are to be found in the way we speak about our research. While Thaiss and Zawacki's focus group informants revealed that "more experienced writers understand that knowing a discipline occurs gradually and involves much more than imitation of forms, templates, and styles" (129), most of the students in their study expressed the kind of anxiety and frustration that, according to the Council of Writing Program Administrators (2003), can lead to overdependence on source material in the first place. (The first thing listed under the heading "What Are the Causes of Plagiarism and the Failure to Use and Document Sources Appropriately?" is "Students may fear failure or fear taking risks in their own work.") Alienation leads to being risk averse, which in turn, ironically, leads to misuse of sources.

All of this explains why my colleagues rejected my suggestion that we develop a source-use policy reflecting disciplinary difference, arguing instead that we should spend more time teaching the ethical component of source use in the first year to reduce the incidence of plagiarism in upper-level classes. Persuaded by their emphasis on ethics, my dean drafted a "contract" that each student signs stating that they have received a copy of the academic integrity booklet and that their first-year seminar instructor has explained it to them. While we have an "administrative resolution" process for first- and second-year students who "unintentionally misuse sources," misuse at the upper level is considered a violation of academic integrity. It is true that the penalty may be mild for such "violations" when the student appears to have acted in ignorance, but charges are still required by our faculty regulations when misuse of any kind is found. Where the *WPA Statement* (Council of Writing Program Administrators 2003) uses the terms *deliberate* to indicate plagiarism and *good faith* to indicate accidental misuse of sources, Drew University (2001) uses *intentional* and *unintentional*. In each case, it is *intent* that is at the heart of this matter. And I think the issue of how and when we use source material in academic writing is a matter that should be discussed in terms of intent; however, not in the current sense of intent to steal, defraud, mislead, or any other ethical or capitalist terms one might insert. Rather, we need to focus on what the author is intending to do by referencing sources and what established members of the discipline intend in the same situation, even if not all of them can articulate it as Thaiss and Zawacki (2006) imply. In other words, we need to focus on *use* of sources rather than *misuse* of sources. It is my contention that as long as our pedagogy, policies, textbooks, software programs, and scholarship continue to focus on the misuse of sources and ignore the larger *intention* of source use itself, we will continue to fail to address the problem of plagiarism in any discipline. Indeed, without consideration of intent, we will also continue to operate with inaccurate definitions of "correct" source use and continue to mystify the real work of the disciplines.

Discipline-specific conventions and in particular source use are the markers of membership in academic disciplines. One must learn them to be a member of a discipline, and in turn they interpellate new members into the values and expectations of that discipline through their very invisibility as ideology and classification as simply "good writing." It is the way we use the words and ideas of others that determines our relationship to them, to their ideas, and to the generation of knowledge. As is evidenced with the case of the passive voice, the speaker plays a different role in each discipline, and the discourse community signals its relationship to that speaker through the way it does or does not invoke his or her name. In some disciplines, especially the sciences, general information matters, and it is much less important to know who discovered it; in others, especially the social sciences, data matter, and the gatherer is identified to allow readers to evaluate the validity of that data (note, though, that the use of initials only in APA prevents us from knowing the gender of those cited); in still others, and especially the humanities, words and creative product are the object of study, and so it matters very much that the creator be named and given appropriate credit. These different relationships have a profound impact on both our work in a specific discipline and our relationship to that work and its dissemination.

The speakers of a discipline are, of course, its actors. They are us if we are already members of the community, and they are who we want to be if we are in the process of joining. As we master the discourse conventions of a discipline, then, we also learn how to take our place in it: how to act appropriately and how to refer to other members. We learn what is valued, and that shapes the way we do research. But we don't learn it from a book or from lectures, and the slow apprenticeship that Russell (1997) describes occurs on multiple levels. We are, in Althusser's (1971) sense of the word, interpellated into the subject-positions necessary to participate in a discipline-specific discourse community through its language and way of speaking itself. The publications of a discipline call readers into specific relationship with texts and each other; they create a community in what might be the most effective ideological apparatus imaginable. We recognize ourselves as members when we can talk the talk in the expected manner without thinking about it; when the language and our ability to communicate in it seem transparent. Indeed, the work is so successful that we are not even aware it is happening — a process that Althusser (1971, 182) describes as ideology working "all by itself." My colleagues were happy to have a general source-use policy even though it contradicted their own practices because they had not been asked to articulate the constructive force of source-use conventions, and I was able to go along with that because I had not done so either. Clearly, as Shirley Rose (1996, 34) has said, a rhetoric of citation practices is very long overdue.

Almost two decades before Rose's call for such a rhetoric, Charles Bazerman (1980, 661) observed that "if students are not taught the skills of creating new statements through evaluating, assimilating, and responding to the prior statements of the written conversation, we offer them the meager choice of being parrots of authority or raconteurs stocked with anecdotes for every occasion," and I would add, "misusers of source material." He ends that statement with "Only a fortunate few will learn to enter the community of the literate on their own." It is, of course, this sentiment that led my colleagues to urge that first-year composition continue to teach the research process, research writing, and generic source use without realizing that it also speaks to discipline-specific conversations. But if we extend Bazerman's point, and Gerald Graff's (2003, 3) arguably similar call that we save students from "cluelessness" by teaching them that "summarizing and making arguments is the name of the game in academia," we see that by focusing on finding and penalizing those who are unable to enter general or discipline-specific discourse communities we continue to fail to create opportunity for more than "a fortunate few" to really enter disciplinary conversation and make meaning within it.

I believe that the use of universal source-use policies and generic instruction in first-year composition or the equivalent actually reduces the ability of students to join the discourse communities of the disciplines and undermines the very goals of composition (to increase communication and help students invent the university). The fact is that academic integrity policies and source-use pedagogies that originate in English departments all too often "present scholarly citation in terms limited to a view of ideas as intellectual property and of scholarly productivity as a factor in a capitalistic economy," as Shirley Rose (1996, 35) so eloquently puts it. She shows how textbooks reinforce that capitalist model of source use with their language of "ownership," "borrowing," "debt," and "intellectual property." They also reinforce an emphasis on form rather than the discursive practices inherent in and inscribed by that form. Source-use instruction has become rote learning of formulae and rules (of thumb and of law). Textbooks and handbooks reproduce lists of rules for every kind of source imaginable in MLA or Chicago style. Some also include APA, CBE, and other style sheets as if one needs only to adjust the format as one moves among disciplines. Many include discussion of how to evaluate sources and determine "appropriate" from "inappropriate" material, but that rarely goes beyond how to evaluate Websites and differentiate online publications from print publications that are available online. The emphasis is on "how to" in specific cases rather than the more difficult know-how of broad interaction with sources. To be fair, of course, textbooks cannot teach students how to act within discourse communities any more than foreign language texts can teach the exact angle to bow, the exact pressure to shake hands (which varies by community anyway), or the manner one greets with kisses. The problem is that unlike language guides and textbooks, writing textbooks suggest that the language of academic discourse does not need to be learned from within a specific context and that cultural practice does not go beyond lists and rules. Instead we penalize for misplaced commas and absent introductory phrases as if that is what counts and there is nothing more to learn.

So we say we are teaching students how to be flexible communicators, but in fact we have set up a disciplinary structure of the other kind in which students are hyperconscious of the rules and thereby less likely to be able to participate in specific discourse communities. They enter the disciplines like tourists clutching their dictionaries and phrase books, and a compulsive fear of "getting it wrong" makes them miss the whole point of "it." This is the very opposite of the goals of the Writing Across the Curriculum (WAC) movement with its emphasis on writing to learn and the discursive freedom that invites students to use writing as a way of making meaning. A major point of WAC was to create ways for students to escape the paralysis brought on by right/wrong binaries and fear of error. Freed from obsessive focus on his or her own correctness, a student can actually listen to others and speak back to them. The parallel with foreign languages may seem a stretch here, but I am going to stick with it because it helps to make apparent what the simplification of our understanding of source use obscures. I think it is harder to enter the discourse community of an unfamiliar academic discipline than to enter that of an unfamiliar nation for precisely this reason. Those readers who are the product of Anglo-American foreign language education will recognize the fear of mispronunciation and punishment. While today the drudgery of drills has largely been replaced by a language immersion approach, the grades are still based on correct pronunciation, spelling, and grammar. And too many students are left functionally monolingual, focusing on form rather than communication and pronunciation rather than engagement.

In 2000 I was in South Africa visiting schools and learning about the Government of National Unity's Curriculum 2005, the ambitious education policy "based on the principles of co-operation, critical thinking and social responsibly . . . [to] empower individuals to participate in all aspects of society" (Manganyi 1997). Part of the curriculum focuses on language, including multilingualism and knowledge of and respect for "cultural and language traditions" to "promote the development of a national identity" by promoting multilingualism to enable "learners to develop and value . . . other languages and cultures in our multi-cultural country and in international contexts" (*Curriculum* 1997). Where possible, students were to study in their "home language" (one of the eleven official languages, which could include English and Afrikaans) or South African Sign Language and learn a "first additional language" and ideally a "second additional language." In the small, very rundown Thaba Jabula Secondary School in Soweto, I visited a ninth-grade classroom where the students were learning Afrikaans, their "second official language" after English, which they spoke fluently. I listened, impressed, and at the break I asked a student how hard it was to learn this language that she told me was actually her fourth language. I admitted that I was finding it impossible to say the name of our Afrikaaner bus driver or, indeed, Gauteng Province where we were. The German version of that *G* sound had eluded me in my middle-school German classes, and this version did so too. She looked at me with concern. "No," she said, "you're worrying about the wrong thing. You don't have to pretend to be Afrikaans. You just have to be able to communicate with them. It doesn't matter how the words sound. If we understand each other, we can work together." Her teacher confirmed this for me. "Yes, perhaps, one day we will all speak each other's languages with each other's accents, but our goal is not to make everyone the same. Each person remains who he is with his own language and accent, but everyone else also understands that language so we can communicate, and then we can also learn about each other."

This is a powerful model as we think about source use and WAC. If disciplinary conventions, including source use, are the languages of each discipline, when source-use instruction focuses on correct pronunciation (avoiding the ill-placed comma, knowing when to italicize a journal title, when to place it in quotation marks, and when to do nothing to it), it leaves us missing the point. Whether instruction is designed to create the opportunity for multilingualism and thereby "invitation into the mental positions of those who think differently from us," as Graff (2003, 13) put it, or whether it is simply advanced conversation within a discipline, if my fear of failure leads me to depend on a phrase book for my Afrikaans sentences or not speak for fear of mangling the *G*, I may never even communicate at all. I will certainly be too busy to meet the glance of my interlocutor, let alone make conversation. The student who depends too heavily on sources for phrases and sentences suffers the same inability.

Reliance on one general English department–generated policy is clearly limiting, yet it is not practical — or desirable — for all students to have to "pretend to be" members of an academic discipline to write college-level papers. A middle ground seems to be to create a sufficient awareness of basic differences and vocabulary for students to be able to communicate in the various "languages" of the disciplines and so have access to the culture and knowledge embedded within them. This, of course, also requires that, as faculty, we give up the notion that there is such a thing as generally agreed-upon "good writing" across the curriculum — give up English department prose as the colonial language — and explore ways to make the languages of our disciplines apparent to us and then to our students without expecting technical perfection or reducing difference to the generic. And this is where WAC can take on a new and more intellectually challenging role in which writing-to-learn ceases to be a general principle that does not necessarily improve writing or thinking (Russell 2001, 259) and becomes a space for demystifying context-specific writing. Russell's reviews suggest that methods for such a pedagogy would include direct instruction in the components of discourse-specific writing, thinking, and source use along with models, guidelines, "classroom talk," and a focus on discipline-specific writing processes (283–91).

Our new goal, Russell concludes, should be to move beyond what we want students to *know* in any given discipline to what we want them to "*do* with the material of the course" (290) and how we want them to do that; or, as Graff (2003) might put it, to give all students the "ability to join an intellectual community that makes sense to them" (274).

If the goal of WAC that we increase communication across the curriculum (also known as CAC) and writing to learn within all parts of it is to be fully realized, we need to retrace and reconsider our history to see how what we focus on now came to dominate, and to listen to the voices that have been ignored and learn from them. Our task in this history is to understand how one discipline — English — came to have an exclusive hold over the notion of "good writing" in all other disciplines. It was WAC that led to the inaccurate definitions and generic institutional plagiarism and source-use policies discussed so far, but it is also within WAC scholarship that we can find more useful ways to think about source use across the disciplines. By retracing our steps, so to speak, we can understand where we lost our way in the shift from writing across the curriculum (WAC) to Writing in the Disciplines (WID) and also refocus our attention on plagiarism across the curriculum in new and productive ways.

The fact that WAC has survived for the last thirty years in still recognizable form is testament to what it has to offer and what it has already delivered. The goal of helping students write to learn and the related goal of reforming pedagogy to include process as well as product have largely succeeded. Writing assignments are sequenced, and students are assigned journals, freewriting, drafts, and revisions across the curriculum. Thanks to WAC, students develop general writing skills that they use to help them articulate what they learn and that, in theory, help them enter different discourse communities. But these skills and strategies were an ideological Trojan horse carrying embedded within them a set of practices that conflict with the disciplinary communities into which they were delivered, the most important being the relationship to sources and the MLA citation method that underpins universal source-use policies and plagiarism detection software.

As we became more immersed in WAC, we began to understand discipline specificity and have often been humbled by the sheer audacity of our project. Susan McLeod (2000) observes:

> when I began my first faculty seminar, I really had no appreciation of the complexity of disciplinary discourse — I assumed that as an English teacher, I knew what good writing was and simply needed to enlighten my colleagues across the disciplines. . . . A passionate, hour-long discussion of the use of the passive voice was one of the most memorable sessions in my own understanding of the social sciences.

I had a similar experience with a laboratory report I tried to write as I collaborated with a colleague in the chemistry department. My colleague could not understand why I was unable to produce the kind of prose she expected of first-year students and I could not believe how difficult it was to write in passive voice that did not sound ugly and disjointed. I learned that there is a world of difference between the passive voice we decry in first-year writing courses and the elegant and informative prose of the hard sciences, but my colleague had to literally rewrite my report before I could get it. For many of us, these experiences led to the move to writing in the disciplines. The question this brief history seeks to understand is why this move did not lead to a rethinking of source use.

Everything we thought we understood about our colleagues turned out to be opaque, and the most opaque of all was source use. I could ask my colleagues what role writing served in their discipline and how it helped to create and disseminate meaning. I could learn that, for some of my colleagues, writing essentially told a story about data (economics) or observation (anthropology), while for others it challenged assumptions (chemistry) or interpretations (history), and for still others it offered interpretation (art history) or connected ideas (sociology). I could also learn that not everyone in those disciplines articulated the role of writing in the same manner, just as my colleagues in English disagree about the role (and importance) of literary analysis. The disciplines in parentheses above could be mixed and matched depending on one's subfield, theoretical or methodological framework, or specific research. At times there seemed to be greater similarity among disciplines than within them. But I never thought to ask about citations and their relationship to source material and the ideas of others. And no one thought to tell me.

While those of us involved in WAC programs (Thaiss and Zawacki's 2006 findings notwithstanding) can talk at great length about the content and purpose of writing, the routine conventions of source use and citation seem like an afterthought. They are often taught at the editing stage of the writing process, and several software programs will even change papers from one format to another as if the issue were really just where to put the punctuation as composition handbooks and software suggest. This afterthought model leads faculty across the country to support a source-use policy that is applicable only to literary studies, because it further obscures the overall discipline-specific differences. Perhaps this model also explains the fact that while there are a few excellent articles on the subject, a very small proportion of the thousands of articles and studies on WAC, WID, CAC, and all their derivatives focus on source use or the discursive nature of research writing within the disciplines. As with the passive voice, perhaps, we think we know what we will find. Or perhaps we do not know how to ask the question and/or our colleagues don't know how to answer it.

Anne Herrington (2000) reminds us that for many, a mission of WAC was "aiming to foster the success of all students, particularly those who for reasons of class, race, or other factors are less likely to succeed." Although we may indeed have largely forgotten this mission, as she suggests, it is never more urgent than in source use where one-size-fits-all policies exclude and discipline some, while somehow permitting others with more advanced and flexible writing skills (what Thaiss and Zawacki call third-stage writers) to enter the discourse of specific disciplines. With the increasing dependence on electronic plagiarism detection, sustained research on source-use practices is long overdue. When we focus not on *how* sources are cited within specific disciplinary discourse communities but on *why* they are cited, we will be in a better position to develop policies and pedagogies that invite students into the discourse of the disciplines rather than disciplining those who do not make it.

Interestingly, if we go back to Bazerman's (1980) article on the relationship between reading and writing, we see the beginning of a thread that could have led to very different source-use policies, and this is where the historical exploration is so important. After summarizing the work of James Britton and his coauthors (1975) in *The Development of Writing Abilities (11–18)* and his comment "source-book material may be used in various ways involving different levels of activity by the writer," Bazerman (1980, 657) observes those "various ways" and "different levels of activity" can be understood as part of an "on-going, written conversation." The fact that he takes great pains to acknowledge the differences between spoken and written conversation indicates what a novel idea this was a quarter of a century ago. By 1996 Shirley Rose could describe the same thing as a "courtship ritual" with no need of justification, but before we move to the recent past we need to really engage with this idea of conversation as Bazerman (1980) approached it. He observes that "conversation requires absorption of what prior speakers have said, consideration of how earlier comments relate to the responder's thoughts, and a response framed to the situation and the reader's purposes" (657). By that definition, my invocation of Russell (1997, 2001), Thaiss and Zawacki (2006), Graff (2003), McLeod (2000), Britton (1975), Bazerman (1980), and Rose (1996) seems to clearly mark this article as a conversation, and we are so used to this idea that it seems somewhat banal even to make the observation.

What makes the observation important is what marks this as a conversation *in the discipline of composition*. That discipline-specific context is marked by much more than my absorbing, considering, and responding to the sources listed above; it is revealed in the way I introduce and cite those sources and the way you will find them presented in the references list (along with the fact that in an early draft of this chapter I called it a "works cited list"). The fact that I wrote this essay using MLA and was then asked to "translate" it to Chicago for this volume also indicates something about the discipline of composition — our emergent but still partial identity *as* a discipline separate from English. But the fact that I assume my readers will understand the irony of this request indicates the same "insider knowledge" as I reveal in my assumption that readers will know what WAC, CAC, WID, and WPA stand for. Bazerman alerted us to this distinction back in 1980 when he wrote:

> The model of conversation even transforms the technical skills of reference and citation. The variety of uses to be made of quotation, the options for referring to others' ideas and information (e.g., quotation, paraphrase, summary, name only), and the techniques of introducing and discussing source materials are the tools which allow the accurate

but pointed connection of one's argument to earlier statements. The mechanics of documentation, more than being an exercise in intellectual etiquette, become the means of indicating the full range of comments to which the new essay is responding. (661)

Although still steeped in the language of afterthought (*"technical* skills of reference and citation" and *"mechanics* of documentation"), Bazerman (1980) was clearly challenging us to look more deeply. Had we done so, our conception of Writing in the Disciplines would have been much more tightly focused on the specific relationship to source material in each discourse community, and our understanding of unintentional plagiarism would be focused on source use rather than *mis*-use.

We had another chance to pick up this thread a decade ago when Shirley Rose (1996) drew on another work of Bazerman (1988) to lead into a Burkean analysis of the conversation within discipline-specific source-use decisions as courtship ritual. She places her analysis in the context of Bazerman's work, observing that Bazerman's "exploration of writers' motives is necessarily limited" and asserting that "a complete rhetoric of citations must be able to address writer's motives and purposes, for these cannot be taken for granted without risk of reducing them to simplistic terms" (38). Through the Burkean lens, Rose sees scholarly citation as "a microcosm of the academic discipline understood as both scene and outcome or cooperative action, the act of citing — collaboration between the author and other authors and between author and reader — serves as a representative anecdote of all written discourse as collaboration" (40). Further, "the scholarly writer's rhetoric builds her identification with both her readers and the other writers she cites in her text as she negotiates for a place in a relatively small and well-defined community" (41).

I'd like to engage in a little analysis of the structure of the last few paragraphs of this paper to help us think more about disciplinary difference. I have quoted heavily from two articles that I consider very significant to this conversation about the history of plagiarism across the curriculum. I have done so with the purpose of demonstrating their relationship and setting a ground for further analysis. If I were to run these paragraphs through some magical software program that would track the percentage of original prose contained therein I'd be done for. I have broken the oft-repeated general rule of thumb that quotation does not make up more than 10 percent of a written paper (at least for the last few paragraphs). And in not citing examples of sources who "oft repeat" advice, I have broken a rule of citation often invoked in composition classes at least. To my credit, I have block-indented a quotation that is over four lines, and I have indicated a source quoted by another source, introduced "borrowed" material so no one is in any doubt as to who is "speaking" at any given time, and not ended a paragraph with a quotation. However, if these paragraphs were part of a psychology paper I would still have breached etiquette because according to APA I should not have quoted at all. I should have summarized or paraphrased. I should also not have included first names, which might focus attention on gender and the impact of the person observing rather than on the observations themselves. For some teachers of mathematics I did not need to cite any sources; I could have simply summarized the general history of the discipline and moved on to my point (ideally several pages ago). But for *this* conversation in *this* discipline I feel that I need to quote for exactly the reasons Rose (1996) argues we use sources at all.

First, she says, we include familiar "words, ideas, and conclusions" of others to remind our readers of our shared knowledge. To quote early WAC scholars is both to give them what my students call "their props" and in so doing, also, to show that I know who is who in the field — or not. Readers who are inclined to respect those "founders" will be more likely to pay attention to my point and to think that I have done my homework. If I did it right, my readers will identify with me and feel that *we* are having a conversation that is important. Indeed, by explaining this I am simply reminding you of what you already know. But I am also, as Rose (1996) further points out, providing you with "a narrative of the process by which [I] arrived at [the] ideas" I discuss in this article. If I am successful, the rhetorical move is as follows: "this is what we already have believed, this is how I propose to challenge or further develop our belief, and you, dear reader, will believe this new way too" (Rose 1996, 41). On the other hand, the fact that I have failed to cite many other scholars in the history of the field could lead some to dismiss me as an upstart rather than a member of the discipline; a follower of footnotes, or what Bazerman (1988) calls "a parrot of authority" (661) rather than a member of this scholarly community to which I presume to speak. "Thus," as Rose puts it, "the citation choices meant to foster identification have the potential for creating division" (41) or outright rejection. If I had cited many sources, you might have assumed I did not know enough to make wise decisions about whom *not* to cite. Conversely, you might have assumed that I am widely read in the field. If I were to cite a source with which you are unfamiliar, Rose's Burkean analysis suggests that I offer you a gift: You can strengthen your relationship to the discourse community and "achieve closer identification with the author" by locating and reading that work (41).

Now let us turn our attention back from one discourse community (ours) to the world of our students. If they include only recent sources, as Rose (1996) observes, we may find them refreshingly up-to-date or depressingly unprepared for the purpose because of their unfamiliarity with historical context. And vice versa. If a student were to explain that Charles Bazerman has written many important books and articles in the field of composition or that David Russell writes about WAC, we would know that she has just learned that fact and does not understand the field sufficiently to know that it is discipline-specific common knowledge. And so on. These rules do not easily lend themselves to handbooks or handouts. They are learned by interacting with a discourse community; by reading as Bazerman (1980) observes and Thaiss and Zawacki (2006) emphasize, but also by trial and error and the comments of others on our work — whether they are the teacher-to-student comments valued by the students in Thaiss and Zawacki's study and in so many others, or the editorial comments and feedback from our colleagues that makes all writing, indeed, a collaboration. Russell's (2001) detailed analysis of naturalistic studies in WAC/WID highlights what many other surveys have reported and what Thaiss and Zawacki found in their study of students; however, those same studies do not all present faculty attitudes to student disciplinary membership in the same way (Russell 2001, 259–98), and this is what indicates that we need more study, especially with regard to the role of source material.

Rose (1996) observes that all too often the sources used by "inexperienced academic writers," and I would add more pressingly novices of a disciplinary discourse, are not "integrated into their texts" to the degree that the students are not integrated into the academic community (43). They may use too many quotations, not enough, or not the right ones; but they also may not introduce those quotations, indicate where paraphrases begin, or provide full citations. They may assume that what they know is common knowledge, or they may assume that what they just learned is not common knowledge. As I did earlier, they may adopt informal prose or inaccurate terminology. But there is a distinction to be made in this list. All mark the writer as an outsider, but only some will result in charges of misuse of sources.

We can focus as much as we like on ethics. Asserting as the WPA statement does that "Ethical writers make every effort to acknowledge sources fully and appropriately in accordance with the contexts and genres of their writing" (Council of Writing Program Administrators 2003), even if we do not classify those who fail as "unethical." To reduce discipline-specific or generic source-use conventions to good and evil, ethical and immoral, is to miss an important pedagogical moment, as many have observed before me. I believe that what we must do instead is remember that South African student learning Afrikaans, and early WAC calls for us to develop strategies to make disciplinary discourse apparent and the connection between discourse conventions and content clear. And then we need to teach those languages. Students may learn general "good writing" in the safe(r) official home language of first-year composition or other first-year and introductory courses, even the first two stages of the research paper as described by Brian Sutton (1997) ("generalized academic writing concerned with stating claims, offering evidence, respecting others' opinions, and learning how to write with authority" [48]); Graff's (2003) summary and argument; and Bazerman's (1988) evaluating, assimilating, and responding to prior arguments. In contrast, in majors, minors, and specializations they must also learn a "first additional language" and a "second additional language" sufficiently that they can enter the culture and knowledge base of a discipline rather than simply learning its facts and remaining "clueless" about the larger issues, concerns, or motives of members of those disciplines. In other words, they need to be taught to really write-to-learn and communicate across the curriculum and in the disciplines. While we should not stop teaching "good writing," we must determine exactly what that is and how a useful form of it may be taught in first-year writing and

WAC classes. But those courses must also begin the process of explaining how and why writing is context specific and the importance of understanding any culture or discipline through its language. It is not the accent that matters, what matters is that we are able to communicate sufficiently for us to learn about ideas. We need to teach students to use sources in dialogue rather than to fear the penalty of misuse in isolation.

REFERENCES

Althusser, Louis. 1971. "Ideology and Ideological State Apparatuses (Notes Towards an Investigation)." In *Lenin and Philosophy and Other Essays*. Trans. Ben Brewster. New York: Monthly Review.

Bazerman, Charles. 1980. "A Relationship Between Reading and Writing: The Conversation Model." *College English* 41 (6): 656–61.

Bazerman, Charles. 1988. *Shaping Written Knowledge: The Genre and Activity of the Experimental Article in Science*. Madison: University of Wisconsin Press.

Britton, James N., et al. 1975. *The Development of Writing Abilities (11–18)*. London: Macmillan.

Carroll, Lee Ann. 2003. *Rehearsing New Roles: How College Students Develop as Writers*. Carbondale: Southern Illinois University Press.

Council of Writing Program Administrators. 2003. "Defining and Avoiding Plagiarism: WPA Statement on Best Policies." http://wpacouncil.org/node/9.

Curriculum 2005: Lifelong Learning for the 21st Century. A User's Guide. 1997. www.polity.org.za/html/govdocs/misc/curr2005.html#foreward.

Drew University. 2001. "College of Liberal Arts Standards of Academic Integrity." www.depts.drew.edu/composition/Academic_Honesty.htm.

Graff, Gerald. 2003. *Clueless in Academe: How Schooling Obscures the Life of the Mind*. New Haven, CT: Yale University Press.

Hare, Victoria Chou, and Denise A. Fitzsimmons. 1991. "The Influence of Interpretive Communities on the Use of Content and Procedural Knowledge." *Written Communication* 8 (3): 348–78.

Herrington, Anne. 2000. "Principles That Should Guide WAC/CAC Program Development in the Coming Decade." *Academic.Writing: Interdisciplinary Perspectives on Communication Across the Curriculum*. http://wac.colostate.edu/aw/forums/winter2000/index_expand.htm.

Manganyi, Chabani. 1997. Foreward. *Curriculum 2005: Lifelong Learning for the 21st Century. A User's Guide*. www.polity.org.za/html/govdocs/misc/curr2005.html#foreward.

McLeod, Susan. 2000. "Principles That Should Guide WAC/CAC Program Development in the Coming Decade." *Academic.Writing: Interdisciplinary Perspectives on Communication Across the Curriculum*. http://wac.colostate.edu/aw/forums/winter2000/index_expand.htm.

Rose, Shirley K. 1996. "What's Love Got to Do With It? Scholarly Citation Practices as Courtship Ritual." *Language and Learning Across the Disciplines* 1 (3): 34–48.

Russell, David. 1997. "Rethinking Genre in School and Society: An Activity Theory Analysis." *Written Communication* 14 (4): 504–54.

Russell, David. 2001. "Where Do Naturalistic Studies of WAC/WID Point?" In *WAC for the New Millennium: Strategies for Continuing Writing-Across-the-Curriculum*, edited by Susan H. McLeod, Eric Miraglia, Margot Soven, and Christopher Thaiss. Urbana, IL: National Council of Teachers of English, 259–98.

Sutton, Brian. 1997. "Writing in the Disciplines, First-Year Composition, and the Research Paper." *Language and Learning Across the Disciplines* 2 (1): 46–57.

Thaiss, Chris, and Terry Myers Zawacki. 2006. *Engaged Writers and Dynamic Disciplines: Research on the Academic Writing Life*. Portsmouth, NH: Heinemann/Boynton Cook.

Walvoord, Barbara E., and Lucille P. McCarthy. 1990. *Thinking and Writing in College: A Naturalistic Study of Students in Four Disciplines*. Urbana, IL: National Council of Teachers of English.

13 Interdisciplinary Work as Professional Development: Changing the Culture of Teaching

JOAN A. MULLIN

There are many lessons to learn about faculty development from writing across the curriculum (WAC) programs, for when they really began to grow in the 1980s, directors of the initiatives were often the first to undertake large-scale faculty development in their institutions. WAC directors had much to offer teaching and learning enterprises then, and many have much to offer now as a result of their experiences with faculty across the disciplines. As teachers of writing who study rhetorical contexts, they quickly learned that only dispensing guidelines and resources — university requirements for taking writing-intensive courses, Web sites on writing in biology or textbooks on writing for film, the top-ten informal writing strategies — does not make a successful WAC program. Unfortunately, there are several WAC programs in the United States today that do exist only as discrete series of rules with little or no effort placed into teaching faculty how writing can be used to teach critical and disciplinary thinking, how writing both shapes and defines a field, and therefore, how students can use writing to read and enter these fields as well as others. Based on nineteenth-century notions of the gentleman scholar, these template-bound programs operate teaching and learning initiatives under the assumption that if faculty are merely given techniques and methods, they will be able to apply them effectively in their classrooms. This strategy flies in the face of both research and experience as they apply not only to faculty development, but also to learning.

For methodologies to evolve, faculty and faculty development facilitators need to shift their teaching paradigms. In the case of disciplinary literacy, they need to make apparent, to themselves and their students, ways to read systems of activity and respond to changing teaching and learning environments they produce. This should be approached collaboratively, so that a director serves as a conduit who both facilitates and benefits from a continual evolution of strategies produced with faculty. As can be seen in this special issue, rather than prescribing ways to teach, faculty developers can best effect

From *Pedagogy: Critical Approaches to Teaching Literature, Language, Composition, and Culture* 8.3 (2008): 495–508.

change by listening, articulating faculty dialogues for further reflection, and facilitating internal change in faculty while modeling teaching practices they and others could adopt. This requires of facilitators a certain disciplinary neutrality, a meta-awareness of their own frames. A WAC developer often claims a department of English, writing, or rhetoric as their home department; as a result, cross-disciplinary programs may become codified through the disciplinary lens of one person and the field or group to which he or she belongs.

SHIFTING AND SIFTING THROUGH PARADIGMS AND DISCIPLINES: THE FACULTY DEVELOPER

Changing paradigms and modeling practices seem relatively simple accomplishments consistent with the strategies outlined in this issue, and the stock and trade of those trained in the analytical and critical traditions of departments of English, writing, and rhetoric. However, I want to use two strands of theoretical language that have helped me think about not just what kinds of faculty development practices I need to implement, but also why my own disciplinary inclinations might make these work — or not. I refer to Krista Ratcliffe's (2005) phrase "rhetorical listening" and to the Bakhtinian (1981) idea of inner and outer dialogue.

Reading Ratcliffe's work, which addresses race, gender, and culture, has made me nonetheless reflect on a barrier met by faculty developers: listening often proceeds out of assumptions about what we will hear and, therefore, how we construct others and our relationship to them. At workshops about writing in the disciplines, for instance, we freely use such terms as "introduction" and "conclusion"; we acknowledge the differences in evidence, in disciplinary "methods" sections; we think we all understand what we mean. And yet, as demonstrated in conversations with faculty, a word as seemingly simple as "discuss" can have different meanings to individuals in different disciplines (Mullin et al. 1998); therefore, no matter what we may think we are understanding, we don't know until our definitions and underlying expectations about these terms are unpacked.

Another example is the issue of plagiarism. In our ongoing research, colleagues and I have found that faculty do agree that wholesale copying of another's work is plagiarism; however, such agreement breaks down when one investigates the individual details of how disciplinary faculty think about adapting others' work, appropriating objects, or taking formulas for granted. These subtle disagreements have made me rethink how I talk about plagiarism not only to faculty, but also to my students. Similarly, when faculty (or students) demonstrate disagreement or disinterest in materials (or when long-term program goals fail to occur), it may be the facilitators who need to change their own assumptions. A perfect example occurred during a recent WAC faculty development workshop given by colleagues in rhetoric and writing; their objective was to give faculty across the disciplines ways to promote critical thinking through peer evaluation and writing. One presenter spoke at length about how short writing assignments help students connect personally with difficult material on the public intellectual in a democracy. Another presenter went on at great length to outline how, in one of her classes, student reflective essays, short in-class writing, portfolio reflections, scaffolding assignments, and peer review help foster writing.

While those in the participant/audience were engaged and asked questions, they also commented in workshop evaluations that there was no way they could adapt such practices to their own content-rich classes — though they were glad to learn that people in writing were doing such good work. The presenters, from a discipline rich in research on collaboration, on reading an audience, on using rhetorical strategies that suit an occasion, had such a strong intellectual connection to their own perspective and expertise that they could not hear their own explanations as disciplinarily bound, and participants could not fit what they heard into their own disciplinary construct: unless facilitators and presenters continually engage in a collaborative reading of their own paradigms, they will not be able to effect change in others.

This is as true in faculty development as it is in the classroom. Lad Tobin (1996) demonstrates how his prejudice toward young men wearing baseball caps blinded him to hearing — really hearing — such students and kept him from reading their work fairly. In the same way, faculty developers who don't truly understand their role as a learner in their own workshops close down the possibility for fostering deep paradigmatic changes they seek in others. Those of us leading faculty toward different pedagogical understandings always have to be aware of how we are forwarding our own agendas, and we have to be flexible and open enough to reconsider our constructions of others and our definitions of their disciplines and ways of teaching. We can do this by actively listening.

AVOIDING THE MISSIONARY, REFUSING THE TEMPLATE

A colleague, relating a conversation among teachers of rhetoric as they designed a WAC program, reported that they decided all they had to do was give faculty rhetorical frames by which they could then analyze and teach disciplinary genres to their students. Terms such as *genre* and *frames* are often used by many faculty development programs that foster workshops on designing assignments or avoiding plagiarism or developing lectures for large classes. However, as Barbara Schneider points out, such generalized approaches presented as panaceas for classroom difficulties often ignore how strategies are defined within, or how they emerge out of, a discipline. Such approaches fail to ask faculty to examine their own individual understandings of learning over which they will lay these generalizable, or even generic, "discipline-specific" methods. The missionaries, believing in their own positions, just expect faculty to accept and apply their ways of doing and being to individual classes, easily transferring the skill of teaching from course to course.

There are two things wrong with this simplistic, messianic approach: one is that it erases disciplinary difference, the other is that it erases teacher difference. In much the same way that traditional teaching is delivered on the premise that all students learn alike, too often faculty development practitioners believe that faculty teach the same — or the same with slight variations. They don't put into practice in their workshops what they ask faculty to do in their classrooms — accommodate different perspectives. This was accounted for by early WAC workshop facilitators Toby Fulwiler, Art Young, and Barbara Walvoord, who engaged faculty as they would their classes, having them write and think in ways their students might, thereby experiencing the pedagogies they might choose to adapt. Somehow, this practice has been lost, perhaps as a result of a faster world in need of quick fixes, perhaps most easily seen in technology workshops where participants learn how to design Web pages, load video and audio, grade papers online, and set up collaborative student groups for discussion. What happens here is what too often happens at most faculty development workshops nowadays: faculty members get talked to, view a demonstration, get a handout or page link, and then are sent home to apply on their own. Even though these seem interactive, such workshops are built on and foster a traditional, missionary form of knowledge transmission: the one who knows brings information for the one who doesn't know to learn and apply — and thus be converted (see McLeod 1989; Bazerman 1991; Jones and Comprone 1993; Segal et al. 1998).

To avoid taking on the missionary identity, anyone who teaches faculty to teach should not only be applying methodology they promote in real classrooms of college students themselves (not something that teaching and learning staff always do), but they should also be partnering with faculty across disciplines to learn how different methodologies apply to specific disciplines, adopting and changing faculty development practices as they do. For me, the benefit of interdisciplinary, listener-oriented faculty partnerships was made evident when I attached myself to a faculty member's art history class, serving in the capacity of a writing tutor to his students, learning what I assumed would be a better way he could adopt WAC strategies in his class. While he certainly did adopt informal in-class writing, I also responded to the visual elements of his discipline, changing writing strategies into visual strategies. By sitting in the class, watching him teach, and listening to students' difficulties both in the class and one-on-one while working with them on their writing, I had to change how I defined *writing*, expanding my understanding to include the visual — which, in 1990, was not yet a part of the vocabulary of WAC, rhetoric or writing classes (Mullin 1998). This experience contributed to the continual, but at least acknowledged, challenge of listening differently to field-specific and content-specific needs of a discipline, of an instructor, and of a particular class on a particular day. That does not mean engaging in a kind of half-listening, that is, waiting for the opportunity to jump in and shape another's disciplines to one's own strategies and expectations. It means listening to try to hear how facilitators might be changed by another's discipline.

By constructing workshops and interactions that are dynamic, that are set up to give faculty experiences that help them explore their disciplinary ways of thinking, their course expectations, and their own styles of teaching and learning, facilitators will learn what faculty assumptions are and how faculty construct their students. Faculty will be able to see fault lines in their assumptions and methodologies and internalize new approaches. Three scholars — Mina Shaughnessy, David Bartholomae, and Mikhail Bakhtin — are useful for understanding paradigm shifts, the processes by which they occur, and why they need to happen. Shaughnessy's *Errors and Expectations* (1977) still stands as a work that alerted many of us to how students' home language affects their ability to succeed in college. Bartholomae (1985) helped us understand how, as students move from class to class, they have to figure out how a historian thinks, what stands for evidence for a biologist, or how a social scientist defines *method* — they are "inventing the university" on their own. Mikhail Bakhtin (1981) articulates the continual play between inner and outer dialogues in which a person engages as he or she comes to grips with new language, new knowledge, and therefore a new (disciplinary) identity.

This research is especially important as more and more of our interdisciplinary work makes universal or missionary claims about writing in a discipline questionable at best. However, while faculty speak eloquently of the challenges in tenure and promotion as they explain their increasingly cross-disciplinary work and publications in journals outside the field, they seem not to recognize the conflicting messages they may be sending students: they tend to look for a "writing in the [generic] discipline" text and ask for rubrics, while unknowingly evaluating student papers out of their own interdisciplinary experiences.[1] The traditional authority of the discipline still holds sway even as experience and practice tell a different story. In a Bakhtinian sense, "authoritative discourse [in this case, of a discipline] may organize around itself great masses of other types of discourses (which interpret it, praise it, apply it in various ways), but the authoritative discourse itself does not merge with these" (Bakhtin 1981: 343). Traditional generic constructions can remain unchallenged unless our internally persuasive voices — ones out of which we construct our world — "enter into inter-animating relationships with new contexts" (345–46). The inner and outer dialogues that need to take place in order to discover, much less accommodate, new disciplinary discourses are the same that need to occur in faculty development. These dialogues are not accomplished when an authoritative word — a discipline, a facilitator's lens — remains unexamined.

Changing a teaching and learning culture does not have to include reading Bakhtin; he and Ratcliffe, Bartholomae, and Shaughnessy would all speak to the need to examine one's "home" language — and the complexity of voices that construct it — by entering into a dialogue with an other that would enable us to hear ourselves by standing a little outside the authoritative discourse. Within a workshop, faculty from various disciplines can provide that distance, critiquing each other's course design, assignments, and methodology from the perspective of learners outside the field. The aha moment comes when they find through this exercise that their students are continually exposed not only to a variety of teaching styles, but also to a variety of language expectations through which they must negotiate (Bartholomae 1985). To adapt

a quote from David Russell and Arturo Yañez (2002: 359): "People act in multiple, interacting systems of activity where writing [teaching and learning]
that seems the 'same' as what one has read or written before is in practice very
different — and not only in the formal features, the 'how' of writing [teaching
and learning]. Lying behind the how are the who, where, when, what and —
most importantly — the why of writing [teaching and learning], the motives
of people engaged in some system of activity." Having experienced the need
to go deeper than merely *how* to write, faculty and facilitators see that their
students need to understand "the who, where, when, what and — most importantly — the why" of a particular pedagogy. They begin to see that students also have to shift from expecting traditional delivery of content in order
to participate within a discipline.

Connecting methodology used in faculty development workshops with
classroom methodology connects, for me, the teaching-learning cycle that is
often broken by the way institutions and faculty development are structured:
curriculum is often created, policy is often established, pedagogy is often developed without equal representation of crucial stakeholders. In the case of
WAC faculty development, input from the learners is often absent from the
workshops and handouts. Represented usually as generalized "students,"
real learners, as they develop within a particular environment (the classroom, the discipline as directed and understood by an instructor), need to be
considered as part of the paradigm shift necessary for changing a teaching
culture.

STUDENT-PARTICIPANTS, NOT CONVERTS

Used to define successful persuasion, Aristotle's rhetorical triangle has been
adapted to stake out the necessity of balancing appeals between text, author,
and audience. To focus only on the author's point of view and its presentation
in a text is to ignore the audience objections, understandings, and assumptions — the communication then fails to accomplish its end. It is useful to
apply this communication construct to faculty development. To concentrate
only on faculty (or workshop facilitator) points of view as they apply to a
constructed classroom (generalized by the facilitator; constructed specifically
or generalized by the faculty) is the same as teaching only two legs of the rhetorical triangle — text and author — and leaving out the real audience (students). Among the reasons that the relationship of instruction to content needs
to be apparent to students is that they tend to resist new teaching strategies as
much as faculty might initially resist them. For both groups, the authoritative
discourse is that of the university's long tradition of instructional delivery.
It is not enough, therefore, to think about changing faculty practices; faculty
development should consider how student expectations about instructional
delivery might also need to be challenged.

For example, years ago, as I began to move from a teacher-centered to an
activity-centered classroom — finding ways for students to take up the speaking, learning, and thinking instead of me performing the speaking, learning,

and thinking — I earned a classic response on end-of-course evaluations: "I don't think the teacher knew very much because she made us do all the work." While I had adopted more activity-oriented teaching strategies that involved students investigating the how, who, what, when, where, and why, the students, my audience, had been expecting content delivery in traditional ways: content in (lecture), content out (test). The result was that audience expectations weren't met, and I as "author," pleased with my own "text" (methods), ended up pretty much talking to myself.

The same thing happens in WAC workshops where faculty often are encouraged to use assigned short, informal writing tasks (through online or print reading responses) or in-class freewriting that address a prompt in order to stimulate engagement with content. As "low-stakes" writing tasks, these are not meant to be graded, but rather to provide opportunities for students to manipulate the vocabulary of a discipline, explore ideas, and try out application of concepts before performing in high-stakes situations (on tests, in research papers). Faculty are told that learning through language is crucial to students' adoption of a system of disciplinary thinking, that using freewriting and reading responses creates safe spaces for the adaptation of a student's language to disciplinary language, and that faculty need to let students experience this language in practice instead of lecturing them. However, students in these faculty members' classes are often operating under the traditional paradigm: they expect lecture and fact production; they become frustrated with what they see as mindless busy-writing; they don't want to hear their classmates talk; they want to know what the teacher wants them to know. That is their teaching-learning paradigm. As a result, teachers get, as I did, negative course evaluations, and negative course evaluations can translate into low merit raises and muted endorsements for tenure or promotion. Whether teaching is central to an institution or not, faculty themselves get frustrated that their attempts at changing pedagogy have failed; they mistrust their own judgment about their new practices, become disillusioned with themselves and their students, cut back on new pedagogies, or just revert back to traditional teaching methods.

Any director in a WAC program has repeatedly seen these phenomena, and he or she may realize that paradigm shifts take time and offer support for faculty that ensures them of the need for patience; directors can also get equally frustrated at faculty's inability to hold the line or their refusal to continue implementing what is considered sound pedagogy. Neither party is completely satisfied, and both might reconsider addressing the third leg of the rhetorical triangle: audience. Whether that audience is the faculty with whom facilitators work or the students with whom faculty work, opening up the strategies behind workshop/classroom pedagogy fosters continuous institutional cultural shifts in teaching and learning. Following are two examples of this: one that shows how facilitators have to practice, rethink, and connect their own classroom activities with disciplinary teaching and learning workshops and one that demonstrates the role students can play in changing the institution's teaching and learning culture.

Listening and Learning from Audience

In the WAC faculty workshops recently conducted, I've used an idea my colleague Susan Schorn and I adopted from colleagues Neill Thew and Magnus Gustafsson (2006). While standing in a circle, faculty are given a numbered list of traditional and contemporary ideas about student writing (see appendix). Each statement is read, and the more strongly the faculty member believes in the statement, the closer to the center of the circle he or she places the number assigned the statement. At the same time, though, faculty are physically indicating their agreement and disagreement by correspondingly moving toward the center or periphery of the circle they are in. While this sounds more like a children's game than an activity in which very high research university faculty would be willing to engage, in every case I have seen and in every subsequent evaluation, faculty enjoy this visual and physical declaration and comparison of their assumptions.

For one, no one has ever asked them to articulate their assumptions about student writing. For another, they are quite astonished to *see* their assumptions, to view faculty they know or those from a range of disciplines disagreeing or agreeing with them about something as "basic" as writing. They begin to ask why: How have they come to construct writing/learning in their particular ways? Are these disciplinary? Personal? Experiential? The power of this exercise lies in how quickly faculty relate their experience with that of students who come into their classes with assumptions about the subject matter, about learning, about them (from Pick-a-Professor or professor.com). They begin to see that student assumptions and attitudes factor into the effectiveness of their classes and that adopting a teaching approach that is dynamic and responsive can change what they most care about: that students learn the content about which they are so passionate.

They also begin to find, within each discipline, ways to talk about these preheld assumptions, to address how students learn as well as what they already think about population geography, Beowulf, or the "mechanical" in engineering. They experience in their interdisciplinary groups the importance of listening to their colleagues-as-students define "exemplify," "propose," "delineate." Lively discussions ensue over these terms, and faculty see they are both disciplinarily loaded and personally imbued with meaning. In the same way, they come to understand that their own students, despite their explanations, may well incorrectly interpret "discuss," even when given examples, because they read the directions through their lens of previous experience. By asking faculty to examine their own personal and disciplinary understandings of assignment terminology, they experience the difficulty students have — and they understand the need to have a quick and similar activity with their students before sending them off with four-page assignment sheets that needlessly attempt to explain terminology — from the faculty member's own viewpoint. The more faculty engage in this ethnographic exploration of their own understanding of students, the more they begin to see how even the traditional lecture might gain new life in their classrooms if they deliver it *with* their audience rather than at them.

PRACTICING WITH INSTEAD OF TALKING AT

While devoting some class time to finding out student assumptions, it is difficult to account for all factors in a classroom population. One other method can assist both teachers and students in changing the dynamic of their practice: using classroom writing mentors. Also called writing fellows, associates, consultants, or tutors, these are graduate or undergraduate students trained as writing tutors who (usually) are linked to a writing-intensive class; they work specifically with students on the writing assigned in the class, but they also work with instructors. A concept started by Tori Haring-Smith at Brown University in the 1980s, several iterations of the original "writing fellows" model have emerged to suit particular theories, contexts, and budgets; however, the use of writing fellows is also closely tied to assumptions about teaching and learning — and some uses of fellows may still support the two-legged, missionary approach that can undermine any pedagogical movement. The way in which writing mentors are used avoids the two-legged trap and fosters change in students and faculty.

When I first had an opportunity to establish a writing center/WAC program and considered using writing tutors in a classroom, there were two models available; one was Haring-Smith's, similar to SI,[2] wherein the writing fellows attend class and work with students, serving as junior teaching assistants. The other model grew out of writing centers: writing tutors are introduced to the class as "their" tutor, may attend a few classes, talk to the instructor about the assignments, and then work with students individually. In order to understand whether linking a tutor to a class would make any difference, I first attached myself as a writing tutor to the art history class.[3] What I learned then, twenty years ago, has continued to develop, but the experience demonstrated to me the need to get inside a discipline, to become familiar with the actual classroom environment, to come to know the teaching personality, and to question my own disciplinary frames. This highlighted for me the interactive nature of classroom work and the need for students, professor, and facilitator (faculty development director or tutor) to mutually engage in the knowledge building within a class: naming writing tutors linked to classroom "writing mentors" better defined this relationship.

Built on the idea of mutual mentoring among the three principals — the writing mentor, student, and instructor — the name underscores the role of "a person who offers support and guidance to another; an experienced and trusted counsellor or friend; a patron, a sponsor" (*Oxford English Dictionary*). A mentor, like a faculty development facilitator, brings expertise; but within a mutual mentoring relationship the mentor also benefits from listening and learning — from being mentored in return by those to whom she is listening.[4] Peer writing mentors act as bridges between instructors and students, translating expectations of the former and questions of the latter to each. They foster communication, and, in the process, open first to themselves and then to each group the purpose behind the pedagogy being used. That may mean explaining to students that, rather than being busy work, response journals or freewriting are rich resources for finding one's own questions to pursue, that they may serve as pieces of a larger paper, that they sharpen summary and thinking skills. It may also mean explaining to faculty, from that peer point of view, that writing a five-page paper can be more challenging for undergraduate students, more in line with developing their novice critical thinking skills within a discipline, and more rewarding to read than a twenty-page paper. What the mentor does is facilitate pedagogical change and effectiveness by serving as a fulcrum for the give and take of teaching and learning within a classroom.

During this process, the student writing mentor herself benefits from the double vision gained from listening to both students and instructor. Situated in what, for her, is a low-stakes learning environment (she doesn't have to take tests, produce papers, demonstrate learning for a grade), the writing mentor learns disciplinary ways of thinking and writing from the inside out — within the context of that class and from that instructor's pedagogical and theoretical point of view. Further, a mentor can communicate her perspective in a nonthreatening way to each of the other two groups because of the positioning of each as mutual mentors. This is why, as my former dean, Richard Lariviere, recognized, peer writing mentors "are the best faculty development we have going." Having requested a writing mentor for his class, he quickly understood the role she played in changing how he thought about students, how he listened to them, and what their potential was for changing the teaching-learning culture (personal communication, 2007). This use of writing mentors not only mutually benefits everyone, but also is another example of how to implement interactive faculty development that addresses all involved in teaching and learning — including the students — and is based on a mutual exploration and expansion of the teaching-learning cycle.

Early data from research in process indicate that by situating mentors *within* the classroom/discipline, a balance between missionary and "going native" is reached as each participant (student-mentor-instructor) weaves together expertise and reflection during the construction of teaching and learning. Each are experts to a point, since each brings something to the table, but they also continually learn from the ever-changing context by which their expertise is shaped. The mentors are mentored — all of them.

Naming can play an important role by constantly reminding the community about the assumptions behind the activity. "Faculty Development," "Teaching and Learning," or "Institutional Excellence" all point to and promote a "center" out of which models emerge rather, perhaps, than an entire culture that emerges out of the institution. "Centers" might also imply a culture of expertise offered or imposed on the needy or wanting rather than a culture of collaborative engagement. By mutually examining our definitions, that which we name and that by which we define learning, by engaging in rhetorical and reflective listening, and by mentoring — that is, teaching and learning — we can move away from a model of teaching as rules, templates, and regulations; we can begin to engage our own assumptions along with those of our students, changing together the definitions that constrain the evolution of what should be our mutual "development."

Appendix: Exploring Writing — Ideas and Ideals

For each statement below, please mark on the circle where you stood.

1. Writing is used to convey knowledge, facts, and ideas.
2. Writing is used to help students learn to think critically.
3. Writing is used to help students complete productive learning tasks.
4. Writing is used to nurture students' talents.
5. Writing is used to help students understand defined goals/outcomes.
6. Writing is used to assess and accredit student abilities and performance.
7. Writing is used to create a safe place for learning to occur.
8. Writing is used to find out what students already know/can do, in order to meet them there.
9. Writing is used to help students extend their understandings of the world.
10. Writing is used to help students develop themselves.
11. What is at the center of the circle for you? "Writing is used . . ."

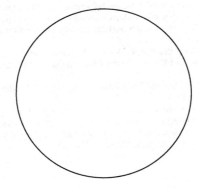

Source: Adapted from Gustafsson and Thew 2006.

NOTES

1. Christopher Thaiss and Terry Meyers Zawacki's (2006) interviews with faculty show this interplay between a "dynamic discipline" and engaged writers.

2. Supplemental instructors are students who are attached to a course after they have taken it in order to help other students succeed. The theories and practices behind this have been most effectively developed through the University of Missouri at Kansas City. See www.umkc.edu/cad/si.

3. I had the good fortune of being in a land-grant state institution where students crossed all ages and generations; therefore, I could take on "peerness" within the classroom.

4. See Mullin and Schorn 2008 and Mullin and Braun forthcoming.

WORKS CITED

Bakhtin, Mikhail M. 1981. *The Dialogic Imagination.* Edited by Michael Holquist and Caryl Emerson. Translated by Michael Holquist. Austin: University of Texas Press.

Bartholomae, David. 1985. "Inventing the University." In *When a Writer Can't Write: Studies in Writer's Block and Other Composing-Process Problems*, ed. Mike Rose, 134–65. New York: Guilford.

Bazerman, Charles. 1991. "The Second Stage of Writing across the Curriculum." *College English* 53, no. 2: 209–12.

Gustafsson, Magnus, and Neill Thew. 2006. "Communication, Reflection, and Assessment across the Curriculum." Preconference workshop, WAC 2006, Clemson, SC.

Jones, Robert, and Joseph J. Comprone. 1993. "Where Do We Go Next in Writing across the Curriculum?" *College Composition and Communication* 44, no. 1: 59–68.

McLeod, Susan H. 1989. "Writing across the Curriculum: The Second Stage, and Beyond." *College Composition and Communication* 40, no. 3: 337–43.

Mullin, Joan. 1998. "Alternative Pedagogy: Visualizing Theories of Composition." In *ARTiculating: Teaching Writing in a Visual Culture*, ed. Eric Hobson, Pamela Childers, and Joan Mullin, 57–71. Portsmouth, NH: Heinemann/Boynton-Cook.

Mullin, Joan, and Paula Braun. Forthcoming. "The Reciprocol Nature of Successful Mentoring Relationships: Changing the Academic Culture." In *Stories of Mentoring, Theories and Praxis*, ed. Michelle Eble and Lynée Lewis Gaillets. West Lafayette, IN: Parlor.

Mullin, Joan, Doug Enders, Neil Reid, and Jason Baldridge. 1998. "Constructing Each Other: Collaborating across Disciplines and Roles." In *Weaving Knowledge Together: Writing Centers and Collaboration*, ed. Carol Peterson Haviland, 153–70. Emmitsburgh, MD: NWCA Press.

Mullin, Joan, and Susan Schorn. 2008. "Challenging Our Practices, Supporting Our Theories: Writing Mentors as Change Agents across Discourse Communities." *Across the Disciplines*. Available at wac.colostate.edu/atd.

Ratcliffe, Krista. 2005. *Rhetorical Listening: Identification, Gender, Whiteness*. Carbondale: Southern Illinois University Press.

Russell, David, and Arturo Yañez. 2002. " 'Big Picture People Rarely Become Historians': Genre Systems and the Contradictions of General Education." In *Writing Selves/Writing Societies: Research from Activity Perspectives*, ed. Charles Bazerman and David Russell, 331–62. Fort Collins, CO: WAC Clearinghouse. wac.colostate.edu/books/selves_societies/russell/russell.pdf.

Schneider, Barbara. 2008. "The Rhetorical Situation: Examining the Framing of Professional Development." *Pedagogy* 8, no. 3: 509–22.

Segal, Judy, Anthony Pare, Doug Brent, and Douglas Vipond. 1998. "The Researcher as Missionary: Problems with Rhetoric and Reform in the Disciplines." *College Composition and Communication* 50, no. 1: 71–90.

Shaughnessy, Mina P. 1977. *Errors and Expectations: A Guide for the Teacher of Basic Writing*. New York: Oxford University Press.

Thaiss, Christopher, and Terry Meyers Zawacki. 2006. *Engaged Writers, Dynamic Disciplines: Research on the Academic Writing Life*. Portsmouth, NH: Boynton/Cook, Heinemann.

Tobin, Lad. 1996. "Car Wrecks, Baseball Caps, and Man-to-Man Defense: The Personal Narratives of Adolescent Males." *College English* 58, no. 2: 158–75.

Theorizing and Researching WAC

Introduction to Part Three

Over the past forty years, scholars have made enormous contributions to WAC theory and research, giving us a rich and deep body of work to guide our field. This is especially true of research into the nature of discourse in the disciplines and professions, and the ways writing works in these fields to produce knowledge. The stream of inquiry commonly referred to as writing in the disciplines (WID) brings the discourse practices of academic, scientific, and professional communities within the purview of WAC inquiry. Additionally, advances in theory and research on learning in cognitive psychology, education, linguistics, and composition have provided WAC practitioners with valuable insights for improving teaching practices, understanding writing processes, making visible the needs of students, and refining claims about the power of writing to foster learning and participation. Our aim in this section is to provide future WAC leaders with essential touchstone pieces.

The first two selections offer theoretical perspectives on the nature and impact of disciplinary discourse on learning, teaching, and research. We begin with Michael Carter's "Ways of Knowing, Doing, and Writing in the Disciplines," which received the 2008 Braddock Award for outstanding article of the year from *College Composition and Communication*. Carter's carefully parsed analysis of metadisciplines and metagenres within and across disciplines situates the specialized learning outcomes associated with particular disciplines in relationship to the kinds of writing students perform in their courses. These large "meta" frames help to illuminate common elements of academic work (e.g., learning outcomes, methodologies, epistemologies) and can assist WAC workshop leaders in facilitating conversations with faculty from across the disciplines regarding the activity systems through which students move and in which they develop. Charles Bazerman's "From Cultural Criticism to Disciplinary Participation: Living with Powerful Words" addresses numerous critiques of WAC's strong emphasis on teaching students to adapt to the conventions, methods, epistemologies, and genres of the disciplines (see, for example, LeCourt in Part One of this volume). He presses WAC leaders to engage even more deeply with the contested and heteroglossic nature of disciplinary conversations, arguing that "[i]t is not the serious attention to disciplinary discourse that restricts our intellectual options *but the refusal to attend* that fosters the hegemony of narrow discourses" (our emphasis). Both Bazerman and Carter make compelling cases for the value of continued and systematic investigation into disciplinary knowledge, genres, and conventions by faculty and students.

From these theoretical perspectives, we turn to Vivian Zamel's "Strangers in Academia: The Experiences of Faculty and ESL Students Across the Curriculum," which provides a recent example of the historical activity of WAC theorists addressing the changing demographics of higher education (see for example, Shaughnessy; Sternglass). Zamel contends that the increase in international students and second language learners demands new approaches to WAC and, in particular, a careful look at the impact of teacher assumptions on pedagogical practice.

Much early WAC work focused on practice, often without rigorous supporting evidence for the claims being made. As the field matures, WAC research is increasing in both quantity and methodological richness. Today, researchers are employing a wide variety of methodologies to investigate many areas central to WAC, including the nature of professional and academic writing and the institutional settings in which these discourses operate; classroom discourse and learning in both general education and courses rooted in disciplinary specialization; student's writing and personal development; faculty writing activities and their relationship to pedagogy; and the impact of technology on teaching with writing and students' literacy practices. The last three articles in this part provide examples of WAC research at the programmatic, institutional, and classroom levels.

Emphasizing the ways in which WAC ideas instantiate themselves in local settings in "'As You're Writing, You Have These Epiphanies': What College Students Say About Writing and Learning in Their Majors," Tom Hilgers, Edna Lardizabal Hussey, and Monica Stitt-Bergh provide an overview of their research on student experiences with writing assignments in writing intensive (WI) courses at the University of Hawaii at Manoa. Their study is an example of WAC research at the programmatic level, one that aims to tease out the nuances of student experiences through interviews. Their results suggest a number of positive outcomes from participation in WI courses, including a greater sense of audience awareness and a wider repertoire of strategies for generating, drafting, and revising texts. Hilgers and his colleagues found that, as students gained more experience with writing in their majors, their goals for writing gradually shifted from satisfying the immediate rhetorical context of the grade toward writing for their own purposes.

Nancy Sommers and Laura Saltz report similar findings in their longitudinal study of student writing development that followed a cohort of Harvard student writers for four years as they progressed through their majors. In "The Novice as Expert: Writing the Freshman Year," they report on what students said about the writing they were asked to do outside of the required composition course, on their analysis of the "artifacts" — assignments, papers, teacher feedback — students brought with them to the interviews, and on the results of surveys they administered. Somers and Saltz wanted to know what might be idiosyncratic from student to student, and what might be generalizable to the transition most students experience in the encounter with unfamiliar academic genres. Their study, like Hilgers et al.'s, reveals the complexity of writing in the academic disciplines and the multiple avenues available to faculty for developing student writing abilities and engaging students in their own writing processes.

In "Innovation Across the Curriculum: Three Case Studies in Teaching Science and Engineering Communication," Jennifer Craig, Neal Lerner, and Mya Poe provide an excellent example of WAC research at the course level, in particular communication intensive courses at MIT. Echoing Carter's position that writing is a form of doing, their chapter describes an ecology of courses and writing tasks aimed at fostering the development of professional identities as students strive to meet target communication competencies, work effectively in teams, and argue with visual data. Their selection provides explanations of the design of the learning outcomes for each class they studied, the methods of implementation, and an assessment of the effectiveness of the various course components. The results are presented in large measure through case studies of individual students who move through these courses. Throughout, the authors point to the many challenges of relating classroom activity to professional practice and underscore the urgency for WAC practitioners to address today's broadening landscape of digital technology and communication activities in the disciplines and professions. Moreover, by its inclusion in the journal *IEEE Transactions in Professional Communication*, the article illustrates the ways in which WAC discourse has been taken up in disciplinary contexts, like engineering.

WORKS CITED

Shaughnessy, Mina P. *Errors and Expectations: A Guide for the Teacher of Basic Writing*. New York: Oxford UP, 1977. Print.
Sternglass, Marilyn S. *Time to Know Them: A Longitudinal Study of Writing and Learning at the College Level*. Mahwah: Erlbaum, 1997. Print.

14 Ways of Knowing, Doing, and Writing in the Disciplines

MICHAEL CARTER

Those of us who work in writing in the disciplines (WID) are aware of a disjunction between the way we conceive the relationship between writing and knowing in the disciplines and the way so many faculty across our colleges and universities conceive that relationship. This disjunction may be quickly summed up as the division between writing in the disciplines and writing outside the disciplines. According to David R. Russell, writing outside the disciplines may be explained in part by the seeming "transparency" of writing: because professors typically learn to write in their disciplines not by any direct instruction but by a process of slow acculturation through various apprenticeship discourses, they are unable to see that writing itself is specific to the discipline. Consequently, faculty in the disciplines continue to conceive of writing as generalizable to all disciplines and therefore distinct from disciplinary knowledge, to be learned as a general skill outside the disciplines (*Writing* 14–20, "Writing Across" 55–56).

It's little wonder, then, that so many faculty in the disciplines complain about being asked to become "writing teachers," arguing that incorporating writing into their classrooms will result in an unacceptable sacrifice of course content. In a model of education understood as the delivery of specialized disciplinary knowledge, writing is considered outside the disciplines, the province of English teachers, and thus unable to play an important role in the disciplines.

The assumptions behind writing outside the disciplines are deeply ingrained in the very concept of the university, based on a particular understanding of the disciplines that has its roots in the transition to the modern American university in the last quarter of the nineteenth century. Under the influence of the German system of higher education, which was founded on *Wissenschaft* or scholarly knowledge, American professors embraced "pure science" as the defining characteristic of the university, an emphasis on rigorous research, typically empirical, and publication in scholarly journals. Unlike the older U.S. college system, in which education was unified, with all stu-

From *College Composition and Communication* 58.3 (2007): 385–418.

dents following the same course of study taught by generalists who could, and often did, shift from one course to another, the new university came to be divided into highly specialized domains of knowledge, each with its own learned societies and journals (Brubacher and Rudy 368; Lucas 179–80; Russell, *Writing* 46–51; Veysey 121–28, 159–73). This movement toward disciplinary specialization was coincident with the demise of rhetoric as a generally required course and the rise of freshman composition as the specific treatment for the poor writing skills of entering students (Connors 3–8; Russell, *Writing* 51–63). This conception of the disciplines as domains of specialized content knowledge, reinforced by the assumption that a writing course outside the disciplines could somehow improve students' writing in the disciplines, has led, as Russell has suggested, to a specialized conception of disciplinary knowledge combined with a generalized conception of writing.

In sharp contrast to writing outside the disciplines, writing in the disciplines is founded on an integrative relationship between writing and knowing. Its roots lie in rhetoric, in which invention has historically played a critical role in both recovering knowledge and generating new knowledge (McKeon; Miller, "The Aristotelian"). The rediscovery of invention in composition (Lauer; Rohman; Young et al.) and the rhetoric-as-epistemic movement (Leff; Scott, "On Viewing," "On Viewing . . . Ten Years Later") provided support for the idea of writing as a way of knowing and learning (Berthoff; Emig; Flower and Hayes; Odell; Reither). WID developed as a response to the recognition that different disciplines are characterized by distinct ways of writing and knowing (Bazerman, "The Second"; Jones and Comprone; Kirscht et al.; McLeod). Thus, a specialized conception of disciplinary knowledge is integrated with a specialized conception of writing.

One way of understanding the distinction I am drawing between writing outside and writing in the disciplines is the difference between knowledge and knowing, that is, disciplines as repositories and delivery systems for relatively static content knowledge versus disciplines as active ways of knowing. Some psychologists describe this distinction as declarative or conceptual knowledge on the one hand and procedural or process knowledge on the other, the difference between knowing that and knowing how (e.g., Anderson). Because the organizing principle of knowledge in the disciplines is typically perceived as conceptual knowledge, faculty and students tend to understand learning in a discipline as a process of obtaining, at least in short-term memory, the particular knowledge base of the discipline. The focus of WID, in contrast, tends to be on procedural knowledge, writing as a way of knowing in a discipline.

Thus, the problem for WID professionals is how to bridge the gap between writing in and writing outside the disciplines, the knowing that and the knowing how. This is not a problem that can be solved by reference to our own discipline's understanding of the relationship between writing and knowing. Rather, we need to be able to conceptualize writing in the disciplines in a way that is grounded in the disciplines themselves, a viable alternative to an understanding of writing as universally generalizable. To address that need, I will draw on the idea of disciplinary ways of doing as a link between ways of writing and ways of knowing in the disciplines (e.g., Herrington; Russell, "Writing to Learn to Do"). In bridging the conceptual gap between knowing and writing in the disciplines, the concept of ways of doing offers the possibility for bridging the outside/in gap as well.

First, I will explore the ties that link ways of knowing, doing, and writing in the disciplines and describe a procedure we have used on our campus to guide faculty in identifying ways of doing in their disciplines. This process helps faculty understand their disciplines as ways of knowing, not just domains of declarative knowledge, and thus to see more readily how writing is related to knowing. Next, I will place these ways of knowing, doing, and writing in the context of North American genre theory, particularly as applied by Carolyn R. Miller, Charles Bazerman, and Russell. This genre theory is useful not only because it establishes a direct connection between writing and doing and thus knowing but also because it points to certain patterns in ways of doing across the disciplines. An advantage of being able to discern these patterns, what I call metagenres and metadisciplines, is that they provide a foundation WID professionals can use for working more effectively with faculty. I illustrate these patterns by drawing on ways of doing and writing identified by faculty at my university. Finally, I place this project within a critique of the modern university and its disciplinary structures of knowledge and consider the idea of knowing, doing, and writing in the disciplines as a basis for postdisciplinary inquiry.

WAYS OF KNOWING, DOING, AND WRITING IN THE DISCIPLINES

Because doing plays a central role in this conception of writing in the disciplines, it may be helpful to understand disciplinary ways of doing and the connection to knowing and writing by looking at an illustration of a concrete form of doing: laboratory experiments. A lab experiment is designed to engage students in a particular way of doing by which they will learn about the scientific concept of the lab and also how to apply an empirical mode of reasoning about the physical world. Thus, the lab experience is a way of doing that is directed toward a way of knowing. It is primarily in writing the lab report, however, that doing becomes knowing. More than merely evidence of having completed the lab and having found the right answers, the lab report frames the doing as a scientific way of knowing: introduction, methods, results, discussion; establishing a hypothesis, testing the hypothesis, accumulating evidence related to the hypothesis, determining whether or not the hypothesis is accepted and why. It provides an opportunity for students to reflect on the relationship between the lab and the scientific concept of the lab and to frame the doing of the lab in the structure of scientific reasoning. This example of a concrete way of doing illustrates the potential relationship that exists among ways of knowing and writing in more abstract ways of doing in the university. From this perspective, writing may be understood as a meta-doing: particular kinds of writing are ways of doing that instantiate particular kinds of doing by giving shape to particular ways of knowing in the disciplines.

It is this relationship among knowing, doing, and writing that is concealed by the disciplinary focus on conceptual knowledge. Doing is the middle term that links writing and knowing in the disciplines. Thus, the challenge in reframing the disciplines as ways of knowing, doing, and writing is to find a means of describing in convincing terms the ways of doing that characterize the disciplines, convincing, that is, to faculty and students in the disciplines. But how do we find such descriptions of the disciplines?

One way is to ask faculty. At my university, we are in the eighth year of an extensive assessment effort based on identifying and measuring outcomes for all the undergraduate programs on campus. This effort is a response both to a mandate from our regional accrediting agency and to a broad recognition that improvement of academic programs requires serious program assessment. Outcomes-based assessment is the process of describing and measuring for each program the skills, knowledge, and other attributes students are expected to demonstrate by the time they graduate. An outcome is what students should be able to do; thus, outcomes describe ways of doing, the procedural knowledge of the disciplines. Faculty are asked first to describe what they expect their majors to be able to do; second to identify what data they will gather, typically students' written work, for determining how well the program has enabled students to achieve the expectations; and third to create and apply a plan for assessing the outcomes. These assessment plans have provided a window onto the ways of doing and associated ways of writing in the disciplines.

Our assessment initiative began by focusing on writing and speaking outcomes and was later melded with a university-wide curriculum assessment initiative. Thus, our Campus Writing and Speaking Program has played an important role in this process, creating an intensive course of action for working with departmental committees to generate outcomes-assessment plans, involving program faculty in the following steps:

- Brainstorming core program values
- Drafting and revising disciplinary outcomes based on those values
- Getting full faculty approval of outcomes
- Brainstorming assessment tools for outcomes
- Drafting and revising assessment procedure
- Getting full faculty approval of assessment procedure

(For a detailed description of this process see Carter.)

In the appendix are two examples, from zoology and psychology, of program outcomes. Notice that each example consists of general goals and specific outcomes, what students are expected to be able to do, along with activities that could be used for teaching and assessing the outcomes. Outcomes, then, are typically written in a way that is both teachable and measurable, to guide teachers in helping students achieve the outcome and to provide implicit criteria that can be used for assessing the extent to which programs have enabled their students to achieve the outcome. Outcomes are demonstrable, that is, they describe what faculty expect their majors to be able to do, ways of doing that are important to the discipline. In the rest of the assessment plans, not included here, faculty identify particular kinds of writing and other learning experiences appropriate to assessing the outcomes. The purpose is to provide faculty with data for making decisions for improving their programs.

The examples illustrate the role of doing in establishing a connection between knowing and writing. For example, the outcomes statement for zoology points to two key disciplinary ways of doing, number 1, being able to engage in scientific inquiry, and number 3, being able to solve problems in zoology. These two ways of doing indicate two important ways of knowing that define the discipline: someone with a degree in zoology should know how to effectively apply scientific reasoning to zoological phenomena and how to solve problems in zoology (the latter a reflection of the large number of majors specializing in fisheries and wildlife management and environmental studies). The kinds of writing that faculty associated with these two sets of outcomes suggest the specialized nature of the outcomes: lab reports, scientific papers, posters, management plans, project proposals, environmental impact statements.

The other three sets of outcomes are more general, not so clearly related to disciplinary ways of doing: being able to generalize information from one context to a related context; to analyze, synthesize, and critique literature in the field; and to write for nonscientific audiences. I would argue that these ways of knowing and doing are more general to the academy. The kinds of writing faculty identified with these outcomes seem to support that argument: homework problems, case studies, essay test questions, literature reviews, annotated bibliographies, critical analyses, articles for newsletters, editorials, summaries — genres that cut across a wide range of disciplines.

Perhaps the most important aspect of the procedure for creating program outcomes is that it is faculty themselves who identify what they expect of their graduates. It is only after these ways of doing have been identified that they are linked to ways of writing, and then not for the sake of writing but for the sake of teaching and assessing the stated outcomes. The disciplinary ways of doing that faculty identify provide a direct link between ways of knowing and ways of writing in the disciplines. Doing enacts the knowing through students' writing, and the writing gives shape to the ways of knowing and doing in a discipline. So instead of focusing only on the conceptual knowledge that has traditionally defined the disciplines, faculty are encouraged to focus also on what their students should be able to do, represented largely in their writing. Having faculty identify disciplinary ways of doing and then assess them through students' writing is a step toward situating writing in, not outside, the disciplines.

GENRES AND METAGENRES

We can easily recognize the lab report I used as an example in the previous section as an academic genre typical of scientific disciplines. It is a response to a particular learning situation marked by a particular way of knowing and doing. But it is also possible to see the lab report as one genre within a broader category of ways of knowing and doing in the disciplines, similar learning situations that call for responses similar to the lab report. The assessment plans, when looked at together, revealed several of these categories of procedural knowledge.

Though declarative knowledge is typically specific to individual disciplines and even to subdisciplines, the procedural knowledge that faculty described tended to be more generic. And because individual academic programs also identified kinds of writing to be used both to teach and assess the outcomes, these patterns of doing were also linked explicitly to written genres. To emphasize the close connection between these disciplinary patterns of doing and particular kinds of writing-that is, each way of doing instantiated in written genres — I call these general ways of doing metagenres.[1]

In her seminal "Genre as Social Action," Carolyn R. Miller defines genre as a typified response to recurrent rhetorical situations. In a later piece, Miller extends her earlier description of genre as "a cultural artifact" to explore the connection between genre and cultures. Genre, she says, occupies a middle position between microlevel and macrolevel forms of analysis, providing a link between particular linguistic processes and particular cultures that both constitute and are constituted by these processes ("Rhetorical Community" 6869). Using the analogy of an anthropologist extrapolating an ancient culture from found artifacts, Miller says that a set of genres "adumbrates a relationship between material particulars, instantiations of a genre in individual acts, and systems of value and signification" in cultures (70).

Another approach to a macrolevel understanding of genre is Bazerman's concept of system of genres, "a complex web of interrelated genres where each participant makes a recognizable act or move in some recognizable genre, which then may be followed by a certain range of appropriate generic responses by others" ("Systems" 96–97). The particular setting that Bazerman investigates is the patent office and the sequence of individual genres that comprise the process of patent applications. Systems of genres provide a concept for understanding the way interrelated genres constitute specific networks of social action. Whereas Bazerman highlights the sequential nature of genres within a system of genres, John Swales points out that in the literature, genre system has been applied to a spectrum of meanings, from established sequences in which genres are typically performed to a loose collection of genres related to each other by a common enterprise (63–64).

Russell builds on the work of Miller and Bazerman in his treatment of genre systems. Drawing on activity theory, Russell situates his understanding of genre within the context of activity systems, structures of human behavior — such as families, religious groups, disciplines, and schools — by which individuals and groups use any number of a variety of means to advance a shared activity ("Rethinking" 510). In activity theory, a written genre may be understood as texts that "are all used to operationalize the same recurring, typified actions of an activity system" (518). Russell uses the idea of genre system as a way of conceptualizing the way various related written genres act within a complex activity system as instruments both to stabilize and to create opportunities to change those activity systems (519–24).

Miller, Bazerman, and Russell address three common themes. First, they define genre as social action, ways of doing and writing by which individual linguistic acts on the microlevel constitute social formations on the macrolevel. Second, they establish the concept of genre set as a collection of related genres. Third, they use the genre set to indicate the role that related genres play in constituting complex social formations. Thus, a genre set may be understood as occupying a level somewhere between the individual genre and the social formation.

As an upper midlevel entity, the genre set is the basis for my use of metagenre, which carries a more particular usage than the loose sense of genre set and less of the connotation of a sequence associated with system of genres. Metagenre signifies a higher category, a genre of genres. Miller's definition of genre as a typified response to a recurrent rhetorical situation directs our attention to certain patterns in the social action of language, patterns of recurring situations and of similar responses to those situations. A metagenre, then, directs our attention to broader patterns of language as social action, similar kinds of typified responses to related recurrent situations. And just as the genre is a dynamic concept, representing a response to a rhetorical situation that both defines and is defined by the situation, a metagenre is also dynamic. In the terminology I've been using thus far, a metagenre indicates a structure of similar ways of doing that point to similar ways of writing and knowing. For example, the lab report may be seen as one of a collection of possible responses to learning situations that call for empirical inquiry, a collection that includes the scientific paper, poster, and project proposal (three of the genres listed by the zoology faculty members for their outcome 1).

Moreover, the idea that genre sets constitute complex social formations is the basis for the concept of the metadiscipline. Together, the genres that compose a metagenre point to a social formation composed of individual disciplines that emphasize the way of doing defined by the metagenre. A metadiscipline, then, is a higher category of disciplines. These broader structures direct our attention away from the specialized conceptual knowledge of individual disciplines, knowledge that is of less significance when diverse disciplines are grouped together, and toward the ways of knowing, doing, and writing common to the disciplines in a metadiscipline.

Thus, the concept of disciplinary ways of knowing, doing, and writing may be understood from three points of view associated with the three themes from Miller, Bazerman, and Russell. The first is the individual discipline. The understanding of genre as social action suggests the strong connection between doing and writing identified by faculty in the disciplines. The ways of doing in the outcomes statements point explicitly to ways of writing and implicitly to ways of knowing. The second point of view is the metagenre. The idea of genre set implies categories of knowing, doing, and writing that cut across disciplines but may be inflected differently in different disciplines and in different contexts. These patterns emerge out of the outcomes identified by faculty in a wide range of disciplines. The third point of view is the metadiscipline. The concept of a relationship between genre sets and complex social formations suggests that disciplines themselves may be grouped according to common ways of knowing, doing, and writing. Each of these three perspectives emphasizes the critical role of writing in the disciplines. In the next two sections, I will explore the concepts of metagenres and metadisciplines.

FOUR METAGENRES

The outcomes statements created by faculty showed that certain ways of doing were repeated in general terms across a variety of disciplines: responses to academic learning situations that call for problem solving, for empirical inquiry, for research from sources, and for performance. These metagenres are based on assessment plans from fifty-one programs from all nine undergraduate colleges at my university. I am also drawing, to a much less extent, on notes taken as I have worked with faculty committees and on other conversations I have had with faculty, which allow me to place the outcomes in the context of intentions expressed by faculty. I cannot claim that these are the only metagenres represented in the data, but these four serve the purpose of illustrating the concept and its application to the academy. And because the data set is limited to programs at my own university (a large, Southern, land-grant institution), the metagenres I survey here may not be generalizable to other institutions. But I believe that what may be generalizable is the idea of academic metagenres and their role in highlighting the critical place of writing in the disciplines.

For each of the four metagenres, I will describe the ways of doing identified by faculty in selected programs, the generic learning situation that defines the metagenre, and the genres that compose the typified responses to the generic learning situation.

Responses to Academic Situations That Call for Problem Solving

Not surprising for a land-grant university with strong engineering and other pre-professional programs, problem solving is the dominant metagenre in the data set. The first example of problem solving as a way of doing comes from the food science program.

> Food science majors should be able to do the following:
> a. identify, define, and analyze a problem: what it is that generates the problem, what is given, what is unknown, and what are the criteria for viable solutions to the problem

b. determine what information is appropriate to solving the problem and then find it, assess its authority and validity, and use it effectively

c. integrate and apply basic science and mathematics as well as food sciences to the solution of problems in food systems

d. offer a range of potential viable solutions to the problem

e. evaluate the solutions according to the established criteria, choose the most viable solution, and make a convincing case for that solution

The second example is from textiles engineering. Engineering programs have been directed to create and evaluate program outcomes by the Accreditation Board of Engineering and Technology (ABET). ABET specifies a series of outcomes that programs are able to define for themselves. Program outcome 3c is generally considered the problem-solving outcome, typically the focus of capstone design courses: "an ability to design a system, component, or process to meet desired needs." Faculty in textiles engineering defined their expectations for students as follows (see appendix for full version):

To demonstrate that graduates have an ability to design a system, component, or process to meet desired needs, they should show that they have a mastery of the design process and that they can apply that process effectively in generating and presenting a design in textiles engineering:

a. problem definition: establishing a problem or need, identifying customer and project requirements, performing market and technical analyses

b. concept generation: converting customer and project requirements to product specifications, generating multiple product options

c. concept selection: comparing product options to product specifications, selecting optimal product option(s)

d. concept refinement: creating and testing prototypes or models; analyzing technical, economic, and environmental viability of design based on prototype or model; selling the product

The descriptions of problem solving in food science and textiles engineering point to a common learning situation and response to that situation. Faculty members create an occasion for students to learn the problem-solving skills appropriate to their fields by applying those skills in situations similar to those students would encounter in their professions. The responses to this common learning situation generally call for students to define a problem, establish parameters for a solution to the problem, generate possible solutions, and identify and justify a recommended solution to the problem.

The metagenre of problem solving is composed of genres named by faculty that share all or most of these features of a typified response to the situation across different disciplines. In Russell's terminology, these genres share the same broad motive, or purpose, which links them in an overall genre system that includes these genres:

- business plans
- feasibility reports
- management plans
- marketing plans
- reports to management
- project reports
- project proposals
- technical memoranda
- technical reports

Responses to Academic Situations That Call for Empirical Inquiry

Empirical inquiry is a way of doing that consists of answering questions by drawing conclusions from systematic investigation based on empirical data. Two examples of empirical inquiry come from microbiology and political science.

Microbiology

Microbiology students should be able to:

a. ask pertinent questions about microbiology, formulate hypotheses based on those questions, and design experiments to test those hypotheses

b. apply deliberate and thorough observational skills to conduct experiments and collect data

c. organize and summarize data and present them in a way that is accurate and comprehensible in both verbal and graphical forms

d. interpret data and draw conclusions that allow the students to support or refute hypotheses and make a case for alternative hypotheses

Political Science

Upon graduation, political science majors should demonstrate an ability to understand and produce quality political science research. Specifically, students should be able to show that they can:

a. identify important research questions

b. identify an existing theory in political science appropriate to the investigation

c. create hypotheses

d. test hypotheses using rigorous empiricism

e. apply appropriate methodologies to collected data

f. explain acquired information in the context of existing knowledge in the field

Looking at metagenres allows us to see similarities among ways of doing across disciplines that are traditionally considered distinct, in this case the natural and social sciences. The similar outcomes in microbiology and political science suggest a common learning situation, one created by faculty to enable students to learn how to apply the empirical research paradigm. Though the research conventions of microbiology and political science differ in significant ways, the faculty in both fields point to similar ways of doing: identifying questions related to the field, establishing a hypothesis for answers to the questions, testing the hypothesis by gathering data based on observations, and drawing conclusions about the hypothesis from the data. The responses to this situation are generally the same. It is not an accident that the outcomes in microbiology correspond to the parts of a scientific report — introduction, methods, results, and discussion. Faculty in political science expect their students to follow a similar model for reporting research. It is the classic way of responding to situations that call for empirical research.

The metagenre of empirical inquiry includes genres such as these:

- laboratory report
- poster
- poster presentation
- research proposal
- research report
- scientific article
- scientific presentation

Responses to Academic Situations That Call for Research from Sources

The two primary distinguishing characteristics of this metagenre are (1) the kind of research that is done, that is, not based on data gathered from independent observations but largely on sources that have their origins elsewhere; and (2) the goal of the research, which typically does not have extrinsic value, such as solving practical problems or investigating hypotheses, but value that is intrinsic to the discipline (more on this below). One example of a way of doing in this metagenre is from history.

History

History majors should be able to:

a. pose an interesting research question about history
b. locate relevant primary and secondary sources for investigating a research question
c. critically evaluate primary and secondary sources in terms of credibility, authenticity, interpretive stance, audience, potential biases, and value for answering the research question
d. marshall the evidence from the research to support a historical argument for an answer to a research question

Another example is from a program in multidisciplinary studies, in which students are expected to bring more than one discipline to bear on their research projects.

Multidisciplinary Studies

Students should be able to develop and apply research skills needed for multidisciplinary projects. Specifically, students should be able to demonstrate that they can:

a. take an interest or problem not contained by a single discipline and mold it into a question that will allow them to explore that interest or problem

b. choose and apply appropriate research methodologies from more than one discipline to address the research question and generate new questions

c. integrate research findings from more than one discipline to form and support a sound argument

d. satisfactorily complete a project that integrates what they have learned in their courses in response to a research question

This metageneric learning situation and response to the situation are more complex than those in the previous metagenres. It is a situation that calls for the very familiar genre of the research paper, which involves a similar way of doing, posing a question, gathering information from resources to answer the question, and making a persuasive case for the answer. However, unlike the other metagenres I have described, the similarity in ways of doing tends to mask the different ways of knowing in the various disciplines.

As I discussed the research paper with faculty in different disciplines, I noticed that they typically described the goals of assigning students to do research in terms that were peculiar to the discipline. Faculty from fields stressing problem solving and empirical research didn't do this; not only were the ways of doing relatively generic across disciplines but also the ways of knowing linked to those ways of doing. It was simply assumed that students in the sciences should know and be able to apply the scientific method or social science methodologies, just as it was assumed that students in engineering and food science should know basic problem-solving skills. In each instance, learning the ways of doing was considered an end in itself, a way of knowing essential to the discipline.

But faculty from disciplines that stress research from sources tend to describe that research not as an end in itself but as a means to an end defined by the individual discipline, a specialized way of knowing. Though the means, i.e., the techniques of doing this kind of research, are clearly metageneric, the ends expressed by faculty in different disciplines were distinct. In literature, for example, the goal is to enable students to read and understand literature from historical, cultural, and theoretical perspectives. It is not just reading literature but learning to write about reading in a way that shapes the act of reading, a way of knowing that marks a literature major. Faculty in religious studies identified the agenda underlying research paper assignments in their field as enabling students to think about religion as a scholarly enterprise. Since most of their students become religious studies majors because they are religious people, the faculty engage them in research in order to guide them in understanding religion itself as more than a confessing experience, a subject of scholarly inquiry to be studied from critical, textual, and historical perspectives. Multidisciplinary studies uses research projects as a way of meeting its goal of encouraging majors to conceive of academic inquiry differently, shifting from seeing a question from the perspective of one discipline to seeing it from the perspective of more than one discipline. In each of these cases, the faculty members use the metageneric research from sources not as an end in itself, that is, not so that students will become experts in doing research, but as a means to a specifically disciplinary end, a distinctive way of knowing that characterizes the discipline.

The genres identified by faculty include the historical narrative from sources, literary criticism, paper, research paper, and research project. The first two are clearly disciplinary genres, but the last three terms, which were used most often, best capture the ambiguous nature of the genres that comprise this metagenre, particularly their lack of correspondence to disciplinary or professional genres in a field, which characterized the previous two metagenres. As such, these may be understood as quintessential academic genres, writing that is used to promote certain ways of knowing and doing without much pretense to practical application beyond the classroom.

Responses to Academic Situations That Call for Performance

The label for this metagenre is intended to denote both the act and the resulting object of a performance, but particularly the primacy of the object as evidence of success in learning to perform the act, the doing of performance. At my university, the disciplines that rely most heavily on this metagenre are in the College of Design. In its assessment guidelines, the college says that its instructional focus is less on conceptual knowledge than on an "enduring understanding, on issues that are at the core of the discipline. These issues are best assessed through *performance* and *artifacts* that are direct evidence of that performance" (emphasis theirs).

Indeed, the outcomes for departments in the College of Design are labeled as "curriculum performance standards," such as this example from the program in art and design:

a. Understanding of basic design principles, concepts, media, and formats in various fine arts disciplines

b. Mastery of basic foundation techniques, particularly as related to specific fine arts fields

c. The ability to conceive, design, and create works in one or more specific fine arts fields

d. Working knowledge of various production methods and their relationship to conceptualization, development, and completion of works of art

e. Understanding the similarities, differences, and relationships among the various fine arts areas

It's interesting to note that these are not really standards for the performance itself, that is, criteria for directly evaluating either the artistic act or the artistic object. Rather, they are an attempt to define the characteristics of what the assessment guidelines call an "enduring understanding" of the discipline of art and design, an understanding that the artifacts indicate. The artifacts — works of art created by students — represent a certain quality of the act of creating the art which itself suggests the students' achievement of the departments' outcomes listed above.[2]

These outcomes, then, differ in one key regard from the others presented here. Instead of describing explicit ways of doing that point toward implicit ways of knowing, in this case the ways of knowing are made explicit and the way of doing implicit. The stress on "enduring knowledge" highlights ways of knowing in contrast to declarative knowledge. It is knowledge that is enacted in performance, generating an artifact that is itself "direct evidence of that performance."

This indirect depiction of a way of doing by the qualities of what is produced by the student may also be found in a discipline outside the College of Design. Here is the primary outcome for the program in rhetoric, writing, and language, which focuses mainly on professional writing, such as technical communication and journalism.

Students in rhetoric, writing, and language:

a. possess a repertoire of writing skills and a familiarity with the conventions governing written discourse in a variety of situations and can apply those skills and conventions creatively and effectively

b. are proficient in designing, writing, and editing documents for various audiences and purposes

c. possess the collaborative skills that allow them to work productively with other writers or specialists to produce effective texts and presentations

Notice that, as in art and design, it is not a particular way of doing that is described here but a set of characteristics of the doer assumed to be represented in the object of the doing. The doing itself is left implicit.

Performance describes a learning situation in which teachers provide opportunities for their students to develop the enduring knowledge necessary for creating the artifacts that are the central focus of students' intended careers. Two features distinguish this learning situation from the previous three. One is that the artifact — what is produced — takes on a heightened status. By way of contrast, faculty and students in engineering understand that the primary locus of engineering lies in solving engineering problems and not in the technical report, which they tend to see as a means of detailing what they did to solve the problem and of recommending solutions. However, designers, artists, journalists, and technical writers see the primary locus of their work as in the artifact itself. The other feature is that these learning situations are opportunities for students to engage in ways of doing that may not lend themselves to explicit description and thus are marked indirectly by qualities of the doer to be represented in the artifact. The learning, then, becomes more of an acquisition of ways of doing than of direct instruction (Krashen). This acquisition tends to occur through the act of creating artifacts that are then critiqued in a way that guides students in the development of enduring ways of knowing. The learning situations are designed to help students acquire the qualities and characteristics that indicate enduring knowledge.

Though the art and design outcomes do not list specific genres, they do refer several times to various "fine arts," presumably drawing, sculpture, painting, multimedia, etc. In rhetoric, writing, and language, the focus is mainly on written performance, including such genres listed by the faculty as documentation, editorials, feature articles, news stories, proposals, and technical reports, but also certain media such as PowerPoint presentations and websites.

The concept of metagenre, based on the idea of genre set in Miller, Bazerman, and Russell, is beneficial not only because it emphasizes the importance of writing in the disciplines but also because it provides a structure WID professionals can use to work with faculty in the disciplines. By highlighting generic patterns of knowing, doing, and writing both within and across disciplines, metagenres underline the critical role that writing can play in helping students participate fully in their disciplines. Learning in the disciplines is much more than banking away conceptual knowledge. WID professionals can use the metagenre to help faculty in the disciplines recognize the broader ways of doing in their own disciplines and to understand how different individual genres can be used as tools for teaching disciplinary ways of doing, a shift in focus from the isolated genre to the metagenre. Enabling faculty to see the broader learning situations of the disciplines may provide the basis for helping them use the various individual genres in a metagenre more strategically throughout the curriculum.

FOUR METADISCIPLINES

Earlier, I pointed out that Miller, Bazerman, and Russell observe a relationship between a set of genres and a social formation that defines and is defined by the set. In contrast to a focus on individual genres, these scholars make the case that looking at the interrelationship among genres that collectively contribute to "operationalizing," as Russell puts it ("Rethinking" 518), complex social formations helps us understand those social formations and the way they are constituted by genres. Here, I am applying that perspective to the genre sets in the academy associated with metagenres. These metagenres highlight broader patterns of disciplinary ways of knowing, doing, and writing that may be thought of as metadisciplines, collections of disciplines that share an emphasis on certain metagenres and are constituted by the various genres within each metagenre.

In my work in helping faculty identify outcomes, it was usually clear where that emphasis lay, from the position an outcome was given in the outcomes statement or from conversations with faculty. However, metadisciplines are not necessarily exclusive; disciplines may belong to more than one metadiscipline. For example, zoology faculty placed empirical research first among its outcomes, as may be expected of a scientific field. But it also included a problem-solving outcome that the faculty evidently believed was of near if not equal importance, a reflection, as I noted above, of the program's focus on preprofessional majors in fisheries and wildlife and environmental studies. In most other cases, though, faculty seemed to value one disciplinary way of doing above others. The composition of metagenres I describe here is not intended to be definitive or generalizable to other institutions. It is a reflection of the data set from my own university and of my own interpretation of disciplinary outcomes statements. It is, thus, an illustration of one way of understanding the pattern of metadisciplines at a university.

Having faculty in the disciplines identify ways of doing and associated ways of writing reveals the extent to which writing is critical to the ways of knowing valued in the disciplines. Broadening the focus to metadisciplines enables WID professionals to identify the larger structures that form the academy and the role that writing plays in constituting those structures. Looking at the academy from the perspective of metadisciplines also tends to further complicate the assumption that disciplines are defined exclusively or even primarily by content knowledge. At the center of each metadiscipline is a way of doing shared by its constituent disciplines despite their differences in content knowledge. Thus, this broader view tends to reduce the emphasis on disciplines as domains of declarative knowledge and highlight the disciplines as ways of doing. And in doing so, it also highlights the integral place of writing in the disciplines. In instantiating the shared ways of doing, writing enacts metadisciplinary ways of knowing. For each of the metadisciplines I describe here, I will list some of the disciplines in my data set that comprise it and identify disciplinary variations I observed.

The genres that comprise the metagenre of problem solving point toward a collection of disciplines that emphasize problem solving as their primary disciplinary way of doing. Disciplines in this metadiscipline include accounting, agricultural and resource economics, animal science, business management, various engineering majors, food science, forestry management, mathematics, pulp and paper science, and psychology. An interesting inclusion in this list is psychology, which, as a social science, would seem to be more appropriately placed with other science programs in empirical inquiry. But as the psychology outcomes indicate, the faculty in that program emphasize students' ability to solve problems, a function of the department's focus on applied psychology.

Variations within the category delineate the different ways in which problem solving is applied in different disciplines within this metadiscipline. First, there are those that stress solving problems by designing a product. Design plays a critical role in engineering, as most engineering programs have a senior design course that acts as a bridge to entering the profession. These courses are usually based on a problem-solving process that leads to a tangible product, an airplane design, a model of a roadway, a piece of machinery, etc. A second variation within this category is disciplines that emphasize the application of specialized knowledge in science or mathematics to solving problems related to the field. Instead of designing a product, food science students, as the outcome above shows, are expected to solve problems by applying what they've learned in their courses as well as in further research in chemistry, microbiology, nutrition, and other sciences. The last variation is problem solving that focuses on gathering information from sources, a way of doing similar to the third metagenre but performed in the context of solving practical problems in a field. An example is agricultural and resource economics, in which students are taught how to find, evaluate, and apply standard economic data to the problems peculiar to that field.

Metadisciplines that share an emphasis on empirical inquiry tend to reside in the sciences, both natural and social, such as anthropology, biology, chemistry, geology, microbiology, political science, and sociology. I have noticed three variations within this metadiscipline. First are those programs that stress hypothetical inquiry, as seen in the examples from microbiology and political science. This kind of doing is typical of what most people associate with science-research that is driven by a hypothesis and is designed to test the hypothesis. But there is another variation that is not hypothetical, which I call descriptive empirical inquiry. For example, I found that most of the lab reports written by geology students are simply descriptions of, say, minerals according to the standard parameters of mineral identification. Faculty noted that much of the professional literature in geology is also descriptive, such as surveying a geological site and the specimens found there. Finally, there is a variation that emphasizes abstract knowledge of methods of inquiry over the actual practice of inquiry. The outcomes statement in anthropology indicates that, although empirical research is critical to the field, students are not actually asked to "do" anthropology. Faculty in that program say it is too difficult and time-consuming for undergraduates to pursue. Thus, the primary genre for teaching students empirical research appropriate to the field is the project proposal.

The metadiscipline composed of disciplines that emphasize research from sources includes history, literature, multidisciplinary studies, philosophy, religious studies, and women and gender studies — generally disciplines in the humanities. As I noted earlier, these disciplines are characterized by a general way of doing but distinct ways of knowing. The primary variation within this metadiscipline accords with the distinct ways of knowing in each discipline.

Performance includes architecture, art and design, graphic design, industrial design, landscape architecture, and language, writing, and rhetoric. It may seem that fields such as industrial design would be better placed in the metadiscipline of problem solving. However, a member of that department said that students don't engage directly in problem solving until graduate school. As undergraduates, the focus of their studies is on learning how to manage the techniques and materials of industrial design, acquiring the "enduring knowledge" of the field they can call upon later for solving problems. My university does not offer a bachelor's degree in music, dance, or theater, but I suspect that these disciplines would also fall within the performance category.

The preponderance of nonwritten performances in art and design and similar programs may seem removed from WID. How could we possibly enhance the work of faculty and students in these fields? However, there is one language-based genre that is crucial to the success of design students, though it never appears explicitly as a program outcome. The assessment document for the College of Design identifies three forms of data for measuring students' achievement of the outcomes: the artifact, a portfolio of artifacts, and the critique. It is the critique that faculty point to as playing an especially important role in evaluating design students, from the very first class to the doctoral defense. Usually oral, though sometimes written, the "crit" involves a presentation of a student's artifact or portfolio that includes an overview of the work, the process and materials involved, and the effectiveness of it in terms of the intended audience or application. This genre typically allows for critiques by faculty and sometimes by other students in response to the student's work.

The critique, then, is itself a performance, or perhaps more accurately a performance about a performance (the artifact or portfolio). It appears to play a significant role, along with the artifact, both in teaching and evaluating enduring knowledge. Learning to manage this genre effectively can have a major impact on a student's success in design, not only in school but also later as a design professional. However, because the critique tends to be an "invisible" genre, there is typically little or no formal instruction and evaluation of the critique itself. WID professionals, perhaps with the aid of colleagues in communication across the curriculum, may be able to work with faculty and students to make the genre more visible, subject to productive instruction and evaluation. Indeed, the critique could also be applied as an effective educational genre in other performance-based curricula.

I suspect that the perspective of the academy provided by metadisciplines would have more immediate value for WID professionals than for faculty in the disciplines. Faculty focused on their own programs may not find that the concept resonates with their needs. For WID faculty, however, the ability to perceive the broader disciplinary formations and to understand the way genres shape and are shaped by those formations offers a rich conception of the integration of writing in the disciplines. This conception also may have practical value. For example, it may be possible to offer workshops for faculty from disciplines within the same metadiscipline in which we help them to see the generic ways of doing and knowing that link their disciplines and then to discover collectively how those ways of doing and knowing are instantiated in writing. In such situations, faculty could learn much about the discourses in their own fields by discovering with each other the similarities and differences of those discourses in other fields.

The metadisciplinary perspective also allows WID professionals to become more aware of the variations within a metagenre among different disciplines, an awareness that may provide a basis for working more effectively with faculty in a single discipline. For instance, understanding the often hidden agendas behind the standard research paper may be useful as we work with faculty and students in metadisciplines that stress research from sources. The similarities in the ways of doing research from sources may obscure the complex disciplinary goal structures behind the research paper. It is important, then, to explore the ways of knowing expected by faculty as well as the more familiar ways of doing. As a rule, the goal is not simply to write a research paper for the sake of learning to manage research from sources but to use the process of doing and writing research to shape a disciplinary way of knowing. A greater awareness of the importance of ways of knowing in the fields allows us to take a more perceptive approach to helping faculty create appropriate learning situations for their students.

CONCLUSION

I began this paper by pointing to the disjunction between writing in and writing outside the disciplines, a result, as Russell suggests, of the tendency of faculty to understand disciplines as domains of specialized knowledge and writing as general across disciplines (*Writing* 14–20, "Writing Across" 55–56). One approach to bridging the gap marked by that disjunction is to focus on ways of doing in the disciplines, a focus that highlights disciplinary ways of knowing and thus offers an alternative to the dominion of declarative knowledge. Doing is the key to connecting knowing and writing in the disciplines. North American genre theory provides a theoretical foundation for conceptualizing the relationship between doing and writing and extending that relationship to metagenres and metadisciplines.

An emphasis on disciplinary ways of doing may allow us to address what Russell refers to as the transparency of writing in the disciplines (*Writing* 14–20, "Writing Across" 55–56). The process described here of encouraging faculty to identify ways of doing and specific ways of writing and assessing the writing, usually with rubrics they have designed, seems to make writing more opaque. Faculty come to understand that what counts as good writing is writing that meets the expectations of faculty in their disciplines. It's also beneficial that all this takes place on their own turf. It is not the writing professional who is telling them what counts as good writing in their fields. The faculty themselves are the experts. And as experts, they also take responsibility for students' writing in their disciplines. Thus, instead of perceiving of WID as asking them to become "writing teachers," they can see that their responsibility for teaching the ways of knowing and doing in their disciplines also extends to writing, which is not separate from but essential to their disciplines. The WID professional becomes an agent for helping faculty achieve their expectations for what students should be able to do.

At my university, we were able to take advantage of outcomes-based program assessment, which initiated and formalized the process of identifying disciplinary ways of doing. Our Campus Writing and Speaking Program played a critical role in that process because we realized early on the potential for linking ways of doing to disciplinary ways of knowing and writing (and speaking). Many other colleges and universities are now or will be participating in outcomes-based assessment, spurred not only by regional accrediting agencies but also by accreditation by professional organizations, most notably ABET but many others as well. This is an opportunity that writing professionals should seize.

But even without a formal assessment process in place, it is still possible when working with faculty to guide them in identifying course or program learning outcomes and helping them incorporate writing as a means of both teaching and evaluating the outcomes. Starting with what students should be able to do can provide a natural link to what they should be able to write. Writing professionals can also do their own analyses of writing in a particular discipline, but this approach may lack the benefit of engaging faculty in identifying disciplinary ways of doing and writing for themselves.

In Russell's history of WID, he notes that the educational system of the old college encouraged a language-rich teaching and learning environment, the recitations that dominated the classroom augmented by the popular and intensely competitive student declamations and debates outside class (*Writing* 38–45). The new university, with its focus on the delivery of highly specialized declarative knowledge and on writing as outside the disciplines, tends to promote a relatively language-poor educational environment. The emphasis on knowing, doing, and writing in the disciplines may be seen as an attempt to return to that earlier language-rich environment when writing and speaking were at the center of education. From another perspective, however, this emphasis may be understood as a part of a broader critique of the modern university and particularly the disciplinary structure of knowledge on which it is founded, a move toward postdisciplinarity or nondisciplinarity (Delanty; Ford; Mourad; Readings; see also Samuels).

For example, Roger P. Mourad argues that the disciplines are based on the epistemology of a preexisting reality that is independent of the inquirer and that may be described through the incremental additions to knowledge about that reality. As an alternative to this understanding of the disciplines, he proposes a postdisciplinary mode of inquiry, which is inquirer-based rather than object-based, meaning that knowledge is local and dynamic rather than universal and incremental, that scholars work in temporary alliances at the intersection of disciplines rather than in disciplines themselves, and that reality is changed by the inquirer rather than independent of the inquirer (77–104). Importantly, this postdisciplinary inquiry would make no distinction among knowledge, research, and teaching. "Teaching," Mourad says, "would become integral to research rather than essentially the after-the-fact transmission of its results. Teaching would not be something one does in addition to or instead of research but something one does through and in the course of research" (105).

Now, I don't want to suggest that the project I am describing in this paper would necessarily spark a revolution in the way we conceive of the university. However, I do think that reconceptualizing the disciplines in terms of meta-genres and metadisciplines is at least an implicit challenge to the disciplines as separate divisions of declarative knowledge. Instead, disciplines may be seen as based on ways of doing and thus ways of knowing and writing, modes of inquiry rather than static territories of knowledge to be more and more thoroughly mapped, a shift in emphasis from knowledge to knowing. And in de-emphasizing the knowledge base of the disciplines, metagenres and meta-disciplines also highlight relationships among the disciplines that are often otherwise obscured, a concept of the disciplines that is much more fluid than the focus on specialized knowledge would suggest.

By questioning the strict boundaries that mark off the disciplines one from another, postdisciplinarity also implicitly questions the assumed dis-junction between the specialized knowledge of a discipline and the general-ized knowledge of writing: the former is not so special; the latter is not so general. It may be, then, that writing is located neither fully in nor fully out-side the disciplines because disciplinary boundaries themselves are porous and in flux; the disciplines are not fixed containers at all. Projecting the disci-plines as ways of knowing, doing, and writing tends to emphasize not dis-junction but junction, the intersections of disciplines, the connection between research and teaching, and the ties between writing and knowing. From this perspective, it is not so much writing in or outside but writing of the disciplines.

Acknowledgments: I would like to recognize the following faculty at my university for their leadership in creating the assessment materials quoted here: Lynn Turner, Food Science; Meredith Davis, Graphic Design; Will Kim-ler, History; Gerry Luginbuhl, Microbiology; David Greene, Multidisciplinary Studies; Andrew Taylor, Political Science and Public Administration; Sharo-lyn Lane, Psychology; Jon Rust, Textiles Engineering; and Jim Gilliam, Zool-ogy. I am grateful to Carolyn R. Miller and David M. Rieder for reading earlier versions of this paper.

NOTES

1. Janet Giltrow has used metagenre in a different sense, a genre in which people write or talk about genre.

2. The outcomes and other quoted material related to assessment in NC State's College of Design is taken from an in-house document, compiled by college faculty, consisting of guiding principles for assessment and goals and performance standards for each department in the college.

APPENDIX: SAMPLE PROGRAM OUTCOMES DOCUMENTS

Department of Zoology: Curricular Outcomes

Students should demonstrate the ability to:

1. engage in clear and careful scientific inquiry. Specifically students should be able to show that they can:

   - ask pertinent questions about zoological phenomena and formulate hypotheses based on those questions, drawing on scientific concepts and principles.

   - apply deliberate and thorough observational skills in conducting an experiment and collecting data to test hypotheses.

   - organize and summarize data and render them in a way that is accurate and comprehensible in both verbal and graphical modes.

   - draw conclusions from data that allow the students to support or refute hypotheses and make a case for alternative hypotheses.

   Evidence for assessment: lab reports, oral or written scientific papers, posters, class activities

2. apply information they have learned in one context to relevant cases in different contexts. Specifically students should be able to show that they can:

   - discern the conceptual similarities that underlie one case and link them to other relevant cases the student is familiar with and to concepts learned in the abstract in class.

   - successfully solve problems in one case by applying concepts and strategies they have derived from previous learning experiences, including both abstract concepts taught in class and other problems they have solved.

   Evidence for assessment: problems assigned for homework, case studies, essay test questions, class activities

3. apply critical thinking skills to solving problems in zoology and related fields. Specifically students should be able to show that they can:

   - identify, define, and analyze a problem: what it is that generates the problem, what is given, what is unknown, and what are the criteria for viable solutions to the problem.

   - read and interpret data and generalize from those data to scientific concepts and principles that can apply to the solution of a problem.

   - apply appropriate scientific concepts and principles to problems in order to provide a range of viable solutions to the problem and design a project for solving the problem.

   - evaluate the solutions according to the established criteria, choose the most viable solution, and make a convincing case for that solution.

   Evidence for assessment: oral or written project proposals, oral or written management plans, problem sets in homework, position statements, essay test questions, environmental impact statements, class activities

4. analyze, synthesize, and criticize scientific literature in the field.

   - distill the important information from scientific articles and describe that information clearly and concisely.

   - read scientific studies critically: assessing the knowns and unknowns, identifying the strengths and weaknesses, evaluating the arguments, and making recommendations for improvement.

   - effectively perform a review of the literature, both in its abbreviated form (as in the introduction of a scientific article) and its extended form. Students should integrate material in an organized fashion and build a logical case concerning the literature. In other words, students should not merely catalogue their sources but instead make an argument using the reading as evidence.

   Evidence for assessment: literature reviews, annotated bibliographies, critical analyses of scientific articles, debates, research papers from scientific sources, oral summaries of articles, class activities

5. communicate scientific information effectively to nonscientific audiences. Specifically students should be able to show that they can:

   - take complex information related to zoology, understand it, and synthesize for non-experts who need to understand and act on the information.

   Evidence for assessment: presentations, newsletters, editorials, lay summaries, class activities

Department of Psychology: Program Outcomes

Upon graduation, psychology majors should be able to:

1. demonstrate an understanding of basic theory and concepts of psychology and the ability to engage in the systematic inquiry into human behavior and experience. Specifically students should be able to show that they can:

   a. demonstrate their knowledge of key psychological theories and concepts.

   b. ask pertinent and productive questions that lead to an analysis of a problem: the source of the problem, the kinds of data needed to solve the problem, and the criteria that must be met for a solution to the problem.

   c. demonstrate an understanding of the data collection process, showing that they know how to collect data for solving problems and how to evaluate those data for their relevance and credibility.

   d. make sound judgments about solutions to problems based on the data they or others have collected.

   e. present data in a way that is accurate and appropriate to the audience.

   f. make a strong case for their judgments based on data, presenting their point logically and clearly.

   Opportunities to guide learning: research proposals, research studies, oral and written lab reports, exams, class discussion

2. discover, understand, manage, and communicate source materials in psychology. Specifically students should be able to show that they can:

   a. find, evaluate, and arrange potential source materials related to a subject.

   b. effectively summarize source materials.

   c. synthesize, analyze, and come to conclusions from multiple source materials.

   d. make an argument for a claim or a proposed action based on source materials.

   e. show that they are skillful consumers of psychology in the popular and scholarly press, analyzing claims, arbitrating among conflicting claims, and recognizing when data confirm or disconfirm hypotheses.

   Opportunities to guide learning: exams, class discussion, summaries, abstracts, literature reviews, research projects, proposals, critical analyses, critiques of proposals, debates, oral presentations

3. work effectively within the complexity and ambiguity that characterize the domains of investigation in the human sciences. Specifically students should be able to show that they can:

   a. handle a broad range of data, both quantitative and qualitative empirical data as well as data from theoretical and philosophical sources.

   b. generate a variety of alternative hypotheses for explaining psychological phenomena.

   c. show that they recognize some of the ways in which researchers, participants, and consumers construct meaning through research paradigms and in psychological settings.

   Opportunities to guide learning: exams, class discussion, research studies, critical analyses of scholarly articles, journal entries

4. generalize theoretical knowledge of psychology to real-world applications. Specifically students should be able to show that they can:

   a. apply core concepts and principles to different life situations.

   b. apply theories of developmental processes and theories of behavior change to situations that require evaluation, maintenance, and/or change.

   c. show that they are aware of subjectivity in psychological research and applications and the potential for imposing their own cultural values on subjects and data.

   d. demonstrate awareness that researchers, agents of change, and participants in research and intervention construct meaning in their world, and that the ways in which individuals construct meaning may well affect the course of research and intervention.

   Opportunities to guide learning: exams, class discussion, homework case reports, reading journals, group case reports, internship project reports, reflective essays or journal entries concerning students' experience with real-world applications

Textiles Engineering: Program Outcomes and Evaluation Criteria

Program Outcomes for Design Component: EC2000 Criterion 3c

To demonstrate that graduates have an ability to design a system, component, or process to meet desired needs, they should show that they have a mastery of the design process and that they can apply that process effectively in generating and presenting a design in textiles engineering:

1. problem definition: establishing a problem or need, identifying customer and project requirements, performing market and technical analyses

2. concept generation: converting customer and project requirements to product specifications, generating multiple product options

3. concept selection: comparing product options to product specifications, selecting optimal product option(s)

4. concept refinement, creating and testing prototypes or models; analyzing technical, economic, and environmental viability of design based on prototype or model; selling the product

Evaluation Criteria for Design Component: EC2000 Criterion 3c

Problem Definition

In their project reports, the team of students should show that they can:

1. establish a problem to be solved or a need to be met by a product on the basis of quantitative data from a market analysis

2. identify specific customer groups for whom the product would solve the problem or meet the need

3. perform a detailed and complete analysis of potential customers' problems or needs based on quantitative information from sources such as surveys, interviews, and reviews of literature

4. describe the project requirements such as parameters related to finances and time and constraints on equipment and raw materials

5. analyze the technology necessary and available for meeting market needs, including a survey of existing technology, potential technology, and technology used by potential competitors

Concept Generation

In their project reports, the team of students should show that they can:

1. convert customer and project requirements into product specifications by the use of quantitative metrics of customer needs

2. identify a suitable number of creative concepts for product options to meet the product specifications

3. effectively demonstrate, using diagrams, sketches, etc., how each of the concepts may function as a product option for meeting product specifications

Concept Selection

In their project reports, the team of students should show that they can:

1. analyze the proposed concepts by quantifying the relationship between the various product options and the product specifications

2. identify and make a convincing case for the optimal product option(s) among all the concepts

Concept Refinement

In their project reports, the team of students should show that they can:

1. create an appropriate and useful prototype, model, or other visual representation of the proposed product

2. use the representation effectively for identifying and proving governing engineering concepts related to the product

3. test the design by performing an industrial design analysis on the product representation (ergonomics, aesthetics, function, etc.)

4. test the design by performing a technical analysis on the product representation (how well it works)

5. test the design by performing an economic analysis (cost/benefit ratio, viability of production, etc.)

6. address the environmental impact of the manufacturing, disposal of by-products, and overall risk to society of the potential product

7. effectively sell the product in terms of its potential economic, technical, and environmental viability

WORKS CITED

Anderson, John R. *Cognitive Psychology and Its Implications* (4th ed.). New York: W. H. Freeman, 1995.

Bazerman, Charles. "Review: The Second Stage in Writing Across the Curriculum." *College English* 53 (1991): 209–12.

———. "Systems of Genres and the Enactment of Social Intentions." *Genre and the New Rhetoric*. Eds. Aviva Freedman and Peter Medway. London: Taylor & Francis, 1994. 79–101.

Berthoff, Ann E. *Forming/Thinking/Writing: The Composing Imagination*. Rochelle Park, NJ: Hayden, 1978.

Brubacher, John S., and Willis Rudy. *Higher Education in Transition: A History of American Colleges and Universities*. 4th ed. New Brunswick, NJ: Transaction Publishers, 1997.

Carter, Michael. "A Process for Establishing Outcomes-Based Assessment Plans for Writing and Speaking in the Disciplines." *Language and Learning Across the Disciplines* 6 (2002): 4–29.

Connors, Robert J. "The New Abolitionism: Toward a Historical Background." *Reconceiving Writing, Rethinking Writing Instruction*. Ed. Joseph Petraglia. Mahwah, NJ: Erlbaum, 1995. 3–26.

Delanty, Gerard. *Challenging Knowledge: The University in the Knowledge Society*. Buckingham, UK: The Society for Research into Higher Education & Open UP, 2001.

Emig, Janet. "Writing as a Mode of Learning." *College Composition and Communication* 28 (1977): 122–28.

Flower, Linda, and John R. Hayes. "The Cognition of Discovery: Defining a Rhetorical Problem." *College Composition and Communication* 31 (1980): 21–32.

Ford, Marcus Peter. *Beyond the Modern University: Toward a Constructive Postmodern University*. Westport, CT: Praeger, 2002.

Giltrow, Janet. "Meta-Genre." *The Rhetoric and Ideology of Genre: Strategies for Stability and Change.* Ed. Richard Coe, Loreli Lingard, and Tatiana Teslenko. Cresskill, NJ: Hampton P, 2002. 187–205.

Herrington, Anne J. "Writing to Learn: Writing Across the Disciplines." *College English* 43 (1981): 379–87.

Jones, Robert, and Joseph J. Comprone. "Where Do We Go Next in Writing Across the Curriculum?" *College Composition and Communication* 44 (1993): 59–68.

Kirscht, Judy, Rhonda Levine, and John Reiff. "Evolving Paradigms: WAC and Rhetoric of Inquiry." *College Composition and Communication* 45 (1994): 369–80.

Krashen, Stephen D. *Second Language Acquisition and Second Language Learning.* New York: Prentice-Hall, 1988.

Lauer, Janice M. "Heuristics and Composition." *College Composition and Communication* 21 (1970): 396–404.

Leff, Michael. "In Search of Ariadne's Thread: A Review of the Recent Literature on Rhetorical Theory." *Central States Speech Journal* 29 (1978): 73–91.

Lucas, Christopher J. *American Higher Education: A History.* New York: St. Martin's, 1994.

McKeon, Richard. "Creativity and the Commonplace." *Rhetoric: Essays in Invention and Discovery.* Ed. Richard Peter McKeon and Mark Backman. Woodbridge, CT: Oxbow, 1987. 25–36.

McLeod, Susan H. "Writing Across the Curriculum: The Second Stage, and Beyond." *College Composition and Communication* 40 (1989): 337–43.

Miller, Carolyn R. "The Aristotelian Topos: Hunting for Novelty." *Rereading Aristotle's Rhetoric.* Ed. Alan G. Gross and Arthur E. Walzer. Carbondale: Southern Illinois UP, 2000. 130–46.

———. "Genre as Social Action." *Quarterly Journal of Speech* 70 (1984): 151–67. Rpt. *Genre and the New Rhetoric.* Ed. Aviva Freedman and Peter Medway. London: Taylor & Francis, 1994. 23–42.

———. "Rhetorical Community: The Cultural Basis of Genre." *Genre and the New Rhetoric.* Ed. Aviva Freedman and Peter Medway. London: Taylor & Francis, 1994. 67–78.

Mourad, Roger P., Jr. *Postmodern Philosophical Critique and the Pursuit of Knowledge in Higher Education.* Westport, CT: Bergin & Garvey, 1997.

Odell, Lee. "The Process of Writing and the Process of Learning." *College Composition and Communication* 31 (1980): 42–50.

Readings, Bill. *The University in Ruins.* Cambridge, MA: Harvard UP, 1996.

Reither, James A. "Writing and Knowing: Toward Redefining the Writing Process." *College English* 47 (1985): 620–28.

Rohman, D. Gordon. "Pre-Writing: The Stage of Discovery in the Writing Process." *College Composition and Communication* 16 (1965): 106–12.

Russell, David R. "Rethinking Genre in School and Society: An Activity Theory Analysis." *Written Communication* 14 (1997): 504–54.

———. "Writing Across the Curriculum in Historical Perspective: Toward a Social Interpretation." *College English* 52 (1990): 52–73.

———. *Writing in the Academic Disciplines, 1870–1990: A Curricular History.* Carbondale, IL: Southern Illinois UP, 1991.

———. "Writing to Learn to Do: WAC, WAW, WAW-WOW!" *Language and Learning Across the Disciplines* 2 (1997): 3–8.

Samuels, Robert. "Re-Inventing the Modern University with WAC: Postmodern Composition as Cultural and Intellectual History." *Across the Disciplines: Interdisciplinary Perspectives on Language, Learning, and Academic Writing* 1 (2004). http://wac.colostate.edu/atd/articles/samuels2004.cfm.

Scott, Robert L. "On Viewing Rhetoric as Epistemic." *Central States Speech Journal* 18 (1967): 9–16.

———. "On Viewing Rhetoric as Epistemic: Ten Years Later." *Central States Speech Journal* 27 (1976): 258–66.

Swales, John. "Language for Specific Purposes." *Annual Review of Applied Linguistics* 20 (2000): 59–76.

Veysey, Laurence R. *The Emergence of the American University.* Chicago: U of Chicago P, 1965.

Young, Richard E., Alton L. Becker, and Kenneth L. Pike. *Rhetoric: Discovery and Change.* New York: Harcourt, 1970.

15

From Cultural Criticism to Disciplinary Participation: Living with Powerful Words

CHARLES BAZERMAN

Critical commonplace now has it that disciplines are socially and rhetorically constructed and that academic knowledge is the product of sociolinguistic activities advancing individual and group interests. In literary studies, we now readily assert that knowledge (at least of the academic kind) is made up out of words and other symbols, that words are made up by people, and that people have their own concerns to look out for — or even worse, that people are so imprisoned by the words they use that the words use the people to reproduce the words. Words almost seem a form of linguistic DNA that ineluctably re-creates itself through the appliance of human beings. Put most simply, you can't trust words to tell you the truth. Such a conclusion, logically unexceptionable within its assumptions, is a great disappointment to any foundational hopes we might have had about the enduring verity and universal authority of the results of our academic labors but is a great encouragement both to the humanist case against the perceived hegemony of sciences (natural and social) and to the radical case against all forms of institutionalized authority that may be perceived as sources of oppression.

This commonplace is precisely critical: rhetorical perception used as a means to distance ourselves from the everyday practice of the world's business in order to reveal and evaluate the hidden mechanisms of life. Indeed, such criticisms can challenge us to remake our world according to our own best lights instead of according to the masked advantage of the few or the imperatives of autonomous symbols beyond the interest of anyone. A much more ancient commonplace dear to the academy also suggests that we only live meaningfully when we have examined our lives. The more precisely we learn how the symbols by which we live have come into place, how they function, whose interests they serve, and how we may exert leverage on them to reform the world, the more we may act meaningfully upon our social desires. Exposing the choice making that lies behind the apparently solid and taken-

From *Writing, Teaching, and Learning in the Disciplines*. Ed. Anne Herrington and Charles Moran. New York: MLA, 1992. 61–68.

for-granted world forces us to address the ethical question of our responsibility for our world.

Criticism, however, is only the beginning of action. Action is a participation, not a disengagement. Participation is the other side of rhetoric: the art of influencing others through language in the great social undertakings that shape the way we live. In the modern world, the academy has become one of the chief institutions of society, in producing socially respected knowledge, in creating concepts and practices that pervade culture and political economy, in advising social leaders, and in educating all. Participation in the academy is a significant means to individual and group influence in the constant reproduction and reshaping of our society. The modern academy is one of the great levers for social change. Disengagement from the academy, unless in the realistic hope of forming some other equally influential and better means of realizing social desires, is withdrawal from great social power, leaving that power in the hands of the very people we criticize for parochialism, narrow interest, and lack of social imagination: the epigoni of the disciplines.

Indeed, the cultural rhetorical critique of disciplinary writing of knowledge tends to bring into prominence the epigonistic formulas that may make the disciplines to seem static things, entrenching outdated beliefs, power and relationships, for such critiques often draw a picture of the current synchronic system of baseline expectations, the seemingly taken-for-granted assumptions that have emerged from the prior negotiations of language. These assumptions necessarily reflect the way things were for those who had influence and power in that negotiation, not the way things are now. Discourse is always in dialectical tension between what came before and new contenders constantly jockeying for voice in any vital communal endeavor. The notion that the rhetoric of a discipline is a uniform synchronic system hides both the historical struggle of heterogeneous forces that lies behind the current apparent regularity and the contemporary contention and complexity of discourse that is played out against the school-taught formulas of current convention. Rhetorical criticism, especially if it is carried out with broad sweeps of condemnation missing the detailed processes of rhetorical struggle, may make disciplines seem purveyors of hegemonic univocality rather than the locales of heteroglossic contention that they are.

Put most bluntly, cultural criticism of disciplines may fall far short of its mark because it believes too readily, and is thus too readily disappointed in, the textbook accounts of disciplinary work — that the disciplines are simply what they represent themselves to be to neophyte students. When we outside any particular discipline discover that a discipline is not all it says it is, does not achieve the irresistible harmony of irrefutable knowledge without serious contention, is not purely separable from its social consequences, and must depend on social forces for its support, we then may too readily believe that the discipline is unredeemably suspect. Yet people who get beyond the 101 textbook in any field begin to learn the complexities of the field, its history, its culture, its production and use of knowledge, its relation to other institutions in society, and its border skirmishes. They also feel and must consciously contend with the constraints and focuses put on their work through the habits, standards, and practices of the discipline, as well as recognize the strains among contending elements in the field and poachers from the neighboring field. In other words they must learn to locate themselves and their work on an ever changing, complex field where communal projects, goals, and knowledge are constantly negotiated from the individual perspectives and interests of participants within and without the field, even as they are all necessarily responsive to those highly powerful but nonetheless fluidly interpreted and reconstituted social facts of disciplinary institutionalization and control.

The overt teachings of a discipline, beginning with textbooks for schoolchildren and continuing through all forms of professional communication may ignore, or even suppress, this knowledge of the many contexts and forces in which the field operates, and which influentially shape the knowledge of the discipline (Latour, *Science*). The overt teachings may pretend that the work of the field is methodologically pure and intellectually isolatable from the messy complexity of the world; such overt teachings of methodological standards may in fact represent only the rhetorical move of one group who has gained the upper hand and is attempting to establish rules that purvey its position. Even when that position of epistemic hegemony may be well institutionalized and entrenched, methodological issues and apparently closed borders always remain available for renegotiation as difficult cases and new foci of concern evolve. Nonetheless, institutionally enforced epistemic standards may lead practitioners to relegate the impure facts of daily life to such backstage forms as jokes, late-night beer talk, or "political strategy" sessions (Gilbert and Mulkay).

Rhetorical analysis of the actual communications of the disciplines opens up and makes more visible these suppressed issues of the dynamics and evolving knowledge production of the disciplines. Rhetorical analysis can make visible the complexity of mutual participation of many people necessary to maintain the large projects of the disciplines, the recognition of the kinds of linguistic practice developed in consonance with the goals of the disciplinary projects, the constant struggle between competing formulations, and the constant innovative edge that keeps the discourse alive. Rhetorical analysis can also open up exclusions and enclosures of discourse to see how and why they are deployed and to question their necessity in any particular case.

But even more rhetorical analysis can provide the means for more informed and thoughtful participation in disciplines so that we can make the disciplines do the best work they were created for, rather than being the self-protecting domains of vested interest and social power that we fear. Rhetorical sophistication allows both insiders to move the discipline effectively and outsiders to negotiate with it and regain decisions that may have been inappropriately enclosed within the expert discourse.

When we teach students the rhetoric of the disciplines, thus, we are not necessarily indoctrinating them unreflectively into forms that will oppress them and others. Such oppressions of the self and others are more likely to occur when individuals learn communication patterns implicitly as a matter of getting along. Explicit teaching of discourse holds what is taught up for inspection, provides the students with means to rethink the ends of the discourse, and offers a wider array of means to carry the discourse in new directions.

The progress of rhetorical self-examination within anthropology provides a striking case in point of how critical examination of discourse can lead to deeper insight into the projects and knowledge of the discipline and to continuing innovation and vitality in the discourse and the disciplinary project, even when critical examination exposes that previous discourse was implicated in social, political, and economic relations that we now disown. Critical historical work on the discourse of anthropology has well demonstrated how the early accounts of anthropologists were part of late-nineteenth-century imperialism, with the United States attempting to subordinate and domesticate the Native American populations through the Bureau of Indian Affairs and European nations spreading their control over the other "primitive" peoples of the world who were being drawn under their political and economic "protection." The genre of ethnography with its authoritative representation of the primitive other, denied direct voice through the suppression of the active role of the native informant in representing the way of life and the elevation of the foreign anthropologist as the objective authority, became a chief textual means for Western societies to objectify the dominated peoples.

Recent critical work on ethnography (Clifford, Clifford and Marcus, Fabian, Geertz, Marcus, Marcus and Cushman, Rosaldo, Tyler) has not only pointed out these intrinsic dynamics of ethnographic texts but has also indicated how ethnography has changed in response to evolving understandings of the relations between "exotic" cultures and the "scientific" culture of the West. However, these revelations, along with the rejection of the social/economic relations of dominance thereby revealed, have not meant an end of the genre of ethnography. People still have multiple needs, both individually and institutionally, to represent their own and each other's lives to each other and for themselves. Questions of who speaks, who owns the discourse, who receives, and for what ends the discourse is carried on have opened up new experimental varieties of ethnography (for example, Rabinow, J. Dumont, Crapanzano) and more sensitive use of all varieties (see, for example, van Maanen). Thus, rather than going out of fashion as discredited, ethnography as a genre has gained new vitality and has spread across the social sciences and even the humanities.

Detailed attention to disciplinary writing does not enslave us to the entrapments of the past but opens up choices for reevaluation and helps us explore the flexible and manifold resources available within traditional disciplinary genres as we understand and reconceive them more deeply. I have found a similar lesson in the response to my study of one of the most restrictive of disciplinary forms as prescriptively imposed by leaders of one discipline attempting to advance a dominant epistemology, theory, and research program. The format of the psychological experimental article as prescribed in the Publication Manual of the American Psychological Association is the result of a self-conscious program of discipline building by behaviorist experimental psychologists over the middle of the twentieth century. In the manual's prescriptions behaviorists have indeed found an appropriate rhetoric for their project based on their assumptions and goals, and growing out of the dynamics of the professional discourse during this period (Bazerman, *Shaping Written Knowledge*, chap. 9). In becoming the official style of the most "scientific" of the social sciences, the APA style has been highly influential throughout all the social sciences. I have found that by analyzing the processes, dynamics, and assumptions of this institutionalization of style, I have not at all served to foster the enclosed dominance of this discourse. Rather professionals and students have largely responded that understanding the implied baggage of the discourse has freed them to make rhetorical choices with greater clarity, whether to continue in the traditional forms, whether to modify them, or whether to abandon them altogether for more conducive discourse for other kinds of projects. The only resistance I have met to the analysis are from those who do not wish to think of their discourse as discourse and claim that their words and arguments carry no freight and are only epiphenomena of their "science." They claim they are writing the only way they could write in consonance with "good science." It is not the serious attention to disciplinary discourse that restricts our intellectual options but the refusal to attend that fosters the hegemony of narrow discourses.

When we do attend to the history and evolution of disciplinary discourses, we see complex heteroglossia, even in the most restricted genres, such as the scientific experimental report. Each newcomer to a field must anew come to understand, cope with, and place him- or herself within the evolving conversation. In studying the development of Isaac Newton's way of discussing his optical findings, a way that would have profound implications for all scientific discourse to follow, I saw Newton working to make sense of the discourses around him, find appropriate ways to address his audiences, respond to the conceptions and objections of his readers, and reforge a new discourse style that would carry overwhelming force on the discourse field that he only gradually came to understand. His final solutions in the compelling "Newtonian style" seemed to suppress all other voices but actually encompassed them in a way that they could not escape to make alternate claims for a century. In examining Newton's rhetoric we move behind the massive social appearance of the supranatural genius Newton, "sailing through silent seas of thought alone," to understand humanistically an individual locating himself among others and finding powerful means to advance his own vision and claims (Bazerman, *Shaping Written Knowledge*, chap. 4). The history of all scientific discourse is built on such individual stories of people each coming to learn to use language effectively and thereby advancing the resources of language.

Once a rhetorical field is highly developed, each individual finds himself in the middle of an intertextual web within which he or she can act only by modifying the intertextuality through new statements. One's goals and activities influence one's idiosyncratic placement and interpretation of that intertextual field. When a modern physicist reads physics articles, he or she reads through the goals of advancing his or her own research project within a competitively structured argument over what claims are to be considered correct and important and how the literature should be added up and moved forward (Bazerman, *Shaping Written Knowledge*, chap. 8). There is constant negotiation among prior statements, new statements, responses, and further work over what constitutes credibility and creditibility (Myers, *Writing*; Latour and Woolgar). By reconstructing the literature around one's own ongoing work and then representing one's new work within that reconstructed matrix of the literature, each person makes the field over fresh and constructs a new place for the self.

Discourse studies of the disciplines aim to understand the evolving dynamics of each disciplinary field and the current state of play into which each new participant enters. Discourse studies of disciplines allow us to design courses that enable students to enter into disciplines as fully empowered speakers rather than as conventional followers of accepted practice, running as hard as they can just to keep up appearances. Even more, discourse studies can provide an enlightened perspective through which students can perceive the professional and disciplinary fields with which they will have to deal as outsiders. It is as important for an ecology activist or a community planner to see into the complexity of the discourse of biologists, geologists, and petrochemical engineers as it is for those professionals to have command of their own discourses.

By taking the discourse of professions and disciplines seriously, we will have the means to help students develop as active, reactive, and proactive members of their communities. With a sense of individual power, they can constantly press at the bit of the disciplinary practices they are trained into or run up against. Seeing through the appearances of the discourse, they can always keep in mind the fundamental goals of the fields in front of them, asking what kind of communication structures, patterns, and rhetorics will best enable the fields to achieve those goals, how they can contribute to those ends as individuals, and in what way the goals achieved through a single disciplinary discourse coordinate (if at all) with other social goals from other forms of social discourse. By understanding how knowledge is constructed, they in their professional lives can best judge what knowledge it is they wish to construct.

This adventure into the power of language in the modern world should not be a far digression for scholars of literary studies, for we have long been examining the power of language to shape the imagination in the religious struggles of the Reformation, the political struggles of the eighteenth century, and the industrial struggles of the nineteenth. Studying disciplinary discourse might mean looking into disciplines and professions we rejected as undergraduates when we chose the life of literary studies, but it certainly takes us no further into arcana than Puritan pamphlet wars, for the disciplines and professions encompass every aspect of our daily life as we near the end of the twentieth century. If we are to create a humane society for the next century, it is precisely the disciplinary and professional words we will have to keep from getting away from us. As much as we understand the powerful words of our society is as much as we will be able to live with and through them.

WORKS CITED

Bazerman, Charles. *Shaping Written Knowledge: The Genre and Activity of the Experimental Article in Science.* Madison: U of Wisconsin P, 1988.

Clifford, James. "On Ethnographic Authority." *Representations* 1.2 (1983): 118–46.

Clifford, James, and George Marcus. *Writing Culture: The Poetics and Politics of Ethnography.* Berkeley: U of California P, 1986.

Dumont, Jean-Paul. *The Head-Man and I.* Austin: U of Texas P, 1978.

———. *Under the Rainbow.* Austin: U of Texas P, 1976.

Fabian, Johannes. *Time and the Other: How Anthropology Makes Its Object.* New York: Columbia UP, 1983.

Geertz, Clifford. *Local Knowledge: Further Essays in Interpretive Anthropology.* New York: Basic, 1983.

———. *Works and Lives: The Anthropologist as Author.* Stanford: Stanford UP, 1988.

Gilbert, G. Nigel, and Michael Mulkay. *Opening Pandora's Box.* Cambridge: Cambridge UP, 1984.

Latour, Bruno. *Science in Action.* Cambridge: Harvard UP, 1987.

Latour, Bruno, and Steve Woolgar. *Laboratory Life: The Social Construction of Scientific Facts.* Beverly Hills: Sage, 1979.

Marcus, George. "Rhetoric and the Ethnographic Genre in Anthropological Research." *Current Anthropology* 21 (1980): 507–10.

Marcus, George, and Dick Cushman. "Ethnographies as Texts." *Annual Review of Anthropology* 11 (1982): 25–69.

Myers, Greg. "The Social Construction of Two Biologists' Proposals." *Written Communication* 2 (1985): 219–45.

———. *Writing Biology.* Madison: U of Wisconsin P, 1990.

Rabinow, Paul. *Reflections on Fieldwork in Morocco.* Berkeley: U of California P, 1977.

Rosaldo, Renato. "Where Objectivity Lies: The Rhetoric of Anthropology." *The Rhetoric of the Human Sciences.* Ed. John Nelson, Allan Megill, and Donald McCloskey. Madison: U of Wisconsin P, 1987.

Tyler, Stephen. *The Unspeakable.* Madison: U of Wisconsin P, 1987.

van Maanen, John. *Tales of the Field: On Writing Ethnography.* Chicago: U of Chicago P, 1988.

16 Strangers in Academia: The Experiences of Faculty and ESL Students Across the Curriculum

VIVIAN ZAMEL

When I go into a classroom these days, I look around and feel like I'm in a different country.

– PROFESSOR OF MANAGEMENT

A few weeks ago a professor came by the reading, writing and study skills center where I tutor. He was with a young Asian woman, obviously one of his students. He "deposited" her in the center, claiming that she desperately needed help with her English. The woman stared into the distance with a frightened, nervous look on her face and tried to force a smile. She handed me a paper she had written on the labor union and asked if I could help her make corrections. After a short introductory discussion, we looked at the paper that we were about to revise — it was filled with red marks indicating spelling, punctuation, and grammar errors; the only written response was something along the lines of "You need serious help with your English. Please see a tutor."

– FROM A TUTOR'S JOURNAL

Students in the lab speak to one another in their own language so that they make sure they know what they are doing. So they may look like they are not listening to the lab teacher. He feels so isolated from them. He feels he has no control, no power. So he may get angry.

– AN ESL STUDENT

These comments show evidence of tensions and conflicts that are becoming prevalent in institutions of higher education as student populations become more diverse. One clear indication that faculty across the disciplines are concerned about the extent to which diverse student populations, particularly students whose native language is not English, constrain their work is the number of workshops and seminars that have been organized, and at which I have participated, in order to address what these faculty view as the "ESL

From *College Composition and Communication* 46.4 (1995): 506–21.

Problem."[1] In the course of preparing to work with faculty, and in order to get a sense of their issues and concerns, I surveyed instructors about their experiences working with non-native speakers of English. As Patricia Laurence has pointed out, though we acknowledge and discuss the diversity of students, "we neglect the 'polyphony'" that represents faculty voices (24). While I did not receive many responses to my request for feedback, those responses that were returned did indeed reflect this polyphony.

Some faculty saw this invitation to provide feedback as an opportunity to discuss the strengths and resources these students brought with them, indicated that ESL students, because of their experience and motivation, were a positive presence in their classes, and noted the contributions ESL students made in discussions that invited cross-cultural perspectives. One professor took issue with the very idea of making generalizations about ESL students. But this pattern of response did not represent the attitudes and perspectives revealed by other faculty responses. One professor, for example, referred to both silent students, on the one hand, and "vocal but incomprehensible students" on the other. But, by far, the greatest concern had to do with students' writing and language, which faculty saw as deficient and inadequate for undertaking the work in their courses. I got the clear sense from these responses that language use was confounded with intellectual ability — that, as Victor Villanueva, recounting his own schooling experiences, puts it, "bad language" and "insufficient cognitive development" were being conflated (11).

In order to demonstrate the range of faculty commentary, I've selected two faculty responses, not because they are necessarily representative, but because they reveal such divergent views on language, language development, and the role that faculty see themselves as playing in this development. I've also chosen these responses because they may serve as mirrors for our own perspectives and belief systems, and thus help us examine more critically what we ourselves think and do, both within our own classrooms and with respect to the larger institutional contexts in which we teach. In other words, although these responses came from two different disciplines, it is critical for each of us to examine the extent to which we catch glimpses of our own practices and assumptions in these texts. The first response was written by an English Department instructor:

> One of my graduate school professors once told me that he knew within the first two weeks of the semester what his students' final grades would be. Recently I had a Burmese-born Chinese student who proved my professor wrong. After the first two essays, there was certainly no reason to be optimistic about this student's performance. The essays were very short, filled with second language errors, thesaurus words, and sweeping generalizations. In the first essay, it was obvious he had been taught to make outlines because that's all the paper was, really — a list. In the second essay, instead of dealing directly with the assigned text, the student directed most of his energy to form and structure. He had an introduction even though he had nothing to introduce. In his conclusion, he was making wild assertions (even though he had nothing to base them

on) because he knew conclusions were supposed to make a point. By the fourth essay, he started to catch on to the fact that my comments were directed toward the content of his essays, not the form. Once he stopped worrying about thesis sentences, vocabulary, and the like, he became a different writer. His papers were long, thoughtful, and engaging. He was able to interpret and respond to texts and to make connections that I term "double face" as a way to comment on the ways in which different cultures define such terms as "respect." Instead of 1 1/4 pages, this essay was seven pages, and it made several references to the text while synthesizing it with his experience as someone who is a product of three cultures. This change not only affected the content of his writing, but also his mechanics. Though there were still errors, there were far fewer of them, and he was writing well enough where I felt it was safe to raise questions about structure and correctness.

This response begins with the recognition that we need to be wary of self-fulfilling prophecies about the potential of students, and indeed this instructor's narrative demonstrates compellingly the dangers of such prophecies. This instructor goes on to cite problems with the student's performance, but he speculates that these problems may have to do with previous instruction, thus reflecting a stance that counteracts the tendency to blame students. Despite the student's ongoing difficulties, the instructor does not despair over the presence of second language errors, over the short essays, the "sweeping generalizations," the empty introduction, the "wild assertions." Instead, this instructor seems to persist in his attempts to focus the student on content issues, to respond to the student seriously, to push him to consider the connections between what he was saying and the assigned reading, to take greater risks, which he succeeds in doing "by the fourth essay." In this, I believe, we see the instructor's understanding that it takes multiple opportunities for students to trust that he is inviting them into serious engagement with the course material, that it takes time to acquire new approaches to written work. What seems to be revealed in this response is the instructor's belief in the student's potential, his appreciation for how language and learning are promoted, his refusal to draw conclusions about intellectual ability on the basis of surface features of language — all of which, in turn, helped the student become a "different writer," a change that affected the content of his writing, that had an impact on the very errors that filled his first papers, that even illuminated the instructor's reading of the assigned texts. This response suggests a rich and complicated notion of language, one that recognizes that language evolves in and responds to the context of saying something meaningful, that language and meaning are reciprocal and give rise to one another.

This response, especially the final section about surface level errors, foreshadows the other faculty response, which was written by an art history instructor and which reveals a very different set of assumptions and expectations:

My experience with teaching ESL students is that they have often not received adequate English instruction to complete the required essay texts and papers in my classes. I have been particularly dismayed when I find that they have already completed 2 ESL courses and have no knowledge of the parts of speech or the terminology that is used in correcting English grammar on papers. I am certainly not in a position to teach English in my classes. (The problem has been particularly acute with Chinese/S. E. Asian students.) These students may have adequate intelligence to do well in the courses, but their language skills result in low grades. (I cannot give a good grade to a student who can only generate one or two broken sentences during a ten-minute slide comparison.)

The first assumption I see in this response is the belief that language and knowledge are separate entities, that language must be in place and fixed in order to do the work in the course. This static notion of language is further revealed by the instructor's assumption that language use is determined by a knowledge of parts of speech or grammatical terminology. Given this belief, it is understandable why she is dismayed by what she characterizes as students' lack of knowledge of grammar, a conclusion she has seemingly reached because her corrective feedback, presumably making use of grammatical terms, has not proven successful. This practice itself is not questioned, however; students or their inadequate English language instruction are held accountable instead. If students had been prepared appropriately, if the gatekeeping efforts had kept students out of her course until they were more like their native language counterparts, her commentary suggests, students would be able to do the required work. There is little sense of how the unfamiliar terms, concepts, and ways of seeing that are particular to this course can be acquired. Nor is there an appreciation for how this very unfamiliarity with the course content may be constraining students' linguistic processes. She does not see, focusing as she does on difference, how she can contribute to students' language and written development, how she can build on what they know. Despite indicating that students may have "adequate intelligence to do well in the course," she doesn't seem to be able to get past their language problems when it comes to evaluating their work, thus missing the irony of grading on the basis of that which she acknowledges she is not "in a position to teach." The final parenthetical statement reveals further expectations about student work, raising questions about the extent to which her very expectations, rather than linguistic difficulties alone, contribute to the "broken sentences" to which she refers.

What we see at work here is in marked contrast to the model of possibility revealed in the first response. What seems to inform this second response is a deficit model of language and learning whereby students' deficiencies are foregrounded. This response is shaped by an essentialist view of language in which language is understood to be a decontextualized skill that can be taught in isolation from the production of meaning and that must be in place in order to undertake intellectual work. What we see here is an illustration of "the myth of transience," a belief that permeates institutions of higher education and perpetuates the notion that these students' problems are temporary and can be remediated — so long as some isolated set of courses or program of instruction, but not the real courses in the academy, takes on the responsibility of doing so (see Rose, "Language"). Such a belief supports the illusion that permanent solutions are possible, which releases faculty from the ongoing struggle and questioning that the teaching-learning process inevitably involves.

In these two faculty responses, we see the ways in which different sets of expectations and attitudes get played out. In the one classroom, we get some sense of what can happen when opportunities for learning are created, when students are invited into a thoughtful process of engaging texts, when students' writing is read and responded to in meaningful and supportive ways. In the other classroom, although we have little information about the conditions for learning, we are told that one way that learning is measured is by technically correct writing done during a 10-minute slide presentation, and this, I believe, is telling. For students who are not adequately prepared to do this work, there is little, the instructor tells us, she can do. Given this deterministic stance, students are closed off from participating in intellectual work.

At the same time that I was soliciting faculty responses to get a sense of their perceptions and assumptions, I began to survey ESL students about what they wanted faculty to know about their experiences and needs in classrooms across the curriculum. I wanted, in other words, to capture the polyphony of students' voices as well. I felt that the work I was engaging in with faculty could not take place without an exploration of students' views, especially since, although faculty have little reservation discussing what they want and expect from students, informing us about their frustrations and disappointments, the students' perspective is one that faculty often hear little about. And since I have become convinced that our role in our institutions ought not to be defined solely by the service we perform for other faculty (either by making our students' English native-like or keeping the gates closed until this is accomplished) but in helping faculty understand the role they need to begin to play in working with all students, the students' perspective was critical.

Within the last two years, I have collected more than 325 responses from first and second year ESL students enrolled in courses across a range of disciplines.[2] I discovered from looking at these responses a number of predominant and recurring themes. Students spoke of patience, tolerance, and encouragement as key factors that affected their learning:

> Teachers need to be more sensitive to ESL students needs of education. Since ESL students are face with the demands of culture adjustment, especially in the classroom, teaches must be patients and give flexible consideration. . . . For example — if a teacher get a paper that isn't clear or didn't follow the assignment correctly, teacher must talk and communicate with the students.

Students articulated the kinds of assistance they needed, pointing, for example, to clearer and more explicitly detailed assignments and more accessible classroom talk:

> In the classes, most teachers go over material without explaining any words that seems hard to understand for us. . . . I want college teachers should describe more clearly on questions in the exams, so we can understand clearly. Also, I think the teachers should write any important information or announcement on the board rather than just speaking in front of class, because sometimes we understand in different way when we hear it than when we read it.

Students spoke with pride about how much they knew and how much they had accomplished through working, they felt, harder than their native English-speaking counterparts did, and they wanted faculty to credit and acknowledge them for this.

> I would like them to know that we are very responsible and we know why we come to college: to learn. We are learning English as well as the major of our choice. It is very hard sometimes and we don't need professors who claimed that they don't understand us. The effort is double. We are very intelligent people. We deserve better consideration . . . ESL students are very competent and deserve to be in college. We made the step to college. Please make the other step to meet us.

At the same time, an overwhelming number of students wanted faculty to know that they were well aware they were having language difficulties and appreciated responses that would help them. But they also expressed their wish that their work not be discounted and viewed as limited. They seemed to have a very strong sense that because of difficulties that were reflected in their attempts at classroom participation and in their written work, their struggles with learning were misperceived and underestimated:

> The academic skills of students who are not native speakers of English are not worse than academic skills of American students, in some areas it can be much better. Just because we have problems with language . . . that some professors hate because they don't want to spend a minute to listen a student, doesn't mean that we don't understand at all.

Students referred to professors who showed concern and seemed to appreciate students' contributions. But the majority of students' responses described classrooms that silenced them, that made them feel fearful and inadequate, that limited possibilities for engagement, involvement, inclusion.

While these students acknowledged that they continue to experience difficulties, they also voiced their concern that these struggles not be viewed as deficiencies, that their efforts be understood as serious attempts to grapple with these difficulties. While faculty may feel overwhelmed by and even resentful of working with such students, these students indicated that they expect and need their instructors to assist them in this undertaking, even making suggestions as to how this can be done. Indeed, the very kind of clarity, accessible language, careful explanation, and effort that faculty want students to demonstrate are the kinds of assistance students were asking of faculty. Without dismissing the concerns of the art instructor, these students nevertheless believed, as does the English instructor, that teaching ought to be responsive to their concerns.

Yet another source of information about students' classroom experiences comes from my ongoing case-study of two students who attended a composition course I taught two years ago and who have met with me regularly since that time to discuss the work they are assigned, their teachers' responses to and evaluation of their work, the classroom dynamics of their courses, the roles they and their teachers play, and the kinds of learning that are expected in their classes.

One of the students who has been participating in this longitudinal investigation is Motoko, a student from Japan who has taken a range of courses and is majoring in sociology. She described courses in which lively interaction was generated, in which students were expected to participate, to write frequent reaction papers and to undertake projects based on first-hand research, to challenge textbook material and to connect this material to their own lived experiences. But in most of her courses the picture was quite different. Lectures were pervasive, classes were so large that attendance wasn't even taken, and short answer tests were often the predominant means of evaluating student work. With respect to one class, for example, Motoko discussed the problematic nature of multiple-choice exams which, she believes, distort the information being tested and deliberately mislead students. In regard to another course, she described what she viewed as boring, even confusing lectures, but she persevered: "Because I don't like the professor, I work even harder. I don't want him to laugh at me. I don't want to be dehumanized. I came here to learn something, to gain something." In yet another course in which only the professor talked, she indicated that she was "drowning in his words." Even a class which assigned frequent written work, which Motoko completed successfully, disappointed her because she had such difficulty understanding the assignments and because her writing was not responded to in what she perceived as a thoughtful, respectful way. Motoko confided that despite her success in this course, she had lost interest in working on her papers.

The other student whose classroom experiences I've been following is Martha, a student from Colombia who, like Motoko, has taken a range of courses, and whose major is biology. Unlike Motoko, who had managed to negotiate "drowning words" and problematic assignments, Martha's sense of discouragement about the purposelessness of much of her work is far more pervasive. With respect to many of her courses, she complained about the absence of writing (which she views as essential for learning), the passive nature of class discussions, contrived assignments that "don't help her think about anything," and the lifeless comments she received. It was in her science courses, however, that she felt the greatest dissatisfaction and frustration. About one chemistry course, she spoke of "just trying to follow the lectures and get a grade in a huge class" that she characterized as a "disaster." She talked of the sense of superiority her professors project, of her inability to learn anything meaningful from assignments which require everyone "to come up with the same information." Her experiences have provoked her to write numerous pieces which reflect her growing sense of despair and which provide a rich commentary on her perspective and experiences. In one of these pieces she has labeled the way professors behave as "academic harassment." In yet another, she questions the purpose of schooling, assignments, and written work: "Each teacher should ask her or himself the next question: Why do I assign a writing paper on this class? Do you want to see creativity and reflection of students or do or want a reproduction of the same book concept?" She is frustrated by the "lack of connections with the material we listen on lectures," the "monotony of the teaching method," the "limited style of questions," the "stressful process of learning." She concludes:

> I have no new words in my lexicon. And how do I know that? From my writing. No fluency. Why? I don't write. I was moving forward and now I'm stagnant. . . . Frustration and lack of interest are the present feelings with my classes because there is not any planned "agenda" to encourage the students to improve ourselves by writing. There is no rich opportunity to break barriers and answer questions to others and also to myself. There is no REACTION and INTERACTION. . . . It does not really matter how many courses the students take in order to improve skills of writing because what it counts is the responsibility encouraged by the teacher's method! the kind of responsibility developed around us is first with *ourselves*! It is an incentive for us to be listened and respected by our writing work! You get into it. Reading provides you grammar. Reading and writing are not separate in the process. It is a combined one. Doble team. Reacting and interacting.

This account, like others Martha has written, reveals her commitment to learning, her insightful understanding of how learning is both promoted and undermined, how writing in particular plays an essential role in this learning, how critical it is for teachers to contribute to and encourage learning. She, like Motoko and the other students surveyed, has much to tell us about the barriers that prevent learning and how these barriers can be broken. And lest we conclude that what these students perceive about their experiences is specific to ESL learners, recent studies of teaching and learning in higher education indicate that this is not the case. For example, Chiseri-Strater's ethnography of university classrooms reveals the authoritarian and limited ways that subject matter is often approached, the ways in which students, even those who are successful, are left silent and empty by the contrived and inconsequential work of many classrooms.

This ongoing exploration of the expectations, perceptions and experiences of both faculty and students has clarified much for me about the academic life of ESL students and what we ought to be doing both within our classrooms and beyond. Given the hierarchical arrangement of coursework within post-secondary schools, given the primacy accorded to traditional discipline-specific courses, it is not surprising that ESL and other writing-based courses have a marginalized position, that these courses are thought to have no authentic content, that the work that goes on in these courses is not considered to be the "real" work of the academy.

This view typically gets played out through coursework that is determined by what students are assumed to need in courses across the curriculum, coursework whose function it is to "guard the tower," to use Shaughnessy's term, and keep the gates closed in the case of students who are not deemed ready to enter ("Diving"). This often implies instruction that focuses on grammar, decontextualized language skills, and surface features of language. And we know from what faculty continue to say about these issues that this is precisely what is expected of English and ESL instruction — and, unfortunately, many of us have been all too ready to comply. Mike Rose speaks to the profoundly exclusionary nature of such a pedagogy and argues that a focus on mechanical skills and grammatical features reduces the complexity of language to simple and discrete problems, keeps teachers from exploring students' knowledge and potential, and contributes to the "second-class intellectual status" to which the teaching of writing has been assigned ("Language" 348). Furthermore, the problematic assumption that writing or ESL programs are in place to serve the academy, that their function is to benefit other academic studies, prevents us from questioning our situation within the larger institution. "Service course ideology," Tom Fox points out, "often leaves the curricular decisions in the hands of those who are not especially knowledgeable about writing instruction," which ultimately means that "political questions — in fact, *any* questions that challenge existing definitions of basic writing — become irrelevant to the bureaucratic task of reproducing the program" ("Basic" 67).

While skills-based and deficit models of instruction bring these kinds of pressures to bear on our work with students, our teaching has further been constrained by composition specialists who make claims about the need for students to adopt the language and discourse conventions of the academy if they are to succeed. David Bartholomae's article, "Inventing the University," is often cited and called upon to argue that students need to approximate and adopt the "specialized discourse of the university" (17). In the ESL literature, a reductive version of this position has been embraced by professionals who maintain that the role that ESL coursework ought to play is one of preparing students for the expectations and demands of discipline-specific communities across the curriculum. Such an approach, however, misrepresents and oversimplifies academic discourse and reduces it to some stable and autonomous phenomenon that does not reflect reality. Such instruction, like coursework shaped by limited conceptualizations of language, undermines *our* expertise and position. And because such instruction privileges and perpetuates the status quo, because it exaggerates the "distinctiveness of academic discourse [and] its separation from student literacy" (Fox, "Basic" 70), such a pedagogy has been characterized in terms of assimilation, colonization, domination, and deracination (Clark; Fox; Gay; Horner; Trimbur).

While there is growing debate about this instructional approach in the field of composition, there have been fewer attempts to problematize this model of teaching in ESL composition, where the norms and conventions of the English language and its discourses have particularly powerful political implications.[3] Hence the need to raise questions about such an instructional focus when it is applied to our work with non-native speakers of English. As I have argued elsewhere, we need to critique approaches that are reductive and formulaic, examine the notion that the language of the academy is a monolithic discourse that can be packaged and transmitted to students, and argue that this attempt to serve the institution in these ways contributes to our marginal status and that of our students.

Those of us who have tried to accommodate institutional demands have, no doubt, found this to be a troubling and tension-filled undertaking, since even when we focus on standards of language use or conventions of academic discourse, students, especially those who are still acquiring English, are not necessarily more successful in meeting the expectations of other faculty. There seems to be little carry-over from such instructional efforts to subsequent work since it is the very nature of such narrowly conceptualized instruction that undercuts genuine learning. As Fox argues, writing teachers who uphold a mythical and fixed set of institutional standards and skills are enacting a pedagogy that, however well-intentioned, is an "unqualifiable failure" ("Standards" 42). Those of us who have resisted and questioned such a pedagogy, embracing a richer and more complicated understanding of how language, discourse, and context are intertwined, may be able to trace the strides students make and to appreciate the intelligence their language and writing reveal, and yet find that this is not extended by other faculty who cannot imagine taking on this kind of responsibility.

We need to recognize that in the same way that faculty establish what Martha calls "barriers" between themselves and students, in the same way that faculty "exoticize" ESL students, we too, especially if our primary work is with ESL students, are perceived as "outsiders."[4] And as long as these boundaries continue to delineate and separate what we and other faculty do, as long as we are expected to "fix" students' problems, then misunderstandings, unfulfilled expectations, frustration, and even resentment will continue to mark our experiences. But this need not be the case. We are beginning to see changes in institutions in response to the growing recognition that faculty across the disciplines must take responsibility for working with all students. Studies, such as the ethnography undertaken by Walvoord and McCarthy, have documented the transformation of faculty from a range of disciplines who became more responsive to the needs of their students as they undertook their own classroom research and examined their own assumptions and expectations.

In my own work with faculty at a number of different institutions, including my own, what first begins as a concern about "underprepared" or "deficient" ESL students often leads to a consideration of the same kinds of pedagogical issues that are at the heart of writing across the curriculum initiatives. But these issues are reconsidered with specific reference to working with ESL students. Together, we have explored our instructional goals, the purposes for assigned work, the means for reading and evaluating this work, the roles that engagement, context, and classroom dynamics play in

promoting learning. Through this collaboration faculty have begun to understand that it is unrealistic and ultimately counterproductive to expect writing
and ESL programs to be responsible for providing students with the language,
discourse, and multiple ways of seeing required across courses. They are recognizing that the process of acquisition is slow-paced and continues to evolve
with exposure, immersion, and involvement, that learning is responsive to
situations in which students are invited to participate in the construction of
meaning and knowledge. They have come to realize that every discipline,
indeed every classroom, may represent a distinct culture and thus needs to
make it possible for those new to the context to practice and approximate its
"ways with words." Along with acknowledging the implications of an essentialist view of language and of the myth of transience, we have considered the
myth of coverage, the belief that covering course content necessarily means
that it has been learned. Hull and Rose, in their study of the logic underlying
a student's unconventional reading of a text, critique "the desire of efficiency
and coverage" for the ways it "limit[s] rather than enhance[s] [students'] participation in intellectual work" (296), for the ways it undermines students'
entry into the academy. With this in mind, we have raised questions about
what we do in order to cover material, why we do what we do, what we
expect from students, and how coverage is evaluated. And if the "cover-the-
material" model doesn't seem to be working in the ways we expected, we ask,
what alternatives are there?

We have also examined the ways in which deficit thinking, a focus on difference, blinds us to the logic, intelligence and richness of students' processes
and knowledge. In *Lives on the Boundary*, Mike Rose cites numerous cases of
learners (including himself) whose success was undercut because of the tendency to emphasize difference. Studies undertaken by Glynda Hull and her
colleagues further attest to how such belief systems about students can lead to
inaccurate judgments about learners' abilities, and how practices based on
such beliefs perpetuate and "virtually assure failure" (325). The excerpt from
the tutor's journal quoted at the beginning of this article, along with many of
the faculty and student responses that I have elicited, are yet other indications
of what happens when our reading of student work is derailed by a focus on
what is presumed to be students' deficiencies. Thus we try to read students'
texts to see what is there rather than what isn't, resisting generalizations about
literacy and intelligence that are made on the basis of judgments about standards of correctness and form, and suspending our judgments about the alternative rhetorical approaches our students adopt.

In addition to working with faculty to shape the curriculum so that it is
responsive to students' needs and to generate instructional approaches that
build on students' competence, we address other institutional practices that
affect our students. At the University of Massachusetts, for example, the Writing Proficiency Exam, which all students must pass by the time they are
juniors, continues to evolve as faculty across the curriculum work together,
implementing and modifying it over time. While the exam is impressive,
immersing students in rich, thematically-integrated material to read, think

about, and respond to, it nevertheless continues to be reconsidered and questioned as we study the ways in which the exam impinges on students' academic lives. And so, for instance, in order to address the finding that ESL students were failing the exam at higher rates than native speakers of English — a situation that is occurring at other institutions as well (see Ray) — we have tried to ensure that faculty understand how to look below the surface of student texts for evidence of proficiency, promoting a kind of reading that benefits not just ESL students but all students. The portfolio option, which requires students to submit papers written in courses as well as to write an essay in response to a set of readings, has proven a better alternative for ESL students to demonstrate writing proficiency. This is not surprising, given that the portfolio allows students to demonstrate what they are capable of when writing is imbedded within and an outgrowth of their courses.

Throughout this work, one of the most critical notions that I try to bring home is the idea that what faculty ought to be doing to enhance the learning of ESL students is *not* a concession, a capitulation, a giving up of standards — since the unrevised approaches that some faculty want to retain may never have been beneficial for *any* students. As John Mayher has pointed out, teaching and learning across college courses are by and large dysfunctional for all students, even those that succeed. What ESL students need — multiple opportunities to use language and write-to-learn, course work which draws on and values what students already know, classroom exchanges and assignments that promote the acquisition of unfamiliar language, concepts, and approaches to inquiry, evaluation that allows students to demonstrate genuine understanding — is good pedagogy for everyone. Learning how to better address the needs of ESL students, because it involves becoming more reflective about teaching, because it involves carefully thinking through the expectations, values, and assumptions underlying the work we assign, helps faculty teach everyone better. In other words, rather than seeing the implications of inclusion and diversity in opposition to excellence and academic standards (as they often are at meetings convened to discuss these issues), learning to teach ESL students, because this challenges us to reconceptualize teaching, contributes to and enhances learning, and for all students. As Gerald Graff has argued in response to those who voice their concerns about the presence of new student populations in their institutions and the negative consequences that this change brings,

> Conservatives who accuse affirmative action programs of lowering academic standards never mention the notorious standard for ignorance that was set by white male college students before women and minorities were permitted in large numbers on campus. It has been the steady pressure for reform from below that has raised academic standards. (88)

Needless to say, given the complexity of this enterprise, these efforts have not transformed classrooms on an institution-wide basis. As is obvious from the surveys and case studies I have undertaken, change is slow, much like the process of learning itself. Shaughnessy referred to the students who entered the CUNY system through open admissions as "strangers in academia" to give us a sense of the cultural and linguistic alienation they were experiencing (*Errors*). In listening to the comments of faculty (note, for example, the comment of the professor of management), it occurs to me that they too are feeling like strangers in academia, that they no longer understand the world in which they work. Janice Neuleib similarly points out that although it is common to view students as "other," as alienated from the academic community, our differing cultural perspectives result in our own confusion and alienation as well.

As we grapple with the kinds of issues and concerns raised by the clash of cultures in academia, we continue to make adjustments which, in turn, generate new questions about our practices. This ongoing dialogue is both necessary and beneficial. Like other prominent debates in higher education on reforming the canon and the implications of diversity, this attempt to explore and interrogate what we do is slowly reconfiguring the landscape and blurring the borders within what was once a fairly well-defined and stable academic community. According to Graff, this is all to the good because this kind of transformation can revitalize higher education and its isolated departments and fragmentary curricula. Within composition, the conflicts and struggles that inevitably mark the teaching of writing are viewed as instructive because they allow students and teachers to "reposition" themselves, raising questions about conventional thinking about instruction and challenging us to imagine alternative pedagogies (Lu; Horner). What Pratt calls the "contact zone," because it represents a site of contestation, is embraced because it enables us to redraw disciplinary boundaries, to reexamine composition instruction, and to revise our assumptions about language and difference.

When faculty see this kind of redefinition as a crisis, I invite them to reconsider their work in light of the way the word "crisis" is translated into Chinese. In Chinese, the word is symbolized by two ideographs — one meaning danger, the other meaning opportunity. Because the challenges that students bring with them may make us feel confused, uncertain, like strangers in our own community, there will be dissonance, jarring questions, ongoing dilemmas, unfulfilled expectations. We can see this reflected in the second faculty response, a response which insists that there are students who don't belong in the academy, that its doors be kept closed. But, as we saw in the first response, perplexities and tensions can also be generative, creating possibilities for new insights, alternative interpretations, and an appreciation for the ways in which these enrich our understanding. Seen from the fresh perspective that another language can provide, the Chinese translation of crisis captures the very nature of learning, a process involving both risk and opportunity, the very process that ideally students ought to engage in, but which we ourselves may resist when it comes to looking at our own practices. But as Giroux urges, teachers must "cross over borders that are culturally strange and alien to them" so that they can "analyze their own values and voices as viewed from different ideological and cultural spaces" (254–55). It is when we take risks of this sort, when we take this step into the unknown, by looking for evidence of students' intelligence, by rereading their attempts as coherent efforts, by valuing, not just evaluating, their work, and by reflecting on the critical relationship between our work and theirs, that opportunities are created not only for students but for teachers to learn in new ways.

NOTES

1. The acronym ESL (English as a Second Language) is used here because it is the commonly used term to refer to students whose native language is not English. Given the inherently political nature of working with ESL learners, it is important to note that at urban institutions, such as the University of Massachusetts at Boston, most of these students are residents of the United States. Furthermore, in the case of a number of these students, English may be a third or fourth language.

2. This investigation of student responses was first initiated by Spack, whose findings were published in *Blair Resources for Teaching Writing: English as a Second Language*. My ongoing survey builds on her work.

3. See, however, the work of Benesch, McKay, Raimes, and Zamel — all of whom have raised questions about the ideological assumptions underlying much ESL writing instruction.

4. I am indebted here to Patricia Bizzell, whom I first heard use the term *exoticize* to characterize how faculty often react towards ESL students.

WORKS CITED

Bartholomae, David. "Inventing the University." *Journal of Basic Writing* 5 (Spring 1986): 4–23.
Benesch, Sarah. "ESL, Ideology, and the Politics of Pragmatism." *TESOL Quarterly* 27 (1993): 705–17.
Chiseri-Strater, Elizabeth. *Academic Literacies: The Public and Private Discourse of University Students.* Portsmouth: Boynton, 1991.
Clark, Gregory. "Rescuing the Discourse of Community." *CCC* 45 (1994): 61–74.
Fox, Tom. "Basic Writing as Cultural Conflict." *Journal of Education* 172 (1990): 65–83.
———. "Standards and Access." *Journal of Basic Writing* 12 (Spring 1993): 37–45.
Gay, Pamela. "Rereading Shaughnessy from a Postcolonial Perspective." *Journal of Basic Writing* 12 (Fall 1993): 29–40.
Giroux, Henry. "Postmodernism as Border Pedagogy: Redefining the Boundaries of Race and Ethnicity." *Postmodernism, Feminism, and Cultural Politics: Redrawing Educational Boundaries.* Ed. Henry Giroux. Albany: State U of New York P, 1991. 217–56.
Graff, Gerald. *Beyond the Culture Wars.* New York: Norton, 1992.
Horner, Bruce. "Mapping Errors and Expectations for Basic Writing: From 'Frontier Field' to 'Border Country.'" *English Education* 26 (1994): 29–51.
Hull, Glynda, and Mike Rose. " 'This Wooden Shack Place': The Logic of an Unconventional Reading." *CCC* 41 (1990): 287–98.
Hull, Glynda, Mike Rose, Kay Losey Fraser, and Marisa Castellano. "Remediation as Social Construct: Perspectives from an Analysis of Classroom Discourse." *CCC* 42 (1991): 299–329.
Laurence, Patricia. "The Vanishing Site of Mina Shaughnessy's *Errors and Expectations.*" *Journal of Basic Writing* 12 (Fall 1993): 18–28.
Lu, Min-Zhan. "Conflict and Struggle in Basic Writing." *College English* 54 (1992): 887–913.
Mayher, John S. "Uncommon Sense in the Writing Center." *Journal of Basic Writing* 11 (Spring 1992): 47–57.
McKay, Sandra Lee. "Examining L2 Composition Ideology: A Look at Literacy Education." *Journal of Second Language Writing* 2 (1993): 65–81.
Neuleib, Janice. "The Friendly Stranger: Twenty-Five Years as 'Other.'" *CCC* 43 (1992): 231–43.
Pratt, Mary Louise. "Arts of the Contact Zone." *Profession* 91 (1991): 33–40.
Raimes, Ann. "Out of the Woods: Emerging Traditions in the Teaching of Writing." *TESOL Quarterly* 25 (1991): 407–30.
Ray, Ruth. "Language and Literacy from the Student Perspective: What We Can Learn from the Long-term Case Study." *The Writing Teacher as Researcher.* Ed. Donald A. Daiker and Max Morenberg. Portsmouth: Boynton, 1990. 321–35.

Rose, Mike. *Lives on the Boundary: The Struggles and Achievements of America's Underprepared*. New York: Free P, 1989.

———. "The Language of Exclusion: Writing Instruction at the University." *College English* 47 (1985): 341–59.

Shaughnessy, Mina. "Diving In: An Introduction to Basic Writing." *CCC* 27 (1976): 234–39.

———. *Errors and Expectations*. New York: Oxford UP, 1977.

Spack, Ruth. *Blair Resources for Teaching Writing: English as a Second Language*. New York: Prentice, 1994.

Trimbur, John. "'Really Useful Knowledge' in the Writing Classroom." *Journal of Education* 172 (1990): 21–23.

Villanueva, Victor. *Bootstraps: From an American Academic of Color*. Urbana: NCTE, 1993.

Walvoord, Barbara E., and Lucille B. McCarthy. *Thinking and Writing in College: A Naturalistic Study of Students in Four Disciplines*. Urbana: NCTE, 1990.

Zamel, Vivian. "Questioning Academic Discourse." *College ESL* 3 (1993): 28–39.

17

"As You're Writing, You Have These Epiphanies": What College Students Say About Writing and Learning in Their Majors

THOMAS L. HILGERS, EDNA LARDIZABAL HUSSEY, AND MONICA STITT-BERGH

The movement known as "writing across the curriculum" (WAC) has evolved throughout its 30-year history. Early on, its advocates emphasized writing as a tool for learning in potentially every context. More recently, some theorists have emphasized the particulars of different contexts and the different demands those particulars place on writers.

In its earliest forms, WAC was part of an effort to use writing to improve student learning across the board (Britton, Burgess, Martin, McLeod, & Rosen, 1975; Emig, 1971). Emerging more or less parallel to the whole language movement and the process movement, WAC was seen positively by some as a restoration of writing's place in learning, but by others as a revisionist attack on traditional educational values such as rules and correctness.

Whole language, the process movement, and WAC all initially were concerned with what were assumed to be basic underlying processes we humans use to find or construct meaning. WAC typically emphasized writing processes (prewriting, drafting, revising, editing) and products (journals, learning logs) that could be adapted to any course. In its infancy, WAC offered a generalist-epistemic approach to learning (Ernst & Newell, 1969; Newell & Simon, 1972; Polya, 1957). At least metaphorically, the emphasis in WAC was on "across," on general processes.

More recent studies of learning and the rise of cognitive science shifted attention from general cognitive skills to skills functioning in contextualized ways (Detterman & Sternberg, 1993; Perkins & Salomon, 1989; Petraglia, 1995). The teaching of general cognitive skills came to be seen as useful only when accompanied by self-monitoring practices that attended to the particulars of varied contexts (Perkins & Salomon, 1989).

Although studies of learning were bringing new attention to contextual differences, composition studies were seeing a renewed interest in rhetoric (e.g., Covino, 1988; Lunsford & Ede, 1984) and an emerging interest in both academic disciplines and professional work sites as rhetorical situations

---

From *Written Communication* 16.3 (1999): 317–53.

(Bazerman, 1981, 1992; Gotswami & Odell, 1985; Herrington, 1985; McCarthy, 1987). Theorists questioned the assumption that first-year writing courses or WAC courses should emphasize general writing skills (Anson & Forsberg, 1990; Odell, 1993; Rorty, 1989; Russell, 1995). Practitioners shifted attention from general goals and general processes to the particulars that define situations as unique, underscoring the postmodernist view that every setting is best seen in terms of its "situatedness." Thus, "writing across the curriculum" seemed to shift toward "writing in specific contexts" or disciplines (WID). This frame of reference generally continues to influence reform movements in writing pedagogy, although many teachers and some theorists continue to emphasize writing as a widely applicable tool for learning (Sorcinelli & Elbow, 1997).

This broadening of emphasis and understanding suggested new sites for inquiring into the effects of WAC instruction. As long as WAC was seen primarily as part of an educational reform effort, WAC outcomes were studied primarily through studies of pedagogical and teacher change. Indeed, up to this day, the most typical evidence of WAC effectiveness involves statements by teachers, often supported by submissions of revised syllabi and assignments that privilege process approaches to learning.

The more recent emphasis on context has spawned significant research on the processes related to learning to write within the academy. Haas (1994), Herrington (1985), McCarthy (1987), and Walvoord and McCarthy (1990) documented the experiences of undergraduates; and Berkenkotter, Huckin, and Ackerman (1994), Kogen (1989), MacDonald (1994), Matalene (1989), Myers (1985), and Reynolds, Matalene, Magnotto, Samson, and Sadler (1995) looked more specifically at how graduate students and professionals are enculturated into particular worlds of writing and writers. Most of these studies, however, were not designed primarily to provide evidence of WAC's effects on the behaviors or thinking of students. In fact, Ackerman (1993) raised important questions about claims of student learning associated with WAC and noted the dearth of studies involving students.

This study was shaped in part by a realization that the history of our own writing program at the University of Hawai'i, although shorter than that of the WAC movement, has paralleled it in certain ways. Our program was devised after a lengthy needs-assessment conducted in the mid-1980s (see Hilgers & Marsella, 1992). The program is built around a graduation requirement of five writing-intensive (WI) classes. When the WI requirement was being phased in (1987–1989), entering freshmen were required to take two, three, or four WI classes to graduate. Beginning with the fall 1990 class, five WI classes were required for a bachelor's degree. (See the Appendix for graduation requirements and a description of WI criteria.)

Although the program is only a decade old, and although the requirement has remained constant, the culture that fosters WI instruction has changed. At the time the program was developed, primary faculty interest was in writing as a mode of learning. Because most of the initial WI classes were developed for first- and second-year students, professors gravitated toward techniques associated with Moffett (1968, 1981), Fulwiler (1987), Elbow (1981), and the like — scholar practitioners very much concerned with writing as a tool for learning. Although the occasional professor would resist this approach because of its apparent distance from course-content concerns, most embraced it at least in theory — in part because professors interested in WAC also wanted to improve teaching.

However, a growing concern during the 1990s has been the special demands of writing within individual majors. (Our campus offers the bachelor's degree through 89 programs; WI courses are typically offered by 75 to 80 programs each semester.) The focus of faculty workshops has become more and more weighted toward inquiry methods of different fields and writing as an artifact of the culture in which it occurs. This reflects the theoretical shift evident in the growing prominence of social constructivism, discourse studies, and even cultural studies.

Furthermore, by the third and fourth years of the program, students were demanding more and more WI courses in their majors. The faculty accommodated this demand; today, approximately 70% of the annual 1,000 WI classes on campus are linked to requirements in the various majors. Indeed, from the program's planning phase, the WI requirement was intended to foster writing experience in the major. The original proposal required that students take two WI courses in their majors; that later was changed to "two upper-division courses" to accommodate students who switch majors late in their college careers. The emphasis on writing in the major is further reflected in graduates' transcripts: Of the 5.9 WI courses now taken by the typical graduate, 3 are from that student's major.

A second prominent feature of our program also parallels a current feature of the WAC movement: WAC offerings are idiosyncratic and nonstandardized. In perhaps half of our majors, specified upper-division courses regularly are offered as WI. In other majors, WI courses are proposed by instructors on a semesterly basis. In both situations, professors have a great deal of latitude in what and how they teach, as long as their practices ultimately conform to the hallmarks of WI courses. Similarly, the order in which students take courses, including WI courses, is far from standardized. Furthermore, beyond majors in which the curriculum is highly structured (e.g., architecture), there is no obvious pattern of sequenced WI assignments either within majors or across lower- and upper-division offerings.

In sum, just as WAC offerings are peculiar to the contexts of sponsoring campuses, our students' WI experiences are peculiar to their individual histories (Marsella, Hilgers, & McLaren, 1992). Across experiences, however, are two somewhat common elements: quantity of writing and size of WI classes. Students do 16 or more pages of writing in at least five of their post-English-100 courses, and their WI experiences occur in classes of 20 or fewer students.

This study was designed to take advantage of the peculiarities of our program and the ways in which its history relates both to the history of the WAC movement and to the issues prominent in discourse studies today. The specific queries in which we engaged were:

1. How does disciplinarity affect students' understanding of writing tasks?
2. What do students nearing completion of the university's WI requirements report that they know about writing?

METHOD

The findings reported here derive from analyses of data elicited via extended interviews. The overall justification for our approach to the research project remains what it was in this study's direct predecessor (Hilgers, Bayer, Stitt-Bergh, & Taniguchi, 1995, pp. 62–64). Once again, we turned to our students as "consumers" of WI classes. Two members of the research team, Hussey and Stitt-Bergh, used a sequence of open-ended questions to gather information from the students.

In pilot work and in the previous study, we found that most students never had been prompted to reflect on their writing experiences across courses. They typically submitted end-of-course evaluations and sometimes wrote short self-assessments at the end of a course, but most had not been asked how their writing related to anything beyond the assignments of a particular course. We believed that encouraging students to be more aware of themselves as writers, and more consciously attentive to how they undertook assignments, would aid our investigation. Therefore, in the current study we decided to ask students to participate in two interviews, one at the beginning of the semester and one near the end. The first interview planted the seeds of reflective attention (Gere, 1991; Schon, 1987) that we planned to harvest during the second interview. It also functioned as a "get-to-know-you" session in which the student became comfortable with the interviewer and with a tape recorder.

Questions in the first interview focused on reasons behind the interviewee's choice of major, important or key learning experiences in the major, attitudes toward writing (in general and in the major), and the student's current WI course in the major. At the end of the first interview, students were asked to select a focal assignment — one assignment from their current WI class that they valued or found interesting — and to consider the following questions as they worked on the assignment:

1. When you first got the assignment, what did you think you had to do?
2. Whenever you worked on the assignment, what decisions did you make?
3. Where in your draft(s) did you have difficulties? (You can mark these areas with Post-it notes or an asterisk.) What were these difficulties?

your draft(s) was it easy for you to write? (You can mark these areas it notes or an asterisk.) Why were these areas easy to write?

d to schedule the second interview after they had completed the ent.

Most of the questions for the second interview involved the student-selected writing assignment: its importance, initial thoughts it provoked, goals and decisions it evoked, difficulties it presented, and feedback the student's work elicited. The final questions of the second interview explored the student's view of writing in his or her major, expectations for writing after graduation, and experiences with the WI requirement in general.

Participants

After students had registered for classes, we identified from computer records a random sample of 246 students who met the following criteria:

1. Had junior or senior standing.
2. Had declared a major in a specified area.[1]
3. Had completed at least four classes in their declared major.
4. Had completed at least three WI courses.
5. Were currently enrolled in at least one WI course in their declared major.

At the beginning of the semester, our office sent students who met the criteria a letter inviting them to participate in the study. The letter, which also described the goals of the study, offered participants $30 for two 90-minute interviews.

Thirty-nine recipients called to schedule an interview. Two of the 39 did not show up for the first interview. Three did not show up for the second interview. Thus, 34 students completed both the first and second interviews and submitted their written assignment, notes, and assignment guidelines (where available).

Data Analysis

Each interview was transcribed by a trained student employee not involved in the study. The two interviewers then used subsets of transcripts to develop a preliminary set of categories that might allow coding of data across interviews. Once a relatively comprehensive and stable set of categories had emerged, the full set of transcripts was coded (using the software program NUD*IST, 1995). At that point, the full research team reviewed both individual transcripts and composite coded data to see if the preliminary categories were comprehensive and parsimonious. Additions, deletions, and modifications of the codes were made at that time. Some codes were eliminated. For example, "Knowing the audience" in the "What was difficult" category was deleted (and responses were recoded) because only two students had mentioned it. Others were added. For instance, "ESL-related" emerged under "What was difficult" because many of the second-language speakers we interviewed believed that writing in a second language presented problems unique to them. Other codes were modified. For example, the category "Suggestions to improve the WI program" initially included "Instructor's attitude, personality, and/or training." Our review of both transcripts and composite data showed that most students were concerned about instructor training, not attitude or personality. Thus, the subcategory was redescribed before transcripts were recoded so that "training" comments remained and the few personality comments were recoded as "other."

To ensure consistency in coding, the interviewers read and coded a sample (at least 25%) of each others' transcripts. Agreement was high (over 80%). To further examine validity and reliability in the coding, we brought in a third reader who was unfamiliar with either the coding scheme or the study and trained him in the coding scheme. He coded a random 25% sample of the transcripts. His codings overall agreed with codings assigned by the primary reader 80% of the time. Where a specific code was assigned differently more than 30% of the time, identifiers associated with the code were discussed and the code descriptor was modified. All transcripts were then recoded using the modified code descriptors.

COMPOSITE PORTRAIT OF INTERVIEWEES

Analysis of each interviewee's records yielded the following composite:

- All interviewees except 1 met the selection criteria. (Transcript data used for selection were tentative. One student who had enrolled in three WI classes had failed to complete one of them successfully. Thus, 1 participant had completed only two WI classes before the interview.)
- Interviewees had completed an average of 4.3 WI classes, from an array of offerings in more than 30 different departments, before the first interview.
- Interviewees' mean grade point average was 3.1 (on a 4-point scale).
- Sixty-one percent had completed at least one WI class in their major before the first interview.
- Forty-four percent had completed at least two WI classes in their major before the first interview.
- Twenty-three percent were enrolled in two WI classes in their major during the semester the interviews were held.
- Sixty percent were between the ages of 23 and 29, 20% were under 23, and 20% were over 29.
- Seventy percent were women.
- Thirty percent spoke English as a second language.

Demographically, the interview group contained a significantly larger percentage of women than did the overall undergraduate population (70% versus 56%). Although the group also reflected a higher percentage of interviewees who spoke English as a second language (30% versus 21%), this difference was not significant.

The distribution of interviewees by college and majors is shown in Table 17-1.

TABLE 17-1   Distribution of Interviewees' Degree Areas

Area	Number of students
Business administration (accounting, finance, management information systems, marketing, travel industry management)	7
Arts & humanities (art, English, history)	9
Mechanical engineering	2
Natural sciences (botany, chemistry, zoology)	6
Social sciences (communication, economics, psychology, speech)	10

FINDINGS

How Does Disciplinarity Affect Students' Understanding of Writing Tasks?

All interviewees were enrolled in at least one 300- or 400-level WI class; in these classes, most writing assignments involved research or experimentation. For more than half of the interviewees, the focal WI class was the capstone course in their majors, and the primary assignment was a lengthy research project. Thus, it is not surprising that 94% of the interviewees chose as their focal task a formal writing assignment that involved doing research.

During the first interview, students typically described taking WI classes in a desired discipline as "more" when compared to taking WI classes as part of their general education or graduation requirements:

- I spend more time and effort writing in mechanical engineering because the classes are more enjoyable. (mechanical engineering major)

- There's more attention to specifics in zoology such as knowing what makes up a nerve cell, whereas outside my major the instructors are getting at general concepts. (zoology major)

- In psychology, I always try to get more references by checking the bibliography or works cited when I'm reading journal articles and I have to write, but I won't go this extra step for courses outside my major. (psychology major)

Other students reported "more stress," "more difficulty," "more technical understanding," and "more reading" in their WI classes in the major.

As we now detail, students generally had vested interests in WI classes in their majors. Because they wanted to succeed in their respective fields, they valued these WI classes more than WI classes outside their majors. When writing in their chosen fields, students were aware that the body of existing knowledge and the conventions of the field were factors in how they researched and wrote. Their perception that specific writing and research tasks were preparing them for their future careers cast a high-stakes aura around writing in the major. They regarded their experiences with research assignments as indicators of probable success in the field.

The Writing Task as a Content-Driven Problem

For all interviewees, the most frequently mentioned issues involved deciding what content to include and how to present that content. Students struggled to determine what information was considered "widely shared knowledge" and therefore did not need to be included, and what information needed to be interpreted and explained in detail. The interviewees also were aware that they had to present their content in ways appropriate to their discipline, but they were unsure what those ways were:

- I had some preconceived notions that the formal lab report was like an English paper. You read whatever you think should be in there. You know, write about opinions rather than what's actually there. I realized that this is not just some book on Shakespeare where you can put your opinions in. It's more how this experiment worked or how this data should be. I had to learn how to be more specific with what I wrote in this course. (chemistry major)

- I knew that adult interactions were important up to this point, but I just had to decide why, and that was hard. Trying to actually sit down and say, well, why really is it that they're important? . . . Finding evidence to support what I wanted to say was the most difficult part. I brainstormed for a couple of days and it was like I was going in circles. I was writing down ideas and different thoughts, but it wasn't really directly related to what I was trying to say. There was a point where I was going through the book and I was trying to find information on why is it important for peer interaction. Is it because they have the same level of thinking or is it because they're aware of their own mental stage? It's like why or why not. . . . I just kept trying to find evidence in the book. (psychology major)

- The final paper you just have to put all four papers together. I think the final paper is a kind of challenge because this is a kind of thing that never happened to me before. We wrote four separate topics, and the final paper, you combined all the papers together. I think maybe you just have to staple all the papers after you revise. But he said, no, he wants a paper with only one topic. . . . How can you go from one time frame to another time frame because you may be talking about 1971–1973, but usually you talk about the '70s then you jump to the '80s? (economics major)

- I had to decide if some information was minor. Should I stick it in or should I leave it out and make it easier for myself? One book had more [information], and two of the books had the same information. Should I add what the third book said or was it just extra stuff? Should I focus on the main uses? (English major)

As newcomers to a discipline, the interviewees lacked thorough knowledge of their fields. However, they were learning that the discipline itself — its body of knowledge and research methods — determined what content they included and how content was organized, developed, and supported.

The Writing Task as a Window Into a Discipline's Methodology

One of the benefits of disciplinary-based research assignments to students was that the assignments helped them learn how to do research. Many or even most of the problems they reported in doing the assignment involved finding information, analyzing data, evaluating the quality of primary and secondary sources, sifting and integrating information, and so forth. From a disciplinary perspective, these are the sorts of skills that often are treated quite directly in the typical graduate methodology course. In contrast, our undergraduate interviewees often associated these problems with the writing assignment itself, in part because very few of their majors provided discrete treatment of methodology issues. After completing the research assignment, students saw themselves as having learned not only about the paper's topic, but about the nature of research in their disciplines:

- This project gave me an idea of what the researchers have to go through to decide what to vary in other people's experiments and not to draw too general conclusions regarding other people's research. I guess it just kind of gave me the idea of what the researchers do and go through. (psychology major)

- [This assignment] helps me to understand basically why you need to research and all this kind of stuff and what type of research is out there. People actually pay money to do research for that kind of stuff. Some of the stuff I thought was so out of the way. Like why would someone want to do research on something so specific that it answers only one question but it can't solve a lot of other questions? [This kind of assignment is important because] just looking at that one article, it's like, "That's stupid." But if you look at other articles that surround it, it's all part of that research. You can show that with this one research you can find out about calcium flowing and then from there you need calcium to move the muscle so without muscle movement you would have diseases like multiple sclerosis and stuff. So, maybe finding out if water flows to that muscle, you can find a cure for multiple sclerosis. It's all a part of a whole. (chemistry major)

- I learned a lot more about these historians that I had studied in class and it was interesting. I was having fun looking up more information about the subject. It was interesting how the opinions about the historians differed. I learned more about their background and how people have analyzed their writing and stuff like that. So, it was really interesting. Now I have a better understanding of what modern history is and that there's not a consensus and it's changing and stuff. I didn't realize how much history changed so much and what the influences were because . . . actually I barely even touched the subject of modern history because it's gone through so many changes and there's so many major influences. (history major)

These students' experiences were different from those of entering freshmen (Hussey, Bayer, Hilgers, & Jones, 1995) who viewed research papers as an exercise in information gathering. Students in this study — in upper-division WI classes in their majors — had acquired a sense of apprenticeship and discovery by participating in a scholarly process that led to a better understanding of investigation methods in a subject area.

The Writing Task as Shaped by Audience Expectations

Part of the difficulties students had dealing with the content and how to present it related to their understanding of the audience. Eighty-two percent of the interviewees saw the instructor who had given the assignment as a primary, or even the exclusive, audience:

- The first [lab report] that I had written was more a specialized genre like for a symposium. I got shot down for that. I got smart and next I asked the TA what it was that he wanted me to write about. So now I know basically what he expects. (chemistry major)

- I knew I was putting in a lot of information into this report because I had to. I knew who I was writing for and I knew what he was looking for. (zoology major)

- I kept thinking if I were the reader, how the writing would make sense to someone else. At the same time there is another motive. I wanted to demonstrate to the teacher the structure of my thinking and my general grasp of the subject. (art major)

Although almost all realized that seeing the teacher as the primary audience was important, 56% of the interviewees also described one or more nonteacher audience(s). Several students had been told by their instructor to write for a hypothetical audience. For example, the mechanical engineering students were instructed to address their memos to "Mr. I. M. Boss." But even in cases in which the instructor did not provide a hypothetical audience, more than half the students created their own. In the professional schools, interviewees often referred to their audience as an individual they believed had specific content knowledge such as a CEO, coworker, or technician. Psychology and chemistry majors often talked about "specialists," and many in the humanities spoke of an "all-purpose" or "generic" reader:

- I'm thinking that this is a business proposal. You are writing to your CEO. He's supposed to know what is turnover rate already, he's supposed to know this and this and this. Do you have to explain to your CEO in situations? He knows everything. You go directly to the point and tell him okay, look, this is our problem. What I'm going to do is this. (travel industry management major)

- I know when you're writing a certain paper, you're to assume that the audience doesn't know anything, but then to me that shouldn't be because when you're writing for a specialist, like on schizophrenia, you're not going to explain what schizophrenia is from the very beginning. But, it's important to know that when you're talking about anorexia nervosa, [to] say which, because there are so many diagnostic criteria for one disease. (psychology major)

- It's always better, I think, to write in a way that anybody can pick up your writing . . . and still be able to follow it. If you think of that somebody as someone who has no knowledge of the subject, that's better than assuming the reader knows something. They may have some background, but you really don't know the extent of their knowledge, and if you presume too much, they may not know what you're writing about. (history major)

Students' conceptions of their audiences played a fundamental role in the choices they made as they worked on their writing. They were aware that the content and how they presented their content depended on the discipline and for whom they were writing.

The Writing Task as an Opportunity to Pursue Personal Goals

Sixty-eight percent of the students claimed they had established their own goals for their focal assignment, goals ranging in nature from creating a "neat layout" to satisfying a burning curiosity about a particular topic. Only 23% of the students stated that getting an "A" or "good grade" was their sole goal. In part, students felt the assignment related to personal goals because most (65%) were allowed to choose a topic that interested them. Furthermore, the fact that the assignment was in their majors, rather than in a general education course, created a presumption of its relevance to personal interests and career goals. The following responses were in answer to the questions, "What were your expectations for writing this assignment? Did you have any goals or purposes for writing this assignment?"

- Well, the topic of this paper relates to politics, economics, and culture in Malaysia. It's interesting to know what a new technology can do on people in general. So, like for example, culture. In Malaysia, it's a multicultural country and it's like with new technology going into the country, there are some people who are not too happy with this because they feel it is against their culture to view certain programs. So, I'm interested to know what their feelings are. (communication major)

- I was curious to know how loud the motorcycle really is and whether it could damage your hearing when you ride it. (mechanical engineering major)

- I wanted to do something different, challenging. . . . I wanted to write an analysis because that film really meant something to me. (psychology major)

- Well, the purpose was that it was due. But I was kind of excited about it because I never really sat down and tried to figure out what the semicolon was for. Another thing, too, was having the chance to read the other person's paper. So I thought I'd brush up on stuff because you kind of go by what you know as far punctuation is. (English major)

The power of writing to give voice to and provide substance for a personally meaningful argument may well be a power that students do not want to give up, once they have experienced it. At the same time, there is a parallel power in the constructs of a genre or a field, a power that results from a collective decision on what is important. Thus, when a student encounters writing assignments that require conformity to external expectations — whether seen as emanating from a professor or from expectations of practitioners within a discipline — the priority attached to personal interest or personal goals can become problematic. This tension is illustrated by one comment from a history major:

> I had to throw out so much stuff, and it was so overwhelming . . . because it was a lot of information. After class, [the instructor] told me to touch on education. But I told him I couldn't see the logic in it and that's why I struggled because I couldn't see what education and family systems have to do with my paper. . . . I was trying to write this paper to please me, so I told him that I'm writing about women, not so much the family and traditional stuff. But he said it would be interesting. So I said OK because it was going to cost me a grade. Later, he wrote that it was an interesting paper, but it was disappointing to me. What I noticed is that when instructors tell you to add more [information] which has nothing to do with what you want to do, you resist. So four chapters out of the paper is me and the other two are what the professor wanted.

This excerpt from an English major also reflects how personal goals conflicted with instructor expectations:

> He teaches us each character should be a reflection of whatever the central argument is. But, I sort of just ignored that. . . . [The professor] always told me that you can't have characters talking on and on. At some point I can say that they talked about this and this for the rest of the evening. But I never did that. . . . In this story, I used a lot of dialogue. I get bothered when I don't get the right sentence of what people would say. It's really important to me. I like to fool around with dialogue because I'm fascinated by the way other people talk. . . . I guess it comes back to like I want to keep this story the way I remembered it. With the central argument, the whole story would naturally change.

Thus, the focal assignment within the major created a situation in which some students had to struggle with and find some approach that allowed them to achieve personal goals and at the same time meet professor and disciplinary expectations.

The Writing Task as Preparation for Postcollege Employment

Sixty-five percent of the interviewees perceived that writing instruction in their majors was preparing them for thinking and writing in the workforce or in graduate school. Students deemed the writing assignments in their majors — program proposals, formal lab reports, critiques of histories, case studies, engineering memos, and so forth — as valuable because they perceived that the reading, drafting, thinking, and revising required to complete the writing tasks were relevant and applicable to their future careers. Forty-seven percent linked the ability to communicate clearly, logically, concisely, and persuasively with professional publication and work-related tasks such as writing reports (e.g., in finance, management, chemistry, psychology) and making presentations (e.g., in marketing, history, engineering):

- With marketing, what I feel, you have to convince a lot of people. So, I feel that marketing is a lot of convincing and a lot of sales, depending on what area of marketing you get into. Communication — verbal, nonverbal, written — requires very good writing skills. (marketing major)

- Writing in [mechanical engineering] is learning to communicate with either your peers, your boss, or the people that work for you. You have to be able to communicate clearly and concisely. Generally, they want something straightforward and to the point, nothing flowery. And they want it in a memo form with maybe a lab report attached to it. (mechanical engineering major)

- A really important part of being a psychologist, I think, is, well — It's emphasized that you do studies or you do research or do journal articles. That's the emphasis in psychology. It seems to me that any time you take a point, you can argue it and create experiments to prove your point or disprove others' points. When you do so — of course, if you're going to publish a journal article, you need these writing skills. (psychology major)

Although 65% of the students anticipated that writing would be a part of their careers or graduate work in general, 55% took this one step further and claimed that the writing experiences in their courses paralleled the writing tasks in their anticipated professional lives. They described types of writing assignments they were learning and perfecting in their majors and noted that they would be doing these same types after they entered the professional world:

- If I was to be a chemist, I would need to write reports and my reports would be similar to these. I would have to know how to write these type of papers to convince someone that my results are good or that this is what they need to know or this is what they need. It may be published, or it may be — say like you're working for a chemical company and you need to impress on someone that this chemical is going to be the wave of the future or is going to be the next AZT or something. (chemistry major)

- I guess it helps to polish my writing skills and express my ideas about my major because when I go to work I will have to write reports like that. If I start working on papers in my major now, I can get myself to be more familiar with the terms and how to approach the reader. (finance major)

- I think most times [on the job] the [management and information systems] major has to talk with the customer and if we need to generate a program, we need to write up a user guide. So writing up a report or a user manual is very necessary for us. Because, for example, if we try to write about the Access program, we need to write up a user manual for the user and then they just look at it. . . . [The professors] give assignments like that for us to do. So, we have to know how to write up in a professional way and be more confident in writing so that we can write up a report to our customer. (management and information systems major)

- If I want to research something, then I'm going to have to do all the data and the calculations like we did here and be able to write a report in this format. If I find something that I can patent, then I'm going to have to be able to distribute a report and the best way to go about that is by getting it published like in the *Journal of the American Chemical Society* thing. You want to be able to get your report in there to show everyone else, hey, this is what I got. You have to be able to communicate in such a way that the other people will be able to follow what you've done and it's got to be coherent and it's got to be a certain format most importantly. (chemistry major)

Overall, the interviewees understood writing in the disciplines as a communicative, frequently persuasive, action. Furthermore, they saw content, method, and audience issues as context- or discipline-related. They also extrapolated from their own experiences how writing functions in their particular fields and in the world outside the university.

WHAT DO STUDENTS NEARING COMPLETION OF THE UNIVERSITY'S WI REQUIREMENTS REPORT THAT THEY KNOW ABOUT WRITING?

Many of the interview questions were designed to gather information about students' understandings of how they completed the focal assignment. Most students articulated, and dealt with, problems associated with process, both the process of getting the assignment done and the process of doing the required research. The interviewees also made general statements about the perceived benefits of writing.

Writers Engage Multiple Resources

Although all interviewees "problematized" their focal assignments, as a group, their subsequent actions revealed no general patterns or sequences. For example, students who sought out their instructors did so for different reasons and at varying stages of their work. Indeed, each student typically created his or her own fluid script and modified it frequently. None of the students viewed writing as a linear process in which he or she regurgitated facts or recorded his or her thoughts on paper. None of them described writing as merely drafting and revising. Instead, students viewed "writing" as a set of problems to be solved and goals to be reached. In solving problems and seeking goals, they backtracked, changed tactics, and engaged multiple sources of information and advice. The sources can be described in four categories: stable texts, persons, previous experience, and emerging texts.

Stable Texts.   The one resource engaged by all the interviewees is what we call "stable texts" (to be distinguished from the "emerging text" that the student is producing and also consulting). The first type of stable text is what the students called "readings": books, journal articles, newspaper articles, class notes, web sites, CD-ROM compilations, and so forth. Seventy-six percent of the student writers talked about readings as playing an important role in their writing process:

- The first thing I did was compare the results to the science data, and there was no published data on the material he gave us, so I searched in the library for things because if you can find a book on whatever you're doing, then you can make other qualitative comparisons. (mechanical engineering major)

- I came to my decisions by doing current research like in the *Honolulu Advertiser* and the *Honolulu Star-Bulletin*. And I went in to locate information on the computer at Hamilton Library. What the governor felt, other politicians [about legalizing prostitution]. (economics major)

- I started thinking about my other classes, so I brought out one of my old books and I started looking through my notes, then I said, oh, Henry VIII was interesting but my old professor didn't really go into depth, so I think I'd like reading about that. (history major)

- I always keep searching through my notes and look for common ideas and as I go along I'll just cross off whatever I already put in the paper so that I don't get confused. That way I can make notations about where I got my information. (zoology major)

The second type of stable text students mentioned — the "assignment sheet" or "paper guidelines" — is privileged because it emanates from the assignment giver. Eighty-two percent referred to such texts to help their decision making:

- I followed it [the assignment sheet] exactly in the beginning, in the first couple of memos. Towards the end, I guess, I didn't really look at it anymore because I had the outline more or less memorized. (mechanical engineering major)

- [The instructor] makes comments like, aren't I repeating myself on these? I had actually gotten this from the handout, the formulas, etc. So, I was following the handout that we got. I think he probably knew that. I think that his point was just because we had it really spelled out for us, maybe we're not supposed to spell it out as much as the handout that we were given for the lab in here. (chemistry major)

Because assignment sheets were associated with instructor expectations, and ultimately with course grades, they were consulted again and again. Students sometimes found the language in assignment guidelines problematic: "Fuzzy" and "sort of ambiguous" were typical descriptors. A simple verb such as *interpret*, readily glided over when read in the clause "we interpret this to mean," becomes problematic when it becomes a procedural command on an assignment sheet, as in "Step 4: Interpret the data."

At the time of the second interview, 94% of the students had received written comments from their instructors — the third type of stable text they consulted. Twenty-five of these students followed their instructors' suggestions when writing their final draft or their next assignment in a series. Seven did not apply the feedback because they saw no reason to do so (e.g., it was on the final draft) or because they did not agree with the instructors' suggestions:

- Like he wrote this — I guess these words gave me the idea to help me write a conclusion because I didn't know how to sort of speculate at the end. He said that you can say, "This suggests that." I didn't think you could give opinions in theses. I thought the conclusion was just a summary of what you wrote before, that's what my friends told me. But he wanted me to make my own speculations, but I didn't really know how to do that. (history major)

- He changed the sentences so we'll work on making this kind of sentence instead of making the sentences wrong. We followed what he told us to change in the first report and then we'd apply all the things he told us to change in another report. (management information systems major)

- I did take into consideration what he said and I did change it according to how he wanted it, but that's because I wanted to get the A and he told me to revise it the way he wanted it and then I'd get an A. But I didn't agree with some of the things. Some of them were good things that I realized I had done wrong. But, some of the other things, like using "therefore," he circled practically all the therefores. I've always written papers that way, so I thought it was okay. The hard part about it was he didn't tell me why and then even if it was wrong I've gotten away with it for a long time. (speech major)

- [His feedback] made me very aware of plagiarizing. He told you to not be so la-di-da with the experiment. He said to state everything about it, state what you know, state what you don't know, and if you don't know it, state why. [The feedback is] going to help me to write the third paper. The third paper, I feel, is a little bit easier than this one. This one was pretty hard. I don't know if it's because I'm used to writing what they want, so that makes it feel easier, or what. . . . A lot of the feedback was helpful in having to focus more as to what I'm supposed to write. (zoology major)

Persons. A desire to better understand the assignment sheet, grading criteria, or written feedback was one of the most frequent reasons students sought out a personal resource: the course instructor. Fifty percent of the students met one-on-one with their instructor to clarify assignment directions or teacher expectations:

- When I first got the assignment I thought it would be a difficult paper to write because I'd have lots of research to do. I thought it would be even more difficult because the instructor wanted lots of current scholarly material which I couldn't find. He explained to me that secondary sources wouldn't be as valuable as primary sources. So I talked to the instructor and he advised me to abstract information from books about past telecommunications and about the present situation from newspapers and journals. I also had questions about the abstract and he said the abstract is like answering the question of the paper. Tell the reader what you are going to examine. (communication major)

- I thought maybe after my first draft I'd go to talk with [the professor]. I realized that he wanted something very innovative, very creative. I realized after speaking with him that he kept giving me lots of hints like when he pointed to parts of my draft and said "This is boring stuff." (travel industry management major)

- He expected us to write a clear, organized paper. . . . Students who are not sure how to write a paper properly, we ask him and he advises us about the structure of the paper. (communication major)

Another personal resource, less authoritative than the course instructor but also less intimidating, was a peer or group of peers. Fifty-nine percent of the students talked with their classmates or friends about their focal assignment or received feedback from them on written drafts. Some instructors encouraged peer interactions in class, especially as students were trying to find research topics or methods. Others provided in-class opportunities for peer feedback on emerging texts. Students, in person, on the telephone, or via e-mail, exchanged hints on how to handle one or another part of the assignment:

- The professor gave me some ideas on how to restate sentences, and I asked my friends questions, like "What do you think this means?" That's how I got my conclusion. Like if I read something about Henry VIII that he fooled around so much, we'd talk about possible reasons. My friends and I always do that even when they're the ones writing papers. Sometimes we go bowling or eat out or go to someone's house. We usually end up talking about our upcoming papers, what they're on. If someone needs help, then we get together and try to help the person. (history major)

- Every time I show my draft to my boyfriend, we just end up arguing over semantics. Like for me it means one thing and for him it means another thing. He just doesn't know. Some lay terms may mean something different in psychology. If I just want to make sure it's grammatically correct, then I'll ask him. (psychology major)

- We'd meet with lab partners during the week after the experiment and just brainstorm about what the experiment was about and to interpret the experiment itself. (zoology major)

- After everyone wrote up their parts to the report, we tried to combine it into one report. Everyone shared ideas on parts that were redundant, parts that were good. We'd try to delete redundant sections or make adjustments on how paragraphs would flow to other paragraphs. We made a lot of changes. (economics major)

- When we came together as a group, the ones working on different projects, we gave each other feedback. Some people changed my grammatical mistakes. If the sentence was not good, they'd change it. (management and information systems major)

Previous Experience. Sometimes before (and sometimes after) consulting with instructors or peers, 71% of the student writers turned to their own accumulated knowledge about the topic or about the format and discipline-specific conventions of the assignment:

- You're likely to put your personal feelings and your objective feelings into the paper without thinking that there may be another possibility. If I believe like China didn't have the technology to produce steel, one thing will be like because I read all the books before that and I have heard people talk about it in my own country. I really have relatives during that period and I already have something that's planted in my mind that it's not efficient because they don't have the technology to produce steel and everyone donates their iron just for this. (economics major)

- I had to see what every other person said because one of the books that I had was a little older and I know from doing other papers that the [Modern Language Association style guide] always updates things. Like now, they say you put one space after the period, not two. So, you know if I had gone back to the book I used in high school it would have been two spaces. (English major)

- For a business proposal, you shouldn't write too many flowery things. You should go right to the point. . . . [Headlines are] part of the business format. It stems out, rather than you put everything. Because later on that's where I'm going to tie it in with mine. Like my corporate balance analysis, I can bring out one-by-one because I'm going to talk about how much is the turnover rate, how much you're going to save, how much the revenue is going to increase, that kind of thing. (travel industry management major)

- I knew the discussion part is just what went on in the experiment, explain about the data, explain why you got that data, and like I said before, trying to influence the person to realize that this is the wrong or right data or however you want to influence that person . . . you explain the theory in the introduction because you bring up the subject and it's like writing a paper. (chemistry major)

Of course, students reviewed what they already had internalized about writers' strategies as they worked to extend or improve their emerging texts. Forty-seven percent of the students consulted stored rules of thumb and assorted prescriptions for achieving success through writing:

- I'm not very good with grammar so I stick with the main points and try not to overemphasize or give opinions. I try to keep it short and specific and I won't elaborate because I tend to make more mistakes. (history major)

- One thing I learned through my English classes is that you have to grab your reader in the first paragraph. If you read someone's paper that's really boring, you're going to read it and by the time you're done, you're not going to know what you read. Where if you have someone tell you a story, at a personal level kind of way, you're going to remember exactly what that story was. (history major)

- When I used to write, I think it was for my philosophy class, well, those classes, you can't just write. You have to read first. You have to read like 20 books before you can even start on a paper. I realized how like this person sees it one way and you really get different pictures. You realize how important the original text is — It's important that you read it through other people's perspectives, but it's not the same as the original's. I really like reading the second literature because it's almost like you're having a dialogue with the other person about your favorite book or author. It also gives you an insight that you never would be able to have on your own. But, it's very different from the original and I guess that's how I learned to be suspicious. Especially when there are so many bad ones written on him — You get really mad because it's really distorted. I just learned not to trust other people's opinions because they have their own agenda too. (psychology major)

Emerging Texts.   Forty-four percent of the students stated that they reread their written drafts to guide them or to make sure that they were being "correct" and making sense:

- I'll finish the paragraph and I'll just keep reading the paragraph over and if I know I don't like it or parts of it, I'll just keep changing it until it ends up into something that I feel sounds the best way I could say it and makes sense. Sometimes, as I was going along and writing the rest of the paper, I would find things that I would say, so I would go back to the intro and think maybe I should change the way I said this part. (botany major)

- As I was writing the paper in the computer I kept looking back to the thesis statement and saying, "Okay, did I cover this point?" "Yes," "Did I cover the next point?" "Yes," "Did I cover the third point?" etc. I sort of went through that sort of progression and it was paragraph by paragraph. I had to follow that same order in the paper so the first part of [the thesis statement] should come in the beginning, the second part should come after that, etc. I tried to follow that format. (art major)

- I will review and review [the data and analysis] until I'm satisfied. I'll go into my conclusion and then look at that part many times until I'm satisfied and then turn it in. (management information systems major)

- I went back and I read through it and tried to see if I could fit more information in and stuff like that. (communication major)

Figure 17-1 summarizes the types of resources students sought out to complete their writing assignment.

FIGURE 17-1   Resources Explicitly Consulted

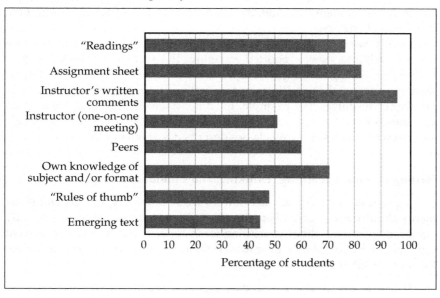

All of the resources previously mentioned potentially influenced both what a student put into a paper and how the student went about writing the paper. However, it is important to distinguish between resources that students engaged and additional determinants of the students' final written text. The shape of the final text, as well as which resources the student consulted, often was determined by exigencies and parameters not fully under the student's control. More than half of the students reported making decisions based on computer center hours, photocopying costs, availability of library books, and so forth:

- I read one book on Laotian textiles that seemed like the only book in English that was around. I was thinking that there's just not enough here for me to write a 10-page paper on. I was either going to have to write everything in that book or I was going to have to change my subject. (art major)

- The original literature I could not get my hands on. . . . They weren't in the library and I didn't want to order it because it was too late in the semester. (psychology major)

- The lab paper we're writing up now is supposed to be an experiment using turtles, but turtles are expensive and we are using a frog heart. But really, a lot of the information that I'm reading in journals is about the human heart. It's really hard to pull this one together. (zoology major)

Although our data did not allow us to determine whether conversations with instructors and peers, written feedback, and so forth, are more significant than such exigencies in shaping a student's decisions, we can say that the external constraints are unavoidable and often become apparent only after a student has problematized a writing assignment and made certain decisions. The constraints change with each subsequent decision. Furthermore, the closer the assignment due date, the more these factors weigh in determining subsequent behavior.

Finally, we found we could grossly quantify the number of different resources each interviewee reported engaging. The average number associated with the focal assignment was 5.7. However, students who had taken a larger-than-average number of WI courses usually reported consulting a greater number of resources. For example, the 5 interviewees who had taken seven WI courses talked of consulting 6.8 resources on the average. And the single student who had taken 12 WI classes described 8 different resources.

Writing Promotes Learning, Thinking, and Confidence

Throughout the interviews, interviewees made summary and general statements about the perceived benefits of writing. First, the students generally agreed that writing about something leads to learning. Ninety-one percent claimed that by completing their focal writing assignment, they learned about the topic or subject:

- When I just made the outline, the paper meant nothing to me and I thought this was going to be a hard paper to write. But, as I was writing — I had read all the stuff and gone to all the classes and knew all the information — but as you're writing, you have these epiphanies and things come to you. It just all seems to fit together. (psychology major)

- It really brings the whole experiment together when you write it up and when you get to see the results, you actually get to see what it is that you did. Once you analyze the data and write it all up and it's a finished product, you can flip through it and see, oh, now I know why I did this. It shows this about this. (mechanical engineering major)

Forty-seven percent of the interviewees believed that, overall, writing is the best way for them to learn:

- When you write an idea or concept and branch off from there into a full essay, it's very different from regurgitating facts because when you're writing something you have to think about how you connect things. (history major)

- I think the writing that I do best is the reflection type. It gives me an opportunity to stop and think through things that I normally wouldn't spend much time thinking about. When I actually write, the ideas become clearer and I can define things for myself. So I think I learn a little bit more about myself through writing. (communication major)

- I can't learn a lot without writing because I may not pay attention in class. But if I need to write, I have to keep my mind on the paper. (finance major)

- I think that good old-fashioned writing is a good way [to learn]. In the end, it really is indicative of what you know about your subject. It's the best way to find out if you know your subject. I think that's why so many teachers choose essay exams. Because they really want you to think and to write something coherent. (history major)

- I think that the writing really puts the icing on the cake where I can really put into perspective what it is I'm supposed to be seeing, what's actually going on, and being able to put that time into thinking about it. (chemistry major)

Second, 35% of the students claimed that writing assignments influence how they think (although "thinking" was not well defined). Often, the ability to think was linked to writing as a way to "organize" and "refine" ideas, become more "analytical," and probe "deeply." Several students also observed that an ability to write seemed to undergird speaking. Experiences with writing helped students internalize conventions of argumentation:

- [Writing] helps me organize my thoughts. . . . Now, when I'm talking to someone, I tend to think "Okay, what are the major points that I want to make in this conversation?" Like if I'm kind of like having some sort of debate. Like if we're all sitting around talking about politics or something, I think about what major points I want to make, what's my back-up for it. (history major)

- I think it helps me to organize my thoughts. You can relate the knowledge or the things that you learned in a more organized format rather than just talking. (travel industry management major)

- [Writing] helps you get a perspective of what you studied. When you read something — Okay, you read it and you sort of understand it, but when you actually have to write about it and tell someone else, in writing, it forces your mind to think of it in a new way. You have to organize your thoughts, you have to make it into some sort of order rather than just thinking on the vast subject. And it forces you to refine your thinking to even more than just having these general ideas. When you have to try to convince someone in writing, it forces you to think a lot sharper . . . it forces you to be even more analytical. (history major)

- I would say that [writing] has helped me think. If I don't write something, I wouldn't really think of a topic that deeply. If you had to research a topic and you had to think about the consequences about it, it would help me think more about the subject. (communication major)

Finally, students claimed that their writing experiences helped boost their confidence in themselves. When directly asked, 76% of the interviewees reported feelings of confidence when writing in their majors:

- I think all the classes and all the writing that I've done here has made me a better writer, but I think maybe after I finish school or whatever, all the writing that I have to do after is going to change and get better. I've reached the point where I'm a good writer now because I think it constantly changes. (communication major)

- If it's performing an experiment for some reason and writing up results on it, I think I'm pretty well prepared to do that. I haven't had to do like a term paper. Anything really long, a big research paper, I'm not sure I would know how to do that. (mechanical engineering major)

- I really have some confidence in my writing ability. Not necessarily because of what I feel. I'm always dissatisfied, but I've gotten enough positive feedback so that I think I'm okay with writing or other people think I'm okay anyway. (history major)

- I know what the format is like. I know how to do research. I know how to do citations. I know the rules and guidelines about writing. (transportation major)

Overall, the interviewees were resourceful, involved, and often deliberate in their writing decisions. They learned to approach writing assignments as problems to be solved and perceived connections between writing and learning.

Discussion

"WAC is uniquely local," Walvoord (1996, p. 68) wrote in her review of more than two decades of the WAC movement. The WAC program at the University of Hawai'i is a local response to faculty and employer perceptions of students' and graduates' writing abilities. Our graduation requirement — five classes designated WI, with a minimum of two from upper-division offerings — reflects two assumptions: writing should be used frequently, and experience with writing should occur throughout a student's college career. Although we have no specific writing-in-the-major requirement, we, as noted in our introduction, have the functional equivalent of WID in that the typical graduate takes an average of three WI courses in his or her major. Thus, upper-division students' experiences — with a variety of writing assignments in a variety of classes, including some in the major — are relevant to issues involving both WAC and WID.

When we add up the findings from this study, the most prominent term in the sum is *confidence* — particularly students' confidence that they can deal with the writing requirements of their majors and their chosen professions. The range and persistence of this finding quite frankly surprised us; not having completed our data analyses when the frequency of comments about confidence became apparent, we initially were not certain that the confidence was well founded. Yet, when we look at the aggregate of student experience, we find that the confidence may have a substantial base. First, students typically had to write in a variety of circumstances and for a variety of real and hypothetical audiences. Second, students either were instructed in, or discovered on their own, different ways to go about doing these writing assignments. Third, they knew how to engage a variety of resources to solve writing problems. Fourth, students became adept using at least embryonic forms of rhetorical problem solving. With rare exceptions, assignment guidelines did not prompt students to "think rhetorically," at least in the global sense. Nonetheless, students did construct audiences (most prominently in professional and science courses), set goals, ask questions about arrangement, and, occasionally, select among alternative approaches. Fifth, students on the brink of graduation were engaged in writing assignments that they believed prepared them for future employment or an advanced degree: More than 80% of the students reported preparedness for writing in their chosen fields.

This was far more than Hussey et al. (1995) found when studying a parallel group of high school students nearing graduation, whose sole rhetorical strategy was typically to "find out what the teacher wants and do that" (p. 3). Also unlike high school seniors, whose typical resource to guide writing was the model five-paragraph theme, students in this study, after multiple WI experiences, were looking to, and accessing, multiple resources. The very fact that they would consult more than one resource suggests that they were operating with rather sophisticated plans for accomplishing both their research and their writing assignments.

A second inescapable finding from this study relates more specifically to our question about the effects of disciplinarity. Our data were not broad enough to document robust differences between WI classes outside and in the major. However, we did find that, whatever the major, students clearly preferred writing experiences involving its courses. True, this was tied to their vision of future work. But it was more than that. It was almost as if doing writing assignments in the major involved making an investment in who the student desired to become; writing, in other words, seemed to be part of professional identity-building. This aspect may prompt student motivation that instructors often report to be missing in general education courses.

Overall, then, WI courses, particularly those in the major, are providing students with rich opportunities to do what professionals do — to observe, gather data, make analyses, and write reports. The in-the-major WI courses also provide students with process-driven structure for doing extended pieces of writing. We hypothesize that a research-related piece of writing is more likely than, for example, a "personal reaction" piece to involve students in the task of sorting through multiple goals. Again, the experience of having multiple goals contrasts positively with the sole archetypical goal of the pre-college student, which is to "please the teacher."

The findings from this study extend beyond our research questions; they also help us see more clearly how our local program objectives are being met. Because our local objectives are part of the larger dialogue on approaches to writing instruction, it seems appropriate to include in this discussion some of what this study tells us about our situation.

The development of the WAC program at the University of Hawai'i was guided by three implicit objectives:

1. To give students opportunities to experience writing as a set of tools for learning.
2. To guide students toward proficiency with the common written genres of their chosen field.
3. To help students situate what they know about writing rhetorically, thus providing them with ready access to writing strategies that may be adapted to meet new needs.

Analyzing our data made us keenly aware that we are well on our way to meeting the first two objectives, but falling short of the third.

Anyone familiar with the literature of WAC knows the emphasis on write-to-learn strategies such as those described by Fulwiler (1981), Walvoord (1986), and many others. In our interviews, students did not mention write-to-learn activities except in infrequent reference to what they had done in lower-division WI (and first-year writing) courses outside their majors. On one hand, that did not surprise us, because the primary focus of this study was a student's experiences with a writing assignment in the major. On the other hand, we were surprised because so much of the training we provided in workshops for our faculty, particularly during the early years of program development, involved the traditional canon of write-to-learn strategies.

Does this mean that our interviewees, involved with relatively traditional research products, were not "writing to learn"? The data reported previously provide little evidence, but the drafts and reading notes that students brought to the second interview showed that students did do exploratory writing, although they may not have labeled it as such. In other words, although instructors of WI courses in the major seldom assigned conventional "write-to-learn" activities, students frequently incorporated exploration into their multifaceted approaches to accomplishing their final drafts. Several of the transcript excerpts illustrate how the writing of a first draft was in part an exercise in exploration and discovery. And the evidence that students perceived themselves as learning content is clear.

It is important also to note that instructors often facilitated exploration and discovery through their construction of a writing assignment. They set multiple deadlines; they invited or insisted on multiple drafts, consultations, reflection, and "re-visioning" of the assignment. What they less frequently did — at least from our examination of assignment sheets — was to connect explicitly the discovery methods that are often implicit in a genre's conventions with the processes in which writer-researchers engage. Nonetheless, a few students appeared to be discovering such connections on their own — often through repeated efforts with assignments in the same genre.

The very fact that students often used genre labels when talking about assignments provides some evidence that our second objective, genre proficiency, plays an important role in WI instructors' design of writing assignments. Another indicator, students' references to discipline-specific conventions, further suggests that at least some students had a sense of how writing functions in their disciplines. Indeed, students' successes with particular genres, especially when accomplished in an environment that included instructors' reminders that "you will be doing this again if you get a job in this field," led students to the kind of confidence we discussed previously.

Overall, then, we see in our data evidence that students clearly gain from our program's combination of WAC and WID approaches. Students get both the variety and quantity of writing experiences associated with WAC and the experiences with particular contexts and genres associated with WID. Nonetheless, we are led to ask "Is this enough?" Is it enough to provide students with experiences in at least five WI classes and to hope that the attention to and frequency of writing will help them to attain the habits of effective writers?

Our interviewees, although confident in their facility with certain genres, seemed unaware that their understanding of genre was limited by the context of a specific classroom, a "controlled circumstance." Furthermore, the difficulties interviewees experienced in discovering appropriate inquiry processes and in solving content problems suggested that they had an essentially superficial understanding of genre: They were versed in format and stylistic conventions and they knew that the writing in their majors was different from other writing they had done, but they generally lacked an understanding of the underlying values and epistemologies that different genres (or even a particular genre) represented. We are, in other words, suggesting that what we have is not quite enough. We are coming up short of our third objective, which is to help students learn strategies they can successfully apply in future circumstances.

However, another aspect of our experience with this study may hint at an approach that offers promise of making our WI requirement more likely to accomplish this third objective. We found that instructors apparently provided little direct instruction on connections between genres and methods of inquiry; only a few students described instructors helping them to understand how researcher-writers develop arguments, interrogate sources, validate findings, and write up results. At the same time, we found that the students are quite ready to see such connections: They frequently seemed to "discover" what they had learned about inquiry methods during the interviews with us.

In other words, it may take just a little pointed prompting to help students recognize connections between writing and inquiring, between genres and epistemologies.

What more might it take to help students achieve proficiency as writers, thinkers, and problem solvers? It might take little more than providing experiences that encourage awareness of what they are doing as they write, and, furthermore, awareness that how what they are doing, even in apparently disparate situations, is ultimately working to solve potentially related sets of epistemological or rhetorical problems.

What would this require of instructors? First, they must help students to situate each new research and writing task among prior experiences and thus to "discover" familiar strategies they might employ or adapt to accomplish the new task. Second, the instructors must foreground the processes of inquiry and validation that professionals in the field might use to accomplish the new task. Third, they must help students come to see connections among inquiry methods, the recording of findings, and the processes of composing a final report. All three of these involve changing emphases far more than changing course content. Ultimately, they require attention to a field's methodology and epistemology — to the generation of research questions, selection of sources, the design of arguments, and the choice of reporting language. Granted, many students will "see" the connections only as they accumulate a wide range of writing and problem-solving experiences. But a mentor's attention to problem definition, alternative solutions, and strategies for crafting an effective solution can help students make connections within an assignment and across assignments.

What would this mean for our particular WAC/WID program? In addition to helping professors foreground aspects of inquiry processes, we might have to ask individual departments to promote a certain amount of sequencing across assignments and even courses — to move from a smorgasbord approach to a fixed-menu approach in at least some majors. Ultimately, it might require greater coordination among faculty members and greater coherence in the curricula of certain majors.

We leave our data with renewed confidence that a hybrid of WAC and WID, with special attention to the ways of writers in each student's chosen major, is well worth the investment our faculty and students are making in WI classes. Nonetheless, we will work to heighten awareness through faculty workshops and to help students acquire a set of habits that will still be useful in approaching problems 25 years from now. In working to improve how WI courses are connected and taught, we will be guided by scholarship in learning, developmental psychology, and rhetoric; and we will continue to ask our students about their experiences.

APPENDIX

Writing-Intensive Requirement

Students who entered the University of Hawai'i (UH) system as freshmen in fall 1990 or later must complete, before they graduate from the Mānoa campus, five WI courses (designated "WI" in each semester's schedule of classes). At least two WI courses must be from courses numbered 300 and above. Students who entered the UH system as freshmen in 1987–1988 must complete, before they graduate from the Manoa campus, two WI courses; in 1988–1989, three WI courses; and in 1989–1990, four WI courses (at least two of which must be numbered 300 and above).

Hallmarks of WI Classes at the University of Hawai'i

1. The course uses writing to promote the learning of course materials. Instructors assign formal and informal writing, both in class and out, to increase students' understanding of course material and to improve writing skills.

2. The course provides interaction between the instructor and students while students do assigned writing; in effect, the instructor acts as an expert and the student as an apprentice in a community of writers. Types of interaction will vary. For example, a professor who requires the completion of long essays may review sections of the essay, write comments on drafts, and be available for conferences. The professor who requires several short papers may demonstrate techniques for drafting and revising, give guidance during the composition of the papers, and consult with students after they complete their papers. (Many professors now use e-mail to provide at least some of this interaction.)

3. Written assignments contribute significantly to each student's course grade.

4. The course requires students to do a substantial amount of writing — a minimum of 4,000 words, or about 16 pages. This may include informal writing. Depending on the course content, students may write analytic essays, critical reviews, journals, lab reports, research reports, reaction papers, and so forth.

5. To allow for meaningful professor-student interaction on each student's writing, the class is restricted to 20 students.

NOTE

1. The majors we specified (e.g., art, business, engineering, history, premed, psychology, speech-communication) attracted the largest numbers of students on campus. We hoped that this specification would increase the likelihood that we would have more than one person per major as informants, because we needed a sample of more than one if we were to do any cross-checking of student perceptions within a given major.

REFERENCES

Ackerman, J. M. (1993). The promise of writing to learn. *Written Communication, 10,* 334–370.
Anson, C., & Forsberg, L. (1990). Moving beyond the academic community: Transitional stages in professional writing. *Written Communication, 7,* 200–231.
Bazerman, C. (1981). What written knowledge does: Three examples of academic prose. *Philosophy of the Social Sciences, 11,* 361–387.

Bazerman, C. (1992). From cultural criticism to disciplinary participation: Living with powerful words. In A. Herrington & C. Moran (Eds.), *Writing, teaching, and learning in the disciplines* (pp. 61–68). New York: Modern Language Association.

Berkenkotter, C., Huckin, T., & Ackerman, J. (1994). Context and socially constructed texts: The initiation of a graduate student in a writing research community. In C. Bazerman & D. Russell (Eds.), *Landmark essays on writing across the curriculum* (pp. 211–232). Davis, CA: Hermagoras Press.

Britton, J., Burgess, T., Martin, N., McLeod, A., & Rosen, H. (1975). *The development of writing abilities.* New York: Macmillan.

Covino, W. A. (1988). *The art of wondering: A revisionist return to the history of rhetoric.* Portsmouth, NH: Heinemann.

Detterman, D., & Sternberg, R. (Eds.). (1993). *Transfer on trial: Intelligence, cognition, and instruction.* Norwood, NJ: Ablex.

Elbow, P. (1981). *Writing with power: Techniques for mastering the writing process.* New York: Oxford University Press.

Emig, J. (1971). *The composing processes of twelfth graders.* Urbana, IL: National Council of Teachers of English.

Ernst, G. W., & Newell, A. (1969). *CPS: A case study in generality and problem solving.* San Diego, CA: Academic Press.

Fulwiler, T. (1981). Showing not telling in a writing across the curriculum workshop. *College English, 43,* 55–63.

Fulwiler, T. (1987). *Teaching with writing.* Portsmouth, NH: Boynton/Cook.

Gere, A. R. (1991). Practicing theory/theorizing practice. In V. A. Chappell, M. L. Buley-Meissner, & C. Anderson (Eds.), *Balancing acts: Essays on the teaching of writing in honor of William F. Irmscher* (pp. 111–121). Carbondale: Southern Illinois University Press.

Gotswami, D., & Odell, L. (Eds.). (1985). *Writing in non-academic settings.* New York: Guilford.

Haas, C. (1994). Learning to read biology: One student's rhetorical development in college. *Written Communication, 11,* 43–84.

Herrington, A. (1985). Writing in academic settings: A study of the contexts for writing in two college chemical engineering courses. *Research in the Teaching of English, 19,* 331–361.

Hilgers, T. L., Bayer, A. S., Stitt-Bergh, M., & Taniguchi, M. (1995). Doing more than thinning out the herd: How eighty-two college seniors perceived writing-intensive classes. *Research in the Teaching of English, 29,* 59–87.

Hilgers, T. L., & Marsella, J. (1992). *Making your writing program work: A guide to good practices.* Newbury Park, CA: Sage.

Hussey, E., Bayer, A., Hilgers, T., & Jones, K. (1995). *Writing in Hawai'i high school senior classes: A glimpse into a few windows* (Office of Faculty Development and Academic Support Report No. 2). Honolulu: University of Hawai'i at Manoa.

Kogen, M. (Ed.). (1989). *Writing in the business professions.* Urbana, IL: National Council of Teachers of English.

Lunsford, A. A., & Ede, L. S. (1984). Classical rhetoric, modern rhetoric, and contemporary discourse studies. *Written Communication, 1,* 78–80.

MacDonald, S. P. (1994). *Professional academic writing in the humanities and sciences.* Carbondale: Southern Illinois University Press.

Marsella, J., Hilgers, T. L., & McLaren, C. (1992). How students handle writing assignments: A study of eighteen responses in six disciplines. In A. Herrington & C. Moran (Eds.), *Writing, teaching and learning in the disciplines* (pp. 174–188). New York: Modern Language Association.

Matalene, C. (Ed.). (1989). *Worlds of writing: Teaching and learning in discourse communities of work.* New York: Random House.

McCarthy, L. P. (1987). A stranger in strange lands: A college student writing across the curriculum. *Research in the Teaching of English, 21,* 233–265.

Moffett, J. (1968). *Teaching the universe of discourse.* Boston: Houghton Mifflin.

Moffett, J. (1981). *Active voice: A writing program across the curriculum.* Portsmouth, NH: Boynton/Cook.

Myers, G. (1985). The social construction of two biologists' proposals. *Written Communication, 2,* 219–245.

Newell, A., & Simon, H. A. (1972). *Human problem solving.* Englewood Cliffs, NJ: Prentice Hall.

NUD*IST 3.0.4d [Computer software]. (1995). Melbourne, Australia: Qualitative Solutions & Research Pty Ltd.

Odell, L. (Ed.). (1993). *Theory and practice in the teaching of writing: Rethinking the discipline.* Carbondale: Southern Illinois University Press.

Perkins, D., & Salomon, G. (1989). Are cognitive skills context-bound? *Educational Researcher, 18*(1), 16–25.

Petraglia, J. (1995). Writing as an unnatural act. In J. Petraglia (Ed.), *Reconceiving writing, rethinking writing instruction* (pp. 79–100). Hillsdale, NJ: Lawrence Erlbaum.

Polya, G. (1957). *How to solve it: A new aspect of mathematical method* (2nd ed.). Garden City, NY: Doubleday.

Reynolds, J., Matalene, C., Magnotto, J., Samson, D., Jr., & Sadler, L. (Eds.). (1995). *Professional writing in context: Lessons from teaching and consulting in worlds of work.* Hillsdale, NJ: Lawrence Erlbaum.

Rorty, R. (1989). *Contingency, irony, solidarity.* Cambridge, UK: Cambridge University Press.

Russell, D. R. (1995). *Writing in the academic disciplines, 1870–1990: A curricular history.* Carbondale: Southern Illinois University Press.

Schon, D. (1987). *Educating the reflective practitioner: Toward a new design for teaching and learning in the professions.* San Francisco: Jossey-Bass.

Sorcinelli, M. D., & Elbow, P. (Eds.). (1997). *Writing to learn: Strategies for assigning and responding to writing across the disciplines.* San Francisco: Jossey-Bass.

Walvoord, B. E. (1986). *Helping students write well: Strategies for all disciplines* (2nd ed.). New York: Modern Language Association.

Walvoord, B. E. (1996). The future of writing across the curriculum. *College English, 58,* 58–79.

Walvoord, B. E., & McCarthy, L. P. (1990). *Thinking and writing in college: A naturalistic study of students in four disciplines.* Urbana, IL: National Council of Teachers of English.

18   *The Novice as Expert: Writing the Freshman Year*

NANCY SOMMERS AND LAURA SALTZ

There is a feeling of loss freshman year, the feeling of not being connected anywhere. For 18 years I lived at home. Now home is not really home anymore, and college isn't really home either.

– Deepak

Seeptember 7, 1997 — a balmy Sunday, the kind of afternoon that New Englanders welcome after late August's gelatinous heat. From an airplane, Harvard Yard appears peaceful, even pastoral. But to the 1,650 freshmen shifting in their folding chairs, the sense of doubt about starting college is palpable.[1] Speaking straight to their opening-day anxieties, Harvard President Neil Rudenstine tries to reassure: "Do not feel surprised if you think you are a displaced person, because that's what you are; and do not worry if all your classmates seem more at home than you, because they are not." As Rudenstine speaks, students look around, many wondering if they will be the admissions committee's *one* mistake.

Throughout the ceremony, dignitaries mount the podium to offer good wishes and advice — remember to create new friends, take intellectual risks, call home — and to remind students that they are becoming part of a great tradition, one that has been shaped by the words of its students. Even months before they arrived on campus, in a letter to the Class of 2001, President Rudenstine had asked the students to consider the role writing might play in their college educations, encouraging them "to write a great deal . . . and experiment with different kinds of writing — because experimentation forces one to develop new forms of perception and thought, a new and more complex sensibility."[2] But how to follow Rudenstine's advice, particularly at the threshold of college, when freshmen are no longer surrounded by the comfort zones of family and structured routines and are suddenly required to manage their time, deciding if they will spend all or none of it studying?

From *College Composition and Communication* 56.1 (2004): 124–49.

Thresholds, of course, are dangerous places. Students are asked as freshmen to leave something behind and to locate themselves in the realms of uncertainty and ambiguity. It doesn't take long for most first-year students to become aware of the different expectations between high school and college writing, that something more is being offered to them and, at the same time, asked of them. The defining academic moment of the first semester is often the recognition, as one freshman put it, that "what worked in high school isn't working anymore." The first year of college offers students the double perspective of the threshold, a liminal state from which they might leap forward — or linger at the door.

THE HARVARD STUDY OF UNDERGRADUATE WRITING

What happens to students as they make their way beyond this threshold? Do they graduate as stronger, more confident writers than they were four years earlier when, as freshmen, they entered college? Do they experience writing as a unique form of learning, as our profession claims, or do they see it as another school assignment, a form of evaluation equal to but more time-consuming than exams? For the 12.4 million college students in the United States, papers are assigned and written in good faith because faculty believe the commonplace that writing teaches students to think. Yet what is missing from so many discussions about college writing is the experience of students. Do students experience writing as learning and thinking and, if so, under what conditions? If we asked undergraduates to describe their experiences in courses *with* and *without* writing assignments, what would we, their teachers, learn? In short, what lessons do students offer us about why writing matters? To answer these questions — to get a glimpse beyond the classroom, behind the page, and between the drafts — the Harvard Study of Undergraduate Writing followed more than 400 students (25%) of the Harvard Class of 2001 through their college careers to see undergraduate writing through their eyes.[3]

Working within the tradition of longitudinal research, our study was designed to collect as many different primary sources of information about students' undergraduate writing experiences as possible, especially the artifacts of their college writing culture: assignments, feedback, papers. We wanted to capture changes and continuities in students' attitudes and writing abilities, information that could be measured through student surveys and gathered through interviews and analysis of student writing. We were particularly interested in the ways in which students talk about writing and how that language shifts over four years.

Three weeks into their first semester, the entire class of 2001 was invited to participate in the study. Participation was voluntary, consisting of five Web-based surveys, two in the freshman year and one in each subsequent year; for completing each survey, students received a coupon for a free pizza. Four hundred twenty-two students joined the study, and 94% of the original sample stayed with it until graduation. From our sample of 422 students, 65 were randomly selected to be part of a subsample, the group we studied in depth.

In addition to completing the surveys, these students were interviewed each semester, and they brought to their interviews each semester's writing, complete with instructor feedback and assignments.

For four years, the study followed a predictable rhythm, with interviews and surveys during the academic year and a hum of activity in the summer as our research team analyzed survey data from 400 students, read the stacks of papers written by the students in the subsample, and then wrote case studies of each student in the subsample to help us synthesize the range of materials assembled. By the end of four years, we had collected more than 600 pounds of student writing, 520 hours of transcribed interviews, and countless megabytes of survey data. Our challenge in following more than 400 students has been to learn as much as possible about individual students, while also keeping in mind the big picture of undergraduate writing with its spectrum of writing practices — to look for patterns across students' undergraduate writing experiences and to learn from each student what might be idiosyncratic and what might be generalizable.

To date, scholars in our field — Marilyn Sternglass, Anne Herrington, Marcia Curtis, and Lee Ann Carroll — have described, through their in-depth case studies, the slow, uneven nature of writing development and demonstrated the value of longitudinal studies to provide a wider perspective than research focused upon just one college course or one undergraduate year. By working with a larger sample and a different set of questions, we hope to extend the conclusions our colleagues have reached about writing development, while also showing the important role the freshman year plays in this development.[4] Whereas these studies have focused attention upon the freshman writing course, we have chosen to look elsewhere in the university, to examine the writing students produce first year in courses other than their required writing course.

The story we tell, then, is of freshman writing at one college, but it is also a larger story about the central role writing plays in helping students make the transition *to* college. We learn much from first-year students about their common struggles and abilities beyond our classrooms: that freshmen who see themselves as novices are most capable of learning new skills; and students who see writing as something more than an assignment, who write about something that matters to them, are best able to sustain an interest in academic writing throughout their undergraduate careers. Whether they enter college as strong or weak writers, freshmen voice the challenge of writing in an unfamiliar genre — the genre of academic writing — in similar ways. On the threshold of college, freshmen are invited into their education by writing.

THE ROLE OF WRITING FRESHMAN YEAR

You can say that you went to lecture or went to discussion section, but when you hold in your hand sixteen papers that you have written your freshman year, then you feel that you have accomplished something.

— JEANNA

> When you are not writing papers in a course, you take more of a tourist's view of
> a subject because you don't have to think in depth about any of the material.
>
> — LISA

In his letter to the Class of 2001, President Rudenstine encouraged students to use college as a time to "write a great deal . . . experiment with different kinds of writing." And Harvard freshmen, for the most part, have multiple opportunities in almost every course to write a great deal. Most find themselves writing anywhere between fourteen and twenty papers their freshman year, in addition to lab reports, response papers, and a range of writing produced outside of class for their extracurricular activities. Humanities and social science students write more than science students, but even science students, some of whom claim to choose their courses to avoid writing, find their freshman year to be writing intensive.

We wanted to understand the role writing plays in the lives of freshmen. Writing is, after all, hard work, especially when students are urged to "experiment": to question, evaluate, and interpret ideas they are trying to comprehend for the first time. The outcome is never certain, especially at the beginning of college, when students feel that their papers are a "shot in the dark," and when they receive feedback such as, "what you say, you say very nicely, but what exactly are you saying?"

At the end of freshman year, we put this question to students: "What would this year have been like if you had not written *any* papers?" "Well," many students responded, "I would have gotten a lot more sleep," or "I would have had a lot more time." But then, as if they couldn't imagine such an alternate universe — "college without papers?" — both strong and weak writers spoke vividly about the many different but complementary roles writing plays in their first year of college. Here is a sample of their responses:

> If I hadn't written, I would have felt as if I was just being fed a lot of information. My papers are my opportunity to think and say something for myself, a chance to disagree.

> Writing adds depth. If I hadn't written, some of the depth of this first year would have been missing. I showed myself to be a credible thinker.

> Once you write a paper, you begin to see so much more; and the more you see, the more interesting the course becomes.

One of the greatest surprises of this study (something for which we were completely unprepared) was the buoyancy of students after a year in which they are asked to refashion themselves as writers, a year in which as novices they need to figure out the expectations of college writing while producing paper after paper. We could imagine students saying that college writing is difficult, that it takes up more time than they ever expected, or that it deprives them of sleep. And we could imagine that students in small seminars, where writing plays a central part, might have been more enthusiastic about writing than students who write papers in large lecture courses. But we were genuinely surprised that students across disciplines and in varying course sizes use similar language when talking about the role of writing freshman year. And we were even more surprised that the comments of the weaker and stronger writers are indistinguishable, except that the weaker writers often speak with even greater passion about the role of writing in helping them make the transition to college, in giving them the confidence "to speak back to the world."

We were also unprepared for the pride of accomplishment that many freshmen experience, the joy of holding in their hands the physical representation of their thinking, the evidence that they have learned something in-depth. Unlike lectures or discussion sections, their papers are concrete, tangible. As one student put it, "I knew nothing about this subject at the beginning of the semester. Now I've written a twenty-five-page paper about it, and everything I have learned is here, stapled together forever." For freshmen, who change so rapidly, writing is a mirror that helps reflect who they are as students, allowing them to see themselves in their own words. One student echoes many when she describes the enormous pleasure of a completed paper:

> The hardest part of writing is when you get the assignment and you think to yourself, "oh, no, oh my goodness — there is no way I'll be able to write this paper." It seems so impossible. You clench your teeth, throw yourself into it, stay up late, and it is awful. Sometimes it is all you can think about. Then, all of a sudden, you have something in your hands. . . . You get this high, seeing that you have actually produced something, something that you actually care about and that you are excited about. You thought you couldn't do it, and you did. And you did it well. Your writing is improving, and your thinking is improving, and you can see it, and hold it in your hands.

The survey data was as consistent as students' interview responses. When we asked our 422 students at the end of their freshmen year, "How important are writing assignments?" they answered with the responses displayed in the following graph (Figure 18-1).

When students indicate that writing assignments are "important" or "very important" because they provide opportunities to become involved with a course (73%), understand and apply the ideas of the course (73%), bring their interests into a course (66%), explore and research new ideas (57%), or discover a new interest (54%), what exactly do we learn?[5] One way to answer this question is to listen to students describe courses where *no* writing is assigned. Courses without papers are most often described as "requirements gotten out of the way" or as encounters with "plops of information" that students are required to "regurgitate on exams" but never digest for themselves. Or as one student reported, "Without writing you don't really belong to a course and don't make it your own."

Probably the most striking metaphor for the experience of taking a class without writing comes from a student who describes a linguistics class in which she felt as if she had been an academic "tourist," never asked "to think

FIGURE 18-1   Freshman Year: How Important Were Writing Assignments in Helping You?

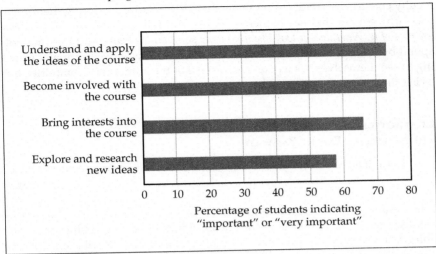

in-depth about any of the material." She went on to explain, "We had exams in the course, but when you have an exam you are answering somebody else's particular questions, not your own. You have to regurgitate the information the professor gives you in response to the question he creates." In imagining a freshman year without writing, students speak directly about the connection between writing and learning: "I did my best learning when writing papers; the ideas I have written about are the ideas I know best," one student comments. Another says, "Writing lets you think and shows you how you think about thinking." In so many of these responses, freshmen equate writing with "in-depth" learning and thinking or note the absence of depth, like our student, the academic tourist, when no writing is assigned. One freshman observes:

> The ideas that I remember, the ideas that I can really grasp, are the ones I have written about. No matter how many lecture notes I have taken, no matter how many lines I have highlighted in my textbooks, it is the texts I have responded to with my own words that I am most able to remember. The process of writing fixes a text in my mind and makes it more than a series of things I have read.

From both interview and survey responses, we learn that writing serves many functions freshman year, both academic and social, to engage students with their learning. These are indeed gratifying responses for faculty across the disciplines who assign writing and spend countless hours responding to the words of their students. More significant, though, is that so few freshmen talk about this kind of learning as an end in itself. The enthusiasm so many freshmen feel is less for writing *per se* than for the way it helps to locate them in the academic culture, giving them a sense of academic belonging. When faculty construct writing assignments that allow students to bring their interests into a course, they say to their students. *This is the disciplinary field, and you are part of it. What does it look like from your point on the map?* And freshmen respond by writing their way into a small corner of academia, gradually learning to see themselves not as the one mistake of the admissions committee but as legitimate members of a college community.

CHARACTERISTICS OF FRESHMAN WRITING: THE NOVICE-AS-EXPERT PARADOX

> I feel as if my ideas have to be so new and exciting — it's college after all.
>
> – EMILY

When one senior was asked to look back at her freshman writing, she commented that in her first year of college she felt as if she were being asked "to build a house without any tools," an apt metaphor to describe the writing experiences of freshmen who often continue to use the same writing hammer they used in high school, even as they realize its inadequacy. Freshmen are required to become master builders while they are still apprentices — to build as they become familiar with the materials and methods of construction. They are asked to develop expertise in new subjects and methodologies, while still learning how to handle the tools of these disciplines and decipher their user's manuals.

Consider the situation of Maura, a first-semester freshman, asked to write the following assignment in a course on comparative religious ethics:

> The final writing assignment should be a five-page paper using the resources of the four religious traditions we have discussed in class to address the puzzle about behavior identified and illustrated by Peter Unger in his book *Living High and Letting Die*. You should, of course, first give a brief account of the puzzle which Unger identifies. Then try to use the resources of Zen Buddhism, Roman Catholicism, Orthodox Judaism, and Early Confucianism to suggest ways of addressing the problems that result from the dispositions which Unger discusses. . . . Finally, ask what we should learn about the proper tasks of Comparative Religious Ethics from Unger.

This is Maura's fourth paper for her religion course and her tenth for the semester, one that requires more from her than all the others because it asks her to "synthesize the ideas and theories of the course and see the big picture." She is asked to perform many tasks at once: identify and explain the puzzle in Unger's argument, which has not been discussed in class; pull forth the underlying assumptions of four religious traditions, three of which she knew nothing about prior to the course; and apply these to Unger's argument — "a huge topic to address in five pages," as Maura notes. Even more difficult, she comments, is the challenge of "imagining how a Zen ethicist or the Pope would respond to Unger, when there are no references to the Pope or to Buddhism in Unger's book." For Maura, who describes herself as "deeply religious," the comparative methodology of the course adds an additional challenge, asking her to see beyond her own faith, to consider "religion as an academic field of study."

Maura's experience reveals much about the paradox of being a freshman writer, of writing simultaneously as a novice and an expert. In asking students to unravel puzzles and see the "big picture" for themselves, assignments such as Maura's ask freshmen to develop expertise in new subjects and methods while still apprentices. When students are new to a topic, they often don't know what information is important or how different pieces of information relate to each other. Everything is given equal weight. Without the benefit of experience, students overestimate or underestimate the importance of a single source and have difficulty synthesizing sources to see the "big picture." As one freshman taking her first medieval history course reports, "I have so much to read, so how do I have time to figure out what I think about any topic?" In the face of so much new information, her response is to write a fourteen-page paper with seventy-six footnotes, including a footnote to document the existence of the Middle Ages. About these footnotes, she comments: "I feel it is safer to use authorities who know what they are talking about."

Reading through 200 pounds of freshman writing, we became aware of the pull and push of forces that produced the words we analyzed. Students are pushed to practice the new conventions of college writing: to consider questions for which they don't have answers, or to write for readers who aren't already converted to their way of thinking, and to accept their own minds as capable of synthesizing and making judgments about dense ideas. And, at the same time, they are pulled by the familiarity of their high school model, their default mode, especially at 3:00 A.M., when the uncertainty of new material and methodologies looms large. Harvard freshmen are given a wide range of writing assignments (to synthesize an entire course in one paper, as Maura is asked to do, or even, as many courses encourage, to "come up with your own topic"), not elementary tasks for students who must construct themselves as authorities in fields about which they know very little. These assignments ask students to work with challenging sources, argue their own ideas, and integrate their arguments into a larger scholarly debate.

In fact, it might seem illogical or unfair to ask novices to perform the moves of experts. One could imagine another pedagogical approach that recognizes freshmen as beginners and asks them to write a series of exercises that are more technically suitable to their skills — to construct paragraphs or two-page reports, instead of being asked to write ten-page arguments, or even not to write at all. Sometimes freshmen themselves wonder about the usefulness of writing papers their first year. In our first survey we asked students, "Why do you think faculty assign writing?" One student responded, "I don't see the point of papers being assigned in college, at least in introductory-level courses . . . students in these courses are extremely unlikely to contribute much to the body of knowledge in a given field. We don't have the depth of knowledge to write about anything substantial."

How do first-year students fashion themselves into authorities when they feel as if they don't have the "depth of knowledge to write about anything substantial"? Our analysis suggests two answers: First, freshmen need to see themselves as novices in a world that demands "something more and deeper" from their writing than high school. Many students feel shaken by the idea of becoming a novice because it involves so much uncertainty, especially those who would prefer to wait to write until they can "contribute to the body of knowledge in a given field." Being a novice, though, doesn't mean waiting meekly for the future, nor does it mean breaking with the past. Rather, it involves adopting an open attitude to instruction and feedback, a willingness to experiment, whether in course selection or paper topics, and a faith that, with practice and guidance, the new expectations of college can be met. Being a novice allows students to be changed by what they learn, to have new ideas, and to understand that "what the teacher wants" is an essay that reflects these ideas.[6]

By contrast, those freshmen who cling to their old habits and formulas and who resent the uncertainty and humility of being a novice have a more difficult time adjusting to the demands of college writing. Even students who come to college as strong writers primed for success have difficulty when they refuse to be novices. These students often select courses to "get their requirements out of the way," blame their teachers for their low grades, and demonstrate an antagonistic attitude toward feedback. They feel as if there is a "secret code" to academic writing or that college itself is a kind of game whose rules — "what the teacher wants" — are kept secret to them, only glimpsed through the cryptic comments they receive on their papers.

Second, we also observed that freshmen build authority not by writing *from* a position of expertise but by writing *into* expertise. As apprentices, they learn to write by first repeating the ideas they encounter in the sources they read and the teachers they admire, using the materials and methods of a course or discipline in demonstrated ways before making them their own.[7] We found that even the strongest freshmen writers were not able to stand back and offer overarching claims or interpretations. The prevalence of the descriptive thesis in freshman writing — the thesis that names or reports on phenomena rather than articulating claims based on an analysis of the evidence — is symptomatic of the novice-as-expert paradox. The ubiquity of the descriptive thesis freshman year suggests that learning happens in stages; ideas need to be ingested before they can be questioned. Students need to immerse themselves in the material, get a sense of the parameters of their subjects, familiarize themselves with the kinds of questions asked of different sets of evidence, and have a stake in the answers before they can articulate analytical theses. All of this takes time, more time than any freshman can possibly devote to a subject. The descriptive thesis is not a flaw in freshman writing but a symptom of a novice working on an expert's assignment.

Similarly, as novices, most freshmen have neither the tools to pry open their sources nor the familiarity with them to ask "why" questions instead of "what" questions. They tend to describe and summarize their sources, letting the sources speak for themselves, wondering, "How do I say something different from what the source already said?" Yet even if freshmen cannot question a source, they find the act of rehearsing and repeating the ideas of a source to be new and validating. Freshmen might not be able to fashion their own tools or even know which tool to use under what condition, but they learn by holding the expert's tools in their hands, trying them out, imitating as they learn. They *may* need seventy-six footnotes to construct a fourteen-page paper the first time they write in a particular discipline. Yet these papers, even when they are derivative and less than ideally constructed, are, in the context of freshman year, highly ambitious and important for future writing development. They give freshmen their first feeling for real academic work. As more expert juniors and seniors, many students talk with equal pride about a different kind of ambition, the counter-intuitive discovery of working with something small, learning to probe deeper and wider, and ultimately saying more. It will be two years and dozens of papers before most students are able to embrace this kind of ambition by finding a genuine question in a source, a gap in the scholarship, the way experts do. Even if asking freshmen to do the work of experts invites imitative rather than independent behavior, it is the means, paradoxically, through which they learn to use writing tools of their own and grow passionate about their work.

CONFRONTING THE NOVICE-AS-EXPERT PARADOX: A COURSE IN MORAL REASONING

> We begin with a story: you are the driver of a trolley car, and you have to decide quickly whether to turn your car and kill one person crossing the tracks, or avoid turning your car and kill five workers. What is the moral principle you use to justify your action? Now imagine you are an observer watching the trolley car from a bridge. You could push a man over the bridge and sacrifice his life to save the five workers. Can you apply the same principle from the first case to the second? What is the moral difference between the two cases?

So begins Professor Michael Sandel on the first day of his moral reasoning course — Justice — introducing students to the methodology of the course, moving back and forth between concrete cases and abstract philosophical principles. Justice, taught each fall semester to 700 students (more than 10,000 since Sandel first taught the course in 1980) is particularly compelling to freshmen, who, at a moment of great transition in their lives, are fascinated by subjects that ask them to contemplate the limits and responsibilities of their new freedom. Moral reasoning gives students a new view of familiar subjects, inspiring freshmen to question their beliefs by steeping them in the historical and philosophical traditions in which these beliefs have been debated.

For a study of undergraduate writing, moral reasoning courses are fascinating. When freshmen identify their best writing experiences, in both our survey and interviews, they talk about these courses more than any others. Even our weakest writers speak passionately about the ways in which these courses changed their thinking, showing them how to "structure and defend" their ideas and giving them a "voice" and "confidence to speak back to the world." One representative student told us, "I feel passionate about the issues in Justice, but if I hadn't written the papers, I would have been shooting out opinions randomly." What is it about the course's methodology that teaches students to "structure and defend" their ideas in writing? How do the writing assignments move students from "shooting out opinions" to giving them the "confidence to speak back to the world?" How, in other words, does it make novices into experts?

Sandel makes clear that the course is not only about the moral reasoning of philosophers but also about the moral reflections of the students in the course. Beyond presenting students with classical and contemporary theories of justice in texts by Aristotle, Kant, Locke, Mill, Nozick, and Rawls and with the application of these theories in arguments about affirmative action, income distribution, and free speech, his lectures challenge students to consider questions such as these: If surrogate motherhood commodifies women's labor, does paid military service do something similar with soldier's bodies? He engages with students one-on-one in lecture, inviting them to provide the criteria to assess or defend their own positions. His goal, as he tells students, is to "awaken the restlessness of reason" by asking them to consider questions that are urgent because "we live some answer to these questions each day." He transforms Sanders Theater, a lecture hall with seating capacity for 1,166 students, into an intimate town meeting of passionate citizens engaged in applying philosophical arguments to real-life situations with real-life consequences.

Like the lectures, the two writing assignments in Justice give students practice in moral reasoning by asking them to enter an existing debate: Should there be a market in human organs? Is the use of race as a factor in identifying criminal suspects morally comparable to the use of race as a factor in college admissions? Students are instructed not to conduct research but to draw on their own critical reflections as informed by the theories presented in the course. In addition to the two seven-page papers, students write two response papers in which they explore the meaning and significance of one sentence or one passage of a philosopher's work by focusing on a specific textual problem or puzzle. All of these writing assignments emphasize an unresolved problem that students must weigh in on, a live debate about textual meaning or a course of action. How do we resolve the paradox in Aristotle's conception of the good life? How can we argue for the use of race in affirmative action but argue against it for racial profiling? In entering a live debate — a conversation in which more than one view is acceptable and for which there are no easy answers — freshmen see that something is at stake in their work, that their writing is not simply "academic."

For students accustomed to the five-paragraph model of writing, entering a debate or unraveling a puzzle represents an entirely new way of writing. To write about philosophy, to practice moral reasoning, is to write in an argumentative mode. Even the texts students analyze are structured as arguments. The assignments encourage students to begin within these arguments by summarizing and assessing them but to move beyond the familiar territory of summary and give "something more" — their own reasoning.

Justice capitalizes on students' paradoxical status as novices. New to philosophical writing, they are also experts who come to the course with their own moral reflections. Students are invited into the enterprise of moral reasoning as colleagues whose ideas and experiences are welcomed, but who need to assess and adjust their thinking as they engage with theorists who have also written about these questions. Students are granted a right to speak out of their expertise, but they are also given the responsibility of considering other interlocutors who "live some answer to these questions each day." Their sense that they are playing in the intellectual big leagues was wonderfully articulated by one student: "To think that I, a freshman, could be asked to find a flaw in Aristotle's reasoning, that it was just me and Aristotle on the page — what a sense of power."

Yet the course recognizes its responsibility to these students, novices who are new to writing philosophical arguments and to the challenging sources of the course. Through a four-page handout developed by Sandel and his teaching assistants, students are introduced to the basic tools for writing philosophical arguments: how to identify debates and disagreements among sources, question and evaluate sources, define key terms, engage counterarguments. They are also given a structure for writing philosophical arguments: begin with a thesis, outline a debate, synthesize competing positions, notice questions and implications which arise from this synthesis, explain how these questions might be answered, offer counterarguments, and propose solutions. In encouraging students to use this structure, which mirrors Sandel's method in his lectures, the course relieves students of the responsibility of inventing the field for themselves.

The Justice assignments are difficult for first-semester freshmen, and those who are most articulate about the challenges are weaker writers, for whom the methods are the newest. The requirement to think critically about a text they are reading for the first time, rather than simply summarize its views, is the most demanding aspect of the assignments. One freshman observed: "These assignments are an entirely new world. I need to argue a point of view, use evidence, and not accept things just because I have read them." Equally challenging, especially for students who come into the course with strong opinions, is to learn how to trust their opinions as a basis for formulating an idea, while at the same time learning the difference between an opinion and an idea.

If Justice is successful in moving students from "shooting out opinions" to "structuring and defending ideas," it is because the course self-consciously addresses the novice-as-expert paradox of freshmen writers. If students feel they have found their "voice" in writing for Justice, it is because the assignments cultivate that voice by insisting they take an active stance toward the texts and ideas they write about. Asking freshmen to enter a debate by identifying disagreements among sources, synthesizing competing positions, and posing counterarguments urges them to practice conceptual moves that push them beyond their high school models. Even if they gravitate toward sources that affirm their opinions or speak from the position of their sources, students gain important practice with the tools of academic argument. In a year of so much uncertainty, freshmen thrive in a course where they are urged to trust their own intuitions, writing their way *into* expertise about something that matters to them.[8]

WRITING THAT MATTERS: A PARADIGM SHIFT

When asked what advice she would give future freshmen, one student responds: "See that there is a greater purpose in writing than completing an assignment. Try to get something and give something when you write." This idea, that a student might "get something" other than a grade and that there might be a "greater purpose in writing than completing an assignment," represents the most significant paradigm shift of the freshman year. When, just three weeks into the freshman year, we asked students, "Why do you think faculty assign writing?" the most common responses focused upon evaluation — "so that professors can evaluate what we know" — and upon an abstract notion that "writing is an important skill in the real world." What is missing from these responses is any sense that students might "get something" other than a grade or career advancement, or that they might "give" something to their professors beyond a rehearsal of the course material. These early responses stand in stark contrast to those given at the end of the year, when so many students report that writing allows them not only to bring their interests into a course but also to discover new interests, to make writing a part of themselves. When students begin to see writing as a transaction, an exchange in which they can "get and give," they begin to see a larger purpose for their writing. They have their first glimmerings of audience; they begin to understand that they are writing for flesh-and-blood human beings, readers who want them to bring their interests into a course, not simply teachers who are poised with red pens, ready to evaluate what they don't know. One student describes her great surprise freshman year when she realizes, after receiving detailed feedback, "someone is actually reading my papers, someone who is trying to understand what I care about in a subject."

If there is one great dividing line in our study between categories of freshmen writers, the line falls between students who continue throughout the year not to see a "greater purpose in writing than completing an assignment" and freshmen who believe they can "get and give" when they write — between students who make the paradigm shift and those who don't. Students who continue to see writing as a matter of mechanics or as a series of isolated exercises tend never to see the ways writing can serve them as a medium in which to explore their own interests. They continue to rely on their high school idea that academic success is reflected in good grades. When one such student is asked about his best writing experience freshman year, he responds, "Do you want me to tell you about the paper I got the best grade on?" If freshmen focus on college writing as a game, where someone else makes up the rules and doles out the grades, it doesn't matter if they write twenty papers or ten. Practice and instruction are, of course, important during freshman year; the more a student writes, the more opportunities she has to become familiar with the new expectations of academic writing and to use writing to discover what is important to her. But it is not practice *per se* that teaches reciprocity. Students who refuse to be novices, who continue to rely on their high school methods and see writing as a mere assignment, often end up writing versions of the same paper again and again, no matter how different their assignments.

What characterizes the experience of freshmen who discover they can "get and give" something in their writing? Looking closely at the ways in which freshmen describe their best writing experiences, we see the crucial role faculty play in designing and orchestrating these experiences, whether by creating interesting assignments, mentoring through feedback, or simply moving aside and giving students freedom to discover what matters to them. The paradigm shift is more likely to occur when faculty treat freshmen as apprentice scholars, giving them real intellectual tasks that allow students to bring their interests into a course.

Yet for freshmen, another force is at work, one that shapes their course selection, engagement with faculty, or choice of writing assignments. In the transitional first year, students often discover themselves as subjects of inquiry when they think about their ethnic, racial, religious, or sexual identities for the first time. One student from New Mexico, for instance, speaks of having "culture shock," the sudden awareness of her culture that comes from leaving it. She describes her first-semester course in Chicano Literature:

> Chicano culture was just something I figured was a part of me, but now I'm really examining it, and trying to form my own identity. I like being in a class where I hear other people's points of view rather than being surrounded by the culture and the stereotypes that I've grown up with. I'm trying to decide for myself what I agree with and what I don't.

Another student speaks of her decision freshman year to learn more about her mother's Italian heritage:

> When I arrived at college, I realized that there is no social group called "Children of Fifth-Generation British Americans," which is what I am on my father's side, but there is an Italian Cultural Club, so I joined the club and got involved. I also started taking Italian and an art history course on Michelangelo, and even wrote about Italian cooking practices in an anthropology paper.

Free to set their own intellectual agendas, many freshmen, particularly those who grew up in relatively homogeneous communities, set off to explore their identities by selecting courses that enable them, however covertly, to study themselves. It is most frequently in these courses that novices discover they can "give and get" something through writing.

When we asked students about their best freshmen writing experience, they described opportunities to write about something that matters to them, whether in Chicano literature or Italian, political science or computer science. Maura, for instance, used many of her freshman papers to think through her doubts about religion and her own social conscience. Since she does not refer to herself in her papers, her professors might not notice the connection between her writing and her religious identity, but she returns in course after course to themes of individuality, responsibility, and culpability. As a senior looking back on her freshman papers, she comments, "I spent much of my freshman year trying to figure out what I am contributing to the world through the study of religion. I was disenchanted by academia and struggled to understand what a life of action versus a life of contemplation would look like. My papers helped me think through some of these issues."

To understand the importance of the paradigm shift freshman year, let's look at the story of one freshman, Jeremy, a deeply religious student for whom academic writing is a medium in which to voice his innermost spiritual doubts.

THE PARADIGM SHIFT: JEREMY

Jeremy grew up on an apple farm in rural Michigan and identifies himself as the first student in thirty-one years to attend Harvard from his high school. He is proud of his status, while at the same time overwhelmed by the range of diverse opinions and beliefs he encounters when he arrives on campus. Dormitory life provides him with his first culture shock: "I arrived in Wigglesworth Hall and met my roommates: an atheist, a Mormon, a Jew, and a Native American. All of them had very different backgrounds and different spiritual beliefs. I grew up as a Mennonite and was taught to see the spiritual world as black and white: either one was a Christian, and on the road to heaven, or one was not, and on the road to hell." This confrontation with diversity and the challenge it poses to his faith spills out of Jeremy's dorm into his course selection and finds its way into almost every paper he writes.

As a high school student, Jeremy thought of writing largely in terms of mechanics (spelling and grammar) and the ability to present facts succinctly. By the end of his first semester at college, however, he believes that writing, like his education generally, should help a student "dig into yourself, dig into your past." He is drawn to courses in comparative religion; the writing assignments are difficult, but they give him many opportunities to "dig," to rethink his most deeply held religious convictions. He describes his best freshman writing experience in one such course, Hindu Myth, Image, and Pilgrimage, where, as he describes it, "we had discussions about *dharma* —

doing what is right — that would spill out of the classroom, into the hallways, continue in the dining hall, and find their way into my papers. I loved writing about something I care about and seeing myself and my voice in my papers." In Jeremy's favorite writing assignment from that class, he is asked to analyze a Hindu image. The following is an excerpt from his paper, entitled "Real Love in the Heart":

> This image is of Hanuman, a devotee of Rama. It is a wall painting in Banaras painted by local artists. In the image Hanuman is opening his heart with his hands. Inside his heart we see Rama and Sita, Hanuman's lord and his wife. . . . This image has stuck in my mind since I first saw it. I have seen many slides, pictures, paintings, and images of Hinduism, but nothing compares to this one for me. I can try to explain many parts of the image and different things I see in it, but nothing can compare to the intangible — the way I feel. I am devoted to Christ and I think that if one were to look into my heart, they could see Christ just as by looking at Hanuman's heart one can see Rama and Sita. This image helped me see the similarities in both my religion and the Hindu religion.

This passage, so clearly written by a novice, reveals the essence of Jeremy's freshman-year questions: How can I express my own beliefs while writing about other religions? And is the spiritual world as black and white as I was brought up to believe? While Jeremy's assignment asks him to analyze an image, he instead outlines *his* process of understanding the image — that he comes to understand and appreciate the image only when he sees how it relates to his religion. He locates the ultimate significance of the image in the way it makes him feel, as if the purpose of the assignment is to explain why he was drawn to the image, preempting any need for analysis. The paper provides a platform on which he can affirm his Christian faith, a way for him to assure himself freshman year that if his family and congregation back home peek into his heart, despite his encounters with diversity and his shaken faith, they will still see his love for Christ.

Jeremy spends his entire freshman year questioning his religious identity, wondering what truths he can hold on to, while discovering writing as a medium through which he can explore his questioning. Trying to figure out who he is and what he believes, he finds every possible chance to insert his personal experience into his work. In an essay about George Orwell for his Expository Writing course, he writes about the ways in which Orwell's questions have influenced him: "Everyone questions everything at college. Each day another thing I used to see as an immovable truth in my life is severely shaken. I often wonder what will last — is there anything absolute that I can hold on to?" During his freshman year, Jeremy's twenty-one papers give him repeated opportunities to practice the "questioning mind-set" that he describes as the key difference between high school and college writing. At the end of the year, he muses, "When you write you can really embrace different ideas and be more open-minded. If you only have true/false or multiple choice exams then everything is black and white. Writing papers lets you think and shows you how you are thinking."

Jeremy's freshman experiences offer us two important lessons. First, though the paradigm shift freshman year is vital for writing development, being passionate about material isn't enough to produce good writing. Personal connection is an important place to start, especially freshman year, for it motivates students and keeps them interested in writing. But the claim that students need to care deeply about a subject to write well simplifies a complex issue. Jeremy's personal investment in his sources propels his writing but prevents him from developing the critical distance he needs to analyze and evaluate them on their own terms or to offer an argument of interest to others, rather than an expression of his personal opinions. We see from his experience that some kinds of distance can be productive for students, especially when they write about strongly held beliefs. Distance helps students see that religious or political positions are debatable and can be argued in an academic context, rather than simply asserted as true.[9]

Second, Jeremy's experiences show us that significant changes in students' attitudes toward writing do not necessarily correspond to changes in the writing itself. The story of the freshman year is not one of dramatic changes on paper; it is the story of changes within the writers themselves. When Jeremy tells us, "writing papers lets you think and shows you how you are thinking," we are surprised when as readers we don't always see his thinking on the page. But writing development isn't always happening on the page during freshman year, an important fact to consider for those who require concrete evidence — a one-time measure at the end of a first-year writing course — as a way to assess student learning. In fact, such gaps between what a student knows about writing and what the student can actually do can be observed throughout all four years, when students are introduced to new disciplinary methods, or when they attempt their first research projects, making it difficult to measure writing development at any *one* point in a student's college career. Nevertheless, changes in attitude and practice freshman year are essential to progress. Only those students who see a greater purpose in their writing are able to sustain an interest in academic writing over their four years of college. And only through a sustained interest can students develop a "questioning mind-set" or acquire the breadth of knowledge necessary to learn the disciplinary approaches that enable them to move from being novices to being experts. Despite the fact that students' passion can prevent them from achieving critical distance, without passion students are unable to make any but small gains in their writing, and they write essays their senior year that are not appreciably different from those they wrote as freshmen.

SUSTAINING INTEREST IN ACADEMIC WRITING

No story about college writing is complete without acknowledging that even with the best pedagogy, some students make very few gains in their writing. For all the students in our study, learning to write has been a slow process, infinitely varied, with movements backward and forward, starts and stops, with losses each time a new method or discipline is attempted. Writing development is painstakingly slow because academic writing is never a student's mother tongue; its conventions require instruction and practice, lots of imitation and experimentation in rehearsing other people's arguments before being able to articulate one's own. The surprise of the study is not that students learn the conventions of academic writing. The surprise is that some students are able to sustain an interest in academic writing throughout college, while others lose interest, despite the quality of their instruction and opportunities to prosper. From a longitudinal perspective what matters is not who is ahead at the end of freshman year (Jeremy clearly was not) but who sustains an interest in academic writing throughout college, moving forward, despite the setbacks. In the big picture of writing development, the story closely resembles Aesop's fable of the tortoise and the hare: those who end the strongest are often the slowest and most encumbered at the start. The longitudinal perspective gives us enough time to ponder why students such as Jeremy, a tortoise, moved forward with his writing, while other students who began college as much stronger writers stalled in their development, content to rely on methods that work reasonably well, replacing old formulas with new ones.

A major conclusion of our study is that students who initially accept their status as novices and allow their passions to guide them make the greatest gains in writing development. As novices who care deeply about their subjects, these students have a reason to learn the methodologies of their chosen disciplines, encouraged to believe that following their own interests is important to their success as students. And as they become more comfortable with these methodologies, they begin to see how disciplinary inquiry can help them build their own fields of expertise. Jeremy, for instance, learns to locate his questions within a wider circle of readers, seeing himself as part of an ongoing critical discussion about what compels people to accept or reject their faiths, a discussion that is legitimate in itself, not just a topic that tells him more about himself. His personal involvement gets redefined as an investment in the academic enterprise of writing prose that is public and shared rather than private and idiosyncratic. The road from personal writing to argument is not easy or quick for Jeremy, or for any of the students in our study, but the accumulation of experience and expertise translates into an academic focus that gives students ownership over their college educations.

The longitudinal perspective offers up another paradox of writing development: what fuels development freshman year is not always enough to sustain it throughout college. While being a novice first year is vital for writing development, being a perpetual novice throughout four years is detrimental. To move forward with their writing, students need to shed the role of novice that was at one time the key to their success. Many of the students who stalled as writers were what we call globetrotters, moving from course to course, constantly breaking new ground in new subjects every time they write, never cultivating the disciplinary expertise in content and method that is necessary to question sources, develop ideas, and comfortably offer interpretations. And while passion is important to fuel writing development, it is not enough to sustain it. If students are only writing to understand their personal experiences, if their expertise comes only from their personal connection with the material, or if they see the personal and academic as opposites, their writing remains a form of self-expression, and they generally lose interest in academic writing by junior year. For Jeremy, who wanted to know what sustains belief after religion, the chance to write about these questions repeatedly in a cluster of courses and through a range of disciplines offered him the opportunity to gain great purchase with his material, while discovering other thinkers interested in similar questions. He was able to move forward with his writing because he learned to ask questions that mattered to him and to others — to have *both* a personal and intellectual stake in these questions.

Studying undergraduate writing lets us inside students' learning, shows us the complexity of a set of experiences called "college writing," and complicates our understanding of the relationship between writing and learning. According to students' own reports, when they do not see a larger purpose for writing other than completing an assignment, when they become complacent, or when they remain perpetual novices throughout college, the conditions for learning or thinking do not always exist. But when students are able to see what they can "get" and "give" through writing, they speak passionately about writing as the heart of what they know and how they learn; writing is not an end in itself but is a means for discovering what matters.

A liberal arts education envisions college as a time for students to learn how to think broadly and deeply, to ask questions and be questioned. To be asked to write in college is to be asked to see farther, wider, and deeper, and ultimately to develop one's own lenses through which to see the world. Writing does not shape a student's education in one course or one year. It is the cumulative practice and sustained instruction — the gaining of expertise — that gives students opportunities to participate in the world of ideas, first as novices and later as experts. The story of the freshman year, then, is the story of students' first steps toward discovering that academic writing can be a generous and democratic exchange. It is the story of the role that writing plays in welcoming students into the academy, showing them they have much to give and much to gain.

Acknowledgments: We would like to thank the Andrew W. Mellon Foundation and Harvard University for funding the Harvard Study of Undergraduate Writing. And we are grateful to many colleagues who read our manuscript and offered us their wise advice: David Bartholomae, Kim Cooper, Marilyn Cooper, Faye Halpern, Cristin Hodgens, Soo La Kim, Emily O'Brien, Maxine Rodburg, Jane Rosensweig, Mimi Schwartz, Suzanne Young, Kathleen Blake Yancey.

NOTES

   1. A note about terminology: though at most colleges the convention is to use the gender-neutral phrase "first-year students," Harvard College retains the term "freshmen."
   2. Rudenstine went on to say in his letter to the Class of 2001: "Whatever your chosen field of study, you will not be able to proceed very far unless you constantly master new vocabularies, experiment with new forms of syntax, and try to see how precisely and sensitively your use of

words can begin to reflect the very best movements of your own mind and imagination operating at their peak."

3. To learn more about the Harvard Study of Undergraduate Writing, please see <http://www.fas.harvard.edu/~expos>.

4. Marilyn Sternglass followed nine students through City College in New York City; Anne Herrington and Marcia Curtis followed four students through University of Massachusetts/Amherst; and Lee Ann Carroll followed twenty students through Pepperdine University in Malibu, California.

5. These numbers are consistent with the findings of Richard Light and his assessment projects at Harvard. In his research, Light looked at writing as one aspect of the entire undergraduate experience. We don't know from Light's research, though, if freshmen were more or less likely than seniors to report levels of engagement with courses that assigned writing.

6. In Lee Ann Carroll's longitudinal study, she describes students as novices but does not argue, as we are here, that for freshmen to move forward with their writing they need to *see* themselves as novices.

7. David Bartholomae has written persuasively about the codes of academic writing and the ways in which students have to "assume privilege without having any" if they are to succeed as academic writers. Our aim here is to show how "assuming privilege" means, often, admitting what you do not know, rather than pretending to possess expertise.

8. Lee Ann Carroll suggests in her study that students prosper when faculty provide "scaffolding" to help them learn the expectations of new disciplines. Sandel's course is an example of *how* scaffolding provides the necessary support for novice writers. Sandel's course is also an example of the kind of "challenging academic setting" that Sternglass suggests students need in order to develop "a greater ability to handle more complex reasoning tasks."

9. Anne Herrington and Marcia Curtis argue for the important role writing plays in helping students locate their spiritual, sexual, and academic identities, demonstrating how the four students in their study were more engaged with their writing when they used their assignments to study themselves. In our study, we also found that students were more engaged with their writing when they used their assignments to figure out what mattered to them personally and intellectually. But we also observed that when students only use writing to study themselves, they become stuck as writers, unable to move forward. Only those students who were able to find a way to connect their interests with those of a discipline, to look beyond the personal to the public, were able to move from being a novice to an expert.

WORKS CITED

Bartholomae, David. "Inventing the University." *When a Writer Can't Write: Studies in Writer's Block and Other Composing Problems.* Ed. Mike Rose. New York: Guilford, 1985.

Carroll, Lee Ann. *Rehearsing New Roles: How College Students Develop as Writers.* Carbondale: SIUP, 2002.

Herrington, Anne J., and Marcia Curtis. *Persons in Process: Four Stories of Writing and Personal Development in College.* Urbana: NCTE, 2000.

Light, Richard J. *Making the Most of College: Students Speak Their Minds.* Cambridge: Harvard UP, 2001.

Sternglass, Marilyn S. *Time to Know Them: A Longitudinal Study of Writing and Learning at the College Level.* Mahwah, NJ: Erlbaum, 1997.

19 Innovation Across the Curriculum: Three Case Studies in Teaching Science and Engineering Communication

JENNIFER L. CRAIG, NEAL LERNER, AND MYA POE

The profession of engineering in the twenty-first century is undergoing numerous changes, notably in the kinds of problems that engineers solve and the associated skill sets that engineers must now have in communication and teamwork [1], [2]. Current educational initiatives such as communication-across-the-curriculum programs attempt to address these changes by integrating communication instruction in engineering courses rather than teaching writing and speaking in "stand alone" technical writing courses [3]–[6]. Many such communication-intensive (CI) curricular changes throughout American universities have been driven by Accreditation Board for Engineering and Technology (ABET) accreditation and by calls for change by the National Academy of Engineering [7]; however, MIT's new communications curriculum was driven almost entirely by alumni feedback. A 1997 survey revealed that while MIT alumni felt that they had received top-notch technical educations, they believed that their lack of training in writing and speaking was a significant hurdle to their professional success [8].

Given this feedback, MIT faculty passed the Communication Requirement, an institute-wide faculty initiative with the intention to integrate "substantial instruction and practice in writing and speaking into all four years and across all parts of MIT's undergraduate program" [8]. Under the Communication Requirement, students are now required to take four CI classes during their undergraduate years, including two CI classes in their majors. CI classes in the majors emphasize communication in the learning of disciplinary content and are taught collaboratively by technical and writing faculty.

Our initial goal at MIT in designing CI instruction was to work with engineering and science faculty to design meaningful, well-defined assignments, use revision and peer review to improve student writing, develop learning goals, and effectively assess student writing. What has also emerged, however, is a move beyond these initial steps to writing and speaking activities that resemble the more advanced challenges of engineering communication that occur in the practice of *doing* engineering [9]. In this way, we have been

From *IEEE Transactions on Professional Communication* 51.3 (2008): 280–301.

able not only to ask "What forms of writing should students be doing?" but also to inquire "What activities encourage students to work and think like professional engineers?" Our particular interest is helping students move from general academic writing or novice approximations of disciplinary writing to internalizing the communication-thinking practices of professional engineers [10]. Thus, our CI classes are not "one size fits all," but rather they are tailored to fit the communication practices of the young professionals in the particular discipline in which we are working. Our collaborative work with engineering and science faculty blends our understanding of writing pedagogy with the expectations of the specific discipline. Currently, every department at MIT offers CI classes in the major, and more than 25 full-time writing instructors work with faculty to help implement writing and speaking instruction in those classes.

One might argue that this considerable commitment of resources makes MIT unique in its approach to integrating communication instruction in engineering classes. However, institutions ranging from large state universities such as North Carolina State University to smaller institutions such as Presbyterian College have active "communication-intensive" programs, albeit using quite different approaches. At some institutions, interested faculty are offered workshops in how to create communication- and writing-intensive instruction. At other institutions, communication-intensive instruction has been added to general education requirements and is supported through writing fellows or writing center tutors. The integrated model we use at MIT is also used effectively at other institutions, although on a smaller scale. As we describe in the MIT case studies that follow, the on-the-ground realities of working with faculty, staff, and students to help them achieve communication and course goals can be easily applied to a wide variety of settings. The importance of helping students meet the target competencies of professional practice, of teaching effective teamwork and collaboration, and of teaching students to understand and argue with visual data are recognized as widespread needs, particularly in the framework of ABET's "engineering criteria" [11]. We believe that our examples attest to the possibilities and challenges in meeting those needs both inside and outside of MIT.

The case studies that we next present describe several key issues that partner with communication tasks. The first case, Learning to Write as a Biological Engineer, examines the ways in which undergraduates in biological engineering may be introduced to the professional writing practices of their emerging discipline. Addressing Teamwork Challenges in Collaborative Communication, the second case, studies the challenges of collaborative communication in aeronautical/astronautical engineering and the ways in which students learn the team skills so central to collaboration. And, finally, Data-Driven Arguments in Biomedical Engineering examines the ways in which biomedical engineers use data and ways to teach students to select data as evidence in visual arguments. In each case, we explain how we rationalize the communication focus for each class, how we implement instruction in each class, and how we assess its effectiveness.

CASE STUDY 1: LEARNING TO WRITE AS A BIOLOGICAL ENGINEER

Rationale for Professional Competencies as Goals

The instructional goal of teaching students to learn to write and speak as engineers implies several things: a certain amount of imprecision as students strive to take on the identities of professionals (and a reminder that they have not yet done so); the acceptance of professional competence as an ultimate goal; the role of a professional mentor to model and teach professional competencies; and a set of fairly defined, "real-world" tasks based on the work that professionals are already doing. In the case study that follows, each of these factors potentially affects the learning that a student might achieve.

Many of the current classes designated as CI at MIT have been mapped on to pre-existing laboratory classes. On one level, this decision makes logistical sense as students have long presented their laboratory work in written or oral forms; the CI requirement offers a structure and instructional support for these established practices. On another level, the tying of communication activities to students' laboratory work represents the ways in which professional practices are a driving force in curriculum and teaching. In other words, the ideals of research and the ways to inculcate students into those ideals have long shaped the undergraduate curriculum at MIT. And these competencies — the ability to undertake independent research or solve problems through sustained inquiry and the ability to communicate the results of those endeavors — are essential to the success of a professional in any science or engineering discipline.

A key component of professionalism as a driving force is the notion of students developing identities as scientists or engineers. The close relationship between identity and learning is theorized under several names, whether called "situated cognition" [12], "cognitive apprenticeship" [13], or "situated learning" [12], and these theories help explain why professionalism can be a powerful curricular and instruction goal as well as a complication for student learning. For instance, Gee sees learning as always rooted in particular sites of practice and says, "Knowing is a matter of being able to participate centrally in practice, and learning is a matter of changing patterns of participation (with concomitant changes in identity)" [12, p. 181]. What this means for students who are learning in laboratory or other professional settings is that tasks need to be as close as possible to those attempted by professionals and that instruction needs to take into account the "communities of practice" that define individual disciplines [14]. This conception of learning leads to a far more dynamic environment than a traditional transformation-of-information model from "knowing" professor to initiate student. Instead, according to Lave, " 'Knowing' is a relation among communities of practice, participation in practice, and the generation of identities as part of becoming part of ongoing practice" [14, p. 157]. Essential to this process is the presence of a mentor to guide student practice toward professional norms. In short, classrooms and laboratories are examples of environments where true professional practice can be found and offer much promise as models for enacting these theories of learning.

When students are writing in these laboratory and classroom contexts, by no means is the trajectory from novice to professional a smooth one. In her study of mechanical engineering students working in groups toward tasks typical of professionals in their field, Dannels found that "students ultimately acted in ways that suggest the prevalence of the academic context" [15, p. 25]. In other words, the group members' identities (and the need to fulfill an assignment in an academic context) strongly determined outcomes. As Dannels notes, "students may have learned how to be professionals in theory, but they did not translate that theory to actual design practices in the classroom" [15, p. 25].

Social theories of learning help explain some of the complications for developing professional identity in engineering education [16]–[18]. The term "discursive identity" [19] can be used to explore "the relationship between language, identity, and classroom learning" in science classrooms. According to Brown, Reveles, and Kelly:

> science learning involves learning to construct one's discursive identity in order to participate in science and its associated discourse. The appropriation of a scientific identity is demonstrated through students' engagement in the classroom conversations, as well as the broader discursive practices that lead to the development of new conceptual knowledge. [19, p. 790]

For undergraduates in a biological engineering class at MIT, these discursive practices include the writing that they are assigned based on the laboratory work they are performing, a context we describe next.

Context for Studying Students' Development of Professional Competencies

Biological Engineering is the newest major course of study at MIT, welcoming its inaugural class in the fall of 2005, and it has proved to be a popular option, with the number of applicants in 2005 exceeding the number of available slots by 50 percent [20]. Laboratory Fundamentals of Biological Engineering (or 20.109 in MIT's numeric language) is the first of two required laboratory classes for students in the major, and as such, offers as an explicit goal that it will help prepare students for subsequent laboratory work, whether in classes or in research labs. Also explicit is the goal of preparing students to be professional biological engineers. For example, the first of four content modules conveys the following to students:

> One major goal we have for this module is to establish good habits for documentation of your work, in your lab notebook and on the [class] wiki. By documenting your work according to the exercises today, you will
>
> • be better research students (in 20.109 and in any research lab you may join)

- be better writers since a clear record of what you've done will improve your data analysis
- be better scientists, since you'll eventually train others to document things this way, too. [21]

This act of consistently placing the work done in this class in terms of larger professional preparation makes the activities key to students' development of professional identities. In a sense, the class is structured so that students will have some exposure to the "hot" areas of research in biological engineering. The four content modules for the spring 2007 semester were genome engineering, biophysical signal measurement, expression engineering, and biomaterial engineering. Each module was led by a faculty member or department researcher, and the lab activities were essentially an opportunity for students to see what it was like to work in that particular lab on that particular topic, albeit under more controlled conditions than independent researchers would find.

Another key aspect of the context for this class and for its assignments is the emerging disciplinary identity of biological engineering itself. The particular focus for much of the student research is in the field known as "synthetic" biology, a line of research that the *New York Times* characterized recently as "an effort by engineers to rewire the genetic circuitry of living organisms" [22]. In more fundamental terms, the approach in synthetic biology is based on using what is known about the genome or genetic code of particular organisms — how particular elements of that code function, what happens if a sequence is missing or is altered — and using what is known to build organisms from the ground up or from the nucleotides that make up DNA.

These tools of synthetic biology provide a key context for the writing students are doing. The first writing assignment (Appendix A) asks students "to write a thoughtful, researched essay exploring how a foundational engineering concept . . . can be applied as a design tool for biological engineering." The research for this essay comes from students' lab work in which they are applying these "foundational" concepts to a virus in an attempt to modify it as it currently exists and build a synthetic version [23]. Thus, the laboratory work acts to generate evidence to support the argument that synthetic biology is a line of research worth pursuing — an argument that was essentially given to the students as they worked from a prewritten abstract.

The second writing assignment in 20.109 (Appendix B) during the spring 2007 semester was a much more conventional write-up of students' laboratory work on the manipulation of a protein complex in yeast. This writing task followed the IMRD pattern (introduction, methods, results, discussion), and for many students its familiarity provided a welcome counterpoint to the first writing assignment. Nevertheless, the perceived familiarity of the genre was not necessarily an ally, as the template form of the laboratory report that students have largely followed in high school laboratory experiences is not the expectation in 20.109. Instead, students are asked to write about their research as scientists would do as they prepare a manuscript for publication. The rhetorical act is thus far more sophisticated than the high school lab template, and students' technical and rhetorical expertise is certainly challenged as they strive to write as biological engineers.

The following student's case study comes from a semester-long research project that examined students' experiences with learning to write in 20.109. Based on an initial survey (Appendix C), one-to-one interviews, observations of class and lab interaction, and examination of written materials, the study looks in particular at students' development of professional identity in a class-room/laboratory context. While the larger study examined four students' experiences in Laboratory Fundamentals of Biological Engineering, what follows focuses on one particular student. In this case, Maxine (not her actual name) represents an engineering student who initially projected a career for herself in the business world rather than in science or engineering. Thus, the professional competencies for writing and speaking have a certain amount of abstraction as mapped onto Maxine's career goals. This lack of direct connection is perhaps more the norm for undergraduates, particularly as career goals shift over time and as class communication assignments can only roughly predict the actual tasks that students will encounter in their futures. Thus, for Maxine the challenges of learning to write like a biological engineer are perhaps emblematic of many engineering students' paths toward professional competencies.

Case Study: Maxine's Struggle to Write Like a Biological Engineer

At the time of this study (spring 2007 semester), Maxine was a sophomore at MIT, part of the second cohort of students to be biological engineering majors. She chose to pursue biological science while in high school after rejecting physics and computer science as possibilities and after reading a great deal on the research in bioinformatics that was being done at MIT. However, both at the start and at the end of the semester, Maxine stated that her future goal was not necessarily to be a research scientist, but instead to work in finance or with a venture capital firm that funds biomedical research. She felt that this type of work would fit well with her self-described attributes: "I really like giving presentations; I love talking. . . . I'm more of a thinker than a hands-on experience [type]. . . . [Laboratory work] is interesting, it's fascinating, but I couldn't do it for a living." This class was also Maxine's first real scientific laboratory experience.

In her answers to a start-of-semester survey on writing experiences and expectations and in her first interview, several responses indicated that Maxine had a fairly sophisticated understanding of what scientific writing might entail and ample experience as a scientific writer. For example, she describes her experiences with writing up scientific content in high school:

> As part of my high school International Baccalaureate program, I was required to write a 22-page mathematics paper. I have also written numerous physics lab write-ups for this same program.

When she gave more specifics on a paper that she identified as a "significant" writing experience, she easily offered technical language:

> I wrote a paper about the kalting problem of Turing's thesis. I took a very mathematical approach to this problem and solved it using Gödel's proof by falsification theorem.

Maxine's sophistication also shows in her response to why she believed 20.109 had been designated as a CI class:

> Biology has a lot of "holes" in it and thus requires the students to constantly question the validity of their research. I think this class has been made a CI to teach students how to properly do that.

In terms of writing goals for the class, Maxine offered the following:

> I hope to analyze large amounts of data and draw logical conclusions, which I can then concisely put down on paper. I hope also to learn to think more creatively, especially in areas such as re-engineering viruses.

Maxine also described a fairly ordered approach as typical to her writing process, one that involved being a "logical writer" but that also met difficulty with getting started (as she searched for a logical framework) and a tendency to be brief or not descriptive enough. In Maxine's words, "I don't like writing a sentence and then describing it for three sentences. I'm not a fan of that."

When it came to the first essay on the genome engineering laboratory work, Maxine struggled to conform to the expectations of the assignment and the time allotted to complete it. As she described, "I was crunched for time and had to just turn something in and hope for the best." Students' first drafts were graded by the writing instructor assigned to the class (who responded in depth to all student writing produced), and Maxine's received a C–, the lowest grade of all students. In his comments to Maxine, the instructor noted that "in revision you need to work on the presentation and logical structuring of the material." In particular, her draft lacked a clear focus, and her examples to frame her argument seemed only loosely connected. In an interview after she had submitted the draft, Maxine described that she had shown the draft to her father, a mathematician, who

> couldn't get past the first page. When I was rereading it, I couldn't believe I wrote it. It had no argument to it. It just flowed here and there and wasn't a very focused argument.

Part of the issue for Maxine and for other students in the class was that the assignment itself, though highly structured, left little potential room for the students to formulate an argument that they were comfortable with and could build on. One of the two faculty instructors for this module noted that the assignment

> was too proscribed ahead of time; the coupling of that structure to the newness of the [lab work] led to essays and a writing experience that . . . I don't know how exciting it was; I know it wasn't that exciting for me [to read].

In a sense, then, the key professional move of culling an argument from the data itself was lost on Maxine. She did feel strongly about the point she wanted to make in this essay: that completely refactoring a genome was a better method for achieving the promise of synthetic biology than other ad hoc approaches to genetic manipulation. However, she admitted that the "problem with arguing for refactoring is that technology hasn't caught up to that yet; it is kind of primitive." This writing task presented several challenges then. First, it required her to argue for a relatively abstract concept based on laboratory work that was not going particularly well. Second, the final faculty reader and grader is a pioneer in this type of research, though the imagined reader was to be fairly broad. As Maxine described,

> Anyone with access to PubMed should be able to read it. There's a lot of scientific information in there that may not be clear to someone who's from a purely mathematical background, but they should still be able to follow through and logically understand what's going on.

The assignment was challenging in that it was very specific and detailed in terms of how to structure the essay and what to include. That detailed structure did not necessarily work well for a writer like Maxine, who needed to figure out a particular focus before she could proceed in a "logical" manner. With the logic of organization already given and the material itself relatively abstract, creating a focused argument was difficult. The content-form relationship was predetermined in a way, unlike a professional scientific writing situation in which the two elements ideally work together. As described by the other instructor for this module,

> The nature of the assignment wasn't polished initially; it was just an awkward assignment where the voice wasn't really all that clear. They just weren't ready to say something.

In Maxine's words:

> I haven't written a paper like the first one before. It was very structured but at the same time it was kind of "Make up your own ideas" and "We want to know what you think." I've actually never had to write such an abstract paper. You don't have very much data backing your arguments in the first place, so your arguments have to be very concise, very precise.

Maxine did feel that her revision to this essay was a success. She noted that "Once my dad was able to follow the entire essay, it was okay." She received a final grade of B.

The second essay also presented challenges for Maxine. This task was to write up the research she had done investigating a protein complex in yeast. However, Maxine realized that this writing was not like the "technical lab reports" she had done in high school. Instead, this was writing a "journal article." As she noted in an interview, "I've never written a biology paper before, especially with the data analysis and writing about yeast and trying to figure out what's going on there."

The technical instructor for this lab module also noted the conflict between these expectations and experiences that students brought from their previous laboratory work, noting that

> I'm surprised that they don't know that what they are trying to do is write a paper that you would find in a journal. For them, I think they still think they are writing a high school laboratory report.

One way to address these expectations was to have students write the sections as homework assignments, which they would submit for instructor feedback. Maxine liked this strategy, noting that "even though the final copy looked nothing like the drafts I submitted, I learned what not to do, and the grades got better and better."

While the technical instructor was a bit surprised by students' expectations of what a "journal article" might entail, she was extremely mindful of the context for this assignment: Students were not writing an article to be submitted for publication; they were writing a research report in which demonstrating mastery of content and mastery of the rhetorical form was key. As she described,

> We try to give them something legitimate that they're writing about, but they don't have a chance to repeat the experiment. I think it is just moving through that realism to artificial framework that's most awkward about the student writing. It is what makes it sound most like student writing to me.

Thus, in the "semiprofessional" context of the classroom, it is essential to remember that student learning is the ultimate goal, not necessarily the advancement of knowledge in a field based on its published research. In this school-based context, however, grades do act as a motivating device and also present some level of disparity for students imagining their instructors as readers/graders. Maxine noted that one instructor was "a very big picture man. As long as you can step outside and see what's going on, he'll give you a good grade." In contrast, she saw the instructor/grader for the lab report as "picky on the details." Nevertheless, that instructor noted that

> I appreciate that this is a student effort; I'm not the editor of *Nature* trying to accept this for publication. It is a little scary to have to say something intelligent about something that someone knows much more than you do.

Writing Assessment in Laboratory Fundamentals of Biological Engineering

As was previously noted, both technical faculty members felt that the first writing assignment would need to change for future semesters. They agreed that the intent of the assignment was sound — to write a focused argument based on the novel research of genome engineering — but indicated a need to find the right balance between structure and openness. The second assignment will largely remain as is: a report, styled like a journal article, about students' lab work; however, the lab content will likely change as faculty try to give students experience with emerging areas of biological engineering research. In addition, faculty note the need to help students better integrate primary literature into their papers, particularly as they discuss unexpected findings or put the research questions themselves into the context of previous research. This sort of professional discursive move is a challenge in this particular environment when students, most of whom are sophomores, simply have not had the experience of reading primary literature, much less mastering the specific body of research in this field.

Nevertheless, the intent of both of these writing assignments was to offer students an opportunity to experience the discursive life of a biological engineer. One of the two faculty members consistently talked about this future outcome and framed her language in terms of students' identities as researchers. In describing the ideal outcome for students learning to write up their research, she said:

> [Students need] to critically evaluate data and to pull loose ends together in a story they can argue — that they can make an argument, an articulate idea that they can express and try to make sense of the work that's in front of them — because that's something they'll have to do; they'll get data back, and they'll say, "What does it mean?" If it has some familiarity, I don't even know if they'll think back to this class, but if the next time that they do it, it feels familiar, that's great. They would have it as part of who they are.

This sense of "who they are," then, is a mix of student and professional identity. Students become novice researchers learning from mentors and from each other. Key elements for this learning in Laboratory Fundamentals of Biological Engineering are lab experiences that approach "authentic" activity. In their lab experiences, students work on new and relevant issues in a new and relevant field, and they have ample opportunities to write up this research, to receive feedback, and to rewrite. These practices fit well the essential conditions for learning that has been described as "cognitive apprenticeship" [13], of which laboratory learning is one type:

> First, students come to understand the purposes or uses of the knowledge they are learning. Second, they learn by actively using knowledge rather than passively receiving it. Third, they learn the different conditions under which their knowledge can be applied. . . . Fourth, learning in multiple contexts induces the abstraction of knowledge, so that students acquire knowledge in a dual form, both tied to the contexts of its uses and independent of any particular context. [13, p. 487]

In Laboratory Fundamentals of Biological Engineering at MIT, the conditions for learning as "cognitive apprenticeship" or as professional experience were certainly present. The experiences of Maxine show the relatively uncertain route toward those goals, hazards that must be recognized and attended to, if the experience is to be successful.

Case Study 2: Addressing Teamwork Challenges in Collaborative Communication

Rationale for a Focus on Teamwork in Collaborative Communication

Engaging in specific writing and speaking tasks, as explored in Case Study 1, introduces students to the criteria of their discourse community. Learning how to produce that communication collaboratively is yet another professional skill they must learn. For engineers, the ability to work successfully in teams is a cornerstone skill that supports high-quality technical work. Of course, engineering students are not strangers to teamwork. By the time they reach their undergraduate courses, they have been active in co-curricular activities, academic projects, and multiple organizations. Yet many of them have not had instruction about team skills, and many of them may not have used those team skills in such fast-paced or complex settings to solve such challenging problems. Although some professors assume that putting students in a group and assigning a project will provide the necessary learning, other faculty understand that, as Lewis, Aldridge, and Swamidass point out, "Students . . . do not appear . . . to acquire teaming skills in the absence of structured experiences designed to develop these competencies" [24, p. 149].

Engineering and science education literature on teamwork abounds in articles, books, and conference papers. Improvement of team skills has been clearly specified in engineering accreditation criteria [25]. Yet even a quick and partial review of that literature demonstrates that educators use the term "teamwork" easily and variously. While it is likely that most educators are referring to the same general abilities, it is worth observing that in some settings, "teamwork" connotes entrepreneurship and creativity, while in other contexts, it connotes leadership or conflict resolution. In some institutions, the emphasis is on understanding learning styles and their effects on interpersonal dynamics and project management [26].

Student definitions may vary as well. In one study that surveyed two groups of students ($N = 2,777$ and $N = 1,157$), findings indicated five factors that contributed to students' understanding of effective teamwork and subsequent behaviors: contributions to the team's work; interactions with teammates; keeping the team on track; expectations of quality; and possession of relevant knowledge, skills, and abilities [27]. Yet in one focus group at MIT, students could not agree on central teamwork skills other than leadership.

Moreover, while some researchers provide a useful starting place for defining teamwork (e.g., [28]), engineering and science faculty may persist in their particular definitions of effective teamwork. Investigating whether or not their definitions and those of their students converge is necessary for efficient interaction and meaningful assessment.

Team skills are important not only because engineers commonly work in design teams or research labs but also because nearly 90% of engineering professionals report collaborative writing and speaking as part of their jobs [29]. Therefore, in the MIT Department of Aeronautics and Astronautics, documents and presentations are often collaboratively created and given, and the team skills that support that work are the subject of discussion and assessment.

In addition to the emphasis on collaborative work, the Department of Aeronautics and Astronautics also preserves the benefits of learning to compose individual documents and presentations because we believe that effective collaboration must be based on strong individual contribution as well as a clear understanding of writing process.

Thus, in an effort to achieve this objective, each capstone course in the department includes individual writing or presentation preparation that then contributes toward a collaboratively written document and/or presentation that reflects the work of the design or research team. Individual faculty members and teaching teams interpret this goal flexibly to meet the pace and scope of the particular project. While some capstone courses work with large design teams, in the case study described here, we focus on a capstone course structured around small teams.

Context and Implementation for Teaching Teamwork in Aeronautics/Astronautics

Experimental Projects Lab I and II (or 16.62x in MIT's numeric language) illustrates one implementation of CI and team-oriented learning objectives. This two-semester course begins as teams of two (and sometimes three) students choose partners, a project, and a project advisor. The projects are primarily proposed by various members of the department faculty although sometimes a student team will create its own project proposal and invite a faculty member to advise them. Generally, the experimental projects are ambitious and rigorous, and time constraints require student teams to work efficiently together.

To define precisely the terms used in this case study description, we use "faculty" to mean the leading professor, an engineering professor in the department. We also use the term to mean the communication instructor who consults on both writing and presentation, and the graduate teaching fellow. The faculty members run the course, give lectures, hold conferences with students, and assign grades. By "advisor," we mean the department member who advises the project because she or he is a subject-matter expert in the area. At times, an advisor is recruited from another discipline, but chiefly the advisors are from the Department of Aeronautics and Astronautics. The advisor meets with the team approximately once a week and advises the members on their experimental process. The technical staff comprises the personnel who run the laboratory and shop facilities and consult on fabrication and implementation issues.

The goal of the first semester is to design a research project to the level of specificity that makes it possible for the team to implement successfully the project during the second semester. The learning objectives for the two semesters are for students to be able to complete the following:

- formulate the success criteria and objectives for an experiment that allows the team to assess a hypothesis;
- develop, as a team, the strategy for the design of the experiment and for data analysis procedures to achieve these objectives;
- implement, as a team and on schedule, the detailed design of the experiment and data analysis;
- execute, as a team and on schedule, the experiment that will assess the hypothesis;
- communicate, orally and in writing, the results of the design process and ultimately the key aspects of the overall project. [30]

Both semesters are based on teamwork, and students collaboratively produce five out of the seven communication products. Students begin with individual writing and individual writing conferences that lay a solid base for collaborative communication work. Lectures given by the communication instructor help students through the writing process. Lectures are grounded in active learning and in the examination of models of past proposals.

In Experimental Projects Lab I, students keep individual lab notebooks, and they individually write two iterations of a design proposal. However, their project work, their meetings with one another and their advisor, and their meetings with the faculty are all done as a team.

Students begin their first semester by collaboratively developing a hypothesis but individually writing design proposals. The collaborative writing of the hypothesis ensures that team members and their project advisor (who is not a member of the teaching team) clearly understand and can communicate their thoughts to one another and to the faculty. After the collaborative hypothesis, students then write individual design proposals in iterations:

(1) The first iteration of the proposal includes an introduction, background, and significance section; the hypothesis; a short literature review; and a technical description of what the experimenters plan to do. Engineering faculty comment on and support the instruction in writing. Before the due date for the first iteration, each student also brings a draft to a 30-minute conference with the communication instructor. The first iterations of the proposal are turned in, commented upon by the communication instructor and by the engineering faculty, graded, and returned to the student. The expectation is that comments on this version will be incorporated into the next revision.

(2) In the second iteration of the proposal, each student adds sections on experimental design; data analysis and error mitigation; project planning (scheduling, budget, facilities needed); and a summary and conclusion. Again, students meet for writing conferences with drafts of their final proposal. The documents are submitted, commented upon, and graded. These final iterations are high stakes writing for the students since their experimental design section must be deemed sound and specific enough for the team to go forward into their second semester.

For the teaching team and the project advisors, the design proposals give a perspective on the ability of each student to conceive of and design experimental research. However, the ability of the team to converge on the design of an experiment also emerges. By reading one student's articulation of the project against his or her partner's proposal, the faculty gain an expanded sense of team functioning. As Loughry, Ohland, and Moore observe, a "major factor accounting for project success [is] the effectiveness of various team processes" [27]. Likewise, other researchers have observed that team difficulties and project problems are linked, but these researchers also conclude that the quality of student written reports is correlated negatively with poor project performance and team dysfunction [31], [32]. Thus, the design proposals and the iterative writing process, along with the periodic team meetings, provide a way not only to mentor students in technical prowess and writing ability but also to investigate potential gaps in team functioning.

The team's first collaborative communication project comes at the end of the first semester when students make a short presentation of their design proposal. Again, the model is that students begin individually on elements of the presentation although they are encouraged to then merge their work. They hear short lectures from the communication instructor. The team practices the presentation with the communication instructor and one or two other teams and receives feedback from both the instructor and their peers. Then, the team makes its presentation and receives questions and comments from the faculty, their advisor, and sometimes their peers. The teaching team grades the oral presentations, and the team members share the grade equally.

In the second semester, Experimental Projects Lab II, the student teams spend little time in the classroom because they are at work in the lab or the shop. The two oral presentations in this term are completed collaboratively, and the final report that describes the entire two-semester experiment is collaboratively written. Again, students receive support through short lectures and writing conferences with the communication instructor.

The challenges in teaching students about collaborative communication divide into issues around content and around process. High-quality content is at the heart of all technical writing and speaking. As students begin to put together a document or a presentation, they often find that the content lacks specificity or is unfocused or (not uncommon) missing. Teasing out the reasons behind these content problems quickly foregrounds team issues around task assignments, lack of consensus, points of confusion, lack of needed skill sets, documentation and scheduling problems, difficulties with responsibility, responsiveness, and basic interpersonal communication. Thus, an early learning objective for students in Experimental Projects Lab I is to understand not only that substance is at the heart of all technical writing and presentation but also that this content is most often produced by strong teamwork. The insistence on substance is reinforced through lectures, through weekly meetings with advisors, through the periodic grading of lab notebooks, and through team meetings with the team members, their advisors, the technical staff, and the faculty. Feedback to the students is explicit, and student teams who are not working in a substantive way find themselves in close conversation with their faculty members and project advisor until the problems are addressed.

Team dysfunction that may have produced these difficulties is also a topic of discussion.

Next, collaborative communication also requires composing processes that may be unfamiliar to students. Student interviews document that most of our students have strong individual writing processes, but collaboratively produced communication involves multiple authors who are completing technical work as they simultaneously represent those technical advances in words and graphics. Several drafts are usually necessary to capture accurately the fast-moving work, yet undergraduate students often tend to avoid the drafting and revision process that is necessary to collaborative work. Moreover, most students have only been recently introduced to technical writing, so they may be unfamiliar and perhaps awkward with the conventions of that style of writing or the organizational demands of a large technical report or presentation. In addition, one or more of the team may have significant writing deficits. To complicate matters, student writers and speakers in teams often struggle to achieve a collective, professional voice.

Lastly, collaborative writing in the twenty-first century brings additional challenges since student writers working on a collaborative document or presentation may be producing it in an asynchronous and distributed manner. Information and partially completed drafts of the document move between writers and editors via email or wikis or through academic management sites. While students may be comfortable with communicating electronically, asynchronously and at a distance, their existing composing and editing practices may not be robust enough to stand up to the organization of a communication with complex information. Moreover, the challenges of electronic, asynchronous, and distributed collaboration expand along with numbers of writers and the scope of the project.

Students faced with collaborative writing tasks need help structuring this interaction to achieve greater coordination [33]. They also need to be guided in adopting a composing style that best fits their team or their work [29]. Because they are unfamiliar with possible ways to divide composition work (horizontal, sequential, stratified), students often fall back on their individual abilities and the linear model [33]. One member assumes the responsibility for writing large parts of and editing the presentation slides or the final report. This style is usually ineffective, inefficient, and inequitable, but it is familiar.

In Experimental Projects I and II, the communication instructor gives guidelines on how to put together a collaboratively written report or presentation and leads a discussion on conflict resolution strategies. Emphasis is placed on more precise documentation, use of style guides, careful division of labor and responsibility, and more realistic scheduling. Additionally, there is discussion about which method or model of composition best fits the team's process. In addition, the communication instructor also reviews presentation slides, organizes "dry runs" or rehearsals, and meets with students and teams for individual writing conferences. Moreover, the communication instructor is available to review presentation slides at any time during the second semester, although many students feel confident in their abilities at that point. Students share the grade for collaborative documents and presentations, so usually students invest a good deal of energy in the collaborative communication process. However, there are instances of "social loafing" and "hitchhiking" that are troublesome for the student teams, detract from the general level of professional accomplishment, and pose problems in assessment for the faculty.

Assessment of Students' Team Skills in Experimental Projects Lab

Assessment of team skills is an important part of helping students develop their skills. Not only is development of team skills part of departmental and institutional accreditation, assessing the effectiveness of team skills also allows faculty to measure those skills and assess their own pedagogical outcomes. However, this is the more challenging task when faculty use collaborative writing and presentation strategies; separating the assessment of team skills from technical and communication ability is not easy.

Faculty want to help each student develop his or her team abilities and to ensure that each student contributes equally to the project. A number of questions arise. Should assessment of team skills be summative or formative? Should assessment of team skills be part of the student grade or not? Self-assessment and student reflection are important, but do these measures qualify as rigorous and valid assessment of team skills? How helpful are self-assessment and peer-assessment to a student? Effective assessment of team skills is challenging, and the need for confidentiality is also demanding; consequently, when working with small teams as in Experimental Projects Lab I and II, team assessment can be so general that it is not truly useful to the students. Some researchers suggest that short, specific peer assessment instruments are most useful in summative rather than formative assessments and when tempered by the professor's own observations (e.g., [27]). But it is not easy to apply this recommendation to large student groups with subsystem design teams that may or may not work closely together. Nor is this conclusion applicable in smaller teams, such as those in Experimental Projects Lab I and II, where confidentiality is difficult to preserve.

Moreover, what do students need to know about team skills? And do team styles vary between disciplines, such as science and engineering? Most students in end-of-semester debriefing sessions in this course have said that lectures on team skills have not been helpful while just a few students have said that learning more about the stages of team formation was useful. In focus groups in a larger three-semester capstone course, students said lectures and readings about teams were not helpful, but students did want some specific advice on how to schedule their technical work. What becomes evident from discussion with student groups is that their definitions of team skills vary widely. Some students focus on conflict resolution, leadership, and interpersonal abilities, and others focus on documentation, scheduling, and division of labor strategies.

How students learn about team skills is not clear either. In a recent focus group, students responded that they learned most from modeling the behavior of more experienced students and from the one-on-one mentoring of their project advisor or professor. Again, this group of students reiterated what an earlier group had said: didactic teaching is not useful to them in developing team skills.

It seems likely that effective teamwork in engineering and the resulting collaborative communication about that work do not arise from a simple list of behaviors to be memorized in a lecture hall but rather from a set of evolving and complex practice-based skills that accompany professional development. A lecture would be easier to give, but it is possible that what is required is ongoing and specific interaction with students who are trying to learn the complex and interlocking elements of effective engineering teamwork. Nor is assessment easily encapsulated. For some contexts, quantitative assessment may be effective; in other contexts, the qualitative and reflective approach may be more useful to young engineers.

Yet for all the challenges, teaching, mentoring, and assessment in teamwork are necessary because of the strong connection between high-quality teamwork, successful research, and sound design work and the collaborative communication in which they are represented. Our students need team skills that range from interpersonal sensitivities to pragmatic project-management abilities. With a comprehensive set of team skills and the awareness that collaboration is a common element of engineering, our students will be able to apply those skills no matter what the specific disciplinary challenges may be.

CASE STUDY 3: DATA-DRIVEN ARGUMENTS IN BIOMEDICAL ENGINEERING

Rationale for Studying How Students Learn to Make Visual, Data-Driven Arguments

With its integration of engineering, medicine, and science, the field of biomedical engineering presents novel research challenges. From technology-development projects that focus on designing and verifying the validity of a new optics imaging device to hypothesis-driven projects that focus on understanding cellular-level changes in tissue scaffolds, the field of biomedical engineering includes perspectives from audiences across many disciplines [34]. Considering this "interdisciplinary challenge," biomedical engineering students must be taught quite varied skills in communicating their research to readers from both science and engineering disciplines.

A central communication skill that is at the core of biomedical engineering research is the effective presentation of data. On one hand, in technology-development projects, researchers use data to convince readers that their design is optimal and feasible. On the other hand, in experimental research, biomedical engineers use data to provide accurate explanations of research findings with detailed explanations of those findings [34]. For experimental researchers, weighing various kinds of data evidence and providing alternative critiques of experimental research findings are central to the practice of conducting research [35], [36]. Furthermore, given this value placed on data argument in experimental research, the effective design of visuals is critical [37], [38].

Nevertheless, when students write research articles, they often do not fully understand how to select and design meaningful plots for their audience [39]. Students tend to make two common errors in their presentation of data: (1) They select poor figures to represent their findings, or (2) they offer little guidance to readers on how to interpret those figures through descriptive captions or supporting textual explanations. As a result, many students mistakenly assume that raw data or a series of similar-looking plots are effective. What students do not yet realize is that pages upon pages of raw data are not only unreadable, pages of raw data also do not guarantee that the research findings are valid. Students may also assume that the "data speak for themselves," and thus, they may offer sparse textual explanations of their designs or findings [40]. However, visuals need meaningful captions and other supporting features to guide readers to the thesis, the main point, of a figure.

In the process of learning to think like professional biomedical engineers in communicating their research results, students must internalize that it is the job of the writer to provide thorough, concise, readable explanations of research findings through visual representations of findings. Scientists and engineers read articles strategically and are unlikely to spend time deciphering overly complicated plots (or prose) [41], [42]. In fact, it is not uncommon for readers to skim the visuals of a research article after reading the title and abstract of the article. In such instances, the visuals presented in the results section are read first, and then the supporting text and other sections of the article are read [43], [44, pp. 30–31].

Overall, the need to argue from data is aligned with the contexts of cases 1 and 2, with professional competencies as a driving curricular force and teamwork/collaboration as an instructional process toward those goals. Through the process of learning how to present research data in clear, readable figures, students must learn how to think and read like professional biomedical engineers, determining how their audience will process visual presentations of data. In their own writing, whether alone or in teams, students must learn how to "translate" raw data into meaningful syntheses of their findings so that readers are given an accurate synopsis of research results. In both writing and visual representation, students must be taught to be mindful of their ethical responsibilities to data collection and analysis. In reading research, students must also learn how to discern the accurate representation of data from potentially fallacious misrepresentations. This last point is particularly important for students to learn if they are to become professional reviewers and journal editors [45]–[47].

In the biomedical engineering course described in this case study, our goal is to teach students how to create meaningful representations of original research findings. Many students who come to this course already know the general structure of a research article. What they lack is an understanding of how to *use* that form to make a valid case for their research findings. Specifically, they lack an understanding of how to read, design, and critique the visual representations of data that are the centerpiece of research articles in biomedical engineering.

Context and Implementation for Teaching Argumentation from Visual Data

Quantitative Physiology: Cells and Tissues (or 6.021J in MIT's numeric language) is a large-lecture, undergraduate course in biomedical engineering. In the course, students study the principles of mass transport and electrical signal generation for biological membranes, cells, and tissues. The course also has several communications-learning goals, including the following: (1) Students will learn to integrate the research and writing processes, and (2) through learning the storyboard approach to selecting and representing quantitative findings, students will learn to present more concise and accurate presentations of their data that give readers confidence in their experimental research.

In Quantitative Physiology, writing is associated with two projects: an experimental project in a wet lab and a theoretical study using computer simulation. Each project lasts approximately five weeks and is carried out in parallel with lectures, recitations, and homework assignments.

Students are introduced to the first project assignment, a microfluidics experiment, approximately three weeks into the course. After selecting a research partner, students write a proposal that describes their proposed lab research. The purpose of the proposal is to ensure that students have well-defined projects before they enter the lab. Without well-defined projects, students will likely gather poor data and, thus, the process of trying to present that data in a meaningful fashion will be frustrating. Even in the proposal stage of the class, the lead technical professor reminds students that the goal of their research is to convey research data accurately, not to make data fit a particular theory:

> When you do your experiment, you may get unexpected results. . . . You should explore unexpected results and try to understand their bases. Your aim should be not simply to reject or accept your hypothesis, but to develop insight into the phenomena. . . . Keep in mind that this is an *experimental* project. Your goal is to characterize *what* happens, not *why* it is happening. Theoretical analyses may support your experimental findings. However, your grade will be primarily based on the reliability of your data. [48]

Within one week, students submit their proposals for review. Initially, approximately 75% of proposals are rejected because the students' research approach is too broad or their methodology is unfocused. After receiving substantial feedback, students revise and resubmit their proposals until their research approach is approved.

While students are in the process of gathering lab data, we provide a lecture on how to take the data they gather in the lab and prepare a written presentation of their findings. This lecture is given collaboratively by the lead technical professor and writing program instructor. In this lecture, we model how professional biomedical engineers think about communicating their findings throughout the data-gathering process.

Given the limited scope of the projects in Quantitative Physiology, we suggest that their principal results can be refined into five or six specific figures, whether hard copies of data obtained in an experiment or simply hand-sketched figures of expected results. The point is to assemble the five or six specific figures into a storyboard, or narrative of the research. The point that we want to stress to students here is that often researchers cannot present every finding within the limited space of a research article. The tension for a researcher is to select meaningful figures without misrepresenting their results.

By developing a storyboard, students also focus on what information is, or is not, important in each of the figures. For each figure, students are asked to identify the two to three points that are most important for the audience to understand. If the list for one figure contains more than three important points, we suggest that the student consider whether the points might be more clearly made with more than one figure. Similarly, if there is only a single interesting point associated with a figure, it might be possible to merge figures to more meaningfully show trends in the findings. The goal in this step is to incorporate all of the interesting results into a logical presentation of the research findings. Figure 19-1 is a storyboard that we use as an example of research from a microfluidics project. It includes the key figures selected for a research article: (a) a figure for the methods section that would be included with a schematic diagram of the microfluidics device; (b) a plot that synthesizes the main findings; (c) data provided in tabular form; and (d) a regression analysis of the findings.

After explaining this model storyboard, we give students a challenge — analysis of several problematic storyboards. The students work with a partner to figure out the problems with the various example storyboards. The challenge has the effect of ensuring that students gain, at least, a rudimentary understanding of the storyboard concept. We revisit the storyboarding concept multiple times after this lecture so that students have multiple opportunities for learning.

After two weeks of lab work by the various groups, students are ready to write a draft of their final report. Once students have completed their research, the teaching assistants review the students' lab notebooks to ensure that the storyboards are suitable. Students then work together to draft a 3,500-word scientific paper. Students submit three copies of their reports, one copy each for the technical staff, writing staff, and peer. We then reconvene one week later at a writing clinic. At the writing clinic, papers are returned, and students speak with reviewers about their comments.

FIGURE 19-1   Sample Storyboard

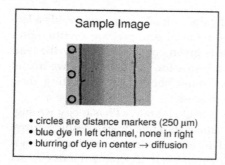

Sample Image

- circles are distance markers (250 μm)
- blue dye in left channel, none in right
- blurring of dye in center → diffusion

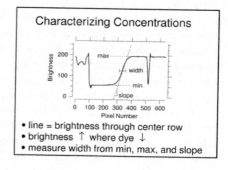

Characterizing Concentrations

- line = brightness through center row
- brightness ↑ where dye ↓
- measure width from min, max, and slope

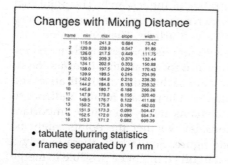

Changes with Mixing Distance

- tabulate blurring statistics
- frames separated by 1 mm

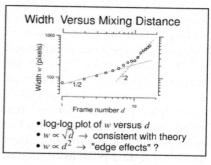

Width Versus Mixing Distance

- log-log plot of w versus d
- $w \propto \sqrt{d}$ → consistent with theory
- $w \propto d^2$ → "edge effects" ?

Source: Used with permission from Dennis Freeman.

As we review the student drafts, we often find that some students do not grasp the storyboard approach that we outline in our communications lecture. As a result, these students' report drafts display little coherence across figures, lack textual explanations, or are poorly designed. We address these issues in our written comments on student papers, our peer-review guidelines, and in a general letter to the class from the lead professor. For example, a comment by a teaching assistant or writing reviewer might point to a problem across several images (e.g., "All of these plots seem to be making the same point but at different concentrations. Can you condense these 8 figures into 4 or even 1 meaningful figure that shows a clear trend in your results?").

The lead technical professor also returns to the idea of the storyboard in summary comments to the class. For example, in fall 2006, the professor wrote the following, along with other comments on how to improve the report drafts:

Create a Storyboard: The most important section of your report is the Results section (this is true for all technical reports). Think of the Results section as a presentation of technical findings that is intended to lead the reader to some set of conclusions. Construct the presentation using figures that build upon each other. The first figure should be close to the raw data (e.g., images, calibration results, etc.). The later figures should show more highly processed results that build on the earlier figures.

Storyboard Method: Start with your figures. Assemble your figures into a storyboard. Associate 2–3 bullet points with each figure. Arrange the figures and bullet points so that each flows naturally into the next.

Common Failure Modes: The Results sections of many of the first drafts seemed to be collections of relatively independent figures that did not build on each other to convey a higher level message. Many Results sections had little text, suggesting that little thought had gone into the purpose of the figures. The first figure in many of the first drafts showed highly processed results (e.g., ratio of swelling in six conditions as a function of concentration of X) that is the main result of the study. This is a bad strategy. Why should a reader believe that the ratio of swelling is the important thing to measure? Why not the difference instead of the ratio? You should show individual swelling relations first, so that the reader can independently come to the conclusion that computing the ratio is a good thing. [49]

After receiving comments from the reviewers, students revise their reports and submit their final manuscripts, along with comments from their peer reviews, within one week. Students' revised, final manuscripts are graded by the same writing and technical faculty who graded their draft reports (Appendix D).

What are the challenges in teaching students how to make arguments with data? The first challenge is having students design projects that will yield useful data. We strongly believe that the best educational research experiences are ones in which students gather original research. Because there are no "right" answers with original research findings, students cannot rely on the faculty to give them the "correct" answer or specific instruction to get the right answer. To ensure that students yield useful data in their lab work, they need help defining their projects. Although the proposal-writing process in Quantitative Physiology requires additional time on the part of the faculty and teaching assistants, the initial time spent reviewing student proposals saves time later in the lab. Rather than helping struggling students redefine poorly defined projects once they are in the lab, the teaching assistants can dedicate more of their time in the lab to helping students decipher their data and to answering more substantive questions about the research process.

Another challenge is getting students to make plausible interpretations of their findings. Students often cling to the idea that they must *prove* a particular theory or that anomalous data mean that their experiment was a failure. By repeatedly reinforcing the idea of the storyboard, we encourage students to move beyond these simple conceptions of scientific research to see how their own data, even if messy or inconclusive, require an explanation that a reader can follow. This approach also helps us remind students that the responsibility of the researcher is to give data a thorough and accurate explanation, not to merely dismiss problematic findings as equipment failure or shoddy research.

A third challenge is getting students to evaluate each other's data critically. Students must be given explicit advice on how to critique data in a peer report and must be rewarded for those efforts. This process includes looking at plots and tables as well as supporting text. As one student observed last year, sometimes it's useful to look at a plot and ask, "Is there anything really useful there?" In order to accomplish this goal of engaged peer review, peer review efforts should be included in the final report grade.

Finally, teaching students to make visual arguments with data in the twenty-first century brings some specific technological challenges. Plots generated in programs like MatLab do not easily import to Microsoft documents, and students who work across platforms often have difficulties sharing figures because images become easily corrupted. We encourage students to generate multiple output forms of their data and to use PDF files. We have also designed specific programs to help students output data from MatLab so that they can focus on data collection and analysis.

Assessment of Student Learning in Quantitative Physiology

In order to understand more about student learning in Quantitative Physiology, we conducted a qualitative study of student learning in the class. Our goal in this small study was to investigate how students' understanding of the research process changed over the semester. We interviewed eight students six times over the course of the semester. Five of the interviews were conducted while students were completing the microfluidics lab project, and one interview was conducted at the end of the semester. We interviewed students five times during one experiment, so we could identify key moments in the learning process. We asked students questions about collecting data, reporting results, collaborating with a partner, and giving/receiving peer review. We also asked them general questions about the scientific research process.

After interviewing students, we coded the data thematically to reveal general trends in the interview responses. At the end of the semester, students saw the research and writing processes as more interrelated. Students no longer thought about research occurring only in the lab and about writing as crafting grammatically correct sentences. Students also learned that analyzing data, creating compelling arguments, and revising their written work require much more time than they originally thought. For example, when we asked students if they discovered any limitations or new possibilities in their data while writing their report, students reported that they found new insights in their data analysis. One student responded:

> I learned that the data can be analyzed in many different ways, with differing results. The important part of data analysis is to objectively analyze the data in a way that is logical and independent of the actual results. I also learned the importance of analyzing seemingly insignificant deviances in the data. You can't just assume that the theories are always correct.

The peer review process was also a valuable way for students also to gain new insights into making arguments with data. For example, another student said this:

> One of the things I realized from the peer review especially is that there are many ways to take data and analyze data, so it is important to justify to the reader why you took a specific approach and why you think it's valid — particularly because it might not seem that obvious to someone else. Also, data presentation matters — both in terms of tables versus figures and text description in Results. Our first draft, we primarily just threw the data at the reader, in the final we tried hard to present it more pointedly.

These comments support our general observations about student writing in Quantitative Physiology. When students revise their reports with feedback from multiple reviewers, the average grade from draft to final increases by approximately one letter grade. From a qualitative assessment perspective, we have found that students' reports are better organized, that the figures they select better convey their research findings, that their figures are clearer because we have addressed issues in visual design such as axes and captions, and that their data analyses include greater attention to detail. As a result of these improvements, we can focus our efforts on further clarifying and refining student understanding of concepts rather than correcting major misunderstandings in report organization and presentation of findings. This has also allowed us to deepen our assessment of student writing to address issues of novelty and conceptual correctness (Appendix D).

We have also found that the focus on storyboarding translates well to oral presentations. For their second project, students give an oral presentation rather than submit a written report. Using the storyboard approach, students are able to design more focused oral presentations of their findings without the common errors found in PowerPoint presentations.

In the field of biomedical engineering, the effective presentation of research results in visual form is an important element in research writing; using reader-expected standards for data representation allows readers from varied disciplinary backgrounds to understand and assess the validity of the findings. Thus, in biomedical engineering classes students need data representation skills that go beyond basic information design. By learning to select key figures of their research findings, integrating those figures into a cohesive storyboard, and critiquing the data in peer manuscripts, students learn one of the most important ways that professional researchers think about communication and research.

CONCLUSION — AND RECURRING QUESTIONS

This article highlights various approaches used in MIT's CI curriculum in trying to generate methods that help students develop the advanced communication thinking skills required of professional engineers today. Using identity as a central concept in a CI course such as Laboratory Fundamentals in Biological Engineering reveals how students struggle to develop a professional identity, even within the space of seemingly simple writing activities in the disciplines and, thus, reveals how we must constantly revise and update our approaches to help students gain a professional identity in that discipline. Using teamwork as a central concept in a CI course such as Experimental Projects Lab I and II has allowed us to explore the connection between successful collaboration in design and communication. Finally, using arguments with data as a central concept in a CI course such as Quantitative Physiology has allowed us to explore the relationship between writing and the data representation and, thus, to change how we teach the process of writing up original research findings.

It is important to note that it is not our intent to create a divide between what is possible at a resource-rich institution such as MIT and other institutions not similarly fortunate. If anything, the questions we raise in these case studies and the limits of our instruction are applicable to many institutions struggling to create meaningful educational opportunities in engineering communication. One significant limit is raised by the very presence of a large cadre of WAC instructors with specific expertise in teaching writing and the subsequent potential for a perceived split between teaching "writing" and teaching "content." Getting engineering faculty more involved in these processes and applying concepts of teamwork and collaboration to the larger enterprise of CI classes at MIT are ongoing challenges.

Our research and the case studies we present here raise other widely applicable questions: What does it mean for educational practice if professional communication competencies and tasks are the goals? How can students and technical faculty best create the conditions for students to learn to be skilled team members? How can engineering students move from mere display of data to making skilled visual arguments based on those data? By no means have we figured out the complete answers to those questions, but we hope that the case studies we present show some potential paths to finding those answers, as well as obstacles in those paths.

Additionally, our inquiry into the teaching of communication at MIT represents "teacher-research" or "action-research" [50] meant both to improve practice and to broaden our knowledge of what it means to learn to communicate as a scientist and engineer. Thus, the sustained research in which we continue to engage — via surveys, focus groups, individual interviews, and analyses of students' work, all in the context of contemporary theories of teaching and learning — are essential activities for communication professionals in any setting.

It is also not our intent for the case studies presented in this article to be the final word on the redesign of communication instruction in engineering education. Our intent, instead, has been to highlight the ways that a commitment to teaching communication within disciplinary frameworks at MIT has brought to the fore three key aspects that require attention: professionalization, teamwork/collaboration, and argumentation. Each of these aspects is present in some degree to all of our CI classes, and each reveals the opportunities and complications for designing communication instruction.

Appendix A

20.109(S07) — Genome Engineering Essay

Assignment

You are asked to write a thoughtful, researched essay exploring how a foundational engineering concept (e.g., abstraction, modularity, insulation, standardization, decoupling) can be applied as a design tool for biological engineering. Your lab work with M13 will provide the context for your argument.

Abstract

This has been written for you to clarify the assignment. You can include this abstract as your own.

> To engineer novel biological systems, we need to change the genetic code of existing biological materials, not by making a few changes as current methods allow us to do but rather by making lots and lots of changes in a fast, cheap, and reliable way. Just as "plug-ins" provide new or improved functions to existing computer programs, the current tools of molecular biology allow for piecemeal modification to genetic programs, adding functionality but often complexity and clumsiness as well. In this essay I will describe two approaches to biological programming, ad hoc adjustment, and complete refactoring, as applied to the simple genome of the bacteriophage M13. With both approaches, I will show how the application of a foundational engineering concept, namely (abstraction, insulation, standardization, decoupling, modularity . . . choose one), enables more reliable and elegant genetic programming and can give rise to a platform with more flexibility and fewer restrictions.

Introduction

From your introduction, your readers expect to find out why your topic is important and why they should be interested in it. To do that, you need to describe the larger context for the work, the ways it's important, and the specific areas your paper will address. There's no need to hide your main point or approach. At the end of the introduction, the reader should want to learn how the foundational idea you've chosen (abstraction, modularity, insulation, standardization, or decoupling) serves a useful purpose and affords great opportunity if incorporated among "best practices" for biological engineers, expecting M13 to be the test case they'll follow.

Launch this section using one of the following quotes, or a personal favorite.

- Today, most software exists, not to solve a problem, but to interface with other software. (I. O. Angell)

- Programming languages should be designed not by piling feature on top of feature, but by removing the weaknesses and restrictions that make additional features appear necessary. (Anonymous, Revised Report on the Algorithmic Language Scheme)
- Programs for sale: Fast, Reliable, Cheap: choose two. (Anonymous)
- Think (design) globally; act (code) locally. (Anonymous)
- Think twice, code once. (Anonymous)
- Weeks of programming can save you hours of planning. (Anonymous)
- Any fool can write code that a computer can understand. Good programmers write code that humans can understand. (M. Fowler, "Refactoring: Improving the Design of Existing Code")
- A program like Microsoft's Windows 98 is tens of millions of lines of code. Nobody can keep that much complexity in their head or hope to manage it effectively. So you need an architecture that says to everyone, "Here's how this thing works, and to do your part, you need to understand only these five things, and don't you dare touch anything else." (C. Ferguson, "High Stakes, No Prisoners; Times Business Press")

Explicitly describe what problem or issue the quote you've chosen highlights and how the point applies to genetic programming as well.

Next . . . well, it's really up to you. You could

- allow one of the more familiar software disasters to illustrate comparable design problems that can be encountered when making biological materials;
- describe some (but not all) current practices in genetic programming and their limitations;
- introduce M13 as the example you've chosen to hack and debug.

Some ideas you may want to introduce are listed but this list is neither exhaustive nor mandatory:

- complexity;
- simplicity;
- refactoring;
- features of good/bad computer programs;
- features of good/bad genetic programs;
- standardization;
- decoupling;
- abstraction;
- usefulness;
- discovery.

Body: Parts 1–3

In these sections you will build off of your introduction to present M13 as an example of the issues you've highlighted. Your readers expect to learn something from what you present; thus, you'll need to supply ample description as well as an analysis of your lab results. Remember your goal is to make a persuasive argument for the concept of abstraction (or modularity, insulation, standardization, decoupling . . .) with evidence from your laboratory experience.

Part 1: How it's built: M13 as a test case

At the conclusion of this section, the reader should have a good understanding of

- the prevalence and diversity of bacteriophage;
- the M13 life cycle (include a figure if you like);
- the size and organization of the genome;
- the proteins encoded by the genome structure (include a figure or table if you like);
- any natural variations to the genome.

End this by highlighting how "engineerable" the natural example seems, and how (abstraction, modularity, insulation, standardization, or decoupling) are key to reliably and predictably accomplishing this.

Part 2: Build to learn: M13 and piecemeal fixes

At the conclusion of this section, the reader should have a good understanding of

- the application of M13 for phage display, cite at least one successful application of this technique;
- the limitations/variations of phage display;
- the modification to the genome that you performed in lab and what useful purpose it could serve;
- your plaque assay and Western data, be it positive or negative (include a figure and table).

End this part by commenting on how fast, cheap, and reliable this approach proved to be. On the scale of other engineering feats, how ambitious was it? How much expertise was required? How can you imagine making it an easier and more robust engineering task?

Part 3: Learn to build: Refactored M13

At the conclusion of this section, the reader should have a good understanding of

- what refactoring is;
- what the rough draft of refactored M13 tried to do;

- which gene (gII, gIX, etc.) you refactored and how you approached/solved the specifics of that problem;

- your plaque assay and Western data, be it positive or negative (include a figure and table).

End this part by commenting on how refactoring compares to ad hoc tweaking and how much or how little promise it holds for building fast, cheap, and reliable biological systems.

Conclusions or Summary

In this section, your readers expect you to tie up the concepts you raised in your introduction with the specific examples you've described in terms of M13. Most important, you need to supply some "future thinking" about the implications of what you've presented, whether for future experimental work or the larger field.

APPENDIX B

20.109(S07) — Expression Engineering Report

Assignment

You are asked to write a formal lab report detailing your work in this module. Specifics for each section of this report are detailed below. General information about formatting the report are mostly addressed here.

Abstract

- Please keep the number of words under 250.
- Do not include references in the abstract.
- Try drafting this section after you've written the rest of the report.
- If you're stuck, start by modifying one crystallizing sentence from each of the sections of your report.
- Please do not plagiarize (accidentally or other) the class wiki. This applies to your entire report.

Introduction

The homework you wrote after the first day of this new module will serve at the heart of your introduction. You should add (at least) one final paragraph to narrow the information "funnel," ending your introduction with a clear description of the problem you're studying and the method you are using. If you would like to preview for the reader your key results and conclusions in the last sentence of your introduction, you may.

Materials and Methods

If you used any kits for any of the manipulations, it is sufficient to cite the manufacturer's directions, e.g., "yeast were transformed according to the Q-biogene transformation kit protocol." Subdivide this section into the following:

(1) Yeast strains and plasmids
- list genotypes and plasmid names when known.

(2) PCR
- include primer design info here;
- include primer sequences, for knockout and for candidate verification;
- include PCR cycling conditions.

(3) Yeast transformation
- include how you selected for transformants;
- include what you did to verify that URA3 was integrated where you thought.

(4) Yeast microarray
- mention kits as relevant, including any deviation from published protocol if any;
- mention how many yeast and how much RNA was used;
- describe array analytical methods in results section rather than in Materials and Methods.

Results: Figures

You should include but are not limited to the following figures and tables:

Figure 1: panel A: table describing transformation results; panel B: agarose gel verifying URA3 insertion.

Figure 2: Spot test images.

Figure 3: Microarray analytics.

Figure 4: Microarray conclusions.

Each figure should be numbered, and should have a title and legend text.

- In paragraph form, describe each figure and the observations you made.
- As much as possible, reserve conclusions about your data for the discussion section. Clearly an exception to this will be which of your deletion candidates was correct, as this information is critical for the next steps in the experiments.

Discussion

You should include but are not limited to:

- conclusions you can draw from your work, including any uncertainties;
- other data (published or personal communications) that support or contradict your conclusions;

- limitations of your work, e.g., what kinds of experiments/controls would have been great to include;
- next experiments you would like to try to extend your findings and strengthen your conclusions.

APPENDIX C

Start of Semester Student Survey For Case 1 — Laboratory Fundamentals of Biological Engineering

Your name: _____

Class standing (check one): ____ FR ____ SOPH ____ JUNIOR ____ SENIOR

Gender: ____ M ____ F

Age: _____

1. What is your primary language for writing and speaking? _____
2. What other languages do you write and speak? _____
3. What have been some of your experiences with writing up scientific content (whether research, lab reports, review articles, etc.)?
4. Describe a significant writing experience, whether in or out of school.
5. What do you struggle with most in your writing?
6. What are your strengths as a writer?
7. What kinds of reading and writing do you do outside of school?
8. What kind of writing do you expect to do after graduation from MIT?
9. Why do you think 20.109 has been designated as a Communications-Intensive class?
10. What are your writing goals for 20.109?

APPENDIX D

Multidimensional Scoring Rubric Used to Grade Student Reports in Quantitative Physiology

10% First Draft of Report

A: Complete report, professionally written.

B: Significant work, but report needs further clarification before final submission.

C: Incomplete descriptions, missing sections, or poor figures.

D: Few results, few figures, few discussion points, report not complete.

5% Critique of Peer Report

A: Several helpful high-level suggestions (e.g., suggesting major restructuring, new figures, . . .) plus probing questions (could your result be caused by . . . ?) plus appropriate low-level comments (e.g., on grammar or graphics).

B: At least one helpful high-level suggestion or probing question plus low-level comments.

C: Helpful low-level comments.

D: Few helpful comments.

15% Report Structure

A: All information is present and is well organized in proper sections, using standard scientific report structure. Appropriate use of source materials. Reader can easily follow from section to section of report.

B: All information is present but poorly organized in no more than one section. Reader may have difficulty following one section of report but generally understands overall report structure.

C: All information is present but multiple instances of misplaced information, and/or repeated minor organizational problems that interfere with report coherence.

D: Information is missing from report, report does not follow standard scientific report structure and/or misuse of source materials. Reader cannot follow overall structure of report.

10% Clarity and Conciseness of Exposition*

A: Content of each paragraph is readable with clear, simple prose and appropriate use of technical language. Each graph clearly supports the prose.

B: Content is readable with minor slips in clarity of a single unclear passage/graph.

C: Major slips in clarity and/or multiple unclear passages/graphs.

D: Repeated wordiness or lack of clarity, poor presentation of visual information, and/or accumulation of stylistic errors that interfere with readability.

*Grades may be reduced for reports that unnecessarily exceed the 10-page (3,500 word) limit.

10% Technical Clarity and Conciseness

A: Methods, Results, and Conclusions are technically clear and concise.

B: Minor lapses in technical clarity or occasional extraneous technical points.

C: Significant lapses in clarity and conciseness, but clear enough to assess results and conclusions.

D: So unclear that results or conclusions cannot be assessed.

20% Conceptual Correctness

A: Thorough investigation of at least one topic, authors demonstrate a clear understanding of this topic, and there are no technical errors.

B: Thorough investigation of at least one topic, and no technical errors.

C: Thorough investigation of at least one topic, but one or more minor technical errors.

D: Investigations are insufficiently thorough (e.g., measured too few cases to support a trend) or contained major technical errors.

30% Insightfulness

> A: Clever experimental design, compelling experimental results, and imaginative analysis.
>
> B: Clever experimental design, compelling experimental results, or imaginative analysis.
>
> C: Acceptable experimental design, adequate experimental results, and acceptable analysis.
>
> D: Unacceptable experimental design, inadequate experimental results, or unacceptable analysis.

Acknowledgment: This research was approved by the MIT Committee on the Use of Human Subjects as Experimental Subjects, and all participants identified have given informed consent for the information presented. The work in Quantitative Physiology was supported by grants from the School of Engineering, the Department of Electrical Engineering and Computer Science, and the Division of Health Sciences and Technology. It was also supported by the National Science Foundation (NSF) VaNTH ERC. The work in teamwork and collaboration was supported by the NSF DUE Grant 0341127 for Rigorous Research in Engineering Education. The authors would like to thank the faculty, who have been their colleagues, contributors, and guides in the courses discussed in this article. The authors also would like to thank the students who have graciously helped them understand more about their learning of science and engineering communication.

REFERENCES

[1] R. Williams. (2003, Jan. 24). Education for the profession formerly known as engineering. *Chronicle of Higher Education.* [Online]. Available: http://chronicle.com/weekly/v49/i20/20b01201.htm

[2] L. Lynn and H. Salzman, "The real global technology challenge," *Change: The Magazine of Higher Learning,* vol. 39, no. 4, pp. 8–13, 2007.

[3] A. Herrington and C. Moran, *Genre Across the Curriculum.* Logan, UT: Utah State Univ. Press, 2005.

[4] C. Anson, Ed., *WAC Casebook: Scenes for Faculty Reflection and Program Development.* New York: Oxford Univ. Press, 2002.

[5] M. Segall and R. Smart, *Direct From the Disciplines: Writing Across the Curriculum.* Portsmouth, NH: Boynton/Cook, 2005.

[6] C. Thaiss and T. M. Zawacki, *Engaged Writers and Dynamic Disciplines: Research on the Academic Writing Life.* Portsmouth, NH: Boynton/Cook, 2006.

[7] National Academy of Engineering, *The Engineer of 2020: Visions of Engineering in the New Century.* Washington, DC: National Academy Press, 2004.

[8] Office of the Communication Requirement at MIT, MIT Undergraduate Communication Requirement: About the Requirement. [Online]. Available: http://web.mit.edu/commreq/background.html

[9] J. Leydens and B. M. Olds, "Publishing in scientific and engineering contexts: A course for graduate students," *IEEE Trans. Prof. Commun.,* vol. 50, no. 1, pp. 45–56, Mar., 2007.

[10] J. Bransford, A. Brown, and R. Cocking, Eds., *How People Learn: Brain, Mind, Experience, and School.* Washington, DC: National Academy Press, 2000.

[11] L. J. Shuman, M. Besterfield-Sacre, and J. McGourty, "The ABET 'professional skills' — Can they be taught? Can they be assessed?" *J. Eng. Edu.,* vol. 94, no. 1, pp. 41–55, 2005.

[12] J. P. Gee, D. Barton, M. Hamilton, and R. Ivanic, Eds., "The new literacy studies: From 'socially situated' to the work of the social," in *Situated Literacies: Reading and Writing in Context*. London: Routledge, 2000, pp. 180–196.

[13] A. Collins, J. S. Brown, and S. E. Newman, "Cognitive apprenticeship: Teaching the crafts of reading, writing, and mathematics," in *Knowing, Learning, and Instruction: Essays in Honor of Robert Glaser*, L. B. Resnick, Ed. Hillsdale, NJ: Erlbaum, 1989, pp. 453–494.

[14] J. Lave, "Teaching, as learning, in practice," *Mind, Culture, and Activity*, vol. 3, no. 3, pp. 149–164, 1996.

[15] D. P. Dannels, "Learning to be professional: Technical classroom discourse, practice, and professional identity construction," *J. Bus. Tech. Commun.*, vol. 14, no. 1, pp. 5–37, 2000.

[16] N. Artemeva, S. Logie, and J. St-Martin, "From page to stage: How theories of genre and situated learning help introduce engineering students to discipline-specific communication," *Tech. Commun. Quart.*, vol. 8, no. 3, pp. 301–316, 1999.

[17] M. J. Luzon, "Genre analysis in technical communication," *IEEE Trans. Prof. Commun.*, vol. 48, no. 3, pp. 285–295, Sep., 2005.

[18] K. Walker, "Using genre theory to teach students engineering lab report writing," *IEEE Trans. Prof. Commun.*, vol. 42, no. 1, pp. 12–19, Mar., 1999.

[19] B. A. Brown, J. M. Reveles, and G. J. Kelly, "Scientific literacy and discursive identity: A theoretical framework for understanding science learning," *Sci. Edu.*, vol. 89, no. 5, pp. 779–802, 2005.

[20] MIT Biological Engineering, Undergraduate and graduate educational programs. [Online]. Available: http://web.mit.edu/be/education/index.htm

[21] Massachusetts Institute of Technology. 20.109(S07): Start-Up Genome Engineering. [Online]. Available: http://openwetware.org/wiki/20.109%28S07%29:Start-up_genome_engineering#Introduction

[22] N. Wade, "Genetic engineers who don't just tinker," *New York Times*, Jul. 8, 2007. [Online]. Available: http://www.nytimes.com/2007/07/08/weekinreview/08wade.html?ref=weekinreview (accessed Jul. 13, 2007).

[23] L. Y. Chan, S. Kosuri, and D. Endy, "Refactoring bacteriophage T7," *Molecular Systems Biology*, vol. 1, 2005, Article 0018.

[24] P. Lewis, D. Aldridge, and P. M. Swamidass, "Assessing teaming skills acquisition on undergraduate project teams," *J. Eng. Edu.*, vol. 82, no. 2, pp. 149–155, 1998.

[25] Engineering Accreditation Commission, *Engineering Criteria 2000: Criteria for Accrediting Programs in Engineering in the United States*, 2nd ed. Baltimore, MD: Accreditation Board for Engineering and Technology, 1998.

[26] L. C. Schmidt, J. A. Schmidt, P. E. Smith, D. I. Bigio, and J. B. Contardo, *Building Engineering Student Team Effectiveness and Management Systems: A Curriculum Guide for Faculty*. Knoxville, TN: College House Enterprises, 2005.

[27] M. L. Loughry, M. W. Ohland, and D. D. Moore. (2007, Jul.). Development of a Theory-Based Assessment of Team Member Effectiveness [Online]. Available: https://engineering.purdue.edu/CATME/E.1.10.pdf

[28] M. W. Ohland, R. A. Layton, M. L. Loughry, and A. G. Yuhasz, "Effects of behavioral anchors on peer evaluation reliability," *J. Eng. Edu.*, vol. 94, no. 3, pp. 319–326, 2005.

[29] K. H. Schulz and D. K. Ludlow, "Incorporating group writing instruction in engineering courses," *J. Eng. Edu.*, vol. 85, no. 3, pp. 227–232, 1996.

[30] Department of Aeronautics and Astronautics, Massachusetts Institute of Technology, Experimental Projects Lab I and II: Subject Syllabus for Spring, 2007.

[31] K. A. Smith, *Teamwork and Project Management*, 3rd ed. New York, NY: McGraw-Hill, 2007.

[32] C. P. Coleman and J. L. Craig, "Using teamwork and communication skills to monitor and strengthen the effectiveness of undergraduate aerospace engineering design projects," *Proc. 2004 American Society for Engineering Education Annual Conf. and Exposition* [Online]. Available: http://www.asee.org/acPapers/2004-713_Final.pdf

[33] P. B. Lowry, J. F. Nunamaker, A. Curtis, and M. R. Lowry, "The impact of process structure on novice, virtual collaborative writing teams," *IEEE Trans. Prof. Commun.*, vol. 48, no. 4, pp. 341–364, Dec., 2005.

[34] R. Coger and H. D. De Silva, "An integrated approach to teaching biotechnology and bioengineering to an interdisciplinary audience," *Int. J. Eng. Edu.*, vol. 15, no. 4, pp. 256–264, 1999.

[35] J. Robinson, "Engineering thinking and rhetoric," *J. Eng. Edu.*, vol. 87, no. 8, pp. 227–229, 1998.

[36] C. Gillen, "Criticism and interpretation: Teaching the persuasive aspects of research articles," *CBE Life Sci. Edu.*, vol. 5, no. 1, pp. 34–38, 2006.

[37] R. Driver, P. Newton, and J. Osborne, "Establishing the norms of scientific argumentation in classrooms," *Sci. Edu.*, vol. 84, no. 3, pp. 287–312, 2000.

[38] E. R. Tufte, *The Visual Display of Quantitative Information*, 2nd ed. Cheshire, CT: Graphics Press, 2001.

[39] J. Fahnestock, "Verbal and visual parallelism," *Written Commun.*, vol. 20, no. 2, pp. 123–152, 2003.

[40] P. B. Childers and M. J. Lowry. (2005). Connecting visuals to written text and written text to visuals in science. *Across the Disciplines* [Online]. Available: http://wac.colostate.edu/atd/visual/childers_lowry.cfm

[41] M. Mathison, S. Mitchell, and R. Andrews, Eds., "'I don't have to argue my design — The visual speaks for itself': A case study of mediated activity in an introductory mechanical engineering course," in *Learning to Argue in Higher Education*. Portsmouth, NH: Boynton/Cook Heinemann, 2000, pp. 74–84.

[42] J. Swales, *Genre Analysis: English in Academic and Research Settings*. New York: Cambridge Univ. Press, 1990.

[43] C. Bazerman, "Physicists reading physics: Schema-laden purposes and purpose-laden schema," *Written Commun.*, vol. 2, no. 1, pp. 3–23, 1985.

[44] C. Berkenkotter and T. Huckin, *Genre Knowledge in Disciplinary Communication: Cognition/Culture/Power*. Hillsdale, NJ: Lawrence Erlbaum Assoc., 1995.

[45] J. Burrough-Boenisch, "International reading strategies for IMRD articles," *Written Commun.*, vol. 16, no. 3, pp. 296–316, 1999.

[46] Office of Research Integrity, US Department of Health and Human Services. RCR educational resources [Online]. Available: http://ori.hhs.gov/education/rcr_resources.shtml

[47] D. Benos, J. Fabres, J. Farmer, J. P. Gutierrez, K. Hennessy, D. Kosek, J. H. Lee, D. Olteanu, T. Russell, F. Shaikh, and K. Wang, "Ethics and scientific publication," *Advanced Physiology Edu.*, vol. 29, no. 2, pp. 59–74, 2005.

[48] D. Freeman. Microfluidics Project Laboratory: 6.021J Quantitative Physiology, Department of Electrical Engineering and Computer Science, Massachusetts Institute of Technology [Online]. Available: http://ocw.mit.edu/NR/rdonlyres/Electrical-Engineering-and-Computer-Science/6021JFall-2004/4D3EE567-3054-425E-B5C870ACEA441AB1/0/micfluiprolab_03.pdf

[49] D. Freeman, Note to students about microfluidics drafts: Quantitative Physiology, Massachusetts Institute of Technology, Cambridge, MA, 2006.

[50] M. Cochran-Smith and S. L. Lytle, *Inside/Outside: Teacher Research and Knowledge*. New York: Teachers College Press, 1993.

PART FOUR

Expanding the Locus of WAC

Introduction to Part Four

The readings included in this section illustrate a WAC principle articulated by program leaders since its inception: to echo Barbara Walvoord, WAC must "dive in or die." That is, WAC must participate in other cross-curricular initiatives and reforms, develop close relationships with writing centers and centers for teaching excellence, and work closely with composition program directors. As the writing students do in their disciplines — and writing itself — are being transformed by e-technologies, Web 2.0, and multimedia, WAC continues to evolve and now encompasses communication across the curriculum (CAC) and electronic communication across the curriculum (ECAC). WAC endures because it adapts and responds to different institutional environments and structures; to new institutional exigencies (e.g., the move to internationalization and the greater numbers of second language writers we meet in our classes); to advances in writing technologies and always expanding communicative spaces; and to ever louder and more incessant calls to assess students' writing competence, typically, and somewhat ironically, in the traditional forms and formats that WAC has all along attended to. In addition to the selections included here, we encourage readers to explore WAC links to service learning (see Jolliffe and Deans), writing fellows and course/curriculum-based tutors (see Haring-Smith and Soven), writing in hybrid and distance courses (see Neff and Whithaus), and the large body of work on "WAC wired" (see Reiss, Selfe, and Young).

The first article in this section, Leslie Roberts's "Writing Across the Curriculum and Writing Centers in Two-Year College English Programs," represents the much smaller body of WAC work in community colleges. In her 2008 survey of WAC programs and writing centers at community colleges in the United States, Roberts describes a mixed picture of success. Her survey shows that WAC programs, primarily in the form of writing courses, linked courses, and learning communities, are a force on only about 20 percent of community college campuses. Perhaps even more disappointing are the high levels of dissatisfaction with existing programs at two-year colleges. Roberts's survey results do provide evidence of the strong relationship between WAC and community college writing centers, which have also served as important allies for WAC program leaders at four-year institutions. The message, how-ever, is clear: a great deal of work remains for faculty and administrators who are interested in investigating how writing across the curriculum can support the achievement of the vocational, transfer, and other goals associated with the unique and valuable missions of community colleges.

Though WAC and writing centers seem to be natural allies, Michael Pemberton's "Rethinking the WAC/Writing Center Connection" reconsiders "this arranged marriage," which, he worries, is a demonstration of administrative expediency rather than a relationship based on a careful analysis of the goals and purposes of the two programs. If WAC rejects the idea of a generalized academic discourse and focuses instead on written genres as situated and so-cially mediated actions, then what role, he asks, should the "generic" writing tutor play? Neither "conscious myopia" about differences nor the "myth of disciplinarity" — that undergraduates are being asked in their assignments to engage in disciplinary conversations — are useful ways to think about the role of writing centers in supporting WAC goals. Instead, Pemberton explains how writing centers can help students by offering them ways out of these "representational dead-ends."

If the writing center is a space for intersecting goals and conversations about the nature of disciplinarity, then Rebecca Nowacek's "Why Is Being Interdisciplinary So Very Hard to Do?" describes both the transformative promise and the pitfalls that inhere in interdisciplinarity. Because interdis-ciplinary learning communities, usually in the form of linked courses, work at the "intersections" of disciplines, she argues, they have the power to trans-form the participants' understanding of disciplinary genres and the activity systems in which they circulate. To frame her analysis of a team-taught inter-disciplinary course, she draws on David Russell and Arturo Yañez's CHAT (cultural historical activity theory) analysis of the writing "double binds" students experienced in an introductory history class. In contrast to the activ-ity system operating in the history example, Nowacek suggests, an interdisci-plinary model gives teachers the opportunity to make the rhetorical dimen-sions of their disciplines visible and to negotiate the contradictions. As she shows, however, the promise of this interdisciplinary pedagogy was under-mined by the three participating teachers' desire to elide difference and em-phasize similarity (Nowacek calls this strategy "convergence and connection") as a way to get along with each other and avoid confusing students.

"Teaching and Learning a Multimodal Genre in a Psychology Course," by Chris Anson, Deanna Dannels, and Karen St. Clair — from composition, communication, and psychology respectively — exemplifies the collaborative goals of communication across the curriculum in its focus on negotiations that occurred around a multimodal assignment. The authors describe and theorize multimodality and hybrid genres to contextualize their analysis of the peda-gogical rational for the assignment, the decisions students made about how to approach the assignment, and the work they turned in, all of which lead the authors to ask questions about whether multimodal genre assignments will help students develop a more complex understanding of the communication genres they will likely encounter in professional contexts.

This section concludes with three very different articles that each ask similar questions about the inclusiveness of WAC pedagogies, how we can best support student writers across the curriculum, and how, as Mike Palmquist's article describes, we might create a campuswide community of writers and teachers of writing. In "Notes on the Evolution of Network Support for Writing Across the Curriculum," Palmquist explains how a focus on creating this community at his institution led to extensive use of networked support for WAC, including the WAC Clearinghouse and multimedia technologies. In tracing the evolution of electronic communication across the curriculum (ECAC) Palmquist shows that, while WAC practitioners did not immediately embrace computers, writing centers moved relatively quickly to provide a wide range of writing services through online writing labs (OWLs), which, subsequently, served as a model for the online writing center he and his colleagues established at Colorado State, featuring MOOs and web forums.

With "Beyond the L2 Metaphor: Towards a Mutually Transformative Model of ESL/WAC Collaboration" by Paul Kei Matsuda and Jeffrey Jablonski, we turn to an increasingly vital WAC imperative to engage with the scholarship and pedagogy of second language (L2) writing. As we think about the ways in which the locus of WAC has expanded, we cannot afford to ignore the growing presence of multilingual, immigrant, and international student writers. Matsuda and Jablonski scrutinize the misconception that learning to write in the disciplines is like learning a second language, a comparison popularized by Lucille McCarthy's "A Stranger in Strange Lands," her study of one student's encounters with the strange languages of disciplinary discourses. While the comparison has been useful for getting L2 and WAC specialists to draw on one another's work, Matsuda and Jablonski argue that it also oversimplifies second language learning and risks further marginalizing L2 writers in our courses and L2 issues in our WAC programs.

Concerns about marginalized writers are also at the center of "Exploring Notions of Genre in 'Academic Literacies' and 'Writing Across the Curriculum,'" an article comparing US WAC to the academic literacies (ACLITS) movement in the UK, written by David Russell and Tiane Donahue in collaboration with scholar-researchers Mary Lea, Jan Parker, and Brian Street from the UK. The chapter describes similarities in the impetus for and ideologies motivating both WAC and ACLITS, that is, the greater numbers of previously excluded groups being admitted to institutions of higher education and a perceived need to standardize their writing. In their analysis of key structural differences, the authors provide valuable insights into the history and underlying reasons for WAC's focus on teaching with writing and ACLITS's on genre theory and language/literacy research. More importantly, the article provides a clear example of how WAC's scholarship addresses urgent areas of interest in higher education around the world.

WORKS CITED

Deans, Tom. "Writing Across the Curriculum and Community Service Learning: Correspondences, Cautions, and Futures." *Writing the Community: Concepts and Models for Service-Learning in Composition.* Ed. Linda Adler-Kassner, Robert Crooksa, and Ann Watters. Washington, DC: AAHE, 1997. 29–38. Print.

Haring-Smith, Tori. "Changing Students' Attitudes: Writing Fellows Programs." *Writing Across the Curriculum: A Guide to Developing Programs.* Ed. Susan H. McLeod and Margot Soven. Newbury Park: Sage, 1992/2000. 123–31. Web. 4 Nov. 2010.

Jolliffe, David. "Writing across the Curriculum and Service Learning: Kairos, Genre and Collaboration." *WAC for the New Millennium: Strategies for Continuing Writing-Across-the-Curriculum Programs.* Ed. Susan H. McLeod, Eric Miraglia, Margot Soven, and Christopher Thaiss. Urbana: NCTE, 2001. 179–99. Print.

McCarthy, Lucille. "A Stranger in Strange Lands: A College Student Writing across the Curriculum." *Research in the Teaching of English* 21 (1987): 233–65. Print.

Neff, Joyce Magnotto, and Carl Whithaus. *Writing Across Distances and Disciplines: Research and Pedagogy in Distributed Learning.* Florence: Routledge, 2007. Print.

Reiss, Donna, Dickie Selfe, and Art Young, eds. *Electronic Communication Across the Curriculum.* Urbana: NCTE, 1998. Web. 22 Apr. 2010.

Russell, David R., and Arturo Yañez. " 'Big picture people rarely become historians': Genre Systems and the Contradictions of General Education." *Writing Selves/Writing Societies: Research from Activity Perspectives.* Ed. Charles Bazerman and David R. Russell. 2003. *The WAC Clearinghouse.* Web. 22 Apr. 2010.

Soven, Margot. "Curriculum-Based Peer Tutors and WAC." *WAC for the New Millennium: Strategies for Continuing Writing-Across-the-Curriculum Programs.* Ed. Susan H. McLeod, Eric Miraglia, Margot Soven, and Christopher Thaiss. Urbana: NCTE, 2001. 200–32. Print.

Walvoord, Barbara Fassler. "The Future of WAC." *College English* 58 (1996): 58–91. Print.

20 Writing Across the Curriculum and Writing Centers in Two-Year College English Programs

LESLIE ROBERTS

INTRODUCTION

In 2005, supported by a CCCC Research Initiative Grant and Two-Year College English Association (TYCA) volunteers, the TYCA Research Initiative Committee distributed the first national survey of two-year college writing programs. This online survey explored two-year college programs and satisfaction within four areas identified in the CCCC grant proposal: Assessment, Technology and Pedagogy, Writing Across the Curriculum and Writing in the Disciplines (WAC/WID), and Teaching Conditions. The goals were to identify shared challenges and effective practices in these key areas, suggest potential areas for research, and provide a foundation for advocacy on local, state, and national levels.

The survey offered seventy-four closed and open-ended questions. To ensure a significant number of responses, TYCA National distributed the survey to all of its members, TYCA Regional Committees contacted colleges in their regions, and the TYCA Research Committee Chair and her assistant contacted colleges in low-response areas. If a college submitted two responses, only the earliest response was included in the survey count. Overall, we received 338 responses from across the nation, so the data reported represent the responses of roughly 338 two-year colleges. All fifty states are represented, with a fairly even breakdown between urban (21%), rural (22%), suburban (27%), and multisite campuses (30%) (Survey Question 4).

Our survey data, we believe, provide a unique snapshot of our profession at work at a particular historical moment. This analysis of the WAC/WID section of the survey, however, is not meant to be definitive or viewed as a reading endorsed by either CCCC or TYCA. As in the other analyses of core sections published in *Teaching English in the Two-Year College* (TETYC), findings presented here are one possible reading of the data, in what we hope to be an ongoing dialogue with teacher-scholars.[1]

From *Teaching English in the Two-Year College* 36.2 (2008): 138–52.

As a graduate student at San Francisco State University (SFSU) in the 1980s, I participated in a local assessment initiative know as JEPET, the Junior English Proficiency Exam, an assessment, devised in response to a study of student writing abilities and undertaken in the 1960s at Dartmouth, which showed that most students were more competent writers just after having completed their first-year writing courses, but that their writing ability steadily declined after that. As a primarily commuter institution, SFSU also had large numbers of transfer students and part-time students, for whom the years between first-year composition completion and junior status could often be greater than two. I taught the first-year composition sequence, as well as the junior-level expository writing course for students who didn't pass JEPET, a course that gave students additional writing experience and instruction, along with what they may have been getting across the rest of the curriculum. At that time, SFSU did not have an integrated WAC program, but it did have this assessment initiative as a way to address the student learning outcomes in written communication beyond general education requirements and the first-year composition sequence. Some of my own first-year composition students needed and could clearly have benefited from more practice and feedback than they had received in the two-semester first-year composition sequence. JEPET failure was not necessarily an indictment of the student's first-year composition experience.

Two decades later, I recalled those experiences as a department chair of English at the Orchard Ridge Campus of Oakland Community College (OCC), when I was asked to comment on the average-to-poor performance of OCC students who had taken the ACT CAAP essay. Although the reasons for poor performance were more complex than I have space to outline here, the chairs of all four campus English departments, as well as the director of the Office of Assessment and Institutional Effectiveness, agreed that the poor showing was not necessarily an indictment of the first-year composition sequence at OCC; instead, we pondered the tendency of skills to deteriorate when they are not used often, which can be the case with part-time students, who take more time to complete even associate's degrees, as well as students whose course-work had not required much writing. How could faculty across the curriculum improve student learning in the area of effective written communication? We needed a coordinated, collegewide WAC program, one that generated faculty interest and provided ongoing professional development for all faculty to increase the amount and types of writing in their classes and to be confident and willing to respond to and assess student writing. What two-year college had a model that we might examine to create such a program? Although I was a member of TYCA for well over a decade, a frequent attendee at CCCC, and a regular reader of *College Composition and Communication* and TETYC, I knew of only one two-year college in the Midwest region with an established, comprehensive, institutionalized WAC program, with fully funded and extensive ongoing professional development for faculty across the disciplines, release time for collegewide coordination, and a curriculum process and general education requirement for students (graduates must have taken at least one writing intensive course in addition to the first-year composition sequence). And, although the one program that I knew of was an impressive one, surely there were more two-year college WAC program models. I was eager when the opportunity presented itself to volunteer to undertake the analysis of the WAC/WID portion for the 2005 TYCA national survey. I saw this as a chance to learn about what I assumed were many WAC initiatives and WAC program assessment models that had been developed or perfected since the 1980s, as well as an opportunity to find a comprehensive model that I could adapt for my institution.

A brief review of the literature recounting the history of WAC and WID initiatives did not deter me; instead, it reminded me that college WAC programs grew out of the writing process movement and came into their own in the 1970s and 1980s (for one review of WAC history, see Fulwiler and Young). In a general sense, WAC encourages faculty in all disciplines to integrate writing into courses in all content areas; faculty in many disciplines share the work of helping students become better writers, avoiding that previously mentioned decline in skills, as well as using writing as a tool for learning. Two-year college WAC programs had been part of the rich history of WAC. In 1987, Stout and Magnotto collected data on WAC efforts by conducting a survey of the 1,270 two-year community colleges in the United States. With a slightly higher response rate than the 2005 TYCA survey response rate, their survey counted 121 respondents who reported that their institution had a WAC program.

Unfortunately, 121 two-year college WAC programs in 1987 appears to have been a heyday of sorts. Although Stout and Magnotto did not report levels of faculty satisfaction with those programs, the sheer number suggests that WAC programs were, at the very least, more prevalent than they appear to be now. Section IV of the 2005 TYCA survey asked ten questions overall about the existence, structure, and overall satisfaction with WAC programs and initiatives and with two-year college writing centers. (See Appendix A.) Although the survey asked a small number of questions with a narrow focus, nonetheless, a few dominant trends among the respondents' comments can be discerned. The majority of the comments suggest the dearth of institutionally integrated, fully funded, coordinated programs as the main reason that a majority of two-year college faculty report being at least somewhat dissatisfied with their institution's approach to integrating WAC. Writing centers were clearly noted as a source of satisfaction, but that satisfaction did not seem to have been prominent in respondents' minds when they reported their overall satisfaction with their institution's approach to WAC/WID.

SURVEY DATA ON WAC/WID PROGRAMS AND INITIATIVES

Faculty in two-year colleges responding to the survey report that WAC is not often delivered as a sustainable program that touches all students in a two-year college. Table 20-1, based on the response to question 40, "Does your college have an institutionally designated Writing Across the Curriculum or

Writing in the Disciplines program?" shows a very small percentage of WAC/WID programs at respondents' institutions. (Some of the explanations for the apparent decline since 1987, at least in institutionalized programs, are discussed later in the essay.)

One of the difficulties faced by two-year colleges is developing college-wide programs that effectively serve students with the variety of goals found at a multiple mission community college. Table 20-2, which indicates the range of responses to question 42, "What programs are directly served if your institution has a WAC/WID program?" shows that, despite the multiple missions of the two-year college, where WAC programs exist, almost twice as many serve transfer students as serve vocational students. (Question 41 was meant to be a follow-up to question 40, in which 63 respondents reported having a WAC program. The number of responses greater than 63 in Table 20-2 is attributed to the fact that respondents were able to mark multiple intents.)

Not all two-year colleges offer honors programs, which likely accounts for the small number of WAC programs that serve honors students, and the comments under "other" did not establish a trend or identify different populations as much as they became a site where respondents began talking about general future plans or past experiences, which they may have repeated or elaborated on when they reached question 48. And, although there were 196

TABLE 20-1   WAC/WID Programs in Two-Year Colleges ($n = 342$)

Type of program	Percentage of colleges	Number of responses
Institutionally designated WAC/WID Program	18	63
No institutionally designated WAC/WID	82	279

At the time of this analysis, 346 responses to the survey had been submitted, but not all 346 answered the questions in this section.

TABLE 20-2   Programs Served by WAC/WID in Two-Year Colleges ($n = 63$)

Program intent	Number of responses	Percentage of responding institutions
Vocational	28	44
Transfer	49	78
Honors	23	37
Other*	25	40

*"Other," in this case, included learning communities and developmental courses or information on plans to develop a program.
Numbers represent those institutions that have a WAC program; however, respondents could mark multiple responses.

comments of some type to the open-ended question about overall satisfaction with the institutional approach to WAC, very few spoke to the demographics of the WAC population or to the issue of satisfaction with which populations were served as a source of dissatisfaction. None celebrated the success or breadth of populations served by an existing program, but a few lamented attempts to establish standards, or lack thereof. "The entire faculty voted to adopt statewide standards for a 'C' paper, but many faculty, especially in the vocational division, give it only lip service." Another response by an English faculty member suggests the problem is that institutions overall, including many faculty, do not envision WAC for Applied Science degree candidates: "A school like ours needs a program that shows how composition MATTERS [emphasis by respondent], even when they want to be landscapers and electricians," and "It is clear that even some of the instructors in non-transfer curriculums feel that writing is not that important."

When the survey was devised, the authors suspected that some faculty were achieving some of the goals of WAC without integrated, institutionalized, collegewide WAC programs. Interdisciplinary learning communities and paired course delivery methods are components of existing WAC programs (those with ongoing professional development, coordination, assessment, and program integration), but they are also common in institutions that don't have the fully integrated program model. Table 20-3 indicates how respondents to question 42 described how their institution's WAC program was delivered. It is possible that the number of respondents grew beyond 63 if, between questions 40 and 42, some respondents answered the question not based on their answer to question 40 or came to believe that their efforts should be labeled a program. Table 20-3, however, assumes that only the 63 respondents who said their institution had a program responded, and respondents are reporting the use of more than one delivery method, accounting for the total response number greater than 63 and total percentages greater than 100 percent. Additional research during Phase II of this project pointed to the fact that some WAC programs are primarily professional development programs for faculty who have not employed any of these delivery strategies.

TABLE 20-3   Delivery Methods among 63 WAC/WID Programs

Delivery method	Number of responses	Percentage of responding institutions
Writing intensive courses	34	54
Linked courses	16	25
Learning communities/academies	23	37
Cluster courses	8	13
Other*	25	40

*Discussed how the program was structured; no alternative delivery methods were identified. Respondents could select more than one delivery method.

The following analysis of comments suggests that whether or not the efforts at an institution are well-coordinated, well-supported, and well-integrated is a key factor in satisfaction, and many respondents comment on the existence of elements, but without coordination. Responses to question 43 (see Table 20-4) show a less bleak version of two-year college WAC. Institutions attempt to deliver WAC or achieve some of WAC's goals with learning communities, writing intensive courses, and service learning initiatives — but without fully institutionalized programs.

WRITING CENTERS AS WAC INITIATIVES

Almost one-third of the nearly 200 open-ended comments about overall satisfaction mention that, although some of these delivery methods made WAC easier to attempt, there was still a need for more elements of a program, including release time for coordination, more attention to scheduling issues, and ongoing staff development. A few comments in particular spoke to the need for a model that better fit the scheduling needs of two-year college students: "We tried learning communities, but adopted a four-year model, which meant that if a student failed or dropped a course, she'd be dropped from the other(s). [. . .] the problem is student scheduling" and "learning communities often have trouble registering students correctly because we don't have an institutionalized procedure for doing so," or "the college has a BIG problem in scheduling linked courses [. . .] composition with other disciplines [. . .] they try, then the problems seem insurmountable, so they quit trying." It is also interesting to note that nearly one-third of the total number of survey respondents' comments in Table 20-4 reported that their institution offered learning communities, yet many of the comments about overall satisfaction in question 48 stated that interdisciplinary cooperation is a barrier to WAC pro-

TABLE 20-4   WAC Activities among Institutions without Programs ($n = 279$)

Delivery method	Number of responses	Percentage of responding institutions
Writing intensive courses	90	32
Linked courses	58	21
Learning communities/academies	108	39
Cluster courses	22	8
Assignments in core composition courses that simulate WAC/WID experiences	67	24
Other*	13	5

*Most comments under "other" discussed program planning or other elements of WAC programs, and there were no clear trends that identified another form of delivery. These "other" comments also mostly spoke to single English courses, writing center workshops, and plans to begin or revive a WAC program. Respondents could check more than one item.

grams. If the culture for interdisciplinary cooperation exists to create and sustain learning communities, perhaps the cooperation is a lesser factor and the real problem lies in willingness to assign or confidence in assessing written work, a deterrent to WAC mentioned in one-third of the comments. (More discussion of the overall satisfaction appears later in this essay.)

As part of the WAC section of the survey, respondents were also asked if their institutions operated writing centers, how those centers were administered (question 44), and what population was served there (question 45). Writing centers were often mentioned as WAC/WID initiatives that are a source of pride for many faculty, and a preponderance of respondents remarked on their institution's successful writing center, highly regarded by students, faculty, and staff alike.

One key factor in a center's success tends to be the administration. Table 20-5 reports the overall findings about what kinds of writer centers exist on two-year college campuses.

Brief follow-up surveys that I conducted with the small number of centers nominated as exemplary pointed to a mix of personnel in the writing center, drawing on full-time and part-time faculty, as well as student tutors, as contributing to success. Staff credentials were also mentioned as important. Pennington and Gardner recommend that writing center directors be English faculty members who have been given release time from a significant part of their loads in preference to directors with no specific training in composition. Comments in the TYCA research initiative survey echoed this preference, and the most satisfied respondents were those whose centers were supervised by English department faculty: "Our center is progressive and effective because the director keeps abreast of methodology and theory in Writing Centers." Sometimes, however, supervising a writing center, in addition to teaching load, is too much for an English faculty member: "Directing the writing center should be a full-time job; our composition program chair is director and has very little time to hire professionals, train tutors, and oversee the center."

The survey also found that almost all writing centers were truly WAC initiatives. Question 45 asked whom the writing center served; Table 20-6 shows the degree to which these centers serve the entire college community.

TABLE 20-5 Writing Centers and Center Directors (*n* = 338)

Center and director	Percentage of colleges	Number of responses
Yes, a center directed by a member of the English language arts faculty	54	181
Yes, but director need not have specialized training in ESL, composition, or English	24	81
No writing center	23	76

TABLE 20-6   Writing Centers as WAC Initiatives ($n = 267$)

Population served	Percentage of colleges	Number of responses
Center serves only ESL	1	2
Center serves only students in college-designated composition or writing program	4	10
Center serves only English language arts students	3	9
Center serves students from all disciplines with writing assignments	92	246

More than two hundred respondents made comments that shine light on the success of two-year college writing centers. Among the many trends, several elements are repeatedly mentioned as keys to success:

- Adequate resources overall and, more specifically, staffing, were key. Many comments praised having directors who were full-time, well-paid tutors with bachelor's or master's degrees in English, in addition to peer tutors: "Ours includes paid and volunteer students, faculty, and community tutors."

- Curriculum variety was desirable. Faculty were most impressed that many centers had a strong online presence for distance education students, and many spoke to the services provided to English Language Learners (ELLs). Successful centers mix services, credit and noncredit, for students and, often, for the larger community.

- Options were also important. Individual tutorials and workshops on high-demand skills were cited as parts of a successful mix: "Our center is pretty innovative. We have an online lab, specialized tutors in ESL, and it serves students from any discipline. We even have some community outreach programs." Another pleased respondent reported: "The writing center offers consultations with any student in any discipline, a variety of writing and grammar workshops, and poetry and short fiction writing contests culminating in a coffeehouse." Some comments suggested expansion from "drop in" tutoring to a more comprehensive model.

- Marketing matters. The image of the center was also mentioned as critical for success, and several respondents mentioned maintaining an image that stresses the fact that the center is not a "fix it" shop. Keeping a high profile and documenting usage were also mentioned as essential means of accountability at institutions with increased competition for limited funds.

WRITING CENTER CHALLENGES

Despite the success of and pride in writing centers, budget cuts were mentioned frequently as the reason why many writing centers are cutting services and struggling to find space in which to operate, along with the staff to tackle projects: "Our writing center is wonderful, but they need more funding to reach more students." "Two people for 10,000. Nuffsaid?" Other challenges mentioned by survey respondents include adapting centers to the needs of ELLs and the growing demands for a virtual presence. Some centers nominated for exemplary practices were noted for having virtual components and service to online students. To meet those needs, respondents stressed finding ways to increase funding and staffing. Further research in the next phase of this project will attempt to examine in more detail how writing centers are serving online and ELL students.

Finding the physical space for expansion was also mentioned as a problem by some respondents. With many community colleges reaching quarter-century birthday marks, infrastructures are stretched and local communities often do not support expanded footprints or provide funds for renovation. Writing centers are too often confined to spaces they have outgrown.

OVERALL SATISFACTION RATES

The survey was designed to allow respondents to think about WAC/WID programs, initiatives such as learning communities that are often not part of integrated institutionalized WAC programs, and writing centers as all being elements of WAC (in questions 40–46) before they were asked in question 47 to indicate overall satisfaction with the college's approach to integrating WAC. Table 20-7 indicates that, despite the satisfaction with writing centers previously reported, the overall satisfaction was low among 333 faculty who rated their institution's approach to integrating WAC.

Fellow TYCA research initiative committee member Patrick Sullivan best characterized the overall nature of the comments by saying that respondents reported experiences that "were like something out of a Greek tragedy, telling a tale of humor and pathos, promise and despair." More than half of the responses expressed marked dissatisfaction with the college's approach to WAC. With 18 percent of 342 reporting that their institution had a WAC program and only 7 percent of 333 reporting being very satisfied with their institution's approach to WAC, a first concern is that even existing programs struggle to win the approval of English faculty or deans, who may have responded to the survey and sometimes lamented their own departmental attitudes and experiences with WAC. "Hard to get commitment from 'either

TABLE 20-7   Overall Satisfaction with Institution's Approach to WAC (*n* = 333)

Overall satisfaction	Percentage of colleges	Number of responses
Very dissatisfied	26	86
Somewhat dissatisfied	38	125
Somewhat satisfied	30	99
Very satisfied	7	23

side,'" one respondent said; others say, "Our faculty are too busy teaching to add WAC responsibilities to their load" and "even though we have a program, I don't know the extent of it." Another critique of an existing program was that "too many of the faculty teaching WAC-designated classes give watered-down writing assignments and offer little if any feedback about the quality of the writing. Not as effective as we had hoped."

Other comments lamented both the practical and theoretical, with the largest number of comments falling into three general and sometimes over-lapping categories: lack of specific kinds of administrative support to initiate or sustain efforts; lack of faculty enthusiasm in multiple disciplines or sup-port beyond English faculty, either to initiate or sustain efforts; and lack of ongoing development or coordination to sustain efforts.

Some lamented the loss of resources, which resulted in the loss of effec-tiveness if not the failure of the entire program: "We had a very strong WAC until the late 1990s when budget cuts led to expanded class size, and hence, less writing in non-English courses." Others cite a culture reluctant to allocate resources, such as release time for coordination, or incentives, such as smaller class size, for new WAC programs: "The English department and the admin-istration have periodically had the conversation about beginning a WAC pro-gram. [. . .] But the current administration doesn't seem to want to designate the time or the resources." In particular, smaller class size for writing inten-sive courses in disciplines characterized as large "lecture" delivery is often rejected. One response described how a particular initiative was truncated: "The college eliminated an entire summer's worth of work to develop a CAC program [. . .] in its place [they] gave release time to a few faculty to float around classes, if asked, to talk about reading and writing (and to point out in a recent accreditation report). Following the accreditation report, those posi-tions were eliminated."

A couple of interesting comments suggested that professional develop-ment for the WAC program needed a stronger focus on writing to explore, promote learning, and encourage critical thinking: "We've had CAC/WAC initiatives both fizzle without doing much to form a culture of writing. I think it's because we've neglected the theoretical dimensions in favor of practi-cal advice." Another response echoed this professional development issue: "Many discipline professors are put off because they think they are supposed to be English teachers [. . .] they aren't told how writing activities can enhance instruction."

One-third of the comments indicated that respondents think WAC is chal-lenged by faculty cooperation issues, including overall willingness to respond in depth to student writing, which was cited as a reason why initiatives fail and why they are not as successful as some might have hoped they would be: "Some faculty resist grading essay questions," and "only rarely does a course outside of English receive a writing emphasis designation [. . .] faculty in other disciplines are reluctant to require substantial writing," which some respondents attribute to "not feeling competent to teach or judge the quality of student writing." Other responses do not highlight confidence, which presumably could be increased with professional development: "Frankly, most other instructors balk at the idea of making the time-consuming act of grading writing a part of their courses" and "most of the other courses don't require much writing and most instructors outside of English use multiple-choice tests for assessment." WID "is led by one member of the English faculty with one course release per semester to coordinate it, but participation by faculty from other disciplines is voluntary, so if they don't want to incorporate writing into their courses, they don't have much incentive to do so." An even more contemptuous suggestion was that "English teachers become the scapegoats for weak [student] writing, and not requiring any writing gives other teachers an edge professionally. They have more time for career-building activities and their students love them and their Scantrons."

A surprisingly large number of comments, which could help explain the decline in actual programs since the previously reported survey in the 1980s, spoke to the frustration of sustaining efforts: "Although a lot of courses require writing assignments, there is no coordination to instill a best practices approach." Another response said, "We used to have one person who coordinated and promoted the WAC/Thinking Across the Curriculum program; since that person left, small pieces of the work have fallen on several different people, with little or no promotion of WI courses." Another comment on the lack of a coordinated program content read, "Our writing in context program is basically a few profs willing to add that designation to their classes with writing required. It's not a 'program,' and it needs a coordinator to evaluate these classes and encourage more linked classes." Others say that integrated and linked courses have results from faculty-to-faculty connections — but still no support for WAC programs.

One comment on a successful program summed up some of the critical elements for success: "I've worked on WAC for years and we have a critical mass of faculty who've received training and are integrating writing into their courses. Students have to take a 'rising junior' test at the 45th credit and need to pass it to graduate. It is an essay based on readings, and it has given a strong push to writing intensive training and courses. It helps that WI courses are all capped at 25 students." Others point to recent assessment initiatives as providing new interest or sustaining interest in WAC: "By assessing writing across the curriculum [. . .] writing in all courses has increased without a mandatory program." It is interesting to note that, in a 1990 publication, Young and Fulwiler identified similar enemies of WAC at many four-year institutions, including resistance from faculty, lack of faculty reward system, and unstable leadership.

ADVOCACY ISSUES AND QUESTIONS FOR FURTHER RESEARCH: WAC/WID PROGRAMS AND INITIATIVES

Responses to the survey's open-ended questions about WAC/WID did not often offer detailed information, or remarks that were positive or celebratory in tone, about the kinds of leadership, training, faculty incentives, or assessment programs needed to support WAC/WID programs. Therefore, Phase II of the WAC/WID portion of the project has focused on those aspects. Comments did suggest that assessment requirements and accreditation visits were generating new interest in WAC/WID programs at some institutions, and several colleagues commented on the college's recent development of rubrics for assessing writing in a variety of courses. One respondent reports that the "institutional writing outcome assessment process, with collection of artifacts scored by teams of faculty, has generated a successful and coopera-tive effort to improve writing across the curriculum." Another says, "We are looking at making effective writing a campus-wide learning outcome." In the follow-up phase, faculty have remarked that WAC program assessment strat-egies — such as grade distribution, course retention, and student surveys of satisfaction — were being examined to judge the efficacy of existing WAC programs. As more colleges reexamine general education programs and stu-dent outcomes assessment, there may be opportunity for WAC initiatives to meet with more success.

Some of the more candid comments suggest that many challenges remain. Working conditions — documented by Section V of the TYCA Research Initia-tive Survey of Writing Programs and reported at CCCC by research initiative committee member Lois Powers — probably may have or continue to have an effect on WAC/WID development and support. Many faculty have experi-enced reduction in travel and professional development funds or release time needed to develop new programs and administer existing ones. Faculty in other departments, with only a handful of full-time faculty and an increasing number of part-time faculty to mentor, find themselves spread too thin, with a small number of full-time faculty in any one department to serve as writing center directors, department chairs, and assessment coordinators: "The teach-ing duties would be acceptable if the Division were not inheriting so many additional duties — like the state-mandated general education assessment of speech, literature, and writing. We are required to assess major parts of our program every single year, and it's extremely wearing. Release time needs to be provided for all of these assessment tasks." "A five-course load [with] 24 students in each course — is a punishing load. In addition, there is no head of department or director of the writing program to supervise and coordinate, so either a few people take on extra responsibilities for no extra pay or things are left undone — like coordination with adjunct faculty, assessment, help for writing intensive faculty, etc." Others lament, "Our WAC program ended when grant funding was no longer available. Our writing faculty are too busy teaching five sections per term to add to their responsibilities" and "teaching five composition courses per semester, English faculty have little time to spearhead WAC training."

Although the final question of the section, question 49, provided respon-dents with the opportunity to identify a two-year college with best prac-tices in WAC/WID, few programs were initially nominated as exemplary by respondents, and even fewer respondents saw this as an opportunity to nominate exemplary writing centers. The research committee conducted brief follow-up e-mail interviews when enough information was provided to make contacts with a faculty member who was knowledgeable about a nominated program, in order to begin designing Phase II of the research project: interviewing WAC program coordinators more thoroughly about the elements and components of successful programs, as well as identifying additional WAC programs and writing centers beyond those nominated in the Phase I survey portion of the project. In these e-mail interviews, comments that helped shape Phase II of the study included how the programs were structured and coordinated, what kinds of professional development both launched and sustained them, and how program assessment was developing. Additional exemplary programs were nominated by these faculty. Interestingly, several faculty in this small sample attributed the institution's success with WAC to the nature of the program's initial development, often characterized as "grassroots, non-formalized, and non-mandated." Success in this case seemed to be predicated on dedication of a small but devoted group, allowing others who were not required to participate also not to feel threatened by this particular use of college resources. Two others were adamant about being supported by a majority of college faculty, and all were united in their insistence on departmental support (whether or not English department members were actually involved in the program). If the college had a writing center as part of a larger Academic Support Center (ASC) separate from the English department, support from that center was deemed crucial as well. Others stressed a systemwide commitment to WAC/WID, which exists in at least two systems (City University of New York and University of Hawaii were noted).

Phase II of the WAC portion of the research initiative, the results of which were previewed at CCCC in New Orleans in April 2008, collected narratives from a dozen institutions with WAC programs that began to clarify these and other areas for further study. To date, more questions remain beyond the scope of the Phase II project: Are WAC efforts more or less prevalent at large, single-campus institutions? at institutions in which developmental or ESL courses are taught in a department separate from the one that teaches the transfer composition sequence? at institutions with larger or smaller adjunct to full-time faculty ratios? at institutions with or without collective bargaining? Can WAC be sustained online? Does the increasing number of online courses suggest a need for effective reading strategies, as well as WAC? What technology issues (such as college e-mail accounts and server space) contribute to use of electronic portfolios? Does faculty knowledge and experience with electronic portfolios provide an environment more ripe for WAC initiatives in the immediate future? Or will electronic WAC portfolios further deepen the "digital divide" and call into question the issues of access that Jody Millward notes in her analysis of the technology portion of the TYCA survey of two-year college writing programs?

THE NEED FOR FURTHER STUDY

Educators in the two-year college face even greater challenges in securing adequate funding, reaching an ever-diverse student body, and assessing the effectiveness of programs for students to whom "success" might mean either moving on to another institution within a year or to full-time employment. Success cannot be measured in terms of numbers of graduates; the future successes of students who participate in programs such as WAC, at a two-year college in particular, cannot always be tracked in subsequent courses and semesters at other institutions. In addition to the diversity of student educational goals, student life circumstances make participating in many programs such as learning communities more difficult than for students at a residential institution. However, Stanley and Ambron were among those who wrote, more than a decade ago, that WAC strategies would be especially beneficial to two-year colleges — challenged by increasingly diverse student populations with vocational, developmental, and transfer goals — and could serve as a solution to the problem of fostering a sense of community in nonresidential, commuter settings. As two-year college faculty continue to revise general education outcomes and create and revise assessment programs, they will be continually reminded that — from the single vocational or developmental course to the full associate degree — effective communication and the critical thinking fostered by writing-to-learn activities are at the heart of the college curriculum. Exemplary WAC/WID programs should be of interest to all two-year college faculty, not just those teaching English.

Phase II of the WAC/WID portion of the TYCA research initiative will identify additional WAC programs and successful centers and delve more deeply into the details of exemplary WAC/WID initiatives.

NOTE

1. I would like to thank the members of the TYCA Research Committee, including David Wong (our research consultant), Lois Powers, Patrick Sullivan, Jane Wagoner, and Sterling Warner, and, for their leadership and attention to this section in particular, Lawrence McDoniel and Jody Millward.

APPENDIX A

Questions 40–49 on the 2005 TYCA National Survey of Two-Year College English Writing Programs dealt with WAC and writing centers.

40. Does your college have an institutionally designated WAC or WID program?

41. If yes, which programs (vocational, transfer, honors, other) are directly served?

42. If yes, how is the program structured? (See options, next question.)

43. If no, does it offer any of the following (writing intensive courses, linked courses, learning communities, cluster courses, assignments in core comp courses that simulate WAC experiences, other)?

44. Does your college have a writing center (directed by ENG faculty, directed by someone without ESL, Comp, or ENG training, no center)?

45. If yes, does the center (serve only ESL, serve only students in a designated program, serve only English/Language Arts, serve students from all disciplines)?

46. Provide additional comments about your writing center.

47. Indicate your satisfaction with your college's approach to integrating WAC (very satisfied, somewhat satisfied, somewhat dissatisfied, very dissatisfied).

48. Comment on your satisfaction with your college's approach to integrating WAC in the disciplines.

49. Identify a two-year college with best practices in administering its WAC program.

WORKS CITED

Fulwiler, Toby, and Art Young. "The WAC Archives Revisited." *Assessing Writing Across the Curriculum: Diverse Approaches and Practices.* Ed. Kathleen Blake Yancey and Brian Huot. Greenwich, CT: Ablex, 1997.

Millward, Jody. "An Analysis of the National 'TYCA Research Initiative Survey Section III: Technology and Pedagogy' in Two-Year College English Programs." *Teaching English in the Two-Year College* 35 (2008): 372–397.

Pennington, Jill, and Clint Gardner. "Position Statement on Two-Year College Writing Centers." *Teaching English in the Two-Year College* 33 (2006): 260–263.

Powers, Lois. "Myth and Reality: The Relationship of Teaching Conditions and the Academic Reality of Two-Year College Teacher-Scholars." Conference on College Composition and Communication. New York, 24 Mar. 2007.

Stout, Barbara R., and Joyce N. Magnotto. "Building on Realities: WAC Programs at Community Colleges." *Writing across the Curriculum in Community Colleges: New Directions for Community Colleges.* Ed. Linda C. Stanley and Joanna Ambron. San Francisco: Jossey-Bass, Inc., 1991.

Young, Art, and Toby Fulwiler. "The Enemies of Writing Across the Curriculum." *Programs That Work: Models and Methods for Writing Across the Curriculum.* Ed. Toby Fulwiler and Art Young. Portsmouth, NH: Heinemann-Boynton/Cook, 1990. 287–294.

21 Rethinking the WAC/Writing Center Connection

MICHAEL A. PEMBERTON

At first glance, it might be difficult to find two writing programs that seem to work together more harmoniously than Writing Across the Curriculum and writing centers. WAC engenders more writing in more classes, and writing centers help students to improve their writing skills and produce, presumably, better papers. Administratively, the two programs are often seen as complementary if not conjoined. If more writing is going to be demanded of more students in more classes, then those students will need additional support services as they work to complete their assignments. And though there may, in some cases, be the money and motivation necessary to create intra-departmental tutorial services for the benefit of students within each major, most often the responsibility for writing assistance either falls on (or is specifically delegated to) the campus writing center.

This approach may appear to have significant merit and may, in fact, be looked on with a good deal of satisfaction by interested parties on all sides. Administrators will likely be pleased because they won't have to create a brand-new support system for WAC; at most institutions, writing centers have generally been in place longer than WAC programs, and in some cases, writing centers may actually have been starting points for early writing across the curriculum efforts (Griffin 400). Faculty will generally be pleased because they have the somewhat illusory impression that writing centers will reduce the additional workload imposed by an increased number of writing assignments. And writing center directors will generally be pleased because their integral role in helping to implement and sustain WAC programs provides the center with more students coming in; an increased sense of budgetary and political security; and, in some cases, additional funding for tutors, supplies, and equipment. Difficulties are generally downplayed, and much of what is written about the relationship between WAC and writing centers concerns itself with descriptions of specific programs and the ways in which instructional articulation is played out. Dinitz and Howe, for example, describe the "evolving partnership" between WAC and writing centers at their respective

From *Writing Center Journal* 15.2 (1995): 116–33.

institutions, suggesting that some of the weaknesses in each institution's models can be fruitfully addressed through the use of "group critiques" (49–50). Ray Wallace, in a similar fashion, details the tutor-training program at the University of Tennessee, Knoxville, stressing the important links that need to be forged between the writing center and the disciplinary faculty; and Carino et al. and Walker echo this point of view. The popular and, perhaps, conveniently pragmatic impression seems to be that writing centers have, in some senses, *always* been writing-across-the-curriculum centers. They have always opened their doors to students working on writing projects for any classes that those students happen to be enrolled in, and they have always had to engage students on a wide variety of topics that vary on a daily, sometimes hourly, basis.

I would like to question, however, whether this arranged marriage between WAC and writing centers, enacted at a growing number of institutions across the country, demonstrates true love and a natural compatibility or merely a disturbing kind of administrative expediency. There are compelling reasons, I think, to reconsider the nature of the relationship between these two programs, particularly when WAC is construed as WID or Writing In the Disciplines.[1]

Though WAC and writing centers have clear pedagogical similarities in their joint focus on text production and writing-as-learning, their underlying epistemologies and resulting assumptions about what qualify as significant rhetorical and textual features remain strikingly different. Much of the current scholarship about WAC programs, for example, focuses on the diverse rhetorics which students are expected to master during their college careers. Drawing from the work of rhetorical and social theorists such as Burke, Foucault, Vygotsky, and Bakhtin, many composition scholars (Bartholomae, Bruffee, and McCarthy, among others) have situated WAC programs in the paradigm of polyvocalism, reflecting the diverse nature of specialized conversations in the "content-area" disciplines and rejecting the notion that a general-purpose "academic discourse" exists. WAC pedagogies often tend, therefore, to address the needs of multiple discourse communities, situated knowledge, and complex, socially-constructed conventions of language by treating each discipline as if it were a separate entity with its own set of practices to be explored.

Writing centers, on the other hand, seem grounded in an opposing set of assumptions, including the widely held tenet of practitioner lore that many aspects of text production (such as tone, awareness of audience, coherence, use of specific detail to support arguments, grammar, etc.) are "generic" in nature and, for the most part, extend across disciplinary boundaries. Tutors who work in writing centers are usually not trained as experts in the rhetoric of a particular discipline (other than their own), and they are expected to work with student writing in a wide variety of disciplines, many of which they may know very little about. Their ability to provide writing assistance to students working in specialized discourse communities often depends upon their ability to draw from their own experiences as writers and readers in a discipline, to work with the aspects of text production they interpret as "common" to virtually all academic texts, and then to apply these common principles to new and possibly unfamiliar academic subjects or genres. In this regard, then, writing center practice operates as if an "academic discourse" does indeed exist, a discourse that can be explained and utilized successfully in student conferences no matter which interpretive community a particular student might be addressing in a given paper. (See, for example, Clark 11–12.)

The epistemologies that inform each of these instructional programs are oppositional but not necessarily in direct conflict. The existence of situationally-embedded, discipline-specific features in academic texts may not, in itself, preclude the possibility that some "transdisciplinary" textual or rhetorical features also exist, features that might be addressed successfully by tutors in a writing center. The need to support generalizations with specific evidence, for example, may display some subtle variations depending upon the discipline and audience addressed in particular texts, but the fact that there must be *some* relationship between generalizations made and evidence offered in support is a feature common to virtually all academic writing. Other "generic" concerns such as sentence- and paragraph-level coherence are also potential subjects for tutorial conferences, and some higher-level rhetorical features which may be shaped only partially by disciplinary conventions — organization, evidence, logical development, tone, introductions, conclusions, etc. — can, perhaps, be discussed acontextually or as "general rules" that must be adapted to specific texts, audiences, or purposes.

Though this *pedagogy of the generic* can be a useful and effective approach for some students, assignments, and contexts (particularly first-year composition courses), I am concerned that it may do a disservice to students who are writing in a multidisciplinary WAC program, particularly because — as I indicated above — the central purpose of writing across the curriculum is to familiarize and train students to become fluent in exactly those discipline-specific rhetorical features that a "generic" writing center pedagogy is geared to overlook. Let me make clear that I do not wish to dismiss the generic pedagogy out of hand; I can envision a number of circumstances — particularly in the case of first-year composition students — when this particular approach and set of tutorial practices might be especially useful and appropriate. But in the context of a writing center that wishes to address the needs of students writing in a WAC program, this approach is insufficient.

My concern over this issue is exacerbated by what I see as compelling evidence that a number of WAC programs often fail to live up to their own foundational principles and slip carelessly into writing pedagogies that provide students, particularly undergraduates, few opportunities to rehearse disciplinary modes of inquiry or forms of discourse. The reasons for these institutional failures are many, but two of the most significant — *conscious myopia* and the *myth of disciplinarity* — may be especially pervasive and worthy of review. As I will show, these failures may actually make it easier for writing centers to work within WAC programs, and they certainly provide some justification for the generic tutorial approach described above. But they paint, I think, an incomplete and somewhat jaundiced picture of how WAC programs and writing centers might work together productively. The differing goals and epistemological perspectives advanced by WAC programs and writing centers will complicate any sort of pedagogical interrelationship we might wish to propose between them. We are obligated, therefore, to consider very carefully what social and instructional roles the writing center and its tutorial staff should assume in conferences with WAC students. These considerations will be the focus of the latter portion of this paper.[2]

Conscious Myopia

One disturbing yet all-too-common way that WAC and writing centers can work together is through a kind of *conscious myopia*, by simply choosing to ignore any problems, pretending they don't exist, or rationalizing them away. For most people, especially the instructors and students who are enmeshed in WAC programs and institutional requirements, this may be the easiest thing to do. Though WAC faculty training programs often work hard to stress the important role faculty play in constructing assignments and guiding students through the conventions of a new discipline, these lessons may be conveniently forgotten after the training is over, especially if they were never fully believed in the first place or if the practicalities of implementing WAC pedagogy appear too complex or burdensome in retrospect (Fulwiler, "How Well" 114–120; Mayher et al. 89). Instructors, students, and tutors may wish to believe that there really *is* such a thing as Writing with a capital "W" that either transcends or can be attended to separately from content issues that are the sole province of the content-area faculty. WAC instructors may require more writing from their students and use writing as a learning tool in their classes, but in spite of assurances from writing specialists that the instructors themselves are the best persons to comment on student writing within a discipline, they may continue to feel a good deal of anxiety about their ability to do so in a useful or helpful way. Reports from faculty workshops tend to bear this out (Kinneavy 15; Knoblauch and Brannon; Mallonee and Breihan). Many successful, publishing academic professionals do not think of themselves as writers and, consequently, doubt their own ability to comment on and respond effectively to student writing. They are also uneasy about spending time on "writing" in their classrooms when there is so much other "material" to be covered in their courses, so the writing center becomes an important resource by default. The refrain is a familiar one: "I don't have time to teach English in my class; that's your job" (Russell 297; Raimes).

And the people who work in writing centers may be perfectly happy to accept this construction of their identity. It does, after all, *give* them an identity as well as a sense of authority and expertise — precious commodities for tutors in otherwise low-paying and low-status jobs. In order to maintain this sense of expertise, tutors may consciously resist the social-constructionist theory that undergirds WAC programs. The social-constructionist paradigm argues, in part, for the distribution of writing expertise within and among the disciplines, locating the sites of textual authority in many diverse fields and interpretive communities. As a result, it also deconstructs and decentralizes the traditionally-accepted, institutionally-constituted authority of the writing center, the writing teacher, and others who claim to know something about "writing" as a subject in itself. Writing center tutors, in this distributed model, are almost never allowed to be authorities or insiders; they are perpetually outside the conversation (not unlike the students they are trying to help), and they will never even be extended an invitation to enter the Burkean parlor. In the face of this disempowering construction of writing center reality, it would be small wonder if the people who work there chose to embrace an alternative construction.

THE MYTH OF DISCIPLINARITY

A second and perhaps more insidious way that WAC programs and writing centers can work together depends on what I call the *myth of disciplinarity* in undergraduate education. As I have indicated above, WAC is grounded, in part, on social-constructionist tenets about knowledge construction, social practices, and education. One of the most important of these tenets is that since different disciplines comprise different discourse communities with different sets of discursive practices, it should be the responsibility of instructors to acquaint students with those practices and associated modes of inquiry. Certainly, this is the case that Art Young makes when he says that

> writing is a social activity; it takes place in a social context. If we want students to be effective communicators, to be successful engineers and historians, then we cannot separate form from content, writing from knowledge, action from context. We should not teach writing generically, in a vacuum, as if it were a skill unconnected to purpose or context. Student writers need to join a community of learners engaged in generating knowledge and solving problems, to join, even as novices, disciplinary conversations and public-policy discussions. WAC programs, therefore, began to stress the role . . . of social context in learning to write and writing to learn. (60–61)

As admirable as these principles might be in theory, in practice the idealistic vision of WAC they present may be just that — an idealistic vision. The truth of the matter may be that on the one hand, undergraduate WAC courses, no matter how well-intentioned, do not and will not offer students the opportunity to participate in disciplinary conversations, and on the other hand, undergraduates are, for the most part, unprepared and unable to do so even if the opportunity were allowed them.

As a general rule, the locus of much undergraduate (and pre-undergraduate) instruction remains rooted in the Freirian "banking model." Instructors and textbooks are regarded as repositories of content information which is disseminated to students, and the students are expected to absorb this information and, on command, to replay — some would say regurgitate — it (Applebee; Nelson; Sherrard; Geisler). This model, of course, ignores the social, cultural, and interpretive forces which shape the knowledge structures that are embraced by a discipline, just as it overlooks the value of collaborative learning as an instructional methodology. Nevertheless, for WAC instructors in the content-area disciplines who are particularly concerned with the issue of "coverage," the banking model is a powerful and persuasive one (Russell 295–7; Waldo 23; Mayher et al. 87). And in keeping with this model, many of the writing assignments that students are asked to complete, even in WAC courses, may not ask students to do more than parrot information gleaned from sources or to "analyze" this information in anything other than a superficial way. My own experience working in writing centers with students from WAC courses indicates that students are often given assignments that allow them to write, for the most part, in pre-disciplinary forms that use the traditional modes of discourse — comparison and contrast, classification, definition, description, etc. — to report or analyze information in generic ways rather than to master the rhetorical conventions of a particular field. A survey of academic writing tasks conducted by Bridgeman and Carlson in 1984 suggests that this practice may, indeed, be widespread. In this study, the researchers investigated "the kinds of writing skills that might be expected of students at entry level, or in early training in their academic fields." Of the ten possible "expected writing skills" to choose from in this survey, seven of the ten were variations on description, comparison and contrast, or summary (255). As David Bartholomae laments, "[m]uch of the written work students do is test-taking, report or summary, work that places them outside the working discourse of the academic community, where they are expected to admire and report on what we do, rather than inside that discourse, where they can do its work and participate in a common enterprise" (144). Though this approach may do a disservice to students and, as Bartholomae claims, be "a failure of teachers and curriculum designers who, even if they speak of writing as a mode of learning, all too often represent writing as a 'tool' to be used by an (hopefully) educated mind" (144), it nevertheless alleviates the problem of discipline-specific rhetorics for tutors in writing centers. Tutors can be trained in the generic modes of discourse, in the structure of argument, in the form of the "standard" research paper, or in the shape of the "typical" lab report, and apply them with some confidence to student papers in political science, biology, chemistry, or sociology. Since undergraduates will not be asked to participate in specialized discourse, tutors need not worry about their own unfamiliarity with it.

Further, there is some evidence that the representations students build about specialized discourses in the early stages of their undergraduate education are relatively naive and that these naive representations impact heavily on the students' own writing (Fulwiler et al. 61; Walvoord and McCarthy; Hare and Fitzsimmons; Geisler). Beginning writers, as Pat Bizzell has noted, are often "unaware that there is such a thing as a discourse community with conventions to be mastered" (230), and as a consequence, students' written texts do little more than duplicate the informational structure of the texts they will be examined on. "Students know intuitively that to do more [than this sort of duplication] would jeopardize their mastery of content knowledge they will be required to demonstrate on tests" (Geisler 42–43). Since undergraduate students are not likely to recognize a rhetorical dimension to knowledge construction in the discipline they are writing for, they are not likely to reproduce that dimension in their own work other than trying to incorporate what they see as the "jargon" of the field. (See, for instance, Schwartz; McCarthy.) If this assessment of students' cognitive representations for specialized discourse is correct, then the disciplinarity problem raised by WAC is once again greatly diminished for writing centers. Since students are not likely to write using discipline-specific discourse conventions, tutors will not have to worry about addressing them. And since instructors will not overtly expect their students to write like experts who are fully conversant with the "commonplaces" of the field (to use Bartholomae's term), tutors need not worry — for the most part — about such deficiencies in student texts.

THE QUESTION OF RESPONSIBILITY

Now, as I said before, these two perspectives on the WAC/writing center relationship are unsettling, partly because they depend upon certain kinds of instructional failure in WAC programs and partly because they depict writing centers as institutions that are willing to embrace these failures and avoid confronting complex, discipline-specific rhetorical issues that would undoubtedly problematize writing conferences. But is the passive role adopted by some writing centers under these circumstances necessarily a bad thing? Is it really the responsibility of a writing center staff to introduce and address matters of disciplinary discourse when WAC courses and their modes-based writing assignments fail to do so? To my mind, the answer is a yes, but a tentative and qualified one. Some research, for example, indicates that even though instructors in the disciplines may give assignments that enable students to fall back on conventional, generic strategies for academic papers learned in high school, those instructors nevertheless may evaluate the papers on the basis of how well they conform to discipline-specific rhetorical standards. (See Faigley and Hansen; Walvoord and McCarthy.) This being the case, then it may very well be the responsibility of writing center tutors to attend to such standards.

The need to attend to matters of disciplinary discourse is even more pronounced when writing centers must support WAC programs which are enacted successfully, when dedicated, progressive instructors work diligently to make their students "insiders" rather than "outsiders," and when students are both enthusiastic and active learners in a new and unfamiliar discipline. But this returns me to my original questions: If WAC is working as it *should*, theoretically, then how do we resolve the opposition between its epistemological assumptions about texts, discourse, and writing and those which inform the operations of writing center practice? If we accept the fact that writing center tutors will never be able to master all the discursive practices of all the disciplines which students are writing in under the auspices of a fully-realized WAC program, then what exactly should the tutors' role be in these writing conferences?[3] What benefits can the writing center and its tutors provide in conferences that would not be more fully realized in meetings with professors or other experts in the field? These questions strike at the heart of what we do in writing centers, and I cannot help but approach them with a certain degree of trepidation. They resist simple answers and all-purpose solutions. I would, however, like to suggest two perspectives — the *environmental* and the *cognitive* — that can provide at least partial and provisionary answers.

ENVIRONMENTAL: THE ROLE OF THE WRITING CENTER

Much has been said and written about the nature of the power and authority relationships which are enacted in tutorial conferences. Though it is sometimes tempting to talk about the writing center conference as if it were completely egalitarian, a site where students and tutors can interact as peers or co-authors, this representation is clearly naive. Characterizations of the writing center as a "rhetorically neutral ground" where tutors "do not have the rhetorical agenda common to one discourse community . . . [and] can thus resist imposing what they value about writing on other departments" (Waldo 18–19) overlook the dynamics of power inherent in any tutoring session. Many power relationships, instantiated along a multitude of dimensions, come into play in all tutorial conferences. Some of these dimensions are economic, some gendered, some cultural, some institutional, and some situational. As John Trimbur and others have remarked, the very term "peer tutor" is itself a contradiction in terms. Students come to the writing center for assistance, and tutors are presumably there — authorized by some sort of institutional power structure — to provide it. Tutors, in the very act of giving suggestions, offering advice, or asking pointed questions, are *de facto* imposing what they value about writing on students and, by implication, on other departments. Nevertheless, the authority granted tutors by their institutional status *as* tutors may be counterbalanced by other dimensions of authority that lean more heavily toward the students. The students, for example, own and control the texts they choose to discuss. They are also likely to know more about the papers' subject matter and discipline-specific conventions than the tutors and therefore be able to speak more knowledgeably about what material is relevant and what is not. The ideal tutorial conference, then, is characterized by *parity*, a balance of power, rather than egalitarianism, where power relationships are either absent or dismissible.

The tutor's very ignorance of discipline-specific subject matter and rhetorical conventions, then, can be seen as an equalizing force in writing center conferences (Hubbuch). Tutors can ask what rhetorical conventions exist for a particular discipline, and students can articulate and explain them, checking at the same time to see that these conventions are being followed in their own texts. The tutor's authority and the student's authority can strike a balance which allows the opportunity for questions and advice (on the tutor's part) and considered judgment (on the student's part). This balance of power is facilitated by the tutor's unique status as an *interested, disinterested other* — someone who attends to and focuses on the students' papers in the context of the tutorial session but who has no real stake in the papers' success or failure. This is quite different from the relationship which is likely to hold between students and instructors, where such a balance of power can rarely be achieved. When conferring with instructors about their papers, students can no longer claim the same authority over the subject matter since the instructor will probably have a greater level of expertise, and they can no longer claim the same control over their texts since the instructor's power to evaluate and grade the final product will exert a tremendous pressure on how rigorously the student will feel compelled to follow the advice given. The student-teacher conferences transcribed and analyzed by Sperling, for example, reveal conspicuous differences in how the instructor, "Mr. Peterson," worked with three students, but they also show the alacrity with which these students were willing to follow the teacher's lead in making revisions to their drafts (136–154; see also Marsella et al. 182–3). What can be concluded from these observations, perhaps, is that although writing center tutors may not be the *best* people to comment on papers produced for courses in WAC programs (in terms of their subject-area knowledge and familiarity with discipline-specific conventions), they may very well be the one quasi-authoritative source that students feel most *comfortable* with, and this, I think, places them and the writing center in an important and worthwhile position.

COGNITIVE: THE ROLE OF THE TUTOR

Cognitive perspectives on the study of writing and conferencing practices also suggest important ways in which WAC and writing centers can work together productively. When writers try to think about or "generate" material that they can use in their writing, they begin by searching their long- and short-term memories, looking for information that can provide them with new ideas, appropriate plans for their writing tasks, or relevant information that can be included in their texts. As writers search their memories, they do so in ways that are both recursive and associational (Hayes and Flower; Flower and Hayes, "Cognitive Process"; Scardamalia and Bereiter). That is, each piece of information they retrieve from their memories becomes, in turn, the basis of a new probe they can use to look for more information. A student writing a paper on the Clinton health plan, for example, might first recall that one of its critical features has to do with catastrophic health coverage for all Americans. This recalled memory ("catastrophic health coverage") is linked, associationally, to the first probe ("the Clinton health plan"), and may, in turn, become the basis for a further memory search. Catastrophic health coverage may bring to mind topics such as medical costs, the insurance industry, or grandma's last stay in the hospital. Each of these may, in turn, lead to further memory searches and further associational chains. The recursive nature of this operation — called "spreading activation" — makes it a powerful search strategy, since it may be modified as needed or redirected to more productive types of search as the goals of the textual plan are themselves met, unfulfilled, or modified.

But this search strategy, in and of itself, may be insufficient to generate the information necessary for successful disciplinary writing. The type and quality of information retrieved from memory are dependent upon the type and quality of the probes which are used to search it, but more fundamentally, these memory probes are dependent upon the nature of the task representation which students construct to guide the search process. Students who do not have functional and productive representations of their writing tasks or textual goals will have difficulty generating ideas or evaluating specific memories for appropriateness. One of the features which distinguishes "novice" from "expert" writers in Flower and Hayes' cognitive model of writing process behaviors is the richness of the task representations which those writers construct for their developing texts. Rich task representations generally take into account factors as audience, rhetorical goals, and alternative views, while less-rich representations are often "writer-based" and egocentric — seemingly unaware of the textual and rhetorical needs of an audience other than themselves. For novice writers whose potential task representations are entirely dependent upon the limited range of textual options and constructions of audience which may be available to them in their own memories, the struggle to become "expert" writers may be a long and tortuous one. Not only will the types of probes they construct to search their memories be limited by their own cognitive processes and perspectives, but the means by which they learn and assimilate new rhetorical strategies will usually be implicit and diffuse, slowly internalized from detectable patterns of reading, writing, and talking behaviors in a discourse community, rather than explicit and focused, derived via an interactive engagement with writing tasks and supportive collaborators.

One important contribution which tutors in writing centers can provide for WAC programs, or more pointedly, for students writing papers in WAC programs, then, is to support and enrich students' cognitive processes by offering them new perspectives for thinking about their tasks (Harris, "Writing Center and Tutoring" 167). When writers confront new writing tasks, they often draw on familiar representations and strategies that have proven useful in the past, hoping that they will prove equally productive in the present. These cognitive constructs may be the result of their previous writing experiences, the social and cultural forces that shape their cognition, or their sense of the rhetorical and discursive conventions they are trying to satisfy. Often these familiar strategies work well for writers; other times — such as when the representations of the writing task are poor or misdirected — they can trap writers in blind alleys.

Writing center conferences can provide opportunities for writers to break out of these representational dead-ends. Each comment, each question, each suggestion or observation made by a writing center tutor can enable student writers to engage their topics in new ways, ways that would not likely occur *sui generis*. Each new probe from a tutor can help writers to break out of conditioned patterns they find themselves immersed in, offering the possibility, on the one hand, of a solution to a perplexing writing problem or, on the other hand, of a dramatic new insight. In this way, a writing tutor's unfamiliarity with discourse conventions can be seen as one of his or her greatest strengths. Not only can the tutors provide access to new pathways and search strategies, but they can also help students to attain what Arthur Koestler has referred to as "bisociative thought" — the ability to discover previously-undetected connections between the knowledge structures of two different fields.

The experience of a tutor in my own writing center can help to illustrate this phenomenon particularly well, I think. As she explains it,

> I was working with a civil engineering student, Rashid, on a paper about housing construction practices in Saudi Arabia, his native country. Rashid had written the paper in conjunction with a survey he planned to conduct when he returned home, a survey which asked questions about personal preferences in architectural style like, "Do you prefer open or enclosed spaces?" and "Do you prefer natural or artificial lighting?" As we worked through the paper and the survey questions, I had to ask Rashid several times to explain some of the construction and architecture terms, since I don't really know much about the field myself. And I also had to ask him to clarify exactly what his point was in the paper. He didn't seem really sure about it either, probably because there were so many questions on so many different topics in the survey that the paper had a lot of trouble pulling them all together. As we kept going through it, I noticed that a lot of the questions had to do with gender issues — "Do you think women should be seen in public?" "What rooms in the house should be for women's use?" — and the like. I thought this was really interesting, given my interest in women's issues, so I started asking him questions about it, and the more we talked, the more he began to see that gender could be a focus for his paper, and he really started to pull it together.

CONCLUDING REMARKS

Ultimately, I think, this is the kind of thinking that WAC — and a college education in general — strive for, and it seems clear that writing centers can play an important role in helping to forge these new, revealing, and insightful connections in student writing. Questions about discourse communities, discursive practices, and discipline-specific conventions will continue to be the subjects of debate in writing centers and in WAC programs (as well they should), but they need not be seen as reasons for despair. Under less-than-perfect circumstances, when WAC programs stray from the principles of writing-in-the-disciplines or writing-to-learn, then writing centers can — if they wish — take a proactive role with students, encouraging them to confront issues of disciplinarity through pointed questions about audience, tone, style, and format.[4] Under more ideal circumstances, when WAC programs are working hard to immerse students in a particular discipline's modes of inquiry and rhetorical tropes, then writing centers should feel confident that their institutional position (the *environmental* role) and their pedagogical practices (the *cognitive* role) can supply significant, concrete benefits to students even though their tutors may not share the content knowledge of the students they work with.

In sum, though WAC programs and writing centers may work well together when there are administrative, institutional, or pedagogical failures involved in their operations, they function together best and most productively when the instructional mission of each is enacted fully, when the epistemological differences between the two programs are seen not as points of contention but as alternative positions of strength.

NOTES

1. For the purposes of this paper, I wish to focus on the difficulties that emerge from WAC programs that are construed as WID, or Writing In the Disciplines, rather than as WTL, or Writing to Learn. Though related in some aspects of their pedagogy, the two WAC approaches have distinctly different goals and generally employ writing for quite different purposes. WAC as Writing to Learn encourages the use of writing as a tool to help students learn subject matter and, often, to make personal connections to their own experience and interests. It employs personal journals, short in-class writing activities, and writing-process teaching strategies to facilitate learning, and since much of the writing students produce as a consequence is relatively short, personal, and ungraded, writing center tutors see relatively little of it. A WID program, on the other hand, though it may use some Writing-to-Learn activities as a part of classroom process, has *professionalization* as its focus, a desire to teach students what it means to write, talk, and think as members of a particular discipline. The writing projects students undertake in these courses may be collaborative, but they are also, presumably, longer, more complex, more centered in the activities of a discipline than those in WTL courses, and writing center tutors are more likely to encounter and engage with the results. When I refer to WAC in this paper, then, I wish to make it clear that I am referring explicitly to the practice of Writing In the Disciplines.

2. I should emphasize once again at this point that the commentary and critique I am advancing are directed specifically at the problems which arise from the epistemological differences between WID classes, with a primary focus on disciplinary discourse and discipline-specific modes of inquiry, and writing centers. It is not my intention to argue that the WID model is or should be adopted by all undergraduate courses, and neither is it my intention to suggest that conscious myopia or the myth of disciplinarity are endemic — or even applicable — to the majority of classes in an undergraduate curriculum. Nevertheless, I would maintain that whenever tutors are asked to work on papers in subject areas that are unfamiliar to them, they will confront difficulties similar to those they would face with WID papers (which would be even more deeply immersed in the language, tropes, and modes of inquiry in the field).

3. I realize, of course, that no tutorial conference will ever be completely generic or limited only to those aspects of writing that can be abstracted from all texts. Each tutor will have a wide range of knowledge that intersects many subject areas to a greater or lesser degree. In this respect, no tutor is likely to be completely ignorant about the topic or field of a given paper. However, to the degree that he or she is unfamiliar with the discipline, generic strategies will undoubtedly play a more prominent role in conferences.

4. Richard Leahy offers a strongly proactive model in his article, "Writing Centers and Writing-for-Learning." He, too, notes that many WAC programs run the risk of "losing sight of writing across the curriculum as a whole," noting that many WAC courses and faculty slip quickly into purely transactional writing assignments that deny students the opportunity to make personal connections with their subject matter. He argues that writing centers can take up the slack, as it were, by actively promoting — among both students and faculty — the value of more expressive writing assignments.

WORKS CITED

Applebee, Arthur N. *Writing in the Secondary School: English and the Content Areas.* Urbana, IL: NCTE, 1981.

Bartholomae, David. "Inventing the University." *When a Writer Can't Write.* Ed. Mike Rose. New York: Guilford Press, 1985. 134–165.

Bizzell, Patricia. "Cognition, Convention, and Certainty: What We Need to Know about Writing." *Pre/Text* 3.3 (1982): 213–243.

Bridgeman, Brent, and Sybil B. Carlson. "Survey of Academic Writing Tasks." *Written Communication* 1.2 (1984): 247–280.

Bruffee, Kenneth A. "Collaborative Learning and the 'Conversation of Mankind.'" *College English* 46.7 (1984): 635–652.

Carino, Peter, Lori Floy, and Marcia Lightle. "Empowering a Writing Center: The Faculty Meets the Tutors." *Writing Lab Newsletter* 16.2 (October 1991): 1–5.

Clark, Irene L. *Writing in the Center: Teaching in a Writing Center Setting.* 2nd ed. Dubuque: Kendall/ Hunt, 1992.

Dinitz, Susan, and Diane Howe. "Writing Centers and Writing-Across-the-Curriculum: An Evolving Partnership?" *Writing Center Journal* 10.1 (1989): 45–51.

Faigley, Lester, and Kristine Hansen. "Learning to Write in the Social Sciences." *College Composition and Communication* 36.2 (1985): 140–149.

Flower, Linda, and John R. Hayes. "The Cognition of Discovery: Defining a Rhetorical Problem." *College Composition and Communication* 31.1 (1980): 21–32.

———. "A Cognitive Process Theory of Writing." *College Composition and Communication* 32.4 (1981): 365–387.

Fulwiler, Toby. "How Well Does Writing Across the Curriculum Work?" *College English* 46.2 (1984): 113–125.

Fulwiler, Toby, Michael E. Gorman, and Margaret E. Gorman. "Changing Faculty Attitudes Toward Writing." *Writing Across the Disciplines: Research Into Practice.* Ed. Art Young and Toby Fulwiler. Portsmouth: Boynton/Cook, 1986. 53–67.

Geisler, Cheryl. "Literacy and Expertise." *Language and Learning Across the Disciplines* 1.1 (1994): 35–57.

Griffin, C. W. "Programs for Writing Across the Curriculum: A Report." *College Composition and Communication* 36.4 (1985): 398–403.

Hare, Victoria Chou, and D. A. Fitzsimmons. "The Influence of Interpretive Communities on Use of Content and Procedural Knowledge in a Writing Task." *Written Communication* 8.3 (1991): 348–378.

Harris, Muriel. *Teaching One-to-One: The Writing Conference.* Urbana, IL: NCTE, 1986.

———. "The Writing Center and Tutoring in WAC Programs." *Writing Across the Curriculum: A Guide to Developing Programs.* Ed. Susan H. McLeod and Margot Soven. Newbury Park: Sage, 1992. 154–174.

Hayes, John R., and Linda S. Flower. "Identifying the Organization of Writing Processes." *Cognitive Processes in Writing.* Ed. L. W. Gregg and E. R. Steinberg. Hillsdale, NJ: Erlbaum, 1980. 3–30.

Hubbuch, Susan M. "A Tutor Needs to Know the Subject Matter to Help a Student With a Paper: ___Agree___Disagree___Not Sure." *The Writing Center Journal* 8.2 (1988): 23–30.

Kinneavy, James L. "Writing Across the Curriculum." *Profession 83.* New York: MLA, 1983. 13–20.

Koestler, Arthur. *The Act of Creation.* New York: Macmillan, 1964.

Knoblauch, C. H., and Lil Brannon. "Writing as Learning Through the Curriculum." *College English* 45.5 (1983): 465–474.

Leahy, Richard. "Writing Centers and Writing-for-Learning." *Writing Center Journal* 10.1 (1989): 31–37.

Mallonee, Barbara C., and J. R. Breihan. "Responding to Students' Drafts: Interdisciplinary Consensus." *College Composition and Communication* 36.2 (1985): 213–231.

Marsella, Joy, Thomas L. Hilgers, and Clemence McLaren. "How Students Handle Writing Assignments: A Study of Eighteen Responses in Six Disciplines." *Writing, Teaching, and Learning in the Disciplines.* Ed. Anne Herrington and Charles Moran. New York: MLA, 1992. 174–188.

Mayher, John S., Nancy Lester, and Gordon M. Pradl. *Learning to Write/Writing to Learn.* Portsmouth: Boynton/Cook, 1983.

McCarthy, Lucille Parkinson. "A Stranger in Strange Lands: A College Student Writing Across the Curriculum." *Research in the Teaching of English* 21.3 (1987): 233–265.

Nelson, Jennie. "This Was an Easy Assignment: Examining How Students Interpret Academic Writing Tasks." *Research in the Teaching of English* 24 (1990): 362–393.

Raimes, Ann. "Writing and Learning Across the Curriculum: The Experience of a Faculty Seminar." *College English* 41.7 (1980): 797–801.

Russell, David R. *Writing in the Academic Disciplines, 1870–1990: A Curricular History.* Carbondale: Southern Illinois UP, 1991.

Scardamalia, Marlene, and Carl Bereiter. "Knowledge Telling and Knowledge Transforming in Written Composition." *Advances in Applied Psycholinguistics: Vol. 2. Reading, Writing, and Language Learning.* Ed. S. Rosenberg. Cambridge: Cambridge UP, 1987. 142–175.

Schwartz, Mimi. "Response to Writing: A College-wide Perspective." *College English* 46.1 (1984): 55–62.

Sherrard, Carol. "Summary Writing: A Topographical Study." *Written Communication* 3 (1986): 324–343.

Sperling, Melanie. "Dialogues of Deliberation: Conversation in the Teacher-Student Writing Conference." *Written Communication* 8.2 (1991): 131–162.

Trimbur, John. "Peer Tutoring: A Contradiction in Terms?" *The Writing Center Journal* 7.2 (1987): 21–28.

Waldo, Mack. "The Last Best Place for WAC: The Writing Center." *Writing Program Administration* 16.3 (1993): 15–26.

Walker, Carolyn. "Communications with the Faculty: Vital Links for the Success of Writing Centers." *Writing Lab Newsletter* 16.3 (November 1991): 11–16.

Wallace, Ray. "The Writing Center's Role in the Writing Across the Curriculum Program: Theory and Practice." *The Writing Center Journal* 8.2 (Spring/Summer 1988): 43–48.

Walvoord, Barbara E., and Lucille P. McCarthy. *Thinking and Writing in College: A Naturalistic Study of Students in Four Disciplines.* Urbana, IL: NCTE, 1990.

Young, Art. "The Wonder of Writing Across the Curriculum." *Language and Learning Across the Disciplines* 1.1 (1994): 58–71.

22 Why Is Being Interdisciplinary So Very Hard to Do?: Thoughts on the Perils and Promise of Interdisciplinary Pedagogy

REBECCA S. NOWACEK

Stanley Fish, in his 1989 essay "Being Interdisciplinary Is So Very Hard to Do," pronounced interdisciplinarity impossible. Defining interdisciplinarity as the attempt to escape "the prison houses of our various specialties to the open range . . . of a general human knowledge," he declared that such a goal "is not a possible human achievement" (237). What passes for interdisciplinarity, Fish argued, is in fact little more than either disciplinary imperialism or the emergence of a new discipline. In the years since, Fish's definition and dismissal of interdisciplinarity have gone largely unchallenged in print. But in practice, interdisciplinarity programs have multiplied at a dizzying pace.

If interdisciplinarity is impossible, what are we to make of the "interdisciplinary" learning communities, first-year seminars, and senior capstone courses that are an increasingly common feature of undergraduate general education programs? By one recent count, over half of current general education reforms include interdisciplinary programs or courses (Ratcliff). Are these programs merely disciplinary imperialism in disguise? Is it possible for anyone, much less students in their first years of undergraduate studies, to engage in authentically interdisciplinary work? By Fish's definition, the answer is no: we cannot, I agree, escape disciplinary constraints for knowledge unfettered by discourse communities. But interdisciplinarity is *not* simply a desire to slip the yoke of disciplinarity. Interdisciplinary work — interdisciplinary teaching, learning, and thinking — is work on the boundaries and intersections of disciplines, work that does not transcend but rather transforms our understanding of disciplines. *[not transforms our understanding]*

Understood in this way, interdisciplinary studies and writing studies can enjoy a mutually beneficial relationship: interdisciplinary classrooms offer a powerful context for writing instruction, and writing instruction offers a powerful means to help students engage in interdisciplinary learning. In this essay I draw on cultural historical activity theory (CHAT) and classroom research to

---

From *College Composition and Communication* 60.3 (2009): 493–516.

explain why interdisciplinary teaching and learning are very difficult, but not impossible, to do. To illustrate, I focus on the challenges faced by participants in a team-taught interdisciplinary course designed to fill general education requirements for first-year university students. Both students and instructors, I argue, must negotiate double binds placed upon them when various disciplines conflict. Those double binds can limit and constrain the work of individuals, but if made an object of reflection, the double bind can also facilitate higher-order thinking about disciplines and the role of writing within them.

Defining Interdisciplinarity

Central to understanding interdisciplinarity is an understanding of disciplinarity. My conception of disciplinarity and thus of interdisciplinarity is informed by recent work in cultural historical activity theory. Drawing on the sociocultural analyses of Vygotsky, Leont'ev, and especially Engeström, CHAT turns our attention from a focus on a single (albeit dynamic) disciplinary discourse community to a view of overlapping and interlocking activity systems. An activity system, in its most basic representation (see Figure 22-1), consists of four elements: a *subject*, either an individual or a collection of people; an *object of* attention and the *motive* (official or unofficial) that drives activity in the system; and the *mediational tools* (cultural and discursive as well as physical) used within the system.

Understood as activity systems, disciplines are not defined solely in contradistinction to one another, though it is true that historically disciplines have often defined and used their objects, motives, and tools in order to stake out institutional turf in relation to one another. Disciplinary activity systems finally take their meaning and definition from the interrelation of subject, tools, and object/motive. The world of human action, in this view, is replete with

FIGURE 22-1 Basic Elements of an Activity System

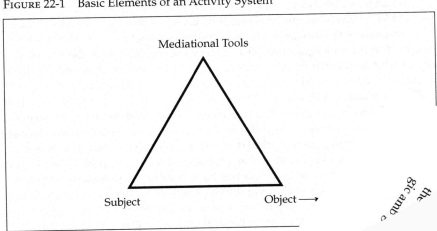

such activity systems; individuals participate often simultaneously in multiple activity systems.

Furthermore, as Russell and Yañez illustrate in their superb CHAT analysis of writing assigned in the general education curriculum, a mediational tool used in one activity system (for instance, the review essay assigned in an undergraduate history class) is often used in other systems (such as the field of professional journalism or the academic discipline of history) but for very different motives. Activity theory helps us to see that borrowed materials are never thoroughly pure or devoid of resonances from other activity systems, and stresses that individuals using mediational tools from one disciplinary activity system within another face a series of complex, unpredictable, and often unconscious negotiations.

Given this view of disciplines, interdisciplinary thought can be understood as the shift from a recognition of the coexistence of multiple but apparently independent activity systems to an awareness of the overlap and interanimation of those activity systems. The defining characteristic of interdisciplinary thought is not freedom from all disciplinary constraints but awareness of the constraints, complements, and interrelations of a limited number of disciplines. Interdisciplinary thought as I am describing it is not somehow more superior, more comprehensive, more pure than disciplinary knowledge — a connotation often found in writings on interdisciplinarity. It is not a transcendent critical consciousness that will liberate us from the dehumanizing constraints of disciplines. Rather, it is a type of abnormal discourse that can empower individuals in limited but powerful ways by making visible previously invisible connections and constraints, even as it may obscure others.

Although interdisciplinarity as I define it is not impossible, it remains very hard to do — and an analysis that focuses on the interdisciplinary classroom as the site of overlapping, interlocking activity systems can help us see why. Such an analysis can also help us see what is powerful — perhaps uniquely, but certainly not inevitably powerful — about the interdisciplinary classroom as a site for writing instruction.

My analyses here draw on and extend the work of Russell and Yañez, who use CHAT to elucidate the challenges of general education courses through their analysis of the difficulties facing students struggling with a book review assigned in an undergraduate Irish history course. Although their focal student Beth had written reviews for her high school history class and a college journalism course, "this similarity proved to be maddeningly deceptive" (347). In actuality, Beth's Irish history course was a new activity system, with different motives and different genre rules. However, Beth and her instructor were slow to recognize those differences, in part because both were unaccustomed to discussing the rhetorical domain of academic literacy. This is not the failing of a single classroom but emblematic of a larger problem in general education: "Unfortunately, we do not have a robust vocabulary for talking about the differences in writing in different activity systems, which can make differences salient — in part because of the patterned isolation and strate-[g]uity the contradiction in general education gives rise to" (354).

Their analysis suggests that teachers need to create opportunities to discuss the rhetorical domains of knowledge in various activity systems. Team-taught interdisciplinary courses offer one such opportunity. The simultaneous presence of multiple instructors heightens the opportunities to be immersed in and discuss the rhetorical dimension of disciplinary expectations. But direct, explicit discussion of similarities and differences among multiple disciplinary ways of knowing is not easy to achieve. In the pages that follow I use the example of one classroom to illustrate the pitfalls and promise of interdisciplinary classrooms.

ONE MEDIATIONAL TOOL, FOUR ACTIVITY SYSTEMS: TEACHING THE THESIS-DRIVEN ESSAY IN "INTERDISC"

The example I provide comes from my observations of a team-taught interdisciplinary course offered to first-year honors students at Villanova University. This was the second in a three-semester sequence designed to fill several general education requirements. The course, known colloquially as Interdisc II, was composed of three distinct three-credit classes — literature, history, and religious studies — in which all eighteen students in the course had to enroll. As Figure 22-2 illustrates, each class period had a disciplinary designation, but professors attended and participated in each other's classes on a regular basis. Sessions with only one professor present were the exception. Because the sessions met back to back in the same room with all the same participants, discussions would sometimes go overtime or segue from one to the next without a break. Generally, though, students kept separate notebooks for each component discipline and spoke of a given class period as belonging to a particular professor. As Figure 22-3 suggests, each professor developed and graded his or her own assignments. Only one assignment — a collaborative, oral final exam — required students to integrate material from the various disciplines and was evaluated by all three professors. Unfortunately, I did not have adequate access to those exams to discuss them here.

FIGURE 22-2   Interdisciplinary Humanities II: A Sample Week Schedule

Monday	Tuesday	Wednesday	Thursday
10–10:50 **History:** Chapter 6 *Middle Ages*	9:30–10:45 **Literature:** *Wife of Bath* (con't)	10–10:50 **History:** excerpts Aquinas' *Treatise on Law*	9:30–10:45 **Religious Studies:** Aquinas' *Summa* (con't)
11–11:50 **Literature:** *Wife of Bath's Prologue* & *Tale*	11–12:15 **Religious Studies:** Aquinas' *Summa*	11–11:50 **Literature:** *The Courtier*	11–12:15 **History:** Chapter 7 *Middle Ages*

FIGURE 22-3   Interdisciplinary Humanities II: The Semester at a Glance

Interdisc Literature II (Professor Olivia S)*	Interdisc History II (Professor Roger B)*	Interdisc Religious Studies II (Professor Thomas H)*
**2–3 pg. on Chaucer	medieval diary	**8–10 pg. on Aquinas
**3–4 pg. on *Faustus*	2 informal response papers	**8–10 pg. comparative
**4–5 pg. open topic	**French Rev. term paper	
take-home midterm take-home final	take-home midterm take-home final	take-home midterm take-home final

The semester culminated in an oral final, taken in groups of three, including presentation of a thesis that integrates information and insights from all three disciplines

*Students addressed their professors by their first names, so I have also
**Indicates assignments described as requiring a thesis

Given the separate but coordinated structure of the course, can Interdisc be considered truly interdisciplinary? Scholars of interdisciplinarity often distinguish between multidisciplinarity, which involves the mere juxtaposition of disciplines, and interdisciplinarity, which, in the words of two highly regarded interdisciplinary studies scholars, "draws on disciplinary perspectives *and integrates their insights*" (Klein and Newell 3, emphasis added). To some extent I have echoed this distinction by arguing that interdisciplinary thought should be understood as a shift from recognizing multiple but apparently independent activity systems to being aware of the overlap among those activity systems.

I describe Interdisc as interdisciplinary for several reasons. First, the professors intentionally organized the syllabus to maximize opportunities to treat related material (for instance, students read Calvin and Milton concurrently) and often went beyond juxtaposition to build on and respond to discussions led by their colleagues. More importantly though, the standard distinction between multidisciplinary juxtaposition and interdisciplinary integration does not sufficiently account for the importance of individual cognition. If, as I have argued, the defining characteristic of interdisciplinary thought is "*awareness of* the constraints, complements, and interrelations of a limited number of disciplines," then we cannot test for the presence of interdisciplinarity by looking at a syllabus. Instead, we must turn to the experience of individuals negotiating the overlaps of various disciplinary activity systems. Given this weakness of the multidisciplinary/interdisciplinary distinction, I prefer to use the term interdisciplinary more broadly as a descriptor of courses that attempt to bring disciplines into dialogue. In such terms, the Interdisc II classroom certainly qualifies as interdisciplinary.

In essence, the students and teachers participating in Interdisc II were really participating in four activity systems: a history class, a literature class, a religious studies class, and the interdisciplinary course that was the sum of those parts. Although the participants in those four systems remained constant, the systems had their own sometimes overlapping, sometimes conflicting objects and motives. But all systems employed (among other tools) the mediational tool of the thesis-driven essay. Tracing the use and representations of the thesis-driven essay by professors and students helps make visible the overlaps and conflicts among the four activity systems and cuts to the heart of what is so challenging and promising about interdisciplinary teaching.

The semester included more than two dozen episodes of explicit writing instruction, distributed among all three disciplines. The Interdisc instructors did not simply assign writing; they worked to teach writing: they sequenced assignments, engaged students in discussions about their expectations, and worked to make some assignments an opportunity for exploration and communication rather than simply evaluation. The history professor assigned reaction papers that were the springboard for in-class discussions. The religious studies professor conferenced with students and wrote copious comments on their ten-page analytical papers. The literature professor frequently assigned in-class freewrites to jumpstart class discussion and encouraged students to revise their formal close-analysis essays. These three professors were not simply reflective and dedicated teachers; they were also committed to teaching with and about writing.

Throughout the semester the instructors stressed the similarities in their expectations regarding thesis. For example, at one point, the literature professor said to the class, "What you are writing in my part of the course, in [the religious studies] part of the course, and I think in most college writing, is the thesis-driven essay." However, with the benefit of hindsight and transcripts it is clear that, despite the effort they put into teaching writing, these three professors meant very different things by the word "thesis" — in CHAT terms, had very different motives — but glossed over those differences in their assignments and class discussions.

Early in the semester, during one of the rare periods when he was the only instructor present, the history professor, Roger (all professor and student names are pseudonyms). distributed a description of his expectations for a term paper on the French Revolution:

> The purpose of the history term paper is to write history from original sources. . . . The textbook will provide an overview for background and a start-up bibliography; you should also look at secondary sources as needed. Remember, however, that the essence of your paper should rely on the primary sources. Your completed paper should not merely narrate an event, but provide an analysis of a question you pose for yourself. At best, it will argue to a conclusion, a thesis. The paper should be approximately 10–15 pages with appropriate documentation and bibliography, written clearly and thoughtfully.

Roger went on to orally explain what he meant by "thesis" and its relationship to "topic."

> Step number one is to pick a topic. Notice step number one is not "I am going to prove that." That's not a topic, that's a thesis. A thesis is an argument. Topic is simply "I am going to write my paper about." So when you tell me your topic, it should be a phrase, not an argument. That comes later. The theory is that you're not sure what the argument is going to be until you've looked at the resources. You don't set out to prove something; you set out to see where the evidence leads you. Okay?

The mediational tool of the thesis essay was given particular meaning and form by Roger's overriding motive of getting students to reason from primary sources by "see[ing] where the evidence leads you" — a methodological approach he associated with the discipline of history.

At the beginning of the next week, the literature professor, Olivia, distributed an assignment asking students to "explain the difference" between a pair of critical comments on one of Chaucer's prologues and to "compar[e] the interpretation of Chaucer each position enables you to make." Like Roger, Olivia initiated a conversation on the difference between thesis and topic, asking students to explain their understanding of the two. The students responded by echoing Roger's language exactly, saying "the topic is the broad overview of what you're doing, your thesis is your argument." As she replied, Olivia initially distinguished topic and thesis much as Roger did: "Yeah, your thesis is your argument. . . . A topic is what you're going to talk about. A thesis is what you personally have to say about it." As she continued, though, she articulated a motive considerably different from Roger's. A thesis, she said, "has to venture something. Peter Elbow, who's a writer about writing I like a lot, says it has to stick its neck out. If it doesn't stick its neck out, it's not a thesis."

Roger wanted students to start with a topic and work their way to a thesis; in fact, he left open the possibility that students might never articulate an explicit thesis: "At best," Roger says in his assignment, the paper "will argue to a conclusion, a thesis." During the last week of the semester, Roger even stated that the thesis "is implicit in the paper" and might not be "expressly written in one place." For Olivia, having a clearly articulated and argumentative thesis in the paper was vital; a topic, which is "what you're going to talk about," cannot replace the thesis, which is "what you personally have to say" about that topic. Olivia's next assignment on Marlowe's *Faustus* also stressed the explicitly argumentative nature of the necessary thesis: "Please remember to . . . advance an argumentative thesis." The mediational tool of the thesis-driven essay was given quite a different meaning by Olivia's overriding motive, which focused more on "stick[ing] its neck out" than on "see[ing] where the evidence leads you."

Olivia's focus on an argumentative thesis offered a striking contrast to the first assignment given by Thomas, the religious studies professor, which was due within a week of the *Faustus* assignment and did not even contain the word "thesis." As Thomas described in the text of his assignment,

> In your paper I want you to recreate the way in which, according to Aquinas, human beings achieve salvation. You will probably want to deal with issues like virtue and habit, grace, original sin, will, free choice, predestination, etc. . . . I want you to make a case for the reasonableness of Aquinas' theology on this issue. Be his defense lawyer. . . . Anticipate objections to the theory and defend Aquinas against them. You should also describe what you feel to be the operative principles or problems around which Aquinas organizes his theology on this issue. What apparently irreconcilable "truths" is he trying to harmonize? . . . [A]t the end you may append your own personal critique as to its failings. What key preconceptions, conclusions, or arguments separate you from Aquinas?

Puzzled by the assignment and attempting to understand whether this paper was to contain any argument, students asked for further explanation in class. One student remarked that "it seems to me that it [asks for] a regurgitation of Aquinas." In response, Thomas used, for the first time, the word "thesis" to describe his paper:

> When you analyze a writer you're just not regurgitating. You're criticizing. It's a critical exercise — it has to be — because you are picking these things out, weighing them, arguing them. There's too much Aquinas for you to put into the paper, so you're going to have to choose, going to have to order, and organize it into an argument. . . . So what you're going to do is present a Thomistic analysis of salvation. And it's very much like what Olivia . . . has been having you do [in in-class freewrites] when you analyze a text and you think like Aquinas. Well, I want you to really think like Aquinas. . . . What ties the system together? What's the most important thing about it? Why does it work or not work? Your thesis will probably come in that sort of a shape. The most important thing for Aquinas about salvation, to understand Aquinas about salvation is. He has a few major principles he's using. He's combining them. And then go through and say: well, given [Aquinas'] understanding of this, salvation works in the following ways. So it is a reconstruction of his argument.

As the assignment suggests and Thomas underscored, his overriding motive was to help students "think like Aquinas." By doing so, he explained, they would come to understand a worldview very different from their own while simultaneously honing their analytical skills. This motive, though, meant that despite Thomas's claim that "it's very much like what Olivia . . . has been having you do when you analyze a text and you think like Aquinas," Thomas's expectations for a thesis were quite distinct from Olivia's and Roger's expectations. Indeed, he modeled a thesis with a Madlib type sentence: "The most important thing for Aquinas about salvation is_____," or "Given [Aquinas'] understanding of _____, salvation works in the following ways." Such a thesis is notable not for the degree that it sticks its neck out, but for the degree that it aptly identifies Aquinas' core assumptions and organizing principles.

Throughout this analysis, I have presented the conflicts among motives and mediational tools as conflicts among disciplinary activity systems. But what evidence is there that the way these instructors represent thesis is representative of their disciplines? This is a question worth asking, for although it has long been an article of faith in the writing in the disciplines (WID) literature that different disciplines have (sometimes profoundly) different ways of knowing and textual conventions, the usefulness of that article of faith has recently come into question. Thaiss has argued that the notion of writing in the disciplines has led to unproductive generalizations that stereotype instructors and mask the richness of their complex and sometimes hybrid disciplinary backgrounds. He proposes a focus on writing in the course (WIC), a change in focus that "would allow researchers to observe the richness of each course context without having to fit that context within the arbitrary category of a so-called discipline" (316). Similarly, Severino and Trachsel report that in the course of examining assignments from a wide variety of disciplines within a college of liberal arts and sciences, they "did not see disciplinary genres acculturating students to distinct patterns of thought" (450). Instead they found "unanticipated but profound differences among *individual* teachers' pedagogies and response preferences," differences that "seemed *unrelated to* the teachers' *disciplinary training*" (453, emphasis added).

So what evidence is there that disciplines, and not just personal preferences, are at work here? Because disciplines are such complex and internally variegated social structures, no individual can be said to be fully representative of an entire discipline. However, the description of the thesis essay provided by each of the Interdisc instructors does resonate with scholarly and popular analyses of how to write in these disciplines. For instance, Thomas's explanation of his expectations for a thesis coincides with the view of writing in religious studies provided in Murphy's *Reasoning and Rhetoric in Religion*. (There are very few scholarly or popular analyses of writing in the disciplines of religious studies or theology at the undergraduate level, though Klemm focuses on the rhetorical strategies of contemporary academic theologians and Yaghjian offers thoughtful analysis of writing in seminary training.) Among the six types of papers Murphy says students are likely to encounter in religious studies and theology classes are research papers ("for example, write a paper on Augustine's theory of the origin of evil" [71]) and analysis papers ("the paper on Augustine's theory of evil becomes an analysis paper when one is asked not only to describe Augustine's position, but to evaluate it or criticize it" [71]).

Thomas's assignment can be easily classified in Murphy's typology as a research paper ("[R]ecreate the way in which, according to Aquinas, human beings achieve salvation. . . . Describe . . . the operative principles or problems around which Aquinas organizes his theology"), with the option of making it an analysis paper ("at the end you may append your own personal critique as to its failings"). Furthermore, Murphy echoes Thomas's in-class discussion of regurgitation versus argument by explaining that although "it might be objected that a research paper does not make any claims because it (ordinarily) contains no explicit arguments — it simply reports on its subject," such objections "overloo[k] the fact that all such descriptions are selective and involve judgment about what is important" and therefore include the "implicit claim not only that what is reported is true but also that it represents

(1) a fair and balanced account of (2) the most important aspects of the subject in question" (72).

While Thomas's representation of thesis fits neatly into a very small body of scholarly analysis of religious studies, Roger's representation of thesis can be contextualized within a vociferous debate in the discipline of history. Poststructuralist views of authorship have sparked ongoing debate about the nature of writing history (see, for instance, White; for a riposte, see Marwick), one that brings particular significance to questions about the roles of narrative and explicit argumentation in history writing. In the wake of poststructuralist theories of authorship, many historians emphasize writing history as active and argumentative. This privileging of explicit argumentation is reflected in the WID literature: Walvoord and McCarthy's Professor Breihan values explicit argumentation and would even on occasion "consciously sacrific[e] subtlety of historical interpretation in order to emphasize the importance of taking a clear stand on an issue" (104), Greene's history of science professor notes that "the first thing to realize about an essay is that it must make an argument" (568), Beaufort's co-author from history asked students to "frame a hypothesis and an argument" (57), and the history professors interviewed by Stockton insisted on the need to "take a stance" and "make an argument" when writing for history (50).

In light of this trend, Roger's insistence that a thesis may not appear at the start of the essay or be explicitly argumentative may appear idiosyncratic rather than disciplinary. But Stockton argues that although the history professors she interviewed claimed to value explicit argument, when responding to papers they rewarded not explicit argument but implicit argument subtly embedded within narrative: "to move beyond expository argument and toward the implicit arguments of narrative is judged to be a mark of growth in student writing" (67). Stockton offers the example of a student with a 4.0 average in her literature major, but who rarely earned higher than a B on her history papers. The student's explicitly argumentative prose, valued in literary studies, was deemed "too forceful" by one of her history professors. Thus, although Roger (who did not align himself with poststructuralist theories) may not represent the most current, common, or popular view of writing in history, his representation of thesis certainly can be contextualized within the discipline's conflicted views of writing.

Resonating with Stockton's claim that explicitly argumentative prose is valued in literary studies, Olivia tells her students that a thesis must "stick its neck out." This allusion to Peter Elbow — who says that the "main point, this incipient center of gravity" of a piece of writing, should "stick its neck out, not just hedge or wonder," and must be "something that can be quarreled with" (20) — also resonates with popular and scholarly analyses of writing literary analysis. The importance of an explicitly argued thesis is stressed in Barnet's *A Short Guide to Writing about Literature*, which explains to students that during the intermediate stages of the writing process "what the thesis of the essay will be — the idea that will be asserted and argued (supported with evidence) — is still in doubt, but there is no doubt about one thing: A good essay will have a thesis, a point, an argument. You ought to be able to state your point in a thesis sentence" (21). A final dimension of this privileging of explicit argument can be seen in the persistence of what Frey termed the "adversary method" and what Wilder more recently has termed the "mistaken critic" topos. Though Frey and Wilder are primarily interested in describing how literary scholars respond to each other's work in order to build knowledge, these methods foreground the necessity of a clear argument articulated early in a literary analysis.

Emphasizing Similarity, Eliding Difference: The Double Bind

Throughout class discussions, the professors stressed the similarities among their expectations for writing, but there was little face-to-face dialogue among them. Exceptions to that trend were rare, but in one such moment two instructors talked together in front of the class about their expectations for a thesis. This interaction occurred during the eleventh week of class and was initiated by Olivia, who spontaneously responded to Roger's advice on developing a thesis:

> ROGER: Think in terms of the distinction now between a topic and a thesis. . . . A topic in a sense is a phrase: I am going to do a paper about blank. A thesis is a declarative sentence that is as particular as possible. . . . [turns to Olivia] What were you going to say?

> OLIVIA: I was going to offer my definition of a thesis. . . . And if this doesn't work for history, this will be an interesting thing for us to find out. When you get to your thesis, you should be able to preface it with the words "I think that" and then complete the sentence. And then when you're all done, to be more sophisticated erase "I think that." But if you can't say "I think that blah blah blah blah blah," it's not a thesis. Does that work for history?

> ROGER: Ah, not too well. Because historians like to think that they're finding reality. So it's not just an opinion.

> OLIVIA: Well, I don't think it has to do with opinion. What I think it has to do with is your personal analysis. . . . That that's what pushes it towards analysis, not opinion.

> ROGER: Mm hmm. I guess I, I think basically we're saying the same thing. I guess I feel more comfortable with it not prefaced by "I think that." That simply what would follow is a declarative sentence in itself.

> OLIVIA: [turning to the class] I want to make sure you guys are clear that you would never hand this in to anyone with the "I think that" still there. But some of you might want to think maybe in other disciplines about that. And I would still say that if you think about it analytically instead of subjectively that might help with history. Right? Because you can't say "I think that the French Revolution." But you can say "I think that a change in sexual mores produced the French Revolution."

> ROGER: I see. Actually it comes out the same because it has to be a declarative sentence.

> OLIVIA: Right. Okay.

This brief exchange illustrates a great deal of what's at stake in team-taught interdisciplinary classrooms. Olivia does open up the possibility that there will be differences in their expectations, and Roger does initially resist what he sees to be a difference in ways of knowing manifest in the textual convention Olivia is proposing. But when they find they agree on the fact that "I think that" should not be in the text, they cease to pursue the possibility that there are further differences. Despite an initial willingness to recognize differences in their motives or their expectations for the mediational tool, the clear tendency is to stress similarities.

This reluctance to discuss differences posed difficulties to students responsible for responding to all three assignments. Roger wanted students to approach texts and make claims as historians would, which for Roger meant allowing the thesis to evolve over time and perhaps reside only implicitly in the final text. Olivia was committed to a version of the thesis-driven essay that was more obviously argumentative. And while Thomas too expected a clear thesis, it was less explicitly argumentative. Ostensibly, the mediational tool of the thesis-driven essay was the same: it went by the same name in each of the three disciplines, and the professors affirmed similarities during discussion. But these similarities were, as Russell and Yañez say, "maddeningly deceptive" and posed considerable challenges to the students enrolled in Interdisc.

The conflicts among motives and mediational tools put the Interdisc students in what Engeström and other CHAT theorists identify as "a psychological double bind." In CHAT terms, a double bind is a scenario in which an individual "receives two messages or commands which deny each other — and the individual is unable to comment on the messages" (Engeström, chapter 3). Double binds are those uncomfortable and perhaps inevitable situations in which individuals experience contradictions within or between activity systems (e.g., between the motives and tools within a single activity system or between the motives of two different activity systems) but cannot articulate any meta-awareness of those contradictions.

In Interdisc, the students received contradictory messages regarding the mediational tool of the thesis-driven essay: the type of thesis valued by any one professor would not necessarily be valued by his or her colleagues, yet students had to write for all three professors. To recognize the differences among the expectations for thesis in the three component disciplines would be to go against the classroom discourse stressing similarities; to ignore the differences would lead students to write less than satisfactory papers. There were few classroom opportunities to reflect on those conflicts, leaving students to come to any meta-awareness of those conflicts on their own.

However, such double binds are a double-edged pedagogical sword. They can be baffling and even incapacitating for individuals, but when these conflicts push individuals to meta-awareness and individuals are able to "make a metacommunicative statement" about the conflict (Engeström, chapter 3), double binds can also facilitate higher-order thinking and critical insight. Engeström describes such outcomes as "learning by expanding." If the double bind is also an opportunity for learning by expanding, the question of how students in Interdisc negotiate the double bind presented by the thesis-driven essay becomes a particularly compelling one.

ONE STUDENT AT WORK: NEGOTIATING AN INTERDISCIPLINARY DOUBLE BIND

Will, a first-year student with a double major in religious studies and philosophy, earned high grades on all three papers under consideration here, and all three professors identified him as one of the most successful students in the class. Analyses of Will's texts indicate that he made subtle but important adjustments to his essays in each discipline. But Will was vexed by the process of moving among the various disciplinary expectations — in part because he relied on a distinction between "research papers" and "analysis papers" that focused solely on mediational tools; he was not able to articulate how the motives of various activity systems might alter those tools.

Will explained that although research and analysis papers are both versions of the thesis-driven essay, each entails a particular writing process and results in a different kind of paper. Analysis papers, as Will described them, are relatively brief, call for a clear "personal opinion," and generally focus on a single text; in CHAT terms, the motive of the analysis paper tool is to make a clear and focused argument. Research papers tend to be longer, address less narrowly defined topics, and require outside research; the motive behind this tool is to demonstrate that outside research has been conducted and applied with some skill to the topic at hand. According to Will, the paper on Marlowe's *Faustus* was an analysis paper; happily, the motive of the analysis paper as he understood it meshed nicely with Olivia's motive of making an argument that "sticks its neck out." Similarly, Will identified the history term paper on the French Revolution as a research paper, and fortunately the motive of a research paper as Will understood it jibed with Roger's motive of encouraging students to use primary texts to develop arguments as historians do. Because these two assignments fell into clearly discernible genres that were able to coexist unproblematically with the expectations of his instructors, they did not challenge Will's sense of what to do or how to do it.

But the Aquinas paper did not fall neatly into either of Will's two genres, and as a result he struggled to develop the thesis for that paper. When asked about the Aquinas paper, Will began by describing the unique writing process it required:

> It was really hard to jump into. . . . I wrote this one actually a little differently than I write a lot of papers. . . . Usually when I've had to do a paper of that length it was more like a research kind of thing where I'd been working on it and studying it with the intent of writing the paper. . . . But this time it was really just like the [analysis] essays I write usually, but a lot longer and covering a lot more material.

Part of what was so different was that despite the fact that he finally had decided it was an analysis paper, Will spent almost no time working on the thesis statement and introductory paragraph: "the intro and conclusion were also very hard. I did those in about five minutes combined, just because I really didn't know what to say in them." For Will, articulating an argumentative thesis was secondary to showing mastery of the component parts of Aquinas' model of salvation.

Differences were evident in the text as well. Whereas the thesis guiding Will's *Faustus* paper made a clear argument about the relationship between the low scenes and the main plot of *Faustus* — "This subplot of *Doctor Faustus* parallels Faustus' own downfall, and his actions toward them mirror the actions taken against him" — the thesis statement of his Aquinas paper surveyed the component parts of Aquinas' model of salvation but did not "stick its neck out." Will identified an important tension in Aquinas' work in the penultimate sentence of his introduction ("This comprehensive discussion ultimately leads to a model of salvation that acknowledges the omnipotence and supremacy of God as well as the importance of humans' contributions to their own futures"), then overviewed the organization of the paper in the final sentence: Will described this thesis as more summary than argument.

But even if he composed this thesis quickly, Will's drafts indicate that his success was more than mere luck. His scribbled marginalia suggest that Will saw his overall purpose as focusing on "the operative principles or problems around which Aquinas organizes his theology." Will's notes also indicate that he believed that he needed to "make a case for the reasonableness of Aquinas' theology" in each area only secondarily. By identifying these operative principles and problems, Will "thought along with Aquinas" — exactly the motive Thomas articulated during his class discussions and interviews.

Despite meeting Thomas's expectations, Will doubted whether this was an appropriate way to write a thesis. In fact, Will described his thesis as "a cop out," as merely "a rehashing or a reformulation" that wasn't "arguing" any one particular point. It was not, in Will's evaluation, particularly "insightful." Whereas analysis papers usually demand something more than "regurgitation," Will said the Aquinas paper was a regurgitation "more than he wanted to let on" since it was only "the structuring, kind of putting it in our own logical flow, that was original."

Will had intuited the differences in the motives among the various activity systems he was being asked to negotiate. But when those differences in motives manifested themselves textually, resulting in differences in the mediation tools (as in the thesis statements), Will second-guessed his work, calling it "a cop out." This denigration of the work he had successfully done suggests how difficult it is for participants — especially students — to negotiate the double binds placed on them when disciplinary activity systems collide. Will wrote successful papers, but intuiting the differences among the activity systems was not sufficient to escape the psychological double bind. Because Will could make no metacommunicative statement about how or why those systems conflicted, he remained puzzled by his success. Despite his good grades, there was no apparent interdisciplinary learning — no move toward awareness of the constraints, complements, and interrelations of these three disciplines. Will's instructors' focus on common features of the mediational tool rather than differing motives of the disciplinary activity systems did nothing to ameliorate this problem.

What if, however, the professors had engaged in meta-level discussions about their expectations for writing and reasoning in their disciplines? What if Will had been explicitly prompted to think about — and provided with a rich vocabulary for describing — these conflicts as productive rather than confining? What if, in other words, these conflicts were made to serve as affordances for learning rather than constraints on it? The type of classroom discussion I am imagining here is reminiscent of Gerald Graff's injunction to "teach the conflicts." "Educational success," Graff argues, can be traced "to the ability of an institution to create a community out of its differences" (172). My analyses of the Interdisc classroom suggest a companion challenge: the ability to engage in meta-reflection on the differences within a community. The Interdisc classroom had great potential to facilitate discussions of the differences among disciplines, but that potential was not fully realized. Why?

WHY BEING INTERDISCIPLINARY IS SO VERY HARD TO DO

Why did these teachers not make clear that the mediational tool of the thesis-driven essay was operating quite differently in their various disciplines? Not because they were thoughtless or inattentive teachers, for they were exceedingly thoughtful and committed. Nor because they were unaware of those differences, for as the exchange between Olivia and Roger shows, they were aware of the differences to at least some degree. Instead, I believe that the lack of attention to disciplinary differences is best explained by the fact that these instructors were experiencing double binds of their own, conflicts among or within the various activity systems in which *they* were participating.

Perhaps the most important double bind facing the three Interdisc instructors was the conflict between the motives of their individual disciplinary activity systems and the activity system of Interdisc itself. As I have argued, the motives that guided these three professors' disciplinary activity systems — to think like a history major, to make pointed arguments based on how language operates in a text, to think along with great religious thinkers — conflicted with one another. But if we shift our attention to the activity system of Interdisc as a whole, the three instructors were able to articulate a shared motive: to stress convergences and connections among the three disciplines. They elaborated this point together in a joint interview:

> OLIVIA: I think there's also a very genuine question in our minds about how much disciplinary difference is the point [of what we do in Interdisc]. . . . It might be interesting to do a little bit more of that with them because I think there are questions there. There are things that literary studies can do that history can't and vice versa. I think all three of us could tell you what some of those things are [but] I'm not sure if the students in the class could.
>
> THOMAS: I think that would be asking a good deal too much of them. . . . We might put a seed in their mind that maybe in some of them, perhaps, at the

end of four years will germinate. . . . This [focus on disciplinary differences] is so abstract for them that I doubt that they could get their minds around it.

OLIVIA: And I think the priority for all of us is precisely the opposite. [The priority] is all the ways in which [students] can do stuff when they see . . . all of the convergences. So since we can't do everything, I think that's more important to all of us.

ROGER: And I think to the extent it's team-taught the effort goes into trying to make the linkages. Not trying to show the differences.

This shared motive to stress similarities grew from several sources. It grew partly from a sense that the students were not cognitively ready for interdisciplinary work; because they lacked sufficient disciplinary exposure, they would not be able to distinguish personal idiosyncrasy from disciplinarity. As Thomas explained on another occasion, "I'm not sure that they can separate us as people from what we do: what is it that Thomas *does* and what is it that's *Thomas*. Until they get another somebody like me to make a comparison, figuring out what the disciplinary differences are becomes a real problem. . . . And I'm just not sure as freshmen they've had enough exposure at the college level to really put flesh and bones on the concept of discipline."

Another motivation for stressing convergences, Roger admitted, was his sense that "now the disciplines seem to be merging in many ways." All three instructors agreed that they might be seen as doing types of history — material history, intellectual history, cultural history. Roger explained that when he taught Interdisc with a different literature professor twenty years earlier, he knew "exactly what the differences [between history and literature] were." Now, with the influx of the New Historicism, cultural studies, and other changes in literary studies, the differences between the disciplines had become, in Roger's words, "fuzzy."

Finally, the motivation to stress convergences sprang from a sense that it offered the students a valuable counterpoint to their usual fragmented experience of the undergraduate curriculum. As Thomas explained:

The way in which the university is organized takes a culture that is a seamless whole and chops it up. And for very good reasons. There are good reasons that's done. But on the other hand, it is an artificial construction, and it's misleading. So, interdisciplinarity — where it works — tries to weave it back together again, so that what they learn in my section suddenly shows up in Milton . . . because the boundaries are not there. Even if we do chop it up [administratively, with separate grades for each component discipline], we try to have the boundaries broken down.

And indeed the students frequently praised how integrated the class was, how often they saw connections among their work for the three disciplines.

Furthermore, instructors working in team-taught interdisciplinary classrooms must fight against another powerful impulse to stress similarities and downplay differences: the tendency to develop what Grossman, Wineburg, and Woolworth term a pseudocommunity. In their study of high school literature and history teachers working together to design an interdisciplinary curriculum, Grossman and colleagues found that participants were eager to get along with their new colleagues and quick to attribute differences of opinion to superficial personality conflicts rather than any fundamental epistemological disagreements. In CHAT terms, the unofficial motive of "getting along" within the larger system of interdisciplinary collaboration conflicts with and generally trumps any effort to recognize the diverse official motives of the various disciplinary activity systems involved.

In such cases, the understandable desire for harmony easily becomes an unfortunate tendency to gloss over legitimate and significant differences. However, Grossman and colleagues argue, only when the participants recognize their epistemological disagreements can they successfully collaborate. Olivia and Roger's in-class exchange about thesis shows the pseudocommunity impulse in action: disagreement was uncomfortable, and they quickly moved toward agreement, avoiding a more difficult but more productive discussion of differences.

Ironically, though, this shared motive of stressing convergences worked directly against the type of meta-discourse on difference that I have argued can make interdisciplinary classrooms powerful contexts for learning and writing in the disciplines. But the difficulty of realizing the potential of the interdisciplinary classroom as a site to explore disciplinary connections cannot be laid solely at the feet of individual instructors who are "too nice" or "insufficiently thoughtful" about their teaching, for the conflicts among the various activity systems place double binds on instructors as well as students. These conflicts are negotiable, to be sure. And if participants can begin to develop a meta-awareness of how and why those conflicts occur, the double binds I have described can even provide opportunities for learning by expanding. Such learning is not easy or inevitable for students or teachers, but if participants can identify and name these double binds, can describe and analyze them, they are better positioned to learn through them.

CONCLUSION: THE PROMISE OF INTERDISCIPLINARY PEDAGOGY

By way of conclusion, I return to a question I posed in the introduction: is it possible for anyone, much less students in their first year of undergraduate studies, to engage in authentically interdisciplinary work? The answer lies in how we define "authentically interdisciplinary work" and how we go about facilitating it. The Interdisc instructors thought that awareness of the disciplines qua disciplines and their differences was too much to ask of first-year students, but Will's experiences suggest that students are expected to negotiate interdisciplinary double binds with or without the benefit of meta-awareness. Fish argues that interdisciplinarity is impossible for anyone — but he stacks the deck by defining interdisciplinarity as the desire to transcend disciplines entirely. But if by interdisciplinary work we mean work that takes place in and becomes aware of the intersections of various disciplinary activity systems, interdisciplinarity is indeed possible and the opportunities for interdisciplinary learning are more prevalent than we often think. To become aware of how disciplinary activity systems interlock is not to have a perfect meta-awareness of disciplinary boundaries. What it means is helping students — and ourselves — make careful and conscious inquiries into what happens when we use tools and motives from one discipline in that of another.

The challenge for interdisciplinary teaching, understood thus, is to help individuals negotiate the conflicts among motives, mediational tools, and other elements of disciplinary activity systems by identifying and naming those double binds, by facilitating opportunities to reflect on and make meta-communicative statements about those conflicts. The double binds that arise when elements of disciplinary activity systems conflict can serve as constraints or as affordances. The brief window I have provided into one team-taught interdisciplinary classroom illustrates how opportunities for discussing and reflecting on these disciplinary collisions arise in such classrooms and why those opportunities are sometimes squandered. While team-taught interdisciplinary classrooms are not the only contexts for such learning, they offer a powerful context for learning about the relationships among various disciplinary activity systems, about the internal logic of those disciplinary activity systems, and about the mediational tools central to those activity systems: in other words, for learning about interdisciplinarity, disciplinarity, and the role of writing in the disciplines.

Acknowledgments: I would like to thank the professors and students of Interdisc II for allowing me into their classroom and sharing their work and ideas so generously. I would also like to thank Deborah Brandt, Virginia Chappell, Krista Ratcliffe, David Russell, and an anonymous *CCC* reviewer for their comments and advice on earlier versions of this manuscript. This research was supported in its early stages by an NCTE Grant-in-Aid and more recently by a Summer Faculty Fellowship from Marquette University.

WORKS CITED

Barnet, Sylvan. *A Short Guide* to *Writing about Literature.* 7th ed. New York: HarperCollins, 1996.

Beaufort, Anne, and John A. Williams. "Writing History: Informed or Not by Genre Theory?" *Genre Across the Curriculum.* Ed. Anne Herrington and Charles Moran. Logan: Utah State UP, 2005. 44–64.

Elbow, Peter. *Writing without Teachers.* New York: Oxford UP, 1973.

Engeström, Yrjo. *Learning by Expanding.* Helsinki, 1987. Mind, Culture, Activity Homepage. Laboratory of Comparative Human Cognition. 10 April 2001. 3 January 2006 <http://lchc.ucsd .edu/MCA/Paper/Engeström/expanding/toc.htm>.

Fish, Stanley. "Being Interdisciplinary Is So Very Hard to Do." *Profession* 89 (1989): 15–22. Rpt. in *There's No Such Thing As Free Speech and It's a Good Thing, Too.* New York: Oxford UP, 1994. 231–42.

Frey, Olivia. "Beyond Literary Darwinism: Women's Voices and Critical Discourse." *College English* 52.5 (1990): 507–26.

Graff, Gerald. *Beyond the Culture Wars: How Teaching the Conflicts Can Revitalize American Education.* New York: W. W. Norton, 1992.

Greene, Stuart. "The Question of Authenticity: Teaching Writing in a First-Year College History of Science Class." *Research in the Teaching of English* 35 (2001): 525–69.

Grossman, Pam, Sam Wineburg, and Stephen Woolworth. "What Makes Teacher Community Different from a Gathering of Teachers?" University of Washington: Center for the Study of Teaching and Policy, December 2000. 3 January 2006 <http://depts.washington.edu/ctpmail/ PDFs/Community-GWW-01-2001.pdf>.

Klein, Julie Thompson, and William H. Newell. "Advancing Interdisciplinary Studies." *Handbook of the Undergraduate Curriculum: A Comprehensive Guide to Purposes, Strategies, Practices, and Change*. Ed. Jerry Gaff and James Ratcliff. San Francisco: Jossey-Bass. 1997. Rpt. in *Interdisciplinarity: Essays from the Literature*. Ed. William H. Newell. New York: College Entrance Examination Board, 1998. 3–22.

Klemm, David. "The Rhetoric of Theological Argument." *The Rhetoric of the Human Sciences*. Ed. John S. Nelson, Allan Megill, and Donald N. McCloskey. Madison: U of Wisconsin P, 1987.

Marwick, Arthur. *The New Nature of History: Knowledge, Evidence, Language*. Hampshire, UK: Palgrave, 2001.

Murphy, Nancey C. *Reasoning and Rhetoric in Religion*. Valley Forge, PA: Trinity P International, 1994.

Ratcliff, James L., et al. *The Status of General Education in the Year 2000: Summary of a National Survey*. Washington. DC: Association of American Colleges and Universities, 2001.

Russell, David R., and Arturo Yañez. "'Big Picture People Rarely Become Historians': Genre Systems and the Contradictions of General Education." *Writing Selves/Writing Societies*. Ed. Charles Bazerman and David R. Russell. 3 January 2006. <http://wac.colostate.edu/books/selves_societies/>. 331–62.

Severino, Carol, and Mary Trachsel. "Starting a Writing Fellows Program: Crossing Disciplines or Crossing Pedagogies?" *International Journal of Learning* 11 (2004/2005): 449–55.

Stockton, Sharon. "Writing in History: Narrating the Subject of Time." *Written Communication* 12.1 (1995): 47–73.

Thaiss, Christopher. "Theory in WAC: Where Have We Been, Where Are We Going." *WAC for the New Millennium: Strategies for Continuing Writing-Across-the-Curriculum Programs*. Ed. Susan H. McLeod et al. Urbana, IL: National Council of Teachers of English, 2001. 299–326.

Walvoord, Barbara E., and Lucille McCarthy. *Thinking and Writing in College: A Naturalistic Study of Students in Four Disciplines*. Urbana, IL: National Council of Teachers of English, 1991.

White, Hayden. *The Content of the Form: Narrative Discourse and Historical Representation*. Baltimore: Johns Hopkins UP, 1987.

Wilder, Laura. "'The Rhetoric of Literary Criticism' Revisited: Mistaken Critics, Complex Contexts, and Social Justice." *Written Communication* 22.1 (2005): 76–119.

Yaghjian, Lucretia B. "Writing Cultures, Enculturating Writing at Two Theological Schools: Mapping Rhetorics of Correlation and Liberation." *Teaching Theology and Religion* 5.3 (2002): 128–40.

23

Teaching and Learning a Multimodal Genre in a Psychology Course

CHRIS M. ANSON, DEANNA P. DANNELS, AND KAREN ST. CLAIR

Increasingly, teachers in courses across a range of disciplines are creating assignments that involve the intersection of oral and written genres. In the past, when pedagogical literature on writing paid attention to oral communication, it did so from the perspective of the support that speaking can lend to a writer's developing text (through one-on-one tutorials, small-group peer conferencing, or reading aloud; see Brooke 1991, 1994; Gere 1990; Murray 1982; Walters 1992; Zoellner 1969). However, until very recently there has been little written on the teaching and learning of multimodal genres that involve both writing and speaking.

In this chapter, we first briefly describe and theorize new genres of communication that bring together writing and speaking in common performative events. In such events, the spoken genre depends upon or intersects with the written genre or vice versa, creating new constraints and new — and often challenging — textual and rhetorical decisions for students. We then turn to an examination of a multimodal assignment one of us (Karen) used in an undergraduate psychology course. We were especially interested in the relationship between the oral and written parts of this assignment, and in the decisions students made about what to present in each mode. In exploring this case of multimodality, we explain Karen's pedagogical rationale for the assignment, analyze the results of students' work, and, through an electronic questionnaire, consider the ways in which the students interpreted and responded to the task. In turn, the results of this descriptive analysis provided the basis for moments of reflection in which Karen considered the implications of the assignment for the further development of her teaching.

Newly emerging technologies are giving rise to unique, blended, "hybrid," and multimodal genres of communication, what Holdstein calls "a type of generic bordercrossing" (1996, 281). In some cases, features of orality are said to be influencing written discourse, as in the rapid-fire exchanges common in Internet chat rooms or Instant Messenger–like systems (Leverenz

From *Genre Across the Curriculum*. Ed. Anne Herrington and Charles Moran. Logan: Utah State UP, 2005. 171–95.

1997). Published essays can take the form of a printed e-mail exchange (Spooner and Yancey 1996). New technologies for visual display, such as PowerPoint and Flash Media, are altering the experience (for both speaker and audience) of conventional oratory (Yancey 2001). And information is increasingly conveyed through multiple media. The genre of the repair manual, for example, may now include written text, still and moving diagrams and pictures, brief video clips, and sound or voice, all enabled by Web-based or CD-ROM technology.

In theorizing the concept of genre in such multimodalities, we are drawn to work that rejects static or form-based conceptions of genre in favor of seeing genre in terms of its functions and actions within particular rhetorical spaces (see Anson and Dannels 2004; Miller 1984; Mountford 2001; Russell 1997). As Amy Devitt (2000) has suggested, genre is "a dynamic social construct, a changing cultural artifact with rhetorical and social functionality. . . . Developing within groups of users, the new genres are also fluid categories that reflect and reify the ideology and values of their users" (18). Genres, in other words, are context-specific manifestations of discursive and rhetorical actions that become normative through repeated use. For this reason, they often emerge as "hybrids" or blends of other genres, simultaneously realizing different forms, functions, and characteristics.

Early work on such permutations typically examined the ways in which a specific communicative event — a speech or a piece of writing — takes on characteristics of another, similar event in the same mode, blurring and blending their two sets of features. Jamieson and Campbell (1982), for example, describe a form of political eulogy that blends two broad rhetorical categories: epideictic and deliberative. The first three parts of the eulogy — acknowledging the person's death, celebrating his or her work in the past tense, and consoling those living — are epideictic in nature. The fourth, bringing the community together in the memory of the dead, is deliberative, a political call to action that focuses on the agendas or unfinished legislation of the deceased. This fourth "subgenre," Jamieson and Campbell suggest, is not a component of a traditional eulogy; it represents a further manifestation.

In classroom settings, students often must complete assignments that similarly vary from canonical forms in ways that relate to a teacher's goals, experiences, and dispositions, as well as to the subject matter at hand. Some varieties of "journal writing," for example, constrain students enough in focus, style, and audience that the writing is no longer highly expressive as conventionally defined by theorists such as Britton et al. (1975) and Elbow (1973). Students used to journal writing in its most expressive manifestation must reorient their assumptions about the genre to match the specific classroom uses of it in each case. Similarly, students used to "saying what they think" after a moment of reflection in a classroom must learn a new variety of this genre when they are the spokesperson for a small group of three or four students, reporting on what the group "thinks" after a breakout session.

This situation becomes even more complex with the addition of different communicative modes (spoken language, written language, visual representations both moving and still, three-dimensional objects, sounds, or other phenomena). Theoretical work in social semiotics suggests we make sense of the world using multimodal resources — not simply linguistic, but pictorial, gestural, choreographical, and graphical, to name a few (Kress and van Leeuwen 1996; Kress and Threadgold 1988; Lemke 2002a, 2002b). Especially in scientific fields, but increasingly in others as well, the communicative patterns of the disciplines are in and of themselves multimodal. As Lemke (1998) puts it:

> Science is not done, is not communicated, through verbal language alone. It cannot be. The "concepts" of science are not verbal concepts, though they have verbal components. They are semiotic hybrids, simultaneously and essentially verbal-typological and mathematical-graphical-operational-topological. The actional, conversational, and written textual genres of science are historically and presently, fundamentally and irreducibly multimedia genres. To do science, to talk science, to read and write science it is necessary to juggle and combine in canonical ways verbal discourse, mathematical expression, graphical-visual representation, and motor operations in the "natural" (including human-as-natural) world. (89)

Perhaps to create a better match between the multimodalities in students' learning and the tasks they complete as part of that learning, assignments across a range of disciplines now increasingly involve such merged representations, which are further enabled by new technologies that bring together text, speech, and visual media. In a teacher-education course at the University of Sydney, for example, students must compose the equivalent of one page in a textbook to be used to teach a concept to students in a particular stage of development. This text must include both visual and verbal elements. In the second phase of the assignment the students are asked to construct a digitized version of the text — a PowerPoint, Hyperstudio, or Web page (Simpson 2003). The students (prospective teachers) engage in such mixed-media assignments so that they can be better prepared to teach the next generation of learners. As the course designers put it, "the literacies involved in schooling and in social life are complex social practices involving the interpretation, production and use of a range of meaning making systems, including language and image. These are negotiated in a range of formats from traditional page-based material to screen-based electronic multi-media."

Similarly, in a Design Fundamentals course at North Carolina State University, students are asked to create a studio book that is a visual, verbal, and written record of the semester, including notes or sketches from required lectures or exhibitions, reflections on required and recommended readings, drawings of ideas and images for the design process, and a scrapbook of handouts and objects or images the students think are important to their design (North Carolina State University 2003a). In a medieval literature course at California Polytechnic University, students are asked to give a presentation that provides a close reading of a particular text. The presentation must be accompanied by a pedagogical handout, which includes an outline of the presentation and any background information. Students are encouraged to be creative in this handout, using illustrations, visual representations of their presentation, and the like, as long as the handout serves pedagogical ends (California Polytechnic University 2003).

For students, performing well on such tasks requires them to understand and interpret these genres within their context of use. We speculate that to begin the process, students apply broad schematic representations to the genre first, placing it into the best-matching "meta-genre" category — general discursive types they have experienced before, often repeatedly. When students are told that they will be required to do an oral presentation on their group project in chemical engineering, for example, their schemas for the meta-genre of oral presentation provide them with some general expectations and conventions for their behavior: stand up in front of the class, explain the project, and so on. Acting on such generalized knowledge, however, is not enough to guarantee them a successful performance. As they practice the speech genre within its context, more specific behaviors or expectations become clear: in an engineering progress report, presenters are often interrupted by the audience (a small group of managers) with questions or requests for clarification, a process often modeled by the teacher in class. Students unfamiliar with this instantiation must learn to "suspend" the progress of their presentation briefly to answer questions, and then, finding where they left off, quickly adjust the remaining presentation to accommodate the information they provided in the answer. As students prepare variations on poster sessions, presentations with accompanying visuals, or Web-based, multimedia assignments, they often need new strategies for deciding what information to convey in what mode, or how to organize it in a compelling and meaningful way for an audience.

The assignment we explore presents specific variations on the meta-genres of the classroom oral presentation and the classroom handout, brought together in a single communicative event. The more specific characteristics and constraints of the assignment — the length of the presentation, the accompaniment of a maximum one-page handout, the goal of extending the course material and informing peers about new concepts and studies — created a unique multimodal form. Because none of the students had ever completed such an assignment, it presented an interpretive challenge that had the potential to reveal much about the need for new methods of instruction and support, and new avenues for research on student learning and performance.

Our exploration of this assignment mirrors the kind of classroom-based assessment procedures encouraged in a view of teaching as reflective practice (see Angelo and Cross 1993; Glassick, Huber, and Maeroff 1997; Rice 1996; Schön 1987). In such a process, faculty systematically collect information about their instruction in order to engage in a "scholarship of teaching," actively investigating the effects of pedagogical decisions and continually improving their instruction. As Angelo (1991) puts it, "the purpose of classroom assessment is to provide faculty and students with information and insights needed to improve teaching effectiveness and learning quality" (17). Consistent with principles of the scholarship of teaching and learning — asking a question related to student learning, gathering data to answer that question, making results public and peer reviewed, and incorporating reflective practice — we create here a collaborative and cross-curricular variation on the typical processes of classroom-based assessment (see AAHE 2003).

In our meetings as a group, we settled on two operative questions that would simultaneously yield some broad speculation about multimodal genres in teaching and learning, and specific, instructionally helpful feedback for Karen in her own postcourse reflections:

- What performative choices did students make when faced with completing a multimodal (combined writing and speaking) assignment?

- Given a carefully articulated, supported, and assessed multimodal assignment, what can we discover about students' learning processes that can provide principles for crafting, supporting, and assessing effective multimodal assignments in the future?

Because Karen played a central role as designer of the assignment in question, as teacher of the course, and as beneficiary — in a direct sense — of her own reflection, we found our roles to be productively mixed. In keeping with investigative designs that encourage such a blending of roles and subject positions (see Fishman and McCarthy 2000), we developed a specific structure for our analysis. Two of us (Chris and Deanna) took the lead in collecting information: Karen's course materials, videotapes of the students' presentations, copies of all their handouts. In her role as instructor, Karen judged the students' performances on the assignment, rating them on a set of criteria and incorporating the results into her final course grades. Chris and Deanna then gathered information from the students through a postcourse online questionnaire. The questionnaire asked students to choose "agree," "disagree," or "not sure" for nine statements about writing and speaking and about the assignment. The statements were followed by twelve open-ended questions focusing on how the student completed the assignment, what they thought Karen was looking for, and so forth (see Tables 23-1 and 23-2). They also coded the videotaped presentations for three features related to successful oratory: strong or weak eye contact with the audience, an extemporaneous style in contrast to a text-bound style (when students read note cards verbatim, for example), and the presence or absence of audience appeals (such as when the speaker asks the audience a direct or rhetorical question at the beginning of the talk). Karen then sent Chris and Deanna her evaluation of the students, including scores on each of the four categories on her rubric, and they figured those results into their analysis. They then presented a summary of their analysis to Karen, who began thinking about the implications of the information for her own teaching and future use of the multimodal assignment.

Engaging in a little genre-bending of our own, we also chose a somewhat unusual way to present the results of this study. As Karen considered the impact of our analysis on her teaching, she wrote brief reflective statements, eventually creating a commentary that appears in italics toward the end of the essay. In this way, she played a kind of hybrid role, at once the coauthor of the main text and the sole author of pedagogical reflections emerging from the analysis.

EXPLORATIONS IN MULTIMODALITY: THE MICROPRESENTATION

The context for our explorations was a special section of Psychology 201 — Controversial Psychological Issues. This general education course is designed, as Karen's syllabus explains, to introduce students to "psychology and contemporary topics to illustrate how psychologists address controversial psychological issues." Karen's course objectives were to:

- refine the student's ability to research, analyze, evaluate, and make decisions about the details of complex contemporary issues in psychology
- improve the student's ability to effectively express views about psychological issues in writing and speaking
- expand the student's knowledge of psychology

Karen's preparation for this section of PSY 201 was supported by two faculty-development initiatives: the First-Year Inquiry Program and the Campus Writing and Speaking Program. In an attempt to reform "transmission" or "conduit" models of education (see Reddy 1979) and give students a more supportive experience, the university enlists faculty to teach First-Year Inquiry (FYI) versions of their courses. The FYI program encourages more hands-on work, more activities and assignments, and greater attention to "guided practice in writing, speaking, listening, asking questions, looking for answers, and evaluating evidence" (NC State 2003b). Participating instructors engage in a series of orientations and workshops designed to acquaint them with principles and methods for active learning, student-centered instruction, and inquiry-guided learning. Section size is capped at twenty to support the more student-centered nature of the course. (In her FYI section of PSY 201, Karen allowed one additional student to enroll, bringing her class size to twenty-one: eleven men and ten women, almost all first-year students. The class represented a mix of fourteen different intended majors.) Supported by her work in the FYI program, Karen's version of PSY 201 engaged students in small-group work and class discussions, and included numerous informal writing and speaking assignments (usually one for each class), which counted for 20 percent of the final grade. Frequent ten-minute quizzes and a final examination provided assessments of learning, and together counted 40 percent of the final grade.

Karen's inclusion of the assignment that is the subject of our inquiry had a more direct genesis in NC State Campus Writing and Speaking Program's faculty seminar, which Karen took during the semester before teaching PSY 201. The semester-long, biweekly seminar is designed to help faculty incorporate both formal and informal writing and speaking into existing courses, with special attention to learning goals, assignment design, and assessment. During the seminar, Karen designed a new, formal, multimodal writing/

speaking assignment: the oral presentation and accompanying one-page handout, which earned students 20 percent of their final grade. Before taking the seminar, Karen had built brief oral presentations into many of her courses, but she had never paired those with a writing assignment in a way that represented a single discourse activity utilizing both oral and written text. Students had occasionally used the board or an overhead projector to punctuate their presentations with something visual, but Karen had not built this systematically into the requirements for the assignment.

In its final version, Karen's assignment description took up three single-spaced pages and included a set of three learning objectives, five recommended steps to complete the assignment, and half a page of suggestions and tips for success. Described throughout as a "formal writing and speaking assignment," it allowed many options for topic choice but placed relatively tight constraints on delivery: students were asked to prepare a micropresentation — a brief oral presentation delivered to the class in no more than four to six minutes — summarizing an article they had located in the psychological literature about a controversial subject such as parental spanking of children, the psychological effects of video-game violence, and the use of electroshock therapy to treat depression. An accompanying written text (only a handout was allowed) had to be no more than a single page in length, designed to highlight, extend, elucidate, or provide examples to support the oral summary. The assignment sheet explained that the handout "is not a written summary of your presentation, nor is it a copy of your presentation notes. It is a visual that helps the audience understand and focus on your presentation. The handout allows elaboration on points; this enables you to provide more information in less time." Students were asked to bring twenty-five copies of the handout.

In addition to the list of five instructional suggestions included in the assignment handout (which we have reproduced as appendix 1), various kinds of classroom support were also foreshadowed in the assignment description: informal writing and speaking assignments to "serve as practice for successfully completing the steps" in the multimodal assignment, opportunities to discuss the students' readings in class, and peer-group work that yielded feedback on the preparation for the presentation. In addition, Karen provided the class with a set of detailed criteria (see appendix 2). These criteria were designed to be formative (helping the students to prepare the assignment) as well as summative (helping her to apply clear, consistent criteria to her grading). Constituting one of four separately scored criteria, the handout category "refers to the quality of your accompanying one-page handout. How well does it accompany your remarks? If you need to add time to your presentation to explain the handout, then the handout is not supporting your presentation. The handout illustrates, elaborates, and clarifies your remarks. A handout riddled with errors, hard to read, confusing, or poorly laid out indicates incomplete work."

To score the presentations, Karen used a rubric matched to the categories in the descriptive criteria.

From the perspective of classroom research, the three of us were interested in how students would respond to this multimodal genre: what would they do to complete the task? How would they conceive of the relationship between their spoken words and the written text? Could we discern anything in their performance or reflections on the experience that would help us to prefigure some new areas for pedagogical development and research on genres in communication across the curriculum?

ASSISTED INQUIRY: CLASSROOM-BASED ASSESSMENT FROM THE OUTSIDE IN

As we reviewed the videotapes of the students' presentations, we were immediately struck by how they used the handout. The class was evenly divided between those who distributed their handouts before starting their presentation and those who waited until it was over. Because Karen had made no recommendations or requirements for whether the audience should have the handout for reference during the talks, we speculated that students construed its purpose differently. Those who provided it at the end were perhaps seeing it as a form of documentation for Karen, or as something the audience could refer to later, while those who began their presentations by circulating the handout may have understood it to be a visual gloss, providing additional detail or allowing the audience to "follow along" as the speaker worked through his or her points.

Survey results confirmed our speculations: students described the purpose of their handout in quite different ways, some to "keep [the] audience on the right track so they could easily follow [the] speech without getting lost or bored," some to "restate" what they presented, and some to "provide a visual aid." A few students clearly used their handout as the equivalent of their talking points, reading from it verbatim. Although 47 percent of students referred to their handouts during the presentation, as many as a third simply handed it out and did not mention it (see Table 23-1).

This key rhetorical and pragmatic difference in the presentations — handout before or after — was mildly correlated to the students' overall grade (with a six-point higher average score among those who circulated their handout in advance of the presentation). In addition, our codings of the videotapes showed a strong relationship to the "before or after" handout order: students who provided their handouts first generally gave livelier presentations, connected more with their audience, and spoke more extemporaneously, sometimes starting their presentation with an audience-directed question. In contrast, students who distributed their handouts at the end were more likely to read their note cards (or the handout itself) aloud, make little or no eye contact with the audience, and use few audience appeals. In two such cases, the students remembered to distribute the handouts only as they were about to take their seats again after their presentation.

Although we might imagine a further connection of these features to questionnaire items that asked students to say whether they liked or thought

TABLE 23-1   Responses to Open-Ended Questions (by percentage)

What was the hardest part about this entire assignment to you?

Getting up in front of the class	40%
Doing the research	27%
Figuring out how to organize the information/what to present	20%
Nothing/overall it was easy	13%

How did you go about writing your accompanying handout?

Focused on key points/made an outline of my talk	60%
Took facts from the Internet	20%
Tried to add more interesting information	20%

How did you go about preparing for the presentation?

I read over the material and created an outline.	40%
I wrote/studied notes about my material.	20%
I practiced aloud (alone or in front of a friend).	26%
I memorized my material.	7%
I didn't prepare at all.	7%

Did you do the handout first, or work on the oral presentation first?

I did the handout first.	33%
I did the presentation first.	67%

Considering everything that you presented to the class, what percentage of that information do you think went into the handout and what percentage went into the presentation?

5% to 10%	40%
20%–50%	47%
80–90%	13%

What percentage of your time went into constructing the handout?

5%–10%	27%
20%–40%	46%
50%–75%	27%

How did you use the handout in your presentation? Did you refer to it, read from it, etc.?

I referred to it as I talked.	47%
I just handed it out.	33%
I read from it.	7%
I used it as a guide.	13%

(continued on next page)

TABLE 23-1   Responses to Open-Ended Questions (by percentage)   (continued)

What purpose did you want the handout to serve? Did it serve that purpose?
Why or why not?

Visual aid for the audience	20%
An outline/summary/restatement of my presentation	40%
Reinforce/back up my major points	13%
Provide information on my topic	27%

If you could decide how to give a presentation in a future class, would you use
an accompanying handout or not? Why or why not?

It would depend on the presentation/information.	33%
Yes (conveys info., helps class to follow, backs up my points)	67%

What do you think your teacher was looking for in the presentation and
handout? That is, what do you think a successful handout and presentation
looked like?

Good connection between presentation and handout	33%
Performance factors: clear, understandable, thought-provoking	33%
Informational factors: hard work, knowledge, evidence of research	33%

If you could have chosen to summarize your article either in writing or in an
oral presentation, which would you have chosen? Why?

Writing (not good at oral/less time to prepare/feels more natural/ can revise)	60%
Oral (not good at writing/can explain better orally/fewer errors/ hate writing)	40%

Are you better at providing information orally or in writing? Why?

Orally (body language, easier than writing, can show emotion)	40%
In writing (easier to organize thoughts, nervous with oral, can revise)	60%

they were good at oral presentations, we did not see a predictable pattern. Students' self-concepts as orators or writers did not appear to be related over-all to these aspects of their presentations. In fact, as shown in Table 23-2, two-thirds of the class indicated that they do not dislike giving oral presentations (with more of them disliking writing assignments), most believe both writing and speaking are important in their planned careers, and most desire more writing and speaking instruction. Yet Table 23-2 shows them to be almost evenly split between those who think they are better at writing versus speaking.

The handouts themselves represented a range of styles, textual density, and use of visuals. For example, Alan's handout, shown in reduced form in

TABLE 23-2   Responses to Yes/No Questions (by percentage)

Questionnaire item	Yes	No	Not sure
I generally dislike giving oral presentations.	33	67	0
I generally dislike doing writing assignments.	47	47	6
Oral presentations will be important in my career.	70	15	15
Writing will be important in my career.	67	13	20
I enjoyed the formal writing/speaking assignment in PSY 201.	60	13	27
The handout helped my oral presentation.	80	13	7
The handouts added significant value to the oral presentations of other students.	67	20	13
I would value additional instruction in how to give effective oral presentations.	80	13	7
I would value additional instruction in how to write effectively.	73	7	20

Figure 23-1, is visually appealing, with mixed font size, sophisticated layout, and a large red and black bar down the left side. He includes a graphic of a brain, and the handout is organized as bulleted points answering a central question at the top of the page. Along the right side of the page, further bulleted points provide examples of the language of diagnostic labeling, the subject of the article he located. In contrast, Kelly's handout on ADHD (Figure 23-2) provides far more text and no visuals. It is organized as bulleted answers to two questions ("What is ADHD?" and "What are the symptoms of ADHD?"). Information about the article itself appears at the very end of the handout, in a five-line paragraph. Most of the text is in the same font size.

The range of styles, formats, density, font types, and other textual and visual elements in the handouts appears to reflect the way that students constructed the relationship between the oral and written components of the task. Karen did not provide examples of handouts, nor any information (beyond what we have already described) about their expected form and content. Considering all the information and suggestions Karen's assignment offered about the presentation — give it a clear structure, don't read it verbatim, use note cards, practice in front of a mirror, and so on (see appendix 1) — this range clearly shows that unfamiliar genres require more instructional support than most teachers are used to providing in content-area courses.

An examination of Karen's scores on the rubric showed no strong or predictable relationships to features of the handouts. However, we noticed a tendency for handouts that began with provocative or interesting questions, followed by an "answer" to the question in the form of well-organized information, to receive higher scores than handouts that simply provided information. This recognition of audience appeals appears to match Karen's overall

Figure 23-1   Alan's Handout

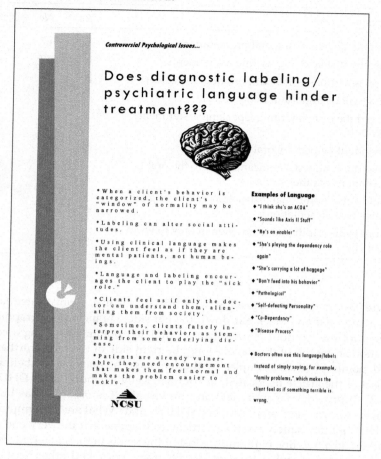

Controversial Psychological Issues...

Does diagnostic labeling/ psychiatric language hinder treatment???

*When a client's behavior is categorized, the client's "window" of normality may be narrowed.

*Labeling can alter social attitudes.

*Using clinical language makes the client feel as if they are mental patients, not human beings.

*Language and labeling encourages the client to play the "sick role."

*Clients feel as if only the doctor can understand them, alienating them from society.

*Sometimes, clients falsely interpret their behaviors as stemming from some underlying disease.

*Patients are already vulnerable, they need encouragement that makes them feel normal and makes the problem easier to tackle.

NCSU

Examples of Language

♦ "I think she's an ACOA"

♦ "Sounds like Axis II Stuff"

♦ "He's an enabler"

♦ "She's playing the dependency role again"

♦ "She's carrying a lot of baggage"

♦ "Don't feed into his behavior"

♦ "Pathological"

♦ "Self-defeating Personality"

♦ "Co-Dependency"

♦ "Disease Process"

♦ Doctors often use this language/labels instead of simply saying, for example, "family problems," which makes the client feel as if something terrible is wrong.

scores on the presentations as well as the students' presentational styles: students who made more eye contact and used extemporaneous styles and audience appeals in their presentations tended more often to organize their handouts around questions. However, Karen's scores on the handouts also indicate as much concern for the clarity of the information as for the visual appeal of the handout per se; one or two well-designed handouts that contained seemingly random pieces of information in "unparallel" form received somewhat lower scores than less visually appealing handouts that were more carefully organized. When considered next to the descriptive rubric shown in appendix 2, these specific aspects of students' performances are most explicitly tied to her suggestions about delivery: demeanor, being both "relaxed and professional," and delivering the presentation "in a way that shows you are interested in your work." Clearly, some students are able to act on these general recommendations and admonitions while others need more explicit or

FIGURE 23-2   Kelly's Handout

ADHD.........

What is attention deficit hyperactivity disorder (ADHD)?

Attention deficit hyperactivity disorder (ADHD) is the most common behavior disorder diagnosed in children and teens. ADHD refers to a group of symptoms that begin in early childhood and can continue into adulthood, causing difficulties at home, at school, at work, and within the community if not recognized and treated.

What are the symptoms of ADHD?

The three groups of ADHD symptoms are:

• **Inattention.** This is the most common symptom. In addition to having difficulty paying attention, people with this ADHD symptom often are unable to consistently focus, remember, and organize. They may be careless and have a hard time starting and completing tasks that are boring, repetitive, or challenging.
• **Impulsiveness.** People who frequently act before thinking may not make sound judgments or solve problems well. They may also have trouble developing and maintaining personal relationships. An adult may not keep the same job for long or spend money wisely.
• **Hyperactivity.** A hyperactive child may squirm, fidget, and climb or run when it is not appropriate. These children often have difficulty playing with others. They may talk a great deal and not be able to sit still for even a short time. Teenagers and adults who are hyperactive don't usually have the more obvious physical behaviors seen in children. Rather, they often feel restless and fidgety, and are not able to enjoy reading or other quiet activities.

Symptoms vary by individual and range from mild to severe.

Symptoms of ADHD can be similar to those of other conditions, such as:

• Learning disabilities.

• Oppositional defiant disorder (ODD).

• Conduct disorder.

• Anxiety disorder.

• Depression.

These conditions are sometimes mistaken for ADHD. They may also occur along with ADHD, which can make diagnosis of the primary problem difficult.
(Information above taken from AOLHealth/ WebMD)

The article that I chose for my presentation was "ADHD, HUNTING, AND EVOLUTION: 'JUST SO STORIES'". In the article, the author is basically giving the reader many bizarre stories that account for ADHD and then he tells why they are faulty and untrue. He then goes on to tell what is the truth about those who have ADHD and why it is true and why the other "Just So Stories" are untrue.

extensive help knowing what they mean and how to apply them to their own performances.

Questionnaire results also suggest few strong consistencies among students, although some general tendencies do emerge from the data. Most students agreed that the handouts helped their own presentations, but were somewhat less sure that they helped the presentations of others. It is not possible to tell whether students felt their own handout helped them as presenters (e.g., to organize information or stay on track) more than it helped their audience; however, almost half said its purpose was to provide an outline or restatement of their presentation, while about one-fifth referred directly to the needs of their audience. The students who saw their handout's purposes in this audience-focused way received the highest overall scores on their presentation, and were among those who connected with their audiences, spoke extemporaneously, and made eye contact.

Students' responses to the questionnaires provide a window into their learning processes as they completed the combined writing and speaking assignments. As shown in Table 23-1, most students worked on the oral presentation first, before creating the handout (67 percent), and spent more time working on it than preparing the handout (73 percent spent one-half to three-quarters of their time preparing the presentation, while only 27 percent spent this amount of time on their handout). Students also used specific processes to prepare the oral presentation and the handout. In preparing for the presentation, students typically read over their material or created an outline (40 percent), or practiced aloud (26 percent). When they created the handout, they typically focused on key points or made an outline for the talk (60 percent). The majority of students also estimated that much less information was provided on the handout than in the presentation. Yet all but one of the handouts provided more text than could be easily read aloud in four to five minutes. Students believe, in other words, that a brief oral presentation conveys far more information than a piece of written text with potentially equal informational and presentational value. These results suggest that, for the most part, students tackled this assignment with the perception that the handout was secondary to the presentation, rather than a tool for structuring or generating the presentation (see Yancey 2001).

Karen's weighting of the grading criteria toward the oral presentation (as well as the usual urgency of having to stand in front of one's peers) no doubt contributed to students' perceptions of its importance relative to the handout. Only one-third of the students explicitly connected the handout to the presentation in describing what they thought Karen was "looking for" in the assignment, in spite of Karen's including this as one of the criteria for success. Yet the majority of students agreed that they would use an accompanying handout for oral presentations in the future if given a chance. We see, then, a complicated relationship between the way that each mode in the assignment is weighted in the evaluation — in this case, not equally — and the overall rhetorical and pragmatic nature of the task. Professionals might understand that the quality of a handout is part of the quality and overall effect of the entire presentation, whereas students interpret this relationship using instructional cues such as how much each part counts, how extensive the suggestions are for each part, and the like.

Our analysis suggests that although students' performances variously interwove or kept separate the oral and written components of the assignment, generally they interpreted them as separate, familiar genres that they were asked to link together. Lacking schemas or operational knowledge for creating a single, multimodal genre in which the written/visual and spoken texts could strategically and artfully reinforce each other, they prepared each as a separate communicative medium. In a few cases, notably among the students who were most aware of the needs of their audience, the merging of the two modalities was fortuitous, but their success did not appear to be a consequence of the instructional support provided for the assignment.

From this perspective, we return to the design and nature of the assignment. In spite of the thorough, carefully presented information Karen provided to the students, and in spite of the direct and indirect instructional activities she crafted to support the assignment, the nature of its complex multimodality also revealed areas for continued instructional development. Certain language in the assignment description, for example, may have suggested the separateness of the two modes even while it was being presented as a single, multimodal task. Including the handout as a separate category in the evaluation rubric, even alongside an explanation pointing to the need for the handout to "support" the presentation, may have led students to divide their attention accordingly when preparing the assignment. Allocating fewer points to the handout relative to the oral presentation likewise suggests an instructional asymmetry between the two. Like the development of a creole from two separate languages, the "evolution" of this multimodal genre may be at a stage when both teachers and students find it easy to revert to more stable and canonical conceptions of each part.

ASSISTED INQUIRY: CLASSROOM-BASED ASSESSMENT
FROM KAREN ST. CLAIR

After participating in the NC State Campus Writing and Speaking Program faculty seminar, I realized that when developing writing and speaking assignments, I need to consider several factors that affect the student's success in completing my assignments: the purpose of the assignments, my plan for guiding students through the assignment, my expectations when evaluating the student's performance, and the student's experience with writing and speaking assignments.

Consequently, for this section of PSY 201 I set out to mirror the course objectives in the formal writing and speaking assignment objectives. I believed the student should be able to apply a course-specific critical thinking process to an empirical or theoretical article concerning a psychological controversy, personalize the critical analysis by reflecting on how the controversy relates to his or her life, and effectively communicate this analysis and reflection. The term "effectively" is, finally, subjective, but specific criteria for evaluating the presentation introduced some objectivity: substance (accuracy and completeness of the information presented), coherence (clarity of the presentation), delivery (timing, evidence of rehearsal), and the handout (quality of support it provides). I prepared a detailed student handout describing the steps to take in completing the assignment, suggestions for successful completion, and how they would receive class support along the way. Reflecting on the analysis now, I recognize that the mixing of writing and speaking requirements in an assignment necessitates even more instruction and support along the way than I planned. Evaluation proved to be difficult; a greater consideration of the student's writing and speaking experiences offers some new insights that could translate into clearer criteria for evaluation.

The results focusing on the order of the handout — something that had not occurred to me to discuss — suggest the need for more time explaining the purpose of the handout (which was to support the information presented) and ways to prepare the handout (use of text and symbols, color and white space). When teaching this course again, not only would I provide stronger suggestions for incorporating the handout throughout the oral presentation, I would change the way I model this expectation by preparing one-page handouts that support or embellish some of my mini-lectures. I would distribute these handouts at the beginning of my presentation and "walk" the students through the points I make by referring to the handout.

The frequent opportunities over the semester for reading, speaking during class, writing informal assignments, and listening to others undoubtedly prepared the students for getting up in front of the group. Being at ease, however, does not necessarily mean skill in relating to the audience. Our analysis suggests that students have difficulty getting away from "doing something for the teacher." Even at the end of a semester, some students continue to "speak to the teacher" and ignore the classmate to whom the response is intended. Students are used to being "taught to" and, clearly, have difficulty making the rhetorical and interpersonal switch to "teach" their classmates. Expecting students to know intuitively the effect of delivery on the audience and to plunge into focusing on its needs and response is probably too high an expectation. Including effective communication as a course and assignment objective requires considerable guidance, modeling, and time for more practice in presentation. A practice I would like to explore further involves the use of "response cards." These small pieces of paper allow students to write comments about each other's presentations. The teacher reserves the editorial privilege to cull thoughtless or unnecessarily harsh comments, and delivers the comments the day following presentations. Perhaps an extension of this technique — using response cards following "practice" oral presentations and allowing for class discussion of specific aspects of presentation style — would provide peer support to reinforce the importance of one's audience.

It is possible, however; that students with less skill at audience appeal and less creative applications for the handout may have better understood their topics and prepared a more thoughtful presentation. My plans to manage the process of the assignment went awry when I set about to evaluate the presentation. Had I read each student's chosen article and carefully helped them work through their presentation outlines, I may have been better able to separate the evaluation criteria: substance, coherence, delivery, and handout. I did require that the chosen article meet my approval to avoid selection of a nonprofessional work. And I required each student to submit an outline of the oral presentation, but this was merely an exercise to keep them on track and avoid last-minute preparations. I found it impossible, however, to recall topics, articles, and outlines when listening to the presentations. Consequently, I was attracted to the delivery and use of the handout over the substance and clarity of points made.

The data also suggest some productive areas to consider when making fair comparisons among the students. Certainly, matching observable evaluation criteria to assignment goals and objectives makes the grading task easier. And arranging for the formal writing and speaking assignment to be counted for only one-fifth on the final grade puts the value of the student's performance on the assignment in perspective. But my expectation for creative, unique presentations made fair evaluations difficult.

The PSY 201 presentations were delivered over three class days. On the second and third day, I found myself grading less stringently than on the first day. In fact, I regraded the first two or three presentations to be fairer. I believe my gradual leaning toward being less stringent reflects my feeling of responsibility for the students' performances. This is not to say that many of the presentations were not what I would describe as "top notch." What I am suggesting is that when a student did not create an eye-catching handout, utilize the handout effectively, deliver the main point of the article, or present his or her reflection on the controversy, I recognized the need to provide a lot more guidance to students to help them through the preparation process.

An ever-present course objective has been to prepare students of psychology for a variety of professional writing and speaking requirements. Although it is undoubtedly true that not all psychologists are skilled at writing and speaking in their work, I nevertheless feel an obligation to expose my students to what has been written and require that they write and speak about the discipline. With that obligation comes the need to state my objectives, guide students through the completion process, and prepare to evaluate what I ask for. All these and consideration of the students' experiences with writing and speaking would not only reduce my own frustrations, but would undoubtedly result in enhanced student outcomes. In the absence of formal study in composition and communication, many teachers in my position face sometimes daunting challenges when we incorporate writing and speaking — even as separate modes — into our classes. The help of experts like Chris and Deanna in "assisted classroom assessment" can reduce those challenges, as has been the case with my own multimodal assignment; but there is obviously much cross-curricular work yet to be done in the face of rapid change in communication, technology, media, and the goals of higher education.

CONCLUSION: GENRE, MULTIMODALITY, AND THE NEED FOR INSTRUCTIONAL DEVELOPMENT

Our limited results suggest that multimodal assignments, although designed to help students to use new and increasingly important communicative strategies that stretch beyond the usual boundaries of canonical classroom forms, are often interpreted by students as separate genres that function to achieve similar goals. In essence, students seem to have difficulty seeing these genres outside of their traditional instantiations ("informative oral report," for example, and "accounting for one's reading in an outline of ideas to be turned in during class"). In this scenario, perhaps students are operating within an academic activity system whose scripts of "handout" and "presentation" position them in a contiguous, not complementary, relationship to one another (Russell 1997). Our informal data also suggest that students were only obliquely aware of ways they could enhance their presentation for their peer audience, perhaps by calling attention to interesting or relevant information in their handouts.

As we discovered in our informal exploration of a relatively simple multimodal assignment, students clearly need to be more fully supported in their acquisition of strategies and skills for communication in an increasingly complex world of discourse. The students' performances ranged from mediocre to excellent, yet almost all of them expressed a desire to receive more instruction in both writing and speaking. And if it is more likely that students will experience complex, multimodal assignments as they move out of general education courses like Karen's and into specialized courses in their majors, the need to establish a base of support early on is clearly an issue for further consideration.

If Karen stands at the end of the WAC continuum where well-informed, diligent faculty reside, it is easy to see the scope of work that remains to be done in faculty development and orientation to communication across the curriculum. Our experiment in "assisted inquiry" finds some affinities with new processes in which peer or outside consultants can offer teachers formative evaluation that is sometimes difficult to collect on one's own; for example, a teacher can't simultaneously be an observer of his or her own teaching, nor is it possible to gather impressions from students that an outsider could using a procedure like small-group instructional diagnosis (see Lewis and Lunde 2001).

But thankfully, not all such formative data collection needs to be externally supported. The process we used to explore and understand students' performances on this task is one that with little alteration could be fruitfully used by any teacher interested in how students interpret and respond to new kinds of assignments. Karen felt that her reflections were considerably enriched by an analysis that, with a few modifications (such as some additional categories on the scoring rubric in the absence of videotapes), could be used by teachers across a range of courses. Such methods promise to bring together the study of new educational genres with their principled application in courses across the varied landscape of higher education.

Finally, not only does our exploration suggest a need for support in students' acquisition of communication skills in multimodal settings, it also raises more complex questions about the nature of genre acquisition and performance. As they become more proficient members of their chosen disciplines where they are increasingly assigned multimodal genres, when do students stop performing within the frameworks of more traditional, single-mode genres? As they move from novice to expert in their disciplines, do they develop more complex and increasingly multimodal understandings of the communication genres that will face them in their professional context? Or are there other constraining aspects of the academic activity system that hamper the acquisition of complex multimodalities? Although our work does not fully answer these questions, our informal exploration suggests that when moving from single to multimodal genre pedagogy, the instructional complexities are also exponentially multiplied. Further research and pedagogy might benefit from increased explorations of these complexities.

APPENDIX 1

Karen's "Suggestions for Success" (as Excerpted from the Assignment)

1. Actively participate in class discussions about articles, the difference between theoretical and empirical research, and evaluating an article's quality.

2. Use information from class discussions on critical thinking, the scientific method, and psychology as guides when carefully reading the article to understand, identify, and critique the author's question, answer, and evidence.

3. Allow time for reflection about what you have discovered from study of the article. Do you agree with the author? Why or why not? How do you relate to the issue? What connections do you have with the author's stand? Do not rush to agree or disagree without being able to articulate why you agree or disagree.

4. Prepare an oral presentation of your work and a supporting handout for distribution by carefully planning and rehearsing.

   a. Consider your audience. Audiences show respect by paying attention to what you have to say; in return, respect them by keeping the focus on your assignment and not on your popularity. The audience expects your presentation to be more interesting than the article. Therefore, an engaging presentation style keeps your audience's attention.

   b. Typically a talk consists of introductory remarks, content or substance of the presentation, and a summary or restatement of the purpose. The substance of your presentation is an oral version of your work on the assignment: identifying the issue, the author's stand, and the author's evidence. Introductory remarks and summary of the purpose are "bookends" for your substance.

   c. No doubt you cannot memorize your presentation, but you are not to read a narrative to your audience. Prepare notes and record them on note cards. Insert talking points (key phrases, words, visual cues) into your notes to guide you through your presentation. Talking points include "check time," "refer to handout," "look at audience." A copy of the presentation notes are turned in to the instructor.

   d. The handout is no more than one page. You can have more than one page if you need to have a chart or diagram or an overhead. Make twenty-five copies of your handout (for each student, the instructor, and possible visitors). The handout is not a written summary of your presentation, nor is it a copy of your presentation notes. It is a visual that helps the audience understand and focus on your presentation. The handout allows elaboration on points; this enables you to provide more information in less time.

   e. Deliver your presentation for four to six minutes. When preparing the presentation, divide it into logical parts and make one note card (or two small) for each part. As you rehearse, time the parts of your presentation so adjustments can be made without sacrificing a whole part.

   f. Rehearse in front of a mirror, standing up. Do it alone until it is perfected. Once the wrinkles are ironed out, deliver the presentation to a trusted listener and ask for suggestions for improvement.

APPENDIX 2

Assignment Criteria Given to Students

Scoring Criteria

1. *Substance*: This category refers to the accuracy of the information presented. Have you thoroughly and appropriately applied the critical thinking process? Have you correctly described the controversial issue and the author's stand on the issue? Do you completely and accurately present the author's evidence? Do not neglect to include your reflections on the issue and the author's stand. If you relate the issue, the author's stand, and the author's evidence but do not provide your reflections about the arguments, then your presentation is incomplete.

2. *Coherence*: This category refers to the clarity of the presentation. Your presentation should be clear enough for your audience to understand. How well does it hang together? Providing minute detail about the author's position and too little detail about your position renders your presentation incoherent or unbalanced. Consider providing context or introductory statements. Would the audience know which part of the assignment you are delivering?

3. *Delivery*: This category refers to the way you deliver your presentation. As you rehearse, consider your demeanor and professionalism. Running out of time (you will be stopped when your time is up, no matter where you are in the presentation), having too much time left, stumbling over your ideas, and losing your place indicate lack of preparation. Be relaxed but professional. Humor is acceptable within reason and when relevant. Delivering your presentation in a way that shows you are interested in your work will likely instill audience engagement and sustained interest.

4. *Handout*: This category refers to the quality of your accompanying one-page handout. How well does it accompany your remarks? If you need to add time to your presentation to explain the handout, then the handout is not supporting your presentation. The handout illustrates, elaborates, and clarifies your remarks. A handout riddled with errors, hard to read, confusing, or poorly laid out indicates incomplete work.

Scoring Scale

Each criterion will be scored on the three-point scale of 3, 2, and 1, which roughly equates to the letter grades of A, B, and C, respectively. Each criterion is weighted equally. The maximum total score is 12. The scores for the criteria are totaled and divided by 12 and multiplied by 100 to yield a percentage score. The percentage score can be compared to the following percentage–letter grade scoring scale: 100–90 = A, 89–80 = B, 79–70 = C.

Any criterion scored 0 would equate to a letter grade of D or F, indicating that the criterion is met at a severely minimal level or not met at all. Should total scoring result in an assignment earning less than the equivalent of a C grade, the student would be obliged to redo the assignment. The new assignment score is subject to a "second-try" reduction in value.

REFERENCES

AAHE 2003. Scholarship of Teaching and Learning Initiative. http://www.aahe.org/.

Angelo, Thomas A. 1991. Ten Easy Pieces: Assessing Higher Learning in Four Dimensions. In *Classroom Research: Early Lessons from Success*, edited by Thomas A. Angelo, 17–31. San Francisco: Jossey-Bass.

Angelo, Thomas A., and Patricia K. Cross. 1993. *Classroom Assessment Techniques: A Handbook for College Teachers*. 2nd ed. San Francisco: Jossey-Bass.

Anson, Chris M., and Dannels, Deanna P. 2004. Writing and Speaking in Conditional Rhetorical Space. In *Classroom Spaces and Writing Instruction*, edited by Ed Nagelhout and Carol Rutz, 55–70. Cresskill, NJ: Hampton.

Britton, James, Tony Burgess, Nancy Martin, Alice McCleod, and Harold Rosen. 1975. *The Development of Writing Abilities (11–18)*. London: Macmillan.

Brooke, Robert. 1991. *Writing and a Sense of Self*. Urbana, IL: NCTE.

———. 1994. *Small Groups in Writing Workshops: Invitations to a Writer's Life*. Urbana, IL: NCTE.

California Polytechnic University. 2003. Medieval assignment. http://cla.calpoly.edu/~dschwart/engl512/512oral.html.

Devitt, Amy J. 2000. The Developing Discipline of Composition: From Text Linguistics to Genre Theory. In *History, Reflection, and Narrative: The Professionalizing of Composition, 1963–1983*, edited by Mary Rosner, Beth Boehm, and Debra Journet, 177–86. Stamford, CT: Ablex.

Elbow, Peter. 1973. *Writing without Teachers*. New York: Oxford University Press.

Fishman, Stephen M., and Lucille McCarthy. 2000. *Unplayed Tapes: A Personal History of Collaborative Teacher Research*. Urbana, IL: NCTE.

Gere, Anne Ruggles. 1990. Talking in Writing Groups. In *Perspectives on Talk and Learning*, edited by Susan Hynds and Donald L. Rubin, 115–28. Urbana, IL: NCTE.

Glassick, Charles E., Mary Taylor Huber, and Gene I. Maeroff. 1997. *Scholarship Assessed: Evaluation of the Professoriate*. San Francisco: Jossey-Bass.

Holdstein, Deborah H. 1996. Power, Genre, and Technology. *College Composition and Communication* 47.2: 279–84.

Jamieson, Kathleen Hall, and Karlyn Khors Campbell. 1982. Rhetorical Hybrids: Fusions of Generic Elements. *Quarterly Journal of Speech* 68: 146–57.

Kress, Gunther, and Terry Threadgold. 1988. Towards a Social Theory of Genre. *Southern Review* 21: 215–43.

Kress, Gunther, and Theo van Leeuwen. 1996. *Reading Images: The Grammar of Visual Design*. London: Routledge.

Lemke, Jay L. 1998. Multiplying Meaning: Visual and Verbal Semiotics in Scientific Text. In *Reading Science: Critical and Functional Perspectives on Discourses of Science*, edited by James Martin and Robert Veel, 87–113. London: Routledge.

———. 2002a. Multimedia Genres for Science Education and Scientific Literacy. In *Developing Advanced Literacy in First and Second Languages*, edited by Mary Schleppegrell and Cecelia Colombi, 21–44. Mahwah, NJ: Lawrence Erlbaum.

———. 2002b. Travels in Hypermodality. *Visual Communication* 1.3: 299–325.

Leverenz, Carrie. 1997. Talk *Is* Writing: Style in Computer-Mediated Discourse. In *Elements of Alternate Style: Essays on Writing and Revision*, edited by Wendy Bishop, 131–39. Portsmouth, NH: Boynton/Cook.

Lewis, Karron G., and J. Povlacs Lunde, eds. 2001. *Face to Face: A Sourcebook of Individual Consultation Techniques for Faculty/Instructional Developers*. 2nd ed. Stillwater, OK: New Forums.

Miller, Carolyn. 1984. Genre as Social Action. *Quarterly Journal of Speech* 70: 151–67.

Mountford, Roxanne. 2001. On Gender and Rhetorical Space. *Rhetoric Society Quarterly* 31.1: 41–71.

Murray, Donald. 1982. The Listening Eye: Reflections on the Writing Conference. In *Learning by Teaching*, 157–63. Portsmouth, NH: Boynton/Cook.

North Carolina State University. 2003a. Design Fundamentals. http://www2.chass.ncsu.edu/cwsp/seminar_reports/toplikar_ex.html.

———. 2003b. First-Year Inquiry. http://www.ncsu.edu/firstyearinquiry.

Reddy, Michael J. 1979. The Conduit Metaphor: A Case of Frame Conflict in Our Language about Language. In *Metaphor and Thought*, edited by Andrew Ortony, 164–201. Cambridge: Cambridge University Press.

Rice, R. Eugene. 1996. *Making a Place for the New American Scholar*. Washington, DC: American Association for Higher Education.

Russell, David R. 1997. Rethinking Genre in School and Society. *Written Communication* 14: 504–55.

Schön, Donald A. 1987. *Educating the Reflective Practitioner.* San Francisco: Jossey-Bass.

Simpson, Alyson. 2003. Textbook assignment. http://www.edfac.usyd.edu.au/staff/simpsona/2003unitoutlines/Undergrad/EDUP4012Multi.html.

Spooner, Michael, and Kathleen Yancey. 1996. Postings on a Genre of Email. *College Composition and Communication* 47.2: 252–78.

Walters, Margaret Bennett. 1992. Robert Zoellner's "Talk-Write Pedagogy": An Instrumental Concept for Today. *Rhetoric Review* 10: 239–43.

Yancey, Kathleen Blake. 2001. A Matter of Design: The Uses of Writing, Speech, and the Visual in Learning across the Curriculum. Plenary address, Conference on Writing across the Curriculum: Writing, Teaching, and Learning in New Contexts, Bloomington, IN, June 1.

Zoellner, Robert. 1969. Talk-Write: A Behavioral Pedagogy for Composition. *College English* 30: 267–320.

24

Notes on the Evolution of Network Support for Writing Across the Curriculum

MIKE PALMQUIST

> If we focus on behavior — behavior we want to change or behavior we want to nurture, such as a traditional practice in the teaching of writing or particular ways of increasing student writing throughout the university community — we begin to look at things in a different way.
>
> – RICHARD YOUNG, INTERVIEW

What would it mean to look at writing across the curriculum (WAC) in a different way? Over the past five years, my colleagues and I have wrestled with our discovery that WAC as it is typically conceptualized — what we have come to think of as "WAC Orthodoxy" — does not work on our campus.[1] Yet we have remained committed to the goals that inform most WAC programs: increased use of writing in disciplinary courses, increased exposure to the conventions and writing strategies employed in various disciplinary communities, and support for faculty who express interest in using writing in their courses. In addition, we have pursued two goals that inform many, although by no means all, WAC programs: direct support for student writers, including those who are not enrolled in WAC courses, and the creation of a campuswide community of writers.

Efforts to meet these goals began at my institution when members of the English faculty started an aggressive program of WAC outreach in the late 1970s. Their efforts ultimately targeted not only faculty at the university, but also public school teachers across Colorado.[2] When I joined the faculty in 1990, WAC seminars were a regular occurrence, and I participated in them enthusiastically. Unfortunately, it was clear by then that our cumulative efforts had resulted in relatively low faculty participation across the university.

From *Inventing a Discipline: Rhetoric Scholarship in Honor of Richard E. Young.* Ed. Maureen Daly Goggin. Urbana: NCTE, 2000. 373–402.

In 1992, reasoning that a new approach was in order, we obtained external funding to explore technological support for WAC (Palmquist, Zimmerman, and Kiefer). Our initial discussions helped us clarify our goals about what our new WAC program should entail, but before we began to implement the program we spent a year evaluating student, faculty, alumni, and workplace perceptions about writing. The results of our exploratory studies challenged our expectations about what our WAC program should ultimately look like (for reports of these studies, see Thomas; Vest, Long, and Anderson; Vest et al.; Zimmerman and Palmquist; Zimmerman et al.).

As we struggled to balance our goals for WAC with what we had learned during our first year of study, we found that the idea of "designing a WAC program" had itself become an obstacle to success. The WAC movement, although fostering diversity in the implementation of individual programs, is informed by a set of expectations — an orthodoxy, if you will — about what a WAC program is, what it does, and who it serves. Perhaps predictably, we found ourselves wrestling with such commonplace issues as whether to focus on writing to learn or on writing in the disciplines, whether to house the program inside or outside the English department, and whether to offer new writing-intensive courses or additional courses in composition, journalism, speech, and technical communication. Unfortunately, we also found that we were at times losing sight of the instructional and institutional goals that had led us to consider designing a WAC program in the first place. Designing the program seemed to have become our primary goal.

Faced with institutional and faculty resistance of various flavors (Couch; Kaufer and Young; McLeod; Soven; Swanson-Owens), we decided to step back from the goal of designing a WAC program per se and focus instead on exploring strategies for reaching the goals that had led us to propose a WAC program. Not surprisingly (in retrospect), we began to enjoy modest success. As Richard Young suggests, we found that focusing on specific goals brought about greater success than focusing on broader issues of program design.

In this essay, I explore how our focus on reaching specific goals — or more accurately, our focus on issues of implementation — has allowed us to create a writing-across-the-curriculum program on a campus that exhibited extraordinary indifference to two decades of previous WAC efforts. Our approach to WAC, as the title of this essay suggests, makes extensive use of network and multimedia technologies. It is also influenced by scholars who have argued that campus writing centers and a direct focus on student writers can play a pivotal role in WAC. In the following sections, I discuss scholarship in each of these areas. I then turn to a discussion of the Online Writing Center at Colorado State University. I conclude with a discussion of future directions in network support for WAC, with attention to the WAC Clearinghouse, a consortium project involving faculty from several colleges and universities.

Unorthodox WAC: Arguments for Direct Student Support

> Because of the uncertainty of our knowledge and the rapidity of change in the field, we believe that constructive change is necessary if any writing program, certainly any WAC program, is to be sustainable. What is stable and persistent as the program evolves is a set of principles that give the program its identity.
>
> – Richard Young and Christine Neuwirth, "Writing in the Disciplines"

If WAC can be said to have an orthodoxy, it lies in its almost unrelenting focus on faculty as a primary audience (Russell). To borrow a phrase from the 1980s, most WAC programs seem to have adopted a trickle-down approach to writing instruction (see Figure 24-1). Seminars and outreach efforts, as a result, are typically targeted at faculty rather than at students. Once faculty have gained a sufficiently robust understanding of how writing can or should be used in their classrooms, they can in turn provide writing instruction — or, at the least, opportunities to write — to their students. As a result, most WAC programs invest heavily in seminars that train faculty to use writing in their classes (Walvoord, "Getting Started"; Young and Fulwiler; Young, "Designing for Change").

This approach has a great deal of merit: if teachers do not assign formal writing or ask students to capture their thinking on paper, then students are much less likely to practice disciplinary conventions or to write to learn. As a result, our WAC efforts include a strong focus on faculty seminars and outreach.

We are concerned, however, about focusing our efforts solely on faculty. Two of the primary goals that have shaped our WAC program are providing direct support for student writers regardless of which courses they are taking and fostering the creation of a campuswide writing community. To meet these goals using a faculty-centered approach would require that most, if not all, faculty on our campus actively participate in our WAC program.

Our experiences, as well as those of other WAC scholars, suggest that such massive participation on the part of faculty at our institution is unlikely. Indeed, despite the tendency of most WAC programs to invest heavily in faculty training and outreach, faculty are the most likely — and typically the

Figure 24-1   A Traditional Top-Down WAC Model

most vocal — sources of resistance to WAC initiatives (Couch; Kaufer and Young; McLeod; Soven; Swanson-Owens). The importance of faculty resistance should not be underestimated; as Susan McLeod points out, it can "gradually wear away even the most firmly established institutional program" (343). Our interviews with faculty and our review of WAC scholarship indicated that faculty resistance typically took one or more of three forms: (1) lack of expertise and/or inclination to teach and respond to writing (Holladay; Strenski), (2) concern that incorporating writing into courses would reduce the amount of instruction provided in the content area (Russell), and (3) programmatic concern about replacing existing courses with writing-intensive courses (an issue of particular importance at public institutions operating under state-mandated ceilings on the number of credits that can be required for graduation).

As we struggled to meet our goals, we found ourselves reflecting on differences between our campus and those on which a faculty-centered approach to WAC has proven successful. In contrast to many smaller, liberal arts colleges, for instance, we found that our faculty as a whole did not seem to focus the majority of their efforts on teaching. The moral force behind the argument that WAC helps students become better writers and thinkers was not compelling to faculty faced with large classes and demanding research agendas. Nor did they welcome our efforts to institute courses that could be team taught by communication and disciplinary faculty or to institute specific courses that focused on communication skills. There simply were not enough "extra" course credits available, they told us, to support our proposals. Finally, we found ourselves faced with a small but rather vocal minority of faculty who expressed disbelief that undergraduates needed additional work on communication. To these faculty, our efforts were at best misguided and at worst a capricious waste of their time.

It seemed clear that a strictly faculty-centered WAC program would not work on our campus: reaching our goals of providing direct support for student writers and creating a campuswide writing community would require a different approach. Over time, our cumulative efforts coalesced into what I have termed an "integrated approach" to WAC (Palmquist et al., "Audience"; see Figure 24-2). Our approach is characterized by the following:

- continued focus on faculty training and outreach
- additional focus on direct support for students
- use of network technology to support access to tutors, teachers, and classmates
- use of the World Wide Web to provide resource materials for writers and instructors
- use of the campus writing center as the visible focus for writing on our campus

As we worked to implement our integrated approach, we found ourselves consulting a range of work, not all of which might initially be seen as compatible. We found ourselves exploring scholarship that views faculty, to

FIGURE 24-2   An Integrated Approach to WAC Program Design

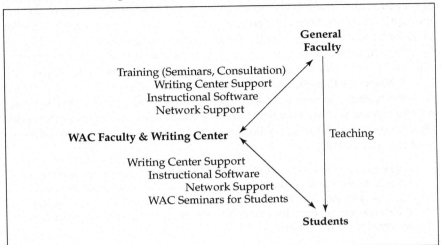

use Richard Young's phrasing, as "agents of change" within the institution. At the same time, we discussed Tori Haring-Smith's "bottom-up" approach to WAC, which views students as the primary audience for WAC efforts.

We also found ourselves persuaded by arguments that the campus writing center — even though it evolved to help students less prepared for college writing — can play an important role in WAC instruction (Griffin; Harris, "Writing"; Holladay; Russell). We found David Russell's observation that the campus writing center could play a central role in a WAC program particularly compelling. Noting that this approach is a "less common model," he observes that it provides "another means of getting around the problem of recruiting faculty whose time and interests may not allow them to restructure their courses to include more writing" (289). Finally, we found ourselves turning to the campus computer network in general — and the World Wide Web in particular — as a vehicle for reaching out to both students and faculty.

TECHNOLOGICAL SUPPORT FOR WRITING ACROSS THE CURRICULUM

> We may be more successful if we shift emphasis away from formal programs to specific things faculty are more likely to accept, like student dialogues via electronic bulletin boards that supplement class work.
>
> — RICHARD YOUNG, INTERVIEW

WAC Scholars Consider Technology

The development of computer support for writing across the curriculum has in some ways paralleled and in other ways lagged behind the adoption of computer support for composition instruction. WAC scholars, like their colleagues in computers and writing, were initially drawn to the potential of using computers to reduce the tedious work of instructing students in grammar and mechanics. In 1984, Muriel Harris and Madelon Cheek, extending the earlier work of Kate Kiefer and Charles Smith on the collegiate version of Writer's Workbench, carried out a project in which they analyzed and subsequently returned papers sent to their writing lab by engineering students. Harris and Cheek observed that the program, which analyzed several aspects of style and mechanics, "allowed us to add into an already overloaded teaching schedule some writing assistance that we could not have offered otherwise" (5). Commenting on the use of the program to support writing across the curriculum, they noted:

> [O]ur use of WRITER'S WORKBENCH generated interest among engineering faculty and encouraged them to consider its potential as a writing tool. This can lead to a stronger interest in writing instruction within their classrooms, drawing them into the writing-across-the-curriculum movement via the computer. (5)

Other WAC scholars also recognized the potential usefulness of computers as a way to draw faculty into a WAC program. In 1988, writing about computers as a way to extend the WAC movement, Gordon and Mansfield recalled, "At a workshop at Drew University in the summer of 1985, Elaine Maimon expressed the hope that the computer would give the writing-across-the-curriculum movement a 'shot in the arm'" (9). Arguing that using computers to carry out disciplinary activities is a form of disciplinary thinking comparable to writing in the discipline, Nicholas Gordon and Susan Mansfield concluded that "it makes sense to expand a writing-across-the-curriculum project into a computers-across-the-curriculum project" (11).

Writing across the curriculum as computer across the curriculum did not, however, gain a foothold in the imagination of most WAC scholars. WAC scholars did not begin exploring in earnest the uses of technology to support WAC until the early 1990s. Even then, as Barbara Walvoord notes in 1996, it would still remain far from the mainstream of the WAC movement. In a call for serious consideration of technology in WAC, she wrote:

> But WAC can no longer just introduce the idea of handwritten journals; it must deal with network bulletin boards, distance learning, and multimedia presentations by both students and teachers, as lines blur between writing and other forms of communication and between classrooms and other learning spaces. ("Future" 72)

Writing Centers and Computers

While WAC scholars have been relatively cautious in their adoption of technological support, their colleagues working in writing centers took note of the potential of computers and computer networks to support their work early in the 1980s. These interests would eventually lead to the development of online writing labs and online writing centers, which have the potential to significantly change the way WAC is implemented and supported on a number of campuses.

Mason expressed a sentiment common to many who saw computers as a means of reducing the tedium of writing instruction. In the *Writing Lab News-letter* in 1982, he argued, "If one has the financial and human resources, one should install a battery of microcomputer stations for CAI [computer-assisted instruction] in the writing lab" (3). Within the year, additional articles appeared in the newsletter discussing CAI and in some cases advocating its use as a replacement for face-to-face tutoring (Southwell).

As computers became more common in writing centers, additional uses were found for them. In 1984, Joan Garcia Kotker discussed the benefits of using computers during tutoring sessions with developmental students, while L. H. Holmes argued one year later that bringing computers into the writing center would help reduce its association with remediation.

Between 1986 and 1989, mirroring a comparable shift in the computers and writing community (Hawisher; Stracke; Sullivan; Weiss), articles began appearing that explored the uses of word processing in the writing center (Crisp; Marshall; Scharton). Also at this time, while the uses of network computing were beginning to be explored in the composition classroom, WAC and writing center scholars began the process that would lead to online writing centers and online writing labs (Kinkead, "Computer Conversations," "Electronic Writing Tutor").

Writing Centers and WAC Programs Move Online

In 1996, Jane Lasarenko noted that she had found "93 self-styled OWLs," or Online Writing Labs. These OWLs fulfill a variety of purposes, ranging from those that serve as little more than online advertisements for campus writing centers, to those that offer online aids such as handouts and links to other online resources, to "Full-Fledged" OWLs, which "offer a complete set of online services, including online manuscript submission and feedback."

The development of OWLs is relatively recent, occurring primarily since 1995, with additional OWLs coming online on a regular basis. The movement toward online writing labs and online writing centers, however, has a comparatively long history. Early work on the concept dates at least to 1987, when Richard Young and Christine Neuwirth proposed to the Buhl Foundation a project that would establish an online writing center to support writing in the disciplines at Carnegie Mellon University. Their proposal, which was expanded significantly and resubmitted in 1988, called for:

- creation of a new first-year writing-in-the-disciplines course that would provide training in "argument for either general and specialized audiences," exposure to "rhetorical forms and methods necessary for effective participation in the upper-level disciplinary courses," and "use of the computer network support system" (10)
- faculty training workshops in writing instruction and use of the computer support system

- creation of a network program that would connect students seeking help with any other student or faculty member who was currently working on the computer network

- access to online consultants (either trained faculty or graduate students) who could provide delayed feedback in situations in which immediate feedback was unavailable or did not sufficiently answer the initial request for help

- access to software that would support writing instruction

Young and Neuwirth's vision of a network-supported writing-across-the-curriculum program, although not funded by the Buhl Foundation, laid out the principles that would later inform the development of many online writing labs and online writing centers. In their proposal, they called attention to functional similarities between their network support system and traditional writing centers, as well as to the potential of the system to help create intellectual communities:

> These are, of course, the traditional and important functions of conventional Writing Centers found at almost every college and university in the country, though in conventional Centers they are carried out between students and consultant face to face. However, because of the computer network, the Support System can perform other functions that cannot be performed by conventional Writing Centers. The most unconventional of these and perhaps in the long run the most important for both the university and the student is the creation of an environment in which collaborative learning can take place spontaneously and freely. The network makes possible the creation of University-wide intellectual communities of students and faculty, admission to which requires only a willingness to participate seriously in any of the on-going, campus-wide dialogues conducted over the network. (11)

When Young and Neuwirth submitted their proposals to the Buhl Foundation, they were at one of the few institutions to possess a computing infrastructure capable of supporting such an endeavor. The experimental Andrew computing system provided access for faculty and students from public labs, offices, homes, and dorm rooms to sophisticated network communication tools and to a now widely adopted file system. In addition, between the mid-1980s and early 1990s, Neuwirth and her colleagues created several software tools that could be used to support writing processes and interaction about writing:

- CECE-Talk, a chat utility that allowed students to collaborate in real time and record a transcript of the discussion (Neuwirth, Palmquist, and Gillespie; Neuwirth, Gillespie, and Palmquist)

- Comments, which allowed students to exchange drafts of papers with classmates and teachers via the network (Neuwirth et al., *Comments*)

- Notes, a hypertext program that supported working from sources (Neuwirth et al., "Notes")

- PREP Editor, which supported commenting in a variety of forms and is the core technology employed in Houghton-Mifflin's CommonSpace software (Neuwirth et al., "Issues")

The Buhl Foundation's decision against funding the project may have delayed the broader movement toward online writing labs and online writing centers, but elsewhere other scholars were also exploring the potential uses of computer networks to support writing instruction. Another early project was Dawn Rodrigues and Kate Kiefer's Electronic Writing Service at Colorado State University (Rodrigues, Kiefer, and McPherson; Rodrigues and Kiefer). Begun in 1989, the project was envisioned as a virtual lab that could be used "as the hub for Writing-Across-the-Curriculum activities" (Rodrigues, Kiefer, and McPherson 3).

The Electronic Writing Service (EWS) provided students, faculty, and staff at the university access to "a variety of computer-assisted writing aids that have been developed or customized by English Department faculty and graduate students, including style analysis programs, prewriting templates, and revision guides" (Rodrigues, Kiefer, and McPherson 3). Writers accessed EWS via electronic mail. Requests for specific documents were listed in the subject line of the message, while requests for style analysis of various kinds were accomplished by inserting the text of the document into the body of the message. The long-term goal of the project was to "expand the EWS by collaborating with other faculty to develop writing aids for courses in all content areas across the curriculum" (3). This goal reflected Kiefer's 1991 vision of the writing classroom of the future, in which the network played a central role in a writing-across-the-curriculum program.

Despite its potential, EWS would enjoy only limited success. Providing network access to Writer's Workbench (which conducted the style analyses for EWS) raised issues about sound use of style analysis programs, noted Kate Kiefer in a 1997 interview:

> Some faculty outside the department wanted to use Writer's Workbench in ways that were inconsistent with our goals as a composition program. And Writer's Workbench is easy to misuse. Unless you have a sensitivity to language or an understanding of what the program can and can't do, you can easily find yourself focusing exclusively on surface issues.

In addition to concerns about how EWS was being used, technical difficulties plagued the project, and it was discontinued in 1991.

In 1991, Purdue University's OWL went online in the form of a similar e-mail request system (Harris, "Hatching"). Unlike the Electronic Writing Service at Colorado State University, however, Purdue's OWL was linked directly to the campus writing center. "E-mail was another way to reach students when we were physically closed," said Muriel Harris, who initiated the project with Dave Taylor (personal interview). Students accessing the Purdue OWL could obtain handouts on various writing issues and interact directly with writing center tutors. Purdue's OWL would shift from a strictly e-mail-based service to a gopher-based system in 1993. In 1994, Purdue's OWL moved to the World Wide Web (http://owl.english.purdue.edu).

Unlike the earlier efforts at Carnegie Mellon and Colorado State University that were designed to provide support for WAC, Purdue's OWL focused primarily on extending the writing center. This focus on the writing center would subsequently mark the majority of efforts to establish online writing labs and online writing centers.

By 1995 a number of writing centers had established an online presence. In addition, Dakota State University's OWL, one of the first in the country, was established because the campus lacked a writing center (Ericsson). A special issue of *Computers and Composition* on "Writing Centers Online," edited by Christine Hult and Joyce Kinkead, came out in 1995. In it several scholars addressed issues related to providing network support for campus writing centers (Harris and Pemberton; Healy; Nelson and Wambeam), online tutoring (Coogan; Jordan-Henley and Maid), and online support for training tutors (Chappell; Johanek and Rickly; Strenski et al.). In the following issue of *Computers and Composition*, a set of related articles, written by scholars affiliated with Michigan Technological University's writing center, critiqued the connection between writing centers and computers, calling attention to the need to foreground the human within an increasingly technological space (George; Grimm; C. Selfe; D. Selfe).

By 1996 the number and variety of OWLs had grown immensely. Writing as part of the Coverweb in the Spring 1996 issue of *Kairos*, J. Paul Johnson observed, "The long list of 'online writing labs,' or OWLs, compiled by the University of Maine's Writing Center Online offers testament to the range of writing services establishing an identity in cyberspace. Clever and memorable as it is, the acronym OWL can hardly begin to describe the work accomplished in this variety of sites." That work includes:

- a gopher or Web site that promotes a "real" writing center (e.g., with photos, hours, location, maps, philosophy statements)
- access to electronic handouts, handbooks, or other local reference material
- access to electronic texts from global net sites
- access to Internet or other network searches
- links to homepages of the local writing community
- a local publishing environment for student writers of electronic texts
- connectivity to local forums or global listservs on writing or writing topics
- links to MOOs and MUSHes for writers
- one-to-one tutorials by means of computer-mediated communication (e.g., private chat rooms, form-based e-mail paper submissions)
- a pointed philosophical mission of redefining traditional notions of academic literacy

Although the movement to put writing centers online had strong roots in the WAC movement, it was clear by the mid-1990s that comparatively little work was being done to provide network support for writing across the curriculum. The visions of network-supported WAC programs put forth by Young and Neuwirth at Carnegie Mellon and Rodrigues and Kiefer at Colorado State University had not yet become reality. After they pulled the plug on the Electronic Writing Service, however, Rodrigues and Kiefer joined with other colleagues and tried a new approach.

WAC ONLINE: THE ONLINE WRITING CENTER AT COLORADO STATE UNIVERSITY

> So much of what's written in WAC seems to be on program design. We need narratives of what's happening.
>
> – RICHARD YOUNG, INTERVIEW

As a graduate student at Carnegie Mellon University in the late 1980s, I worked closely on several research projects with Richard Young, Christine Neuwirth, and David Kaufer. The majority of these projects focused on the impact of technology on writing and writing instruction. As a result, I was familiar with their thinking about the role computers could play in WAC. When I joined the faculty at Colorado State University in 1990, I shared those ideas with my new colleagues, who had been working toward the same goals.

The Online Writing Center at Colorado State University is in many ways a product of the work conducted in the late 1980s at the two universities. Although we could not have predicted the particular form it has taken (the World Wide Web, among other things, was still years away), it is informed by many of the same goals.

In 1991, following the demise of the Electronic Writing Service, Don Zimmerman and I began collaborating with Kate Kiefer and Dawn Rodrigues on a successor to the program. We envisioned a project that would provide closer links to the writing center, direct support for students as well as faculty, and resource materials that writers could consult as needed. In 1992, after several attempts to obtain funding, we received support from the Colorado Commission on Higher Education (Palmquist, Zimmerman, and Kiefer).

Our funding supported the study of computer support for writing instruction and the development and assessment of a network-supported, writing-across-the-curriculum program.[3] We spent the first year conducting baseline assessments of writing needs and attitudes on our campus and in the engineering professions (the target audience for our initial WAC efforts; for reports of these studies, see Thomas; Vest et al.; Zimmerman and Palmquist; Zimmerman et al.). In the second year, we began developing and assessing alternative designs for the Online Writing Center, using Asymetrix Multimedia ToolBook as a development platform. In the third year, we concentrated our efforts on developing content for the Online Writing Center. In the fourth year, we shifted our development efforts to the World Wide Web and began direct support of writing in courses in electrical, civil, and mechanical engineering. In the final year of external funding, we expanded our support for courses to other departments across the university.

The Online Writing Center emerged by 1997 on our campus as a highly visible means of supporting writing across the curriculum (see Figure 24-3). We are enjoying success in attracting participation not only from faculty who have responded to our previous WAC efforts (seminars, outreach), but also from some who had resisted those efforts. The central strategy we have used in enlisting support for the Online Writing Center is to position it as an extension of the classroom and a service to teachers and students. Perhaps the most

FIGURE 24-3   Colorado State University's Online Writing Center Homepage

important technique contributing to this strategy is the online assignment, a variation of the syllaweb concept (the practice of putting course syllabi and other materials on the World Wide Web).

The online assignment, as we have implemented it, attempts to replicate (in an abbreviated form) the product and process of giving a writing assignment. In a classroom, an instructor typically hands out the assignment, discusses its key points, and answers student questions about the assignment. Occasionally, the instructor will also provide example texts and point students to additional resources that might be of use in completing the assignment. On the Online Writing Center, we provide the equivalent of the assignment sheet, add commentary from the instructor on key points of the assignment, in some cases provide annotated example texts, and provide links to resources that students can use to complete the assignment (see Figures 24-4 and 24-5).

In addition to online assignments and annotated example texts, we also provide a wide range of materials that support composition instruction, technical communication instruction, and writing in the disciplines. These reference materials, implemented as hierarchically structured hypertexts with cross-links, function as online textbooks (see Figure 24-6). In some cases, such as our reference unit on argumentation, written by Donna LeCourt, they exceed five hundred screens in size. Most of the reference materials provide direct support for students, but several, including an extensive unit on writing across the curriculum written by Kate Kiefer, provide support for faculty.

FIGURE 24-4   An Online Writing-in-the-Disciplines Assignment

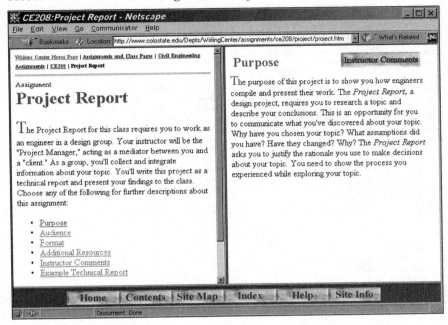

FIGURE 24-5   An Annotated Example Text

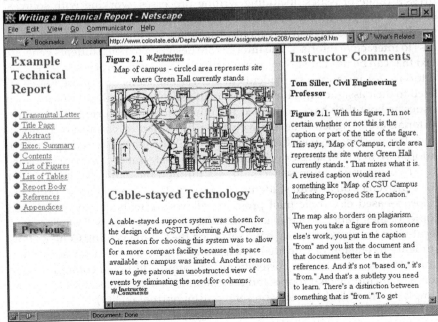

FIGURE 24-6   A Reference Unit on Audience

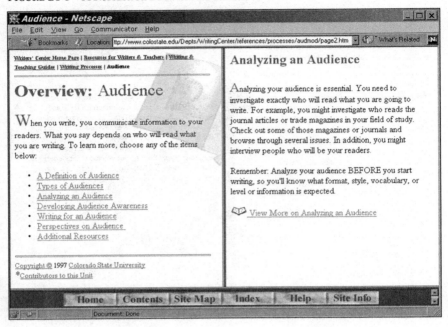

As this essay is being written, fifty-two reference units are available on the Online Writing Center, with several in preparation. Reference materials address a range of issues, including writing processes, working with sources, speeches and presentations, types of documents, and critical reading.

In addition to reference materials, the Online Writing Center also offers access to interactive tutorials. The tutorials are designed to help students generate text that can be used at various points in their composing processes. Invention tutorials, for instance, ask students to answer questions or explore issues related to their assignments. Revision tutorials ask them to analyze critically such issues as how they have addressed their audience or supported their claims. Tutorials are designed to be relatively brief, but writers can return to a tutorial and start working on it at the point they left it. When they have completed the tutorial, writers can save or print their text, or paste it into a word processor.

Two communication services offered through the Online Writing Center have proven popular with students and faculty. The "Send a Paper" program, a forms-based electronic mail program, allows students to send text-based copies of their papers to a teacher or writing center tutor. Class "Web Forums," located on the class pages we have set up on the Online Writing Center, allow students to engage in threaded discussions of issues related (or sometimes unrelated) to class. We are currently investigating additional communication services, including chat rooms and the potential of VRML-based MOOs (more simply, interactive chat rooms presented using virtual reality).

A final set of materials available through the Online Writing Center is external links. We have provided links to our university library, to library databases, and to various library services on and off campus. We have also provided an extensive set of links to Web-based materials for writers and teachers. These include links to other online writing centers and to WAC sites.

As we have worked on the Online Writing Center, we have found our greatest success working with individual faculty and students (Palmquist, Kiefer, and Zimmerman). A faculty member who experiences success with the Online Writing Center has proven to be our best way of enlisting additional faculty in that department. We have also found success through making presentations to faculty groups and administrators. After a recent presentation to our university's leadership forum, for instance, I was approached by several faculty who expressed interest in putting their writing assignments online.

More important in terms of the long-term success of the program, presentations to faculty and administrators have helped us secure long-term funding for the program. Following a series of presentations in the winter and spring of 1996, our university administration approved a new tenure-track faculty line to direct our writing center and head up WAC efforts on campus. In the following year, we sought approval (and received strong indications that we would be successful) for base funding for our writer/programmer and a graduate teaching assistant to support further development of the Online Writing Center. One of the keys to our success in attracting institutional funding for our program has been the strong support of our department chair, our dean, and our associate deans. Keeping them informed of our efforts has been a high priority throughout the project, and we are now seeing the benefits associated with that decision.

Similarly, our interactions with individual students have proven to be the foundation for positioning the Online Writing Center as the focus of a campuswide community of writers. Students who have had good experiences after submitting a paper by means of electronic mail or who have found our reference units or tutorials helpful have begun to spread the word about the Online Writing Center. A sizable number of first- and second-year students have learned about the Online Writing Center through its use in our composition program. And a growing number are being exposed to it through disciplinary courses. Our interactions with students in our courses, in the campus writing center, and online suggest that a growing number of students are becoming aware of — and are starting to use on a regular basis — the resources available through the Online Writing Center.

THE FUTURE OF NETWORK SUPPORT FOR
WRITING ACROSS THE CURRICULUM

> What is going to keep this movement from going the way of other movements that Russell has chronicled over the past century?
>
> – RICHARD YOUNG, INTERVIEW

As we have worked to develop the Online Writing Center — and, more to the point, to develop a working writing-across-the-curriculum program on our campus — we have constantly found ourselves faced with questions about where to go next. The decision to focus on students has been extremely important in the long-term development of our program, for instance, as has the decision to shift the project to the World Wide Web. Focusing on students has meant that we have had to confront directly the issue of large numbers of papers coming across the network to tutors in our writing center. Our tutors initially resisted the idea of commenting by means of e-mail. They argued that they could do a better job face to face. We agreed with them, but pointed out that many of the students sending the papers would not come to the writing center in the first place; reaching out to them electronically would both help them with their writing and potentially provide them with the incentive to come in for face-to-face discussions.

We also found ourselves facing the question of what to do when a faculty member teaching a class of eighty students wanted to require all of his students to send their biweekly writing assignments to our tutors. We have resolved that issue for now, largely by pointing out that we did not have the tutoring resources to support mass submissions of papers for review, but we know we will face it again, and we are working to secure funding for additional tutors, either from central administration sources or from the departments who make heavy use of the tutoring services offered by the writing center.

One of the logical extensions of our goal to directly support students is to provide WAC seminars for students. In 1997 we began those seminars, offering them through the campus writing center. Graduate student interns, taking a tutoring course for credit under the direction of our writing center director, Laura Thomas, have been involved in developing the workshops, as have our regular tutors. The materials they have developed for the seminars are being used as the basis for expanding existing or writing new reference materials for the Online Writing Center.

Additional projects we are exploring involve the use of database programs to make it easier for faculty to update assignments on the Online Writing Center — something that must now be done manually by our writer/programmer, Luann Barnes. Our university is in the midst of evaluating products that might be used to accomplish this task. Our hope is that the product selected by the university committee conducting the evaluation will be compatible with our current design. We are also interested in evaluating the use of work-group software that will allow us to more easily exchange and comment on student writing, and scheduling software that will allow students to more easily set up face-to-face meetings with tutors.

One of the most intriguing projects we are currently pursuing is the WAC Clearinghouse (http://wac.colostate.edu/index.cfm), a Web site that is being developed with the involvement of several scholars from around the country, among them Christine Hult, Bill Condon, Gail Hawisher, Martin Rosenberg, Kate Kiefer, Linn Bekins, Paul Prior, and Sharon Quiroz. Like other WAC sites on the Web, such as WAC Page, maintained by Larry Beason at Eastern Washington University (http://webarchive.org/web/19970415020337/http://ewu66649.ewu.edu/WAC.html), and the Computer-Supported Communication Across the Curriculum site maintained by Donna Reiss (http://web archive.org/web/19980113002109/http://www.tc.cc.va.us/tcresourc/faculty/ tcreisd/dreiss/ecacsite.htm), the WAC Clearinghouse provides information about WAC issues and concerns. It also provides a discussion forum for a range of WAC issues, a place to share scholarship on WAC, and resources on teaching and program design.

As increasing numbers of WAC scholars begin to explore network support for WAC, we are seeing additional innovations in program design and implementation. Some of these are discussed in publications that focus on electronic support for writing across the curriculum, such as the edited collection *Electronic Communication Across the Curriculum* (Reiss, Selfe, and Young), while others appear as essays in journals (Walvoord, "Future") and new collections addressing mainstream WAC issues (e.g., an essay by Reiss and Young in a collection by McLeod and Miraglia on the future of WAC, under consideration for publication). Other reports of innovations in network support for WAC have been or will be discussed in workshops and presentations at recent and upcoming national WAC conferences.

The Online Writing Center represents an approach to WAC that seems to have strong potential for long-term success. Exploring ways to make it easier for faculty to use writing in their courses appears as though it would work in situations in which faculty are at least willing to consider using writing. As we have found, however, each campus faces its own set of challenges. On our campus, many of the more common approaches to WAC did not enjoy the success they did elsewhere. As a result, I have no illusions that our approach will necessarily translate well to other institutions. But I am confident that the principle of identifying specific behaviors we want to change is more likely to bring about long-term success than focusing on creating a general program. I am also confident that the benefits of network communication will play an increasingly important role in the design of existing and new WAC programs. If so, we will have made clear progress toward looking at WAC in new ways.

NOTES

1. I would like to thank my colleagues for their support, goodwill, and insights as we have worked together on this project: Kate Kiefer, Don Zimmerman, Dawn Rodrigues, David Vest, Luann Barnes, Michel Muraski, Steve Reid, Donna LeCourt, Tom Siller, Laura Thomas, Lauren Myracle, Laurel Nesbitt, Stephanie Wardrop, Brenda Edmands, and Kathy Zellers. I am grateful for comments on drafts of this essay from Kate Kiefer, Donna LeCourt, and Donna Reiss. And I am particularly indebted to Richard Young for his thoughtful responses to this essay, for his insights into the process of creating and maintaining successful WAC activities, and for his friendship.

2. The Writing-to-Learn Project began at Colorado State University in 1984 when Kate Kiefer, Steve Reid, Jean Wyrick, and Bill McBride began meeting with high school language arts teachers. Later that year, they expanded their efforts to teachers from other disciplines. The project continued through the 1980s and ultimately involved elementary through high school teachers from seven school districts across Colorado.

3. The Transitions study followed four teachers and 187 students in eight classrooms. Each teacher taught the same course in a traditional and a computer-supported writing classroom. We interviewed students and teachers, collected student drafts, collected teaching materials and logs, observed the classrooms, collected network communications, and surveyed students. A complete report of the study is found in Palmquist, Kiefer, Hartvigsen, and Godlew's *Transitions: Teaching Writing in Computer-Supported and Traditional Classrooms*.

WORKS CITED

Beason, Larry. "WAC Page." Eastern Washington University. <http://ewu66649.ewu.edu/WAC .html>.

Chappell, Virginia A. "Theorizing in Practice: Tutor Training 'Live from the VAX Lab.'" *Computers and Composition* 12 (1995): 227–36.

Coogan, David. "E-Mail Tutoring, a New Way to Do New Work." *Computers and Composition* 12 (1995): 171–81.

Couch, Ruth. "Dealing with Objections to Writing Across the Curriculum." *Teaching English in the Two-Year College* 16 (1989): 193–96.

Crisp, Sally. "You Can Teach an Old Dog New Tricks: Observations on Entering the Computer Age." *Writing Lab Newsletter* 11.3 (1986): 12–14.

Ericsson, Patricia. "WAC Learns to Fly: The Birth of an OWL." Computers and Writing Conference. Columbia, MO. 22 May 1994.

George, Diana. "Wonder of It All: Computers, Writing Centers, and the World." *Computers and Composition* 12 (1995): 331–34.

Gordon, Nicholas, and Susan Mansfield. "Computers Across the Curriculum: A Confluence of Ideas." *Computers and Composition* 6 (1988): 9–13.

Griffin, C. W. "Programs for Writing Across the Curriculum: A Report." *College Composition and Communication* 36 (1985): 398–403.

Grimm, Nancy Maloney. "Computer Centers and Writing Centers: An Argument for Ballast." *Computers and Composition* 12 (1995): 323–29.

Haring-Smith, Tori. *A Guide to Writing Programs: Writing Centers, Peer Tutoring Programs, and Writing-Across-the-Curriculum.* Glenview, IL: Scott, 1987.

Harris, Muriel. "Hatching an OWL (Online Writing Lab)." *ACE Newsletter* 9.4 (1996): 12–14.

———. Telephone interview. 1997.

———. "The Writing Center and Tutoring in WAC Programs." McLeod and Soven 154–74.

Harris, Muriel, and Madelon Cheek. "Computers Across the Curriculum: Using WRITER'S WORKBENCH for Supplementary Instruction." *Computers and Composition* 1 (1984): 3–5.

Harris, Muriel, and Michael Pemberton. "Online Writing Labs (OWLs): A Taxonomy of Options and Issues." *Computers and Composition* 12 (1995): 145–59.

Hawisher, Gail E. "Studies in Word Processing." *Computers and Composition* 4 (1986): 6–31.

Healy, Dave. "From Place to Space: Perceptual and Administrative Issues in the Online Writing Center." *Computers and Composition* 12 (1995): 183–93.

Holladay, John. "Institutional Project Grant: A Report on Research into Writing-Across-the-Curriculum Projects." Report no. JC880422. Monroe County Community College, MI. ERIC 1987. ED 298 995.

Holmes, Leigh Howard. "Expanding Turf: Rationales for Computers in Writing Labs." *Writing Lab Newsletter* 9.10 (1985): 13–14.

Johanek, Cindy, and Rebecca Rickly. "Online Tutor Training: Synchronous Conferencing in a Professional Community." *Computers and Composition* 12 (1995): 237–46.

Johnson, J. Paul. "Writing Spaces: Technoprovocateurs and OWLs in the Late Age of Print." *Kairos* 1.1 (1996). <http://english.ttu.edu/kairos/1.1/index.html>.

Jordan-Henley, Jennifer, and Barry M. Maid. "Tutoring in Cyberspace: Student Impact and College/ University Collaboration." *Computers and Composition* 12 (1995): 211–18.

Kaufer, David, and Richard Young. "Writing in the Content Areas: Some Theoretical Complexities." *Theory and Practice in the Teaching of Writing: Rethinking the Discipline.* Ed. Lee Odell. Carbondale: Southern Illinois UP, 1993. 71–104.

Kiefer, Kate. "Computers and Teacher Education in the 1990s and Beyond." *Evolving Perspectives on Computers and Composition Studies: Questions for the 1990s.* Ed. Gail E. Hawisher and Cynthia L. Selfe. Urbana, IL: NCTE, 1991. 113–31.

———. Personal interview. 1997.

Kiefer, Kate, and Michael Palmquist. "WAC Clearinghouse." Colorado State University. <http:// aw.colostate.edu/resource_list.htm>.

Kiefer, Kate, and Charles Smith. "Textual Analysis with Computers: Tests of Bell Laboratories' Computer Software." *Research in the Teaching of English* 17 (1983): 201–14.

Kinkead, Joyce. "Computer Conversations: E-mail and Writing Instruction." *College Composition and Communication* 38 (1987): 337–41.

———. "The Electronic Writing Tutor." *Writing Lab Newsletter* 13.4 (1988): 4–5.

Kotker, Joan Garcia. "Computers and Tutors." *Computers and Composition* 1 (1984): 6–7.

Lasarenko, Jane. "PR(OWL)ING AROUND: An OWL by Any Other Name." *Kairos* 1.1 (1996). <http://english.ttu.edu/kairos/1.1/index.html>.

Marshall, Rick. "Word Processing and More: The Joys and Chores of a Writing Lab Computer." *Writing Lab Newsletter* 11.10 (1987): 1–4.

Mason, Richard G. "Computer Assistance in the Writing Lab." *Writing Lab Newsletter* 6.9 (1982): 1–5.

McLeod, Susan H. "Writing Across the Curriculum: The Second Stage, and Beyond." *College Composition and Communication* 40.3 (1989): 337–43.

McLeod, Susan H., and Margot Soven, eds. *Writing Across the Curriculum: A Guide to Developing Programs.* Newbury Park: Sage, 1992.

Nelson, Jane, and Cynthia A. Wambeam. "Moving Computers into the Writing Center: The Path to Least Resistance." *Computers and Composition* 12 (1995): 135–43.

Neuwirth, Christine M., Terilyn Gillespie, and Michael E. Palmquist. *A Student's Guide to Collaborative Writing with CECE-Talk: A Computer Network Tool.* Pittsburgh: Carnegie Mellon U, Center for Educational Computing in English/Annenberg-CPB, 1988.

Neuwirth, Christine M., David S. Kaufer, Ravinder Chandook, and James H. Morris. "Issues in the Design of Computer Support for Co-Authoring and Commenting." *Proceedings of the Conference on Computer-Supported Cooperative Work.* Los Angeles: ACM, 1988. 183–95.

Neuwirth, Christine M., David S. Kaufer, Rick Chimera, and Terilyn Gillespie. "The Notes Program: A Hypertext Application for Writing from Sources Texts." *Hypertext '87 Proceedings.* Chapel Hill: ACM, 1987. 345–65.

Neuwirth, Christine M., David S. Kaufer, Gary Keim, and Terilyn Gillespie. *The Comments Program: Computer Support for Response to Writing.* Pittsburgh: Carnegie Mellon U, CECE-TR-3, Center for Educational Computing in English, 1988.

Neuwirth, Christine M., Michael E. Palmquist, and Terilyn Gillespie. *An Instructor's Guide to Collaborative Writing with CECE Talk, A Computer Network Tool.* Pittsburgh: Carnegie Mellon U, Center for Educational Computing in English, 1988.

Palmquist, Mike, Kate Kiefer, James Hartvigsen, and Barbara Godlew. *Transitions: Teaching Writing in Computer-Supported and Traditional Classrooms.* Greenwich, CT: Ablex, 1998.

Palmquist, Mike, Kate Kiefer, and Donald E. Zimmerman. "Creating Community through Communication Across the Curriculum." *Electronic Communication Across the Curriculum.* Ed. Donna Reiss, Dickie Selfe, and Art Young. Urbana, IL: NCTE, 1998. 57–72.

Palmquist, Mike, Dawn Rodrigues, Kate Kiefer, and Donald E. Zimmerman. "Enhancing the Audience for Writing Across the Curriculum: Housing WAC in a Network-Supported Writing Center." *Computers and Composition* 12 (1995): 335–53.

Palmquist, Mike, Donald E. Zimmerman, and Kate Kiefer. *Colorado State Center for Research on Writing and Communication Technologies.* Proposal to Colorado Commission on Higher Education Programs of Excellence. July 1992.

Reiss, Donna. "Computer-Supported Communication Across the Curriculum." Tidewater Community C. <http://www.tc.cc.va.us/tcresourc/faculty/tcreisd/dreiss/ecacsite.htm>.

Reiss, Donna, Dickie Selfe, and Art Young, eds. *Electronic Communication Across the Curriculum.* Urbana, IL: NCTE, 1998.

Rodrigues, Dawn, and Kate Kiefer. "Moving toward an Electronic Writing Center at Colorado State University." *Writing Centers in Context: Twelve Case Studies.* Ed. Joyce A. Kinkead and Jeanette G. Harris. Urbana, IL: NCTE, 1993. 216–26.

Rodrigues, Dawn, Kate Kiefer, and S. McPherson. "English Department Offers Electronic Writing Service." *Vector* 7.5 (1990): 3–4, 16.

Russell, David R. *Writing in the Academic Disciplines, 1870–1990: A Curricular History.* Carbondale: Southern Illinois UP, 1991.

Scharton, Maurice. "The Third Person: The Role of the Computer in Writing Centers." *Computers and Composition* 7 (1989): 37–48.

Selfe, Cynthia L. "Three Voices on Literacy, Technology, and Humanistic Perspective." *Computers and Composition* 12 (1995): 309–10.

Selfe, Dickie. "Surfing the Tsunami: Electronic Environments in the Writing Center." *Computers and Composition* 12 (1995): 311–23.

Southwell, M. G. "Computer-Assisted Instruction in the Comp-Lab at York College/CUNY." *Writing Lab Newsletter* 7.8 (1983): 1–2.

Soven, Margot. "Conclusion: Sustaining Writing Across the Curriculum Programs." McLeod and Soven 189–97.

Stracke, Richard. "The Effects of a Full-Service Computer Room on Student Writing." *Computers and Composition* 5 (1988): 51–56.

Strenski, Ellen. "Writing Across the Curriculum at Research Universities." *Strengthening Programs for Writing Across the Curriculum.* Ed. Susan H. McLeod. *New Directions for Teaching and Learning* 36. San Francisco: Jossey-Bass, 1988. 31–41.

Strenski, Ellen, and TA-TALKers. "Virtual Staff Meetings: Electronic Tutor Training with a Local E-Mail Listserv Discussion Group." *Computers and Composition* 12 (1995): 247–55.

Sullivan, Patricia. "Human-Computer Interaction Perspectives on Word-Processing Issues." *Computers and Composition* 6 (1989): 11–33.

Swanson-Owens, Deborah. "Identifying Natural Sources of Resistance: A Case Study of Implementing Writing Across the Curriculum." *Research in the Teaching of English* 20 (1986): 69–97.

Thomas, Laura H. "Educating Electrical Engineers for Workplace Communication: A Qualitative Study." MA thesis. Colorado State U, 1994.

Vest, David, Marilee Long, and Thad Anderson. "Electrical Engineers' Perceptions of Communication Training and Their Recommendations for Curricular Change: Results of a National Survey." *IEEE Transactions on Professional Communication* 39 (1996): 38–42.

Vest, David, Marilee Long, Laura H. Thomas, and Michael E. Palmquist. "Relating Communication Training to Workplace Requirements: The Perspective of New Engineers." *IEEE Transactions on Professional Communication* 38 (1995): 11–17.

Walvoord, Barbara E. "The Future of WAC." *College English* 58 (1996): 58–79.

———. "Getting Started." McLeod and Soven 12–31.

Weiss, Timothy. "A Process of Composing with Computers." *Computers and Composition* 6 (1989): 45–59.

Young, Art, and Toby Fulwiler. *Writing Across the Disciplines: Research into Practice.* Upper Montclair, NJ: Boynton/Cook, 1986.

Young, Richard E. "Designing for Change in a Writing-Across-the-Curriculum Program." *Balancing Acts: Essays on the Teaching of Writing in Honor of William F. Irmscher.* Ed. Virginia A. Chappell, Mary Louise Buley-Meissner, and Chris Anderson. Carbondale: Southern Illinois UP, 1991. 141–60.

———. Telephone interview. 1997.

Young, Richard E., and Christine M. Neuwirth. "Writing in the Disciplines: Computer Support for Collaborative Learning." Proposal to the Buhl Foundation. May 1988.

Zimmerman, Donald E., and Michael E. Palmquist. "Enhancing Electrical Engineering Students' Communication Skills." *Proceedings of the IEEE International Professional Communication Conference.* Philadelphia: IEEE, 1993. 428–31.

Zimmerman, Donald E., Michael E. Palmquist, Kathleen E. Kiefer, Marilee Long, David Vest, Martha Tipton, and Laura H. Thomas. "Enhancing Electrical Engineering Students Communication Skills — The Baseline Findings." *Proceedings of the IEEE International Professional Communication Conference.* Banff, Canada: IEEE, 1994. 412–17.

25

Beyond the L2 Metaphor: Towards a Mutually Transformative Model of ESL/WAC Collaboration

PAUL KEI MATSUDA AND
JEFFREY JABLONSKI

Learning to write in the disciplines is often difficult because students tend to be unfamiliar with discipline-specific writing practices, such as linguistic and discourse conventions, audience expectations as well as dominant cultural and epistemological assumptions. To many undergraduate and graduate students, the experience of learning to write in various academic contexts is akin to learning a new language. To characterize this experience, the analogy of "writing in the disciplines as a second language" has been invoked by some writing across the curriculum (WAC) specialists.

We want to argue, however, that the second-language metaphor — or, for short, the L2 metaphor — needs to be approached critically because writing in the disciplines, after all, is not the same as learning a second language. Our first goal in this paper, then, is to critically examine the "WID as a second language" metaphor and consider its implications for WAC programs. Specifically, we want to argue for a critical approach to the use of this metaphor because, as we will discuss, its broad and uncritical use can mask the complexity of second-language learning and can lead to the marginalization of second-language writers in WAC programs as well as in the professional discourse of composition studies in general. By critiquing the use of the L2 metaphor in composition studies, however, we do not mean to suggest that second-language studies has nothing to offer WAC specialists; on the contrary, we believe that specialists in both WAC and English as a second language (ESL) have much to learn from one another. Our second goal, then, is to consider mutually beneficial ways of achieving interdisciplinary collaboration between WAC and ESL specialists.

THE USES OF THE L2 METAPHOR IN COMPOSITION STUDIES

In general, the L2 metaphor is useful because it can encourage specialists in composition studies to learn from second-language studies. As Tony Silva, Ilona Leki, and Joan Carson (1997) recently argued in "Broadening the Perspective

From *Academic.Writing*, 1 (2000).

of Mainstream Composition Studies," insights from second-language acquisition and ESL writing pedagogy "could help composition studies develop a more global and inclusive view of writing" (p. 402). In *Understanding ESL Writers* (1992), Leki also wrote that "in certain ways theories about and insights into second-language acquisition may be useful for all writing teachers, since writing researchers, theorists, and teachers have pointed out that even in one's native language, learning to write is something like learning a second language" (p. 10).

A prime example of the use of the L2 metaphor by a WAC specialist can be found in "Stranger in Strange Lands" (1987), Lucille Parkinson McCarthy's classic study of a college student writing in various disciplinary classrooms. In this study, McCarthy characterized the experience of Dave, a white, middle-class college student, by comparing it to the process of learning a second language — or second languages. She wrote:

> As I followed Dave from one classroom writing situation to another, I came to see him, as he made his journey from one discipline to another, as a stranger in strange lands. In each new class Dave believed that the writing he was doing was totally unlike anything he had ever done before. This metaphor of a newcomer in a foreign country proved to be a powerful way of looking at Dave's behaviors as he worked to use the new languages in unfamiliar academic territories. (p. 234)

The L2 metaphor gives WAC specialists a way of explaining to teachers across the disciplines — or, in McCarthy's words, " 'native speakers' of discipline-specific language — just how foreign and difficult their language is for student newcomers" (p. 262). Indeed, the L2 metaphor seems to provide a useful way of capturing student writers' experience in ways that no other metaphor can.

McCarthy is by no means the only one to notice the usefulness of the L2 metaphor in composition studies. In the late 1970s and the early 1980s, the L2 metaphor became popular among teachers and researchers of basic writing, including Mina P. Shaughnessy. In *Errors and Expectations* (1977), a groundbreaking study of basic writing, Shaughnessy invoked the metaphor of academic English as a second language, referring to basic writers learning to write in college as "strangers in academia" (p. 3). She saw an analogical relationship between the two groups of students because basic writers, "however different their linguistic backgrounds, are clearly colliding with many of the same stubborn contours of formal English . . . that are also troublesome to students learning English as a second language" (p. 92). For this reason, she sought in her work to apply "ESL approaches in the teaching of English to natives" of the United States (1976, p. 162). For instance, she tried to improve writing teachers' attitudes toward basic writers by adapting "the view a teacher is more likely to have toward a foreign student learning English" (1977, p. 121). She continued:

> [The ESL student's] errors reflect upon his linguistic situation, not upon his educability; he is granted by his teacher the capability of mastering English but is expected in the course of doing so to make errors in English; and certain errors, characteristic errors for natives of his language

who are acquiring English as a second language, are tolerated far into
and even beyond the period of formal instruction simply because they
must be rubbed off by time. (p. 121)

Shaughnessy's work was influential in pointing out the relevance of second-
language research and pedagogy to writing instruction for basic writers, as a
number of studies that explored this issue in the late 1970s and the 1980s cited
Errors and Expectations as a point of departure for their effort.

In *Teaching Writing as a Second Language* (1987), for instance, Alice S. Horning extended Shaughnessy's use of the L2 metaphor in her effort to develop a
theory of writing acquisition by applying insights from second-language acquisition research. She contended that "Basic writers develop writing skills
and achieve proficiency in the same way that other adults develop second-
language skills, principally because, for basic writers, academic, formal, written English is a new and distinct linguistic system" (p. 2). She explained:

> They are, moreover, newcomers to the academic community of a college
> or university, and while their native language may or may not be some
> dialect of English, formal written English is quite foreign to them. They
> must master both the language and culture of academia, and they face
> many of the same intellectual and psychological challenges that confront
> other second-language learners. (p. 2)[1]

Barry M. Kroll and John C. Schafer (1978) also attempted to apply error
analysis in ESL to basic writing research. In "Error Analysis and the Teaching
of Composition," they argued that "consideration of the issues involved in
the evolution of error-analysis in ESL can contribute, both theoretically and
methodologically, to [composition specialists'] study of the errors students
make in written composition." Specifically, they argued that composition
specialists could use "a sophisticated terminology for discussing error" developed by second-language researchers to "promote the type of interdisciplinary work that we see as crucial to the advancement of composition theory and
research" (p. 248).

PROBLEMATIZING THE L2 METAPHOR

Despite Kroll and Schafer's argument for interdisciplinary cooperation, however, the relationship between composition and second-language specialists
has thus far been limited, for the most part, to the occasional borrowing of
theoretical and practical insights. These borrowing practices are problematic,
however, because they often construct and represent second-language scholarship in limited ways and may diminish the potential for further collaboration and mutual growth. For instance, the application of ESL pedagogy in
composition studies has often focused on the problem of errors, giving the
impression that the field of second-language writing is concerned almost exclusively with students' errors, whereas the study of errors is only a small
part of the growing body of second-language writing scholarship.

Furthermore, the use of the L2 metaphor can also mask the complexity of
second-language learning. As McCarthy (1987) acknowledged, students who

have the same ethnic and class backgrounds as their teachers are "actually in a privileged position in terms of [their] potential for success" in figuring out the teachers' tacit expectations (p. 262). And if writing in various disciplines is more difficult for students from different ethnic and class backgrounds, it is even more so for second-language writers who do not even share the linguistic background — a point that is often forgotten in the age of "institutionalized" critique based on race, class, and gender. Yet, when the L2 metaphor is used as a way of explaining the difficulty of learning to write in the disciplines for native English speakers, there is no language left to explain the experience of second-language writers, who are literally learning a second language in addition to learning various disciplinary "languages." In other words, the use of the L2 metaphor, which seems to encourage interdisciplinary cooperation between WAC and ESL specialists, could also be contributing to the marginalization of second-language issues in WAC programs. It could also be affecting the ability of ESL specialists to effectively communicate the needs of second-language writers with instructors across the disciplines.

The disciplinary relationship reflected in the current use of the L2 metaphor seems to be what Matsuda (1998) has called the "division of labor model" (p. 104).[2] In this model, the two "disciplines" are considered to be independent and discrete, each taking on a different responsibility: ESL specialists are expected to work only with ESL students — which is more or less accurate — and writing specialists, including WAC specialists, are to be concerned with non-ESL students only. The obvious problem with this division is that writing specialists in composition studies remain unprepared to work with ESL students who, after finishing ESL courses, are also enrolled in writing programs at all levels. Such borrowing of insights from second-language studies without considering the needs and interests of second-language writers or specialists is ultimately an inadequate appropriation.

Another problem with this model is epistemological. That is, the borrowing practices that we have discussed are based on the assumption that the interdisciplinary exchange of knowledge can take place without affecting the knowledge being borrowed or the dynamics of knowledge in the two disciplines. Such a view of the interdisciplinary relationship seems epistemologically naive and its consequences to second-language students and specialists ethically problematic. In the next section, then, we propose what we call a mutually transformative model of interdisciplinary collaboration between second-language studies and writing across the curriculum, which can help challenge the limited conceptions of the relationship between ESL and WAC.

TOWARDS A MUTUALLY TRANSFORMATIVE MODEL OF ESL/WAC COLLABORATION

The mutually transformative model is a view of interdisciplinary interaction that recognizes the dynamic and fluctuating nature of knowledge and fields. This view of the interdisciplinary relationship sees both the knowledge being borrowed and the fields that are involved to be affected by the interaction. In the context of the WAC/ESL relationship, this model helps us see that WAC can borrow from ESL but it also affects the disciplinary and institutional practices of both WAC and ESL in ways that may never have been anticipated or wanted. Traditionally, as we have shown, this change has been focusing on altering WAC practices to better serve the needs of native English speakers in WAC programs without considering how second-language students or specialists are affected in relation to WAC practices.

The mutually transformative model suggests that WAC specialists, in incorporating second-language perspectives, need to recognize how second-language students and specialists are affected by this inevitable relationship — inevitable not only because the L2 metaphor provides a way of incorporating second-language perspectives in WAC practices but also because ESL students are often subjected to WAC practices. The model can also encourage WAC specialists to realize the need to develop WAC programs in ways that reflect this awareness.

What, then, do WAC specialists need to do to move beyond the problematic interdisciplinary relationship that is reflected in the current use of the L2 metaphor as we have outlined? First, WAC specialists need to pay more attention to the presence and needs of second-language writers in WAC programs. It has generally been assumed that ESL programs exist to provide remedial instruction to second-language writers for a certain period of time so that they can function effectively in other academic environments — including writing intensive courses in their majors. However, second-language "problems" do not somehow disappear after a few semesters of instruction. For this reason, many second-language writers will continue to require support throughout their academic career and beyond. To meet the needs of these students effectively, WAC specialists need to recognize their presence and to learn from second-language specialists in addressing the needs of those students.

Second, in engaging in interdisciplinary interactions with second-language studies — or, for that matter, any other disciplines — WAC specialists need to pay more attention to the implications of such interactions on many levels, including disciplinary, programmatic, and individual. To this end, WAC specialists, before engaging in any interdisciplinary interaction, might develop a disciplinary equivalent of an environmental-impact statement, which reflects a thorough consideration of the consequences of such an interaction — just as engineers do before they begin projects that are potentially hazardous to the surroundings. For example, if a WAC program is to incorporate an ESL component, it should be done in ways that are informed by a careful examination of the structures and goals of ESL programs as well as WAC programs. Another example, at the disciplinary level, is to critically reflect on the interdisciplinary borrowing of knowledge by asking questions such as: What are we gaining? At what (and whose) cost? What are we overlooking? How can we make it beneficial for everyone involved?

However, assessing the impact of WAC specialists' actions on second-language issues is difficult because the interests and concerns of ESL specialists are not always apparent to WAC specialists. For this reason, WAC specialists should make an effort to move from the interdisciplinary borrowing approach to a more participatory approach. In other words, any such interaction should start with a dialogue between specialists from both fields. Opening up WAC programs to diverse and innovative perspectives is not new; in fact, it is virtually axiomatic (Maimon, 1992; Walvoord, 1992). WAC specialists can profitably apply this philosophy to the context of the WAC/ESL relationship as well.

There are a number of ways that the ESL/WAC collaboration might be initiated. For instance, ESL specialists can be invited to participate in the process of designing and developing WAC programs that are sensitive to the needs of second-language students. At institutions where WAC programs are administered by a committee, ESL specialists may be invited to join the committee to represent the needs and interests of ESL specialists and students. At institutions where WAC programs are administered by an individual director, ESL specialists may be called upon as outside consultants. Conversely, WAC specialists can also make efforts to participate in the development of English for academic purposes programs — a unit within the ESL program that aims at preparing ESL students for language and writing demands across the disciplines.

Collaboration is also important in incorporating an ESL component into existing WAC programs or vice versa. The involvement of specialists from both WAC and ESL programs in coordinating such development is crucial so that duplicating services can be avoided. When programs offer services with similar goals, they often risk being consolidated by higher-level administration in order to conserve limited resources — without consulting those who are involved in the programs.

WAC and ESL specialists can also work together to create joint programs within writing centers or instructional development centers. Some instructional development centers provide funding for initiatives to develop unique and innovative programs. An advantage of this approach is that it will allow for the development of innovative programs without threatening the existing institutional structure. As McLeod (1997) has pointed out, creating a new interdisciplinary program with a unique structure may make it "vulnerable to the administrative ax" (p. 68). To achieve collaboration without losing the institutional status that both programs worked hard to establish, WAC and ESL programs should attempt to do so without abandoning the existing program structures. By working together in the service of improving teaching and learning, WAC and ESL could also conserve resources by sharing hard-to-come-by grant funding and aid one another in securing increased institutional status (McLeod, 1997).

At the disciplinary level, more dialogue between WAC and ESL specialists needs to take place at conferences and symposia as well as publications in both composition studies and second-language studies. In that vein, we see our own collaboration as a starting point for a movement toward more mutually transformative interaction between WAC and ESL specialists.

CONCLUSION

Donna LeCourt (1996) suggests that faculty across the disciplines are open to making their discourses more accessible to students who have been traditionally excluded from academia. ESL students, as Vivian Zamel (1995) points out, are one of those groups of students whose presence is increasingly felt. By collaborating with ESL specialists in incorporating second-language issues into WAC practices, WAC specialists can play an even greater role in further democratizing discourses across the curriculum.

NOTES

1. Horning's discussion of second-language acquisition research is somewhat dated. For a more up-to-date review of second-language acquisition research and its implications for composition studies, see Silva, Leki, and Carson.

2. For a history of the creation of the disciplinary division of labor between composition studies and second-language studies, see Matsuda (1999).

REFERENCES

Horning, Alice. (1987). *Teaching writing as a second language.* Carbondale, IL: Southern Illinois UP.

Kroll, Barry M., & Schafer, John C. (1978). Error-analysis and the teaching of composition. *College Composition and Communication, 29,* 242–248.

LeCourt, Donna. (1996). WAC as critical pedagogy: The third stage? *Journal of Advanced Composition, 16,* 389–405.

Leki, Ilona. (1992). *Understanding ESL writers: A guide for teachers.* Portsmouth, NH: Boynton/Cook.

Maimon, Elaine P. (1992). Preface. In Susan H. McLeod & Margot Soven (Eds.), *Writing across the curriculum: A guide to developing programs* (pp. ix–xiv). Newbury Park, CA: Sage.

Matsuda, Paul Kei. (1998). Situating ESL writing in a cross-disciplinary context. *Written Communication, 15,* 99–121.

Matsuda, Paul Kei. (1999). Composition studies and ESL writing: A disciplinary division of labor. *College Composition and Communication, 50,* 699–721.

McCarthy, Lucille Parkinson. (1987). A stranger in strange lands: A college student writing across the curriculum. *Research in the Teaching of English, 21*(3), 233–265.

McLeod, Susan H. (1997). WAC at century's end: Haunted by the ghost of Fred Newton Scott. *Writing Program Administration, 21*(1), 67–73.

Shaughnessy, Mina P. (1976). Basic writing. In Gary Tate (Ed.), *Teaching composition: 10 bibliographical essays* (pp. 137–167). Fort Worth, TX: Texas Christian UP.

Shaughnessy, Mina P. (1977). *Errors and expectations: A guide for the teacher of basic writing.* New York: Oxford UP.

Silva, Tony, Leki, Ilona, & Carson, Joan. (1997). Broadening the perspective of mainstream composition studies: Some thoughts from the disciplinary margins. *Written Communication, 14,* 398–428.

Walvoord, Barbara E. (1992). Getting started. In Susan H. McLeod & Margot Soven (Eds.), *Writing across the curriculum: A guide to developing programs* (pp. 12–31). Newbury Park, CA: Sage, 1992.

Zamel, Vivian. (1995). Strangers in academia: The experiences of faculty and ESL students across the curriculum. *College Composition and Communication, 46,* 506–521.

26 Exploring Notions of Genre in "Academic Literacies" and "Writing Across the Curriculum": Approaches Across Countries and Contexts

DAVID R. RUSSELL, MARY LEA, JAN PARKER, BRIAN STREET, AND TIANE DONAHUE

The SIGET IV panel on genre in Writing Across the Curriculum (WAC) and "academic literacies" (ACLITS) has set rolling a discussion of the similarities and differences in the two traditions, the former originating in the US in the early 1970s, the latter originating in England in the early 1990s. This paper maps out some elements of each in relation to the other and to genre, which we hope will set in motion further discussions and cross-fertilization.

At first glance, the two seem very different. As their respective titles suggest, one is about writing and the other about literacies. The term WAC means efforts to improve students' learning and writing (or learning through writing) in all university courses and departments (with some attention to school and adult education as well). The term "writing in the disciplines" (WID) is also used, somewhat synonymously, but suggests greater attention to the relation between writing and learning in a specific discipline. (For an overview and bibliography on WAC, see Bazerman, Little, Bethel, Chavkin, Fouquette, & Garufis, 2005.)

ACLITS is about *literacies* in higher education, primarily. In the UK, literacy has been more traditionally associated with school and adult learning, rather than the university. Indeed, there is still a strongly held belief amongst most UK university teachers that literacy needs to be attended to before students embark upon higher education studies (a view that is shared by many — perhaps most — US university teachers). ACLITS is working to change that view of literacy by taking social practices approaches to multiple and plural literacies, often associated with "New Literacy Studies" (Street, 1996).

WAC is twenty years older, and much larger and sprawling, encompassing many — and, often, dissenting — voices within it. Some 2,400 articles and

From *Genre in a Changing World*. Ed. Charles Bazerman, Adair Bonini, and Débora Figueiredo. Fort Collins: The WAC Clearinghouse and Parlor Press, 2009. 395–423.

books on WAC have been published since 1975, with some 240 empirical studies. ACLITS is much younger, relatively smaller, and more focused and coherent. Though the object of both is similar — academic writing — the purposes are different. WAC is primarily a pedagogical reform movement. Despite being practitioner led, ACLITS has focused on research and theory thus far, describing practices and understanding them theoretically. It is just entering into large-scale pedagogy and reform efforts.

At first glance at least, the two also appear to come from rather different intellectual worlds. WAC comes out of US "rhetoric and composition," a field that arose out of the professionalization of teachers of first-year university general writing courses in the 1970s — with very much a humanities bent — and located in English departments primarily, with relatively little contact with linguistics. ACLITS comes primarily out of studies in language, literacy and ethnography, with a focus on descriptive studies of specific literacy practices, and has no particular disciplinary home.

These differences are magnified by the very different systems of higher education they inhabit. The US system emphasizes late specialization, with a period of "general education" in the first two years of university, and writing in several disciplines. In the UK students have tended to specialize early and write for one discipline, although recently "modular" courses have involved more "mix" of disciplines and therefore more switching of written genres (Lea & Street, 1998, 2006). In the UK assessments of students almost always involve extensive written work, whereas in the US assessments are often multiple choice. The primary difference is that the US has a ubiquitous, required general writing course in higher education, first-year composition, which deeply colors the whole enterprise of WAC.

Yet there are important similarities. Both ACLITS and WAC took their impetus from widening participation, as it is called in the UK, or admission of previously excluded groups in the US. The US has for decades had a system of mass education, whereas the UK is really only beginning "massification." So both WAC (in the 1970s) and ACLITS (in the 1990s) began as a response to an influx of new students.

Ideologically both are oppositional, attempting to reform higher education and make it more open. And both use writing/literacy to resist deeply entrenched attitudes about writing, and about students and disciplines. Both attempt to move beyond elementary skills (and thus remedial or deficit) models of writing to consider the complexity of communication in relation to learning.

And in terms of research, there is a strong element of ethnographic research in North America, that owes much to Dell Hymes and Shirley Brice Heath and that complements British traditions of anthropology and applied linguistics (see Heath & Street, 2008). And ACLITS has from the beginning been influenced by North American WAC research by Bazerman, Bartholomae (1986), Russell and others.

And in the last 10 years, North American WAC programs have begun to speak of themselves in terms of multimodal "communication across the curriculum" (CAC), in part a response to the New London Group and its interest in new media, which was also influential for ACLITS.

We organize this paper around parallel descriptions of each tradition under the headings historical origins, institutional positions, theory and research about genre, and finally pedagogy using genre. We conclude by drawing out a number of comparisons between the two for further dialog.

HISTORICAL ROOTS

ACLITS Origins

The notion of "academic literacies" has its roots in a body of practice-based research and literacy theory that became significant in the UK during the 1990s. Until this time little attention had been paid to issues of student writing, the general assumption — although rarely articulated — being that students would learn how to write through their tacit acculturation into the norms and conventions of single subject disciplinary frames (Ivanic & Lea, 2006). Hounsell (1988) had previously looked at problems students encountered when confronted with the unfamiliar discourses of the university. He identified academic discourse as "a particular kind of written world, with a set of conventions, or 'code,' of its own." He illustrated how students needed to be sensitive to different disciplinary ways of framing in their writing, and highlighted the tacit nature of academic discourse calling for its features to be made more explicit to students. (See also the Australian research of Ballard & Clanchy, 1988.) This focus on explicit acculturation into disciplinary codes and discourses shared much in common with the earlier work of Bizzell (1982) and Bartholomae (1986) in the US, which as we will see, grew out of the US WAC movement that began in the 1970s.

By the early 1990s, UK higher education was experiencing a fundamental change with unprecedented expansion in the sector and the consequences of the 1992 Education Act, which abolished the binary divide between polytechnics and universities, bringing them together for both administrative and funding purposes under one government funded body. In practical terms this meant increasing numbers of students and class sizes with no concomitant expansion in resources. One response was the creation of "study skills" and "learning support" centers, where students were able to receive one-on-one or small group support which their lecturers were no longer in a position to provide. It was among those practitioners working with students in such centers that the early roots of the field of academic literacies research began to emerge (much as in the US in the 1970s, the work of Mina Shaughnessey grew out of work with students identified as under-prepared and began serious interest in writing development). Increasingly frustrated with the limitations of simplistic surface- and skills-based models of student writing in their work with students, they began to look both for more workable and theorized explanations of the problems being encountered by student writers. As practitioner-researchers, they found themselves at the interface between theory and practice and their early publications often reflected this intersection (Ivanic, 1998; Jones, Turner, & Street, 1999; Lea, 1994; Lea & Street, 1998, 1999; Lea & Stierer, 1999; Lillis, 1999, 2001).

The dearth of literature on student writing coming out of the UK at that time meant that these researcher-practitioners often looked to the US for theoretical framing for their work. Particularly influential was Bazerman's early work (1988). Although his concern had been with the texts produced by established academic writers, UK researchers found this a particularly useful framing with which to think about undergraduate student writing. In particular his claim that writing matters because the different choices around what and how we write results in different meanings, underpinned the framing for both research and practice with student writers. With the expansion of higher education and increasing numbers of adult students entering UK universities as "non-traditional" entrants in the early 1990s, Bazerman's analysis provided a fruitful way of exploring how these students brought their own knowledge and experience to the construction of the writing they were required to undertake for assessment (Lea, 1998). Examining the object under study, the literature of the field, the anticipated audience and the author's own self in the writing of mature students laid bare the ways in which engaging with academic knowledge could conflict with other more familiar "ways of knowing." For Ivanic and her colleagues at Lancaster University (Clark & Ivanic, 1991), adopting principles of critical language awareness provided a further theoretical orientation from which to view so called problems with student writing.

This backdrop provided a foundation for the contested approach which has become associated with academic literacies research during the last decade, examining in detail students' struggles with meaning making and the nature of power and authority in student writing (Ivanic, 1998; Lea, 1994; Lea & Street, 1998; Lillis, 1997). In part this was influenced by related developments in critical linguistics (Fairclough, 1989). Work on critical language awareness in schools (Fairclough, 1992) seemed particularly pertinent to the new higher education context. In 1996 Street published an innovative chapter on academic literacies which both challenged academic convention (by incorporating the original texts of others rather than integrating them into his own work with conventional referencing) and foregrounded questions of "academic literacies." The perspective taken by Street (1996) in this publication sat within a body of work that had become known as the "New Literacy Studies" (NLS). Street's seminal contribution to NLS had been made earlier when he distinguished between autonomous and ideological models of literacy (Street, 1984). He had argued that whereas an autonomous model of literacy suggests that literacy is a decontextualized skill, which once learned can be transferred with ease from one context to another, the ideological model highlights the contextual and social nature of literacy practices, and the relationships of power and authority which are implicit in any literacy event. Literacy, then, is not something that once acquired can be effortlessly applied to any context requiring mastery of the written word. Writing and reading practices are deeply social activities; familiarity with and understanding these practices takes place in specific social contexts, which are overlaid with ideological complexities, for example, with regard to the different values placed on particular genres of written texts. Following this perspective, NLS, with its roots in sociolinguistics and linguistic anthropology, conceptualizes writing and reading as contextualized social practices.

Until the mid-1990s New Literacy Studies had been concerned with school-based, community, and workplace literacies, primarily of people in different cultural contexts, notably Iran, South Africa, and Latin America (Street, 2001) but had not paid any attention to literacies in the university "at home." Although the early work of, for example Lea (1994) and Lillis (1997), had conceptualized writing as contextualized social practice explicitly challenging deficit models of writing, neither at that time situated their work explicitly in the NLS tradition nor made reference to "academic literacies," as such. However, Lea (1994) did illustrate the multiplicity of discourses in the academy, an important distinction from the use of the term discourse in the singular. Ivanic also foregrounded the use of different and competing discourses in her study of mature students (Ivanic, 1998). Overall, what characterized this emerging body of work was its specific focus on student writing as social practice and recognition of the multiplicity of practices, whether these were conceptualized as discourses or literacies. The use of the term "literacies," rather than "discourses" (the framing more commonly provided by the US writers in the college composition field), gradually became more prevalent in the UK literature. This was not merely because of its association with a theoretical framing provided by the NLS, but because the focus of concern was student writing, rather than spoken language; the term *discourse* being associated more commonly with the use of spoken rather than written language at that time.

Research by Lea and Street (1998), building on the NLS methodological approach but also on Lea's practitioner experience, introduced new theoretical frames to a field which was, at the time, still predominantly influenced by psychological accounts of student learning (e.g., Gibbs, 1994). Rather than frame their work in terms of "good" and "poor" writing, Lea and Street suggested that any explanation needed to examine faculty and student expectations around writing without making any judgments about which practices were appropriate. Drawing on the findings from an empirical research project conducted in two very different universities, they examined student writing against a background of institutional practices, power relations, and identities, with meanings being contested between faculty and students, and an emphasis on the different understandings and interpretations of the writing task. Findings from their research suggested fundamental gaps between students' and faculty understandings of the requirements of student writing, providing evidence at the level of epistemology, authority, and contestation over knowledge, rather than at the level of technical skill, surface linguistic competence, and cultural assimilation. Based on their analysis of their research data, they explicated three models of student writing. These they termed study skills, socialization, and academic literacies. The study skills model is based on the assumption that mastery of the correct rules of grammar and syntax, coupled with attention to punctuation and spelling, will ensure student competence in academic writing; it is, therefore, primarily concerned with the surface features of text. In contrast the academic socialization model assumes students need to be acculturated into the discourses and genres of particular disciplines and that making the features and requirements of these explicit to students will result in their becoming successful writers. In some respects the third model, academic literacies, subsumes many of the features of the other two; Lea and Street (1998) point out that the models are not presented as mutually exclusive. Nevertheless they argue that it is the academic literacies model which is best able to take account of the nature of student writing in relation to institutional practices, power relations, and identities, in short to consider the complexity of meaning making which the other two models fail to provide.

The explication of the three models proposed by Lea and Street has been drawn upon very widely in the literature on teaching and learning across a range of HE [higher education] contexts (see, e.g., Thesen & van Pletzen, 2006, on South Africa) and calls for a more in-depth understanding of student writing and its relationship to learning across the academy, thus offering an alternative to deficit models of learning and writing based on autonomous models of literacy.

WAC Origins

The WAC movement's origin in the US in the 1970s can only be understood in light of the century-old US tradition of university-level "composition" courses, required of almost all first-year university students. These courses were taught in English departments and traditionally mixed the teaching of literary texts with skills-based instruction in writing, often with a remedial stigma attached (deficit model). In the late 1970s, composition teachers professionalized the teaching of writing, developing their own MA and PhD programs in rhetoric and composition (that is, the teaching of university-level writing). They developed several strands of research drawn from both the humanities (i.e., classical rhetoric) and the social sciences (e.g., education), and pushed composition teaching beyond literary analysis and "skills and drills."

As with ACLITS in the 1990s, the rise of the WAC movement in the late 1970s and early 1980s (Russell, 1991) was a response to the influx into higher education of previously excluded groups, through open admissions policies in public institutions. One response was to radically rethink the remedial or deficit model of writing and found writing centers, special curricula, and systematic research into the differences between student and teacher perceptions of error — much as with ACLITS research in the mid-1990s. Another approach was to enlist teachers from other disciplines to improve students' writing — and learning: the WAC movement.

The early theoretical inspiration for the WAC movement in the US came directly from a British educational theorist and reformer, James Britton, and his colleagues at the University of London Institute of Education, who coined the term WAC (Russell, 1991) as part of their efforts to improve writing in the disciplines in secondary education. Britton and his colleagues (1975) viewed writing (and talk) as a gradually developing accomplishment, thoroughly bound up with the particular intellectual goals and traditions of each discipline or profession, not as a single set of readily-generalizable skills learned once and for all. They also theorized writing in terms of disciplinary learning and personal development, not discrete, generalizable skills. And they used Vygotsky (among others) to theorize it. In Britain, the Language across the Curriculum or Language Awareness movements (as they were called) did not last long or have a great impact on secondary schools, and almost none in HE at the time (although see Ivanic, 2004, for more recent attention to Critical Language Awareness), but their ideas were picked up by the fledgling WAC movement in the US — mainly in higher education.

In the early 1980s, the dominant model of writing research was cognitive. But by the mid-1980s, a few US researchers began to use ethnographic methods to explore writing development as a cultural-historical phenomenon. As with the ACLITS in the late 1990s, the Ethnography of Communication was the inspiration. The seminal article was by Lucille McCarthy, a PhD student of Dell Hymes. Her 1987 article "A Stranger in Strange Lands" followed one student as he went to courses in four disciplines, and as the title suggests, McCarthy found that the differences in disciplinary writing practices and communities were much more important to the student than the similarities, a theme pursued by Lea and Street (1998) in their account of UK students' switching between courses in modular degrees.

Classroom practice in general composition courses began to change as well in the 1980s. "WAC textbooks" in first-year composition courses began to appear, which taught the genres of writing in the social and natural sciences — not as formulas to be followed, ordinarily, but as indices of the ways of knowing, the epistemology and social actions, of knowledge domains or disciplines.

Research into social dimensions of the disciplines and professions — how and why professionals write — complemented textual research. A large strand of research into the genres of professional and academic research writing began (e.g., Bazerman, 1988; Berkenkotter & Huckin, 1995). Some compared student writing to that of professionals. For example, Geisler's (1994) work on expert and student texts in philosophy, *Academic Literacy and the Nature of Expertise*, exposed philosophers' ways of writing, thinking, and being, in relation to the discursive moves of students writing in philosophy courses. And an educational reform movement swept US HE.

INSTITUTIONAL POSITIONS

WAC Institutionally

Institutionally, WAC has been focused in programs within individual universities (and some secondary schools). It is a higher education reform movement, but without a centralized national organization, though it does have a loosely organized special interest group associated with the professional organization for composition, the Conference on College Composition and Communication (CCCC). Despite this, it has had wide influence in HE over the last 30 years. Perhaps one third of US institutions have some WAC program, in a vast number of forms (McLeod & Soven, 1992). Many WAC programs also include some curricular structure(s) to provide continuity. Institutions or departments often designate certain courses as "writing intensive" or "writing extensive" and require students to take certain ones (or a certain number of them) to graduate. Other universities have "linked" courses in which some or all of the students in a course in a discipline take a parallel course in writing, which uses the content of the disciplinary course and is planned in conjunction with it. More rarely, departments organize a sequence of writing tasks and student support that extends throughout their curriculum, from first year to last, to consciously develop students' writing (and often other communication modes). Some universities have required all departments to develop such a sequence. All these curricular forms are almost always in addition to first-year composition courses, though some universities require freshman "seminars" instead: a first-year writing course taught by staff in various disciplines with subjects for writing drawn from their disciplines (Monroe, 2006).

Almost all WAC programs include organized efforts to develop awareness of writing among teachers in the disciplines and their competence in supporting students in their writing. Many institutions have interdisciplinary workshops and seminars for academic teaching staff from all disciplines on writing development. There they not only discuss the particular needs and resources for their students' writing but also how writing works differently in each of their disciplines, how it brings students to deeper involvement with the unique ways of knowing in each — the epistemology of each — and how students can be helped to write to learn as they learn to write in a field (in Britton's famous phrase, now a slogan). Teaching staff learn to design and sequence assignments, communicate expectations, and give feedback. And since 1993 there has been a biennial national (now international) conference that draws about 500 faculty members from a great range of disciplines, institutions, and countries.

Finally, WAC programs are often connected with or part of a writing center or centers (often attached to a student support unit). Tutors (graduate or undergraduate students, typically) give individual or small group help to students. Sometimes tutors are drawn from various disciplines. Sometimes there are discipline-specific writing centers. And sometimes there are tutors assigned to specific courses (usually large lectures) to help students with their writing and learning. These centers have tried to avoid the remedial or deficit model of writing by helping all students with their writing — and, in some centers, even teaching staff who are writing research articles.

All of these efforts struggle with a range of institutional attitudes and structures that militate against WAC: reductive and remedial concepts of student writing (particularly that writing is a set of general skills to be mastered in the ubiquitous first-year general writing courses), demands on faculty time for research, large enrollments in many courses, and so on (Walvoord, 1997).

After 30 years, it is still an uphill battle, but because so many academics in the US have been exposed to the idea of WAC — through attending workshops or teaching writing-intensive courses, for example — WAC has become part of the institutional landscape of higher education in the US.

ACLITS Institutionally

In the UK, "writing-intensive" (though not writing conscious) undergraduate courses were traditionally the preserve of Oxford and Cambridge, where teaching was based on individual teaching by faculty members supervising student writing, or as it was perceived, student disciplinary learning, in weekly one-on-one sessions. The post-1992 expansion, entailing large class sizes and an increasingly diverse student body, and the growth of themed, interdisciplinary modular curricula resulted in more attention to writing as meaning making and as a social practice. This has led to movements such as Writing Development in Higher Education (biennial conferences since 1995) and more recently the WAC-influenced Thinking Writing project and new, US style, writing centers (for these and other examples see Ganobcsik-Williams, 2006).

ACLITS has influenced all of these efforts. However, as illustrated above, ACLITS, although primarily practitioner led, has tended to be more focused on theory and research. Indeed there have been questions raised in the literature about the value of the framing offered by academic literacies research for pedagogy. Lillis (2006) suggests that we need to develop an academic literacies pedagogy which places the nature of dialogue at its centre and that more specifically we should be thinking about how we can develop and validate alternative spaces for writing and meaning making in the academy. Lea (2001) suggests that the principles emerging from academic literacies research can be taken up in different institutional contexts. She illustrates this through a case study of a postgraduate course in teacher education delivered online.

From a practitioner perspective the provision of support based on any particular set of principles is unusual. Nevertheless, many practitioners do draw on the general framing offered by the academic literacies perspective, albeit not explicitly. The biennial Writing Development in Higher Education conference draws together those working across settings in the field of writing support, who are adopting a social practice model of writing. A number of institutions have pursued programs for supporting students and their teachers, often in relation to widening participation. These developments are frequently initiated by educational development units and supported by some form of student learning center. Although both of these generally have a broad brief of which writing is only a part, taken together they are generally the most important institutional sites for writing development in the UK. While educational development units work directly supporting faculty with issues of teaching and learning, including student writing, the brief of most student learning centers is to work only with students. Coupled with the fact that the latter is often low status, hourly paid work and the academic credibility of the former is continually under threat as universities are increasingly reluctant to employ educational developers on academic contracts, the kinds of approaches suggested by Lillis and Lea are few and far between.

THEORY AND RESEARCH: THE ROLES OF GENRE

ACLITS Theory and Research Using Genre

Issues of genre are central to the three models of student writing outlined above (skills, socialization, and academic literacies). Each of these models is implicitly associated with a different orientation to the notion of genre. In terms of study skills, genre would be conceptualized primarily in relation to surface features and form; academic socialization would be associated with the conceptualization of genre in terms of established disciplinary norms for communication, given primarily by the texts written by academics within a disciplinary community. The empirically grounded academic literacies perspective is aligned with a view of genre as social practice rather than genre knowledge in terms of disciplinary communication per se, although this is by its very nature central to the social practice perspective.

Research in the field has uncovered the range of genres engaged in by students across the university, with variation evident not just in terms of the discipline or specific departmental or module requirements for student writers. For example, genre variation is evident in terms of the individual predispositions of individual university teachers and in relation to specific assignments (Lea & Street, 1998; see also Lea & Street, 1999, 2006). The contribution of the theoretical and methodological framing offered by social anthropology and applied linguistics is central to this understanding of genre types as they emerge in the detailed everyday encounters around writing in particular institutional contexts. Much of the research has been undertaken through an ethnographic lens which provides the opportunity to make the familiar strange, to approach everyday practices around student writing as an area of study without bringing to this judgments about the nature of that writing (see Heath & Street, 2008). Through such a lens a range of genres become visible and opened up for scrutiny, not just those that are given by either generic academic writing requirements or by the discipline. For example, researchers have examined feedback on students' written work and the implications for meaning making and issues of identity (Ivanic, 1998, 2004; Lea & Street, 1998; Lillis, 2001). Stierer (1997, 2000) has examined the nature of assignment questions for master's level students and the implications of the ways in which these are framed for students' understanding of assignment questions. Lea (2006) has explored the textual nature of online student debates and how students integrate these into their assignments. Street and colleagues have explored the issue of "genre switching" amongst pre-university students being prepared for university entry in Widening Participation courses at King's College London (Scalone & Street, 2006; Lea & Street, 2006 — see below).

The findings of the type of detailed research signaled above suggests, then, that genre questions arise in consideration of the range of texts and practices which are integral to any understanding of student writing — and how best to support it — rather than being merely concerned with disciplinary considerations, such as "how to write in History," "how to reference in Psychology," "how to develop an argument in English."

As we have already discussed above, ACLITS has tended to focus on unpacking micro-social practices, such as "gaps" between student and lecturer perceptions of particular writing activities, often embedded deeply in traditions of essayist literacy and the assessment of writing. Researchers in this tradition have also focused on theorizing and researching new genres of writing in HE teaching, in different modes and media (see below), and on the ways in which students are called upon — often implicitly — to switch between different genres and modes (which also raises the more general issue of how genre and mode are theorized in relation to other traditions of genre analysis and multimodal studies). Arguably what distinguishes academic literacies research from WID is its tendency to focus at this micro level and also upon the different interpretations and understandings of genres of the participants in any particular writing encounter in the university. Drawing on the kind of framing provided by Berkenkotter and Huckin (1995), genres emerge in the relationship between the creation of texts and their associated practices in any particular context. Not only do they vary across disciplines, subjects and/or fields of study but also in text types (e.g., academic assignments, faculty feedback/marginalia, email).

This approach to genre draws a range of texts and practices into the academic literacies frame, rather than concentrating on student essay writing per se. The focus on the minutiae of texts and practices in understanding meaning making is given by the ethnographic roots of this field, and particularly Hymes' (1974) ethnography of communication, resulting in the foregrounding of an institutional perspective which takes precedence over a disciplinary or subject based focus. This may indeed be the most important distinction between the different traditions being explored in this chapter, despite their evidently common theoretical and, in part, methodological roots. As the landscape of higher education has changed over the last decade, with increased emphasis on professional rather than purely academic study and concomitant attention to new genres of writing in the academy, the theoretical framing offered by academic literacies research is becoming increasingly valuable in terms of both research and practice. For example, Creme (2008) is concerned with learning journals as transitional genres bridging a gap between students' personal worlds and the rigorous discipline-based genres embedded in more conventional essay writing. (Student journal writing is also a strategy used by the Widening Participation Program at King's College London, described below).

A number of practitioner-researchers are also underpinning their work in new multimodal environments for learning with principles offered by academic literacies research. Walton and Archer (2004) illustrate the limitations of teaching web searching skills in a South African context, if teachers do not understand the explanations and interpretations that their students are bringing to reading the web. They suggest that students already have to be in command of subject discourses and understand the genres they encounter online in order to make their searching worthwhile; supporting students in using the web in their studies requires sensitivity to the students' background and prior experience. This perspective mirrors that offered by the early findings in the field but has application to online learning. McKenna (2005) examines how students' use of hypertext challenges the linear construction of argument in academic writing. She suggests that this environment offers students the possibility to take up new subject positions not possible in more conventional essayist genres. The focus is less upon disciplinary genre knowledge and more upon issues of subjectivity and agency and the ways in which these both rub up against and challenge and subvert conventional academic genres.

WAC Theory and Research Using Genre

WAC research has taken two complementary directions: one investigating the writing of professionals in various disciplines and professions; another focused on student writing in the disciplines — especially the role of writing in learning (Russell, 1997). Concepts of genre have been central in theory and research in both. (See Klein, 1999, and Newell, 2006, for reviews of quantitative studies of writing to learn; see Russell, 2001, and Bazerman et al., 2005, for reviews of qualitative studies of student writing in HE).

Some studies have viewed genre in traditional form-based terms, as collections of identifiable features and conventions (e.g., contrastive rhetoric; the genre studies reviewed in Klein, 1999). However, in the past two decades, new ways of thinking about genre in student writing — growing out of the study of the genre and activity of professional writing — emphasize the activity of genre (Bazerman, 1988). This approach is rooted in C. Miller's (1984, 1994) theory of genre as social action. Genres are "typified rhetorical actions based in recurrent situations" (1984, p. 159). The researcher's focus shifts from the text itself to the relationship between the text and the activity of people in situations where texts are used in regularized — typified — ways. Genres are not merely forms of words, but forms of life, socio-cultural regularities that stabilize-for-now (but never finally) our interactions (Schryer, 1993).

In the late 1980s, the concept of genre as social action was combined with Vygotskian cultural-historical activity theory, which sees the relation between thought and language (and learning and writing) in social as well as cognitive terms. Cultural tools such as speaking and writing mediate our interior thoughts as well as our external social interactions. Genres, as typified ways of interacting with tools, can be seen as ways of coordinating joint activity and regulating thought (Russell, 1997; Bazerman, 2009). For Bazerman and Russell (2003), as the signs on a page mediate between relationships and people, so do genres; texts are "attended to in the context of activities" and can only be studied in their "animating activities" — production, reception, meaning, and value, "embedded in people's uses and interpretations."

Quantitative studies of student writing using genre have tended to see genres in the older, form-based way, and to look at their effects in more strictly cognitive rather than social cognitive terms. They focus on the requirements genres pose for searching out and organizing information, structuring relationships among ideas and with audiences, and controlling stance toward content (Bazerman, 2009; Klein, 1999; Newell, 2006). These studies show that students engage in different processes when they have the expectations of one genre rather than another (student newspaper, in-class essay, registrar's form).

Qualitative studies of student writing have tended to take an activity or social action approach to genre as they describe student writing and students' writing and learning. In the last dozen years, theories of genre systems (Bazerman, 1994; Russell, 1997) or networks (Prior, 2009) or ecologies (Spinuzzi, 2003), informed by cultural historical activity theory, have been applied to understanding professional work and its relationship to education (e.g., Smart 2006; Winsor 2003). Contexts such as organizations or institutions are viewed as complex activity systems mediated by complex systems of intertextual genres, through which knowledge circulates and activity is mediated in intersubjective networks (Prior, 2009; Russell & Yañez, 2003). Research on genre has traced the relationships between academic writing/activity and the writing/activity of other systems, such as home, professions, hobbies, etc. (e.g., Prior, 1998; Russell & Yañez, 2003), and its effects on both writing and identity. Genre is seen as offering direction or motive to activity, as well as pathways to new identities for participants. Indeed, longitudinal studies of students in HE (Beaufort, 2007; Wardle, 2007; Sommers, 2004; Donahue, 2008) have described the genres that students acquire as they learn in the disciplines, within various institutional contexts.

PEDAGOGY AND GENRE

WAC and Pedagogy

WAC pedagogical theory, research, and practice are well developed and take two basic directions: implicit and explicit. The most common view among teachers in the disciplines (and most WAC experts, very likely) is that students learn to write new genres primarily through writing in authentic contexts, such as their courses in the disciplines. And the focus of the WAC movement is on encouraging writing, feedback (teacher or peer), and revision or repetition. In this view, students learn to write by writing.

A strong theoretical argument for this view has been made by a group of Canadian researchers, and supported with a long series of qualitative studies that fail to show transfer of genre knowledge from academic to workplace contexts (Dias, Freedman, Medway, & Paré, 1999). They theorize that genre knowledge is tacit and only acquired unconsciously as part of some purposeful, communicative activity in the context where the genre is used. Students "pick it up" without being explicitly taught a genre.

There are three well-articulated approaches in North America to explicit teaching, which inform much teaching of writing and, often, WAC as well. The first might be termed "genre acquisition," teaching in an explicit (though not necessarily presentational) way certain generic "moves" or conventions of genres, derived from analysis of the genres (either textual or contextual or both). This is the most common approach in North American second language teaching (English for Special Purposes/English for Academic Purposes). The goal is to provide linguistic resources that students need. For example, Swales' analysis of the generic moves of academic research article introductions is taught to L2 graduate students explicitly, along with a good deal of reading and analysis of introductions, structured practice writing them, and so on. This approach has been used rather little in WAC or first language teaching, perhaps because there are fundamental differences between first and second language learners (see Carter, Ferzli, & Weibe, 2004). (A somewhat similar approach, Systemic Functional Linguistics, is even less common in North America.)

A second approach (Devitt, 2004; Bawarshi, 2003) is to teach "genre awareness" as distinct from (but related to) genre acquisition. Students first rhetorically analyze familiar genres whose contexts they have experienced, then move to less or unfamiliar genres that are related to them (antecedent genres, usually), studying both the form and aspects of the context, always trying to "keep form and context intertwined" (Devitt, 2004, p. 198). They then do "genre ethnography" of some context in which the genre is used (see Johns, 2002). Devitt argues that teaching genre awareness, rather than particular skills, will facilitate transfer, as previously learned genres become antecedent genres for further learning and practice of related genres (Devitt, p. 202ff). This approach has been used mainly in general writing courses (first-year composition, technical communication, etc.) where there are students from a variety of disciplines and the teacher is not expert in all of them. Students do research in the target context and its genres. The teacher helps them become good researchers into genre. But the teacher does not teach a specific genre to the students.

A third approach, sometimes termed "New Rhetorical," is to teach a genre explicitly, but in the process of performing a rhetorical action in its target context of use — which is the situation in disciplinary classrooms, typically. In the process of doing some discipline-specific learning activity, students also get explicit instruction in genre. But the instruction is not confined to teaching stages or moves or conventions; it also attempts to teach the logic of communication in terms of the logic of the learning/disciplinary activity — the "why" and "where" and "when" of a genre as well as the "what" and "how" of it. For example, Carter et al. (2004) developed an online tool for teaching the laboratory report genre in science and engineering education. LabWrite leads students through the process of doing and representing (textually, mathematically, and graphically) the laboratory activity as they are doing it. The goal of instruction is not to teach "the genre" or "writing" but to teach scientific concepts and scientific method using genre as a mediational means. The genre is a tool for doing and learning science in the context of the course-specific laboratory. A comparison group study found that students who used LabWrite wrote lab reports that chemistry teachers rated as "significantly more effective" in (1) learning the scientific concept of the lab and (2) learning to apply scientific reasoning. The students also (3) developed a significantly more positive attitude toward writing lab reports than the comparison group. This is the only comparison group study to show explicit instruction effective in teaching a genre to L1 adults.

The second question — genre's relationship to writing to learn — has been explored empirically primarily with younger students. Efforts to substantiate the claim that the act of writing per se improves learning were not successful. Instead, research found that the kinds (or genres) of writing students do and the conditions in which they do it matter a great deal. MacDonald and Cooper (1992) found that university literature students who kept academic journals structured by discipline-specific questions did better on exams than students who kept unstructured personal journals on their reading. Indeed, the largest literature review to date of controlled comparison studies of writing to learn, Klein (1999), found that the most effective approaches were those based on genre, but the studies are few and still inconclusive. Klein describes the theory of how genre supports learning thus: "writers use genre structures to organize relationships among elements of text, and thereby among elements of knowledge" (p. 203).

However, as noted above, these quantitative studies of student writing using genre have tended to see genres in the older, form-based way, and to look at their effects in more strictly cognitive rather than social cognitive terms. They look at study questions, journals, and essays, not discipline-specific tasks. And as Bazerman (2009) points out, "The effects seem to be associated with the specific nature of tasks, with study questions leading to increased recall and essays associated with connecting ideas (see also Newell, 2006; McCutcheon, 2007). This pattern, as Bazerman points out, is reminiscent of Scribner and Cole's (1981) finding that the "cognitive effects of literacy were varied and tied to the institutionally embedded practices which literacy was used for." Bazerman goes on to theorize that Vygotsky's (1978, 1986) concept that learning precedes development may explain the way genre may facilitate the development of higher-level discipline-specific ways of knowing, as well as low-level task-specific knowledge (2009).

Finally, critical pedagogy has also influenced WAC on genre. Beginning with Mahala (1991), some teachers and theorists have called for WAC to embrace the wider critical pedagogy movement, in various ways (see Bazerman et al., 2005 for a summary). One line of critique and reform calls WID "assimilationist" and emphasizes the importance of valuing students' non-academic language and genres, especially those drawn from ethnic or class backgrounds, which academic genres often exclude (Delpit, 1993; Villanueva, 2001; McCrary, 2001).

Another line of critique and reform emphasizes students' individual voice, and questions whether academic discourse in the disciplines provides students with the authority and stance they need to preserve and express a personal voice, to assert their authority over the disciplinary genres — and to resist simply reproducing the dominant ideologies of the disciplines (Mahala, 1991; Halasek, 1999; LeCourt, 1996). These arguments often call for students to write personal or non-academic genres in the disciplinary classrooms. Elbow (1998) even argues that students best develop an intellectual stance for writing academic discourse by writing non-academic genres. And in a broader sense, Malinowitz's (1998) feminist critique argues that WID should challenge the established boundaries of disciplines and genres of academic writing, as third wave feminism has done.

Responses to these critiques emphasize (1) that the very power of the disciplines makes it important to understand them — and understanding is a necessary precondition to intelligently critiquing and/or resisting them, (2) that learning new ways of thinking and acting can enrich and expand one's identity, and (3) that critiques of the disciplines from the point of view of the humanities prejudge what students will find most valuable for their ethical and personal development (Bazerman, 1992, 2002). McLeod and Maimon (2000) argue that WAC itself is "quietly subversive" as it resists the banking (transmission) model of education and encourages teachers to make students active and critical learners rather than passive recipients of knowledge. Finally, disciplines themselves are not monolithic and each contains critical elements with it, with which WAC can and does engage.

There is then lively theoretical debate and much pedagogical experimentation and research on genre in WAC pedagogy, and discussions of pedagogy and genre between ACLITS and WAC approaches seem a fertile ground for producing new strains of pedagogical thought and action.

ACLITS and Pedagogy

Although the development of a pedagogic dimension of academic literacies is still in its infancy, increasing attention is being paid to the pedagogical significance of the specific application of theory and research on academic literacies, in which genre is an explicit pedagogical consideration.

Indeed, the seminal work of the ACLITS researchers referred to above has brought some very basic issues — of academic identity, of the status of academic knowledge, of whether and which genres of academic writing should be distinguished and valued — into the wider pedagogical debate.

One such debate is over assessment practices and their effect on learning. In researching and questioning feedback practices and the setting and implementation of marking (grading) criteria, ACLITS has highlighted some interesting preconceptions and hidden agendas. Shay (2008) suggests that seeing assessment as a social practice has masked deep disciplinary and sub-disciplinary divisions between ideas of whether knowledges, knowledge-making practices or disciplinary "insiderdom" are being judged. Several projects reported at the European Association of Teachers of Academic Writing 2007 (e.g., Wrigglesworth & McKeever on "Developing Academic Literacy in Context," and Coffin et al. on "Genre-Based Pedagogy for Discipline-Specific Purposes") reported that teachers' attempts to make assessment criteria more explicit had concealed rather than revealed assessment practices. An ACLITS approach revealed the concealment, but more clearly needs to be done to change pedagogic practice.

Two basic premises about ACLITS research, however, are that we need to be concerned with all the texts in the academy, not just student writing, and that focus on student writing alone has masked the need to focus on the range of genres (in various and intertwined media), not just those written genres which are dominant in terms of assessment (see Lea & Street, 1998; Lea, 2001; Stierer, 1997; Lea and Stierer, 2007).

A narrow focus on assessment glosses over the question of whether normative genres should be resisted. Both students and academics may resist genres that have become part of their context; whether they in practice can and do resist is an interesting question. For, if genres appear in particular contexts but then become themselves part of the context and can in fact be resisted, should we be teaching students to conform or resist? Lillis (2001) calls for dialogue and interaction around texts and suggests "exploring ways in which alternative meaning making practices in writing can be institutionally validated." Burke and Hermserschmidt (2005) take a similar approach; Creme (2008) suggests something similar in her "transitional writing." But how do we then deal with the fact that new genres tend to get quickly drawn into the academy, e.g., assessing learning journals (see Creme & Hunt, 2002)?

Debates such as these have become particularly pertinent as new genres of writing are taking their place in the academy. These spaces have the potential to offer a range of possibilities for explicating academic literacies principles and empowering student writers in contrast to the more essayist genres. However, a word of caution is necessary in that institutions are constantly trying to tie down new genres for assessment. For example, UK HE, under mandate from the government, is developing rigid assessment criteria based on those which have been associated with essay writing and applying these uncritically to more personal and reflective genres of writing, which were originally conceptualized as formative writing spaces. ACLITS offers possibilities to resist this focus on writing for assessment, pointing to academic writing's potential to develop, e.g., academic identity, disciplinary meaning making, and pedagogic autonomy.

There are currently perhaps two generally accepted pedagogic models of academic writing: in one, writing is regarded as a personal act of meaning making; the other sees writing as a demonstration of the acquisition of institutional, subject or disciplinary knowledge and insiderdom. The first is largely transformatory — certainly of the individual and potentially if communicated to the disciplinary and academic community, of that community's meaning-making processes. The second is concerned with disciplined writing, in at least two senses: with the writing and the control of what John Bean (1996) called "expert insider prose." Whatever the possibilities of the first, academics work with institutional pressures at all levels to use the second, controlling, expert model. So feedback practices tend to a default "correction" model, while the student struggling to make and communicate meaning is seen as a problem; summative assessment criteria are linked to disciplinary and professional benchmarks and genre study used to identify dominant conventions, codes, and criteria.

Students can indeed be taught both about genres and about how to resist them (Devitt, 2009). However, ACLITS research draws attention to academic writing beyond the classroom, chiming with WAC's model of a continuum between student, doctoral and faculty writing (Monroe, 2002). ACLITS research is perhaps more problematizing, showing that beyond the individual teacher's classroom, institutional pressures circumscribe and define what can be written — written, or a least accepted as "disciplined" for the purpose of being awarded a master's or PhD and being published to the academic community. In Europe, South Africa, and Australia, an academic performance culture has gone beyond the demand to publish to the demand that publication be in a "rigorous" journal — peer-reviewed, of course, but also one accepting the role of, and accepted as, disciplinary gatekeeper. (A pressure that some academic journals are publicly resisting, publishing "alternative" critical writing in its own right and as embedded in disciplinary journal articles — see Creme, 2008, and Creme & Hunt, 2002 — publishing Essays and New Voices, and in Special Issue "Calls" welcoming "alternative forms of writing and experimentation with form, and different ways of giving voice.")

At a time when UK and European university policy makers, research funding and assessment bodies seem to be demanding generic and normalized academic writing, ACLITS research illuminates both the pragmatics and problematics of genre and/in academic writing.

Conclusion: Toward Further Dialog

Comparisons are difficult, first because (as we said in the introduction) WAC and ACLITS are doing different things, and secondly because the US WAC movement is large and diverse, with so many currents and conflicting strands that it is difficult to make generalizations about it. But perhaps a good place to begin is with genre theory and research methods.

The ACLITS perspective, coming out of Ethnography of Communication and Applied Linguistics, views genre as social practice rather than genre knowledge in terms of disciplinary communication per se, and its analysis is meant to unpack micro-social practices, such as "gaps" between student and teacher perceptions of particular writing activities, often embedded deeply in traditions of essayist literacy and the assessment of writing. Ethnographic methods show how genre types emerge in the detailed everyday encounters around writing in particular institutional contexts and how genre switching may be a hidden feature of pedagogy.

Not surprisingly, the ACLITS perspective on genre is perhaps closest to the sorts of WAC research that come out of linguistic anthropology and ethnomethodology. This includes the work of Dell Hymes' student McCarthy (1987) and her work with Fishman (2000, 2002), Herrington and Moran's (2005) research on new genres, and most especially the work of Prior (1998) and his group, who unpack the "laminated" micro-processes of student writing through longitudinal text analysis combined with ethnographic observation. Prior (2009), along with Spinuzzi (2003) and others (Prior, Hengst, Roozen, & Shipka, 2006; Prior & Shipka, 2003), look for the surprising ways writing is embedded in genres that do not reach official status or even, sometimes, conscious recognition, and that emerge in and out of the multimodal spaces of composing (Post-it notes, marginal drawings, and so on). And they look for pedagogical possibilities in these.

The dominant North American perspective sees genre not as social practice (from the point of view of the Ethnography of Communication) but as social action, from a rhetorical and speech act perspective (Bazerman, 2004). This has no counterpart in ACLITS, nor does the North American research on writing in the professions toward which students move. This research may sometimes use ethnographic methods, but may also use a range of other methods: content, discourse, intertextual, rhetorical, or speech act analysis — looking at texts (even large numbers of texts) in contexts that are often viewed in historical, rhetorical, or other sociological terms rather than anthropological or ethnographic terms.

One consistent tendency in genre research in both ACLITS and WAC (apart from cognitive research on writing-to-learn in psychology) is that both are concerned to go beyond a linguistic "needs analysis" and pedagogical provision of the kind that, for example, English for Academic Purposes (EAP) has emphasized (important as these are) and look further at the wider aspects of the learning situation, in terms not only of disciplinary epistemology and methods, but also of student identity, social positioning and resistance, gender, and so on, as well as in terms of wider institutional factors.

In terms of pedagogy, ACLITS, though it has a practitioner-led aspect, has tended to be more focused on theory and research, and the relationship of writing support and "academic literacies" approaches has been less defined and institutionalized than WAC in the US. The descriptive tendency (reserving judgment, as in the best ethnographic tradition) has only begun to enter the crucible of political change on the ground in teaching and in institutional politics. WAC, by contrast, has for three decades striven to work with individual faculty and courses, to influence departmental curricula and institutions. As ACLITS begins to expand and institutionalize its interactions with teaching staff in other disciplines, it will be mutually beneficial to compare notes.

As we noted, there have been repeated calls for WAC to resist institutional practices and traditions that limit student writing and learning, calls which resonate with Lillis' (2001) call for ACLITS to develop an academic literacies pedagogy which places the nature of dialogue at its center and considers how to develop and validate alternative spaces for writing and meaning making in the academy. In WAC the ideological valences of writing pedagogies have been a source of controversy, as we noted, whereas it has been endemic to the ACLITS approach from the outset given its rooting in New Literacy Studies and the "ideological model" of literacy. Research on teachers who take an explicitly political approach in the WAC classroom have found resentment and counter-resistance among students (Seitz, 2004) and most WAC programs take a much more indirect approach to institutional change. (This explains why US WAC programs may appear to be "academic socialization," in Lea and Street's terms, but are in fact about much more.) Thus far, ACLITS seems to be taking a nuanced path, not fronting the political in the classroom or asking students themselves to directly challenge existing structures, generic or otherwise, but rather respecting their vulnerable institutional position, as in Street and colleagues' work with the King's College widening participation project. These experiments will give US advocates of critical pedagogy and their opponents something to think about. Similarly, the successes and failures of US critical pedagogy applied to the disciplines might prove instructive to ACLITS.

Future dialog might proceed on many issues and congruencies, but with healthy scholarly caution. Because WAC is older by two decades, North Americans may have to resist a feeling of déjà vu and consider both the institutional differences that lie behind findings and the ways in which findings are only superficially similar. For example, Creme's (2008) analysis of learning journals as transitional genres bridging personal and discipline-based genres sounds much like the decade-long US experiments with journals and learning logs (MacDonald & Cooper, 1992), but Creme's approach rests on rather different assumptions and a different HE system. Indeed, ACLITS approaches to journals might overcome a number of (in hindsight) naïve assumptions that led the move toward journals to fade, in large part, in WAC.

Similarly, the major efforts of ACLITS on assessment research, particularly "diversifying assessment" beyond the academic essay, resonate strongly with the major efforts in the US toward alternative assessment (in new or hybrid genres), which were pioneered in WAC research and practice, particularly in the mid-1990s in the journal *Assessing Writing*.

And the multimodal, multi-literacies approach of ACLITS finds its counterpart in the Communications Across the Curriculum programs that emerged in the US in the last ten years, new versions of (or successors to) WAC programs (Hocks, 2001). But clearly there is a different valence to the concept of multi-literacies in the UK and CAC in the North America.

Similarly, there is much potential in terms of reaching beyond HE to other educational levels. ACLITS is now becoming much involved in what in the UK is called further education and what in the US is called adult education or lifelong learning. WAC has not been much focused on this (despite much research on this in adult literacy in education departments), apart from some work in community colleges, and might learn much from the research of Ivanic and her colleagues, for example.

Both ACLITS and WAC have been interested in the transition from secondary to higher education, but have not developed major collaborative efforts with secondary schools, either for research or pedagogical experimentations, apart from some work in the 1990s in the US (Farrell-Childers, Gere, & Young, 1994) and some recent work on Widening Participation in the UK that has included support for pre-university students (see above). And perhaps most importantly, neither ACLITS nor WAC have much developed a dialog with the international EAP/ESP community of second-language research and teaching, which has its own varied theories of genre and approaches to teaching, often existing side-by-side with first-language efforts in universities or even departments.

Finally, we hope that this mapping of ACLITS and WAC will further discussion, not only between the US and UK, but also with other countries. While both ACLITS and WAC treat genre in social and cultural terms, there are fundamental differences in approaches to and development of genre theory, research, and pedagogy, which deserve fuller exposition and continuing mutual reading of each others' work and dialog on it.

REFERENCES

Ballard, B., & Clanchy, J. (1988). Literacy in the university: An "anthropological" approach. In G. Taylor, B. Ballard, V. Beasley, H. K. Bock, J. Clanchy, & P. Nightingale (Eds.), *Literacy by Degrees* (pp. 7–23). Milton Keynes, United Kingdom: Society for Research into Higher Education/Open University Press.

Bartholomae, D. (1986). Inventing the university. In M. Rose (Ed.), *When a writer can't write: Studies in writer's block and other composing-process problems* (pp. 134–166). New York: Guilford Press.

Bawarshi, A. S. (2003). *Genre and the invention of the writer: Reconsidering the place of invention in composition.* Logan: Utah State University Press.

Bazerman, C. (1988). Shaping written knowledge: The genre and activity of the experimental article in science. Madison: University of Wisconsin Press.

Bazerman, C. (1992). From cultural criticism to disciplinary participation: Living with powerful words. In A. Herrington & C. Moran (Eds.), *Writing, Teaching, and Learning in the Disciplines* (pp. 61–68). New York: MLA.

Bazerman, C. (1994). *Constructing experience.* Carbondale: Southern Illinois University Press.

Bazerman, C. (2002). Distanced and refined selves: Educational tensions in writing with the power of knowledge. In M. Hewings (Ed.), *Academic writing in context* (pp. 23–29). Birmingham, United Kingdom: University of Birmingham Press.

Bazerman, C. (2004). Speech acts, genres, and activity systems: How texts organize activity and people. In C. Bazerman & P. Prior (Eds.), *What writing does and how it does it: An introduction to analyzing texts and textual practices* (pp. 309–339). Mahwah, New Jersey: Erlbaum.

Bazerman, C. (2009). *Genre and cognitive development: Beyond writing to learn.* In C. Bazerman, A. Bonini, & D. Figueiredo, *Genre in a Changing World* (pp. 279–294). Fort Collins, Colorado: WAC Clearinghouse and Parlor Press.

Bazerman, C., Little, J., Bethel, L., Chavkin, T., Fouquette, D., & Garufis, J. (2005). *Reference guide to writing across the curriculum.* West Lafayette, Indiana: Parlor Press.

Bazerman, C., & Russell, D. R. (Eds.). (2003). Writing selves/writing societies: Research from activity perspectives. Retrieved from Colorado State University, The WAC Clearinghouse and Mind, Culture, and Activity: http://wac.colostate.edu/books/selves_societies

Bean, J. C. (1996). *Engaging ideas: The professor's guide to integrating writing, critical thinking, and active learning in the classroom.* San Francisco: Jossey-Bass.

Beaufort, A. (2007). *College writing and beyond: A new framework for university writing instruction.* Logan: Utah State University Press.

Berkenkotter, C., & Huckin, T. N. (1995). *Genre knowledge in disciplinary communication: Cognition/culture/power.* Hillsdale, New Jersey: Erlbaum.

Bizzell, P. (1982). Cognition, convention, and certainty: What we need to know about writing. *PRE/TEXT, 3*(3), 213–244.

Britton, J., Burgess, T., Martin, N., McLeod, A., & Rosen, H. (1975). *The development of writing abilities (11–18).* London: Macmillan.

Burke, P., & Hermserschmidt, M. (2005). Deconstructing academic practices through self-reflexive pedagogies. In B. Street (Ed.), *Literacies across educational contexts: Mediating learning and teaching* (pp. 346–367). Philadelphia: Caslon Press.

Campbell, P. (Ed.). (2008). *Measures of success: Assessment and accountability in adult basic education.* Edmonton, Alberta, Canada: Grass Roots Press.

Carter, M., Ferzli, M., & Weibe, E. (2004). Teaching genre to English first-language adults: A study of the laboratory report. *Research in the Teaching of English, 38*(4), 395–413.

Clark, R., & Ivanic, R. (1991). Consciousness-raising about the writing process. In C. James & P. Garrett (Eds.), *Language awareness in the classroom* (pp. 168–185). London: Longman.

Coffin, C. (in press). Genre-based pedagogy for discipline-specific purposes. *Proceedings of EATAW.*

Creme, P. (2008). A space for academic play: Student learning journals as transitional writing. *Arts and Humanities in Higher Education 7*(1), 49–64.

Creme, P., & Hunt, C. (2002). Creative participation in the essay writing process. *Arts and Humanities in Higher Education, 1*(2), 145–166.

Delpit, L. (1993). The politics of teaching literate discourse. In T. Perry & J. W. Fraser (Eds.), *Freedom's plough: Teaching in the multicultural classroom* (pp. 285–295). New York: Routledge.

Devitt, A. J. (2004). *Writing genres.* Carbondale: Southern Illinois University Press.

Devitt, A. (2009). Teaching critical genre awareness. In C. Bazerman, A. Bonini, & D. Figueiredo, *Genre in a Changing World* (pp. 337–351). Fort Collins, Colorado: WAC Clearinghouse and Parlor Press.

Dias, P., Freedman, A., Medway, P., & Paré, A. (1999). *Worlds apart: Acting and writing in academic and workplace contexts.* Mahwah, New Jersey: Erlbaum.

Donahue, C. (2008). *Ecrire à l'université: Analyse comparée.* Villeneuve d'Ascq, France: Presses Universitaires du Septentrion.

Fairclough, N. (1989). *Language and power.* London: Longman.

Fairclough, N. (Ed.). (1992). *Critical language awareness.* New York: Longman.

Farrell-Childers, P. B., Gere, A. R., & Young, A. P. (1994). *Programs and practices: Writing across the secondary school curriculum.* Portsmouth, New Hampshire: Boynton/Cook.

Fishman, S. M., & McCarthy, L. P. (2000). *Unplayed tapes.* New York: Teachers College Press.

Fishman, S. M., & McCarthy, L. P. (2002). *Whose goals? Whose aspirations? Learning to teach underprepared writers across the curriculum.* Logan: Utah State University Press.

Ganobcsik-Williams, L. (Ed). (2006). *Teaching academic writing in UK higher education: Theories, practice and models.* London: Palgrave/Macmillan.

Geisler, C. (1994). *Academic literacy and the nature of expertise: Reading, writing, and knowing in academic philosophy.* Hillsdale, New Jersey: Erlbaum.

Gibbs, G. (Ed.). (1994). *Improving student learning: Theory and practice.* Oxford: Oxford Center for Staff Development.

Halasek, K. (1999). *A pedagogy of possibility: Bakhtinian perspectives on composition studies.* Carbondale: Southern Illinois University Press.

Heath, S. B., and Street, B. (2008). *On ethnography: Approaches to language and literacy research.* New York: Teachers College Press.

Herrington, A., & Moran, C. (Eds.). (2005). *Genre across the curriculum.* Logan: Utah State University Press.

Hocks, M. (2001). Using multimedia to teach communication across the curriculum. *WPA: Writing Program Administration, 25*(1–2), 25–43.

Hounsell, D. (1988). Towards an anatomy of academic discourse: Meaning and context in the undergraduate essay. In R. Saljo (Ed.), *The written world: Studies in literate thought and action* (pp. 161–177). Berlin: Springer-Verlag.

Hymes, D. H. (1974). *Foundations in sociolinguistics: An ethnographic approach.* Philadelphia: University of Pennsylvania Press.

Ivanic, R. (1998). *Writing and identity: The discoursal construction of identity in academic writing.* Amsterdam: John Benjamins.

Ivanic, R. (2004). Discourses of writing and learning to write. *Language and Education, 18*(3), 220–245.

Ivanic, R., & Lea, M. R. (2006). New contexts, new challenges: The teaching of writing in UK higher education. In L. Ganobcsik-Williams (Ed.), *Teaching academic writing in UK higher education: Theories, practice and models.* London: Palgrave/Macmillan.

Johns, A. M. (Ed.). (2002). *Genre in the classroom: Multiple perspectives.* Mahwah, New Jersey: Erlbaum.

Jones, C., Turner, J., & Street, B. (Eds.). (1999). *Students writing in the university: Cultural and epistemological issues.* Amsterdam: John Benjamins.

Klein, P. D. (1999). Reopening inquiry into cognitive processes in writing-to-learn. *Educational Psychology Review, 11*(3), 203–270.

Lea, M. R. (1994). "I thought I could write until I came here": Student writing in higher education. In G. Gibbs (Ed.), *Improving student learning: Theory and practice* (pp. 216–226). Oxford: Oxford Center for Staff Development.

Lea, M. R. (1998). Academic literacies and learning in higher education: Constructing knowledge through texts and experience. *Studies in the Education of Adults, 30*(2), 156–171.

Lea, M. R. (2001). Computer conferencing and assessment: New ways of writing in higher education. *Studies in Higher Education, 26*(2), 163–182.

Lea, M. R., & Stierer, B. (1999). *Student writing in higher education: New contexts.* Buckingham, United Kingdom: Open University Press/SRHE.

Lea, M. R., & Stierer, B. (2007, December). *Writing as professional practice in the university as workplace.* Paper presented to the Society for Research into Higher Education Annual Conference, Brighton, United Kingdom.

Lea, M. R., & Street, B. (1998). Student writing in higher education: An academic literacies approach. *Studies in Higher Education, 23*(2), 157–172.

Lea, M. R., & Street, B. (1999) Writing as academic literacies: Understanding textual practices in higher education. In C. N. Candlin & K. Hyland (Eds.), *Writing: Texts, processes and practices* (pp. 62–81). London: Longman.

Lea, M. R., & Street, B. (2006). The "academic literacies" model: Theory and applications. *Theory into Practice, 45*(4), 368–377.

LeCourt, D. (1996). WAC as critical pedagogy: The third stage? *JAC: A Journal of Composition Theory, 16*(1), 389–405.

Lillis, T. M. (1999). Whose common sense? Essayist literacy and the institutional practice of mystery. In C. Jones, J. Turner, & B. Street (Eds.), *Student writing in university: Cultural and epistemological issues* (pp. 127–147). Amsterdam: John Benjamins.

Lillis, T. M. (2001). *Student writing: Access, regulation, desire.* London: Routledge.

Lillis, T. (1997). New voices in academia? The regulative nature of academic writing conventions. *Language and Education, 11*(3), 182–199.

MacDonald, S. P., & Cooper, C. M. (1992). Contributions of academic and dialogic journals to writing about literature. In A. Herrington & C. Moran (Eds.), *Writing, teaching, and learning in the disciplines* (pp. 137–155). New York: MLA.

Mahala, D. (1991). Writing utopias: Writing across the curriculum and the promise of reform. *College English, 53*(7), 773–789.

Malinowitz, H. (1998). A feminist critique of writing in the disciplines. In S. C. Jarratt & L. Worsham (Eds.), *Feminism and composition studies: In other words* (pp. 291–312). New York: MLA.

McCarthy, L. P. (1987). A stranger in strange lands: A college student writing across the curriculum. *Research in the Teaching of English, 21*(3), 233–265.

McCrary, D. (2001). Womanist theology and its efficacy for the writing classroom. *College Composition and Communication, 52*(4), 521–552.

McCutcheon, D. (2007). Writing and cognition: Implications of the cognitive architecture for learning to write and writing to learn. In C. Bazerman (Ed.), *Handbook of research on writing* (pp. 451–470). Mahwah, New Jersey: Erlbaum.

McKenna, C. (2005). Words, bridges and dialogue: Issues of audience and addressivity in online communication. In R. Land & S. Bayne (Eds.), *Education in cyberspace* (pp. 91–140). London: Routledge.

McLeod, S. H. (1988). *Strengthening programs for writing across the curriculum.* San Francisco: Jossey-Bass.

McLeod, S. H., & Soven, M. (1992). *Writing across the curriculum: A guide to developing programs.* Newbury Park, California: Sage.

McLeod, S. H., & Maimon, E. (2000). Clearing the air: WAC myths and realities. *College English, 62*(5), 573–583.

Miller, C. R. (1984). Genre as social action. *Quarterly Journal of Speech, 70*(2), 151–176.

Miller, C. R. (1994). Rhetorical community: The cultural basis of genre. In A. Freedman & P. Medway (Eds.), *Genre and the new rhetoric* (pp. 67–78). New York: Taylor & Francis.

Monroe, J. (Ed.). (2002). *Writing and revising the disciplines.* Ithaca, New York: Cornell University Press.

Monroe, J. (Ed.). (2006). *Local knowledges, local practices: Writing in the disciplines at Cornell.* Pittsburgh: University of Pittsburgh Press.

Newell, G. E. (2006). Writing to learn: How alternative theories of school writing account for student performance. In C. A. MacArthur, S. Graham, & J. Fitzgerald (Eds.), *Handbook of writing research* (pp. 235–247). New York: Guilford Press.

Prior, P. (1998). *Writing/disciplinarity: A sociohistoric account of literate activity in the academy.* Mahwah, New Jersey: Erlbaum.

Prior, P. (2009). *From speech genres to mediated multimodal genre systems: Bakhtin, Voloshinov, and the question of writing.* In C. Bazerman, A. Bonini, & D. Figueiredo, *Genre in a Changing World* (pp. 17–34). Fort Collins, Colorado: WAC Clearinghouse and Parlor Press.

Prior, P., Hengst, J., Roozen, K., & Shipka, J. (2006). "I'll be the sun": From reported speech to semiotic remediation practices. *Text and Talk, 26,* 733–766.

Prior, P., & Shipka, J. (2003). Chronotopic lamination: Tracing the countours of literate activity. In C. Bazerman & D. Russell (Eds.), *Writing selves, writing societies* (pp. 180–238). Fort Collins: The WAC Clearinghouse.

Russell, D. R. (1991). *Writing in the academic disciplines, 1870–1990: A curricular history.* Carbondale: Southern Illinois University Press.

Russell, D. R. (1997). Rethinking genre in school and society: An activity theory analysis. *Written Communication, 14*(4), 504–554.

Russell, D. R. (2001). "Where do the naturalistic studies of WAC/WID point: A research review." In S. McLeod, E. Miraglia, M. Soven, and C. Thaiss (Eds.), *WAC for the New Millennium* (pp. 259–298). Urbana, IL: NCTE.

Russell, D. R., & Yañez, A. (2003). "Big picture people rarely become historians": Genre systems and the contradictions of general education. In C. Bazerman & D. R. Russell (Eds.), *Writing selves/writing societies: Research from activity perspectives* (pp. 331–362). Retrieved from Colorado State University, The WAC Clearinghouse and Mind, Culture, and Activity: http://wac.colostate.edu/books/selves_societies

Scalone, P., & Street, B. (2006). Academic language development program (widening participation). *British Studies in Applied Linguistics, 20,* 121–136.

Schryer, C. F. (1993). Records as genre. *Written Communication, 10*(2), 200–234.

Scribner, S., & Cole, M. (1981). *The psychology of literacy.* Cambridge, Massachusetts: Harvard University Press.

Seitz, D. (2004). *Who can afford critical consciousness? Practicing a pedagogy of humility.* Cresskill, New Jersey: Hampton Press.

Shay, S. (2008). Beyond social constructivist perspectives on assessment: The centering of knowledge. *Teaching in Higher Education, 13*(5), 595–605.

Smart, G. (2006). *Writing the economy: Activity, genre, and technology in the world of banking.* London: Equinox Publishing.

Sommers, N., & Saltz, L. (2004). The novice as expert: Writing the freshman year. *College Composition and Communication, 56*(4) 124–149.

Spinuzzi, C. (2003). *Tracing genres through organizations: A sociocultural approach to information design.* Cambridge, Massachusetts: MIT Press.

Street, B. (1984). *Literacy in theory and practice.* Cambridge: Cambridge University Press.

Street, B. (1996) Academic literacies. In D. Baker, C. Fox, & J. Clay (Eds.), *Challenging ways of knowing: Literacies, numeracies and sciences* (pp. 101–134). Brighton, United Kingdom: Falmer Press.

Street, B. (Ed.). (2001). *Literacy and development: Ethnographic perspectives.* Routledge: London.

Stierer, B. (1997). *Mastering education: A preliminary analysis of academic literacy practices within master-level courses.* Milton Keynes, United Kingdom: Education Center for Language & Communications, Open University.

Stierer, B. (2000). Schoolteachers as students: Academic literacy and the construction of professional knowledge within master's courses in education. In M. R. Lea & B. Stierer (Eds.), *Student writing in higher education: New contexts* (pp. 179–195). Buckingham, United Kingdom: Society for Research into Higher Education/Open University Press.

Thesen, L., & van Pletzen, E. (Eds.). (2006). *Academic literacy and the languages of change.* London: Continuum.

Villanueva, V. (2001). The politics of literacy across the curriculum. In S. McLeod, E. Miraglia, M. Soven, & C. Thaiss (Eds.), *WAC for the new millennium* (165–178). Urbana, Illinois: NCTE.

Vygotsky, L. (1978). *Mind in society: The development of higher psychological processes.* Cambridge, Massachusetts: Harvard University Press.

Vygotsky, L. (1986). *Thought and language.* Cambridge, Massachusetts: MIT Press.

Walton, M., & Archer, A. (2004). The web and information literacy: Scaffolding the use of web sources in a project-based curriculum. *British Journal of Educational Technology, 35*(2), 173–186.

Walvoord, B. E. F. (1997). *In the long run: A study of faculty in three writing-across-the-curriculum programs.* Urbana, Illinois: NCTE.

Wardle, E. (2007). Understanding "transfer" as generalization from FYC: Preliminary results of a longitudinal study. *WPA Journal, 31*(1/2), 65–85.

Winsor, D. A. (2003). *Writing power: Communication in an engineering center.* Albany: State University of New York Press.

Wrigglesworth, J., & McKeever, M. (in press). Developing academic literacy in context. *Proceedings of EATAW.*

PART FIVE

Assessing WAC

Introduction to Part Five

Though in the early years of the WAC movement assessment stood as a peripheral concern to student learning and faculty development, perhaps no other area of activity engages current WAC leaders more. As we strive to both prove and improve program effectiveness, assessment serves our needs at multiple levels. Because WAC programs, institutions of higher education, and the public have a stake in the evaluation process, no single assessment method can give us all of the information needed to make arguments about the effectiveness of our programs. Rather, as the selections in Part Five demonstrate, we can employ multiple methodologies in a continuing cycle of evaluation and improvement.

Because WAC programs, in their missions and structure, include a high degree of local adaptation, our assessment methods must also be developed at the local level, focusing on the classroom and the curriculum, on learning and teaching, and on the interaction between learning and teaching. WAC program assessment is "as much about faculty development — about how faculty develop and monitor their teaching and about how their understanding of learning changes — as it is about student development," Kathleen Yancey and Brian Huot suggest in their introduction to *Assessing Writing Across the Curriculum: Diverse Approaches and Practices*. While the specific focus of a program assessment will depend on its institutional and evaluative context, as Yancey and Huot note, the central goal of assessment is "always formative," with enhanced teaching and learning and ongoing program development as the focus (11). All of the articles in this section take this formative goal as a given of good program assessment, even as they demonstrate a rich variety of approaches, methods, and locations.

In the first article in this section, "Assessing Writing in Cross-Curricular Programs: Determining the Locus of Activity," Chris Anson presents a robust and useful framework for evaluating the opportunities for WAC programs to assess the effectiveness of their work, particularly in the area of student learning and development. The departmental or academic program level, he argues, provides the greatest potential to use assessment to engage faculty in discussions of the writing-related issues that matter most to them and to their students. Writing intensive (WI) courses, for example, which are implemented at the departmental level, remain the most common, complex, and often problematic instantiation of WAC.

And, indeed, WI classrooms have been the subject of a great deal of assessment activity. In "Merging a Culture of Writing with a Culture of Assessment: Embedded, Discipline-Based Writing Assessment," Terry Myers Zawacki and Karen Gentemann describe a WAC assessment process carried out at the departmental level and focused on student writing in WI courses in the disciplines. They show how the conversations that occur among departmental faculty around student writing, while prompted in part by a state mandate, can be made useful in advancing writing and learning outcomes for students in the discipline and for fostering transformative cross-curricular exchange.

In "The Writer's Personal Profile: Student Self-Assessment and Goal Setting at Start of Term," Tracy Ann Robinson and Vicki Tolar Burton provide a tool for student self-assessment that, at the same time, offers faculty and program directors a unique student perspective on what students are learning in WI courses. The authors suggest that certain kinds of assessment activities — such as having students reflect on their strengths and weaknesses, set specific and realistic writing goals, and self-assess during as well as at end of term — can be carried out in ways that directly benefit the individual student writer, in addition to providing useful data for administrators, program leaders, and faculty.

Barbara Walvoord's analysis of the role of faculty in assessment, "From Conduit to Consumer: The Role of WAC Faculty in WAC Assessment," outlines seven roles that faculty can play, progressing from least empowered to most empowered, although none is mutually exclusive: conduit, convert, changer, case, creator, collaborator, and client–customer. Each role, she suggests, allows WAC professionals to ask questions about "what we are assessing, why we are assessing it, the implications of those choices, and where each might be most and least useful." Her chapter includes a case study that illustrates how a single WAC program can combine various kinds of assessment and varied faculty roles to integrate multiple perspectives and satisfy different stakeholders. From the beginning, Walvoord argues, faculty engagement has been the "heart" and "life" of WAC, so we must think carefully about how we construct faculty roles in our assessments and what these constructions imply for our mission and programmatic goals.

We conclude with Martha Townsend's resource-rich overview of WAC program weaknesses and strengths — a must-read for anyone interested in WAC program development, direction, and sustainability. In "WAC Program Vulnerability and What to Do About It: An Update and Brief Bibliographic Essay," Townsend provides key references to the major voices in WAC across the years who have addressed, based on hard-earned lessons, the elements that have proven critical to the success of WAC programs.

WORKS CITED

Yancey, Kathleen, and Brian Huot. "Introduction — Assumptions About Assessing WAC Programs: Some Axioms, Some Observations, Some Context." *Assessing Writing Across the Curriculum: Diverse Approaches and Practices.* Ed. Kathleen Yancey and Brian Huot. Greenwich: Ablex, 1997. Print.

27 Assessing Writing in Cross-Curricular Programs: Determining the Locus of Activity[1]

CHRIS M. ANSON

INTRODUCTION

Historically, writing-across-the-curriculum (WAC) programs emerged in the United States from localized efforts at smaller colleges with a focus on student learning and high-quality pedagogy (Russell, 1991, p. 282). Early scholarship tended to be preoccupied with advocacy, program description, and recommendations for implementation (see Anson, Schwiebert, & Williamson, 1993 for an overview). As a result, generalized theories of WAC and an urge to redistribute writing across the curricular landscape pushed into the background important considerations of institutional context (type, size, population, and available resources) and the relationship between the structure of the program and specific institutional missions and goals. So important was the need to sell the idea that writing is, to use Janet Emig's words, "a powerful tool for learning," and so focused was the call to support it in all subject areas, that proponents theorized little about possible differences in emphasis, programmatic orientation, or intellectual activity in diverse settings. As WAC developed, variations in approach — writing across the curriculum, writing to learn, writing in the disciplines, and more recently electronic communication across the curriculum — led to the perception that programs were diversifying; but rarely were those differences tied explicitly to the analysis of institutional context and the role of WAC programs within those contexts. With increasing pressure to determine the effectiveness of writing (and writing instruction) within and across various contexts in our educational institutions, we need clearer and more generative models for implementation and assessment.

This essay offers a heuristic for understanding and locating writing assessment activities in the context of cross-curricular programs. The heuristic is based on two loci, one focusing on the "space" within the institution at which assessment activity takes place, the other focusing on the nature of the assessment activity itself: its scope, agency, and purposes. When these two

From *Assessing Writing* 11.2 (2006): 100–12.

loci are brought together, a matrix of potential activity within the institution is created, providing a way to understand and evaluate existing programs and resources as well as a method for determining new points of articulation or emphasis. A case is made for the potential of the *department* or *academic program* to create reforms across entire campuses in the area of WAC.

WHERE WAC HAPPENS: CONTEXTS OF ACTIVITY

As Nagelhout and Rutz (2004) have pointed out, classrooms can be conceptualized as both literal and metaphorical spaces — static, physical locations as well as activity convergers with a "stunning variety of connections" to the other social and communicative networks these physical locations enable and rely on (p. 7). From such a spatial perspective, "writing across the curriculum" ranges from a single act of writing within a specific teacher's classroom to sophisticated writing-intensive programs in which scores of teachers assign and respond to writing in "certified" courses that adhere to various requirements for numbers and lengths of papers, revisions, and the percentage of a grade that is decided by written products.

In its formative years, WAC was far less programmatic than individualistic. Advocates to whom the job of literacy instruction fell — usually those in English departments or composition programs — used a workshop approach to help teachers in other disciplines to incorporate writing into their instruction for a variety of purposes (see Fulwiler & Young, 1982; Young & Fulwiler, 1986). Motivated by an interest in student learning and a conviction that writing plays an important role in intellectual development and career preparation, teachers adopted classroom strategies and adapted them to their own needs, as suggested by a number of pedagogically-oriented publications that offered ideas for teachers in various disciplines (e.g., Gere, 1985).

In Figure 27-1, these individual initiatives appear on a line that defines the institutional and instructional contexts where WAC takes place. Representing a continuum of engagement, the line is defined mainly by the institutional source of the activity and its complexity. Although specific teachers who incorporate writing into their individual courses are engaged in something far from simplistic, the continuum is designed to reveal a scale of institutional activity centers, moving gradually from isolated efforts to more collective efforts at higher administrative and curricular levels.

Early WAC programs often relied on a grassroots approach that theoretically could spread across a campus without formal mechanisms either to ensure the consistency of the initiative or to assess its impact. The context of activity in this approach is a lone teacher who assigns and supports writing in his or her course, outside of any systematic emphasis on writing. The collective efforts of such individuals often amount to a "program" on many campuses even though it may lack a clearly identified central office, budget line, or higher-level organizational context such as a committee. In such cases, a loose confederation of energetic and committed individuals is entirely responsible for generating the activity of WAC. Attention to writing in discipline-

FIGURE 27-1   Contexts of Activity

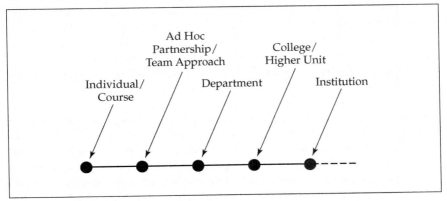

based courses can also occur with no collective effort at all; at institutions that admit they do not have a WAC program, it is always possible to find teachers who have learned about or experimented with writing in their courses in a completely isolated way, with no opportunities for collaboration.

As we move along the line in Figure 27-1, we also move outward from an individual effort to some modest collaboration, most often in the form of a partnership, a team-teaching situation, a linked course, or what Maimon (2001) calls "*ur*-learning communities" (p. ix). In a more formalized configuration of such partnerships, writing experts may be hired to support individual faculty, as is practiced in the Cain Project at Rice University, where trained consultants "work closely with faculty in science and engineering to plan and implement communication instruction in existing courses" (Rice University, n.d.). Also included are curriculum focus groups in which program leaders enlist a handful of faculty from different disciplines to work on their own courses collectively, usually over a semester or an entire year (see Miami University of Ohio, n.d.).

When a grassroots movement or scattered, unsupported effort is ineffective at changing the landscape of an entire institution, the context of activity sometimes shifts to the far right of the continuum, jumping over departmental or collegiate contexts. Many WAC programs in the United States, for example, are managed at the institutional level by a centralized unit. The University of Hawai'i at Manoa has one of the oldest writing-intensive programs in the United States. Students there must take five WI courses from over 400 certified WI courses offered in 70 departments (University of Hawai'i at Manoa, n.d.). Started in 1987, the University of Missouri at Columbia's program is almost as old and almost as large, with over 250 certified WI courses annually supporting a two-course requirement (University of Missouri, n.d.). These and other successful WI programs oversee the consistency of the writing requirement and its distribution across the campus, and provide plentiful faculty development and other activities to support the requirement.

At large universities, the *college* as a context of activity (see Figure 27-1) has not been very fully explored. In some cases, especially at universities characterized by a "silo" mentality where larger units operate with some autonomy, entire colleges can opt out of participating in a WAC effort because it presents too many obstacles or too little perceived value. Conversely, a specific college may decide to innovate on its own, looking to the intellectual connections among its cluster of departments and disciplines for support and affirmation. A highly successful example of a college as a context for WAC engagement is *AgComm*, a program located in the College of Agriculture at Iowa State University (Iowa State University, n.d.). With the help of WAC experts, this college took the initiative to saturate its curriculum with communication activities (both writing and speaking). Initially, it set up a system in which each course was allotted a certain number of communication credits based on the intensity of students' experience in writing and/or speaking. Each department in the college then decided how many of these special credits students needed to accumulate before they could graduate with a major. The program was so successful that eventually the credit system was dropped; students were getting far more experience, in most cases, than anyone cared to count.

Also relatively unexplored as a context of systematic WAC activity is the individual department. In this decentralized approach, each department or program is responsible for deciding how much writing students should do and of what types, and where in the major these experiences should take place. In this way, attention to and improvement of communication abilities becomes the province of each group of disciplinary experts, who see the relationship between their students' success and their own curricular and pedagogical efforts. Rather than an institution-wide requirement imposed from above without regard for disciplinary or departmental differences, this model is sensitive to local needs and contexts, encouraging faculty to shape their own emphases and requirements. Unlike the scattershot, individualistic model, however, it is driven by the collective agreements and curricular decisions of an entire department or undergraduate program. Understanding writing on their own terms — and on the terms of their disciplines and interests — motivates faculty leaders and creates a desire for programmatic success. For example, as part of a project focusing on writing in the majors, WAC leaders at George Mason University have helped departments across the institution to develop rubrics based on commonly assigned papers and projects. Although responding to a state mandate, this project gives "valuable information about . . . students' writing abilities but also, and perhaps more importantly, provides a venue for faculty to talk about their goals and expectations for student writers" (George Mason University, n.d.).

Regardless of the model chosen for implementation or consultation, questions about the effectiveness of a WAC program ought to provide the formative information that structures its programming. How are writing activities assessed? How do program leaders find out what's working well or not well? How can departments figure out where curricular deficiencies exist in students' preparation? In order to imagine kinds and levels of such assessment, we need another axis, this one representing a continuum from the most local and classroom-based to the most sophisticated and systematic forms of assessment, research, and inquiry.

How WAC Is Assessed: Levels of Inquiry

Figure 27-2 depicts a continuum of assessment activity starting at the most local and teacher-specific level and moving up to the most systematic, sophisticated kinds of research on writing and student learning, particularly but not necessarily large-scale research.

Much integration in WAC takes place without much conscious attempt to investigate its role and nature in teaching. Principled uses of writing can be found on every campus, but teachers' sense of the effects of writing is mostly tacit, arising from the routines of teaching (for example, reading a set of student papers in response to a new assignment and noticing textual or discursive features that appear to have been prompted by the assignment). The role of tacit knowledge in teaching has been much debated (see the dialogue between Shulman, 1987a,b and Sockett, 1987), but in spite of the relationship of tacit knowledge to the quality of teaching, it is difficult or impossible to

FIGURE 27-2   Levels of Inquiry

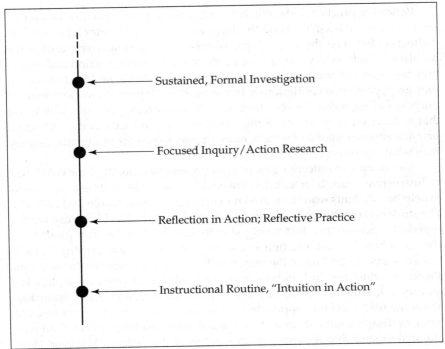

- Sustained, Formal Investigation
- Focused Inquiry/Action Research
- Reflection in Action; Reflective Practice
- Instructional Routine, "Intuition in Action"

engage in systematic *assessment* of one's methods without bringing what is tacit into consciousness. As Sockett (1987) puts it, tacit knowledge "finds expression in the knower's performance without a self-conscious awareness," although it may still be "describable and observable by others." At this level of inquiry, then, the principles and processes of WAC may be said to be embedded in the daily routines of a specific teacher, and assessed according to the principles of "intuition in action" — that is, "an immediate experience of a teaching situation in its entirety, without any need or possibility of distance, analysis or sequencing" (Johansson & Kroksmark, 2004, p. 377). Dissemination of intuitive knowledge often takes the form of narrative or "lore," an important if sometimes unreliable form of knowledge production (see Schubert & Ayers, 1999; Witherell & Noddings, 1991; especially Schubert, 1991; and Brody, Witherell, Donald, & Lundblad, 1991).

Only a few steps from this tacit form of assessment are levels of inquiry that educational theorists call *reflection in action* and *reflective practice*. Reflection in action generally refers to the capacity to think about and build new understandings of something while doing it. As Schön (1983) puts it:

> the practitioner allows himself to experience surprise, puzzlement, or confusion in a situation which he finds uncertain or unique. He reflects on the phenomenon before him, and on the prior understandings which have been implicit in his behavior. He carries out an experiment which serves to generate both a new understanding of the phenomenon and a change in the situation. (p. 68)

Reflective practice finds affinities with reflection-in-action but involves a kind of stepping back from and thinking about an activity after it is over. The distinction between these two types of reflection, especially concerning the problem introduced by varying amounts of time between action and reflection, has been the object of some debate (see Eraut, 1994), and for this reason they are represented contiguously in Figure 27-2. However, it is clear that for purposes of assessing the results of an action or strategy — especially when that is reflected in written text that must be read and analyzed — reflective practice appears to offer teachers more opportunities for systematic inquiry than what can be accomplished "on one's feet."

An example of reflective practice as an assessment method for WAC may be instructive. "Judith" uses brief, low-stakes, overnight writing assignments to help her students read the material in her course more deeply and critically. The students sometimes complain that the assignments feel like "busy work," especially because they factor only slightly into students' course grades. Yet she has a hunch — an intuition — that the assignments are causing gains in students' understanding of the material. To explore this hunch, the next time she teaches the class she builds brief, in-class quizzes into the course plan. The quizzes ask students to explain concepts in the readings, make assertions about the readings and support those assertions with specific examples, and agree or disagree with statements made about the readings and explain why. She makes sure that the quizzes do not repeat the tasks in her short, low-stakes writing assignments. Students then take quizzes at various points during the course, half of them on readings that do not have low-stakes writing assignments attached to them, and the other half on readings that do have these assignments. She does an informal content analysis of the quiz results based on a simple scoring rubric, and finds that when the students write about the readings, they answer questions with more specificity and accuracy than when they do not write about them. She can then share the results of this informal research with the students in order to help them to see the value of the assignments, and/or she can share her findings with colleagues.

As we move up the axis in Figure 27-2, the generally informal investigations and experiments practitioners conduct as part of their work give way to more systematic and change-yielding processes known as *action research*. Action research generally refers to a cluster of research methodologies designed to explore questions and produce change in iterative cycles, with each cycle refining or extending the results of previous cycles. One key feature of action research that distinguishes it from reflective practice is its collaborative nature. As Kemmis and McTaggart (1988) define it:

> Action research is a form of collective self-reflective enquiry undertaken by participants in social situations in order to improve the rationality and justice of their own social or educational practices, as well as their understanding of those practices and the situations in which the practices are carried out. . . . The approach is only action research when it is collaborative, though it is important to realise that action research of the group is achieved through the critically examined action of individual group members. (pp. 5–6)

If Judith were interested in formalizing her research, she might begin working with a small group of colleagues, perhaps in her department, to investigate overall learning of course content with and without the informal writing. Under the provisions of action research, she and her colleagues would develop a plan of critically informed action (low-stakes writing) to improve current practice (learning of the course content and student engagement in the material). Members of the group would then actively experiment with informal writing in the classes using a deliberate and controlled method. They would observe their actions individually and collectively, and gather evidence systematically enough to allow careful evaluation. Observations can include reflective journal entries or other qualitative information. Finally, group reflection is essential to interpreting the results of observations and the structuring of further cycles of action. Interpretation is usually more systematic and rigorous than what takes place in the routines of teaching (see Zuber-Skerrit, 1992).

Positioned at the highest reaches of the axis and familiar to most educators, formal research meets strict empirical standards and is carefully and rigorously set up, often after a small-scale pilot study. Formal research studies must be replicable (able to be conducted in exactly the same way in a different context); aggregable (able to build on prior research and included in a meta-analysis); and reliable (see Haswell, 2005). Because the focus of the present analysis is on single institutions, high-level research and assessment is shown to take place within them; however, much WAC inquiry also takes place across institutions or in the broader realm of higher education, workplace settings, or public writing, suggesting that the continuum does not end at the institution's boundaries. Such research might include investigations of the transition students make as writers between secondary education and college.

McCarthy's (1987) well-known study of students' writing at Loyola College serves as an example of research at this inter-institutional level. McCarthy studied the writing experiences of three undergraduate students during their freshman, sophomore, and junior years. She focused more intensively on Dave, one of the subjects, shadowing him as he attended classes and struggled with the various writing assignments in them. Her carefully structured study, which involved a combination of methodologies including ethnographic observations and interviews, text analysis, and composing-aloud protocols, was one of the first major pieces of research to reveal the ways in which students are challenged to write in different discursive communities and the difficulties they often have transferring their writing skills and strategies from one context to the next. Clearly, the thoroughness of this analysis, its adherence to the strictest principles of formal research, and the length of time devoted to it place it in a different category than the sorts of scholarship and reflective practice represented in other points along the axis.

Extending our fictitious WAC instructor Judith's interests in the role of informal writing in students' learning from assigned readings, we can imagine a more elaborate, sustained study that would represent this level of formality in research and assessment. Attending to concerns such as teacher effect and other instructional variables, Judith might set up several sections of the same course with identical curricula. Serving as the control group, students in one set of courses would not do low-stakes writing assignments focusing on the reading material. Students in the other, experimental group would do informal writing assignments for every major reading. All other aspects of the courses would remain the same. More sophisticated analyses could then look at differences in student performance across a range of tasks, including tests of knowledge, formal papers or written essay exams, attitudes toward the subject matter, or even retention of information over time. Again, based on the level of formality, the somewhat more "externalized" nature of the researcher, and the adherence to sophisticated methodologies, such a study stands in contrast to the primarily teacher-focused, less generalized inquiries involved in reflective practice and action research.

CHOICE OF LOCI: THE POTENTIAL OF DISCIPLINARY AND DEPARTMENTAL ACTIVITY

Merging the two axes described in Figures 27-1 and 27-2 — contexts and levels of inquiry — creates a matrix of potential activity at different levels, focusing not just on the implementation of writing but also on systematic explorations of how well it works educationally. The matrix allows us to define both the "sites" of activity and the kinds and goals of research. This is not to suggest that a form of reflective practice in one teacher's classroom is any less important than a survey of campus-wide practices conducted by an office of institutional research. Each serves an important purpose in the context of higher education and in the goals of achieving excellence through inquiry.

Yet although it is possible to find highly successful efforts to support and assess WAC that represent various positions in such a matrix, it is useful to consider how well different options can effect major and lasting changes across entire colleges and universities. Such a critique can help us to structure WAC programs and use writing assessment strategies at the most appropriate and effective levels.

Figure 27-3 shows three positions in the matrix. The first might involve a single teacher, working in the context of a college course, engaging in reflective practice by exploring classroom-based questions about the role of writing in teaching and learning. The second might involve a group of teachers who are engaged in action research, cycling between phases of active experimentation, observation and data analysis, and collective reflection. The third depicts a position in which institutional-level research of a highly formal and sustained nature might involve data collection and analysis from students across an entire campus, either longitudinally or at a particular moment in time.

The positions at the bottom left corner of the matrix — teacher-generated, classroom-based efforts to assess and innovate with writing or simply pay attention to it in the instructional routines of teaching — has the advantage

FIGURE 27-3   Three Positions in the Matrix

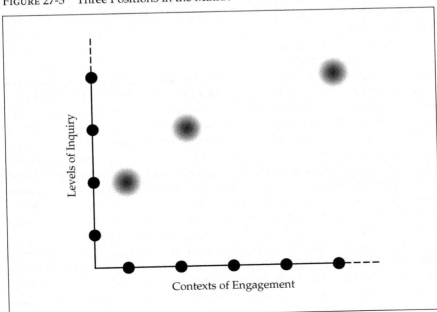

Levels of Inquiry

Contexts of Engagement

of individualized improvements in courses and permanent change through greater levels of expertise and experience in individual teachers. Clearly, however, what such an arrangement gains from the passion of its advocates it often loses from a lack of institutional support and long-term sustenance. The departure of leaders within the group or competing pressures for time can result in dissolution or malaise. Without a systematic effort, students gain writing experience arbitrarily, depending on their choice of courses. Some students graduate without exposure to multiple genres of discourse or opportunities to use writing in the service of their learning, while others may leave with greater preparation by virtue of their experiences, including major sustained and well-supported writing projects. On the level of pedagogical improvement, teacher-generated and classroom-focused reflective practice is highly desirable, but short of legislating it across a campus, it will not yield broad reforms.

Because of its similarly localized focus, the second option shown in Figure 27-3 also suffers from a lack of generalizability to the rest of a campus in which a group of colleagues may engage in action research. The changes that such collaborations engender can be transformative, yet this kind of process, even when replicated semester after semester, may not create widespread, lasting integration of writing across the curriculum or lead to change in the entire teaching culture of the institution. Unless there exists some institutionalized method of disseminating the results of the team's work, its assessment efforts remain too circumscribed to bring about institutional reforms on a broader basis.

The third position shown in Figure 27-3 moves the "activity" of teaching and assessing writing to an institutional level (commonly, as previously mentioned, in the form of writing-intensive programs linked to institutional assessments of writing ability). Although such programs are a popular and viable way to ensure that writing reaches into all parts of the campus, they seed WAC selectively and try to assess it too broadly. As several scholars have pointed out, the institutional writing-intensive model needs continued reinforcement and monitoring because it is not based on a "sea change" but on a curricular requirement carried out by select faculty. At its most vulnerable, it can lead non-WI faculty to teach courses — guilt-free — with little or no writing (see White, 1990; Holdstein, 2001). The problem of intrinsic motivation for supporting writing is not addressed on an institutional level; rather, the institution requires and usually supports the *expectation* of engagement. And because the program is built on the foundation of an institutional requirement, many stakeholders believe that its success should be widespread and measurable, without understanding that dozens of other variables (including the extent to which students are exposed to writing in *non-WI* classes) can affect both programmatic and individual assessments of improvement.

At very small colleges, articulation between campus-wide efforts and the efforts of individual teachers is possible and desirable, perhaps best exemplified by the internationally known, interconnected initiatives at Alverno College in Milwaukee, Wisconsin, which include digital portfolios, ability-based instruction, a strong focus on writing and speaking in all courses, outcomes-based assessment, major faculty-development work, and a student "assessment-as-learning" program that focuses on assessment in action (see Alverno College for Women, n.d.). Yet most institutions of higher education are structured into departments, divisions, or other units representing, at the very least, clusters of disciplines and more often individual departments with specialized missions, curricula, and faculty. Consequently, there is considerable unexplored potential for creating WAC programs at the place where the departmental context of engagement intersects with investigations ranging from relatively informal to more sustained and rigorous (see Figure 27-4). This potential arises from shared understandings about the field, the role of writing in it, the goals of the department, and ways that these goals might be assessed. As an activity center, the department provides an intellectual space where new ideas, methods, and results can be shared for the benefit of the faculty and the students. Most departments are of a scale that allows individual faculty members to share their own strategies and classroom-based research, yet the department as a whole can structure and manage an effort more programmatically.

North Carolina State University, for example, has established a model of program improvement and assessment in which every academic department has created learning outcomes for its undergraduate majors (see Anson, Carter, Dannels, & Rust, 2003; North Carolina State University, n.d.). Embedded

FIGURE 27-4   The Department as Locus of Change

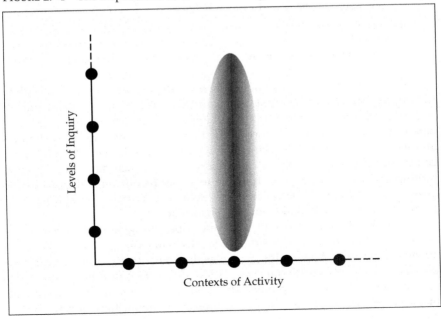

within these are outcomes for students' writing and speaking abilities. Based on what the *faculty* in the department believe should be the abilities of students who graduate with a degree in that discipline, the outcome statements drive a process of continuous program assessment and review, with small annual assessment efforts leading up to major portfolio summaries every seven years. The process of negotiating and articulating outcomes leads to faculty investment by tapping into what the department cares about in student learning and achievement.

One of the learning outcomes in the Department of Philosophy and Religion, for example, focuses on the development of broad disciplinary knowledge for Religious Studies majors.

Upon graduation, Religious Studies majors should demonstrate:

1. An awareness of and appreciation for the diversity of religious perspectives. Specifically, students should be able to demonstrate that they:

   a. are familiar with the variety of religious beliefs and practices in the world and can describe them fairly and accurately;

   b. are familiar with the interaction between religion and culture in various traditions.

The second outcome references writing and speaking abilities directly:

2. An ability to think and write critically about religion. Specifically, students should be able to demonstrate that they:

   a. can describe and analyze elements of religious traditions;

   b. can assess academic writings on religion;

   c. can make an effective and valid argument about religion, one that successfully establishes a premise and supports the premise with appropriate and persuasive evidence (Campus Writing and Speaking Program).

By initially articulating *learning* outcomes, departments inevitably realize the importance of writing. First, communication is central to all disciplines; no student can be considered competent until and unless he or she can participate in the written and oral work of the field, as demonstrated by Religious Studies' focus on critical thinking and writing. Second, many learning outcomes are best assessed through written products, which means that even if writing is not thought to directly relate to a specific outcome, the process of assessment will make it relevant (and reveal new ways that writing can play a formative role in reaching the outcome instructionally).

By itself, of course, creating outcomes does not guarantee a change in action. Based on their own experience, faculty will easily guess that students are not uniformly achieving the outcomes they have created (since it is never the case that faculty create outcomes below the current threshold of student achievement). Yet faculty opinions about writing are notoriously mixed and inconsistent, which yields a sense of uncertainty about how effectively the outcomes are being achieved. At this point, it makes little sense to rush to implementation strategies until some systematic assessment is conducted across the program or department. One department at North Carolina State University, for example, found that students were not doing as well as expected on one outcome, which concerned the ability to break down verbal statements of problems into their components in order to figure out what is given, what is known from prior experience, and what is not known. Once the outcome was assessed, faculty could turn to curricular and pedagogical questions: where and how could that intellectual activity be practiced and reinforced? Is it something that ought to come early in the curriculum or later on, or should it be scaffolded throughout students' coursework? How does it fit into different required and elective courses?

The Religious Studies program assesses its outcomes, including those given above, in a number of ways best suited to the needs, interests, and dispositions of its faculty. Portfolios of student work (papers and essays from appropriate courses identified by faculty) provide the "space" within which several outcomes are assessed. Faculty meetings provide another context for faculty to discuss impressions of student work, with analysis of typical products serving as the basis for more concrete ideas about improvements in the curriculum or the need for faculty development in the area of assignment design, grading, and supporting writing.

In a localized, outcomes-based model such as this, it is difficult to avoid questions of assessment because no principled curricular progress can be made without knowing something about the status quo. Yet in WAC programs whose context of engagement is the individual classroom or the entire institution, systematic assessment is often lacking. In the first case, the WAC activities are so embedded within a teacher's pedagogy that assessment of their effectiveness operates tacitly; in the second case, the complexity and highly general nature of an institutional WAC program militate against global assessments beyond usually uninformative, highly generic writing skills.

Figure 27-4 shows a focus within the band of activities at the department or program level, yet the band extends vertically from individual classroom assessment efforts to more formal programs of research. For example, just as individual faculty are sharing the results of their own efforts in a collective way in departmental meetings or focus groups, unit-wide assessments can be set up to look systematically across the entire major, using either representative sampling of work or collecting evidence from every student, perhaps as part of a curricular requirement such as a portfolio of work. If a curriculum revision is supposed to scaffold students' learning of discipline-specific writing conventions, then a formal longitudinal research project could begin with baseline data from students in all four years of the program, and then compare the results of annual assessments over time to gauge the level of improvement on this outcome. At the same time, an individual faculty member might be experimenting with techniques directly focusing on the classroom application of the outcome through reflective practice, or a team of teachers could engage in action research toward the same end.

Although North Carolina State University has found much to recommend departmentally-focused WAC implementation, such programs are not without their challenges. Departments are not all evenly committed to the processes described above, and intra-departmental conflicts sometimes work against agreement about assessment or implementation practices. Some departments, especially in fields with clear career trajectories for graduates, are intrinsically motivated to ensure that their students achieve their outcomes, while for others, especially in the humanities, the relationship between outcomes and the wide variety of things students do after graduation makes outcomes seem less important. Some departments are well positioned to conduct formal assessments of outcomes, while others may lack the expertise and resources to do so effectively. For this reason, it is important for such a model to stress *continuous* program review and assessment, so that unnecessary burdens do not fall all at once on busy faculty (as they often do in periodic accreditation reviews). It is also important to build a "culture" of teaching and assessing writing by providing opportunities and rewards for faculty to become involved.

CONCLUSION: TOWARD EFFECTIVE ASSESSMENT THROUGH INSTITUTIONAL ARTICULATION

In a departmentally-focused model such as the one at North Carolina State University, it may seem that other positions in the matrix are abandoned in favor of localized efforts. Although major *changes* take place at the departmental or programmatic level, *opportunities* to learn about teaching and assessing writing are available at other positions as well. Ideally, a campus-wide effort needs to create opportunities for articulation, even in the context of a dominant structure of departmentally-owned and controlled efforts to improve undergraduate writing. In such a model, activities are encouraged and sponsored at as many positions in the matrix as resources allow. Organizationally, an institution benefits from a program or center to help coordinate such multiple efforts. North Carolina State's Campus Writing and Speaking Program, for example, is the supporting unit for many activities focusing on writing, including campus-wide workshops; a monthly lecture series; departmental consultations (especially on outcomes assessment); a faculty seminar in which up to fifteen faculty work over a full semester to redesign specific courses they teach in order to enhance the role of communication in them; a grants program to bring together departmental teams in action-research projects; and an "Assisted Inquiry" program that provides direct consultation to individual faculty interested in classroom-based research (assistance in design, IRB approvals, data collection and analysis, and publication of the results). At the same time, many other units on campus are also supporting increased attention to writing, including the Faculty Center for Teaching and Learning, the Freshman Writing Program, the Division of Undergraduate Academic Programs, Campus Writing and Speaking Tutorial Services, and the library system.

Articulation among and between the assessment and implementation activities also allows for the cross-fertilization of ideas. As a departmentally-based team conducting formal research on students' writing abilities in the major hears the results of an informal inquiry from a teacher in another department, perhaps through a lecture series, the team's research is informed in new ways. Or, as the results are shared of a major, institutionally-sponsored survey on the types and amounts of writing students are doing across campus, a small group of faculty engaged in action research on their courses can begin folding in some data about what they can reasonably expect students' experiences in writing to have been before taking the courses they are teaching. With central support from a program or center for the dissemination of these efforts — through a Web portal, document publications, campus research report series, lectures and presentations, and other means — the focus on writing becomes an integral and ongoing part of the institutional culture.

NOTE

   1. This essay is a merged and revised version of two addresses: "From Outcomes to Input: Entrusting Departments to Improve Writing," keynote address, 7th Annual Symposium on Innovative Teaching, Simon Fraser University, Burnaby, British Columbia, Canada, May 18, 2005; and "Permanent Change: Motivation, Ownership, and Continuous Local Assessment of Writing and Speaking," First International Conference on Enhancing Teaching and Learning Through Assessment," Hong Kong, China, June 15, 2005.

REFERENCES

Alverno College for Women. (n.d.). *For educators.* Retrieved May 7, 2006. From http://www.alverno.edu/for_educators/index.html.
Anson, C. M., Carter, M., Dannels, D., & Rust, J. (2003). Mutual support: CAC programs and institutional improvement in undergraduate education. *Journal of Language and Learning Across the Disciplines, 6* (3), 26–38. Retrieved from http://wac.colostate.edullad/v6n3/anson.pdf.
Anson, C. M., Schwiebert, J. E., & Williamson, M. M. (1993). *Writing across the curriculum: An annotated bibliography.* Westport, CT: Greenwood.
Brody, C. M., Witherell, C., Donald, K., & Lundblad, R. (1991). Story and voice in the education of professionals. In: C. Witherell & N. Noddings (Eds.), *Stories lives tell: Narrative and dialogue in education* (pp. 257–278). New York: Teacher's College Press.
Eraut, M. (1994). *Developing professional knowledge and competence.* London: Falmer.
Fulwiler, T., & Young, A. (Eds.). (1982). *Language connections: Writing and reading across the curriculum.* Urbana, IL: National Council of Teachers of English.
George Mason University. (n.d.). *Assessing WAC/WID.* Retrieved May 7, 2006. From http://wac.gmu.edu/program/assessing/phase4.html.
Gere, A. R. (Ed.). (1985). *Roots in the sawdust: Writing to learn across the disciplines.* Urbana, IL: National Council of Teachers of English.
Haswell, R. H. (2005). NCTE/CCCC's recent war on scholarship. *Written Communication, 22* (2), 198–223.
Holdstein, D. H. (2001). "Writing across the curriculum" and the paradoxes of institutional initiatives. *Pedagogy, 1* (1), 37–52.
Iowa State University. (n.d.). *AgComm.* Retrieved on May 7, 2006. From http://www.agcomm.iastate.edu/admin/isuagcomm.html.
Johansson, T., & Kroksmark, T. (2004). Teachers' intuition-in-action: How teachers experience action. *Reflective Practice, 5* (3), 357–381.
Kemmis, S., & McTaggart, R. (Eds.). (1988). *The action research planner.* Melbourne: Deakin University.
Maimon, E. (2001). Preface. In: S. H. McLeod, E. Miraglia, M. Soven, & C. Thaiss (Eds.), *WAC for the new millennium: Strategies for continuing writing-across-the-curriculum programs.* Urbana, IL: National Council of Teachers of English.

McCarthy, L. P. (1987). A stranger in strange lands: A college student writing across the curriculum. *Research in the Teaching of English, 21* (3), 233–265.

Miami University of Ohio. (n.d.). *Center for writing excellence: Learning communities.* Retrieved May 9, 2006. From http://www.units.muohio.edu/cwe/Learn_Community.html.

Nagelhout, E., & Rutz, C. (2004). *Classroom spaces and writing instruction.* Cresskill, NJ: Hampton Press.

North Carolina State University. (n.d.). *Campus writing and speaking program.* Retrieved May 7, 2006. From www.2.chass.ncsu.edu/cwsp.

Rice University. (n.d.). *The Cain project in engineering and professional communication.* Retrieved May 7, 2006. From http://www.owlnet.rice.edu/~cainproj/about.html.

Russell, D. R. (1991). *Writing in the academic disciplines, 1890–1990: A curricular history.* Carbondale, IL: Southern Illinois University Press.

Schön, D. A. (1983). *The Reflective Practitioner: How professionals think in action.* London: Temple Smith.

Schubert, W. H. (1991). Teacher lore: A basis for understanding praxis. In: C. Witherell & N. Noddings (Eds.), *Stories lives tell: Narrative and dialogue in education* (pp. 207–233). New York: Teacher's College Press.

Schubert, W. H., & Ayers, W. C. (Eds.). (1999). *Teacher lore: Learning from our own experience.* Troy, NY: Educator's International Press.

Shulman, L. S. (1987a). Knowledge and teaching: Foundations of the new reform. *Harvard Educational Review, 57,* 1–22.

Shulman, L. S. (1987b). Sounding an alarm: A reply to Sockett. *Harvard Educational Review, 57,* 473–482.

Sockett, H. T. (1987). Has Shulman got the strategy right? *Harvard Educational Review, 57,* 209–219.

University of Hawai'i at Manoa. (n.d.). *Manoa writing program.* Retrieved on May 7, 2006. From http://mwp01.mwp.hawaii.edu/overview.htm.

University of Missouri. (n.d.). *Campus writing program.* Retrieved on May 7, 2006. From http://cwp.missouri.edu/.

White, E. (1990). The damage of innovations set adrift. *AAHE Bulletin, 43* (3), 3–5.

Witherell, C., & Noddings, N. (1991). *Stories lives tell: Narrative and dialogue in education.* New York: Teacher's College Press.

Young, A., & Fulwiler, T. (Eds.). (1986). *Writing across the disciplines: Research into practice.* Portsmouth, NH: Boynton/Cook.

Zuber-Skerrit, O. (1992). *Action research in higher education: Examples and reflections.* London: Kogan Page Ltd.

28

Merging a Culture of Writing with a Culture of Assessment: Embedded, Discipline-Based Writing Assessment

TERRY MYERS ZAWACKI AND
KAREN M. GENTEMANN

I t is no secret that the federal government, state governments, regional accrediting agencies, and specialized accrediting agencies all believe that assessment will address the apparent demand for "accountability." Never mind that "assessment" is not the equivalent of "testing," but is rather a philosophy about education, albeit accompanied by an emerging consensus of what constitutes good methodology and best practice. The philosophy, simply stated, is that student learning is the purpose of teaching and that much of student learning can be demonstrated, and, further, if a good assessment is conducted, corrections or changes can be made to enhance the learning experience for students. Central to assessment is the concept that faculty own the curriculum. The individual instructor in his or her classroom does not stand alone, however. Program faculty must establish coherence in the curriculum by agreeing upon the contribution of each part and sharing a sense of direction and purpose for the student and the learning experiences.

So, it is ironic that those who are calling for accountability are championing assessment, and those who have so much to gain from it are so much less enthusiastic. The purpose of this article, then, is to demonstrate that, given an approach developed by faculty to improve the educational experience for students, assessment can lead to greater understanding among faculty about their goals and expectations for student writers, which provides, in turn, an impetus to improve teaching and student learning.

George Mason University (or Mason), home to both of the co-authors, is situated in Fairfax, Virginia, a state that very early on embraced the idea that assessment could be used for improvement purposes while also providing information to state legislators and to the public that would demonstrate that publicly supported institutions were fulfilling their obligations to its citizens. In 1985, Virginia legislators directed SCHEV, the State Council of Higher Education for Virginia, to investigate means to measure student achievement. Shortly thereafter, SCHEV directed Virginia's public institutions to develop

From *Assessment in Writing.* Ed. Marie C. Paretti and Katrina Powell. Tallahassee: Assn. of Institutional Research, 2009. Assessment in Disciplines Series. 4. 49–64.

plans for assessing institution-defined student outcomes. More than a decade later, in 2001, SCHEV issued new guidelines that required all institutions to develop definitions of six specific learning competencies and plans for assessing them, with reporting to begin two years later.

What made both mandates unusual, if not unique, is that both allowed each institution to develop its own assessment plans; the mandate, then, was designed with great flexibility so that plans could match assessment procedures with institutional missions and cultures. There were no demands for standardized testing and no one method was identified as the norm for the state. Even when the State Council determined that assessment in the state needed to be refocused on six competencies — written communication, oral communication, information technology, scientific reasoning, quantitative reasoning, and critical thinking — SCHEV continued to allow institutional flexibility in defining these skills and determining how best to assess them. In this article, we will provide the specific context and motivations for creating an assessment of writing that is discipline-based and embedded in the curriculum, and that is congruent with the George Mason culture.[1]

COURSE-EMBEDDED ASSESSMENT AND MASON'S CULTURE OF WRITING IN DISCIPLINES

The commitment to course-embedded assessment is both practical and philosophical. From a practical perspective, removing assessment from the curriculum proved not to work at Mason. Early attempts to have students take standardized tests, specifically the Academic Profile and Major Field Achievement Tests (MFAT)[2] failed, chiefly because of the demographics of our student population and the use value for our faculty. Of the over 17,000 undergraduate students Mason enrolls, just over 4,000 live on campus. Further, a typical graduating class is composed of 60 percent transfer students, the majority of whom work off campus. For these students, there were no inherent incentives for spending additional time on campus taking standardized tests. For the teaching faculty, the tests provided little information they could use to change the way they taught or what they taught.[3] One of the primary reasons these tests did not serve as an impetus for examining the curriculum is that the faculty had no role in conceptualizing or creating the tests (although they were reviewers) and were passive receivers of the results. Further, these tests were "assessment" tests, something perceived as being outside the realm of faculty responsibility.

Philosophically, there were and remain many reasons for the course-embedded commitment. As we explained earlier, the point of conducting an assessment is to improve teaching and learning. This happens when faculty own the assessment process, with both the process and the results contributing to their understanding of the effectiveness of the curriculum, and, for the purposes of this article, the effectiveness of writing instruction in and across courses in the curriculum. Further, when faculty have a stake in the results, they are more inclined to use the information generated by the assessment to make changes both in the curriculum and in their own courses. Thus, faculty must be involved, at some level, in developing and participating in the process, and, whatever their role, they must be vested in knowing the results of the assessment. These are the principles that Karen, as director of Institutional Assessment since 1988, has long endorsed and that made her enthusiastic about the writing assessment plan proposed to the State Council, which entails a holistic scoring process using student papers collected from an upper-division writing-intensive (WI) course in the major and assessed by faculty teaching in that major.

Given a strong culture of writing in the disciplines at Mason, which is described later, we were well poised to respond to the 2001 mandate when it came to assessing students' writing competence. As director of our nationally recognized Writing Across the Curriculum (WAC) program, Terry was eager to lead an assessment effort that would focus not only on student writing in the majors but would also allow for a wider discussion of teachers' expectations for student writers and how these are conveyed to students through assignments, comments on papers, grades, and grading criteria. Because all of our students must fulfill a writing-intensive requirement, the plan also made practical sense in that we would be able to include our transfer students among those whose writing was being assessed. We also had practicality in mind when we decided to assess randomly selected papers written in response to only one representative assignment in the course rather than for several different assignments or even course portfolios. While portfolios may have given us a fuller picture of students' competence at writing in multiple genres, we knew that most faculty would be unlikely to accept an invitation to spend a day or more reading and assessing stacks of portfolios, particularly when the papers included in the portfolio would likely require discussion of the different assignment purposes and contexts. Our choice of a single sample of writing has limitations, of course: students might respond differently to different stimuli; the writing from any given student could be less than that student's best effort. Nonetheless, our methods mitigate against many other sources of error, such as a general lack of student motivation (students are typically motivated when papers are part of the course grade); an unrepresentative sample (papers were randomly selected); and rater bias (raters were trained and papers were rated anonymously).

WRITING ACROSS THE CURRICULUM (WAC) AT GEORGE MASON

Before we describe the specifics of the assessment plan we designed, with the assistance of the Provost-convened Writing Assessment Group, we want to give some background on WAC at Mason and the genesis of the plan, which was developed a year prior to the state mandate. Along the way, we'll also provide a theoretical context, based in composition studies, for our approach. Mason's WAC program dates back to 1978, when the first teaching-with-writing workshops were offered to faculty across disciplines with funding support from the deans of several colleges; in 1980, interested faculty attended a summer institute, sponsored by a grant from the state's Funds for Excellence in Higher Education program. The Faculty Senate convened the WAC committee in 1990 and in 1993 voted to require one upper-division writing-intensive course for all majors, in addition to an advanced composition course focused on writing in disciplines (e.g., writing in humanities, social sciences, natural sciences, business, and technology). While these courses, along with first year composition, constitute the curricular requirements for the WAC program (http://wac.gmu.edu/), our goals are realized through a variety of "writing-infused" majors and courses and through our extensive and ongoing faculty development efforts. The writing assessment workshops we planned would be, in many ways, a continuation of these efforts, with the required writing-intensive (WI) course(s) in the major offering a context-appropriate venue for assessing students' competence as college writers.

The year before we received the 2001 mandate to assess writing, we already had begun to set in place a process for determining the effectiveness of the WI requirement. We were motivated, in part, by a new general education program that specifically called for the assessment of written communication. With the support of the Provost's Office, Terry and Karen convened the Writing Assessment Group (WAG) that included representatives from each of the colleges, appointed by the respective deans. The group decided that our first step should be to find out what writing tasks faculty typically assign and their satisfaction with students' ability to achieve those tasks; to that end, we designed and circulated a survey to all undergraduate faculty (see http://wac.gmu.edu/assessing/assessing_student_writing.php#part1). WAG then developed a proposal in response to the state mandate in which we defined student writing competence very generally as the ability to use writing to discover, to learn, and to express knowledge. We explained that, while there are some shared criteria for good writing across disciplines, we recognized that different disciplines have distinct goals and priorities for student writers. Thus, we proposed to embed the assessment in required WI courses using papers selected by faculty in the major and a rubric developed by faculty through participation in a holistic scoring workshop.

Institutions in Virginia may choose a variety of ways to comply with the state requirement to assess writing competence; the approach taken by George Mason fits with and reflects our strong WAC culture, which is built on the premise that, because genres and conventions reflect disciplinary exigencies for writing, faculty in the discipline are most suited to help students become competent writers in their majors. Further, they are the most qualified to evaluate their students' writing competence; thus, our belief that assessment should be embedded in ongoing curricular activities, not conducted apart from the curriculum.[4] (See Figure 28-1 for an overview of the complete process for assessing and reporting writing competence.)

WRITING ASSESSMENT AND WRITING IN THE DISCIPLINES, THEORY AND PRACTICE

Our choice to embed assessment in the upper-division WI course with responsibility for the process given to faculty in the major is also supported by theory and research on writing assessment and writing in the disciplines

FIGURE 28-1   George Mason University Writing Assessment Process

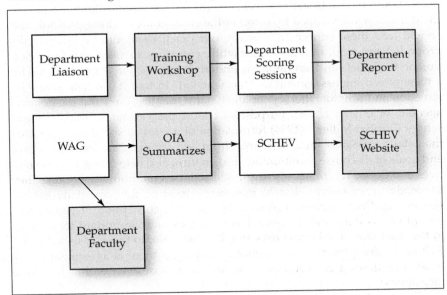

(WID). Charles Cooper and Lee Odell's 1977 collection, *Evaluating Writing: Describing, Measuring, Judging,* continues to be useful for developing writing assessment plans and procedures, particularly Cooper's chapter on the "Holistic Evaluation of Writing." Cooper uses the term "holistic" to describe any procedure that seeks to qualify rather than quantify the features of a piece of writing. A holistic scoring process entails comparing papers against others in the group to develop a basis for making judgments about quality. The comparison often results in a list of features — primary traits — that may be used to develop a scoring rubric. Although some do not consider primary trait scoring as a holistic process, Cooper is more inclusive in suggesting that this kind of scoring still requires attention to "the special blend of audience, speaker role, purpose, and subject required by that kind of discourse and by the particular writing task." Furthermore, the scoring rubrics are "constructed for a particular writing task set in a full rhetorical context," as is the case in our departmental scoring workshops. This kind of scoring, Cooper suggests, will "very likely have an indirect impact on the way teachers give writing tasks and respond to them," which makes it "potentially the most useful" of all the evaluation processes he describes (p. 11). Besides being useful for informing pedagogical change, Cooper argues emphatically that raters from similar backgrounds who devise their own scoring guides "on the spot" through conversations about student writing samples can achieve very high scoring reliability (p. 19).

More recently, we also turn to the guiding principles Brian Huot (2002) lays out in *(Re)Articulating Writing Assessment for Teaching and Learning,* which reiterates many of the values we described in our introduction: the assessment should be site-based and locally controlled, with questions and assessment measures developed by those in the community; writing professionals should lead these efforts; and, finally, our practices should be theoretically grounded, practical, and carried out with a conscious awareness of and reflection on the beliefs and assumptions underlying our actions.[5] Huot argues for a view of writing assessment as "social action" in that it can help shape instruction and promote literacy for all students, not just carry out the political agendas of others. Huot's purposeful use of the key term "social action" echoes Carolyn Miller's (1984) formulation of genres as social actions rather than static forms; as such, they arise from and adapt to the shared motives and goals of discourse communities and, in turn, also help to shape those motives and goals. Yet, Miller also argues, discourse communities, because they are made up of many different members, are also "fundamentally heterogeneous and contentious" (1994, p. 74). Miller's conception of genres and disciplines as fluid and dynamic has been especially important to writing-in-the-disciplines (WID) theorists and, by extension, to those of us assessing writing in disciplines, as we cannot assume that there is agreement about what constitutes a correct way of writing across or even within the same disciplines.[6]

These points were borne out in the cross-disciplinary training workshops we describe next and in departmental assessment workshops; in both, faculty initially used the same general terminology to describe the features of good writing but discovered, as they elaborated on the terms in discussing the student samples, that they often disagreed about the specifics. The scoring rubrics reflect these differences across disciplines, as we'll explain, and they also reflect, in the way the criteria were ordered on the page, the different disciplinary values faculty placed on some features in relationship to others.

Training workshops. Once the WAG proposal was accepted by SCHEV, our assessment efforts began with a series of training workshops for a cross-curricular group of faculty members who had been appointed by their chairs to lead departmental writing assessment efforts with assistance from WAG members. The first training workshops were led by Terry and two WAG members from the English department: Ruth Fischer, former director of Composition, and Chris Thaiss, the creator and former director of the WAC program. In these training workshops, the leaders used sample papers collected from students in the advanced composition course we mentioned earlier, which is focused on writing from research. Students across all summer sections of the course, regardless of their major, were given the same "review of the literature" assignment and were asked to submit a second copy of their paper with no name attached to be used for assessment purposes. This assignment was chosen for the training workshops because most upper-division students are assigned research papers of one kind or another in their major and most faculty are familiar with the genre even though many may not do the kind of experimental research that is typically reported in a research review.

In the training workshops, the leaders modeled the holistic process described earlier by having faculty participants (a) read four of the sample literature review papers against each other, (b) describe the traits for "good" writing that were demonstrated (or not) in the papers, (c) group these traits into larger, more general categories, and, (d) finally, arrive at a set of criteria to be included on the scoring rubric. (For a detailed explanation of the holistic scoring rationale and process, see documents available at http://wac.gmu .edu/assessing/rationale.pdf and http://wac.gmu.edu/assessing/holistic .pdf) The sample papers for the training workshops had been selected carefully to represent different majors and a range of writing abilities. While the workshop leaders hoped that the literature review assignment and the papers that had been selected would lead to interesting cross-disciplinary discussions of expectations for writing, all of us were surprised by the disagreements that emerged and the valuable insights both we and the faculty in attendance gained from the conversations that ensued. We expected, for example, that faculty might have different views regarding the construction and placement of a thesis, appropriate evidence, and the seriousness of certain kinds of errors. However, faculty from different disciplines also differed significantly in their definitions of concise prose, the kind of research information that must be cited, and the appropriate voice and style for academic writing. In one workshop, for example, several faculty members from the humanities were strongly at odds with others from the sciences about the long and "exceedingly dull" opening paragraphs of the literature review that introduced the writer's hypothesis for a psychology lab report. They preferred the "fresh voice" of the autobiographical introduction for a review of the research on body image and female athletes, which the science faculty dismissed as irrelevant and inappropriate.

It is not difficult to understand why faculty from different disciplines might disagree about the features of good writing nor why they might be surprised to discover that their disagreements extend to features they assume to be characteristic of good academic writing across disciplines. While faculty certainly understand that there are significant epistemological differences among disciplines, they often do not see the ways in which these differences influence prose styles and other written conventions, believing instead that good writing is good writing across the curriculum. David Russell (1997) calls this the "myth of transparency," by which he means that, because the written conventions in a discipline are learned very gradually by its apprentices as an integral part of the discourse, the process of writing becomes transparent with both genres and conventions appearing to be "unproblematic renderings of the fruits of research" (pp. 16–17). That helps to explain why many of the workshop faculty marked the psychology paper down for its "tedious" writing style and lack of transitions between sections, while others criticized the "flowery" prose and overly complex sentences in a humanities paper. One valuable outcome of this training workshop, then, was the realization on the part of the cross-disciplinary faculty that they did not necessarily share the same values for acceptable student writing nor even assign the same meanings to the terms they were using on the rubric.

Departmental rubrics and scoring. These differences can be seen most clearly in a comparison of the departmental rubrics faculty subsequently developed when they met to assess papers from the writing-intensive (WI) course in their own majors. To illustrate, we'll compare the first two criteria on the scoring rubrics for WI courses in government and international affairs, biology/ecology, and business. Because all government courses above the 300-level are designated writing-intensive and so fulfill the requirement, the papers to be assessed were drawn from political theory courses across several concentrations for which all students were given the same assignment prompt (though the prompt differed in the material to be discussed). After reading and discussing four sample papers to derive the traits to be included on the rubric, the government and international affairs faculty decided that the first criterion on the list should address the content of the argument itself and whether it was "clear, complex, original; showed knowledge of the material, conceptual sophistication and engagement with the topic; and demonstrated the ability to recognize multiple perspectives." The second criterion addressed the form of the argument, including a "well-stated thesis," logical evidence, balanced paragraphs, and relevant conclusion.

Although the biology faculty assessing papers from the writing-intensive ecology lab course used considerably different language to describe their top criterion, like the government and international affairs faculty, they also wanted papers to demonstrate a conceptual understanding of the discipline. Their rubric begins with this criterion, which also addresses the formal structure of an experimental report: "Demonstrates understanding of scientific writing: Abstract summarizes key points and sections; understands what needs to be cited; each section has content appropriate to the section; graphics integrated into and integral to the paper; discussion section synthesizes results with literature; evidence of analytical thinking." The second criterion on the rubric assessed the content, i.e., how well the student used research data ("relevant information," "correct and accurate paraphrasing") and employed technical terminology, among other features.

In sharp contrast, business faculty who participated in scoring papers from the gateway business models WI course and from several other writing-infused core courses decided that the ability to follow formatting instructions and write error-free prose was critical to a student's success in the major. Further, they agreed that a student's failure to perform satisfactorily on this criterion would mean that the paper overall could not be considered competent. This insistence on adhering to format guidelines for prescribed genres (e.g., memo, executive summary) and writing correct prose reveals the importance placed on writing appropriately for the workplaces that students will encounter. Tellingly, the second criterion on the rubric — audience, tone, and style — is also focused on a reader's reception of the text and, by extension, of the writer him/herself. Content features move to third place on their rubric. It's interesting to note that, while biology faculty ordered the criteria on their rubric much differently than business faculty and placed much less emphasis on audience, they decided that papers receiving an "unacceptable," as compared to a "less than satisfactory," rating on any one criterion must be deemed unacceptable in overall writing competence. This decision reflects their strongly held belief that reasoning scientifically and the ability to report information accurately in scientific formats are foundational criteria for students of the discipline. Interestingly, government and international affairs, biology, and business faculty were all concerned about many students' practice of quoting excessively and/or inappropriately from sources.

While faculty in their own departmental workshops may have agreed upon the criteria to be included on the rubrics and the weight to be given to each item, this is not to say that they were in complete agreement about whether and how papers satisfactorily fulfilled these criteria. Government and international affairs faculty, for example, discovered, to their surprise, that many of them were teaching students to write thesis statements in a form that was unsatisfactory to others. After some discussion about each other's preferences for a thesis, they decided to include the following elaboration in parenthesis after the "Form of Argument" criterion: "(Note: Some would like a thesis paragraph to lay out a framework for the argument to follow; others noted that the 'conclusion' should not come in the first paragraph.).". In a workshop assessing the writing in portfolios[7] from the capstone nursing course, faculty were similarly surprised when they realized that almost a third of them had given an unsatisfactory score on "Style and Mastery of Mechanics and Grammar" to a portfolio that the others had ranked satisfactory or more than satisfactory. When Terry probed with faculty the reasons for the disparity in scores, those giving unsatisfactory scores explained that the long, complex sentences (termed "run-ons") were not appropriate in a field where precise, concise communication to audiences of doctors, patients, administrators, and/or the public was the chief goal. Others argued, however, that two of the portfolio papers — a reflection paper and the "paradigm case" assignment (a personal narrative about a nursing experience) — lent themselves to a more complex writing style, which this particular portfolio demonstrated with great success. To give another example, in almost a replay of the run-on discussion in the nursing workshop, faculty from the health/recreation major used the term "run-on" to describe "elaborate sentences, i.e., those containing more than three clauses," which, they conceded, after hearing the differing opinions of colleagues, might be acceptable for certain concentrations and/or genres in the major. Disagreements like those in nursing and health/recreation reveal how important it is to assess writing not just in the context of the discipline but also in the context of a particular course with the learning and writing goals for any given assignment being taken in consideration.[8]

But how does one explain disagreements among faculty, like those in government and international affairs in regard to thesis statements, where faculty are assessing papers in the same genre, in this case position papers, a genre that is central to political discourse? Faculty expectations for student writers and their standards for good writing derive from a complex mix of variables, not just the discipline, Terry and co-author Chris Thaiss (2006) suggest in *Engaged Writers and Dynamic Disciplines: Research on the Academic Writing Life*. Their conclusions are based on interviews with faculty from 14 different disciplines and data from departmental assessment workshops and student focus groups. Variables include faculty's often-opaque understanding of general standards for academic writing; conventions of disciplines and also sub-disciplines; institutional and departmental cultures; and faculty's personal writing goals for students and idiosyncratic likes and dislikes (pp. 60, 95). While evidence of these variables can be seen in teachers' assignments and responses to student writing — by students, certainly, and by writing researchers — faculty are often unaware of their own preferences and how these might differ from others in the same field, and so they rarely explain them to students.[9] Far from being a negative aspect of the assessment process, the disagreements that surface among faculty in the departmental workshops prove to be good opportunities for faculty development, as they result in a better understanding of each other's expectations and a clearer articulation of the agreed-upon scoring criteria, as the thesis discussion described above illustrates. Further, the conversations that occur around the merits of the sample papers and the features to be included on the rubrics also lead to wider discussions about the appropriateness of particular assignments for achieving learning outcomes, and, even more broadly, the appropriateness of the designated WI course itself for helping students to achieve the writing and learning outcomes for the curriculum.

USING ASSESSMENT FOR FACULTY, COURSE, CURRICULAR CHANGE

In addition to giving faculty a clearer understanding of their own expectations for student writers and how these may differ from the expectations of others in the same discipline and across disciplines, the workshops also help faculty acquire a more precise language for expressing their expectations to students. While the scoring rubrics are posted on many department websites as a guideline for evaluating student writing, faculty are always encouraged to adapt the rubrics to reflect the specific writing goals of their assignments as well as their own stylistic preferences. The recognition that they do have stylistic preferences — whether embedded in the discipline, as the nursing example illustrates, or derived from other contexts, e.g., "rules" they learned in school — has been enlightening for many faculty, especially those who have been annoyed at their colleagues' seeming ability to overlook the errors that they find so distracting. In the workshops, these annoyances are aired and some agreement is reached about which errors can be tolerated and which must result in an overall unsatisfactory score. Interestingly, while faculty are often most vocal in their complaints about the number of errors students commit in their writing, in workshop discussions of sample papers other features of the written text, e.g., "an understanding of scientific reasoning," emerge as top priorities in scoring students' writing competence. Discussions like these extend from the papers at hand to the ways teachers grade papers and whether they are spending too much of their time correcting errors and not enough time explaining higher order concerns related to the quality and structure of the students' arguments.

In workshops where faculty find that they are dissatisfied with students' scores on a number of the criteria on the rubric they've devised, the discussion often turns to the assignment itself and/or the course from which the assignment came. Sometimes the assignment is pinpointed as a possible cause of the students' problems if it isn't clearly worded or hasn't required students to demonstrate the thinking and writing skills faculty think are important to assess. Occasionally, the content of the WI course and its place in the curriculum is scrutinized as a possible reason for students' inability to fulfill expectations articulated on the rubric. This was the case, for example, with the WI course for information technology, where an initial attempt to assess student writing was unsuccessful because faculty determined the assignment for which the papers were written did not elicit the skills they considered critical to students' success as writers in their majors. Nor did the designated WI course give students the opportunity to learn those skills in an appropriate context. This discovery led to a change in the course to be designated WI and, subsequently, a second assessment workshop focused on papers from that course. A similar discovery was made by dance faculty who are looking at the overall curriculum to determine which course(s) might be most appropriate for the WI designation depending upon their students' professional goals, which, for dance, might range from dancing professionally, choreographing dance, or writing about dance.

The Mason business school has also used the assessment process for their own ends as a way to improve student writing in courses throughout the curriculum as well as to gather data to report to their accrediting body, the Association to Advance Collegiate Schools of Business (AACSB). After meeting to read sample papers to develop a rubric, a business faculty task force exchanged electronic versions of the rubric to produce a more nuanced articulation of each of the criteria (see http://wac.gmu.edu/assessing/rubrics/SOM_Rubric_07.pdf). In a subsequent scoring session, the task force evaluated 51 papers from a range of core courses in the major. According to their report, they achieved an 82 percent inter-rater reliability on what had initially seemed to many of them to be a very subjective process. The task force also reported its pleasure in seeing the higher-than-expected number of satisfactory scores for overall competence. But they also recognized the challenges they faced in determining how the student writers of papers deemed "not competent" overall managed to have passed successfully both the advanced composition course and the business gateway WI course.

From the perspective of a composition professional, one possible response to the business task force is to point out that all writers may struggle and have trouble formulating their ideas clearly in writing when writing about unfamiliar content, for unfamiliar audiences, and in contexts that are likewise unfamiliar. Over time, and with practice, most writers become proficient in meeting the rhetorical and discursive demands of a given writing situation, even though these are rarely spelled out explicitly. Students, then, do not learn how to write in college once and for all in, say, a required composition course. Rather, to gain proficiency, rhetorical flexibility, and confidence, they need sustained practice in writing in their majors, across courses, and for different teachers. This is not a one-way process; when teachers explain to students, and to themselves, their expectations for student writing and the multiple contexts from which they may derive, students will be better equipped to fulfill those expectations. The rubrics that faculty develop in the assessment workshops are a step in this direction.

How Assessment Results Are Reported and Utilized

As a further commitment to faculty development and course and curricular change, the WAG, with Karen's endorsement, decided not to report each department's assessment results to the state as individual units, so that no department would be embarrassed if their assessment results did not meet their expectations. Rather, each unit analyzed their own data and reported to WAG in a standard format in which evaluations were summarized as percentages in categories of *high competence, competence,* and *needs improvement.* In some cases, units used slightly different terminology, e.g., *more than satisfactory, satisfactory, unsatisfactory,* but all scales were grouped into three categories. As part of the internal report, departmental assessment leaders, with WAG assistance, also analyzed and summarized as percentages the scores on each of the criterion on the rubric, which were rated with the same three-part scale. All of this information was given back to the department in a report that also included recommendations for faculty to help students improve their writing and, in some cases, for faculty to change aspects of particular courses and/or the curriculum. For purposes of reporting to SCHEV, the Office of Institutional Assessment utilized the common criteria across rubrics and aggregated the data from all departments that had conducted the assessment, thus preserving the confidentiality of all units. At the same time, the state was provided with sufficient information to judge the compliance of George Mason with the assessment mandate (details of the George Mason writing assessment reports are available at https://assessment.gmu.edu/StudentLearningCompetencies/ Written/index.cfm).

A few years into our assessment process, WAG members interviewed the liaisons from each unit who had participated in the training workshops to identify changes that had been made as a result of participating in the writing assessment. We found that the most common improvements included the sharing of the departmental writing rubrics among faculty, particularly with new and adjunct faculty, and posting the rubrics on department websites for students and others to view. Some departments had developed training workshops for teaching assistants focused on how to use the rubrics and the scoring process to calibrate their evaluations of and responses to students' writing; others added additional writing requirements to existing courses in order to give students more opportunities to engage in writing. Harder to determine is the impact on faculty teaching. Did those who participated in the assessment process make changes in their writing assignments to better elicit the kind of writing they had identified as important? Did faculty share the rubrics in their classes with students so they would have a standard to work towards? This information was harder to capture, but as we will soon begin the second cycle of writing assessment, we intend to examine not only changes in student outcomes, but in faculty practices in the classroom.

One of the ways we plan to continue focusing on the centrality of faculty development in the assessment of writing is to utilize wiki web pages as we revisit existing rubrics and create new ones for units that have not yet been through the process. By doing so, we should be able to encourage more faculty to participate in the development and final approval of any given rubric. Talks are also under way about how to incorporate the assessment of critical thinking, one of our required state competencies, with the assessment of writing. To date, we have assessed critical thinking through oral presentations, but we feel we can expand our writing assessment workshops so that critical thinking becomes a part of rubric development, allowing each unit to assess both student writing and critical thinking using the some sample of papers.

We also plan to continue a tradition started a few years ago when we held a Celebration of Writing reception after being recognized by *US News and World Report* for our exemplary WAC program. All faculty who regularly teach WI courses and/or who participated in the assessment process were invited to the reception where they were thanked by the President of the university and the Provost for their commitment to improving student writing. The celebration began with the creation of posters representing the work of each unit that had assessed writing. At the request of the President, the posters were next displayed in the atrium of the central administration building for a meeting of the Board of Visitors. Individual departments and the bookstore also displayed posters.

WHAT'S NEXT?

While the U.S. Department of Education continues to try to expand No-Child-Left-Behind legislation to include students in higher education, state higher education authorities can and do feel the need to be at the forefront of this political pressure, which has resulted in requirements and proposed legislation to further ensure "accountability" from state institutions. In Virginia, this has taken the form of additional reporting requirements by colleges and universities to include the "value added" that institutions are providing their students. "Competence" in the previously identified six core areas will no longer be sufficient to demonstrate accountability. Institutions must now report change in student attainment from a given point, presumably at matriculation, to some later date in the students' college career. What this means for the assessment of writing in the state is that students will likely either be tested or will provide a sample of student work that will be compared to a later test or sample of work. While the final guidelines have not been adopted as of this writing, there is no doubt that some kind of pre/post comparison will become central to future assessment in Virginia. Will faculty continue their commitment to assessing writing as well as other important areas? At George Mason, we are committed to the course-embedded, faculty-driven approach we have described in this article. But the strain on faculty will be evident as we move to this next stage.

Meanwhile, regional accrediting agencies, as well as specialized accrediting bodies such as AACSB and the Commission on Collegiate Nursing Education (CCNE) also continue to examine and revise their requirements so that the assessment of student learning is now a critical focal point of the self-studies done in preparation for reaccreditation. The Southern Association of Colleges and Schools (SACS), for example, requires institutions to identify the "student learning outcomes for educational programs," including general education, and assess "whether it achieves these outcomes" (see http://sacscoc .org). Written communication, along with critical thinking, are nearly always identified as basic competencies within general education, as well as the major. Thus, the importance of developing effective strategies for assessing writing is nearly universal. No institution can ignore the need to focus on effective methods for assessing and improving writing among its students.

The opportune circumstance of the beginning of the Mason writing assessment program, i.e., the prior decision by the Faculty Senate to require all students to take designated intensive-writing courses in the major, gave us the foundation to develop a faculty-owned, discipline-specific writing assessment program. The culture of writing that took root and provided political support for institutionalizing WI courses began many years prior to the WI policy decision. The relentless effort of many individuals, but particularly Chris Thaiss, mentioned earlier, and Terry Zawacki, nurtured a sense of common responsibility across disciplines to develop and support student writing. The compatibility of this culture of writing with a culture of assessment in which we routinely use information to reflect on where we are, where we want to be, and how to get there has resulted in a thriving, sustainable program of writing assessment. Improved student writing should be the reward we will document as we begin a second cycle of assessing writing.

NOTES

1. It should be noted that all assessment at George Mason takes place in the curriculum; students are not tested outside of the classroom. In some cases, questions are included in final exams that are used for broader assessment purposes (scientific and quantitative reasoning); in others, computer-based modules are completed as part of course requirements (information technology). Groups of faculty using collaboratively agreed-upon rubrics review both written and oral work in critical thinking, oral communication, and written communication.

2. Both the Academic Profile and the MFAT are products of the Educational Testing Service (ETS). The Academic Profile was replaced in 2005 by the Measure of Academic Proficiency and Progress (MAPP).

3. The MFAT, which is discipline-specific, was more meaningful for department faculty, but for the most part, it tended to reinforce shared beliefs about student ability rather than serve as a spotlight on the curriculum. (The one exception to this was the poor showing on one area of an MFAT that encouraged a department to continue offering a course in a subfield they had been considering eliminating.)

4. Given time and resources, our preference would be to begin the assessment process by meeting with disciplinary faculty to articulate writing outcomes for students and then using these outcome statements to guide and inform the assessment process. The work being done by Michael Carter and colleagues at North Carolina State offers one of the best models we know for this ap-

proach. For a description of the process and the results thus far, see http://www2.chass.ncsu.edu/CWSP/outcomes.html

5. See also the important body of work on writing assessment produced by Edward White, e.g., *Teaching and Assessing Writing: Recent Advances in Understanding, Evaluating, and Improving Student Performance* (1994), and Richard Haswell, e.g., *Gaining Ground in College Writing* (1991) and his edited collection *Beyond Outcomes: Assessment and Instruction Within a University Writing Program* (2001). For university practices focused on writing-in-the-disciplines, see Barbara Walvoord's *Assessment Clear and Simple: A Practical Guide for Institutions, Departments, and General Education* (2004), in which she makes a strong case for course-embedded procedures.

6. For fuller explanations of these theories, see, also, the work of Amy Devitt (2004) on genres and Charles Bazerman and David Russell (2002) on activity theory.

7. Nursing faculty chose to assess portfolios rather than single papers to fulfill both the SCHEV mandate and the requirements of the Commission on Collegiate Nursing Education (CCNE).

8. An overarching goal for the paradigm case assignment, for example, is to help nursing students gain confidence in their own authority and intuitions about patients by telling and sharing their own care-giving stories.

9. In turn, as Terry and Chris Thaiss learned from the student focus groups they conducted as part of their research, students across disciplines generally considered teachers to be idiosyncratic and unpredictable in their comments and grades on papers (Thaiss & Zawacki, 2006, pp. 108–110).

REFERENCES

Bazerman, C., & Russell, D. R. (2002). Writing selves/writing societies: Research from activity perspectives. *Perspectives on Writing.* Retrieved July 30, 2009, from the WAC Clearinghouse at http://wac.colostate.edu/books/selves_societies/

Cooper, C. (1977). Holistic evaluation of writing. In C. Cooper, & L. Odell (Eds.), *Evaluating writing: Describing, measuring, judging* (pp. 3–22). Urbana, IL: National Council of Teachers of English.

Devitt, A. (2004). *Writing genres.* Carbondale, IL: Southern Illinois University Press.

Haswell, R. (1991). *Gaining ground in college writing: Tales of development and interpretation.* Dallas, TX: Southern Methodist University Press.

Haswell, R. (Ed.). (2001). *Beyond outcomes: Assessment and instruction within a university writing program.* Westport, CT: Ablex.

Haswell, R., & McLeod, S. (1997). WAC assessment and internal audiences: A dialogue. In K. Yancey & B. Huot (Eds.), *Assessing writing across the curriculum: Diverse approaches and practices* (pp. 217–236). Greenwich, CT: Ablex.

Huot, B. (2002). *(Re)Articulating writing assessment for teaching and learning.* Logan, UT: Utah State University Press.

Miller, C. (1984). Genre as social action. *Quarterly Journal of Speech, 70,* 151–167.

Miller, C. (1994). Rhetorical community: The cultural basis of genre. In A. Freedman, & P. Medway (Eds.), *Genre and the new rhetoric.* Bristol, PA: Taylor and Francis.

Russell, D. (1997). Rethinking genre in school and society: An activity theory analysis. *Written Communication, 14*(4).

Thaiss, C., & Zawacki, T. M. (2006). *Engaged writers and dynamic disciplines: Research on the academic writing life.* Portsmouth, NH: Heinemann.

Walvoord, B. (2004). *Assessment clear and simple: A practical guide for institutions, departments, and general education.* San Francisco: Jossey-Bass.

White, E. (1994). *Teaching and assessing writing: Understanding, evaluating, and improving student performance.* San Francisco: Jossey-Bass.

Yancey, K., & Huot, B. (Eds.). (1997). *Assessing writing across the curriculum: Diverse approaches and practices.* Greenwich, CT: Ablex.

29 The Writer's Personal Profile: Student Self-Assessment and Goal Setting at Start of Term

TRACY ANN ROBINSON AND
VICKI TOLAR BURTON

INTRODUCTION

> Assessment . . . means gathering information in a way that shows genuine respect for individuals in the classroom. To respect people, we must listen to them — pay attention to what they have to say about their situation. (Beeson & Darrow, 1997, p. 98)

One of the paradoxes of higher education's current practice of placing heavy emphasis on program and curriculum assessment is that while such assessment can certainly lead to system improvements, it can also compromise student learning by narrowing the instructional focus (as instructors work to prepare students for success in specified measurable learning outcomes) and by diverting valuable teaching time to required assessment. Another problem with assessments for continuous improvement is that they typically are conducted at the end of a given course, so the students completing the assessments don't themselves benefit from their feedback. And in undergraduate WAC/WID programs, which are targeted to faculty support and development, both the assessment activities and resulting improvements tend to be faculty-centered. Many WAC/WID program administrators rely on faculty to identify student writing issues and program weaknesses; direct feedback from students is less commonly solicited.

In this article we address these paradoxes and problems as we argue for a different approach to WAC/WID program assessment, one that prioritizes student learning over data gathering and that gives WI (writing intensive) students greater control and responsibility for their own learning experience than is usually possible in a pre-set curriculum.

Central to our argument is a new research-based self-assessment tool, the Writer's Personal Profile (WPP), a start-of-term questionnaire to support writing and learning in upper-division writing intensive (WI) courses. Intended for use by students close to graduation, the WPP invites respondents to reflect

From *Across the Disciplines* 6 (2009).

on their college writing experiences, their strengths and weaknesses as writers, and the role of writing in their future careers. Then, based on these reflections, students set personal writing goals that will serve them in their post-graduation workplace and toward which they will work throughout the WI course. As well as laying the groundwork for their forthcoming course experience, the WPP also establishes a baseline reference for students' self-evaluation of their writing progress both during and at the end of the term.

In a research study conducted in 23 WI classes across seven colleges at Oregon State University, we found that at the same time students who complete this profile are learning through self-reflection and directing their own experience via personal goal setting, they are also generating a body of information that their instructor can use to target course content and assignments more specifically to the current cohort of students. Moreover, such "unfiltered" student input generates some surprising findings that constitute assessment data useful for WI program improvement.

In this article, then, we describe the institutional and scholarly contexts for our study, the study methodology, selected findings relevant to WI courses, programmatic applications of the study's findings, and best practices for using the Writer's Personal Profile to improve WI teaching and learning.

Institutional Context for the Study

Oregon State University is a mid-size (20,000 students) Research I Land-, Sea-, Space-, and Sun-Grant institution at which undergraduates must complete at least one upper-division writing intensive course in their major. This WI requirement, in place since 1989, is supported by the OSU Writing Intensive Curriculum (WIC) Program through which a half-time director (a professor of English with specialization in rhetoric and composition studies) offers faculty consultations on course development, reviews proposed WI courses, and provides faculty development for WI course instructors and others who wish to use more writing in their courses. Faculty teaching WI courses are encouraged but not required to take the five-session introductory WIC seminar offered each fall. The WIC Program supports approximately 125 WI courses across the university. In addition to seminars, the program offers a rich website with resources for WI faculty and students (http://wic.oregonstate.edu); a quarterly newsletter on the teaching of writing; speakers and workshops on writing throughout the year; development grants for courses and departments; and a number of other activities. The WIC Program director works collaboratively with the university's writing center, library staff, and the first-year writing and other university programs.

But even with this robust and active WIC program, some WI instructors remain uninformed about our program requirements and WI pedagogies, and they may not articulate writing outcomes for their courses. Academic advisors may also be uninformed about the WIC requirement. Hence, many students begin their WI course unsure of its purpose and what they can expect to gain from it.

While nothing short of committed and concerted university-wide attention can fully resolve this problematic situation, a more realistic approach is to address it through strategies applied within individual WI classrooms. This, then, is the motivation for development and implementation of the Writer's Personal Profile, which constitutes a grassroots approach to pedagogical transformation by serving these four functions:

- Helping students gain a more complete understanding of what, exactly, a WI course is and what they can expect to give to and gain from the course; end-of-term WPP reviews also help outgoing students recognize the value of their course participation.

- Helping WI instructors get to know their incoming students as writers, facilitating their efforts to set reasonable and relevant course expectations and teach to their students' self-identified writing needs.

- Including students in the outcomes-setting process for their WI course and encouraging them to consider the elements of personal motivation, engagement, and personal responsibility for their learning experiences to enhance their gains as course participants.

- Enhancing the perceived value of these upper-division courses by increasing their visible contribution to college students' successful transition into the professional workplace.

Scholarly Context for the Study

In considering the future of self-assessment, Boud (1995) argues:

> Self-assessment can be viewed not as a distinct element of teaching and learning, but in relation to reflection, critical reflection and metacognitive practices. It is part of that set of activities which encourage students to take responsibility for their own learning, monitor their learning plans and activities, process their studying and assess their effectiveness. Self-assessment then would become something which is embedded in courses, designed from the very start to assist students with their learning. (p. 215)

The scholarly context for development of the WPP includes cross-disciplinary research on student self-evaluation and reflection, the relationship between goal setting and learning, and self-efficacy development related to writing instruction and learning in general. Important connections between student self-evaluation and enhanced learning at all stages of schooling are noted throughout the education literature (see for example Boud, 1995; Buehl, 1996; Hobson, 1996; and MacGregor's 1993 collection of essays on this topic). Likewise, composition research such as that reported in Smith and Yancey (2000), Young (2000), O'Neill (1998), and Silva, Cary, and Thaiss (1999) has demonstrated a positive association between reflective self-assessment and writing skills development at all levels.

In addition, educators, psychologists, and academic success specialists have discovered that conscious goal setting enhances learning and task performance in academic, professional, and other arenas (see for example Eppler & Harju, 1997; Fenwick & Parsons, 2000; Kanar, 2004; Locke, 1996; Schunk, 2003; and Zimmerman, 1998). As a participatory, self-empowering learning strategy, goal setting tends to increase students' motivation, responsibility-taking, and engagement in a given learning experience (see observations of researchers such as Anderson, Billone, Stepien, & Yarbrough, 1996; Brophy, 1987; Chang and Lorenzi, 1983; and Locke, 1996). Moreover, successful completion of goals tends to heighten self-efficacy beliefs, which also influence the levels of motivation and engagement students bring to their learning experiences (Schunk, 1990, 2003; Zimmerman, 1998). As defined by social cognitive theorist Albert Bandura (1986), self-efficacy beliefs are "people's judgments of their capabilities to organize and execute courses of action required to attain designated types of performances" (p. 391). Frank Pajares (2002), who quotes Bandura's definition, adds that "self-efficacy beliefs provide the foundation for human motivation, well-being, and personal accomplishment. This is because unless people believe that their actions can produce the outcomes they desire, they have little incentive to act or to persevere in the face of difficulties."

Recognizing and valuing the many benefits of reflective self-evaluation and conscious goal setting — and of the agency and instrumentality cultivated through these activities — the Writer's Personal Profile places these two activities front-and-center in the WI classroom. In doing so, the tool helps edge undergraduates away from "empty vessel" learning behavior and into a participatory, horizontal student-teacher relationship model more characteristic of adult learners and "educationally powerful learning environments" (Chickering & Reiser, 1993).

STUDY METHODOLOGY

The primary objective of this study was to pilot the WPP in a variety of WI courses across the university to see how instructors and students used it and how it served these two clienteles. The intent was to draw from these observations to develop a set of best practices and recommendations that could guide future tool use. Study phases included developing and pre-testing the profile and obtaining IRB approval for its use as a research instrument; recruiting faculty participants; administering the profile and collecting and compiling the results; and completing the WPP assessment activities, including end-of-term follow-up with students and faculty debriefings.

The writing profile is constructed as a survey comprising both multiple-choice and short-answer questions related to the areas of emphasis in our WI curriculum. To close the exercise, students are invited to set two personal writing goals for their WI course. These goals — which should be specific, realistic, and achievable within the course time frame — need not align with the specified course outcomes; more important, the goals should aim at bridging gaps between students' current writing competencies and those they anticipate needing as writers in their intended careers. The researchers consulted with the university's survey research center staff in formulating and presenting these questions (an extended discussion of which appears in Chapter 2 of Robinson's 2006 thesis). The tool was then pre-tested in five WI classes and with a group of writing center assistants prior to its design and contents being finalized for the formal study. As a formal research effort that involved human subjects, this study was awarded approval by the university's internal review board (IRB).

Twenty-two of the 50 Oregon State faculty slated to teach WI courses during the study term (winter 2004) accepted our invitation for study participation; among them, 23 WI sections, with enrollments ranging from 6 to 61 students, were represented. Participating faculty ranged from full professors to adjunct instructors and included a two-person teaching team. About two-thirds of the faculty participants had previously completed the WIC introductory seminar and/or other faculty training; several were teaching a WI course for the first time; and two were teaching multiple sections of the same WI course.

Paper copies of the WPP were distributed to participating faculty on the first day of the study term, and they were asked to administer the WPP during the first week of the term. We also provided them with a script that covered the necessary points regarding informed consent and guarantee of respondent anonymity, but beyond that they were free to administer the WPP as they saw fit, e.g., as an in-class or take-home assignment, with a request for alternative ID to allow student–survey matching by the instructor (but not by us), and so forth.

A total of 256 undergraduates, or about half of the available subjects in the participating WI sections, completed the WPP at start of term. Per human subject research requirements, student participation was always voluntary, but some participating faculty sought their students' involvement more actively than others. After collecting their students' WPPs, the instructors forwarded the profiles to us. Participants' responses were collated in an Excel data table; collective class results were sent to the respective instructors both for their own review and, if desired, for distribution of class results to their students. The completed hard copies of the profile were also returned to the instructors for possible subsequent use during the course and for end-of-term student review.

Assessment of the questionnaire's effect on student participation and learning and on faculty's teaching experience included an end-of-term writing self-evaluation for use by all students enrolled in the participating courses (not just those who had completed the profile). Faculty were also asked to complete a debriefing questionnaire and to participate in a face-to-face debriefing interview after the study term ended. Based on student and instructor feedback, the tool was refined, and recommendations for best practices in using the tool were developed.

RESULTS

The full study results (available in Robinson, 2006) are copious and varied and can be interpreted from a number of perspectives. Here, however, we limit our discussion to results that revealed the tool's usefulness for students and teachers, those that pointed the way to best practices, and those that just simply surprised us.

Results: Student Self-Reflection and Goal Setting

One purpose of the study was to learn more about students' self-reflection and goal setting as they begin a challenging upper-division writing intensive course in their major. Some salient findings about student self-reflection and goal setting included the following:

- All students could opt out of participating in the study, but some teachers requested or required that students complete the WPP as a classroom activity. Not surprisingly, students were more likely to complete the survey if it was presented as an in-class exercise rather than as an optional, take-home assignment. In other words, despite what we know (and communicate to students) about the benefits of self-reflection and goal setting, that argument in itself may not be sufficiently persuasive to motivate students to use the WPP entirely of their own volition.

- Most students who did complete the WPP took it seriously and made a good-faith effort to answer all questions, including the open-ended ones asking about their writing strengths and weaknesses. This seemed to be true whether or not they were being given credit for WPP completion.

- Virtually all WPP respondents set personal writing goals, most of which met the criteria of being specific, realistic, and achievable within the course time frame. But this is where the commonalities ended. The goals set by study participants covered the entire range of writing categories used to characterize the open-ended responses.[1] While the majority of goals were related to writing skills typically targeted in WI courses in the disciplines (e.g., ideas and content, organization, clarity and conciseness, and genre knowledge), a surprisingly large percentage focused on skills that many WI instructors believe upper-division students should be carrying with them into the course. For example, 16 percent of the goals were writing-process related (i.e., dealt with issues of time management, proofreading/revising, collaborative work, peer review, or getting started), 9 percent addressed conventions such as punctuation, spelling, and grammar, and 6 percent targeted sentence fluency and word choice skills.

- To get feedback on student experience with the WPP, another self-assessment was administered at the end of the study term to students in participating WI sections. This self-assessment could be taken by all students (not just those who had completed the WPP), but it did include questions targeted to WPP-takers. Some instructors gave their students an opportunity to review their WPPs before completing the end-of-term assessment. Students who did so collectively reported more growth as writers and saw more usefulness for the start-of-term tool than students who did not review their WPP responses before completing the end-of-term assessment. Perhaps the most striking difference in responses from these two groups pertained to personal writing goal achievement. Of those who did review their original WPPs, 42 percent reported having made significant progress toward their writing goals, while only 14 percent of non-reviewers reported significant progress. These results suggest that at the end of their WI experience, the students' completed WPPs may function as a benchmarking tool that reminds them where they started from and hence enables them to more precisely gauge their progress during the term.

Results: Instructor Use of the WPP and of Student Data

Most faculty reviewed the WPP responses, both on the individual forms and in the compiled data set, and this effort prompted several of them to modify teaching approaches, assignment design, and/or responding practices. What they found most helpful and/or surprising about their students' responses varied by instructor, but a majority valued the insights gained on their students': (1) perceptions of their strengths and weaknesses as writers and of their research paper writing skills and deficits; (2) expectations of whether/how this course would help their writing; and (3) their personal writing goals.

Most faculty appear to have initially overlooked the goal-setting aspect of the WPP and opportunities for integrating that important aspect into their WI course. However, in the debriefing phase of the study, many instructors engaged with the idea of goal setting and with following up on writing goals students set during the term, as well as with identifying external resources that would support students' goal achievement. At the end of the study, most instructors also expressed interest in using the WPP in future WI classes, planning to make it a required assignment and to take fuller advantage of the tool by using it as a basis for discussion and follow-up throughout the term. They also planned to place more focus on the goal-setting aspect of the WPP.

Results: Support Needed for Instructors Using the WPP

Feedback from faculty participants suggested a number of ways that the OSU WIC Program could support WI instructors using the WPP. Such support includes faculty orientation and training on best practices for using the WPP, making the WPP available on Blackboard so that results can be aggregated easily by teachers, providing a "toolbox" of writing and learning resources that teachers can offer in support of students' personal writing goals, and offering faculty development opportunities focused on genre and characteristics of "good writing" in various fields and disciplines.

Results: Understanding Advanced Writers

In addition to its benefits for students and faculty, the WPP also has secondary use as a vehicle for information gathering and program assessment for WI program directors, college deans and department heads, curriculum developers, and others who seek to more accurately characterize advanced college writers. While we would not suggest that data from our pilot study of 23 WI courses can be generalized to represent all Oregon State students (much less those at other universities), our data does have a number of uses at the program level. We see potential contributions in three main areas.

- The first area is verifying (or complicating) assumptions about incoming WI students' prior college-level writing experience. For example, a surprising study finding for us was that only about 40 percent of the upper-division WIC students who completed the WPP had taken first-year writing at Oregon State University. As is undoubtedly true at many universities, OSU faculty tend to imagine their students' experience here as starting in the freshman year and continuing on through to graduation. Consequently, many base their expectations of upper-division students' writing skill sets on an assumption of a common first-year writing experience. Our data contradicts that assumption and has been a good reminder to faculty of the wide variety of first-year writing experiences (or lack thereof) their majors may actually have had.

- A second area in which the WPP provides programmatic data is in confirming or complicating guiding WAC principles that inform WI program policies and practices. One such principle is the privileging of writing-to-learn (WTL) as a learning approach — a practice that has already been questioned by some members of the composition and education communities (see for example Ackerman, 1993; Ochsner & Fowler, 2004; and Smagorinsky, 1995). One WPP question lists a number of WTL strategies and asks students to indicate which of these they have tried previously and which have been helpful to their learning. Most of our study respondents acknowledged experience with some WTL strategies (most frequently note-taking, outlining or idea grouping, brainstorming, freewriting, and summarizing). Asked about the helpfulness of these activities in learning course material, however, respondents' opinions varied widely, with typical WAC WTL strategies such as response journals and impromptu in-class writing receiving the lowest ratings. For example, 98 percent of the respondents who had tried note-taking considered this practice useful to their learning, but only about half of those who reported prior experience with in-class WTL activities also reported finding them helpful.

    While this difference may simply reflect students' perceptions that they are tested on material in class notes and that therefore notes are more useful, it may also indicate that different WTL approaches are more useful in some disciplines than in others. While, as Bazerman et al. (2005) point out, the efficacy of specific WTL strategies has been investigated in certain disciplines (biology, physics, mathematics, and nursing, for example), further cross-disciplinary research could yield evidence of which WTL strategies are effective in which disciplines — and perhaps also which do not work in any discipline.

    Our study also raised questions about another WAC staple, peer review. MacAllister (1982) cites research showing that "peer responses to writing can be just as effective as responses made by instructors," and other researchers, including Sims (1989), have cited benefits associated with peer review. However, WPP respondents expressed an ambivalence toward peer review similar to that documented in studies by Artemeva and Logie (2002), Chuck and Young (2004), Helfers, Duerden, Garland, and Evans (1999), and Saito and

Fujita (2004). WPP respondents indicated a general distrust of peer review, especially as compared to feedback on a draft from the instructor. We remain committed to the use of peer review in WI courses, but our results suggest that students may carry baggage of past negative peer review experiences into their advanced writing courses. WI teachers may therefore need to debrief students on the best and worst of peer review, model strong reviewing for the class, and offer assignment-specific guidelines for peer review. We would like to encourage more research on student attitudes toward the effectiveness of peer review when all of these efforts have been accomplished. Will students continue to view their peers' feedback with the same degree of ambivalence and distrust?

Results on revision were surprising in a different way. Citing Sommers (1980) and Crowhurst (1986), Beeson and Darrow (1997) report a prevailing belief among scholars that "students . . . generally see revision as merely 'cleaning up' a text" (p. 105). But our study results suggest that many incoming upper-division WI students have a more comprehensive notion of revision than Beeson and Darrow's observation suggests. Fifty-seven percent of our respondents showed an understanding that substantive editing and reworking of content and organization is part of revising rather than limiting their definition to sentence-level copyediting, style issues, and cleaning up of grammatical errors. It is also interesting that in their definitions, students applied the idea of "correcting" not only to language issues but also to ideas, content, and organization. These results suggest that student views of revision at the upper division may differ from those of first-year writers, a possibility that merits further investigation.

- The third major area in which WPP data can contribute to WI program assessment is in helping to identify areas for innovation and improvement in faculty training and program direction. For example, in examining questions that shed light on program goals and purposes, we found that most incoming WI students who anticipate improving as writers expect their improvement to occur in "high-level" areas such as ideas and content, organization, and knowledge of workplace writing genres, expectations consistent with WI program goals. On the other hand, what respondents identified as their principal writing weakness (and frequently also cited as a goal for improvement) seems somewhat at odds with standard WI agendas. Twenty-six percent of these responses focused on standard writing conventions (e.g., faulty punctuation, spelling, capitalization, paragraph breaks, grammar and usage), almost twice as many as the two next-most-frequently cited areas of concern, content and organization.[2]

As is typical of undergraduate WAC and WID programs nationwide, Oregon State's WIC Program does not emphasize conventions-related instruction in WI courses and encourages faculty not to think of themselves as the "grammar police." This stance aligns with the vision and espoused purposes of the broader WAC movement and is also consistent with the current nationwide de-emphasis of grammar in writing instruction at all levels of schooling, a trend whose roots are documented and critiqued by Kolln and Hancock (2005) but supported by many others. Given that grammatical correctness is one of the most important ingredients of effective workplace writing (see for example Anderson, 1985; Gray, Emerson, & MacKay, 2005; Jones, 1994; and National Commission on Writing, 2005), upper-division college undergraduates' lack of confidence in their grammar skills, as expressed in their WPP responses, raises significant questions about how well our students have been served by the "anti-grammar" trend in American education. Students' concerns about conventions also suggest that our WIC Program might look for ways to help them shore up these skills prior to graduation.

BEST PRACTICES FOR USING THE WRITER'S PERSONAL PROFILE

Once the study was completed and we saw that results indicated the positive impact of the instrument for teaching and learning, we were eager to expand the tool's use to other WI courses at the university. One early change involved renaming the instrument. Although it had been called the Start-of-Term Writing Questionnaire (STQ) during the study, we wanted a name that would be more student-centered and settled on the Writer's Personal Profile (WPP). We also worked with the university's Technology Across the Curriculum program to design a version of the WPP that could be administered electronically through Blackboard. The research study showed the importance of requiring WPP completion by all students rather than making it an optional exercise. For teachers who prefer the electronic version, the questionnaire is uploaded into Blackboard as a test, and students complete it there. Students can save their answers for future review and print out copies for themselves and their instructor.

The teacher can also download the aggregate Blackboard data into an Excel spreadsheet and analyze it to obtain an overview of the class as writers — information that can then be shared with the course participants. Students may also be asked to consolidate their data onto a one-page summary sheet, which is available on the WPP website.

With new awareness of class needs and experiences, the teacher can integrate the results into the course, for example by referring to students' responses in lectures or discussions of writing, in writing conferences, or as part of writing assignment feedback. We see the completion of the assessment feedback loop as a rich opportunity to use reflective self-evaluation and goal setting to shape students' experience in their WI course. And not surprisingly, various faculty use the results in differing ways.

A faculty member in mechanical engineering, for example, shares the aggregated strengths, weaknesses, and goals with the class and then asks students, in pairs, to design strategies by which each writer can achieve her or his individual writing goals. A business professor categorizes the students' personal writing goals and discusses these categories with the class. Then, during in-class peer review sessions, he displays the categories on the overhead projector to remind students of issues they may want to address. An English teacher uses the WPP as a conversation starter in writing conferences with students, inviting them, for example, to talk more about preparing to write in their chosen career field. She finds that discussing self-identified writing strengths and weaknesses enables students to share particular concerns they may have about writing and identify strategies for dealing with those concerns. And teachers who use a process memo with the submission of each assignment have asked students to restate their two writing goals on the process memo and indicate how they addressed the two goals in writing the current assignment.

Other best practices based on faculty feedback include asking students to self-assess their writing goals and strategies at mid-term and then again at the end of the course. The end-of-term assessment can ask students not only to look back at their growth as writers in the course but also to look ahead and set writing goals for their future academic work and their careers. Another practice is to allow time in the course for discussion/follow-up of the students' responses. Especially recommended are "goals check-in" activities that students do either on their own, in conference with the instructor, or as a group activity. Checking in with students not only makes it clear that their instructor really is holding them accountable for accomplishing their goals, but also gives students an opportunity to bring up any difficulties they are encountering as they work toward those goals. Instructors may be able to suggest strategies and point to resources for resolving difficulties.

We encourage faculty to build time into the course syllabus for an in-class, end-of-term review by each student of his/her WPP, preferably in conjunction with some kind of end-of-term writing evaluation activity.

IMPLICATIONS FOR PROGRAM BUILDING

Our research indicates that the Writer's Personal Profile is used most effectively when faculty have some training and orientation to the instrument before they use it. Our current training model is one two-hour session that introduces the WPP, suggests best practices for its use, and explains the technical aspects of administering it on Blackboard. In our faculty training, the first thing faculty do is complete the WPP themselves, perhaps imagining themselves as a student in the class, or taking the opportunity to reflect on their own writing goals and struggles. This personal experience invariably increases their engagement with the tool and triggers ideas on how to use it in their classes. As we introduce the tool's potential for students and its possible impact on teaching, we especially emphasize the goal-setting opportunities and encourage faculty to return to the goals throughout the term, as described above. We are also developing online training modules on best practices for using the WPP, and we are integrating WPP training into our introductory seminar for WI faculty.

The data we gathered have given us a rich collection of new, specific knowledge of what WI writers at our institution need and want, and we have tailored faculty development experiences to support those needs. Here are a few examples of programmatic activities that have already been initiated in response to WPP results:

- **Faculty seminars on frequent errors, proofreading, and editing.** As mentioned previously, problems with standard writing conventions was the most frequently mentioned writing weakness among 256 student respondents. To support WI teachers in responding to these problems, we are offering faculty seminars on Lunsford and Connors' (and now Lunsford and Lunsford's) studies of most frequent errors in student writing, as well as workshops on proofreading and editing. In addition, the OSU WIC Program website (http://wic.oregonstate.edu) contains student grammar guides using examples from various disciplines. And to broaden the base of support for student writers in this area, we have discussed their concerns with our first-year and professional writing program and writing center staff.

- **Department presentations on time management of writing.** Students' self-assessment of their problems with research writing highlighted numerous areas in which students (and therefore their teachers) need support. Across the board, time management of writing was the top student-identified problem. Although process writing, itself a staple of the OSU WIC Program, implies forced time management, we are investigating other strategies that can be used by WI teachers and students, and we are offering presentations that focus on time management of department-specific writing projects.

- **Support for development of visual communication pedagogies.** Another highly ranked problem for writers of research papers was "incorporating and citing tables and figures." To address this issue we have awarded a WIC development grant to a faculty member studying effective use of visuals, and we offer seminars in which instructors with expertise in this area share their approaches.

- **"Surviving Your WIC Course" website for students.** In part in response to study findings, we have developed a website (http://wic.oregonstate.edu/survivalguide/) for students that addresses the challenges of completing a major writing project.

FUTURE DIRECTIONS, INCLUDING THE IRB CONUNDRUM

Some readers may recall that in 2004, the Oregon State University Writing Intensive Curriculum Program and Center for Writing and Learning collaborated to produce the film *Writing Across Borders*, in which international students discuss how they were taught to write in their home cultures and how they have had to adjust to write in an American university. With funding from internal grants, we were able to give away the first 1,000 copies of the film at various writing conferences. In a similar spirit, we have decided to set the Writer's Personal Profile free — to make it available not only to Oregon State faculty but also to colleagues at other institutions. The Writer's Personal Profile website (http://wic.oregonstate.edu/OSU/WPP.htm) contains a print version of the WPP and instructions for creating a Blackboard version, a link to the original thesis study, a handout on best practices for WPP use, and a sample end-of-term assessment. The survey and related WPP documents are copyrighted, so they cannot be reproduced for profit, but users are invited to adapt the questions to local needs. We hope that colleagues who gather data using the WPP will let us know what they learn — and how use of the tool impacts teaching and learning at their institutions.

As we have shared our data at conferences, many people have suggested that it would be useful for us to collect data on all the future Writer's Personal Profiles completed for OSU WIC courses. We agree that this would be a worthy task, but it would also be a labor-intensive one for which our university's program does not have personnel or funding. Further, in any ongoing research study using "human subjects," students completing the WPP must agree to be part of the study, and completion of the survey must be optional, which contradicts what we found to be a best practice for use of the instrument. Making the WPP part of an ongoing formal research study also adds responsibilities for WI instructors. And frankly, it is hard enough already to persuade faculty to take on use of the WPP, which many overworked colleagues see as "one more thing." To ask them to administer human subjects protection might close the show. So, at least for now, we continue to work for program improvement by using the results of the research study and by responding to expressed needs of faculty, but we are not collecting the WPP data from current classes. Individual WI faculty may be collecting WPP data for their own use.

We conclude by offering our thoughts on future research issues inspired by — or contested by — the Writer's Personal Profile. We are encouraged by student responses to goal setting for writing improvement, and we would like to see more research done on the impact of self-assessment, goal setting, and metacognition on college writers' development, especially as they approach graduation. Along with the findings of Hilgers et al. (1999) that 68 percent of students interviewed had established personal goals for their focal WI assignment (p. 330), and Thaiss and Zawacki's findings that some students in their study shaped disciplinary writing assignments to meet personal goals (pp. 118–119), our findings suggest the use of goal setting by student writers as a promising line for future research.

Another promising research area might involve examining canonical strategies of WAC teaching, for example various types of writing-to-learn assignments and the use of peer review, which have undergone little scrutiny as they are used across the disciplines. We would particularly like to see more studies of the effectiveness of specific WTL strategies in a variety of disciplines, especially in light of the question Klein (1999) raises in his review of the research on cognitive processes in writing to learn: "*When* writing contributes to learning, *how* does it do so?" (p. 206). And we would like to know more about how teachers assess the effectiveness of a given WAC strategy in their own classes and how they tend to view and act on student self-reported information (as used in our study). Is student self-report always the best measure of how well these strategies are working?

Even more than prompting additional WAC and WID research, we hope to prompt teachers of WI courses from across the disciplines to consider the powerful potential of self-assessment at the start of WI courses for advanced student writers — both as that self-assessment attunes students to the writing tasks ahead (not only within their course but also onward into their careers) and as students' feedback and goal setting help teachers attune their course to specific students in a specific class. Self-assessment not only helps students grow but also helps them realize they are growing. And their input helps teachers reflect on current teaching practices and make changes with intention. Such habits of organic assessment and improvement are at the heart of excellence in teaching and learning.

NOTES

1. These categories include "citing sources," "clarity and conciseness," "conventions," "genre," "ideas and content," "organization," "personal traits," "sentence fluency," "voice," "word choice," "writing process," "writing-to-learn," and "general." For a detailed description and examples of responses for each of these categories, see "Classification of Open-ended Student Responses" in Chapter 3 of Robinson (2006).

2. It is important to note that we (and the students) are using the term "conventions" the way it is used in Oregon public education, which is as one of the seven categories on which K–12 student writing is assessed (see Oregon Department of Education, 2005). This category refers to "standard writing conventions (e.g., punctuation, spelling, capitalization, paragraph breaks, grammar and usage)" and the degree to which errors in those areas impede readability. This use of the term diverges significantly from its meaning in much WID scholarship, where it typically signifies the discursive approaches specific to a given discipline (for example, "the conventions of writing in engineering").

REFERENCES

Ackerman, John M. (1993). The promise of writing to learn. *Written Communication, 10,* 334–370.

Anderson, Kristena, Billone, Christine, Stepien, William, & Yarbrough, Kathleen (1996). *Increasing Students' Responsibility for Their Own Learning.* Master's thesis, St. Xavier University.

Anderson, Paul V. (1985). What survey research tells us about writing at work. In Lee Odell and Dixie Gotswami (Eds.), *Writing in nonacademic settings* (pp. 67–78). New York: Guilford.

Artemeva, Natasha, & Logie, Susan (2002). Introducing students to intellectual teamwork: The teaching and practice of peer feedback in the professional communication classroom. *Language and Learning Across the Disciplines: A Forum for Debates Concerning Interdisciplinary, Situated Discourse Communities, and Writing Across the Curriculum Programs (LLAD), 6,* 62–85.

Bandura, Albert (1986). *Social foundations of thought and action: A social cognitive theory.* Englewood Cliffs, NJ: Prentice Hall.

Bazerman, Charles, Little, Joseph, Bethel, Lisa, Chavkin, Teri, Fouquette, Danielle, & Garufis, Janet (2005). *Reference guide to writing across the curriculum.* West Lafayette, IN: Parlor Press and the WAC Clearinghouse. Retrieved from http://wac.colostate.edu/books/bazerman_wac/

Beeson, Larry, & Darrow, Laurel (1997). Listening as assessment: How students and teachers evaluate WAC. In Kathleen Blake Yancey & Brian Huot (Eds.), *Assessing writing across the curriculum: Diverse approaches and practices* (pp. 97–121). Greenwich, CT: Ablex.

Boud, David (1995). *Enhancing learning through self assessment.* London: Kogan Page.

Brophy, Jere (1987). Synthesis of research on strategies for motivating students to learn. *Educational Leadership, 45,* 40–48.

Buehl, Doug (1996). Improving students' learning strategies through self-reflection. *Teaching and Change, 3,* 227–243.

Chang, Grace Shing-Yung, & Lorenzi, Peter (1983). The effects of participative versus assigned goal setting on intrinsic motivation. *Journal of Management, 9,* 55–64.

Chickering, Arthur W., & Reiser, Linda (1993). *Education and identity* (2nd ed.). San Francisco: Jossey-Bass.

Chuck, Jo-Anne, & Young, Lauren (2004). A cohort-driven assessment task for scientific report writing. *Journal of Science Education and Technology, 13,* 367–376.

Crowhurst, Marion (1986). Revision strategies of students at three grade levels. *English Quarterly, 19,* 216–226.

Eppler, Marion A., & Harju, Beverly L. (1997). Achievement motivation goals in relation to academic performance in traditional and nontraditional college students. *Research in Higher Education, 38,* 557–573.

Fenwick, Tara J., & Parsons, Jim (2000). *The art of evaluation: A handbook for educators and trainers.* Toronto: Thompson Educational Publishing.

Gray, F. Elizabeth, Emerson, Lisa, & MacKay, Bruce (2005). Meeting the demands of the workplace: Science students and written skills. *Journal of Science Education and Technology, 14,* 425–435.

Helfers, Christine, Duerden, Sarah, Garland, Jeanne, & Evans, D. L. (1999). An effective peer revision method for engineering students in first-year English courses. In *Proc. 29th ASEE/ IEEE Frontiers in Education Conference,* 10–13 November 1999, San Juan, Puerto Rico (pp. 13a6-7–13a6-12). Retrieved from http://ieeexplore.ieee.org/ielx5/6763/18097/00840323.pdf?arnumber=840323

Hilgers, Thomas L., Hussey, Edna Lardizabal, & Stitt-Bergh, Monica (1999). "As you're writing, you have these epiphanies": What college students say about writing and learning in their majors. *Written Communication, 16*(3), 317–353.

Hobson, Eric H. (1996). Encouraging self-assessment: Writing as active learning. In Tracey E. Sutherland & Charles C. Bonwell (Eds.), *Using active learning in college classes: A range of options for faculty* (pp. 45–58). New Directions for Teaching and Learning 67. San Francisco: Jossey-Bass.

Jones, Elizabeth A. (1994). Defining essential writing skills for college graduates. *Innovative Higher Education, 19,* 67–78.

Kanar, Carol C. (2004). *The confident student.* Boston: Houghton-Mifflin.

Klein, Perry (1999). Reopening inquiry into cognitive processes in writing-to-learn. *Educational Psychology Review, 11,* 203–270.

Kolln, Martha, & Hancock, Craig (2005). The story of English grammar in United States schools. *English Teaching: Practice and Critique, 4,* 11–31. Retrieved from http://education.waikato.ac.nz/research/files/etpc/files/2005v4n3art1.pdf

Locke, Edwin A. (1996). Motivation through conscious goal setting. *Applied and Preventative Psychology, 5,* 117–124.

MacAllistor, Joyce (1982). Responding to student writing. In C. Williams Griffin (Ed.), *Teaching writing in all the disciplines* (pp. 59–65). New Directions for Teaching and Learning 12. San Francisco: Jossey Bass.

MacGregor, Jean (Ed.) (1993). *Student self-evaluation: Fostering reflective learning.* New Directions for Teaching and Learning 56. San Francisco: Jossey-Bass.

National Commission on Writing for America's Families, Schools, and Colleges. (2005). *Writing: A powerful message from state government.* College Board.

Ochsner, Robert, & Fowler, Judy (2004). Playing devil's advocate: Evaluating the literature of the WAC/WID movement. *Review of Educational Research, 74,* 117–140.

O'Neill, Peggy (1998). From the writing process to the responding sequence: Incorporating self-assessment and reflection in the classroom. *Teaching English in the Two-Year College, 26,* 61–70.

Oregon Department of Education (2005). Student scoring guide 2003–2004: Writing, CIM. Retrieved from http://www.ode.state.or.us/teachlearn/testing/scoring/guides/student/hswrtg.pdf

Pajares, Frank (2002). Overview of social cognitive theory and of self-efficacy. Retrieved from http://www.des.emory.edu/mfp/eff.html

Robertson, Wayne (Director). (2005). *Writing across borders* (DVD). Corvallis, OR: Oregon State University Writing Intensive Curriculum Program and Center for Writing and Learning.

Robinson, Tracy Ann (2006). Charting their own course as writers: A study of writing-intensive students' self assessment and goal setting at start of term. Master's thesis, Oregon State University. Retrieved from http://hdl.handle.net/1957/1939

Saito, Hidetoshi, & Fujita, Tomoko (2004). Characteristics and user acceptance of peer rating in EFL writing classrooms. *Language Teaching Research, 8,* 31–54.

Schunk, Dale H. (1990). Goal setting and self-efficacy during self-regulated learning. *Educational Psychologist, 25,* 71–86.

Schunk, Dale H. (2003). Self-efficacy for reading and writing: Influence of modeling, goal setting, and self-evaluation. *Reading and Writing Quarterly, 19,* 159–172.

Schunk, Dale H., & Zimmerman, Barry J. (Eds.) (1998). *Self-regulated learning: From teaching to self-reflective practice.* New York: Guilford.

Silva, Mary Cipriano, Cary, Ann H., and Thaiss, Christopher (1999). When students can't write: Solutions through a writing-intensive nursing course. *Nursing and Health Care Perspectives, 20,* 142–145.

Sims, Gerald K. (1989). Student peer review in the classroom: A teaching and grading tool. *Journal of Agronomy Education, 18,* 105–108.

Smagorinsky, Peter (1995). Constructing meaning in the disciplines: Reconceptualizing writing across the curriculum as composing across the curriculum. *American Journal of Education, 103,* 160–184.

Smith, Jane Bowman, & Yancey, Kathleen Blake (Eds.) (2000). *Self-assessment and development in writing.* Cresskill, NJ: Hampton.

Sommers, Nancy (1980). Revision strategies of student writers and experienced adult writers. *College Composition and Communication, 31,* 378–388. Reprinted in Villanueva, Victor (Ed.) (2003), *Cross-talk in comp theory: A reader* (2nd ed.) (pp. 43–54). Urbana, IL: NCTE.

Thaiss, Chris, & Zawacki, Terry Myers (2006). *Engaged writers and dynamic disciplines: Research on the academic writing life.* Portsmouth, NH: Boynton/Cook Heinemann.

Young, Elizabeth (2000). Enhancing student writing by teaching self-assessment strategies that incorporate the criteria of good writing. Doctoral dissertation, Rutgers University Graduate School of Education.

Zimmerman, Barry J. (1998). Developing self-fulfilling cycles of academic regulation: An analysis of exemplary instructional models. In Dale H. Schunk and Barry J. Zimmerman (Eds.), *Self-regulated learning: From teaching to self-reflective practice* (pp. 1–19). New York: Guilford.

30

From Conduit to Customer: The Role of WAC Faculty in WAC Assessment

BARBARA E. WALVOORD

Writing-across-the-curriculum (WAC) programs construct assessment in many different ways, and with many different meanings. It is, therefore, important to be conscious of the implications of various kinds of WAC assessment and to choose among them knowingly and deliberately. In thinking back over my 25 years as a WAC director and assessor and while reading the literature on WAC assessment, I am amazed by the shifting roles that faculty members play in WAC assessment and by the fact that I've never read a thorough analysis of these roles and their implications. I believe a careful consideration of these roles is crucial to any WAC program that embarks on assessment.

Faculty play seven roles in WAC assessment. The fact that they all begin with "C" shows, I believe, that configurations of the cosmos confirm their correctness: *Conduit, Convert, Changer, Case, Creator, Collaborator,* and *Client–Customer.*

There is a general progression in these roles from least empowered to most empowered roles for faculty. However, I do not want to judge which role is "best," because different ones will be most appropriate for different purposes. The roles are not mutually exclusive, nor always found in "pure" form. However, analyzing them separately can make us more aware of the fundamental assumptions underlying our assessment and keep us from being naive or from making choices that embody assumptions we do not want.

I will concentrate on faculty roles because, though student learning is the goal of WAC programs, faculty have usually been WAC's immediate audience, their change its immediate goal, and their loyalty is its lifeblood. For each type of faculty role, I will suggest what we are assessing, why we are assessing it, the implications of those choices, and where each might be most and least useful. At the end of the chapter, I illustrate how various types might be combined in an institution's WAC assessment program.

From *Assessing Writing Across the Curriculum: Diverse Approaches and Practices.* Ed. Kathleen Yancey and Brian Huot. Greenwich: Ablex, 1997. 15–36.

I define as "assessment" any study, whether it is called "research" or "assessment," that seeks to determine the outcomes of WAC. For this analysis, I'll draw on the WAC literature and on my own experience at three institutions where I've been WAC director and at several hundred more where I've been a consultant, assessor, or workshop leader over the last 25 years.

CONDUIT

One role for faculty in WAC assessment is the Conduit. In Conduit studies, the assessor seeks to know whether, as a result of a WAC experience, identifiable WAC beliefs or strategies come out the other end. Questionnaires, syllabi, assignments, and classroom observation by students or researchers are the usual data. These studies assume that the greater the percentage of faculty who are practicing WAC strategies or beliefs, the more successful the program.

This model is based on the foundationalist assumption that there is a reality out there, and that the assessor's job is to find it: Are the folks REALLY using WAC? Eblen (1983) notes that "self reports may blend respondents' beliefs and intentions with actual practice" (p. 347). In the Conduit study, that is bad. The goal is to determine actual practice, untainted by faculty beliefs and intentions. Thus, syllabi and assignment sheets, classroom observation by outsiders, or questionnaires to students about classroom practices are regarded as stronger data than faculty self-report or as being necessary to validate faculty self-report.

One published example of a conduit study is Smithson and Sorrentino's 1987 investigation of 13 of the 18 faculty who had attended a workshop at Virginia Polytechnic Institute and State University. The faculty indicated their agreement, on a Likert scale, with WAC principles and classroom practices that the authors of the test had formulated (e.g., "Writing cannot be used to teach concepts in the subject disciplines but only to test if concepts have been learned" p. 338). This survey was administered four times in a pre-post test design: (a) before the workshop; (b) immediately after the workshop; (c) after 10 weeks; and (d) after 5 years. At the 10-week and 5-year points, 10 of the faculty also responded in writing to queries such as "Did you continue to use writing to teach your subject?" and "If you use fewer methods now than you did during your first quarter after the workshop, which ones have you dropped and how soon after the workshop did you stop using them?" (Note also that WAC is defined as "methods" — bounded entities to be counted.) The authors found that, even 5 years after the workshop, the faculty reported using more of the writing strategies than they had before the workshop. (Note the implication: the longer the time, the greater the success.) In addition, this study used student reports to corroborate faculty self-reports. Two hundred thirty-eight students in 10 classes reported their teachers' use of methods the assessors had defined, such as "shared his/her writing with the class" and "used peer evaluation of drafts" (p. 340). Eighty-six percent of the students stated that the teacher provided for peer evaluation of drafts.[1]

Conduit assessment offers several advantages for this purpose. First, the results of such studies, taken within their paradigm, suggest that assessors can find identifiable WAC strategies and beliefs after a faculty member's WAC experience. Second, it produces quantifiable data that can be easily and quickly communicated to a broad spectrum of internal and external audiences. Such a paradigm is familiar and powerful for the media, the business and governmental communities, and often for educators as well. Third, if conducted by questionnaire to faculty, Conduit studies are relatively easy and cheap to perform. The faculty have a limited role and need not be asked for significant time involvement.

However, in its pure form, the Conduit model has limitations that may be more or less serious depending on one's goals. (In pointing out these limitations, I'm analyzing the Conduit paradigm, not necessarily criticizing the studies I've mentioned.) In Conduit studies, the assessor defines what counts as WAC beliefs and strategies; the *assessor's* voice dominates. If faculty are quoted, it's within strictly limited frames. If faculty are not using WAC strategies, readers do not learn why, or what faculty are doing instead. It's a yes or no distinction: Faculty either do or do not adhere to what the assessors define as WAC — which is the presumed goal.

The assessor is assumed to be the neutral, objective collector of data. Assessors typically do not describe their own roles, interests, stances, or political contexts for the study. Much current thinking in WAC and other fields challenges the assumption of "objectivity" in an assessor or researcher; accordingly, if WAC programs assume this "objective" role for the assessor, they will want to acknowledge that fact and know their reasons for choosing the paradigm.

Further, when the assessors, not the faculty respondents, define WAC strategies or beliefs, two dangers arise. One is that the questions will mean different things to the responders than the assessor thought they would. On a Likert-scale question, it is hard to state a belief in such a way as to gather reliable and valid information about whether people actually hold that belief. You would think strategies such as "journals" would be easier to test than beliefs, but they, too, have danger. In a forthcoming study of WAC outcomes, my colleagues and I found that the word "journal," for example, might be quite differently interpreted, even by faculty who had attended workshops where journals were heavily emphasized. Further, our data suggest that faculty are not always very sure, or very concerned about, which teaching strategies would be classified as WAC and which would not. The faculty who come to WAC may be involved, as well, in other kinds of growth experiences, and they sometimes don't even remember whether an idea came to them from a WAC source or some other source. Conduit assessment tends to ignore all this.

A second danger of having the assessor define WAC is that WAC classroom strategies may not be the most enduring or important outcomes of WAC. My and my colleagues' forthcoming study suggests that WAC faculty constantly change their classroom *strategies* anyway — both before and after

WAC workshops. The more enduring outcomes, and the ones many faculty state are most important, may be philosophies of teaching and learning, general guidelines for classroom practice, or a model of the learning community experienced in a WAC workshop or writing response group. These qualities are harder, however, to measure than observable teaching strategies.

In addition to silencing the faculty and giving the assessor the privilege of defining WAC and of being the "objective" data collector, Conduit studies also imply a "training" model. For example, the WAC program "trains" faculty to do something that the leaders and researchers assume to be good. The more of it that faculty do and the longer they continue to do it after the WAC training, the more successful WAC is.

The issue of faculty change is problematic in Conduit assessment. Faculty are supposed to change once, when they come into WAC, but then stop changing, or at least not change beyond the boundaries of what the assessors would define as WAC beliefs and practices. The Conduit paradigm implicitly assumes that if faculty are not doing WAC, they have backslid, resisted, or stood still. Whether they might have developed something better than the assessor's version of WAC, given their situations, is not entertained. Conduit research also does not fully acknowledge that a set of pedagogical practices and philosophies might work better in one situation than in another.

A final issue in Conduit assessment — as in every other kind of assessment — is how do we know that WAC is "good." In every type of assessment, I've seen cases where WAC was merely *assumed* to be good. But when the assessors try to demonstrate that WAC is good, their mode of doing so may affect, and be affected by, the role that faculty play in assessment. Conduit studies, in accord with their foundationalist assumptions, typically define "good" as that which results in measurable student learning. The strategies, not the teacher, are assumed to be the cause of the learning. Thus, if the strategies result in student learning, then teachers who adopt the strategies should be producing student learning.

Conduit studies typically measure student learning directly or indirectly: (a) They may directly measure student learning in the classrooms of the faculty who are being assessed or (b) They may measure faculty behavior that the research literature suggests will result in student learning.

As regards the first option, direct measurement of student learning, the field is littered with corpses (see Klaus, 1982; Young & Fulwiler, 1986, for the difficulties; see MacDonald & Cooper, 1992, for a more successful example). A variation is to measure students' *perceptions* of their own learning (see Marsalla, Hilgers, & McLaren, 1992).

Indirect measures, measuring teacher behavior, depend on a research literature that establishes the efficacy of WAC strategies. Then, if one's own faculty can be shown to be following those strategies, one can reasonably assume that student learning is occurring. Attempts to establish student learning as a result of WAC strategies per se have been very mixed, thus leading Ackerman, in 1993, to state that research on student outcomes had yet to show conclusively that WAC practices enhance student learning. However, a broader body of education literature is useful here. That body of research strongly suggests that student "involvement" is the key to student learning, and that having students engage interactively with each other, with the teacher, and with the subject, in modes such as writing, enhances student learning (Angelo, 1993; Astin, 1985; Chickering & Gamson, 1987; Kurfiss, 1987). On the basis of this research, the National Center for Educational Statistics (1995) has recently suggested that, instead of trying in every case to measure student learning directly, assessors may measure the faculty behaviors that this national body of research suggests will enhance student learning.

Conduit assessment, then, may simply assume WAC teaching strategies to be good, or it may try to establish that they are good because they result in student learning, measured either directly or indirectly. Either way, the faculty member's role is that of Conduit. The assessor's gaze is fixed on measurable student learning or faculty behaviors that result in learning. The strategies are assumed to be the key to the learning. The faculty member is a conduit for the WAC strategies.

In my own WAC program, I have used Conduit studies for particular goals and audiences. But, I always want to be aware of their limitations: lack of power and authority for the faculty member, the absence of the faculty member's voice, the dominance of the "objective" voice of the researcher, the foundationalist assumptions, the "training model," the assumption that WAC is the only catalyst for change, the issue of faculty change itself (i.e., its meaning, its value, and its role in WAC outcomes), and the problematic definition of "good." The Conduit paradigm can be modified in actual practice to transcend or minimize some of these limitations, or the Conduit model can be combined with other models in an assessment program. The end of this article shows an example of such combining.

CONVERT

The Convert role places more emphasis on the richness of the faculty member's lived experience, and it changes the basis of authority for claims that WAC is "good." Fundamentalist Christian religion is the analogy: The *preacher* may talk about the benefits of salvation or publish surveys about how many folks adhere to the religion, but nothing can match the power of the *convert herself*, who stands up in the congregation and testifies, "I was a sinner, and now I am saved."

Published examples of WAC "testimonial" literature, authored by discipline faculty, appear in disciplinary journals (search ERIC under "writing instruction," "higher education," and the name of the discipline) and within various edited collections (e.g., Fulwiler & Young, Eds., 1990; Parker & Goodkin, 1987; Griffin, Ed., 1982; Thaiss, Ed., 1983). Testimonials published for a wider audience are the tip of the iceberg; the underwater base is the wealth of information from local sources: campus WAC newsletters, local and regional conferences, campus WAC assessment reports, and WAC workshop brochures ("Former participants say . . .").

The usual aim of Convert assessment is to persuade unbelievers or to help other faculty implement WAC. Faculty testimonial accounts are sometimes cast in a "how to" frame: here's the classroom strategy I use, here's how to do it, and here are its results. They are sometimes cast in a narrative frame: here's what happened to me as a result of the workshop. Faculty authors may present actual classroom assignment sheets, syllabi, student work, or student evaluations, which are used as concrete models or, as in Conduit assessment, as evidence to back up the speaker's self-report. The faculty member's own persuasiveness and passion, or evidence of student learning in his or her own classroom, are typically the basis of the speaker's claim that WAC is "good."

Sometimes faculty converts report struggle, disappointment, change, adaptation, or abandonment of WAC strategies. These are similar to the religious convert's description of past sins: A necessary part of the genre, to be followed by accounts of how faculty eventually saw the light, adopted WAC strategies, and how well these work in the classroom.

I am not saying that Convert accounts are false or that genre influence is wrong. The influence of genre is always present in discourse. Some faculty *do* experience WAC as a kind of conversion experience that *does* change their practices and beliefs, as my and my colleagues' forthcoming study demonstrates. Further, testimonials can powerfully move an audience as Conduit studies rarely can. They allow the hearer to identify with the testifier as a person "like me." Such stories can transfix a board of trustees, a Rotary Club, and many other kinds of internal and external audiences. The "how to" element can be both useful and persuasive to other faculty. The testifier role may be the first opportunity for a faculty member to speak publicly on behalf of WAC, thus leading to further, more complex leadership roles. Convert accounts give faculty a voice. Convert accounts probably merit a place in every WAC program's assessment mix; I have used them in my own WAC programs.

However, to construct assessment around the degree to which someone is converted is to fall into some of the same assumptions as the Conduit role: the faculty member should ideally follow "our" model; the workshop or other WAC experience is the one important point of significant change, and after that, we hope the WAC faculty will stay on the true road and not backslide. The "testifier" role can be powerful for faculty in assessment, but can also be a limited one. WAC assessors who use it need to be aware of its limitations.

CHANGER

WAC assessors can move away from the "our model" limitations of the Conduit and Convert studies by focusing on faculty change and WAC's impact on change, without trying to define what kind of change it should be. Through questionnaire or interview, the assessor asks faculty open-ended questions about change and about WAC's role in spurring change. Change itself, rather than "our model" or specific beliefs and strategies, now becomes the implied goal of a WAC program and the object of its assessment. The faculty member is cast as "Changer." The frequent goal of such assessment is to demonstrate that the WAC program has produced beneficial results; the typical audiences are administrators and funders.

One published Changer study is Eble and McKeachie (1985). During the late 1970s and the 1980s, the Bush foundation supported faculty development, including a number of WAC programs at 24 institutions of higher education in Minnesota and North and South Dakota. Eble and McKeachie asked, via questionnaires, a random sample of faculty at these institutions: "Did [the faculty development program] have an effect on teaching?" Of 455 faculty, 383 responded; 78 percent of those replied "Yes." In Kalmbach and Gorman's 1986 study at Michigan Technological University, 82 percent of the 90 respondents said their teaching of writing had improved since the workshop. The definitions of "effect" and "improve" were left to the faculty members. (See Beaver & Deal [1990] for another "changer" study.)

Changer studies allow freedom for faculty interpretation of WAC and of effective classroom strategies. The faculty member is given the power to define what "change" is and whether WAC has spurred change. I've used Changer studies for reporting to my administrators and Board that X percent of the faculty who have been through a WAC workshop reported they had "changed their teaching in some way." It works, politically, if the administrators, board members, or other audiences see change as a valid goal.

The Changer model may still be foundationalist, however, and audiences may ask for confirming evidence that these changes REALLY occurred. Like the Conduit model, the Changer model may devalue faculty voices as "self-report."

The Changer model also reifies change for its own sake. What about the faculty member who was doing much of this from the beginning, and so reports little change? Does she count as a "failure" in the assessment? Or what about the faculty member who has another style and philosophy worked out, who is effective with it in the classroom, and who decides not to change it? And how about the possibility that change could be for the worse?

Further, a "did you or didn't you change?" questionnaire, like the "did you or didn't you use WAC?" Conduit questionnaire, may fail to provide rich detail about the complexity of classrooms and faculty lives.

CASE

To discover in more detail what is happening in the classroom and to get away from questionnaire or testimonial, one can go into the classroom for direct observation. A growing number of WAC case studies are doing just that. The "case study" *research method* can be broader than assessment per se (although it can contribute to assessment), and it can be broader than the faculty role I have called "Case." In the Case role, the faculty member remains the object of the assessor's gaze. The case often focuses on problems or difficulties, not on testimony of success. Assessors may use cases to explore troubling issues and to inform program improvement.

The Case role, like the Convert role, highlights the faculty member's lived experience. However, the faculty member's role may still be quite limited.

When Pulitzer Prize–winning journalist and teacher Don Murray agreed to have his composing practices observed as a case study by Berkenkotter (1983), he wrote an end piece to Berkenkotter's report, which he entitled "Response of a Laboratory Rat." Just so. Unlike Berkenkotter's study, many WAC classroom case studies don't give the rat a chance to speak. The assessor's is the voice of authority: Observed details and quotations from the teacher are framed to support the assessor's conclusions. Despite their seeming candor about classroom realities, case studies can still privilege the voice of the outside assessor, silence the teacher, and resemble the Conduit and Convert paradigms in which the assessor knows best and in which change is desired only in the direction the assessor defines.

Some recent published case assessments have cast the faculty in two roles: (a) "resistor" to WAC ideas or (b) well-intentioned but unsuccessful. In one "resistor" case study, Swilky (1992) followed two faculty during the semester after a WAC workshop. She details the suggestions she gave them and notes ways in which they either "resisted" or "adopted" what she calls "my ideas." Her practice of referring to the teachers by their first names casts them as research subjects, not professionals whose words are being cited by a colleague. She points out the dissonance between what "Robert," the teacher, has stated as a goal and what she, the researcher, perceives actually happens: "By maintaining this approach to responding to student texts, Robert works against his goal of assisting students. . . ." (p. 58).

However, "*Robert's*" views on this perceived dissonance are absent. Did he *intend* to work against his own goal? Has his goal changed? What was his reasoning? The researcher uses quotations from Robert's letters to her to illustrate what she calls "both positive and negative resistance." Positive resistance she defines as "productive responses that question the agendas that reformers impose on others"; negative resistance is "unproductive opposition" (p. 51). But the judgments about positive and negative are the researcher's. Swilky acknowledges the possibility of positive resistance and concludes that "different determinants, including personality, assumptions, beliefs, and institutional conditions, affect teachers' decisions about pedagogical priorities." However, she explores these determinants not from the teacher's point of view, but from her own view. She does not question the value or rightness of the ideas she gives to the teachers. The article is strangely split, in this way, with a nod to the teachers' concerns, but within a dominant paradigm of researcher-controlled WAC orthodoxy against which teachers are counted as "resistors." Because "my ideas" still form the goal, the assessor's emphasis is on whether "my ideas" are adopted or not, rather than on the teacher's own goals and theories, the teacher's ongoing growth and change, career patterns, or ways of interpreting the data.[2] While WAC literature about student learning increasingly acknowledges the productivity or at least the legitimacy of learners' resistance to received authority (Chase, 1988; Mortensen & Kirsch, 1993; Trimbur, 1989), in "resistance" studies there is little acknowledgment that in a WAC workshop, WAC is the received authority, and "resistance" to authority may be an appropriate, even desirable, stance for a teacher–learner.

Several other published case studies highlight not so much the teacher as resistor, but the ways in which teachers' good intentions for writing may go awry in the classroom. Marshall (1984) investigates two high school class-rooms — one in science, one in social studies — where the teachers delib-erately tried to use writing for learning and themselves had led in-service workshops for their colleagues about using writing. The social studies teacher, Marshall concludes, mainly accomplished his goals. In the science class, how-ever, students' ways of handling the assignment subverted the teacher's goals. The focus of the study is on "how successful were [the teachers] in meeting their objectives?" (p. 168). The objectives, then, are supposedly the teachers', as interpreted by the researcher. But the judgments about success are Mar-shall's. The teachers' voices, their judgments about their success — or about his judgment — do not enter; nor do student voices, except in short quotes framed by the researcher. Despite the seemingly detailed analysis of the class-room, the teacher is silenced; the outside assessor is in control.

Johnstone (1994) details a college geology class where the teacher, though a strong advocate of WAC among his colleagues, does not achieve his learn-ing goals because, the researcher judges, he does not integrate journals effec-tively into his class but keeps them peripheral, relying mainly on lecture and multiple-choice testing. The responsibility for the classroom failure is placed squarely on the teacher, but his voice is oddly absent. We do not learn from his perspective his rationale for doing what he did or even whether he concurred with the researcher's judgment.

Case studies of how WAC is used by teachers in the classroom are useful to assist in program planning, to share with faculty in workshops, and to make WAC programs humble and realistic after listening to Convert stories. However, Case assessment may fail to focus squarely or fully on why the teachers did what they did, from their point of view. It casts them as resistors or as well-meaning, by the assessor's judgment. Their voices, judgments, rea-sons, and conclusions are often still missing. They are still the object of the assessor's gaze. The assessment does not present the teachers richly to us as creators of meaning, as people who are struggling in often skillful ways to realize their own goals, and to juggle multiple constraints in the classroom. This more powerful teacher role emerges in the "Creator" model.

CREATOR

In the next three types of assessment (Creator, Collaborator, and Client–Customer), both the faculty member and the assessor assume quite different roles than any we have discussed so far. These roles may challenge some fun-damental assumptions that WAC assessors have usually made.

In the Creator role, the faculty member is regarded by the assessor not as an implementor of assessor-defined WAC activities, but as a creator who will make something new, perhaps unexpected, from WAC, and who has the right to do so without judgment by the assessor. Such studies may use case study research methods, but the faculty role is quite different from what I have called the Case.

A model for understanding teachers in the Creator role is provided by Carneson (1994), who studied elementary and secondary school teachers in Britain. In his diagram, teachers are shown working among many diverse and even conflicting forces. At the base of the diagram is the teacher's accountability to the self, to professional colleagues, school management, students, parents, friends, family, and community. The teacher then moves through a "framing matrix" composed of many different perspectives and theories of teaching, not just those of a particular project like WAC. Finally, in the classroom, with all its constraints and stimuli, teachers try to maximize control over elements that are in turn controlling them.

Carneson's model is similar in spirit to the view of teachers proposed by Hargreaves (1988), who also works in K–12. Research suggests, Hargreaves notes, that learning is enhanced by student involvement — by what might broadly be called the interactive classroom. Yet most teaching is "transmission" teaching that relies on lecture and keeps the student passive. Most current theories about why transmission teaching is so widespread are "psychologistic," says Hargreaves — that is, they blame teachers' personal qualities or lack of competence. On that basis, proposed remedies are to select better teachers and to train them better. But Hargreaves counters with what he calls a "sociological" explanation for the dominance of "transmission" teaching.

> The framework I want to propose rests upon a regard for the importance of the active, interpreting self in social interaction; for the way it perceives, makes sense of and works upon the actions of others and the situation in which it finds itself; the way it pursues goals and tries to maximize its own (often competing) interests; the way it pursues these things by combining or competing with other selves; the way it adjusts to circumstances while still trying to fulfil or retrieve its own purposes — and so forth. In this view, teachers, like other people, are not just bundles of skill, competence and technique; they are creators of meaning, interpreters of the world and all it asks of them. They are people striving for purpose and meaning in circumstances that are usually much less than ideal and which call for constant adjustment, adaptation, and redefinition. Once we adopt this view of teachers or of any other human being, our starting question is no longer why do teachers fail to do X [as in WAC "resistor" studies], but why do they do Y. What purpose does doing Y fulfil for them? Our interest, then, is in how teachers manage to cope with, adapt to and reconstruct their circumstances; it is in what they achieve, not what they fail to achieve. (p. 216)

Hargreaves' theory of teacher change is made more explicit later in his article:

> All teaching takes place in a context of opportunity and constraint. Teaching strategies involve attempts at realizing educational goals by taking advantage of appropriate opportunities and coping with, adjusting to, or redefining the constraints. (p. 219)

To Hargreaves' notion that teachers seek to realize educational goals, Raymond, Butt, and Townsend (1992) add the teacher's goal of creating a self:

> The process of teacher development has to be understood in relation to personal sources, influences, issues and contexts. While changes in status and institutional mandates provide both possibilities for, and limitations to, . . . development, there is also a deeper, more personal struggle to carve a . . . self. . . . Professional development is, in this sense, an enactment of a long process of creating self, of making and living out the consequences of a biography. (p. 149)

This Creator model represents an important shift from Swilky's and Swanson-Owens' focus on "resistance" and the causes of resistance to WAC. The Creator model focuses on assessing why the teacher does what she or he does. It recognizes that teachers often have very sensible reasons for decisions and are motivated by multiple, powerful forces and loyalties. There's a recognition that teachers are deeply rooted in their own pasts and that they have philosophies, outlooks, and investments that shape their use of new ideas. The assessor attempts to illuminate the reasons, goals, and principles that guide teachers' actions and development. In the pure form of Creator assessment, the assessor gives up the sole right to judge what is "good" in the teacher's situation because the goal of assessment is to research teacher behavior and rationale, not to pass judgment on it.

Once an assessor shifts to a view of the faculty member as creator, then a collaboration — rather than a subject–object relationship — becomes possible. So Creator and Collaborator roles tend to appear together. The next part of my discussion discusses both of them.

COLLABORATOR

In Collaborator assessment, the assessor not only views the faculty member as Creator, but also collaborates with the faculty member in establishing the goals, methods, models, and/or uses of the assessment itself.

One version of the Creator–Collaborator role is provided by Guba and Lincoln's (1989) "fourth generation evaluation." Such evaluation eschews the foundationalist assumptions we noted as characteristic of conduit and convert research, in favor of a social constructivist paradigm. Evaluation is "created through an interactive process that includes the evaluator . . . as well as the many stakeholders" (p. 8). The evaluator and the other stakeholders collaborate to create the meaning of the evaluation. To ensure effective action based on the evaluation, Guba and Lincoln recommend "negotiation" to arrive at a course of action on which multiple stakeholders can agree (p. 10). This is very different from the Conduit, Convert, and Case paradigms where the assessor defines what is "WAC" and what is "good." Creator and Collaborator studies may use the methods of the "case study," but they transcend the Case role for faculty as I have defined it.

McCarthy and Fishman's collaborative work provides a published example of the faculty member as Creator and Collaborator. In several articles published over several years, McCarthy, a writing specialist, and Fishman, a philosopher significantly influenced by WAC, examine Fishman's teaching as it grows and changes over several years (Abbott, Bartlet, Fishman, & Honda, 1992; Fishman, 1985, 1989, 1993; Fishman & McCarthy, 1992, 1995, 1996; McCarthy, 1991; McCarthy & Fishman, 1991, in press). What emerges is the story of a teacher's journey whose outcome the writing specialist does not pretend to know or control, but for which she, and their interaction, provide a rich resource.[3] McCarthy the researcher watches keenly and collects data as this fascinating development unfolds. Each collaborator learns from the other. Readers of their accounts learn the complexity of the human journey, share Fishman's reasoning about his classes, and come to understand how he balances conflicting needs, adapts ideas he reads or hears, seizes opportunities, juggles constraints, shapes goals and changes them, combines paradigms and philosophies, but always insists on his own right to determine what is "good" for him and his classroom. The assessment is his.

It's true that only Fishman's class is studied, not McCarthy's, so it's not a completely reciprocal exchange of roles. Further, McCarthy's voice as the framer, explainer, and outside investigator is dominant in some of their pieces. They struggle with issues of equality and authority in their collaboration, as they admit. But their study goes as far as any I know within WAC literature to approach the Creator–Collaborator model.

Another study where teachers' voices enter as coauthors, and their growth, rather than their resistance or conversion, become the focus, is a 1991 study of four college classrooms by me and McCarthy and our college-level teacher–collaborators from four disciplines. The teachers, all former WAC workshop participants, collaborated with McCarthy and me, the outside researchers, to study the "difficulties" that arose in their classrooms where WAC workshop ideas were being implemented in various ways. The point of the study is not "resistance" in the teachers, but the mutual efforts of teacher and outside researcher to learn what was happening in the classrooms and to make pedagogical changes of the teachers' own choosing. Our study suggests that WAC methods discussed in a workshop may work more or less well in actual classrooms and that classroom research is one way for the teacher to gain fuller insight on which further pedagogical changes can be based. In the biology classroom, for instance, Anderson (the teacher), and I (the outside researcher) trace over 4 years Anderson's pedagogical changes and the subsequent rise in the quality of students' scientific experiments and reports.[4]

My own work, then, and that of McCarthy, Fishman, Anderson, and other colleagues moves along a continuum toward assessing not the adoption of particular WAC-defined agendas, but rather more generally how teachers change over time, what factors influence those changes, and how particular events such as a WAC workshop fit into personal journeys, into broader institutional contexts, and into career-long growth patterns — that is, why teachers do Y, not why they fail to do X. The work increasingly privileges faculty voices and relies on collaboration with faculty for the creation of knowledge.

If we translate the Creator–Collaborator roles into campus assessment, perhaps the most difficult aspect for WAC programs is the loss of "our model" or "our ideas" as the standard against which faculty behavior is measured.

The Creator and Collaborator roles require that faculty themselves shape the standard. If assessment is determining whether a program is meeting its goals, then the goal of a WAC program must be not to operationalize WAC as WAC assessors understand it, but to assist faculty members in their own growth as they understand it. WAC leaders provide a certain kind of expertise; faculty provide other kinds. WAC leaders may take a facilitative role, managing the WAC budget, planning workshops and other aspects, but faculty must be acknowledged as full partners in the overall endeavor. WAC leaders may suggest new ideas, but faculty members themselves are the final arbiters of whether these ideas will "work" for them or not. WAC leaders may be facilitators of the growth process, but faculty must grow in their own direction. Assessment in such a program, then, seeks to determine whether faculty-directed, faculty-owned growth has resulted from WAC's activities.

"Yes," you might say, "but isn't there good growth and bad growth? Isn't teaching with WAC better than teaching without WAC?" Yes, perhaps, for some or many situations. But the assessor can't finally determine that. In this situation, the assessor begins with the commitment to a faculty-owned WAC: The only effective WAC is WAC that the teacher has made her own and the only effective changes in teaching are the changes that the teacher herself has constructed. Results of this kind of assessment are stories of growth and change, presented without assessor judgment, often told by multiple voices. The difficulty, of course, is that such results are difficult to present in meaningful ways to the Rotary Club or the Podunk City News, or even sometimes to one's own colleagues and administrators. So, like the other roles, this one also may be softened, adapted, or combined with others.

CLIENT–CUSTOMER

Related to the collaborator role is the Client–Customer. In this role, the faculty member is clearly in charge of deciding what is needed. The faculty member comes to WAC for expertise or services, but is assumed to be free to use the advice or service in whatever way she or he sees fit. If service to the Client–Customer is the goal of WAC, then assessment of WAC outcomes would measure not adherence to "our ideas" or growth defined by "our" models, but rather whether or not the Client–Customer believes WAC has contributed to whatever he or she needed. WAC assessment measures how WAC succeeds as a consultant.

One force that will drive this role in the future is the student outcomes assessment that faculty and institutions now must conduct for accrediting agencies, legislatures, and boards. In the past, WAC leaders have needed to do assessment in order to justify their budget requests and defend their right to exist or their plans for new initiatives. But the faculty who were being assessed had no particular stake in how the evaluation turned out. In most disciplines, faculty did not usually have to submit to rigorous assessment of their own teaching, certainly not in terms of student outcomes. (Disciplines that prepare students for licensure are the exception.) As that changes, faculty will seek help in assessing student learning. With new urgency, they will want to know the outcomes of their classroom strategies, including but not limited to WAC strategies. Departments and programs such as General Education will need to document student outcomes.

They may ask WAC to help with this assessment. After all, WAC programs and workshops have traditionally offered help with assigning grades and with classroom research. The potential of WAC strategies for contemporary assessment is illustrated by Thomas Angelo and K. Patricia Cross's *Classroom Assessment* (1993), a widely used publication. WAC proponents will find much that is familiar, particularly the "one-minute paper" and other forms of informal writing. WAC has called these strategies "journals" or "expressive writing" and has focused on their use as "writing to learn." Cross and Angelo recommend some of the same strategies but focus on their utility for assessment, that is, for telling the teacher how well learning is progressing.

Another example of WAC's potential for assessment is how my colleagues and I in 1985 began showing teachers in the disciplines how to use Primary Trait Analysis (PTA), which was developed for the National Assessment of Educational Progress and described by Richard Lloyd-Jones (1977) in the literature that composition specialists read. In my and my colleagues' 1991 study of teaching and student learning in four disciplines, PTA functioned as a research tool. But now the potential of PTA for contemporary assessment is becoming more clear. Not only can teachers use PTA to assess student learning in their classrooms, but departments and institutions can use it in their assessment processes. Other WAC leaders and I are beginning to do workshops and consulting under the "assessment" flag, not the "WAC" flag. For example, as WAC director on my own campus, I have been asked to work with one of the branch campuses to help them assess student learning in their General Education program. That job feels very much like a consultancy to me. It is clear that they are requesting my services; they are the Clients–Customers. It is THEY who have to figure out how to assess General Education in their college, and it is THEY who will be held accountable by the administration, the accrediting agency, and the board for doing so.[5]

It seems to me that the strength of this Client–Customer role is the power it gives to faculty. There are limitations and challenges as well, however. One limitation may be that the client's framework does not fully utilize what WAC has to offer. A too-narrow focus on assessment as product, for example, may blur WAC's important insights into the role of writing in discovery. The client's agenda may not include the kind of thoroughgoing transformation of the academy that WAC's vision has often embodied.

Another limitation is that, as in the Creator–Collaborator roles, WAC gives up power to the faculty member. Once again, WAC leaders will be tempted to say, "Yes, but isn't teaching with WAC actually better than teaching without WAC?" and they will have to answer, "Perhaps, but it's the faculty member who must determine that, who must create meaning from what we offer."

One challenge of the Client–Customer role is to define WAC's own role in this new relationship. Will WAC be co-opted by faculty or departments who want WAC to collaborate in showing success? More broadly, Guba and Lincoln (1989) discuss the close relationship that often exists between assessor and assessed. How can assessment be best constructed to help WAC handle that relationship?

The Creator, Collaborator, and Client–Customer roles, then, represent a radically new approach for WAC. They bring their own benefits and limitations and their own uses and challenges.

COMBINING FACULTY ROLES IN A CAMPUS WAC ASSESSMENT PROGRAM: A CASE STUDY

To illustrate how various kinds of WAC assessment, with varied faculty roles, can be combined by a single WAC program, I will describe the program I know best: the one I directed at the University of Cincinnati (UC) from 1991 to 1996. Equally complex stories of WAC assessment could be told about other campuses. Two that can be followed over a period of time through published works include Michigan Technological University (Flynn, Jones, Shoos, & Barna, 1990; Fulwiler, 1981, 1984, 1988; Fulwiler & Young, 1982, 1990) and the University of Hawaii at Manoa (see the bibliography in Hilgers, Bayer, Stitt-Bergh, & Taniguchi, 1995). These programs have constructed WAC in complex and multivocal ways, combining the faculty roles I have discussed and integrating multiple points of view.

In fall of 1991, I was hired as director of a 3-year-old WAC program funded on year-by-year "one-time" funds out of the provost's office. Its primary activity had been workshops for faculty. End-of-workshop freewrites by faculty had shown high faculty satisfaction, but little other assessment had been done. The legislature and board were sharply reducing the university's funding and were highly critical of how undergraduate education was being conducted. As I saw it, the program needed four things immediately: (a) as the new director, I needed to establish good rapport with the faculty who had attended workshops and who now were the "heart" of the WAC program; (b) UC's WAC needed to collect outcome evidence that could be used in a campaign for permanent funding, or even just to ensure the year-by-year funding, especially if we got a new provost; (c) UC's WAC could prove its usefulness by providing the president with ammunition in his effort to prove to the legislature, board, and media that UC was working hard on undergraduate education and making some changes; and (d) I needed to do all this with limited time, staff, and money.

Because we thought change was a valued goal for us and for other audiences, the WAC Committee and I designed a simple yes or no question in the Changer mode: "Did you make any changes in your teaching as a result of the workshop?" A second question asked, "What changes did you make?" To avoid taking total control of the definition of changes, we left the second question open-ended for the first half of our sample. From those first answers we composed a list of strategies such as "added more writing to the course" and "sequenced assignments in a different way." The second half of our sample were given this list of strategies and were asked to mark the ones they had used. Thus, this part of the questionnaire was Conduit research, asking faculty whether they had used WAC strategies the assessors named, but with a twist: We had given faculty some power to define the strategies we would name. We queried 117 people — 89 percent of the workshopped faculty still on campus — so we had a good sample size. Ninety-nine percent of the faculty queried answered that they had made some changes. The most frequent change they reported was to add more writing. We used that information widely and with good effect for internal and external audiences.

Further, the committee and I used a method of administering the questionnaire that helped us strengthen our evidence within the foundationalist paradigm, to gather some of the richness of faculty experience, and to help me get to know the WAC faculty. We invited all the workshopped faculty to lunch-time discussion groups of six to eight people. We asked them to bring syllabi or course materials for a discussion of what WAC had meant to them and what they would suggest for WAC's future. At these lunches, faculty filled out the questionnaire and then just talked about their WAC experiences. Faculty who did not come to the lunch groups we contacted by phone. These discussions yielded several things. First, we could argue that the syllabi and course materials, as well as the experience of talking about one's use of WAC before a group of colleagues, some of whom might know something about one's teaching, would serve to curtail exaggeration or wishful thinking in the "self-report" questionnaire about changes. Second, we got a list of converts and testifiers, that is, faculty who had benefitted from WAC and who were good at talking about the benefits to faculty colleagues. We later invited these faculty to testify in the media, in our own WAC newsletter, and as presenters at future faculty workshops. We also identified faculty who would help us with various WAC projects. Third, people really did share with us their problems and disappointments as well as what had worked well for them, thus helping to improve our program.

Finally, these conversations made us increasingly dissatisfied with the limitations of the Conduit, Convert, and Changer modes and stimulated us to think about how to conduct assessment in which the faculty members played more powerful roles. We began to read and to discuss other modes. The result was a study of WAC faculty on three campuses reported in the forthcoming book by me, Hunt, Dowling, and McMahon. In that book, we try to move toward the Creator and Collaborator roles. But, after all this, in my fifth year at UC, a public relations consultant hired by the university to help publicize its work came to interview me about WAC. It was hard to make the three-campus study, with its qualitative results, its rich faculty voices, and its complex outcomes of WAC, seem usable to him. He wanted numbers. So I went back to the 99 percent of faculty who had changed their teaching after a WAC workshop. Aha! said his face, now we're getting somewhere. I think this story illustrates my point that an individual WAC program might mix the faculty roles and research paradigms, choosing whichever meets both the needs of one's audiences and one's own personal and professional integrity.

I also want to emphasize integrity. Integrity is a tough issue in a postmodern world and within a social constructivist paradigm. I believe, however, that it is important to work out the ethical implications of one's assessment. At UC, we used several paradigms and faculty roles, depending on the needs of our program and our audiences: Ya want numbers, I give ya numbers; ya want stories, I give ya stories. But we have tried to follow the "rules" of each paradigm, never to falsify data, always to be candid about what we see as strengths and weaknesses of our data, and always to respect the rights and needs of our faculty and students, even in, or perhaps especially in, paradigms where they play circumscribed roles.

One thing is very clear to me: WAC assessment is becoming more complex, more varied, and more self-aware. As WAC programs face a complex and challenging future,[6] WAC assessors need to think carefully about how they construct faculty roles in their assessment and about what those faculty roles imply for WAC's mission, its goals, its identity, and its relationships with the faculty colleagues who from WAC's beginning have been its heart and its life.

NOTES

1. Other published Conduit studies are Goetz (1990), Kalmbach and Gorman (1986), Hughes-Weiner and Jenson-Chekalla (1991), and Braine (1990).

2. Similar in many ways is Deborah Swanson-Owens' (1986) case study of two high school teachers with whom she worked for a semester on a project to use writing.

3. Models for such collaboration are described by McCarthy and Walvoord (1988) and by Cole and Knowles (1993).

4. For another study that attempts to present WAC faculty members' experiences from the "Creator/Collaborator" perspective, see my and my co-authors' 1997 NCTE study *In the Long Run: A Study of Faculty in Three Writing-Across-the-Curriculum Programs.*

5. The strategies I and my colleagues are developing for assessment are further explored in a monograph manuscript by me and Virginia Johnson Anderson, tentatively titled *Using the Grading Process for Assessment.*

6. See my 1996 essay on the Future of WAC.

REFERENCES

Abbott, M. M., Bartlet, P. W., Fishman, S. M., & Honda, C. (1992). Interchange: A conversation among the disciplines. In A. Herrington & C. Moran (Eds.), *Writing, teaching, and learning in the disciplines* (pp. 103–118). New York: MLA.

Ackerman, J. (1993). The promise of writing to learn. *Written Communication, 10,* 334–370.

Angelo, T. A. (1993). A teacher's dozen: Fourteen general, research-based principles for improving higher learning in our classrooms. *AAHE Bulletin, 45*(8), 3–13.

Angelo, T. A., & Cross, K. P. (1993). *Classroom Assessment Techniques.* 2nd ed. San Francisco: Jossey-Bass.

Astin, A. (1985). *Achieving educational excellence.* San Francisco: Jossey-Bass.

Beaver, J. F., & Deal, N. (1990). *Writing across the entire curriculum: A status report on faculty attitudes.* Paper presented at the annual meeting of the Northeastern Educational Research Assn., Ellenville, NY, October 31 through November 2.

Berkenkotter, C., & Murray, D. (1983). Decisions and revisions: The planning strategies of a publishing writer, and response of a laboratory rat — or, being protocoled. *College Composition and Communication, 34,* 156–172.

Braine, G. (1990). Writing across the curriculum: A case study of faculty practices at a research university. ERIC ED 324 680.

Carneson, J. (1994). Investigating the evolution of classroom practice. In H. Constable, S. Farrow, & J. Norton (Eds.), *Change in classroom practice* (pp. 101–112). London and Washington DC: Falmer Press.

Chase, G. (1988). Accommodation, resistance and the politics of student writing. *College Composition and Communication, 39*, 13–22.

Chickering, A. W., & Gamson, Z. F. (1987). Seven principles for good practice in undergraduate education. *AAHE Bulletin, 39*(7), 3–7.

Cole, A. L., & Knowles, J. G. (1993). Teacher development partnership research: A focus on methods and issues. *American Educational Research Journal, 30*, 473–495.

Constable, H. (1994). Introduction: Change in classroom practice: The need to know. In H. Constable, S. Farrow, & J. Norton (Eds.), *Change in classroom practice* (pp. 1–10). London and Washington, DC: Falmer Press.

Eble, K. E., & McKeachie, W. J. (1985). *Improving undergraduate education through faculty development.* San Francisco: Jossey-Bass.

Eblen, C. (1983). Writing across the curriculum: A survey of university faculty views and classroom practices. *Research in the Teaching of English, 17*, 343–348.

Fishman, S. M. (1985). Writing-to-learn in philosophy. *Teaching Philosophy, 8*, 331–334.

Fishman, S. M. (1989). Writing and philosophy. *Teaching Philosophy, 12*, 361–374.

Fishman, S. M. (1993). Explicating our tacit tradition: John Dewey and composition studies. *College Composition and Communication, 44*, 315–330.

Fishman, S. M., & McCarthy, L. P. (1992). Is expressivism dead? Reconsidering its romantic roots and its relation to social construction. *College English, 54*, 647–661.

Fishman, S. M., & McCarthy, L. P. (1995). Community in the expressivist classroom: Juggling liberal and communitarian visions. *College English, 57*, 62–81.

Fishman, S. M., & McCarthy, L. P. (1996). Teaching for student change: A Deweyan alternative to radical pedagogy. *College Composition and Communication, 47*, 342–366.

Flynn, E., Jones, R. W., with Diane Shoos and Bruce Barna (1990). Michigan technological university. In T. Fulwiler & A. Young (Eds.), *Programs that work* (pp. 163–180). Portsmouth, NH: Boynton/Cook.

Fulwiler, T. (1981). Showing not telling in a writing across the curriculum workshop. *College English, 43*, 55–63.

Fulwiler, T. (1984). How well does writing across the curriculum work? *College English, 46*, 113–126.

Fulwiler, T. (1988). Evaluating writing across the curriculum programs. In S. McLeod (Ed.), *Strengthening programs for writing across the curriculum* (pp. 61–76). San Francisco: Jossey-Bass.

Fulwiler, T., & Young, A. (Eds.) (1982). *Language connections: Writing and reading across the curriculum.* Urbana, IL: National Council of Teachers of English.

Fulwiler, T., & Young, A. (Eds.) (1990). *Programs that work.* Portsmouth, NH: Heinemann, Boynton/Cook.

Goetz, D. (1990). *Evaluation of writing-across-the-curriculum programs.* Paper presented at the annual meeting of the American Psychological Assn., Boston, August 10–14. ERIC ED 328 917.

Griffin, C. W. (Ed.) (1982). *Teaching writing in all disciplines.* New Directions for Teaching and Learning No. 12. San Francisco: Jossey-Bass.

Guba, E. G., & Lincoln, Y. S. (1989). *Fourth generation evaluation.* Newbury Park, CA: Sage.

Hargreaves, A. (1988). Teaching quality: A sociological analysis. *Curriculum Studies, 20*, 211–231.

Hilgers, T. L., Bayer, A. S., Stitt-Bergh, M., & Taniguchi, M. (1995). Doing more than "thinning out the herd": How eighty-two college seniors perceived writing-intensive classes. *Research in the Teaching of English, 29*, 59–87.

Hughes-Weiner, G., & Jensen-Chekalla, S. K. (1991). Organizing a WAC evaluation project: Implications for program planning. In L. C. Stanley & J. Ambron (Eds.), *Writing across the curriculum in community colleges.* New Directions for Community Colleges No. 73. San Francisco: Jossey-Bass.

Johnstone, A. C. (1994). In B. Johnstone & V. Balester (Rev. Eds.) (1994). *Uses for journal keeping: An ethnography of writing in a university science class.* Norwood, NJ: Ablex.

Kalmbach, J. R., & Gorman, M. E. (1986). Surveying classroom practices: How teachers teach writing. In A. Young & T. Fulwiler (Eds.), *Writing across the disciplines* (pp. 68–85). Monmouth, NJ: Boynton/Cook.

Klaus, C. (1982, Spring). Research on writing courses: A cautionary essay. *Freshman English News, 11*, 3–14.

Kurfiss, J. (1987). *Critical thinking.* ASHE-ERIC Higher Education Report. Washington, DC: The George Washington University, School of Education and Human Development.

Lloyd-Jones, R. (1977). Primary trait scoring. In C. Cooper & L. Odell (Eds.), *Evaluating writing: Describing, measuring, judging* (pp. 33–66). Urbana, IL: National Council of Teachers of English.

MacDonald, S. P., & Cooper, C. R. (1992). Contributions of academic and dialogic journals to writing about literature. In A. Herrington & C. Moran (Eds.), *Writing, teaching, and learning in the disciplines* (pp. 137–155). New York: MLA.

Marsalla, J., Hilgers, T. L., & McLaren, C. (1992). How students handle writing assignments: A study of eighteen responses in six disciplines. In A. Herrington & C. Moran (Eds.), *Writing, teaching, and learning in the disciplines* (pp. 174–190). New York: MLA.

Marshall, J. D. (1984). Process and product: Case studies of writing in two content areas. In A. Applebee (Ed.), *Contexts for learning to write: Studies of secondary school instruction* (pp. 149–168). Norwood, NJ: Ablex.

McCarthy, L. (1991). *Multiple realities and multiple voices in ethnographic texts.* Paper presented at the annual Conference on College Composition and Communication, Boston, March 21–23. ERIC ED 332210. *Research in Education* Oct.

McCarthy, L. P., & Fishman, S. M. (1991). Boundary conversations: Conflicting ways of knowing in philosophy and interdisciplinary research. *Research in the Teaching of English, 25,* 419–468.

McCarthy, L. P., & Fishman, S. M. (In Press). A text for many voices: Representing diversity in reports of naturalistic research. In G. E. Kirsch & P. Mortensen (Eds.), *More than data: Ethics and representation in qualitative studies of literacy.* Urbana, IL: National Council of Teachers of English.

McCarthy, L. P., & Walvoord, B. E. (1988). Models for collaborative research in writing across the curriculum. In S. H. McLeod (Ed.), *Strengthening programs for writing across the curriculum* (pp. 77–89). New Directions for Teaching and Learning No. 36. San Francisco: Jossey-Bass.

Mortensen, P., & Kirsch, G. E. (1993). On authority in the study of writing. *College Composition and Communication, 44,* 556–572.

National Center for Education Statistics (1995). *College student learning: Identifying college graduates' essential skills in writing, speech and listening, and critical thinking.* Washington, DC: U.S. Department of Education.

Parker, R., & Goodkin, V. (1987). *The consequences of writing: Enhancing learning in the disciplines.* Montclair, NJ: Boynton/Cook.

Raymond, D., Butt, R., & Townsend, D. (1992). Contexts for teacher development: Insights from teachers' stories. In A. Hargreaves & M. G. Fullan (Eds.), *Understanding teacher development* (pp. 143–161). New York: Teachers College Press.

Smithson, I., & Sorrentino, P. (1987). Writing across the curriculum: An assessment. *Journal of Teaching Writing, 6,* 325–342.

Swanson-Owens, D. (1986). Identifying natural sources of resistance: A case study of implementing writing across the curriculum. *Research in the Teaching of English, 20,* 69–97.

Swilky, J. (1992). Reconsidering faculty resistance to writing reform. *WPA: Writing Program Administration, 16,* 50–60.

Thaiss, C. (Ed.) (1983). *Writing to learn: Essays and reflections on writing across the curriculum.* Dubuque, IA: Kendall-Hunt.

Trimbur, J. (1989). Consensus and difference in collaborative learning. *College English, 51,* 602–616.

Walvoord, B. E. (1996). The future of writing across the curriculum. *College English, 58,* 58–79.

Walvoord, B. E., & Anderson, V. J. (In preparation). *Using the grading process for assessment* (working title).

Walvoord, B. E., Hunt, L., Dowling, H. Fil, Jr., & McMahon, J. (1997). *In the long run: A study of faculty in three writing-across-the-curriculum programs.* Urbana, IL: National Council of Teachers of English.

Walvoord, B. E., & Dowling, H. Fil, Jr., with J. Breihan, V. Johnson Gazzam, C. E. Henderson, G. B. Hopkins, B. Mallonee, & S. McNelis (1990). The Baltimore area consortium. In T. Fulwiler & A. Young (Eds.), *Programs that work* (pp. 273–286). Portsmouth, NH: Boynton/Cook.

Walvoord, B. E., & McCarthy, L. P., with V. Johnson-Anderson, J. R Breihan, S. Miller-Robison, and A. K. Sherman (1991). *Thinking and writing in college.* Urbana, IL: National Council of Teachers of English.

Young, A., & Fulwiler, T. (Eds.) (1986). *Writing across the disciplines: Research into practice.* Montclair, NJ: Boynton-Cook.

31 WAC Program Vulnerability and What to Do About It: An Update and Brief Bibliographic Essay

MARTHA TOWNSEND

INTRODUCTION — UPDATE

Two years ago I had the honor of being Carol Rutz's interviewee for her annual series on WAC leaders in [*The WAC Journal*]. With that honor, though, came a good deal of intimidation. My interview followed those of John Bean, Chris Anson, and Bill Condon, a prestigious lineup to be sure. There was a factor beyond these esteemed colleagues' reputations, however, that contributed to my intimidation: I chose to speak frankly about an issue that was foremost in my professional life at that moment — the possible demise of the WAC program that my colleagues and I had guided for over fifteen of its twenty years.[1]

In her introduction, Carol describes the interview as having a "subtext [that] might require an elegy for Missouri's wonderful, long-standing WAC/ WID program" (43).[2] At the time of my interview, Campus Writing Program (CWP) had for several years been under pressure to make changes that CWP staff, members of the Campus Writing Board, and writing-intensive (WI) faculty found unsettling. Indeed, the scenario was sufficiently dire that it was difficult to imagine that the Program could survive. Among the issues CWP faced were physical relocation of our office, loss of our well-established tutorial component to another campus entity, pressure to implement assessment procedures that were contrary to acknowledged best practices, and strained relations with the administrator to whom we reported.

Remarkably, however, MU's Campus Writing Program has not only survived, but, following two years of excellent interim leadership, is undergoing a renaissance. The hire of a new permanent director is pending; two new staff members who serve as liaisons to WI faculty have been hired; a new administrator has been appointed to whom the Program reports; and there has been no lessening in the number or quality of WI courses being offered. The future of CWP looks very bright indeed. Reporting these developments, as an update

From *The WAC Journal* 19 (2008): 45–62.

to the 2006 interview, gives great pleasure to all of us who were associated with CWP.

Former CWP staff is crafting a local history of the Program, with which we have a combined forty-four years of involvement. In it, we speculate on factors that may have led to our successful Program's difficult period and its subsequent recovery. But the larger point is that CWP is not alone among WAC programs that experience vulnerability. If faculty resistance to WAC is legion, programmatic vulnerability is just as common. In 1991 David Russell posited that "on an institutional basis, WAC exists in a structure that fundamentally resists it" (295).

Perhaps one of the best-known devolutions of a well-established WAC program is that of the English Composition Board (ECB) at the University of Michigan. Founded in 1979 and perhaps the earliest WAC program at a major university, it became a prototype for numerous programs around the country. It acquired a solid reputation for, among other things, the scholarly productivity of the non-tenure-track associates who worked with it. Despite ECB's widely respected work and its success at Michigan, however, the program was dismantled quickly and easily by Michigan administrators who had other priorities. A similar example is the writing program directed by Chris Anson at the University of Minnesota, about which he has written, "What strikes me . . . is how easily all the things that have taken so much negotiation, planning and hard work are dismantled" ("Who" 168).

Other examples abound, as anyone who reads WPA-L or WAC-L can attest. In 1994, Ed White comments on the phenomenon, as well, in writing about WAC programs that rely on "flagged" courses, which are specially designated with a "W," or "WI," and the like. "The 'W' program usually begins with a strong vote of confidence from the faculty and the administration," White writes, "since its advantages are many and obvious. . . . But the 'W' program is filled with traps for the unwary and usually leads to unimagined fiasco" (161). He goes on to describe in grim detail one of many such programs he has seen over the years that failed to live up to its initial expectations. The net result, he reports, was "less writing throughout the new curriculum, cynical faculty, mocking students, [and] graduates even less prepared to do critical thinking and writing than before" (163).

There already exists a good body of literature that speaks to how and why WAC programs struggle, along with various sources for addressing the problems. This essay summarizes several of the representative sources, the "classics" as it were, and then offers additional suggestions not found in earlier work, suggestions that could perhaps enable WAC programs to avoid, manage, and/or overcome their vulnerabilities.

WAC programs, it is good to remind ourselves, are highly idiosyncratic. It is an axiom within WAC initiatives that if WAC is to be successful it must respond to the exigencies of each institution — mission of the school, fiscal resources, student demographics, and faculty governance, to mention a few. Toby Fulwiler pointed out, in 1988, the challenges that WAC's idiosyncrasy presents for *evaluating* WAC programs. This idiosyncrasy also makes it difficult to prescribe a one-size-fits-all set of suggestions for *sustaining* WAC. Inasmuch as this essay cannot be a comprehensive "how to" manual, readers are encouraged to delve more deeply into all of the literature and to call on their counterparts at similar programs who are nearly always willing to lend an ear and share experience.

Compelling reasons exist to consolidate some of the old with some of the new at this moment in WAC's history. By most accounts, the number of WAC programs is growing; and, many institutions are looking to revitalize existing programs. At the 2008 Writing Across Research Borders conference, for example, Chris Thaiss delivered preliminary results from the national and international WAC surveys he and his colleagues are engaged in. To date, they have 1,250 respondents from the U.S. and 207 international respondents from 47 countries. Sue McLeod's 1987 WAC survey indicates that 418 institutions at that time had WAC programs.[3] The current number is 608, an increase of 48 percent. Plus, 209 recent respondents indicate that their institutions are planning to begin WAC programs. Of the Ph.D.-granting institutions represented, 59 percent report having WAC programs of some kind. And surprisingly, a large number of programs are directed by tenured faculty.[4] Research from WAC programs was well represented at sessions throughout the three-day conference.

WAC PROGRAM VULNERABILITY AND POSSIBLE SOLUTIONS — THE EARLY LITERATURE

The seven citations in this section — a partial list, to be sure — each address WAC program vulnerability and possible solutions in different ways. They appear in chronological order.

In "Evaluating Writing Across the Curriculum Programs" in *Strengthening Programs for Writing Across the Curriculum* (1988), Fulwiler itemizes seven "obstacles" to evaluating WAC programs. He notes that these obstacles are "inherent in the programs themselves" (62). That is, program vulnerability and evaluation are integrally interconnected. The seven obstacles are as follows: WAC means different things at different institutions; WAC programs are result oriented, not research oriented; WAC programs grow, evolve, and mutate at alarming rates; WAC program administration varies from institution to institution; measures that are quick and dirty do not seem to prove much; WAC programs are amorphous and open ended; and evaluating successful WAC programs is as complicated as evaluating good teaching or successful learning (63–64). Fulwiler follows with five "dimensions" that could provide measurable data (or, as I read it, suggestions for addressing potential vulnerability): the institution's community of scholars; pedagogy; improving student learning; improving student writing; and improving faculty writing (65–72). His overarching suggestion is to "look at everything that is happening at your university (everything within your capability and resources, that is), document it, and see what patterns emerge when you study this information" (72).

Just two years later, in the concluding essay to *Programs That Work: Models and Methods for Writing Across the Curriculum* (1990), co-editors Fulwiler and Art Young itemize six "enemies" of WAC: uncertain leadership; English department orthodoxy; compartmentalized academic administration; academe's traditional reward system, which does not value teaching; testing and quantification; and entrenched attitudes (287–294). The challenge for WAC, they say, "is to change attitudes, ways of thinking, and academic structures" — no easy feat, as anyone who works in any sector of academe knows (294). Still, they point out, the fourteen programs featured in *Programs That Work* managed to do so to some degree. The key is developing "a more or less permanent structure whereby writing-across-the-curriculum advocacy is ever renewed and expanded" (294).

Margot Soven's concluding chapter in *Writing Across the Curriculum: A Guide to Developing Programs* (1992), which she co-edited with Sue McLeod, points to the "road-blocks" and "dangers" WAC faces, in spite of the many positive outcomes that programs produce. Among them are cynical faculty who have given up on students and efforts to help them; English department faculty, in particular, who don't trust that discipline-based faculty will follow through on writing instruction; and administrators who look to WAC programming as a means of saving money spent on writing instruction (135–136). Soven's chapter embeds two other often-cited sources: Ed White's "The Danger of Innovations Set Adrift" and Mike Rose's myth of transcience. In the former, White describes various WAC program innovations undertaken at one institution and then adopted by another, unsuccessfully. "In each case," Soven notes, "the cause of failure was imagining that ideas that work well at one institution can be transported to another without considerable attention to the substructures in place at the school" (136). Soven quotes Russell who describes the myth of transcience — "the convenient illusion that some new program will cure poor student writing, that there is a single pedagogical solution to complex structural issues" (qtd in Soven 136) — as "perhaps the most insidious threat to WAC." Soven ends the chapter with yet another sobering problem: a great deal of any WAC program's success relies on the person directing it. But she also offers a possible solution. "The hidden danger to writing across the curriculum may not be faculty burnout but writing administrator burnout; the cure is the mutual support and encouragement writing program administrators provide to one another" (136).

In addition to Soven's concluding chapter, McLeod and Soven's entire 1992 volume warrants inclusion in this list. Although not structured as a "problems and solutions" manual, the book includes twelve chapters, along with appendices, by experienced WAC program developers, each of whom address various components of WAC programming. The book is now out of print, but was published on the World Wide Web in 2000 and can be downloaded from the WAC Clearinghouse.

John Ackerman, not writing as a proponent of WAC but instead calling attention to one of its weaknesses, nonetheless, informs readers how a shortcoming can be re-cast to better ends. In "The Promise of Writing to Learn"

(1993), he writes about one of WAC's most prominently espoused pedagogies, noting that writing-to-learn is widely acclaimed, but little proved. " '[W]riting as a mode of learning' (Emig, 1977)," he says, "is at best an argument yet to be made" (334). Most of his essay demonstrates the lack of research WAC proponents can marshal for this pedagogy, yet he does not mean to "untrack or devalue teachers and advocates of WAC who have found ways to invigorate their teaching, classrooms, and professional status with write-to-learn practices" (362). Rather, he suggests posing the question of how writing enhances learning differently: "How, why, and with what consequence do you and your students carry on the work of daily classroom, disciplinary, or everyday practices?" (363).

Writing in observation of WAC's twenty-fifth anniversary in 1995, Barbara Walvoord (1996) argues that, "the 'enemies' frame may limit WAC's responses to the complexities of its next quarter century" (58). Instead, she suggests that seeing WAC within the paradigm of social movements is a more positive way to frame the challenges, each of which then suggests a possible solution: work with other movement organizations; define WAC's relationship to institutional administration; define WAC's relationship to technology; reexamine the meaning of key terms; and deal with assessment (68–74). The advantage of this framing, she suggests, "is the power that [social] movements sometimes have to change individuals, to change a culture" (74).

Eric Miraglia and Sue McLeod also write in celebration of WAC's twenty-fifth anniversary, and they present results from a 1995 survey of WAC programs. This survey looked at mature WAC programs to see what factors might account for programmatic staying power or, conversely, demise. "Whither WAC? Interpreting the Stories/Histories of Enduring WAC Programs" (1997) is useful, then, for three key findings that lead to WAC program longevity: administrative support, including funding; grassroots and faculty support; and strong, consistent program leadership (48)."Cast in negative terms, the bottom line could hardly be simpler: lack of administrative support and lack of funding are the two most oft-cited causes of program discontinuance" (50). Faculty disinterest ranked third among cited causes for discontinuance (52). And, a "significant subset of respondents" tied absence or departure of a director to a program's discontinuance (54). These findings, both positive and negative, point to what WAC programs need in order to endure.[5]

WAC Program Vulnerability and Possible Solutions — Recent Literature

In this section, bibliographic sources are embedded within a list of characteristics that describe successful WAC programs.[6] Not all of these characteristics must be obtained for programs to become successful, but a combination of some of them certainly does, and the first three are absolutely essential. Again, the axiom applies that each institution must grow the program that works within its own constraints and possibilities. These characteristics derive from WAC literature, from CCCC and WPA annual conferences and workshops, from WAC-L and WPA-L exchanges, and from my observations of over twenty years of working in and consulting for WAC programs in the U.S. and abroad. For the most part, these sources are post-2000. Rather than appearing in chronological order, citations are included under the entry to which they pertain. Entries appear under Institutional, Classroom and Teaching, and Program levels.

CHARACTERISTICS OF SUCCESSFUL WAC PROGRAMS

Institutional Level

1. Strong Faculty Ownership of the Program.   Grassroots and faculty support is one of Miraglia and McLeod's three key findings from the 1995 survey on mature WAC program longevity, cited above. Such things as faculty-requested help to use writing in their teaching, faculty-established policies for writing requirements, and faculty representation on writing committees are signs that faculty care about student writing and want WAC to succeed. In the University of Missouri's case, faculty concern about student writing led to the formation of its WAC program, and faculty ownership resides in the Program's proactive governance organization, the Campus Writing Board.[7] Conversely, as Miraglia and McLeod point out, when faculty are disinterested, WAC programs wither. In "Enlivening WAC Programs Old and New" (2007), Joan Mullin and Susan Schorn describe how UT Austin's program needed rejuvenating after it had begun to run on "auto-pilot" because WAC course approval was relegated to staff, leaving faculty out of the loop (5–6).

2. Strong Philosophical and Fiscal Support from Institutional Administrators, Coupled with Their Willingness to Avoid Micromanagement.   Administrative support, with funding, is another of Miraglia and McLeod's key findings from the 1995 survey. WAC programs require influential officers who understand that writing is much more than grammar and correctness, officers who are willing to advocate for good writing instruction at all levels of institutional decision making. Administrators must take an active role in securing resources for adequate staffing and program operation; they should not see WAC as an easy or cost-effective substitute for composition. At the same time, if administrators interfere with day-to-day management of the program, faculty will perceive an inappropriate top-down meddling with curriculum, which is traditionally faculty's purview. Maintaining a healthy balance is critical.

3. One and Two Above, in Combination.   Neither is sufficient without the other; both must be present and operate synchronistically. If either faculty or administration is unwilling or disinterested, the WAC program will likely fail. This point recalls Fullan and Miles's Lesson Six in "Eight Basic Lessons for the New Paradigm of Change" summarized by McLeod and Miraglia in *WAC for the New Millennium: Strategies for Continuing Writing-Across-the-Curriculum Programs* (2001): "both top-down and bottom-up strategies are necessary" (20).

4. Symbiosis with the Institution's Mission and Linkages with Other Programs.   One of the enduring lessons from the 1990 Bryn Mawr Summer Institute for Women in Higher Education Administration is tying programs firmly to institutions' mission statements. Thus, Missouri's Campus Writing Program selected four university missions that intersected closely with our WAC work, which we then highlighted in on-campus publications. (See Townsend, 2001, 250–253.) In "A Reflective Strategy for Writing Across the Curriculum: Situating WAC as a Moral and Civic Duty" (2003), John Pennington and Robert Boyer describe how their Catholic, liberal arts college situates WAC as a moral and civic duty, a strategy that "complements our mission to provide for a values-centered curriculum" (87). In "Transforming WAC through a Discourse-Based Approach to University Outcomes Assessment" (2005), John Bean and his co-authors describe how Seattle University's Strategic Plan assessment mandate provided the impetus to reform writing and critical thinking. In "The Future of WAC" (1996), Barbara Walvoord recommends that WAC programs establish closer relationships with campus leaders in technology, assessment, administration, and even with other social movements. Obviously, any WAC program should articulate with its institution's composition program, so that students see the writing requirement(s) as parts of a whole, rather than disconnected items to be checked off a graduation requirement list.

5. Autonomy, Focus, and Goals.   WAC programs require a clear understanding of what they aim to accomplish and an appropriate measure of autonomy that allows them to do it. Walvoord advocates "constant clarification of goals at both the national and local levels" (67). Recognizing the success that Clemson and North Carolina State universities had experienced when incorporating communication into their WAC programs, staff at Missouri debated whether we could add communication to our overall program goals. Ultimately, we decided that we lacked sufficient personnel and resources; keeping our WAC focus allowed us to maintain the strength of our current work. Lillian Bridwell-Bowles's fairly new CXC program at Louisiana State University, on the other hand, is making excellent progress with *four* emphases (written, oral, visual, technological) that it undertook from the very outset. Wendy Strachan's *Writing-Intensive: Becoming W-Faculty in a New Writing Curriculum* (2008) describes how the lack of autonomy adversely affected Simon Fraser's newly developed writing-intensive program. When an administrative mandate required it to integrate into an already existing teaching and learning center, the new partners "discovered they had less in common than had been hoped or assumed," and the forced integration created a "concretely diminished visibility of the [writing-intensive] unit as an individual entity with a distinctive, campus-wide mission" (227–229).

6. A Reward Structure That Values Teaching.   Faculty need to perceive that their work is valued by their colleagues, departments, institutions, and disciplines. Those who haven't previously used writing as part of their pedagogical repertoire will undoubtedly experience an increase in workload, if for no other reason than they are restructuring their teaching practices. The rewards are often not immediate or concrete, especially at research extensive institutions where the most notable rewards come from publication. The work begun by Ernest Boyer and the Carnegie Foundation for the Advancement of Teaching in the 1990s, now popularly known as the scholarship of teaching and learning (SOTL), is making inroads on some campuses. The lesson from Strachan (admittedly a single example) seems to be to work closely with teaching and learning programs, but not be subsumed by them. As the University of Missouri's case has shown, WAC can succeed in research extensive environments, but those leading the programs have to work harder and be prepared to counter more opposition. Stipends for attending workshops, individualized consultation with WAC leaders afterward, and TA support can provide meaningful incentives and demonstrate institutional support.

Classroom and Teaching Level

7. Ongoing Faculty Development.   Once WAC programs are up and running, administration may look to reduce fiscal support on the grounds that the faculty development component has been accomplished. Not so. Faculty change institutions or drop away from their WAC involvement; new ones arrive; previously uninvolved faculty become interested; committed WAC faculty want new ideas or a more sophisticated understanding of how writing and learning intersect. The need for faculty development never goes away. An effective resource, cited by WAC personnel across the U.S., is John Bean's *Engaging Ideas: The Professor's Guide to Integrating Writing, Critical Thinking, and Active Learning in the Classroom* (1996). We give a copy to every faculty member who attends our semi-annual workshop and we base workshop sessions on selected readings. Another resource is Chris Anson's *The WAC Casebook: Scenes for Faculty Reflection and Program Development* (2002) with dozens of examples based on real WAC problems. Specific answers aren't provided, but plenty of suggestions for discovering them are. Faculty who are drawn to teaching with writing are often the same ones drawn to teaching with technology. "WAC Wired: Electronic Communication Across the Curriculum" (2001) by Donna Reiss and Art Young is a good source for helping WAC leaders to hone that connection if they haven't already.

One of the most important components of faculty development is creating relationships between the WAC program and the faculty who are doing the teaching. Campus Writing Program personnel eagerly invested time in getting to know the faculty in the disciplines who were doing the hard work in the trenches. Exiting a local bank recently, I ran into an animal science professor, T. Safranski, who we had worked with. Acknowledging the transition the Program is undergoing, he lamented that, "If I went over to CWP's office right now, no one would know who I am." WAC programs can — and should — become welcoming places where faculty can go to talk about teaching, particularly if their departments or colleagues don't value those conversations. These relationships are an often-overlooked aspect to faculty development, one that can be difficult to explain to administrators, but which experienced WAC leaders understand.

8. Low Student-to-Instructor Ratio, with TA Help if Necessary. Even with the best advice on managing the paper load that accompanies writing-based teaching, WAC faculty still need time to read and respond to student papers. Granting that many variables enter into the equation, the optimum class size is likely fifteen to twenty-five students per instructor. If conditions require larger enrollments, graduate teaching assistants, preferably from the same discipline as the course, should be employed. This kind of work for faculty and TAs, though, is far from intuitive, as Lisa Higgins and Virginia Muller point out in "An Other Teacher's Perspective: TAs in the WI Classroom" (1994). They offer a list of eleven questions the professor and TA should discuss. Beth Finch Hedengren recommends that professors read her *TA's Guide to Teaching Writing in All Disciplines* (2004) with their TAs. Each chapter has a "Working with Your Professor" section with suggestions for discussing the content.

9. Integration of Writing Assignments with Course Goals; Student Engagement. If there is one single principle that applies to all WAC teaching, it is that the writing assignments (whatever form they take) must reinforce course learning goals. It follows that the writing must conform to the instructor's comfort level with using a variety of assignments. Bean's *Engaging Ideas* is an excellent source for showing faculty the myriad ways they can integrate writing into their discipline-based teaching. Mary Segal and Robert Smart's co-edited *Direct from the Disciplines: Writing Across the Curriculum* (2005) shows how faculty members from eleven different disciplines developed WAC courses at Quinnipiac University. The faculty examples range from "fairly modest" to "more radical" (5–6); Art Young describes the book as "reader friendly . . . a welcome contribution to faculty in specific disciplines" (Back Cover). Katherine Gottschalk and Keith Hjortshoj's *The Elements of Teaching Writing: A Resource for Instructors in All Disciplines* (2004) is also a useful resource.

Closely related to student writing and learning is higher education's relatively recent focus on student engagement. Nearly all of the researchers in this field tout writing as one of the top means of ensuring student engagement. George Kuh, the developer of the National Survey of Student Engagement, and his co-authors of *Student Success in College: Creating Conditions That Matter* (2005) are unequivocal: "Writing across the curriculum encourages interdisciplinary efforts and challenges students to think critically and holistically about their assignments. Required coursework in writing ensures that everyone benefits from the extensive writing experience, and discipline-specific writing helps students realize the importance of writing well in their future professions" (185). *In Making the Most of College: Students Speak Their Minds* (2001), Richard Light writes, "Of all skills students say they want to strengthen, writing is mentioned three times more than any other" (54). He notes that the relationship between the amount of writing for a course and students' level of engagement is "stunning . . . The simple correlation between the amount of writing required in a course and students' overall commitment to it tells a lot about the importance of writing" (55–56). In separate publications in 1992 and 1993, Alexander Astin reports that "[Writing] proved to have significant effects on nine of the 22 general education outcomes" (38) and that "the number of courses taken that emphasize the development of writing skills is positively associated with self-reported growth [in a number of areas] . . . The pattern certainly reinforces the idea that the current emphasis on 'writing across the curriculum' is a positive force in undergraduate education today" (243). In *Our Underachieving Colleges: A Candid Look at How Much Students Learn and Why They Should Be Learning More* (2006), former Harvard University president Derek Bok affirms that "good writing — like critical thinking — will never be a skill that students can achieve or retain through a single course [like first-year composition] . . . sustained improvement will require repeated practice" (98). These few examples represent only a small portion of the support for WAC available in the literature on engagement and student success.

Programmatic Level

10. *Knowledgeable, Diplomatic WAC Program Leadership and Staff.* Faculty in the disciplines need access to well-informed WAC specialists when they are designing writing assignments and grading criteria, coordinating assignments with course goals, and matching the myriad WAC pedagogies to their own teaching styles. At the same time, well-trained WAC personnel must be confident enough to sublimate their own knowledge when working with faculty who are, of course, the experts in their own disciplines. Strong, consistent program leadership, as Miraglia and McLeod's survey demonstrated, is key to WAC program longevity. WAC programs require more than just a director; they also require staff members who, Strachan argues, need to be highly qualified and permanent. "Short-term hiring and turnover of [staff]," she says, "means loss of experience and continuity, a loss that can weaken an initiative . . ." (233). As Mullin and Schorn point out, WAC leaders must be able to recognize when programs have stagnated and then be willing to renew and re-invigorate when those signs occur. It takes strong leaders to acknowledge, as they did, that, "We needed . . . a renewal of the institution's WAC culture" (6).

11. *Budget and Resources.* This characteristic, from the Miraglia and McLeod survey and embedded above in item two, bears repeating as a separate item. High-quality higher education is not cheap, and high-quality WAC programs do not develop without adequate resources, which the administration must provide. WAC, however, should not be a hard sell. Academe as a whole, along with virtually every discipline, avows the necessity for graduates to communicate clearly. Writing is at the center of general education and of every disciplinary major higher education offers. Writing is one of the few universally agreed upon aspects of a quality education. Among the resources WAC programs need are a well-staffed writing center; leadership and staff plus professional development for them, to ensure they stay current in the field; incentives and instructional materials for faculty development; a campus WAC newsletter; and perhaps awards for exemplary student writing.

12. Research Agenda.   Every WAC program, no matter how modest, should undertake some effort to conduct research about the work it is doing. In-house publication of positive findings can reinforce and reward faculty accomplishments. Conversely, negative findings presented sensitively can enable classroom improvement. Student voices and opinions can be included in these reports. Conference presentations and refereed publications by WAC personnel and WAC instructors can positively impact WAC program credibility, especially at research-oriented institutions. Chris Thaiss and Terry Myers Zawacki's *Engaged Writers and Dynamic Disciplines: Research on the Academic Writing Life* (2006) is an excellent example of two WAC WPAs who studied the faculty and students in their program and report on what they learned. Administrators take note when WAC programs contribute new knowledge to the field. At the very least, the WAC program itself should model to its constituents the same intellectual curiosity and critical inquiry that WAC courses are intended to foster in students.

13. Flexible but Sound Guidelines, if Flagged Courses Are Used.   Criteria for certifying "W" courses if they are part of the curriculum must be flexible enough to accommodate all disciplines, rigorous enough to ensure course and programmatic integrity, and be informed by current theories and best practices within the field. Daunting though this may sound, numerous programs have arrived at workable standards. Not surprisingly, these guidelines tend to be somewhat similar across programs. An overview of features that typify "W" courses as reported by Christine Farris and Raymond Smith appears in Townsend's 2001 article "Writing Intensive Courses and WAC," along with the guidelines used by the University of Missouri since 1984.

14. Regular Internal Assessment Combined with Periodic External Program Review.   The assessment culture that permeates higher education now may mean that these essential functions are less overlooked in WAC programs than was formerly the case. Often, institutions have regular cycles for *departmental* reviews; *programs,* however, can sometimes slip through the cracks, so WAC WPAs may need to lobby for administrators to commission and pay for external program reviewer visits. Institutional re-accreditation can be one impetus for requesting an external review. Internal assessment should be part of any WAC program's ongoing agenda. William Condon's "Accommodating Complexity: WAC Program Evaluation in the Age of Accountability" (2001) is an excellent place to start. "Integrating WAC into General Education: An Assessment Case Study" describes how Missouri's Campus Writing Program used both a new general education initiative and hiring a new director as impetus for internal and external reviews. (See Townsend, 1997.) Administrators will sometimes urge WAC leaders to give writing competence tests as part of the WAC program's assessment agenda. Resist strongly. In "Dangerous Partnerships: How Competence Testing Can Sabotage WAC" (2005), Doug Brent calls his attempt to link competence testing and WAC a "total failure" (87), noting that "their seemingly complementary approaches . . . mask some deeply divided pedagogical assumptions that threaten to undermine the benefits of a WAC program" (78).

15. *Patience and Vigilance.* When all is said and done, WAC "attempts to reform pedagogy more than curriculum. . . . It asks for a fundamental commitment to a radically different way of teaching, a way that requires personal sacrifices, given the structure of American education, and offers personal rather than institutional rewards" (Russell, 1991, 295). WAC programs and commitments grow slowly, and reforms take time. WAC leaders must be simultaneously patient and perseverant while programs evolve.

Conclusion

Strachan's *Writing-Intensive* is the most recent and most in-depth account of a WAC program's vulnerability. Her narrative will make for instructive reading for WAC WPAs and for graduate students in WAC WPA training or seminars — as would all of the entries in the bibliography. But because many of Strachan's points mirror the situation Missouri's Campus Writing Program experienced not long ago, the positive update at the beginning of this essay is all the more meaningful to report. It has been seventeen years since David Russell (in 1991) wrote, "[W]ithout structural changes to integrate writing into the disciplinary fiber of institutions, without a commitment to permanent change in the way academia values writing in pedagogy, WAC programs will always work against the grain" (304). Based on some of the sources above, one could say his cautionary words have been validated once again. But in those WAC programs that have found solutions to the particular vulnerabilities they have experienced, those of us who practice, promulgate, and research WAC can find ample encouragement and inspiration to move ahead with our work enthusiastically.

ENDNOTES

1. At the time of my interview I had accepted an offer to develop a new WID program at another university and was stepping down from my Campus Writing Program directorship at the University of Missouri. During a one-year hiatus in the English Department at MU, I realized that after fifteen years of WAC/WID program administration a shift in my career was warranted, and I am now a regular faculty member in my department. My CWP colleagues, Marty Patton and Jo Ann Vogt, also left CWP after twelve- and seventeen-year tenures respectively. Marty is also fully in MU's English Department, and Jo Ann is now director of Indiana University's Writing Center.

2. The distinctions between WAC and WID aren't crucial for this article. Rather than the "WAC/WID" formulation, I simply use "WAC" to refer to programs that may have characteristics of either or both.

3. See "Writing Across the Curriculum: The Second State, and Beyond," *College Composition and Communication* Vol. 40 (October 1989): 337–343.

4. Chris Thaiss, Tara Porter, and Erin Steinke, "The International WAC/WID Mapping Project: Objectives and Current Results," Writing Research Across Borders conference, Session E16, University of California-Santa Barbara, February 22, 2008. See http://mappingproject.ucdavis.edu for more information.

5. All three of Miraglia and McLeod's findings are reflected in the six reasons that MU's Campus Writing Program was seen as having been sustained. Steve Weinberg, a journalist and member of CWP's 1992 Internal Review Committee, wrote in *The Chronicle of Higher Education* (June 16, 1993, B2–B3) that CWP had likely survived because the program has a regular line in the campus budget and the support of the provost; has a staff housed outside in English, and is therefore perceived as belonging to the whole campus; has a director and staff who are specialists in WAC; offers TA and faculty development skillfully; students learn in first-year composition about MU's larger writing requirement; and faculty members see the rewards from their extra work.

6. This list reframes and enlarges on an earlier version for W-flagged courses. (See Townsend, 2001, 242–245.) Thanks to Lynn Bloom for the assignment that led to the 2001 concept and to Wendy Strachan for the inspiration to add "levels" and broaden the characteristics to WAC programs generally.

7. Marty Patton is the first in our Program to have pointed this out.

WORKS CITED

Ackerman, John M. "The Promise of Writing to Learn." *Written Communication* Vol. 10, No. 3 (1993): 334–370.

Anson, Chris M. *The WAC Casebook: Scenes for Faculty Reflection and Program Development.* New York: Oxford University Press, 2002.

Anson, Chris M. "Who Wants Composition? Reflections on the Rise and Fall of an Independent Program." *Field of Dreams: Independent Writing Programs and the Future of Composition.* P. O'Neill, A. Crow, and L. W. Burton, Eds. Logan: Utah State University Press, 2002. 153–169.

Astin, Alexander W. *What Matters in College? Four Critical Years Revisited.* San Francisco: Jossey-Bass, 1993.

Astin, Alexander W. "What Really Matters in General Education: Provocative Findings from A National Study of Student Outcomes." *Perspectives* Vol. 22, No. 1 (Fall 1992): 23–46.

Bean, John C. *Engaging Ideas: The Professor's Guide to Integrating Writing, Critical Thinking, and Active Learning in the Classroom.* San Francisco: Jossey-Bass, 1996.

Bean, John, David Carrithers, and Theresa Earenfight. "Transforming WAC through a Discourse-Based Approach to University Outcomes Assessment." *The WAC Journal* Vol. 16 (2005): 5–21.

Bok, Derek. *Our Underachieving Colleges: A Candid Look at How Much Students Learn and Why They Should Be Learning More.* Princeton: Princeton University Press, 2006.

Brent, Doug. "Dangerous Partnerships: How Competence Testing Can Sabotage WAC." *The WAC Journal* Vol. 16 (2005): 78–88.

Condon, William. "Accommodating Complexity: WAC Program Evaluation in the Age of Accountability." *WAC for the New Millennium: Strategies for Continuing Writing-Across-the-Curriculum Programs.* Susan H. McLeod, Eric Miraglia, Margot Soven, and Christopher Thaiss, Eds. Urbana, IL: National Council of Teachers of English, 2001.

Fulwiler, Toby. "Evaluating Writing Across the Curriculum Programs." *Strengthening Programs for Writing Across the Curriculum.* Susan McLeod, Ed. San Francisco: Jossey-Bass, 1988. 61–75.

Gottschalk, Katherine and Keith Hjortshoj. *The Elements of Teaching Writing: A Resource for Instructors in All Disciplines.* Boston: Bedford/St. Martin's, 2004.

Hedengren, Beth Finch. *A TA's Guide to Teaching Writing in All Disciplines.* Boston: Bedford/St. Martin's, 2004.

Higgins, Lisa and Virginia Muller. "An Other Teacher's Perspective: TAs in the WI Classroom." *The Writery: Newsletter of the Campus Writing Program* Vol. 1, No. 2 (October–November 1994): 1–2. http://cwp.missouri.edu/cwpinfo/newsletter.htm.

Kuh, George D., Jillian Kinzie, John H. Schuh, Elizabeth J. Whitt, and Associates. *Student Success in College: Creating Conditions That Matter.* San Francisco: Jossey-Bass, 2005.

Light, Richard J. *Making the Most of College: Students Speak Their Minds.* Cambridge: Harvard University Press, 2001.

McLeod, Susan H. and Margot Soven, Eds. *Writing Across the Curriculum: A Guide to Developing Programs.* Newbury Park, CA: Sage Publications, 1992.

McLeod, Susan H., and Margot Soven, Eds. *Writing Across the Curriculum: A Guide to Developing Programs.* WAC Clearinghouse Landmark Publications in Writing Studies, 2000. http://wac.colostate.edu/aw/books/mcleod_soven/

McLeod, Susan H., Eric Miraglia, Margot Soven, and Christopher Thaiss, Eds. *WAC for the New Millennium: Strategies for Continuing Writing-Across-the-Curriculum Programs.* Urbana, IL: National Council of Teachers of English, 2001.

Miraglia, Eric and Susan H. McLeod. "Whither WAC? Interpreting the Stories/Histories of Enduring WAC Programs." *WPA* Vol. 20, No. 3 (1997): 46–65.

Mullin, Joan and Susan Schorn. "Enlivening WAC Programs Old and New." *The WAC Journal* Vol. 18 (2007): 5–13.

Pennington, John and Robert Boyer. "A Reflective Strategy for Writing Across the Curriculum: Situating WAC as a Moral and Civic Duty." *The WAC Journal* Vol. 14 (2003): 87–100.

Reiss, Donna and Art Young. "WAC Wired: Electronic Communication Across the Curriculum." *WAC for the New Millennium: Strategies for Continuing Writing-Across-the-Curriculum Programs.* Susan H. McLeod, Eric Miraglia, Margot Soven, and Christopher Thaiss, Eds. Urbana, IL: National Council of Teachers of English, 2001. 52–85.

Russell, David. "Writing Across the Curriculum in Historical Perspective: Toward a Social Interpretation." *College English* Vol. 52 (1990): 52–74.

Russell, David. *Writing in the Academic Disciplines, 1870–1990: A Curricular History.* Carbondale: Southern Illinois University Press, 1991.

Rutz, Carol. "Martha 'Marty' Townsend: A Different Kind of Pioneer." *The WAC Journal* Vol. 17 (2006): 43–51.

Safranski, T. Personal Communication. January 2008.

Segal, Mary T. and Robert A. Smart, Eds. *Direct from the Disciplines: Writing Across the Curriculum.* Portsmouth, NH: Boynton/Cook Heinemann, 2005.

Soven, Margot. "Conclusion: Sustaining Writing Across the Curriculum Programs." *Writing Across the Curriculum: A Guide to Developing Programs.* Susan H. McLeod and Margot Soven, Eds. WAC Clearinghouse Landmark Publications in Writing Studies, 2000, 132–136. http://wac.colostate.edu/aw/books/mcleod_soven/

Strachan, Wendy. *Writing-Intensive: Becoming W-Faculty in a New Writing Curriculum.* Logan: Utah State University Press, 2008.

Thaiss, Chris and Terry Myers Zawacki. *Engaged Writers and Dynamic Disciplines: Research on the Academic Writing Life.* Portsmouth, NH: Boynton/Cook Heinemann, 2006.

Townsend, Martha A. "Integrating WAC into General Education: An Assessment Case Study." *Assessing Writing Across the Curriculum: Diverse Approaches and Practices.* Kathleen Black Yancey and Brian A. Huot, Eds. Greenwich, CT: Ablex, 1997. 159–172.

Townsend, Martha A. "Writing Intensive Courses and WAC." *WAC for the New Millennium: Strategies for Continuing Writing-Across-the-Curriculum Programs,* Susan H. McLeod, Eric Miraglia, Margot Soven, and Christopher Thaiss, Eds. Urbana, IL: National Council of Teachers of English, 2001. 233–258.

Walvoord, Barbara. "The Future of WAC." *College English* Vol. 58, No. 1 (1996): 58–79.

White, Edward M. *Teaching and Assessing Writing, Second Edition.* San Francisco: Jossey-Bass, 1994.

White, Edward M. "The Damage of Innovations Set Adrift." *AAHE Bulletin* Vol. 3 (1990): 3–5.

Young, Art and Toby Fulwiler, "The Enemies of Writing Across the Curriculum," *Programs That Work: Models and Methods for Writing Across the Curriculum.* Toby Fulwiler and Art Young, Eds. Portsmouth, NH: Boynton/Cook, 1990. 287–294.

SELECTED READINGS AND RESOURCES

ADDITIONAL READINGS BY PART

Part One: Charting the WAC Movement

Ambron, Joanna. "History of WAC and Its Role in Community Colleges." *Writing Across the Curriculum in Community Colleges.* San Francisco: Jossey-Bass, 1991. 3–8. Print.

Bazerman, Charles. "The Second Stage in Writing Across the Curriculum." *College English* 53 (1991): 209–12. Print.

Bazerman, Charles, and David Russell, eds. *Landmark Essays on Writing Across the Curriculum.* Davis: Hermagoras, 1994. Print.

Bazerman, Charles, Joseph Little, Lisa Bethel, Teri Chavkin, Danielle Fouquette, and Janet Garufis. *Reference Guide to Writing Across the Curriculum.* West Lafayette: Parlor Press and the WAC Clearinghouse, 2005. Print.

Griffin, C. W. "Programs for Writing Across the Curriculum: A Report." *College Composition and Communication* 36.4 (1985): 398–403. Print.

Jones, Robert, and Joseph Comprone. "Where Do We Go Next in Writing Across the Curriculum?" *College Composition and Communication* 44.1 (1993): 59–68. Print.

Kinneavy, James. "Writing Across the Curriculum." *Profession* 83 MLA (1983): 13–20. Print.

Kruse, Otto. "Origins of Writing in the Disciplines: Traditions of Seminar Writing and the Humboldtian Ideal of the Research University." *Written Communication,* 23.3 (2006): 331–52. Print.

Mahala, Daniel. "Writing Utopias: Writing across the Curriculum and the Promise of Reform." *College English* 53 (1991): 773–89. Print.

Maimon, Elaine. "WAC: Past, Present and Future." *Teaching Writing in All Disciplines.* Ed. C. W. Griffin. San Francisco: Jossey-Bass, 1982. 67–82. Print.

Maimon, Elaine. "Writing in All the Arts and Sciences: Getting Started and Gaining Momentum." *WPA: Writing Program Administration* 4 (Spring 1981): 9–13. Print.

Malinowitz, Harriet. "A Feminist Critique of Writing in the Disciplines." *Feminism and Composition Studies: In Other Words.* Ed. Susan Jarratt and Lynn Worsham. New York: MLA, 1998. 291–312. Print.

McLeod, Susan. "Defining Writing Across the Curriculum." *WPA: Writing Program Administration* 11 (Fall 1987): 19–24. Print.

McLeod, Susan. "The Foreigner: WAC Directors as Agents of Change." *Resituating Writing*. Eds. Joseph Janangelo and Kristine Hansen. Portsmouth, NH: Boynton, 1995. 108–16. Print.

McLeod, Susan. "Writing Across the Curriculum: The Second Stage, and Beyond." *College Composition and Communication* 40.3 (1989): 337–43. Print.

McLeod, Susan, and Elaine Maimon. "Clearing the Air: WAC Myths and Realities." *College English* 62.5 (2000): 573–83. Print.

McLeod, Susan, and Margot Soven, eds. *Composing a Community: A History of Writing Across the Curriculum*. West Lafayette: Parlor Press, 2008. Print.

Miraglia, Eric, and Susan McLeod. "Whither WAC? Interpreting the Stories/Histories of Enduring WAC Programs." *Writing Program Administration* 20.3 (Spring 1997): 46–65. Print.

Parker, Robert. "The 'Language Across the Curriculum' Movement: A Brief Overview and Bibliography." *College Composition and Communication* 36.2 (May 1985): 173–77. Print.

Russell, David. "Writing Across the Curriculum in Historical Perspective: Toward a Social Interpretation." *College English* 52.1 (Jan. 1990): 52–73. Print.

Stout, Barbara R., and Joyce N. Magnotto. "Writing across the Curriculum at Community Colleges." *New Directions for Teaching and Learning* 36 (1988): 21–30. Print.

Thaiss, Chris, and Tara Porter. "The State of WAC/WID in 2010: Methods and Results of the U.S. Survey of the International WAC/WID Mapping Project." *College Composition and Communication* 61.3 (Feb. 2010): 535–70. Print.

Walvoord, Barbara Fassler. "The Future of WAC." *College English* 58 (1996): 58–91. Print.

Part Two: Practicing WAC

Ackerman, John. "The Promise of Writing to Learn." *Written Communication* 10.3 (1993): 334–70. Print.

Bridgeman, Brent, and Sybil B. Carlson. "Survey of Academic Writing Tasks." *Written Communication* 1.2 (1984): 247–80. Print.

Britton, James, Tony Burgess, Nancy Martin, Alex McLeod, and Harold Rosen. *The Development of Writing Abilities*. London: Macmillan, 1975. Print.

Connor-Greene, Patricia, Catherine Mobley, Catherine E. Paul, Jerry A. Waldvogel, Liz Wright, and Art Young, eds. *Teaching and Learning Creatively: Inspirations and Reflections*. West Lafayette: Parlor, 2006. Print.

Fulwiler, Toby. *The Journal Book*. Portsmouth: Boynton, 1987. Print.

Fulwiler, Toby, and Art Young, eds. *Language Connections: Writing and Reading Across the Curriculum*. Urbana: National Council of Teachers of Writing, 1982. *The WAC Clearinghouse*. Web. 22 Apr. 2010.

Herrington, Anne, and Charles Moran, eds. *Writing, Teaching, and Learning in the Disciplines*. New York: MLA, 1992. Print.

Hirsch, Linda, and Carolina DeLuca. "WAC in an Urban and Bilingual Setting: Writing-to-Learn in English y en Español." *Language and Learning Across the Disciplines* 6.3 (August 2003): 61–73. *The WAC Clearinghouse*. Web. 21 June 2010.

Hirsch, Linda, Joanne Nadal, and Linda Shohet. "Adapting Language Across the Curriculum to Diverse Linguistic Populations." *Writing Across the Curriculum in Community Colleges.* Eds. Linda Stanley and Joanna Ambron. San Francisco: Jossey-Bass, 1991. 71–78. Print.

Jablonski, Jeffrey. *Academic Writing Consulting and WAC: Methods and Models for Guiding Cross-Curricular Literacy Work.* Cresskill: Hampton, 2006. Print.

Johns, Ann M. "ESL students and WAC Programs: Varied students and diverse needs." *WAC for the New Millennium: Strategies for Continuing Writing-Across-the-Curriculum Programs.* Ed. Susan McLeod, Eric Miraglia, Margot Soven, and Christopher Thaiss. Urbana: NCTE, 2001. 141–64. Print.

Kiefer, Kate. "Integrating Writing into Any Course: Starting Points." *Academic .Writing* (2000). *The WAC Clearinghouse.* Web. 21 June 2010.

Thaiss, Christopher, ed. *Writing to Learn: Essays and Reflections on Writing Across the Curriculum.* Dubuque: Kendall, 1983. Print

Weiser, Irwin. "Local Research and Curriculum Development: Using Surveys to Learn about Writing Assignments in the Disciplines." *The Writing Program Administrator as Researcher.* Ed. Shirley Rose and Irwin Weiser. Portsmouth: Boynton, 1999. 95–106. Print.

Part Three: Theorizing and Researching WAC

Beaufort, Anne. *College Writing and Beyond: A New Framework for University Writing Instruction.* Logan: Utah State UP, 2007. Print.

Beaufort, Ann. "Developmental Gains of a History Major: A Case for Building a Theory of Disciplinary Writing Expertise." *Research in the Teaching of English* 39.2 (2004): 136–85. Print.

Bergmann, Linda, and Janet S. Zepernick. "Disciplinarity and Transference: Students' Perceptions of Learning to Write." *WPA: Writing Program Administration* 31.1–2 (Fall/Winter 2007): 124–49. Print.

Canagarajah, A. Suresh. *Critical Academic Writing and Multilingual Students.* Ann Arbor: Multilingual Matters, 2002. Print.

Carroll, Lee Ann. *Rehearsing New Roles: How College Students Develop as Writers.* Carbondale: Southern Illinois UP, 2002. Print.

Carter, Michael. "The Idea of Expertise: An Exploration of Cognitive and Social Dimensions of Writing." *College Composition and Communication* 41.3 (1990): 265–86. Print.

Casanave, Christine Pearson. *Writing Games: Multicultural Case Studies of Academic Literacy Practices in Higher Education.* Mahwah: Erlbaum, 2002. Print.

Chiseri-Strater, Elizabeth. *Academic Literacies: The Public and Private Discourse of University Students.* Portsmouth: Boynton, 1991. Print.

Emig, Janet. *The Web of Meaning: Essays on Writing, Teaching, Learning, and Thinking.* Portsmouth: Boynton, 1983. Print.

Emig, Janet. "Writing as a Mode of Learning." *College Composition and Communication* 28 (1977): 122–28. Print.

Fishman, Stephen, and Lucille McCarthy. "When Writing-to-Learn Is Not Enough." *Crossing the Curriculum: Multilingual Learners in College Classrooms.* Ed. Vivian Zamel and Ruth Spack. Mahwah: Erlbaum, 2004. 145–62. Print.

Geisler, Cheryl. *Academic Literacy and the Nature of Expertise.* Hillsdale: Erlbaum, 1994. Print.

Haswell, Richard H. *Gaining Ground in College Writing: Tales of Development and Interpretation.* Dallas: Southern Methodist UP, 1991. Print.

Haviland, Carol Peterson, and Joan Mullin. *Who Owns This Text? Plagiarism, Authorship, and Disciplinary Cultures.* Logan: Utah State UP, 2009. Print.

Herrington, Anne J., and Marcia Curtis. *Persons in Process: Four Stories of Writing and Personal Development in College.* Urbana: NCTE, 2000. Print.

Hilgers, Thomas, Ann Shea Bayer, Monica Stitt-Bergh, and Megumi Taniguchi. "Doing More Than 'Thinning Out the Herd': How Eighty-Two College Seniors Perceived Writing-Intensive Classes." *Research in the Teaching of English,* 29.1 (1995): 59–87. Print.

Huot, Brian. "Finding Out What They Are Writing: A Method, Rationale and Sample for Writing-Across-the-Curriculum Research." *WPA: Writing Program Administration* 15 (1992): 31–40. Print.

Jarratt, Susan, Elizabeth Losh, and David Puente. "Transnational Identifications: Biliterate Writers in a First-Year Humanities Course." *The Journal of Second Language Writing* 15 (2006): 24–48. Print.

Jolliffe, David, ed. *Writing in Academic Disciplines.* Norwood: Ablex, 1988. Print.

Leki, Ilona. "Coping Strategies of ESL Students in Writing Tasks across the Curriculum." *TESOL Quarterly* 29.2 (Summer 1995): 235–60. Print.

Leki, Ilona. "Meaning and Development of Academic Literacy in a Second Language." *Multiple Literacies for the 21st Century.* Ed. Brian Huot, Beth Stroble, and Charles Bazerman. Cresskill: Hampton, 2004. 115–28. Print.

Leki, Ilona. "Negotiating Socioacademic Relations: English Learners' Reception by and Reaction to College Faculty." *Journal of English for Academic Purposes* 5 (2006): 136–52. Print.

Lunsford, Andrea, and Lisa Ede. "Representing Audience: Successful Discourse and Disciplinary Critique." *College Composition and Communication* 47.2 (May 1996): 167–79. Print.

Marsella, Joy, Thomas Hilgers, and Clemence McLaren. "How Students Handle Writing Assignments: A Study of Eighteen Responses in Six Disciplines." *Writing, Teaching and Learning in the Disciplines.* Ed. Anne Herrington and Charles Moran. New York: MLA, 1992. 174–88. Print.

McCarthy, Lucille. "A Stranger in Strange Lands: A College Student Writing across the Curriculum." *Research in the Teaching of English* 21 (1987): 233–65. Print.

McCarthy, Lucille, and Stephen Fishman. "An ESL Writer and Her Discipline-Based Professor: Making Progress Even When Goals Don't Match." *Written Communication* 18.2 (2001): 180–228. Print.

Monroe, Jonathon, ed. *Writing and Revising the Disciplines.* Ithaca: Cornell UP, 2002. Print.

Prior, Paul A. *Writing/Disciplinarity: A Sociohistoric Account of Literate Activity in the Academy.* Mahwah: Erlbaum, 1998. Print.

Russell, David, and Arturo Yañez. "'Big Picture People Rarely Become Historians': Genre Systems and the Contradictions of General Education." *Writing Selves/Writing Societies.* Ed. Charles Bazerman and David R. Russell. Fort Collins: The WAC Clearinghouse and Mind, Culture, and Activity, 2003. 331–62. Print.

Russell, David R. "Where Do the Naturalistic Studies of WAC/WID Point To?" *WAC for the New Millennium: Strategies for Continuing Writing-Across the Curriculum Programs.* Eds. Susan McLeod, Eric Miraglia, Margot Soven, and Christopher Thaiss. Urbana: NCTE, 2001. 259–98. Print.

Santos, Terry. "Professors' Reactions to the Academic Writing of Nonnative-Speaking Students." *TESOL Quarterly* 22.1 (1988): 69–90. Print.

Soliday, Mary. "Reading Student Writing with Anthropologists: Stance and Judgment in College Writing." *College Composition and Communication* 56:1 (Sept. 2004): 72–93. Print.

Sommers, Nancy, and Laura Saltz. "Across the Drafts." *College Composition and Communication* 58:2 (2006): 248–57. Print.

Spack, Ruth. "The Acquisition of Academic Literacy in a Second Language: A Longitudinal Case Study." *Written Communication* 10 (1997): 235–61. Print.

Sternglass, Marilyn S. *Time to Know Them: A Longitudinal Study of Writing and Learning at the College Level.* Mahwah: Erlbaum, 1997. Print.

Swales, John. "Discourse Communities, Genres, and English as an International Language." *World Englishes* 7.2 (1988): 211–20. Print.

Thaiss, Chris, and Terry Myers Zawacki. *Engaged Writers and Dynamic Disciplines: Research on the Academic Writing Life.* Portsmouth, NH: Boynton, 2006. Print.

Thaiss, Chris, and Terry Myers Zawacki. "Questioning Alternative Discourses: Reports from the Disciplines." *ALT DIS: Alternative Discourses and the Academy.* Ed. Christopher Schroeder, Helen Fox, and Patricia Bizzell. Portsmouth: Boynton, 2002. 80–96. Print.

Tinberg, Howard. *Border Talk: Writing and Knowing in the Two-Year College.* Urbana: NCTE, 1997. Print.

Walvoord, Barbara, and Lucille McCarthy. *Thinking and Writing in College: A Naturalistic Study of Students in Four Disciplines.* Urbana: NCTE, 1990. Print.

Young, Art, and Toby Fulwiler, eds. *Writing Across the Disciplines: Research into Practice.* Upper Montclair: Boynton, 1986. Print.

Zamel, Vivian. "Questioning Academic Discourse." *Negotiating Academic Literacies: Teaching and Learning Across Languages and Cultures.* Ed. Vivian Zamel and Ruth Spack. Mahwah: Erlbaum, 1998. 187–98. Print.

Zamel, Vivian, and Ruth Spack, eds. *Crossing the Curriculum: Multilingual Learners in College Classrooms.* Mahwah: Erlbaum, 2004. Print.

Part Four: Expanding the Locus of WAC

Barnett, Robert W., and Jacob Blumner. Eds. *Writing Centers and Writing Across the Curriculum Programs: Building Interdisciplinary Partnerships.* Westport: Greenwood, 1999. Print.

Bridwell-Bowles, Lillian, Karen E. Powell, and Tiffany Walter Choplin. "Not Just Words Any More: Multimodal Communication across the Curriculum." *Across the Disciplines* 6 (January 2009). *The WAC Clearinghouse.* Web. 21 June 2010.

Deans, Tom. "Writing Across the Curriculum and Community Service Learning: Correspondences, Cautions, and Futures." *Writing the Community: Concepts and Models for Service-Learning in Composition.* Ed. Linda Adler-Kassner, Robert Crooks, and Ann Watters. Washington, DC: AAHE, 1997. 29–38. Print.

Hall, Jonathan. "WAC/WID in the Next America: Redefining Professional Identity in the Age of the Multilingual Majority." *The WAC Journal* 20 (Nov. 2009). *The WAC Clearinghouse.* Web. 21 June 2010.

Haring-Smith, Tori. "Changing Students' Attitudes: Writing Fellows Programs." *Writing Across the Curriculum: A Guide to Developing Programs.* Ed. Susan H. McLeod and Margot Soven. Newbury Park: Sage, 1992/2000. 123–31. *The WAC Clearinghouse.* Web. 21 June 2010.

Harris, Muriel. "The Writing Center without a WAC Program: The DeFacto WAC Center/Writing Center." *Writing Centers and Writing Across the Curriculum Programs: Building Interdisciplinary Partnerships.* Ed. Robert Barnett and Jacob Blumner. Westport: Greenwood, 1999, 89–104. Print.

Hocks, Mary E. "Using Multimedia to Teach Communication Across the Curriculum." *WPA: Writing Program Administration* 25.1–2 (2001). 25–43. Print.

Jolliffe, David A. "Writing across the Curriculum and Service Learning: Kairos, Genre and Collaboration." *WAC for the New Millennium: Strategies for Continuing Writing-Across-the-Curriculum Programs.* Ed. Susan McLeod, Eric Miraglia, Margot Soven, and Christopher Thaiss. Urbana: NCTE, 2001. 86–108. Print.

Matsuda, Paul Kei. "Situating ESL Writing in a Cross-Disciplinary Context." *Written Communication* 15.1 (1998): 99–121. Print.

Mullin, Joan. "Writing Centers and WAC." *WAC for the New Millennium: Strategies for Continuing Writing-Across-the-Curriculum Programs.* Ed. Susan McLeod, Eric Miraglia, Margot Soven, and Christopher Thaiss. Urbana: NCTE, 2001. 179–99. Print.

Neff, Joyce Magnotto, and Carl Whithaus. *Writing Across Distances and Disciplines: Research and Pedagogy in Distributed Learning.* Florence: Routledge, 2007. Print.

Palmquist, Mike. "A Brief History of Computer Support for Writing Centers and Writing Across the Curriculum Programs." *Computers and Composition.* 20.4 (2003): 395–419. Print.

Palmquist, Mike, Dawn Rodrigues, Kate Kiefer, and Donald E. Zimmerman. "Enhancing the Audience for Writing Across the Curriculum: Housing WAC in a Network-Supported Writing Center." *Computers and Composition* 12 (1995): 335–53. Print.

Reiss, Donna, and Art Young. "WAC Wired: Electronic Communication Across the Curriculum." *WAC for the New Millennium: Strategies for Continuing Writing-Across-the-Curriculum Programs.* Ed. Susan H. McLeod, Eric Miraglia, Margot Soven, and Christopher Thaiss. Urbana: NCTE, 2001. 52–85. Print.

Reiss, Donna, Dickie Selfe, and Art Young, eds. *Electronic Communication Across the Curriculum.* Urbana: NCTE, 1998. Print.

Severino, Carol, and Trachsel, Mary. "Theories of Specialized Discourses and Writing Fellows Programs." *Across the Disciplines* 5 (March 2008). *The WAC Clearinghouse.* Web. 21 June 2010.

Severino, Carol, and Trachsel, Mary. "Starting a Writing Fellows Program: Crossing Disciplines or Crossing Pedagogies?" *International Journal of Learning* 11 (2004): 449–55. Print.

Soven, Margot. "Curriculum-Based Peer Tutors and WAC." *WAC for the New Millennium: Strategies for Continuing Writing-Across-the-Curriculum Programs.* Ed. Susan H. McLeod, Eric Miraglia, Margot Soven, and Christopher Thaiss. Urbana: NCTE, 2001. 200–32. Print.

Waldo, Mark L. "The Last Best Place for Writing Across the Curriculum: The Writing Center." *WPA: Writing Program Administration* 16.3 (1993): 15–23. Print.

Wallace, Ray. "The Writing Center's Role in the Writing Across the Curriculum Program: Theory and Practice." *Writing Center Journal* 8.2 (1988): 43–48. Print.

Wardle, Elizabeth A. "Can Cross-disciplinary Links Help Us Teach 'Academic Discourse' in FYC?" *Across the Disciplines* 2 (July 2004). *The WAC Clearinghouse.* Web. 21 June 2010.

Zawacki, Terry Myers, and Ashley Williams. "Writing Within Interdisciplinary Learning Communities." *WAC for the New Millennium: Strategies for Continuing Writing-Across-the-Curriculum Programs*. Ed. Susan McLeod, Eric Miraglia, Margot Soven, and Christopher Thaiss. Urbana: NCTE, 2001. 109–140. Print.

Part Five: Asssessing WAC

Anson, Chris. "Toward a Multidimensional Model of Writing in the Academic Disciplines." *Writing in Academic Disciplines*. Ed. David Jolliffe. Norwood: Ablex, 1988. 35–88. Print.

Bean, John C., David Carrithers, and Theresa Earenfight. "Transforming WAC through a Discourse-Based Approach to University Outcomes Assessment." *WAC Journal* 16 (Sept. 2005): 5–21. Print.

Bean, John C. "Evaluating Teaching in Writing-Across-the-Curriculum." *Evaluating Teachers of Writing*. Ed. Christine Hult. Urbana: NCTE, 1994. 147–66. Print.

Carter, Michael. "A Process for Establishing Outcomes-Based Assessment Plans for Writing and Speaking in the Disciplines." *Language and Learning Across the Disciplines* 6 (2002): 4–29. Print.

Hawthorne, Joan I. "Student Perceptions of the Value of WAC." *Language and Learning Across the Disciplines* 3 (Oct. 1998): 41–63. Print.

Lovitt, Carl, and Art Young. "Portfolios in the Disciplines: Sharing Knowledge in the Contact Zone." *New Directions in Portfolio Assessment: Reflective Practice, Critical Theory, and Large-Scale Scoring*. Ed. Laurel Black, Donald Daiker, Jeffrey Sommers, and Gail Stygall. Portsmouth: Heinemann, 1994. 334–46. Print.

Peters, Brad, and Julie Fisher Robertson. "Portfolio Partnerships Between Faculty and WAC: Lessons from Disciplinary Practice, Reflection, and Transformation." *College Composition and Communication* 59.2 (December 2007): 206–36. Print.

Walvoord, Barbara, Linda Lawrence Hunt, H. Fil Dowling, and Joan D. McMahon. *In the Long Run: A Study of Faculty in Three Writing-Across-the-Curriculum Programs*. Urbana: NCTE, 1997. Print.

Yancey, Kathleen, and Brian Huot, eds. *Assessing Writing Across the Curriculum: Diverse Approaches and Practices*. Greenwich: Ablex, 1997. Print.

How To Do WAC

Resources for Starting and Sustaining a WAC Program:

Anson, Chris M., ed. *The WAC Casebook: Scenes for Faculty Reflection and Program Development*. New York: Oxford UP, 2002. Print.

Fulwiler, Toby, and Art Young, eds. *Programs that Work: Models and Methods for Writing across the Curriculum*. Portsmouth: Boynton, 1990. Print.

McLeod, Susan H., ed. *Strengthening Programs for Writing Across the Curriculum*. San Francisco: Jossey-Bass, 1998. *The WAC Clearinghouse*. Web. 22 Apr. 2010.

McLeod, Susan, Eric Miraglia, Margot Soven, and Christopher Thaiss. *WAC for the New Millennium: Strategies for Continuing Writing-Across-the-Curriculum Programs*. Urbana: NCTE, 2001. Print.

McLeod, Susan H., and Margot Soven, eds. *Writing Across the Curriculum: A Guide to Developing Programs*. Newbury Park: Sage, 1992. *The WAC Clearinghouse*. Web. 22 Apr. 2010.

Soven, Margot. *Write to Learn: A Guide to Writing across the Curriculum*. Cincinnati: South-Western, 1996. Print.

Thaiss, Christopher. *The Harcourt Brace Guide to Writing Across the Curriculum*. Fort Worth: Harcourt, 1998. Print.

Resources for Teaching with Writing Across the Disciplines

John Bean, *Engaging Ideas: The Professor's Guide to Integrating Writing, Critical Thinking, and Active Learning in the Classroom*. San Francisco: Jossey-Bass, 1996. Print.

Bullock, Richard. *The St. Martin's Manual for Writing in the Disciplines: A Guide for Faculty*. New York: Bedford, 1994. Print.

Gottschalk, Katherine, and Keith Hjortshoj. *The Elements of Teaching Writing: A Resource for Instructors in All Disciplines*. Boston: Bedford, 2004. Print.

Hedengren, Beth Finch. *A TA's Guide to Teaching Writing in All Disciplines*. New York: Bedford, 2004. Print.

Howard, Rebecca Moore, and Sandra Jamieson. *The Bedford Guide to Teaching Writing in the Disciplines: An Instructor's Desk Reference*. Boston: Bedford, 1995. Print.

Walvoord, Barbara. *Helping Students Write Well: A Guide for Teachers in All Disciplines*. New York: MLA, 1982. Print.

ONLINE WAC RESOURCES AND JOURNALS

WAC Clearinghouse: http://wac.colostate.edu/index.cfm

The WAC Journal: http://wac.colostate.edu/journal/ (also available in print)

Across the Disciplines: Interdisciplinary Perspectives on Language, Learning, and Academic Writing: http://wac.colostate.edu/atd/*

International WAC Network: http://mappingproject.ucdavis.edu/ or http://wac.colostate.edu/network/

Special Issues of Interest

From Across the Disciplines

March 29, 2008. Rewriting Across the Curriculum: Writing Fellows as Agents of Change in WAC
Guest editors: Brad Hughes and Emily B. Hall
http://wac.colostate.edu/atd/fellows/index.cfm

---

*In January 2004, *Academic.Writing* and *Language and Learning Across the Disciplines* merged to form *Across the Disciplines*. Issues of *Academic.Writing* and *Language and Learning Across the Discplines* are archived at:
    http://wac.colostate.edu/atd/archives.cfm?showatdarchives=aw
        (for *Academic.Writing*)
    http://wac.colostate.edu/atd/archives.cfm?showatdarchives=llad
        (for *LLAD*)

January 19, 2009. Writing Technologies and Writing Across the Curriculum:
Current Lessons and Future Trends
Guest editor: Karen J. Lunsford
http://wac.colostate.edu/atd/technologies/index.cfm

December 3, 2009. Writing Across the Curriculum and Assessment:
Activities, Programs, and Insights at the Intersection
Guest editors: The Florida State University Editorial Collective
(Kathleen Blake Yancey; Emily Baker; Scott Gage; Ruth Kistler;
Rory Lee; Natalie Syzmanski; Kara Taczak; and Jill Taylor)
http://wac.colostate.edu/atd/assessment/index.cfm

From **Language and Learning Across the Disciplines***

Issue 2.2: Special Issue on the History of WAC, September 1997

Issue 3.2: Special Issue on Communications Across the Engineering
Curriculum, July 1999

Issue 4.3: Special Issue on Service Learning, October 2000

Issue 5.1: Special Issue on WAC and Nursing, April 2001

Issue 5.3: Special Issue on WAC in International Contexts, February 2002

Issue 6.2: Special Issue on Poetry Across the Curriculum, June 2003

---

*PDFs of all of these special issues are available at http://wac.colostate.edu/atd/
archives.cfm?showatdarchives=llad

ABOUT THE EDITORS

Terry Myers Zawacki directs George Mason University's highly ranked Writing Across the Curriculum Program and also leads the cross-university writing assessment initiative. Her publications include the coauthored *Engaged Writers and Dynamic Disciplines: Research on the Academic Writing Life* and articles on writing centers and writing fellows, alternative discourses, writing in learning communities, feminism and composition, writing assessment, and second language writers in the disciplines, the latter the focus of her current research and her keynote address at the tenth International WAC conference in 2010. Zawacki is a member of the Consultants Board of the International WAC Network and a section editor for the Writing Fellows pages of the WAC Clearinghouse. She also serves on the editorial board of *Across the Disciplines: Interdisciplinary Perspectives on Language, Learning, and Academic Writing* and is on the Publications Review Board for the *Digital Books* series on the WAC Clearinghouse. In addition, she is the WID specialist for the Hacker handbook series published by Bedford/St. Martin's, among these *A Writer's Reference* and *The Bedford Handbook.* She is an associate professor of English.

Paul M. Rogers is an assistant professor of English at George Mason University and the associate director of the Northern Virginia Writing Project. His recent scholarship includes "Traditions of Writing Research" (Routledge, 2010) coedited with Charles Bazerman and "Writing and Knowledge Making: Insights from a Historical Perspective" in *Writing in Knowledge Societies* (Parlor Press, in press). He was a 2008 recipient of the K. Patricia Cross Award for leadership in higher education, and a corecipient of the 2009 Janet Emig Award for research in English education. He is cochair of the 2011 International Writing Research Conference — Writing Research Across Borders II.

ACKNOWLEDGMENTS (*continued from page iv*)

INDEX